Test Item File 2

Edward Scahill
University of Scranton

MICROECONOMICS
Second Edition

R. Glenn Hubbard
Anthony O'Brien

Upper Saddle River, New Jersey 07458

VP/Editorial Director: Natalie Anderson
Acquisitions Editor: David Alexander
Assistant Editor: Christina Volpe
Associate Managing Editor: Suzanne DeWorken
Senior Operations Specialist: Arnold Vila

Pearson Prentice Hall[TM] **is a trademark of Pearson Education, Inc.**

10 9 8 7 6 5 4 3 2 1

ISBN-13: 978-0-13-813289-7
ISBN-10:   0-13-813289-5

Preface

Edward Scahill of the University of Scranton prepared the test bank to accompany microeconomics. This test bank includes 2,000 multiple-choice questions, true/false, short-answer, and graphing questions. There are questions to support each key feature in the book. Test questions are annotated with the following information:

- Difficulty: 1 for straight recall, 2 for some analysis, 3 for complex analysis
- Type: multiple-choice, true/false, short-answer, essay
- Topic: the term or concept the question supports
- Skill: fact, definition, analytical, conceptual
- Learning objective
- AACSB (see below)
- Page number
- Special feature in the main book: chapter-opening business example, *Economics in Your Life, Solved Problem, Making the Connection, Don't Let this Happen to You!* and *An Inside Look.*</BL>

The Association to Advance Collegiate Schools of Business (AACSB)

The test bank authors have sought connected select test bank questions to the general knowledge and skill guidelines found in the AACSB standards.

What is the AACSB?

AACSB is a not-for-profit corporation of educational institutions, corporations, and other organizations devoted to the promotion and improvement of higher education in business administration and accounting. A collegiate institution offering degrees in business administration or accounting may volunteer for AACSB accreditation review. The AACSB makes initial accreditation decisions and conducts periodic reviews to promote continuous quality improvement in management education. Pearson Education is a proud member of the AACSB and is pleased to provide advice to help you apply AACSB Learning Standards.

What are AACSB Learning Standards?

One of the criteria for AACSB accreditation is the quality of the curricula. Although no specific courses are required, the AACSB expects a curriculum to include learning experiences in such areas as:

- Communication
- Ethical Reasoning
- Analytic Skills
- Use of Information Technology
- Multicultural and Diversity
- Reflective Thinking

These six categories are AACSB Learning Standards. Questions that test skills relevant to these standards are tagged with the appropriate standard. For example, a question testing the moral questions associated with externalities would receive the Ethical Reasoning tag.

How Can Instructors Use the AACSB Tags?

Tagged questions help you measure whether students are grasping the course content that aligns with AACSB guidelines noted above. In addition, the tagged questions may help instructors identify potential applications of these skills. This in turn may suggest enrichment activities or other educational experiences to help students achieve these skills.

The test bank was checked for accuracy by Rachael Small of the University of Colorado, Boulder.

TestGen

The computerized TestGen package allows instructors to customize, save, and generate classroom tests. The test program permits instructors to edit, add, or delete questions from the test banks; edit existing graphics and create new graphics; analyze test results; and organize a database of tests and student results. This software allows for extensive flexibility and ease of use. It provides many options for organizing and displaying tests, along with search and sort features. The software and the test banks can be downloaded from the Instructor's Resource Center (www.prenhall.com/hubbard).

Table of Contents

Chapter 1 Economics: Foundations and Models

1.1 Three Key Economic Ideas

1. Consider the following two factors:
   a. A study conducted by Forrester Research estimates that between 2000 and 2015, 3.3 million jobs in the United States will have been outsourced.
   b. Over this same period, the number of jobs expected to be created is more than 450 million and the number of jobs due to all causes is estimated at 430 million.

   These statements suggest that
   A) it is highly likely that the average person will lose her job due to outsourcing.
   B) the likelihood that the average person will lose her job due to outsourcing is large small to losing her job due to other causes.
   C) the likelihood that the average person will lose her job due to outsourcing is very small compared to losing her job due to other causes.
   D) the US is not creating jobs fast enough to offset jobs lost due to outsourcing and other causes.
   Answer: C
   Diff: 2   Type: MC   Page Ref: 3/3
   Topic: Three key economic ideas
   Skill: Analytical
   Objective: LO1: Explain these three key economic ideas: People are rational. People respond to incentives. Optimal decisions are made at the margin.
   AACSB Coding: Reflective Thinking
   Special Feature: Economics in YOUR life!: Are You Likely to Lose Your Job to Outsourcing?

2. The study of economics arises due to
   A) money.
   B) scarcity.
   C) greed.
   D) resources.
   Answer: B
   Diff: 1   Type: MC   Page Ref: 4
   Topic: Three key economic ideas
   Skill: Conceptual
   Objective: LO1: Explain these three key economic ideas: People are rational. People respond to incentives. Optimal decisions are made at the margin.
   AACSB Coding: Reflective Thinking
   Special Feature: None

3. Which of the following statements is true about scarcity?
    A) Scarcity refers to the situation in which unlimited wants exceed limited resources.
    B) Scarcity is not a problem for the wealthy.
    C) Scarcity is only a problem when a country has too large a population.
    D) Scarcity arises when there is a wide disparity in income distribution.
    Answer: A
    Diff: 1   Type: MC   Page Ref: 4/4
    Topic: Three key economic ideas
    Skill: Definition
    Objective: LO1: Explain these three key economic ideas: People are rational. People respond to incentives. Optimal decisions are made at the margin.
    AACSB Coding: Reflective Thinking
    Special Feature: None

4. The basic economic problem of scarcity
    A) has always existed and will continue to exist.
    B) will eventually disappear as technology continues to advance.
    C) is a problem only in developing economies.
    D) does not apply to the wealthy in society.
    Answer: A
    Diff: 1   Type: MC   Page Ref: 4/4
    Topic: Three key economic ideas
    Skill: Conceptual
    Objective: LO1: Explain these three key economic ideas: People are rational. People respond to incentives. Optimal decisions are made at the margin.
    AACSB Coding: Reflective Thinking
    Special Feature: None

5. By definition, economics is the study of
    A) how to make money in the stock market.
    B) how to make money in a market economy.
    C) the choices people make to attain their goals, given their scarce resources.
    D) supply and demand.
    Answer: C
    Diff: 1   Type: MC   Page Ref: 4/4
    Topic: Three key economic ideas
    Skill: Definition
    Objective: LO1: Explain these three key economic ideas: People are rational. People respond to incentives. Optimal decisions are made at the margin.
    AACSB Coding: Reflective Thinking
    Special Feature: None

6. What is an economic model?
    A) It is a description of an economic issue that includes all possible related information.
    B) It is a description of an economic issue based on official government information.
    C) It is a detailed version of some aspect of economic life used to analyze an economic issue.
    D) It is a simplified version of some aspect of economic life used to analyze an economic issue.
    Answer: D
    Diff: 1   Type: MC   Page Ref: 4/4
    Topic: Three key economic ideas
    Skill: Definition
    Objective: LO1: Explain these three key economic ideas: People are rational. People respond to incentives. Optimal decisions are made at the margin.
    AACSB Coding: Reflective Thinking
    Special Feature: None

7. Where do economic agents such as individuals, firms and nations, interact with each other?
    A) in public locations monitored by the government.
    B) in any arena that brings together buyers and sellers.
    C) in any physical location people where people can physically get together for selling goods, such as shopping malls.
    D) in any location where transactions can be monitored by consumer groups and taxed by the government.
    Answer: B
    Diff: 1   Type: MC   Page Ref: 4/4
    Topic: Three key economic ideas
    Skill: Conceptual
    Objective: LO1: Explain these three key economic ideas: People are rational. People respond to incentives. Optimal decisions are made at the margin.
    AACSB Coding: Reflective Thinking
    Special Feature: None

8. The term "market" in economics refers to
    A) a place where money changes hands.
    B) a legal institution where exchange can take place.
    C) a group of buyers and sellers of a product and the arrangement by which they come together to trade.
    D) an organization which sells goods and services.
    Answer: C
    Diff: 1   Type: MC   Page Ref: 4/4
    Topic: Three key economic ideas
    Skill: Definition
    Objective: LO1: Explain these three key economic ideas: People are rational. People respond to incentives. Optimal decisions are made at the margin.
    AACSB Coding: Reflective Thinking
    Special Feature: None

9. Economists assume that individuals
    A) behave in unpredictable ways.
    B) will never take actions to help others.
    C) prefer to live in a society that values fairness above all else.
    D) are rational and respond to incentives.
  Answer: D
  Diff: 1   Type: MC   Page Ref: 5/5
  Topic: Three key economic ideas
  Skill: Conceptual
  Objective: LO1: Explain these three key economic ideas: People are rational. People respond to incentives. Optimal decisions are made at the margin.
  AACSB Coding: Reflective Thinking
  Special Feature: None

10. Which of the following best describes an assumption economists make about human behavior?
    A) They assume that individuals act rationally all the time in all circumstances.
    B) They assume that rational behavior is useful in explaining choices people make even though people may not behave rationally all the time.
    C) They assume that people take into account the question of fairness in all decisions they make.
    D) They assume that individuals act randomly.
  Answer: B
  Diff: 2   Type: MC   Page Ref: 5/5
  Topic: Three key economic ideas
  Skill: Conceptual
  Objective: LO1: Explain these three key economic ideas: People are rational. People respond to incentives. Optimal decisions are made at the margin.
  AACSB Coding: Reflective Thinking
  Special Feature: None

11. Economists assume that rational people do all of the following except
    A) use all available information as they act to achieve their goals.
    B) undertake activities that benefit others and hurt themselves.
    C) weigh the benefits and costs of all possible alternative actions.
    D) respond to economic incentives.
  Answer: B
  Diff: 2   Type: MC   Page Ref: 5/5
  Topic: Three key economic ideas
  Skill: Conceptual
  Objective: LO1: Explain these three key economic ideas: People are rational. People respond to incentives. Optimal decisions are made at the margin.
  AACSB Coding: Reflective Thinking
  Special Feature: None

12. Your roommate, Serafina, a psychology major, said, "The problem with economics is that it assumes that consumers and firms always make the correct decision. But we know that everyone's human, and we all make mistakes." Do you agree with her comment?
    A) Yes, I agree with her. One cannot make predictions about economic behavior because in reality people make incorrect choices in many situations.
    B) I disagree with her. Economics does not study correct or incorrect behaviors but rather it assumes that economic agents behave rationally, meaning they make the best decisions given their knowledge of the costs and benefits.
    C) Yes, I agree with her. Economic theory should allow for irrational behavior so that we can have more reliable predictions.
    D) I disagree with her. If we cannot assume that decisions are correct, then we will not be able to examine the moral implications of these decisions.
    Answer: B
    Diff: 2   Type: MC   Page Ref: 5/5
    Topic: Three key economic ideas
    Skill: Analytical
    Objective: LO1: Explain these three key economic ideas: People are rational. People respond to incentives. Optimal decisions are made at the margin.
    AACSB Coding: Analytic Skills
    Special Feature: None

13. Consider the following statements:
    a.   Car owners purchase more gasoline from a gas station that sells gasoline at a lower price than other rival gas stations in the area.
    b.   Banks do not take steps to increase security since they believe it is less costly to allow some bank robberies than to install expensive security monitoring equipment.
    c.   Firms produce more of a particular DVD when its selling price rises.

    Which of the above statements demonstrates that economic agents respond to incentives?
    A) a only.
    B) b only.
    C) c only.
    D) a and b.
    E) a, b, and c.
    Answer: E
    Diff: 3   Type: MC   Page Ref: 5/5
    Topic: Three key economic ideas
    Skill: Conceptual
    Objective: LO1: Explain these three key economic ideas: People are rational. People respond to incentives. Optimal decisions are made at the margin.
    AACSB Coding: Analytic Skills
    Special Feature: None

14. In the first six months of 2003, branches of Commerce Bank in New York City were robbed 14 times. The New York City Police recommended steps the bank could take to deter robberies, including the installation of plastic barriers called "bandit barriers." The police were surprised the bank did not take their advice. According to a deputy commissioner of police, "Commerce does very little of what we recommend. They've told our detectives they have no interest in ever putting in the barriers."

    It would seem that Commerce bank would have a strong incentive to install "bandit barriers" to deter robberies. Why wouldn't they do it?
    A) The banks would rather delay installation of any theft deterring equipment in anticipation of new lower cost innovations in the security devices market.
    B) The banks must have weighed the cost of installing bandit barriers against the benefits and decided that they have "no interest in ever putting in the barriers".
    C) The banks are concerned that "bandit barriers" would send the wrong message to customers –– that the bank is unsafe.
    D) The banks probably resent any interference from the police department.
    Answer: B
    Diff: 2   Type: MC   Page Ref: 5/5
    Topic: Three key economic ideas
    Skill: Conceptual
    Objective: LO1: Explain these three key economic ideas: People are rational. People respond to incentives. Optimal decisions are made at the margin.
    AACSB Coding: Reflective Thinking
    Special Feature: None

15. Over the past decade, health plans have sought to contain rising health care costs by raising premiums and encouraging the use of lower-cost generic drugs. Recently, some health insurers have implemented plans that involve lowering or eliminating co-payments on medications for chronic illnesses.
Source: Vanessa Fuhrmans, "New Tack on Copays: Cutting Them", Wall Street Journal, Tuesday, May 8 2007, Page D1.

Which of the following best explains why employers and health insurers might choose to adopt this radical approach?
    A) These health plans are trying to persuade employers and consumers to bear a greater share of rising health care costs.
    B) They believe that this will give consumers incentives to take better care of their health which in turn, will enable health plans to save even more money by preventing costly health crises down the road.
    C) Health insurers have an incentive to institute plans that promote equity.
    D) Health insurers are finally recognizing that many, especially the elderly, are not getting the care they need.
Answer: B
Diff: 2   Type: MC   Page Ref: 5/5
Topic: Three key economic ideas
Skill: Analytical
Objective: LO1: Explain these three key economic ideas: People are rational. People respond to incentives. Optimal decisions are made at the margin.
AACSB Coding: Analytic Skills
Special Feature: None

16. In Austria, per child, an Austrian woman can get up to 48 months of pension benefits and is guaranteed a maternity allowance two months before and after she gives birth. Further, the Austrian government gives monthly payouts ranging from $132 to $547, depending on the age of offspring and offers generous tax benefits for families with children. How will these benefits affect a woman's decision to have children?

    A) These incentives will have no effect on having children; the decision to have children is a social and psychological decision, not an economic decision.
    B) These incentives will encourage only less educated women to have more children.
    C) These incentives will encourage only women with high opportunity costs to have more children.
    D) These incentives will encourage women to have children and increase the birth rate.
Answer: D
Diff: 2   Type: MC   Page Ref: 5/5
Topic: Three key economic ideas
Skill: Analytical
Objective: LO1: Explain these three key economic ideas: People are rational. People respond to incentives. Optimal decisions are made at the margin.
AACSB Coding: Analytic Skills
Special Feature: Making the Connection: Will Women Have More Babies if the Government Pays Them To?

17. In the United States and in most European countries, aging populations and declining birthrates threaten public finances. As the population ages, there are fewer workers paying taxes relative to the number of retired people receiving government benefits. Which of the following government policies would not help reduce the pressure on public finances?

   A) offer financial incentives to increase the birthrate

   B) reduce taxes paid by current workers so that they an save for their future

   C) reduce retiree benefit payments

   D) raise the retirement age

   Answer: B

   Diff: 2   Type: MC   Page Ref: 5/5
   Topic: Three key economic ideas
   Skill: Analytical
   Objective: LO1: Explain these three key economic ideas: People are rational. People respond to incentives. Optimal decisions are made at the margin.
   AACSB Coding: Analytic Skills
   Special Feature: Making the Connection: Will Women Have More Babies if the Government Pays Them To?

18. What does the term "marginal" mean in economics?

   A) the edge of a market

   B) an additional or extra

   C) illegal

   D) secondary

   E) trivial

   Answer: B

   Diff: 1   Type: MC   Page Ref: 6/6
   Topic: Three key economic ideas
   Skill: Definition
   Objective: LO1: Explain these three key economic ideas: People are rational. People respond to incentives. Optimal decisions are made at the margin.
   AACSB Coding: Reflective Thinking
   Special Feature: None

19. A grocery store sells a bag of potatoes at a fixed price of $2.30. Which of the following is a term used by economists to describe the money received from the sale of an additional bag of potatoes?
    A) marginal revenue
    B) gross earnings
    C) pure profit
    D) marginal costs
    E) net benefit
    Answer: A
    Diff: 1   Type: MC   Page Ref: 7/7
    Topic: Three key economic ideas
    Skill: Conceptual
    Objective: LO1: Explain these three key economic ideas: People are rational. People respond to incentives. Optimal decisions are made at the margin.
    AACSB Coding: Reflective Thinking
    Special Feature: None

20. Economics promote which of the following as the way to make the best decision?
    A) Continue an enjoyable activity as long as you do not have to pay for it.
    B) Continue an enjoyable activity until it is no longer enjoyable.
    C) Continue an enjoyable activity until you cannot afford to pursue it.
    D) Continue an enjoyable activity up to the point where its marginal benefit equals its marginal cost.
    Answer: D
    Diff: 2   Type: MC   Page Ref: 7/7
    Topic: Three key economic ideas
    Skill: Conceptual
    Objective: LO1: Explain these three key economic ideas: People are rational. People respond to incentives. Optimal decisions are made at the margin.
    AACSB Coding: Reflective Thinking
    Special Feature: None

21. Marginal analysis involves undertaking an activity
    A) until its marginal costs start declining.
    B) only when its marginal benefits are positive.
    C) until its marginal benefits equal marginal costs.
    D) only if its marginal costs are greater than its marginal benefits.
    Answer: C
    Diff: 1   Type: MC   Page Ref: 7/7
    Topic: Three key economic ideas
    Skill: Conceptual
    Objective: LO1: Explain these three key economic ideas: People are rational. People respond to incentives. Optimal decisions are made at the margin.
    AACSB Coding: Reflective Thinking
    Special Feature: None

22. The revenue received from the sale of an additional unit of a product
    A) is a marginal benefit to the firm.
    B) is called profit.
    C) is called gross sales.
    D) is called a net gain.
    Answer: A
    Diff: 2   Type: MC   Page Ref: 7/7
    Topic: Three key economic ideas
    Skill: Definition
    Objective: LO1: Explain these three key economic ideas: People are rational. People respond to incentives. Optimal decisions are made at the margin.
    AACSB Coding: Reflective Thinking
    Special Feature: None

23. Making optimal decisions "at the margin" requires
    A) making decisions according to one's whims and fancies.
    B) making consistently irrational decisions.
    C) weighing the costs and benefits of a decision before deciding if it should be pursued.
    D) making borderline decisions.
    Answer: C
    Diff: 1   Type: MC   Page Ref: 7/7
    Topic: Three key economic ideas
    Skill: Conceptual
    Objective: LO1: Explain these three key economic ideas: People are rational. People respond to incentives. Optimal decisions are made at the margin.
    AACSB Coding: Reflective Thinking
    Special Feature: None

24. If the marginal cost of producing a television is constant at $200, then a firm should produce this item
    A) only if the marginal benefit it receives is greater than $200 plus an acceptable profit margin.
    B) as long as the marginal benefit it receives is just equal to or greater than $200.
    C) as long as its marginal cost does not rise.
    D) until the marginal benefit it receives reaches zero.
    Answer: B
    Diff: 2   Type: MC   Page Ref: 7/7
    Topic: Three key economic ideas
    Skill: Conceptual
    Objective: LO1: Explain these three key economic ideas: People are rational. People respond to incentives. Optimal decisions are made at the margin.
    AACSB Coding: Reflective Thinking
    Special Feature: None

25. Making "how much" decisions involve
    A) calculating the total benefits of the activity and determining if you are satisfied with that amount.
    B) calculating the total costs of the activity and determining if you can afford to incur that expenditure.
    C) calculating the average benefit and the average cost of an activity to determine if it is worthwhile undertaking that activity.
    D) determining the additional benefits and the additional costs of that activity.
    Answer: D
    Diff: 2   Type: MC   Page Ref: 6/6
    Topic: Three key economic ideas
    Skill: Conceptual
    Objective: LO1: Explain these three key economic ideas: People are rational. People respond to incentives. Optimal decisions are made at the margin.
    AACSB Coding: Reflective Thinking
    Special Feature: None

26. Which of the following is an example of a "how much" decision?
    A) The Pleasantville movie theatre is open only in the evenings. The theatre's manager is debating whether to add daily matinee shows.
    B) The Zhous have demolished their old home and are debating whether to build a ranch-style house or a Craftsman home.
    C) You're planning to hold a graduation party and must decide between having your party catered or having a pot-luck.
    D) Chelsea has withdrawn from the swim team to take up a full-time job.
    Answer: A
    Diff: 2   Type: MC   Page Ref: 6/6
    Topic: Three key economic ideas
    Skill: Conceptual
    Objective: LO1: Explain these three key economic ideas: People are rational. People respond to incentives. Optimal decisions are made at the margin.
    AACSB Coding: Reflective Thinking
    Special Feature: None

27. The extra cost associated with undertaking an activity is called
    A) net loss.
    B) marginal cost.
    C) opportunity cost.
    D) foregone cost.
    Answer: B
    Diff: 1   Type: MC   Page Ref: 7/7
    Topic: Three key economic ideas
    Skill: Definition
    Objective: LO1: Explain these three key economic ideas: People are rational. People respond to incentives. Optimal decisions are made at the margin.
    AACSB Coding: Reflective Thinking
    Special Feature: None

28. Cassie's Quilts alters, reconstructs and restores heirloom quilts. Cassie has just spent $800 purchasing, cleaning and reconstructing an antique quilt which she expects to sell for $1,500 once she is finished. After having spent $800, Cassie discovers that she would need some special period fabric that would cost her $200 in material and time order to complete the task. Alternatively, she can sell the quilt "as is" now for $900. What is her marginal benefit if she sells the quilt "as is" now?
    A) $100
    B) $900
    C) She makes a marginal loss of $600, not a marginal benefit.
    D) The marginal benefit cannot be determined.
    Answer: B
    Diff: 2   Type: MC   Page Ref: 7/7
    Topic: Three key economic ideas
    Skill: Analytical
    Objective: LO1: Explain these three key economic ideas: People are rational. People respond to incentives. Optimal decisions are made at the margin.
    AACSB Coding: Analytic Skills
    Special Feature: None

29. Cassie's Quilts alters, reconstructs and restores heirloom quilts. Cassie has just spent $800 purchasing, cleaning and reconstructing an antique quilt which she expects to sell for $1,500 once she is finished. After having spent $800, Cassie discovers that she would need some special period fabric that would cost her $200 in material and time in order to complete the task. Alternatively, she can sell the quilt "as is" now for $900. What is the marginal cost of completing the task?
    A) $200
    B) $500
    C) $1,000
    D) $1,000 plus the value of her time
    Answer: A
    Diff: 2   Type: MC   Page Ref: 7/7
    Topic: Three key economic ideas
    Skill: Analytical
    Objective: LO1: Explain these three key economic ideas: People are rational. People respond to incentives. Optimal decisions are made at the margin.
    AACSB Coding: Analytic Skills
    Special Feature: None

30. Cassie's Quilts alters, reconstructs and restores heirloom quilts. Cassie has just spent $800 purchasing, cleaning and reconstructing an antique quilt which she expects to sell for $1,500 once she is finished. After having spent $800, Cassie discovers that she would need some special period fabric that would cost her $200 in material and time in order to complete the task. Alternatively, she can sell the quilt "as is" now for $900. What should she do?
    A) She should cut her losses and sell the quilt now.
    B) It does not matter what she does; she is going to take a loss on her project.
    C) She should purchase the period fabric, complete the task and then sell the quilt.
    D) She should not do anymore work on the quilt because she has already spent too much time on it and has not been paid for that time.
Answer: C
Diff: 3   Type: MC   Page Ref: 7/7
Topic: Three key economic ideas
Skill: Analytical
Objective: LO1: Explain these three key economic ideas: People are rational. People respond to incentives. Optimal decisions are made at the margin.
AACSB Coding: Analytic Skills
Special Feature: None

Scenario 1-1

Suppose a cell-phone manufacturer currently sells 20,000 cell-phones per week and makes a profit of $5,000 per week. A manager at the plant observes, "Although the last 3,000 cell phones we produced and sold increased our revenue by $6,000 and our costs by $6,700, we are still making an overall profit of $5,000 per week so I think we're on the right track. We are producing the optimal number of cell phones."

31. *Refer to Scenario 1-1.* Using marginal analysis terminology, what is another economic term for the incremental revenue received from the sale of the last 3,000 cell phones?
    A) gross earnings
    B) marginal revenue
    C) sales revenue
    D) gross profit
Answer: B
Diff: 1   Type: MC   Page Ref: 7/7
Topic: Three key economic ideas
Skill: Definition
Objective: LO1: Explain these three key economic ideas: People are rational. People respond to incentives. Optimal decisions are made at the margin.
AACSB Coding: Reflective Thinking
Special Feature: None

32. ***Refer to Scenario 1–1.*** Using marginal analysis terminology, what is another economic term for the incremental cost of producing the last 3,000 cell phones?

    A) marginal cost
    B) operating cost
    C) explicit cost
    D) Any of the above terms are correct.

Answer: A

Diff: 1   Type: MC   Page Ref: 7/7
Topic: Three key economic ideas
Skill: Definition
Objective: LO1: Explain these three key economic ideas: People are rational. People respond to incentives. Optimal decisions are made at the margin.
AACSB Coding: Reflective Thinking
Special Feature: None

33. ***Refer to Scenario 1–1.*** Had the firm not produced and sold the last 3,000 cell phones, would its profit be higher or lower, and if so by how much?

    A) Its profit will be $6,700 higher.
    B) Its profit will be $700 higher.
    C) Its profit will be $700 lower.
    D) Its profit will be $6,000 lower.

Answer: B

Diff: 2   Type: MC   Page Ref: 7/7
Topic: Three key economic ideas
Skill: Analytical
Objective: LO1: Explain these three key economic ideas: People are rational. People respond to incentives. Optimal decisions are made at the margin.
AACSB Coding: Analytic Skills
Special Feature: None

Table 1-1

Hours Open	Total Revenue (Dollars)
1	$35
2	60
3	80
4	92
5	100
6	105

Eva runs a small bakery in the village of Roggerli. She is debating whether she should extend her hours of operation. Eva figures that her sales revenue will depend on the number of hours the bakery is open as shown in the table above. She would have to hire a worker for those hours at a wage rate of $12 per hour.

34. *Refer to Table 1-1.* Using marginal analysis, determine how many hours should Eva extend her bakery's hours of operations?
    A) 2 hours
    B) 3 hours
    C) 4 hours
    D) 5 hours
    E) 6 hours
    Answer: C
    Diff: 3   Type: MC   Page Ref: 7/7
    Topic: Three key economic ideas
    Skill: Analytical
    Objective: LO1: Explain these three key economic ideas: People are rational. People respond to incentives. Optimal decisions are made at the margin.
    AACSB Coding: Analytic Skills
    Special Feature: None

35. *Refer to Table 1-1.* What is Eva's marginal benefit if she decides to stay open for two hours instead of one hour?
    A) $60
    B) $95
    C) $25
    D) $36
    Answer: C
    Diff: 2   Type: MC   Page Ref: 7/7
    Topic: Three key economic ideas
    Skill: Conceptual
    Objective: LO1: Explain these three key economic ideas: People are rational. People respond to incentives. Optimal decisions are made at the margin.
    AACSB Coding: Analytic Skills
    Special Feature: None

36. ***Refer to Table 1-1.*** What is Eva's marginal cost if she decides to stay open for two hours instead of one hour?
    A) $12
    B) $24
    C) $71
    D) $36
    Answer: A
    Diff: 2   Type: MC   Page Ref: 7/7
    Topic: Three key economic ideas
    Skill: Conceptual
    Objective: LO1: Explain these three key economic ideas: People are rational. People respond to incentives. Optimal decisions are made at the margin.
    AACSB Coding: Analytic Skills
    Special Feature: None

37. Soo Jin shares a one-bedroom apartment with her classmate. Her share of the rent is $700 per month. She is considering moving to a studio apartment which she will not have to share with anyone. The studio apartment rents for $950 per month. Recently, you ran into Soo Jin on campus and she tells you that she has moved into the studio apartment. Soo Jin is as rational as any other person. As an economics major, you rightly conclude that
    A) Soo Jin did not have a choice; her roommate was a slob.
    B) Soo Jin figures that the additional benefit of having her own place (as opposed to sharing) is at least $250.
    C) Soo Jin figures that the benefit of having her own place (as opposed to sharing) is at least $950.
    D) the cost of having one's own space outweighs the benefits.
    Answer: B
    Diff: 2   Type: MC   Page Ref: 7/7
    Topic: Three key economic ideas
    Skill: Analytical
    Objective: LO1: Explain these three key economic ideas: People are rational. People respond to incentives. Optimal decisions are made at the margin.
    AACSB Coding: Analytic Skills
    Special Feature: None

38. All economic questions arise from the fact that resources are scarce.
    Answer: ◉ True   False
    Diff: 1   Type: TF   Page Ref: 4/4
    Topic: Three key economic ideas
    Skill: Conceptual
    Objective: LO1: Explain these three key economic ideas: People are rational. People respond to incentives. Optimal decisions are made at the margin.
    AACSB Coding: Reflective Thinking
    Special Feature: None

39. Scarcity is a problem that will eventually disappear as technology advances.
    Answer: True   ○ False
    Diff: 1   Type: TF   Page Ref: 4/4
    Topic: Three key economic ideas
    Skill: Conceptual
    Objective: LO1: Explain these three key economic ideas: People are rational. People respond to incentives. Optimal decisions are made at the margin.
    AACSB Coding: Reflective Thinking
    Special Feature: None

40. The term "market" refers only to trading arrangements that have been approved by the government.
    Answer: True   ○ False
    Diff: 1   Type: TF   Page Ref: 4/4
    Topic: Three key economic ideas
    Skill: Conceptual
    Objective: LO1: Explain these three key economic ideas: People are rational. People respond to incentives. Optimal decisions are made at the margin.
    AACSB Coding: Reflective Thinking
    Special Feature: None

41. The sales revenue a seller receives from the sale of an additional unit of goods is called the marginal benefit.
    Answer: ○ True   False
    Diff: 1   Type: TF   Page Ref: 7/7
    Topic: Three key economic ideas
    Skill: Definition
    Objective: LO1: Explain these three key economic ideas: People are rational. People respond to incentives. Optimal decisions are made at the margin.
    AACSB Coding: Reflective Thinking
    Special Feature: None

42. Marginal benefit is the benefit that your activity provides to someone else.
    Answer: True   ○ False
    Diff: 1   Type: TF   Page Ref: 7/7
    Topic: Three key economic ideas
    Skill: Definition
    Objective: LO1: Explain these three key economic ideas: People are rational. People respond to incentives. Optimal decisions are made at the margin.
    AACSB Coding: Reflective Thinking
    Special Feature: None

43. If it costs Sinclair $300 to produce 3 suede jackets and $420 to produce 4 suede jackets, then the difference of $120 is the marginal cost of producing the 4th suede jacket.
Answer: ⊙ True   False
Diff: 1   Type: TF   Page Ref: 7/7
Topic: Three key economic ideas
Skill: Conceptual
Objective: LO1: Explain these three key economic ideas: People are rational. People respond to incentives. Optimal decisions are made at the margin.
AACSB Coding: Reflective Thinking
Special Feature: None

44. Suppose the extra cost to Apple Computer of producing another iPod is $270. Then, Apple should not produce this unit if it can only sell it for $270.
Answer: True   ⊙ False
Diff: 2   Type: TF   Page Ref: 7/7
Topic: Three key economic ideas
Skill: Analytical
Objective: LO1: Explain these three key economic ideas: People are rational. People respond to incentives. Optimal decisions are made at the margin.
AACSB Coding: Analytic Skills
Special Feature: Solved Problem: Apple Computer Makes a Decision at the Margin

45. Assume that Apple computer can earn an additional $81 million of revenue from making 300,000 more iPods. What must the additional cost of producing these 300,000 be to make the additional output economically rational?
Answer: The additional cost of the 300,000 extra iPods must be no more than $81 million to make the production of these extra units economically rational.
Diff: 2   Type: SA   Page Ref: 7/7
Topic: Three key economic ideas
Skill: Conceptual
Objective: LO1: Explain these three key economic ideas: People are rational. People respond to incentives. Optimal decisions are made at the margin.
AACSB Coding: Analytic Skills
Special Feature: Solved Problem: Apple Computer Makes a Decision at the Margin

46. Identify three factors that limit the number of jobs that can move from developed countries to countries such as India and China.

Answer: The factors include:

1. Relatively few workers in India and China are qualified for and capable of working for multinational firms.

2. Poor protection of intellectual property in these countries limits the willingness of firms to locate in developing nations.

3. Poor infrastructure limits a firm's ability to run their operations efficiently. For example, many potential workers live in isolated areas far removed from major cities and airports.

Diff: 2   Type: SA   Page Ref: 18-9/18-9
Topic: Three key economic ideas
Skill: Analytical
Objective: LO1: Explain these three key economic ideas: People are rational. People respond to incentives. Optimal decisions are made at the margin.
AACSB Coding: Analytic Skills
Special Feature: An Inside Look: Should the United States Worry about High-Tech Competition from India and China?

1.2   The Economic Problem that Every Society Must Solve

1. The three fundamental questions that any economy must address are
   A) What will be the prices of goods and services; how will these goods and services be produced; and who will receive them?
   B) What goods and services to produce; how will these goods and services be produced; and who receives them?
   C) Who gets jobs; what wages do workers earn; and who owns what property?
   D) How much will be saved; what will be produced; and how can these goods and services be fairly distributed?

Answer: B

Diff: 1   Type: MC   Page Ref: 8/8
Topic: The economic problem that every society must solve
Skill: Conceptual
Objective: LO 2: Discuss how an economy answers these questions: What goods and services will be produced? How will the goods and services be produced? Who will receive the goods and services?
AACSB Coding: Reflective Thinking
Special Feature: None

2. Every society faces economic tradeoffs. This means
   A) some people live better than others do.
   B) not everyone can have enough goods to survive.
   C) producing more of one good means less of another good can be produced.
   D) society's output cannot be made available to all.
   Answer: C
   Diff: 1   Type: MC   Page Ref: 8/8
   Topic: The economic problem that every society must solve
   Skill: Definition
   Objective: LO 2: Discuss how an economy answers these questions: What goods and services will be produced? How will the goods and services be produced? Who will receive the goods and services?
   AACSB Coding: Reflective Thinking
   Special Feature: None

3. Society faces a tradeoff in all of the following situations except
   A) when deciding who will receive the goods and services produced.
   B) when deciding what goods and services will be produced.
   C) when deciding how goods and services will be produced.
   D) when some previously unemployed workers find jobs.
   Answer: D
   Diff: 2   Type: MC   Page Ref: 8/8
   Topic: The economic problem that every society must solve
   Skill: Conceptual
   Objective: LO 2: Discuss how an economy answers these questions: What goods and services will be produced? How will the goods and services be produced? Who will receive the goods and services?
   AACSB Coding: Reflective Thinking
   Special Feature: None

4. Which of the following statements is false?
   A) Anytime you have to decide which action to take you are facing an economic tradeoff.
   B) Tradeoffs do not apply when the consumers purchase a product for which there is
      excess supply, such as a stock clearance sale.
   C) Every individual, no matter how rich or poor, is faced with making tradeoffs.
   D) Economics is a social science that studies the tradeoffs we are forced to make because
      of scarcity.
   Answer: B
   Diff: 2   Type: MC   Page Ref: 8/8
   Topic: The economic problem that every society must solve
   Skill: Conceptual
   Objective: LO 2: Discuss how an economy answers these questions: What goods and services will be produced? How will the goods and services be produced? Who will receive the goods and services?
   AACSB Coding: Reflective Thinking
   Special Feature: None

5. Which of the following is not an example of an economic tradeoff that a firm has to make?
    A) whether it is cheaper to produce with more machines or with more workers
    B) whether it is to outsource the production of a good or service
    C) whether or not consumers will buy its products
    D) whether it should produce more of its product
    Answer: C
    Diff: 1   Type: MC   Page Ref: 8/8
    Topic: The economic problem that every society must solve
    Skill: Conceptual
    Objective: LO 2: Discuss how an economy answers these questions: What goods and services will be produced? How will the goods and services be produced? Who will receive the goods and services?
    AACSB Coding: Reflective Thinking
    Special Feature: None

6. Opportunity cost is defined as
    A) the benefit of an activity.
    B) the monetary expense associated with an activity.
    C) the highest valued alternative that must be given up to engage in an activity.
    D) the total value of all alternatives that must be given up to engage in an activity.
    Answer: C
    Diff: 1   Type: MC   Page Ref: 8/8
    Topic: The economic problem that every society must solve
    Skill: Definition
    Objective: LO 2: Discuss how an economy answers these questions: What goods and services will be produced? How will the goods and services be produced? Who will receive the goods and services?
    AACSB Coding: Reflective Thinking
    Special Feature: None

7. The Coffee Nook, a small cafe near campus, sells cappuccinos for $2.50 and Russian tea cakes for $1.00 each. What is the opportunity cost of buying a cappuccino?
    A) 2 1/2 Russian tea cakes
    B) 2/5 of a Russian tea cake
    C) $2.50
    D) $1.00
    Answer: A
    Diff: 1   Type: MC   Page Ref: 8/8
    Topic: The economic problem that every society must solve
    Skill: Conceptual
    Objective: LO 2: Discuss how an economy answers these questions: What goods and services will be produced? How will the goods and services be produced? Who will receive the goods and services?
    AACSB Coding: Reflective Thinking
    Special Feature: None

8. Ted quits his $60,000-a-year job to be a stay-at-home dad. What is the opportunity cost of his decision?
    A) 0 since he will no longer be earning a salary
    B) depends on the "going rate" for stay-at-home dads
    C) at least $60,000
    D) the value he attributes to the joy of parenting
    Answer: C
    Diff: 1   Type: MC   Page Ref: 8/8
    Topic: The economic problem that every society must solve
    Skill: Conceptual
    Objective: LO 2: Discuss how an economy answers these questions: What goods and services will be produced? How will the goods and services be produced? Who will receive the goods and services?
    AACSB Coding: Reflective Thinking
    Special Feature: None

9. The distribution of income primarily determines which of the fundamental economic questions?
    A) What goods and services are to be produced?
    B) How the goods and services are to be produced?
    C) Who will receive the goods and services produced?
    D) How to plan the economy?
    Answer: C
    Diff: 2   Type: MC   Page Ref: 8/8
    Topic: The economic problem that every society must solve
    Skill: Conceptual
    Objective: LO 2: Discuss how an economy answers these questions: What goods and services will be produced? How will the goods and services be produced? Who will receive the goods and services?
    AACSB Coding: Reflective Thinking
    Special Feature: None

10. Which fundamental economic problem was 3Com, a leading U.S. high-tech firm, addressing when it decided to move its computer network switch manufacturing operations to China?
    A) Where to produce?
    B) How to produce?
    C) What to produce?
    D) For whom to produce?
    Answer: B
    Diff: 1   Type: MC   Page Ref: 8/8
    Topic: The economic problem that every society must solve
    Skill: Conceptual
    Objective: LO 2: Discuss how an economy answers these questions: What goods and services will be produced? How will the goods and services be produced? Who will receive the goods and services?
    AACSB Coding: Reflective Thinking
    Special Feature: Chapter Opener: What Happens When U.S. High-Technology Firms Move to China?

11. Automobile manufacturers produce a range of automobiles such as sports utility vehicles, luxury sedans, pickup trucks and compact cars. What fundamental economics question are they addressing by making this range of products?
    A) How to produce goods that consumers want?
    B) Why produce a variety of automobiles?
    C) What to produce?
    D) Who to produce automobiles for?
Answer: C
Diff: 1   Type: MC   Page Ref: 8/8
Topic: The economic problem that every society must solve
Skill: Conceptual
Objective: LO 2: Discuss how an economy answers these questions: What goods and services will be produced? How will the goods and services be produced? Who will receive the goods and services?
AACSB Coding: Reflective Thinking
Special Feature: None

12. Consider the following economic agents:
    a.   the government
    b.   consumers
    c.   producers

    Who, in a modern mixed economy, decides what goods and services will be produced with the scarce resources available in that economy?
    A) the government
    B) producers
    C) consumers
    D) consumers and producers
    E) the government, consumers and producers
Answer: E
Diff: 1   Type: MC   Page Ref: 9/9
Topic: The economic problem that every society must solve
Skill: Definition
Objective: LO 2: Discuss how an economy answers these questions: What goods and services will be produced? How will the goods and services be produced? Who will receive the goods and services?
AACSB Coding: Reflective Thinking
Special Feature: None

13. The decision about what goods and services will be produced made in a market economy is made by
    A) lawmakers in the government voting on what will be produced.
    B) workers deciding to produce only what the boss says must be produced.
    C) producers deciding what society wants most.
    D) consumers and firms choosing which goods and services to buy or produce.
    E) consumers dictating to firms what they need most.

Answer: D
Diff: 1   Type: MC   Page Ref: 9/9
Topic: The economic problem that every society must solve
Skill: Definition
Objective: LO 2: Discuss how an economy answers these questions: What goods and services will be produced? How will the goods and services be produced? Who will receive the goods and services?
AACSB Coding: Reflective Thinking
Special Feature: None

14. Which of the following is correct about the economic decisions consumers, firms, and the government have to make?
    A) Governments may face the problem of shortages but not scarcity in making economic decisions.
    B) Only individuals face scarcity; firms and the government do not.
    C) Firms and the government face scarcity, individuals only face shortages.
    D) Each faces the problem of scarcity which necessitates tradeoffs in making economic decisions.

Answer: D
Diff: 1   Type: MC   Page Ref: 9/9
Topic: The economic problem that every society must solve
Skill: Conceptual
Objective: LO 2: Discuss how an economy answers these questions: What goods and services will be produced? How will the goods and services be produced? Who will receive the goods and services?
AACSB Coding: Reflective Thinking
Special Feature: None

15. Why is it necessary for all economic systems to not only provide people with goods and services, but also restrict them from getting as much of these goods and services as they wish?
    A) Failure to do this could reduce the efficiency of the system by producing some goods and services that are not as highly valued as others.
    B) Failure to do this could lead to an inequitable allocation of goods and services produced.
    C) Failure to do this could lead to drastic shortages of good and services.
    D) Failure to do this could reduces efficiency and leads to an inequitable allocation of output.
    Answer: A
    Diff: 3   Type: MC   Page Ref: 10/10
    Topic: The economic problem that every society must solve
    Skill: Analytical
    Objective: LO 2: Discuss how an economy answers these questions: What goods and services will be produced? How will the goods and services be produced? Who will receive the goods and services?
    AACSB Coding: Analytic Skills
    Special Feature: None

16. How does a market system prevent people from getting as many goods and services as they wish?
    A) Governments interfere with the market mechanism to influence the allocation of goods and services.
    B) In a market system, firms can charge any price they want thus, preventing poor people from getting as many goods and services as they wish.
    C) The market system allocates goods and services to those who are able to pay for those products and therefore income is a limiting factor.
    D) The government imposes taxes on those who earn beyond a certain amount of income.
    Answer: C
    Diff: 2   Type: MC   Page Ref: 10/10
    Topic: The economic problem that every society must solve
    Skill: Conceptual
    Objective: LO 2: Discuss how an economy answers these questions: What goods and services will be produced? How will the goods and services be produced? Who will receive the goods and services?
    AACSB Coding: Reflective Thinking
    Special Feature: None

17. Who receives the most of what is produced in a market economy?
    A) Lawmakers and other politically favored groups.
    B) Those who are willing and able to buy them.
    C) Everyone receives an equal amount.
    D) People who earn the highest incomes.
    Answer: B
    Diff: 1   Type: MC   Page Ref: 10/10
    Topic: The economic problem that every society must solve
    Skill: Conceptual
    Objective: LO 2: Discuss how an economy answers these questions: What goods and services will be produced? How will the goods and services be produced? Who will receive the goods and services?
    AACSB Coding: Reflective Thinking
    Special Feature: None

18. How are the fundamental economic decisions determined in Cuba?
    A) Individuals, firms, and the government interact in a market to make these economic decisions.
    B) These decisions are made by the country's elders who have had much experience in answering these questions.
    C) The government decides because Cuba is a centrally planned economy.
    D) The United Nations decides because Cuba is a developing economy.
    Answer: C
    Diff: 1   Type: MC   Page Ref: 9/9
    Topic: The economic problem that every society must solve
    Skill: Factual
    Objective: LO 2: Discuss how an economy answers these questions: What goods and services will be produced? How will the goods and services be produced? Who will receive the goods and services?
    AACSB Coding: Reflective Thinking
    Special Feature: None

19. How are the fundamental economic questions answered in a market economy?
    A) The government alone decides the answers.
    B) Individuals, firms, and the government interact in markets to decide the answers to these questions.
    C) Households and firms interact in markets to decide the answers to these questions.
    D) Large corporations alone decide the answers.
    Answer: C
    Diff: 2   Type: MC   Page Ref: 9/9
    Topic: The economic problem that every society must solve
    Skill: Conceptual
    Objective: LO 2: Discuss how an economy answers these questions: What goods and services will be produced? How will the goods and services be produced? Who will receive the goods and services?
    AACSB Coding: Reflective Thinking
    Special Feature: None

20. Which of the following is a problem inherent in centrally planned economies?
    A) There are no problems and everyone, including consumers, is satisfied.
    B) There is too much production of low-cost, high-quality goods and services.
    C) Production managers are more concerned with satisfying government's orders than with satisfying consumer wants.
    D) Unemployment is too high.
    Answer: C
    Diff: 2   Type: MC   Page Ref: 9/9
    Topic: The economic problem that every society must solve
    Skill: Conceptual
    Objective: LO 2: Discuss how an economy answers these questions: What goods and services will be produced? How will the goods and services be produced? Who will receive the goods and services?
    AACSB Coding: Reflective Thinking
    Special Feature: None

21. All of the following contributed to the downfall of the Soviet Union in 1991 except
    A) public dissatisfaction with low living standards and political repression.
    B) an inability to produce low-cost consumer goods that households wanted.
    C) lack of high-quality goods and services.
    D) lack of a strong dictator who can coordinate economic activities.
    Answer: D
    Diff: 2   Type: MC   Page Ref: 9/9
    Topic: The economic problem that every society must solve
    Skill: Factual
    Objective: LO 2: Discuss how an economy answers these questions: What goods and services will be produced? How will the goods and services be produced? Who will receive the goods and services?
    AACSB Coding: Reflective Thinking
    Special Feature: None

22. When goods and services are produced at the lowest possible cost, _____ occurs.
    A) allocative efficiency
    B) productive efficiency
    C) equity
    D) efficient central planning
    Answer: B
    Diff: 1   Type: MC   Page Ref: 10/10
    Topic: The economic problem that every society must solve
    Skill: Definition
    Objective: LO 2: Discuss how an economy answers these questions: What goods and services will be produced? How will the goods and services be produced? Who will receive the goods and services?
    AACSB Coding: Reflective Thinking
    Special Feature: None

23. Productive efficiency is achieved when
    A) firms add a low profit margin to the goods and services they produce.
    B) firms produce the goods and services that consumers value most.
    C) firms produce goods and services at the lowest cost.
    D) there are no shortages or surpluses in the market.
    Answer: C
    Diff: 1   Type: MC   Page Ref: 10/10
    Topic: The economic problem that every society must solve
    Skill: Definition
    Objective: LO 2: Discuss how an economy answers these questions: What goods and services will be produced? How will the goods and services be produced? Who will receive the goods and services?
    AACSB Coding: Reflective Thinking
    Special Feature: None

24. When production reflects consumer preferences, _____ occurs.
    A) allocative efficiency
    B) productive efficiency
    C) equity
    D) efficient central planning
    Answer: A
    Diff: 1   Type: MC   Page Ref: 10/10
    Topic: The economic problem that every society must solve
    Skill: Definition
    Objective: LO 2: Discuss how an economy answers these questions: What goods and services will be produced? How will the goods and services be produced? Who will receive the goods and services?
    AACSB Coding: Reflective Thinking
    Special Feature: None

25. Allocative efficiency is achieved when
    A) goods and services are fairly distributed among consumers in an economy.
    B) firms produce the goods and services that consumers value most.
    C) firms produce goods and services at the lowest cost.
    D) there are no shortages or surpluses in the market.
    Answer: B
    Diff: 1   Type: MC   Page Ref: 10/10
    Topic: The economic problem that every society must solve
    Skill: Definition
    Objective: LO 2: Discuss how an economy answers these questions: What goods and services will be produced? How will the goods and services be produced? Who will receive the goods and services?
    AACSB Coding: Reflective Thinking
    Special Feature: None

26. Which of the following contributes to the efficiency of markets?
    A) Governments play an active role in the day-to-day operations of markets.
    B) Markets are able to bring about an equitable distribution of goods and services.
    C) Markets promote equal standards of living.
    D) Markets promote competition and voluntary exchange.
    Answer: D
    Diff: 2   Type: MC   Page Ref: 10/10
    Topic: The economic problem that every society must solve
    Skill: Conceptual
    Objective: LO 2: Discuss how an economy answers these questions: What goods and services will be produced? How will the goods and services be produced? Who will receive the goods and services?
    AACSB Coding: Reflective Thinking
    Special Feature: None

27. Which of the following statements is true about competition in a market?
    A) Competition forces firms to outsource the production of their labor-intensive products.
    B) Competition forces firms to undercut their selling price, thus benefiting consumers who will be able to purchase products at the lowest price possible.
    C) Competition forces firms to produce and sell products as long as the marginal benefit to consumers exceeds the marginal cost of production.
    D) Competition forces firms to add only low profit margins to their costs of production.
    Answer: C
    Diff: 2   Type: MC   Page Ref: 10/10
    Topic: The economic problem that every society must solve
    Skill: Conceptual
    Objective: LO 2: Discuss how an economy answers these questions: What goods and services will be produced? How will the goods and services be produced? Who will receive the goods and services?
    AACSB Coding: Reflective Thinking
    Special Feature: None

28. Voluntary exchange increases economic efficiency
    A) because neither the buyer nor the seller would agree to a trade unless they both benefit.
    B) because voluntary exchange only takes place with government permission.
    C) because it is free and consequently does not cost anything.
    D) because it allows wealthy individuals to act altruistically and give to the poor.
    Answer: A
    Diff: 1   Type: MC   Page Ref: 10/10
    Topic: The economic problem that every society must solve
    Skill: Conceptual
    Objective: LO 2: Discuss how an economy answers these questions: What goods and services will be produced? How will the goods and services be produced? Who will receive the goods and services?
    AACSB Coding: Reflective Thinking
    Special Feature: None

29. Which of the following generates productive efficiency?
    A) competition among sellers
    B) competition among buyers
    C) government inspectors
    D) government production rules and regulations
    Answer: A
    Diff: 1   Type: MC   Page Ref: 10/10
    Topic: The economic problem that every society must solve
    Skill: Conceptual
    Objective: LO 2: Discuss how an economy answers these questions: What goods and services will be produced? How will the goods and services be produced? Who will receive the goods and services?
    AACSB Coding: Reflective Thinking
    Special Feature: None

30. Which of the following generates allocative efficiency in a market economy?
    A) national government intervention
    B) voluntary exchange between buyers and sellers
    C) United Nations rules for competition
    D) equity
    Answer: B
    Diff: 1   Type: MC   Page Ref: 10/10
    Topic: The economic problem that every society must solve
    Skill: Conceptual
    Objective: LO 2: Discuss how an economy answers these questions: What goods and services will be produced? How will the goods and services be produced? Who will receive the goods and services?
    AACSB Coding: Reflective Thinking
    Special Feature: None

31. Which of the following is a result of a market economy?
    A) environmental protection
    B) an equal income distribution
    C) agreement on equity
    D) voluntary exchange
    Answer: D
    Diff: 1   Type: MC   Page Ref: 10/10
    Topic: The economic problem that every society must solve
    Skill: Conceptual
    Objective: LO 2: Discuss how an economy answers these questions: What goods and services will be produced? How will the goods and services be produced? Who will receive the goods and services?
    AACSB Coding: Reflective Thinking
    Special Feature: None

32. Selling tickets to graduation ceremonies has long been a tradition among students at institutions that limit the number of guests. Suppose your classmate, Heidi purchased two tickets for $40 each. Is this transaction economically efficient?
    A) No, people should never be allowed to sell items they received for free.
    B) Yes, it was a voluntary exchange that benefited both parties.
    C) No, Heidi paid too much for the tickets.
    D) Yes, it is efficient only from the perspective of the seller and not from the perspective of the buyer.
    Answer: B
    Diff: 2   Type: MC   Page Ref: 10/10
    Topic: The economic problem that every society must solve
    Skill: Conceptual
    Objective: LO 2: Discuss how an economy answers these questions: What goods and services will be produced? How will the goods and services be produced? Who will receive the goods and services?
    AACSB Coding: Analytic Skills
    Special Feature: None

33. In economics, the term "equity" means
    A) everyone has an equal standard of living.
    B) the hardest working individuals consume all they want.
    C) only elected officials have high standards of living.
    D) economic benefits are distributed fairly.
    Answer: D
    Diff: 1   Type: MC   Page Ref: 10/10
    Topic: The economic problem that every society must solve
    Skill: Definition
    Objective: LO 2: Discuss how an economy answers these questions: What goods and services will be produced? How will the goods and services be produced? Who will receive the goods and services?
    AACSB Coding: Reflective Thinking
    Special Feature: None

34. Which of the following is motivated by an equity concern?
    A) Some US colleges have cut back on merit scholarships since these programs siphon money from need-based programs, thus harming lower-income students with greater financial need.
    B) Following the removal of subsidies in urban water use, household demand for water decreased quite significantly in Bogor, Indonesia.
    C) In November 2003, the Federal Communications Commission implemented the "local number portability" rule which gives cell phone customers the option of keeping their number when they switch carriers within the same geographic region.
    D) The United States protects intellectual property rights, allowing inventors to prevent others from using their inventions without payment.

Answer: A
Diff: 3   Type: MC   Page Ref: 10/10
Topic: The economic problem that every society must solve
Skill: Conceptual
Objective: LO 2: Discuss how an economy answers these questions: What goods and services will be produced? How will the goods and services be produced? Who will receive the goods and services?
AACSB Coding: Reflective Thinking, Ethical Reasoning
Special Feature: None

35. Which of the following is motivated by an efficiency concern?
    A) In December 2006, the Bush administration restarted a short-term housing assistance program for victims of Hurricane Katrina.
    B) Each year, the University of Notre Dame conducts a lottery to parcel out the 30,000 seats available to contributors, former athletes and parents in the 80,000-seat stadium.
    C) The United Network for Organ Sharing advocates a system of rationing scarce kidneys that would favor young patients over old in an effort to wring more life out of donated organs.
    D) The federal government's housing choice voucher program assists very low-income families, the elderly, and the disabled to afford decent, safe, and sanitary housing in the private market.

Answer: C
Diff: 3   Type: MC   Page Ref: 10/10
Topic: The economic problem that every society must solve
Skill: Conceptual
Objective: LO 2: Discuss how an economy answers these questions: What goods and services will be produced? How will the goods and services be produced? Who will receive the goods and services?
AACSB Coding: Reflective Thinking, Ethical Reasoning
Special Feature: None

36. Which of the following is not an example of an efficiency-equity tradeoff faced by economic agents?

    A) According to an article by in the American Journal of Public Health by Edward Kaplan and Michael Merson of Yale University School of Medicine, the federal government's current method of allocating HIV-prevention resources is not cost-effective. Instead of allocating resources to states in proportion to reported AIDS cases, resources should flow first to those activities that prevent more infections per dollar and then to less and less effective combinations of programs and populations until funds are exhausted, even if it means that some populations would be left without any prevention services.

    B) Concerned about the falling birth rate, the French government has pledged more money for families with three children, in an effort to encourage working women to have more babies.

    C) The growing demand for corn by ethanol producers has led to a surge in the price of tortillas, a staple in the Mexican diet. To quell public outcry over rising tortilla prices, the Mexican government released government corn stocks at prices well below the market, and pressured states to impose price ceilings on tortillas.

    D) Some US colleges cut back on merit scholarships since these programs siphon money from need-based programs, thus harming lower-income students with greater financial need.

    Answer: B
    Diff: 3   Type: MC   Page Ref: 10/10
    Topic: The economic problem that every society must solve
    Skill: Analytical
    Objective: LO 2: Discuss how an economy answers these questions: What goods and services will be produced? How will the goods and services be produced? Who will receive the goods and services?
    AACSB Coding: Analytic Skills, Ethical Reasoning
    Special Feature: None

37. Which of the following correctly describes the relationship between economic efficiency and economic equity?
    A) They are both automatically achieved in a free market economy.
    B) They always call for opposite outcomes.
    C) There is no conflict between the two goals.
    D) There is often a trade-off between the two.

    Answer: D
    Diff: 2   Type: MC   Page Ref: 10/10
    Topic: The economic problem that every society must solve
    Skill: Conceptual
    Objective: LO 2: Discuss how an economy answers these questions: What goods and services will be produced? How will the goods and services be produced? Who will receive the goods and services?
    AACSB Coding: Reflective Thinking
    Special Feature: None

38. The government makes all economic decisions in a centrally planned economy.
    Answer: ⊙ True   False
    Diff: 1   Type: TF   Page Ref: 9/9
    Topic: The economic problem that every society must solve
    Skill: Conceptual
    Objective: LO 2: Discuss how an economy answers these questions: What goods and services will be produced? How will the goods and services be produced? Who will receive the goods and services?
    AACSB Coding: Reflective Thinking
    Special Feature: None

39. When voluntary exchange takes place, both parties gain from the exchange.
    Answer: ⊙ True   False
    Diff: 1   Type: TF   Page Ref: 10/10
    Topic: The economic problem that every society must solve
    Skill: Conceptual
    Objective: LO 2: Discuss how an economy answers these questions: What goods and services will be produced? How will the goods and services be produced? Who will receive the goods and services?
    AACSB Coding: Reflective Thinking
    Special Feature: None

40. A college must decide if it wants to offer more evening and weekend classes. This decision involves answering the economic question of "for whom to produce".
    Answer: True   ⊙ False
    Diff: 1   Type: TF   Page Ref: 9/9
    Topic: The economic problem that every society must solve
    Skill: Conceptual
    Objective: LO 2: Discuss how an economy answers these questions: What goods and services will be produced? How will the goods and services be produced? Who will receive the goods and services?
    AACSB Coding: Reflective Thinking
    Special Feature: None

41. One desirable outcome of a market economy is that it leads to a more equitable distribution of income.
    Answer: True   ⊙ False
    Diff: 1   Type: TF   Page Ref: 10/10
    Topic: The economic problem that every society must solve
    Skill: Conceptual
    Objective: LO 2: Discuss how an economy answers these questions: What goods and services will be produced? How will the goods and services be produced? Who will receive the goods and services?
    AACSB Coding: Reflective Thinking
    Special Feature: None

42. What is the difference between economic efficiency and equity?

Answer: Economic efficiency is concerned with maximizing the value of output that can be generated by a given resource base while equity deals with the distribution of society's total output among the sectors and individuals of society.

Diff: 2   Type: SA   Page Ref: 10/10
Topic: The economic problem that every society must solve
Skill: Definition
Objective: LO 2: Discuss how an economy answers these questions: What goods and services will be produced? How will the goods and services be produced? Who will receive the goods and services?
AACSB Coding: Reflective Thinking
Special Feature: None

43. Define productive efficiency. Does productive efficiency imply allocative efficiency? Explain.

Answer: Productive efficiency is an efficiency criterion that describes a situation in which goods and services are produced at the lowest possible cost. It does not imply allocative efficiency which is a criterion associated with producing goods and services that consumers value most. For example, a manufacturer may be able to produce typewriters at the lowest possible cost of say, $200 but this does not necessarily mean that consumers are willing to pay $200 for a typewriter.

Diff: 3   Type: SA   Page Ref: 10/10
Topic: The economic problem that every society must solve
Skill: Definition, Conceptual
Objective: LO 2: Discuss how an economy answers these questions: What goods and services will be produced? How will the goods and services be produced? Who will receive the goods and services?
AACSB Coding: Analytic Skills
Special Feature: None

44. Define allocative efficiency. Explain the significance of this concept in economics?

Answer: Allocative efficiency is an efficiency criterion that describes a situation where the marginal benefit (or marginal valuation) of the last unit purchased is equal to the marginal cost of producing that unit. In other words, allocative efficiency occurs when production reflects consumer preferences. This is a significant concept in that all societies face scarcity which necessitates that societies make choices about what goods and services to produce. To maximize society's wealth, resources must flow to their highest valued use. This value is determined by consumers.

Diff: 3   Type: SA   Page Ref: 10/10
Topic: The economic problem that every society must solve
Skill: Definition, Conceptual
Objective: LO 2: Discuss how an economy answers these questions: What goods and services will be produced? How will the goods and services be produced? Who will receive the goods and services?
AACSB Coding: Reflective Thinking
Special Feature: None

1.3   Economic Models

1. Economic models do all of the following except
    A) answer economic questions.
    B) portray reality in all its minute details.
    C) make economic ideas explicit and concrete for use by decision makers.
    D) simplify some aspect of economic life.
    Answer: B
    Diff: 1   Type: MC   Page Ref: 11/11
    Topic: Economic Models
    Skill: Definition
    Objective: LO 3: Understand the role of models in economic analysis
    AACSB Coding: Reflective Thinking
    Special Feature: None

2. Which of the following is part of an economic model?
    A) assumptions
    B) norms
    C) opinions
    D) preferences of economic agents
    Answer: A
    Diff: 1   Type: MC   Page Ref: 11/11
    Topic: Economic Models
    Skill: Definition
    Objective: LO 3: Understand the role of models in economic analysis
    AACSB Coding: Reflective Thinking
    Special Feature: None

3. Which of the following statements is false about positive economic analysis?
    A) Positive analysis uses an economic model to estimate the costs and benefits of different course of actions.
    B) Positive analysis uses an economic model to estimate the costs and benefits of different course of actions.
    C) There is much more disagreement among economists over positive economic analysis than over normative economic analysis.
    D) Unlike normative economic analysis, positive economic analysis can be tested.
    Answer: C
    Diff: 2   Type: MC   Page Ref: 14/14
    Topic: Economic Models
    Skill: Conceptual
    Objective: LO 3: Understand the role of models in economic analysis
    AACSB Coding: Reflective Thinking
    Special Feature: None

4. Which of the following is a positive economic statement?
   A) Everyone should live at the same standard of living.
   B) If the price of gasoline rises, a smaller quantity of it will be bought.
   C) The government should close income tax loopholes.
   D) U.S. firms should not be allowed to outsource production of goods and services.
   Answer: B
   Diff: 2   Type: MC   Page Ref: 14/14
   Topic: Economic Models
   Skill: Conceptual
   Objective: LO 3: Understand the role of models in economic analysis
   AACSB Coding: Reflective Thinking
   Special Feature: None

5. Which of the following is a positive economic statement?
   A) People should not buy SUVs.
   B) The government should mandate electric automobiles.
   C) Scarcity necessitates that people make trade–offs.
   D) Foreign workers should not be allowed to work for lower wages than the citizens of a country.
   Answer: C
   Diff: 2   Type: MC   Page Ref: 14/14
   Topic: Economic Models
   Skill: Conceptual
   Objective: LO 3: Understand the role of models in economic analysis
   AACSB Coding: Reflective Thinking
   Special Feature: None

6. Which of the following is a normative economic statement?
   A) Rising global demand for diesel and heating oil has led to increases in the price of crude oil.
   B) With falling home prices and rising mortgage interest rates, the amount of foreclosures has increased.
   C) The federal government is considering raising the gasoline tax to promote the use of public transportation.
   D) Fashion designers should be allowed to copyright designs to promote innovation.
   Answer: D
   Diff: 2   Type: MC   Page Ref: 14/14
   Topic: Economic Models
   Skill: Conceptual
   Objective: LO 3: Understand the role of models in economic analysis
   AACSB Coding: Ethical Reasoning
   Special Feature: None

7. Which of the following is a normative economic statement?
   A) The price of gasoline is too high.
   B) The current high price of gasoline is the result of strong worldwide demand.
   C) When the price of gasoline rises, the quantity of gasoline purchased falls.
   D) When the price of gasoline rises, transportation costs rise.
   Answer: A
   Diff: 2   Type: MC   Page Ref: 14/14
   Topic: Economic Models
   Skill: Conceptual
   Objective: LO 3: Understand the role of models in economic analysis
   AACSB Coding: Reflective Thinking
   Special Feature: None

8. Which of the following statements best characterizes the disagreements between Paul Samuelson and Jagdish Bhagwati in the debate about over outsourcing?
   A) Their disagreements are grounded in positive economic analysis. They disagree about the model and the assumptions used in the model.
   B) Their disagreements are grounded in positive economic analysis. They disagree about the relevant economic statistics used in the model.
   C) Their disagreements are grounded in normative economic analysis. They disagree over how to interpret the relevant economic statistics.
   D) Their disagreements are grounded in normative economic analysis. They disagree over the types of jobs lost to outsourcing.

   Answer: C
   Diff: 2   Type: MC   Page Ref: 13/13
   Topic: Economic Models
   Skill: Analytical
   Objective: LO 3: Understand the role of models in economic analysis
   AACSB Coding: Analytic Skills
   Special Feature: Making the Connection: When Economists Disagree: A Debate over Outsourcing

9. The economic analysis of minimum wage involves both normative and positive analysis. Consider the following consequences of a minimum wage:
   a.   The minimum wage law causes unemployment.
   b.   A minimum wage law benefits some groups and hurts others.
   c.   In some cities such as San Francisco and New York, it would be impossible for low-skilled workers to live in the city without minimum wage laws.
   d.   The gains to winners of a minimum wage law should be valued more highly than the losses to losers because the latter primarily comprises businesses.

   Which of the consequences above are positive statements and which are normative statements?
   A) A, b, and c are positive statements and d is a normative statement.
   B) A and b are positive statements, c and d are normative statement.
   C) Only a is a positive statement, b, c and d are normative statements.
   D) A and c are positive statements, b and d are normative statements
   Answer: B
   Diff: 2   Type: MC   Page Ref: 14/14
   Topic: Economic Models
   Skill: Analytical
   Objective: LO 3: Understand the role of models in economic analysis
   AACSB Coding: Analytic Skills
   Special Feature: Don't Let This happen to YOU!: Don't Confuse Positive Analysis with Normative Analysis

10. "A decrease in the price of digital cameras will decrease the demand for camera film." This statement is an example of a positive economic statement.
    Answer: ⊚ True   False
    Diff: 1   Type: TF   Page Ref: 14/14
    Topic: Economic Models
    Skill: Conceptual
    Objective: LO 3: Understand the role of models in economic analysis
    AACSB Coding: Reflective Thinking
    Special Feature: None

11. "The distribution of income should be left to the market" is an example of a positive economic statement.
    Answer: True   ⊚ False
    Diff: 1   Type: TF   Page Ref: 14/14
    Topic: Economic Models
    Skill: Conceptual
    Objective: LO 3: Understand the role of models in economic analysis
    AACSB Coding: Reflective Thinking
    Special Feature: None

12. Policies based on normative economic ideas tend to increase economic efficiency and improve equity.

Answer: True   ○ False

Diff: 2   Type: TF   Page Ref: 14/14
Topic: Economic Models
Skill: Conceptual
Objective: LO 3: Understand the role of models in economic analysis
AACSB Coding: Reflective Thinking
Special Feature: None

13. What is the difference between positive economic analysis and normative economic analysis? Give one example each of a positive and normative economic issue or question or statement.

Answer: Positive economic analysis is concerned with what is. Positive economic analysis reaches conclusions based on verifiable statements. Normative economic analysis, on the other hand, is concerned with what ought to be. Normative analysis reaches conclusions based on opinions. (Students will give many different examples.)

Diff: 2   Type: SA   Page Ref: 14/14
Topic: Economic Models
Skill: Definition, Conceptual
Objective: LO 3: Understand the role of models in economic analysis
AACSB Coding: Reflective Thinking
Special Feature: None

1.4   Microeconomics and Macroeconomics

1. Which of the following is a microeconomics question?
   A) How much will be saved and how much will be produced in the entire economy?
   B) What will the level of economic growth be in the entire economy?
   C) What factors determine the price of carrots?
   D) What determines the average price level and inflation?

Answer: C

Diff: 2   Type: MC   Page Ref: 15/15
Topic: Microeconomics and Macroeconomics
Skill: Conceptual
Objective: LO 4: Distinguish between microeconomics and macroeconomics
AACSB Coding: Reflective Thinking
Special Feature: None

2. The branch of economics which studies how households and firms make choices, interact in markets and how government attempts to influence their choices is called
    A) macroeconomics.
    B) microeconomics.
    C) positive economics.
    D) normative economics.
Answer: B
Diff: 1   Type: MC   Page Ref: 15/15
Topic: Microeconomics and Macroeconomics
Skill: Definition
Objective: LO 4: Distinguish between microeconomics and macroeconomics
AACSB Coding: Reflective Thinking
Special Feature: None

3. Which of the following is a macroeconomics question?
    A) What determines the inflation rate?
    B) What determines the production of DVDs?
    C) What factors determine the price of carrots?
    D) What determines the wage of auto workers?
Answer: A
Diff: 2   Type: MC   Page Ref: 15/15
Topic: Microeconomics and Macroeconomics
Skill: Conceptual
Objective: LO 4: Distinguish between microeconomics and macroeconomics
AACSB Coding: Reflective Thinking
Special Feature: None

4. The branch of economics which studies the behavior of entire economies and policies that affect the economy as a whole is called
    A) public economics.
    B) microeconomics.
    C) macroeconomics.
    D) normative economics.
Answer: C
Diff: 1   Type: MC   Page Ref: 15/15
Topic: Microeconomics and Macroeconomics
Skill: Definition
Objective: LO 4: Distinguish between microeconomics and macroeconomics
AACSB Coding: Reflective Thinking
Special Feature: None

5. Examining the conditions that could lead to a recession in an economy is an example of macroeconomics topic.
Answer: True   False
Diff: 1   Type: TF   Page Ref: 15/15
Topic: Microeconomics and Macroeconomics
Skill: Conceptual
Objective: LO 4: Distinguish between microeconomics and macroeconomics
AACSB Coding: Reflective Thinking
Special Feature: None

6. According to a Wall Street Journal article, there are nearly 75,000 patients in the U.S. awaiting kidney transplants. To move more people off the wait list, economists along with computer experts and surgeons are developing a market for kidney swapping. This is an example of a macroeconomics topic.
Source: Laura Meckler, "Kidney Swaps Seen as a Way to Ease Donor Shortage", Wall Street Journal, page A1, Oct 15, 2007.
Answer: True   ⊚ False
Diff: 1   Type: TF   Page Ref: 15/15
Topic: Microeconomics and Macroeconomics
Skill: Conceptual
Objective: LO 4: Distinguish between microeconomics and macroeconomics
AACSB Coding: Reflective Thinking
Special Feature: None

7. How does the study of microeconomics differ from that of macroeconomics? Give one example each of an issue studies in microeconomics and in macroeconomics.
Answer: Microeconomics is the study of how household and businesses make choices, how they interact in markets, and how the government attempts to influence their choices while macroeconomics is the study of the economy as a whole including topic like unemployment, inflation and economic growth. (Students will give many different examples.)
Diff: 2   Type: SA   Page Ref: 15/15
Topic: Microeconomics and Macroeconomics
Skill: Definition, Conceptual
Objective: LO 4: Distinguish between microeconomics and macroeconomics
AACSB Coding: Reflective Thinking
Special Feature: None

1.5   A Preview of Important Economic Terms

1. Which of the following statements is true about profit?
   A) Profit refers to the revenue received from the sale of a quantity of goods.
   B) Profit is calculated by multiplying price and quantity sold.
   C) The terms "accounting profit" and "economic profit" can be used interchangeably.
   D) Profit is the difference between revenue and cost.
Answer: D
Diff: 2   Type: MC   Page Ref: 16/16
Topic: A Preview of some important economic terms
Skill: Definition
Objective: LO 5: Become familiar with important economic terms
AACSB Coding: Reflective Thinking
Special Feature: None

2. Human capital refers to
   A) the money people have.
   B) the machines workers have to work with.
   C) the accumulated skills and training workers have.
   D) the wealth people have.
   Answer: C
   Diff: 1   Type: MC   Page Ref: 16/16
   Topic: A Preview of some important economic terms
   Skill: Definition
   Objective: LO 5: Become familiar with important economic terms
   AACSB Coding: Reflective Thinking
   Special Feature: None

3. Which of the following is an example of an activity undertaken by an entrepreneur?
   A) designing your landscaping for your new home
   B) holding a position as the president of a liberal arts college
   C) running for the president of the United States
   D) starting your own pet sitting business
   Answer: D
   Diff: 1   Type: MC   Page Ref: 16/16
   Topic: A Preview of some important economic terms
   Skill: Definition
   Objective: LO 5: Become familiar with important economic terms
   AACSB Coding: Reflective Thinking
   Special Feature: None

4. Which of the following is counted as "capital" in economics?
   A) the money people have
   B) the machines workers have to work with
   C) the accumulated skills and training workers have
   D) the wealth people have
   Answer: B
   Diff: 2   Type: MC   Page Ref: 16/16
   Topic: A Preview of some important economic terms
   Skill: Conceptual
   Objective: LO 5: Become familiar with important economic terms
   AACSB Coding: Reflective Thinking
   Special Feature: None

5. Technology is defined as
    A) the process of developing and revising models.
    B) new innovations and creations.
    C) the processes used to produce goods and services.
    D) the process of recycling products.
    Answer: C
    Diff: 1   Type: MC   Page Ref: 16/16
    Topic: A Preview of some important economic terms
    Skill: Definition
    Objective: LO 5: Become familiar with important economic terms
    AACSB Coding: Reflective Thinking
    Special Feature: None

6. Which of the following statements about economic resources is false?
    A) Economic resources include financial capital and money.
    B) Economic resources are also called factors of production.
    C) Economic resources are used to produce goods and services.
    D) Some economic resources are human-made while others are found in nature.
    Answer: A
    Diff: 1   Type: MC   Page Ref: 16/16
    Topic: A Preview of some important economic terms
    Skill: Definition
    Objective: LO 5: Become familiar with important economic terms
    AACSB Coding: Reflective Thinking
    Special Feature: None

7. In the market for factors of production, firms earn income by selling goods and services to households.
    Answer: True   ⊘ False
    Diff: 1   Type: TF   Page Ref: 16/16
    Topic: A Preview of some important economic terms
    Skill: Conceptual
    Objective: LO 5: Become familiar with important economic terms
    AACSB Coding: Reflective Thinking
    Special Feature: None

8. One example of human capital is the amount of savings that you have.
    Answer: True   ⊘ False
    Diff: 1   Type: TF   Page Ref: 16/16
    Topic: A Preview of some important economic terms
    Skill: Conceptual
    Objective: LO 5: Become familiar with important economic terms
    AACSB Coding: Reflective Thinking
    Special Feature: None

9. What is the difference between an invention and an innovation?

Answer: An invention is the development of a new good or a new process for making a good. An innovation is the practical application of an invention. Innovation could also refer to any significant improvement in a good or in the means of producing a good.

Diff: 1   Type: SA   Page Ref: 15/15
Topic: A Preview of some important economic terms
Skill: Conceptual
Objective: LO 5: Become familiar with important economic terms
AACSB Coding: Reflective Thinking
Special Feature: None

1.6 Appendix: Using Graphs and Models

1. If a graph has a line that shows the amount of outsourcing in the last ten years, it is known as
    A) a pie chart.
    B) a time series graph.
    C) a demand curve for outsourcing.
    D) a supply curve of outsourcing.

Answer: B

Diff: 1   Type: MC   Page Ref: 26/26
Topic: Appendix: Using Graphs and Formulas
Skill: Definition
Objective: Appendix: Review the use of graphs and formulas
AACSB Coding: Reflective Thinking
Special Feature: None

2. Two-dimensional graphs have a horizontal and a vertical axis and are used in economics to illustrate
    A) relationships between two economic variables.
    B) one variable.
    C) a flow chart.
    D) a pie chart.

Answer: A

Diff: 1   Type: MC   Page Ref: 27/27
Topic: Appendix: Using Graphs and Formulas
Skill: Definition
Objective: Appendix: Review the use of graphs and formulas
AACSB Coding: Reflective Thinking
Special Feature: None

3. If a straight line passes through the point $x = 14$ and $y = 3$ and also through the point $x = 4$ and $y = 10$, the slope of this line is
    A) negative 11 divided by 6.
    B) seven tenths.
    C) negative seven tenths.
    D) 6 divided by 11.
   Answer: C
   Diff: 2   Type: MC   Page Ref: 27/27
   Topic: Appendix: Using Graphs and Formulas
   Skill: Analytical
   Objective: Appendix: Review the use of graphs and formulas
   AACSB Coding: Reflective Thinking
   Special Feature: None

4. How can the influence of a third variable be shown on a two-dimensional graph?
    A) by allowing the relationship to be nonlinear
    B) by allowing the position of the relationship line or curve to shift on the graph
    C) by drawing a third axis coming out of the two axes
    D) by super-imposing the third variable on the two-dimensional graph
   Answer: B
   Diff: 3   Type: MC   Page Ref: 28/28
   Topic: Appendix: Using Graphs and Formulas
   Skill: Conceptual
   Objective: Appendix: Review the use of graphs and formulas
   AACSB Coding: Analytic Skills
   Special Feature: None

5. Which of the following statements is false?
    A) An inverse relationship has a negative slope value.
    B) A direct relationship has a positive slope value.
    C) A curved line has slope values that change at every point.
    D) A straight line has a slope of zero.
   Answer: D
   Diff: 2   Type: MC   Page Ref: 28/28
   Topic: Appendix: Using Graphs and Formulas
   Skill: Conceptual
   Objective: Appendix: Review the use of graphs and formulas
   AACSB Coding: Reflective Thinking
   Special Feature: None

6. The relationship between sales and revenue is
    A) an inverse relationship.
    B) a direct relationship.
    C) a negative relationship.
    D) independent.
    Answer: B
    Diff: 1   Type: MC   Page Ref: 28/28
    Topic: Appendix: Using Graphs and Formulas
    Skill: Conceptual
    Objective: Appendix: Review the use of graphs and formulas
    AACSB Coding: Reflective Thinking
    Special Feature: None

7. Suppose when the price of laptops fall, college students buy more laptops. This implies that
    A) there is a positive relationship between laptop prices and quantities purchased by
       college students.
    B) there is a negative relationship between laptop prices and quantities purchased by
       college students.
    C) there is a direct relationship between laptop prices and quantities purchased by college
       students.
    D) there is a one-to-one relationship between laptop prices and quantities purchased by
       college students.
    Answer: B
    Diff: 1   Type: MC   Page Ref: 28/28
    Topic: Appendix: Using Graphs and Formulas
    Skill: Conceptual
    Objective: Appendix: Review the use of graphs and formulas
    AACSB Coding: Reflective Thinking
    Special Feature: None

8. If the price of gasoline was $1.25 a gallon and it is now $2.25 a gallon, what is the percentage
   change in price?
    A) 4.4 percent
    B) 8 percent
    C) 44 percent
    D) 80 percent
    Answer: D
    Diff: 1   Type: MC   Page Ref: 33/33
    Topic: Appendix: Using Graphs and Formulas
    Skill: Analytical
    Objective: Appendix: Review the use of graphs and formulas
    AACSB Coding: Reflective Thinking
    Special Feature: None

9. In 2001, Hooverville consumed 205,000 tons of sugar. In 2002, sugar consumption rose to 245,000 tons. Calculate the percentage change in sugar consumption.
    A) 8.37%
    B) 11.95%
    C) 19.51%
    D) 26.33%
Answer: C
Diff: 1   Type: MC   Page Ref: 33/33
Topic: Appendix: Using Graphs and Formulas
Skill: Conceptual
Objective: Appendix: Review the use of graphs and formulas
AACSB Coding: Reflective Thinking
Special Feature: None

10. At a recent company meeting, Geraldine Erwin, sales manager of Dastoria, a flavored beverage producer announced, "We have increased our sales by 8 percent in just six months." Suppose six months ago, its sales amounted to $452,000, what is the value of its sales today?
    A) $36,160
    B) $488,160
    C) $415,840
    D) $565,000
Answer: B
Diff: 1   Type: MC   Page Ref: 33/33
Topic: Appendix: Using Graphs and Formulas
Skill: Conceptual
Objective: Appendix: Review the use of graphs and formulas
AACSB Coding: Reflective Thinking
Special Feature: None

Figure 1-1

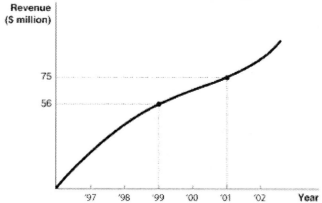

11. *Refer to Figure 1-1.* Using the information in the figure above, calculate the percentage change in sales of alcoholic beverages between 1999 and 2001.
    A) 33.9%
    B) 19%
    C) 25.3%
    D) 13.4%
Answer: A
Diff: 1   Type: MC   Page Ref: 33/33
Topic: Appendix: Using Graphs and Formulas
Skill: Conceptual
Objective: Appendix: Review the use of graphs and formulas
AACSB Coding: Reflective Thinking
Special Feature: None

Figure 1–2

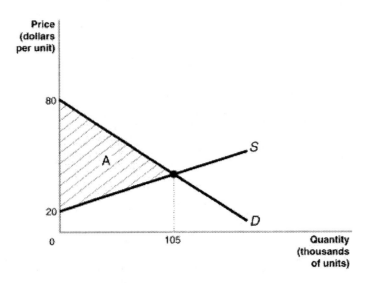

12. *Refer to Figure 1–2.* Calculate the area of the triangle *A*.
    A) $8.4 million
    B) $3.15 million
    C) $6.3 million
    D) $2.1 million
    Answer: B
    Diff: 1   Type: MC   Page Ref: 33/33
    Topic: Appendix: Using Graphs and Formulas
    Skill: Conceptual
    Objective: Appendix: Review the use of graphs and formulas
    AACSB Coding: Analytic Skills
    Special Feature: None

Figure 1-3

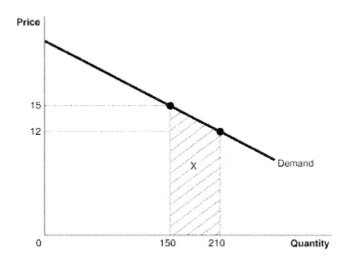

13. *Refer to Figure 1-3.* Calculate the area of the trapezoid X.
    A) $270
    B) $720
    C) $810
    D) $2,520
   Answer: C
   Diff: 2   Type: MC   Page Ref: 33/33
   Topic: Appendix: Using Graphs and Formulas
   Skill: Conceptual
   Objective: Appendix: Review the use of graphs and formulas
   AACSB Coding: Analytic Skills
   Special Feature: None

Figure 1–4

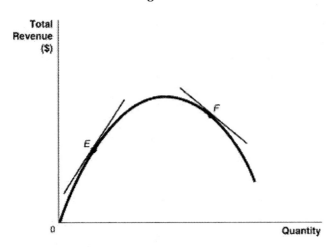

14. *Refer to Figure 1–4.* Which of the following statements is true?
    A) The slope of the tangent at X is positive and the slope of the tangent at Y is negative.
    B) The slope of the tangent at X is negative and the slope of the tangent at Y is positive.
    C) The slope of the tangent at X and the slope of the tangent at Y are negative.
    D) The slope of the tangent at X and the slope of the tangent at Y are positive.
    Answer: A
    Diff: 1   Type: MC   Page Ref: 31/31
    Topic: Appendix: Using Graphs and Formulas
    Skill: Conceptual
    Objective: Appendix: Review the use of graphs and formulas
    AACSB Coding: Analytic Skills
    Special Feature: None

15. What is the "omitted variable" problem in determining cause and effect?
    A) It is a problem that arises when an insignificant variable is given too much weight in an economic analysis leading to skewed conclusions about cause and effect.
    B) It is a problem that arises when a significant variable is not given enough weight in an economic experiment leading to skewed conclusions about cause and effect.
    C) It is a problem that arises when an insignificant economic variable that should have been omitted is included in an economic experiment leading to false conclusions about cause and effect.
    D) It is a problem that arises when an economic variable that affects other variables is omitted from an analysis and its omission leads to false conclusions about cause and effect.
    Answer: D
    Diff: 1   Type: MC   Page Ref: 30/30
    Topic: Appendix: Using Graphs and Formulas
    Skill: Definition
    Objective: Appendix: Review the use of graphs and formulas
    AACSB Coding: Reflective Thinking
    Special Feature: None

16. What is the "reverse causality" problem in determining cause and effect?
    A) It is a problem that occurs when one concludes that a change in variable X caused a change in variable Y when in actual fact, it is a change in variable Z that caused a change in variable Y.
    B) It is a problem that occurs when one observes that a change in variable X caused a change in variable Y which caused a change in variable Z and concludes that a change in variable X caused a change in variable Z.
    C) It is a problem that occurs when one concludes that a change in variable X caused a change in variable Y when in actual fact, it is a change in variable Y that caused a change in variable X.
    D) It is a problem that arises when two variables are inter-connected so that a change in variable X causes a change in variable Y, and a change in variable Y causes a change in variable X.

Answer: C
Diff: 1   Type: MC   Page Ref: 30/30
Topic: Appendix: Using Graphs and Formulas
Skill: Definition
Objective: Appendix: Review the use of graphs and formulas
AACSB Coding: Reflective Thinking
Special Feature: None

17. The prevalence of Alzheimer's dementia is very high among residents living in nursing homes. A student concludes that it is likely that living in nursing home causes Alzheimer's dementia. What is the flaw in the student's reasoning?
    A) The student has failed to take into account other causes of Alzheimer's disease.
    B) The student is drawing a false conclusion; he is confusing cause and effect.
    C) The student is using an inadequate sample size.
    D) The student is drawing a false conclusion by making the mistake of omitting critical variables such as the age and gender of the residents.

Answer: B
Diff: 2   Type: MC   Page Ref: 30/30
Topic: Appendix: Using Graphs and Formulas
Skill: Conceptual
Objective: Appendix: Review the use of graphs and formulas
AACSB Coding: Analytic Skills
Special Feature: None

18. You explain to your friend, Haslina who runs a catering service called "Meals in a Zip" about an economic theory asserts that consumers will purchase less of a product at higher prices than they will at lower prices. She contends that the theory is incorrect because over the past two years she has raised the price of her catered meals and yet has seen a brisk increase in sales. How would you respond to Haslina?

    A) Haslina is right; she has evidence to back her claim. The theory must be erroneous.
    B) I will explain to her that she is making the error of reverse causality: it is the increase in demand that has enabled her to raise her prices
    C) I will explain to her that there are some omitted variables that have contributed to an increase in her sales such as changes in income.
    D) Haslina is making the mistake of assuming that correlation implies causation.

    Answer: C
    Diff: 2   Type: MC   Page Ref: 30/30
    Topic: Appendix: Using Graphs and Formulas
    Skill: Conceptual
    Objective: Appendix: Review the use of graphs and formulas
    AACSB Coding: Reflective Thinking
    Special Feature: None

19.

Table 1–2

Year	Flat–panel TV sets (millions)
2003	1.00
2004	1.5
2005	7.3
2006	12.7
2007*	20

Refer to Table 1–2. The table above shows the sales and projected sales (*) of flat–panel television sets in North America. Present the information using a bar graph.

Answer:

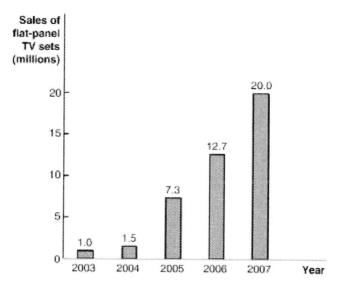

Diff: 1 *Type: SA* *Page Ref: 25/25*
Topic: Appendix: Using Graphs and Formulas
Skill: Conceptual
Objective: Appendix: Review the use of graphs and formulas
AACSB Coding: Analytic Skills
Special Feature: None

Chapter 2   Trade-offs, Comparative Advantage, and the Market System

2.1   Production Possibilities Frontiers and Opportunity Costs

1. Scarcity
    A) stems from the incompatibility between limited resources and unlimited wants.
    B) can be overcome by discovering new resources.
    C) can be eliminated by rationing products.
    D) is a bigger problem in market economies than in socialist economies.
    Answer: A
    Diff: 2   Type: MC   Page Ref: 38/38
    Topic: Production Possibilities Frontier and Opportunity Costs
    Skill: Conceptual
    Objective: LO 1: Use a production possibilities frontier to analyze opportunity costs and trade–offs
    AACSB Coding: Reflective Thinking
    Special Feature: None

2. In 2002, BMW made a tactical decision to use a robot to attach the gearbox to the engines of its vehicles instead of using two workers as it had done previously. The robot method had a higher cost but installed the gearbox in exactly the right position. In making this decision, BMW
    A) faced no tradeoffs because the robot method increased efficiency.
    B) faced a tradeoff between higher cost and lower precision (in installing the gearbox in exactly the right position)
    C) adopted a negative technological change because it replaced workers with robots.
    D) eroded some of its competitiveness in the luxury car market because of its increased cost of production.
    Answer: B
    Diff: 2   Type: MC   Page Ref: 36/36
    Topic: Production Possibilities Frontier and Opportunity Costs
    Skill: Analytical
    Objective: LO 1: Use a production possibilities frontier to analyze opportunity costs and trade–offs
    AACSB Coding: Analytic Skills
    Special Feature: Chapter Opener: Managers Making Choices at BMW

3. The principle of opportunity cost is that
   A) in a market economy, taking advantage of profitable opportunities involves some
      money cost.
   B) the economic cost of using a factor of production is the alternative use of that factor
      that is given up.
   C) taking advantage of investment opportunities involves costs.
   D) the cost of production varies depending on the opportunity for technological
      application.

Answer: B
Diff: 2   Type: MC   Page Ref: 38/38
Topic: Production Possibilities Frontier and Opportunity Costs
Skill: Conceptual
Objective: LO 1: Use a production possibilities frontier to analyze opportunity costs and trade-offs
AACSB Coding: Reflective Thinking
Special Feature: None

4. The production possibilities frontier shows
   A) the various products that can be produced now and in the future.
   B) the maximum attainable combinations of two products that may be produced in a
      particular time period with available resources.
   C) what an equitable distribution of products among citizens would be.
   D) what people want firms to produce in a particular time period.

Answer: B
Diff: 2   Type: MC   Page Ref: 38/38
Topic: Production Possibilities Frontier and Opportunity Costs
Skill: Conceptual
Objective: LO 1: Use a production possibilities frontier to analyze opportunity costs and trade-offs
AACSB Coding: Reflective Thinking
Special Feature: None

5. The production possibilities frontier model shows that
   A) if consumers decide to buy more of a product its price will increase.
   B) a market economy is more efficient in producing goods and services than is a centrally
      planned economy.
   C) economic growth can only be achieved by free market economies.
   D) if all resources are fully and efficiently utilized, more of one good can be produced
      only by producing less of another good.

Answer: D
Diff: 2   Type: MC   Page Ref: 38/38
Topic: Production Possibilities Frontier and Opportunity Costs
Skill: Conceptual
Objective: LO 1: Use a production possibilities frontier to analyze opportunity costs and trade-offs
AACSB Coding: Analytic Skills
Special Feature: None

6. The production possibilities frontier model assumes all of the following except
    A) labor, capital, land and natural resources are fixed in quantity.
    B) the economy produces only two products.
    C) any level of the two products that the economy produces is currently possible.
    D) the level of technology is fixed and unchanging.
    Answer: C
    Diff: 2   Type: MC   Page Ref: 38/38
    Topic: Production Possibilities Frontier and Opportunity Costs
    Skill: Conceptual
    Objective: LO 1: Use a production possibilities frontier to analyze opportunity costs and trade-offs
    AACSB Coding: Reflective Thinking
    Special Feature: None

7. The attainable production points on a production possibility curve are
    A) the horizontal and vertical intercepts.
    B) the points along the production possibilities frontier.
    C) the points outside the area enclosed by the production possibilities frontier.
    D) the points along and inside the production possibility frontier.
    Answer: D
    Diff: 2   Type: MC   Page Ref: 38/38
    Topic: Production Possibilities Frontier and Opportunity Costs
    Skill: Conceptual
    Objective: LO 1: Use a production possibilities frontier to analyze opportunity costs and trade-offs
    AACSB Coding: Reflective Thinking
    Special Feature: None

8. The unattainable points in a production possibilities diagram are
    A) the points within the production possibilities frontier.
    B) the points along the production possibilities frontier.
    C) the points of the horizontal and vertical intercepts.
    D) the points outside the production possibilities frontier.
    Answer: D
    Diff: 2   Type: MC   Page Ref: 38/38
    Topic: Production Possibilities Frontier and Opportunity Costs
    Skill: Conceptual
    Objective: LO 1: Use a production possibilities frontier to analyze opportunity costs and trade-offs
    AACSB Coding: Reflective Thinking
    Special Feature: None

Figure 2–1

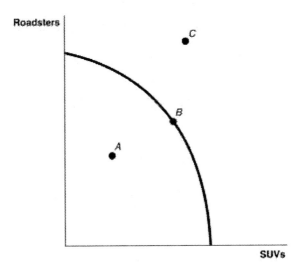

9. *Refer to Figure 2–1.* Point *A* is
    A) technically efficient.
    B) unattainable with current resources.
    C) inefficient in that not all resources are being used.
    D) the equilibrium output combination.
Answer: C
Diff: 1   Type: MC   Page Ref: 38/38
Topic: Production Possibilities Frontier and Opportunity Costs
Skill: Conceptual
Objective: LO 1: Use a production possibilities frontier to analyze opportunity costs and trade–offs
AACSB Coding: Reflective Thinking
Special Feature: None

10. *Refer to Figure 2–1.* Point *B* is
    A) technically efficient.
    B) unattainable with current resources.
    C) inefficient in that not all resources are being used.
    D) the equilibrium output combination.
Answer: A
Diff: 1   Type: MC   Page Ref: 38/38
Topic: Production Possibilities Frontier and Opportunity Costs
Skill: Conceptual
Objective: LO 1: Use a production possibilities frontier to analyze opportunity costs and trade–offs
AACSB Coding: Reflective Thinking
Special Feature: None

11. *Refer to Figure 2–1.* Point C is
    A) technically efficient.
    B) unattainable with current resources.
    C) inefficient in that not all resources are being used.
    D) is the equilibrium output combination.
    Answer: B
    Diff: 1   Type: MC   Page Ref: 38/38
    Topic: Production Possibilities Frontier and Opportunity Costs
    Skill: Conceptual
    Objective: LO 1: Use a production possibilities frontier to analyze opportunity costs and trade–offs
    AACSB Coding: Reflective Thinking
    Special Feature: None

12. In a production possibilities frontier model, a point inside the frontier is
    A) allocatively efficient.
    B) productively efficient
    C) allocatively inefficient.
    D) productively inefficient.
    Answer: D
    Diff: 1   Type: MC   Page Ref: 38/38
    Topic: Production Possibilities Frontier and Opportunity Costs
    Skill: Conceptual
    Objective: LO 1: Use a production possibilities frontier to analyze opportunity costs and trade–offs
    AACSB Coding: Reflective Thinking
    Special Feature: None

13. Bella can produce either a combination of 60 silk roses and 80 silk leaves or a combination of 70 silk roses and 55 silk leaves. If she now produces 60 silk roses and 80 silk leaves, what is the opportunity cost of producing an additional 10 silk roses?
    A) 25 silk leaves.
    B) 2.5 silk leaves.
    C) 55 silk leaves.
    D) 10 silk leaves
    Answer: A
    Diff: 2   Type: MC   Page Ref: 39/39
    Topic: Production Possibilities Frontier and Opportunity Costs
    Skill: Conceptual
    Objective: LO 1: Use a production possibilities frontier to analyze opportunity costs and trade–offs
    AACSB Coding: Analytic Skills
    Special Feature: None

14. If the production possibilities frontier is linear, then
    A) opportunity costs are decreasing as more of one good is produced.
    B) it is easy to efficiently produce output.
    C) opportunity costs are increasing as more of one good is produced.
    D) opportunity costs are constant as more of one good is produced.
    Answer: D
    Diff: 2   Type: MC   Page Ref: 39/39
    Topic: Production Possibilities Frontier and Opportunity Costs
    Skill: Conceptual
    Objective: LO 1: Use a production possibilities frontier to analyze opportunity costs and trade-offs
    AACSB Coding: Reflective Thinking
    Special Feature: None

Figure 2-2

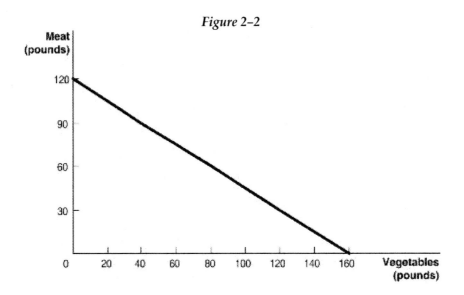

Figure 2-2 above shows the production possibilities frontier for Mendonca, an agrarian nation that produces two goods, meat and vegetables.

15. *Refer to Figure 2-2.* What is the opportunity cost of one pound of vegetables?
    A) 3/4 pounds of meat
    B) 1.2 pounds of meat
    C) 1 1/3 pounds of meat
    D) 12 pounds of meat
    Answer: A
    Diff: 2   Type: MC   Page Ref: 40/40
    Topic: Production Possibilities Frontier and Opportunity Costs
    Skill: Conceptual
    Objective: LO 1: Use a production possibilities frontier to analyze opportunity costs and trade-offs
    AACSB Coding: Analytic Skills
    Special Feature: Solved Problem: Drawing a Production Possibilities Frontier for Rosie's Boston Bakery

16. *Refer to Figure 2-2.* What is the opportunity cost of one pound of meat?
    A) 3/4 pounds of vegetables
    B) 1.6 pounds of vegetables
    C) 1 1/3 pounds of vegetables
    D) 16 pounds of vegetables
    Answer: C
    Diff: 2   Type: MC   Page Ref: 40/40
    Topic: Production Possibilities Frontier and Opportunity Costs
    Skill: Conceptual
    Objective: LO 1: Use a production possibilities frontier to analyze opportunity costs and trade-offs
    AACSB Coding: Analytic Skills
    Special Feature: Solved Problem: Drawing a Production Possibilities Frontier for Rosie's Boston Bakery

17. *Refer to Figure 2-2.* Suppose Mendonca is currently producing 60 pounds of vegetables per
    period. How much meat is it also producing, assuming that resources are fully utilized?
    A) 45 pounds of meat
    B) 75 pounds of meat
    C) 80 pounds of meat
    D) 100 pounds of meat
    Answer: B
    Diff: 2   Type: MC   Page Ref: 40/40
    Topic: Production Possibilities Frontier and Opportunity Costs
    Skill: Conceptual
    Objective: LO 1: Use a production possibilities frontier to analyze opportunity costs and trade-offs
    AACSB Coding: Analytic Skills
    Special Feature: Solved Problem: Drawing a Production Possibilities Frontier for Rosie's Boston Bakery

18. *Refer to Figure 2-2.* The linear production possibilities frontier in the figure indicates that
    A) Mendonca has a comparative advantage in the production of vegetables.
    B) Mendonca has a comparative disadvantage in the production of meat.
    C) the tradeoff between meat and vegetables is constant.
    D) it is progressively more expensive to produce meat.
    Answer: C
    Diff: 2   Type: MC   Page Ref: 40/40
    Topic: Production Possibilities Frontier and Opportunity Costs
    Skill: Conceptual
    Objective: LO 1: Use a production possibilities frontier to analyze opportunity costs and trade-offs
    AACSB Coding: Analytic Skills
    Special Feature: Solved Problem: Drawing a Production Possibilities Frontier for Rosie's Boston Bakery

19. A production possibilities frontier with a bowed outward shape indicates
    A) the possibility of inefficient production.
    B) constant opportunity costs as more and more of one good is produced.
    C) increasing opportunity costs as more and more of one good is produced.
    D) decreasing opportunity costs as more and more of one good is produced.
    Answer: C
    Diff: 2   Type: MC   Page Ref: 42/42
    Topic: Production Possibilities Frontier and Opportunity Costs
    Skill: Conceptual
    Objective: LO 1: Use a production possibilities frontier to analyze opportunity costs and trade-offs
    AACSB Coding: Reflective Thinking
    Special Feature: None

20. Increasing opportunity cost along a bowed out production possibilities frontier occurs because
    A) of inefficient production.
    B) of ineffective management by entrepreneurs.
    C) some factors of production are not equally suited to producing both goods or services.
    D) of the scarcity of factors of production.
    Answer: C
    Diff: 2   Type: MC   Page Ref: 42/42
    Topic: Production Possibilities Frontier and Opportunity Costs
    Skill: Conceptual
    Objective: LO 1: Use a production possibilities frontier to analyze opportunity costs and trade-offs
    AACSB Coding: Reflective Thinking
    Special Feature: None

21. The slope of a production possibilities frontier
    A) has no economic relevance or meaning.
    B) is always constant.
    C) is always varying.
    D) measures the opportunity cost of producing one more unit of a good.
    Answer: D
    Diff: 1   Type: MC   Page Ref: 42/42
    Topic: Production Possibilities Frontier and Opportunity Costs
    Skill: Conceptual
    Objective: LO 1: Use a production possibilities frontier to analyze opportunity costs and trade-offs
    AACSB Coding: Reflective Thinking
    Special Feature: None

22. Increasing marginal opportunity cost implies that
    A) the more resources already devoted to any activity, the payoff from allocating yet more resources to that activity increases by progressively smaller amounts.
    B) the more resources already devoted to any activity, the benefits from allocating yet more resources to that activity decreases by progressively larger amounts.
    C) that rising opportunity costs makes it inefficient to produce beyond a certain quantity.
    D) the law of scarcity.
Answer: A
Diff: 2   Type: MC   Page Ref: 42/42
Topic: Production Possibilities Frontier and Opportunity Costs
Skill: Conceptual
Objective: LO 1: Use a production possibilities frontier to analyze opportunity costs and trade-offs
AACSB Coding: Reflective Thinking
Special Feature: None

23. If opportunity costs are constant, the production possibilities frontier would be graphed as
    A) a ray from the origin.
    B) a positively sloped straight line.
    C) a negatively sloped curve bowed in toward the origin.
    D) a negatively sloped straight line.
Answer: D
Diff: 1   Type: MC   Page Ref: 40/40
Topic: Production Possibilities Frontier and Opportunity Costs
Skill: Conceptual
Objective: LO 1: Use a production possibilities frontier to analyze opportunity costs and trade-offs
AACSB Coding: Reflective Thinking
Special Feature: None

Figure 2–3

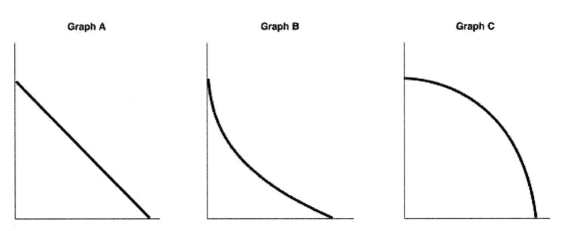

24. ***Refer to Figure 2–3.*** Carlos Vanya grows tomatoes and strawberries on his land. His land is equally suited for growing either fruit. Which of the graphs in Figure 2–3 represent his production possibilities frontier?

    A) Graph A
    B) Graph B
    C) Graph C
    D) Either Graph A or Graph B
    E) Either graph B or Graph C

Answer: A
Diff: 2   Type: MC   Page Ref: 40/40
Topic: Production Possibilities Frontier and Opportunity Costs
Skill: Conceptual
Objective: LO 1: Use a production possibilities frontier to analyze opportunity costs and trade–offs
AACSB Coding: Reflective Thinking
Special Feature: None

25. ***Refer to Figure 2–3.*** Carlos Vanya grows tomatoes and strawberries on his land. A portion of his land is more suitable for growing tomatoes and the other portion is better suited for strawberry cultivation. Which of the graphs in Figure 2–3 represent his production possibilities frontier?

    A) Graph A
    B) Graph B
    C) Graph C
    D) either Graph A or Graph B
    E) either graph B or Graph C

Answer: C
Diff: 2   Type: MC   Page Ref: 42/42
Topic: Production Possibilities Frontier and Opportunity Costs
Skill: Conceptual
Objective: LO 1: Use a production possibilities frontier to analyze opportunity costs and trade–offs
AACSB Coding: Reflective Thinking
Special Feature: None

26. An outward shift of a nation's production possibilities frontier can occur due to
    A) a reduction in unemployment.
    B) a natural disaster like a hurricane or bad earthquake.
    C) a change in the amounts of one good desired.
    D) an increase in the labor force.
    Answer: D
    Diff: 2   Type: MC   Page Ref: 43/43
    Topic: Production Possibilities Frontier and Opportunity Costs
    Skill: Conceptual
    Objective: LO 1: Use a production possibilities frontier to analyze opportunity costs and trade-offs
    AACSB Coding: Reflective Thinking
    Special Feature: None

27. An outward shift of a nation's production possibilities frontier represents
    A) economic growth.
    B) rising prices of the two goods on the production possibilities frontier model.
    C) an impossible situation.
    D) a situation in which a country produces more of one good and less of another.
    Answer: A
    Diff: 1   Type: MC   Page Ref: 43/43
    Topic: Production Possibilities Frontier and Opportunity Costs
    Skill: Conceptual
    Objective: LO 1: Use a production possibilities frontier to analyze opportunity costs and trade-offs
    AACSB Coding: Reflective Thinking
    Special Feature: None

28. Economic growth is represented on a production possibilities frontier model by the production possibility frontier
    A) shifting outward.
    B) shifting inward.
    C) becoming steeper.
    D) becoming flatter.
    Answer: A
    Diff: 1   Type: MC   Page Ref: 43/43
    Topic: Production Possibilities Frontier and Opportunity Costs
    Skill: Conceptual
    Objective: LO 1: Use a production possibilities frontier to analyze opportunity costs and trade-offs
    AACSB Coding: Reflective Thinking
    Special Feature: None

29. Without an increase in the supplies of factors of production, how can a nation achieve economic growth?
    A) by producing more high- value goods and less of low-value goods
    B) through technological advancement which enables more output with the same quantity of resources
    C) by lowering the prices of factors of production
    D) by increasing the prices of factors of production
    Answer: B
    Diff: 2   Type: MC   Page Ref: 43/43
    Topic: Production Possibilities Frontier and Opportunity Costs
    Skill: Conceptual
    Objective: LO 1: Use a production possibilities frontier to analyze opportunity costs and trade-offs
    AACSB Coding: Reflective Thinking
    Special Feature: None

30. Which of the following would shift a nation's production possibilities frontier inward?
    A) discovering a cheap way to convert sunshine into electricity
    B) producing more capital equipment
    C) an increase in the unemployment rate
    D) a law requiring workers to retire at age 50
    Answer: D
    Diff: 2   Type: MC   Page Ref: 43/43
    Topic: Production Possibilities Frontier and Opportunity Costs
    Skill: Conceptual
    Objective: LO 1: Use a production possibilities frontier to analyze opportunity costs and trade-offs
    AACSB Coding: Analytic Skills
    Special Feature: None

Figure 2-4

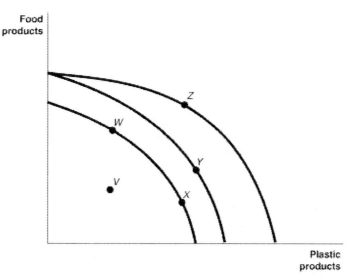

Figure 2-4 shows various points on three different production possibilities frontiers for a nation.

31. ***Refer to Figure 2-4.*** A movement from X to Y
     A) could be due to a change in consumers' tastes and preferences.
     B) could occur because of an influx of immigrant labor.
     C) is the result of advancements in food production technology only, with no change in the technology for plastic production.
     D) is the result of advancements in plastic production technology only, with no change in food production technology.
     Answer: B
     Diff: 2   Type: MC   Page Ref: 43/43
     Topic: Production Possibilities Frontier and Opportunity Costs
     Skill: Conceptual
     Objective: LO 1: Use a production possibilities frontier to analyze opportunity costs and trade-offs
     AACSB Coding: Analytic Skills
     Special Feature: None

32. ***Refer to Figure 2-4.*** A movement from Y to Z
     A) represents an increase in the demand for plastic products.
     B) could occur because of general technological advancements.
     C) is the result of advancements in food production technology.
     D) is the result of advancements in plastic production technology.
     Answer: D
     Diff: 2   Type: MC   Page Ref: 43/43
     Topic: Production Possibilities Frontier and Opportunity Costs
     Skill: Conceptual
     Objective: LO 1: Use a production possibilities frontier to analyze opportunity costs and trade-offs
     AACSB Coding: Analytic Skills
     Special Feature: None

33. *Refer to Figure 2–4.* Consider the following events:
    a.   an increase in the unemployment rate
    b.   a decrease in a nation's money supply
    c.   a war that kills a significant portion of a nation's population

    Which of the events listed above could cause a movement from *Y* to *W* ?
      A) a, b and c
      B) a and b only
      C) a and c only
      D) a only
      E) c only
    Answer: E
    Diff: 2   Type: MC   Page Ref: 43/43
    Topic: Production Possibilities Frontier and Opportunity Costs
    Skill: Conceptual
    Objective: LO 1: Use a production possibilities frontier to analyze opportunity costs and trade–offs
    AACSB Coding: Analytic Skills
    Special Feature: None

34. *Refer to Figure 2–4.* Consider the following movements:
    a.   from point *V* to point *W*
    b.   from point *W* to point *Y*
    c.   from point *Y* to point *Z*

    Which of the movements listed above represents economic growth?
      A) a, b, and c
      B) b and c only
      C) a only
      D) b only
    Answer: B
    Diff: 2   Type: MC   Page Ref: 43/43
    Topic: Production Possibilities Frontier and Opportunity Costs
    Skill: Conceptual
    Objective: LO 1: Use a production possibilities frontier to analyze opportunity costs and trade–offs
    AACSB Coding: Analytic Skills
    Special Feature: None

35. **Refer to Figure 2–4.** Consider the following events:
   a.   a decrease in the unemployment rate
   b.   general technological advancement
   c.   an increase in consumer wealth

   Which of the events listed above could cause a movement from V to W ?
     A) a only
     B) a and b only
     C) b and c only
     D) a, b, and c.
   Answer: A
   Diff: 2   Type: MC   Page Ref: 43/43
   Topic: Production Possibilities Frontier and Opportunity Costs
   Skill: Conceptual
   Objective: LO 1: Use a production possibilities frontier to analyze opportunity costs and trade–offs
   AACSB Coding: Analytic Skills
   Special Feature: None

36. **Refer to Figure 2–4.** Consider the following events:
   a.   a reduction in the patent protection period to no more than 2 years
   b.   a war that destroys a substantial portion of a nation's capital stock
   c.   the lack of secure and enforceable property rights system

   Which of the events listed above could cause a movement from W to V?
     A) a only
     B) a and b only
     C) a and c only
     D) b and c only
     E) a, b, and c
   Answer: C
   Diff: 2   Type: MC   Page Ref: 43/43
   Topic: Production Possibilities Frontier and Opportunity Costs
   Skill: Conceptual
   Objective: LO 1: Use a production possibilities frontier to analyze opportunity costs and trade–offs
   AACSB Coding: Reflective Thinking
   Special Feature: None

37. The Great Depression of the 1930s with a large number of workers and factories unemployed would be represented in a production possibilities frontier graph by
    A) a point inside the frontier.
    B) a point outside the frontier.
    C) a point on the frontier.
    D) an intercept on either the vertical or the horizontal axis.

    Answer: A
    Diff: 2   Type: MC   Page Ref: 43/43
    Topic: Production Possibilities Frontier and Opportunity Costs
    Skill: Conceptual
    Objective: LO 1: Use a production possibilities frontier to analyze opportunity costs and trade–offs
    AACSB Coding: Reflective Thinking
    Special Feature: None

38. Suppose there is some unemployment in the economy and society decides that it wants more of one good. Which of the following statements is true?
    A) It is not possible to achieve this unless technology advances.
    B) It can increase output without giving up another good by employing more resources.
    C) It will have to increase resource supplies.
    D) It will have to give up production and consumption of some other good.

    Answer: B
    Diff: 2   Type: MC   Page Ref: 43/43
    Topic: Production Possibilities Frontier and Opportunity Costs
    Skill: Conceptual
    Objective: LO 1: Use a production possibilities frontier to analyze opportunity costs and trade–offs
    AACSB Coding: Reflective Thinking
    Special Feature: None

39. If society decides it wants more of one good and all resources are fully utilized, then
    A) it is unable to do this unless technology advances.
    B) additional resource supplies will have to be found.
    C) it has to give up some of another good and incur some opportunity costs.
    D) more unemployment will occur.

    Answer: C
    Diff: 2   Type: MC   Page Ref: 43/43
    Topic: Production Possibilities Frontier and Opportunity Costs
    Skill: Conceptual
    Objective: LO 1: Use a production possibilities frontier to analyze opportunity costs and trade–offs
    AACSB Coding: Reflective Thinking
    Special Feature: None

40. According to the production possibility model, if more resources are allocated to the production of physical and human capital, then all of the following are likely to happen except
    A) fewer goods will be produced for consumption today.
    B) the production possibilities frontier will be shift outward in the future
    C) future economic growth is enhanced.
    D) the country's total production will fall.

Answer: D

Diff: 2   Type: MC   Page Ref: 43/43
Topic: Production Possibilities Frontier and Opportunity Costs
Skill: Conceptual
Objective: LO 1: Use a production possibilities frontier to analyze opportunity costs and trade–offs
AACSB Coding: Analytic Skills
Special Feature: None

Figure 2–5

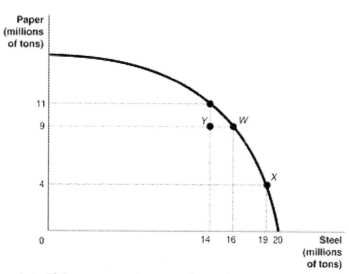

41. *Refer to Figure 2–5.* If the economy is currently producing at point Y, what is the opportunity cost of moving to point W?
    A) 2 million tons of steel
    B) zero
    C) 9 million tons of paper
    D) 16 million tons of paper

Answer: B

Diff: 2   Type: MC   Page Ref: 43/43
Topic: Production Possibilities Frontier and Opportunity Costs
Skill: Conceptual
Objective: LO 1: Use a production possibilities frontier to analyze opportunity costs and trade–offs
AACSB Coding: Analytic Skills
Special Feature: An Inside Look: BMW Managers Change Production Strategy

42. ***Refer to Figure 2–5.*** If the economy is currently producing at point *W*, what is the opportunity cost of moving to point *X*?

    A) 3 million tons of steel

    B) 19 million tons of steel

    C) 5 million tons of paper

    D) 9 million tons of paper

Answer: C

Diff: 1   Type: MC   Page Ref:

Topic: Production Possibilities Frontier and Opportunity Costs

Skill: Conceptual

Objective: LO 1: Use a production possibilities frontier to analyze opportunity costs and trade–offs

AACSB Coding: Analytic Skills

Special Feature: An Inside Look: BMW Managers Change Production Strategy

43. In a report made to the US Congress in 2001, the National Academy of Sciences cautioned that if fuel economy encourages the production of smaller and lighter cars, "Some additional traffic fatalities would be expected." This statement suggests that

    A) US auto manufacturers are more concerned about producing fuel efficient cars to compete with their Japanese and South Korean rivals than about consumer safety.

    B) there is a tradeoff between safety and fuel economy.

    C) society should value safety more highly than fuel economy.

    D) society should value fuel economy more highly than consumer safety because of the long term environment benefits generated by less gasoline use.

Answer: B

Diff: 2   Type: MC   Page Ref: 43/43

Topic: Production Possibilities Frontier and Opportunity Costs

Skill: Conceptual

Objective: LO 1: Use a production possibilities frontier to analyze opportunity costs and trade–offs

AACSB Coding: Reflective Thinking

Special Feature: None

44. Suppose your expenses for this term are as follows: tuition: $5,000, room and board: $3,000, books and other educational supplies: $500. Further, during the term, you can only work part–time and earn $4,000 instead of your full–time salary of $10,000. What is the opportunity cost of going to college this term, assuming that your room and board expenses would be the same even if you did not go to college?

    A) $5,500

    B) $8,500

    C) $11,500

    D) $14,500

Answer: C

Diff: 3   Type: MC   Page Ref: 43/43

Topic: Production Possibilities Frontier and Opportunity Costs

Skill: Analytical

Objective: LO 1: Use a production possibilities frontier to analyze opportunity costs and trade–offs

AACSB Coding: Analytic Skills

Special Feature: None

45. The opportunity cost of taking a semester–long economics class is
    A) the cost of tuition and fees only.
    B) the value of the time spent in the classroom.
    C) zero because there is no admission charged if you are enrolled in the course.
    D) equal to the highest value of an alternative use of the time and money spent on the class.
    E) the knowledge and enjoyment you receive from attending the class.
Answer: D
Diff: 2   Type: MC   Page Ref: 43/43
Topic: Production Possibilities Frontier and Opportunity Costs
Skill: Conceptual
Objective: LO 1: Use a production possibilities frontier to analyze opportunity costs and trade–offs
AACSB Coding: Reflective Thinking
Special Feature: None

Figure 2–6

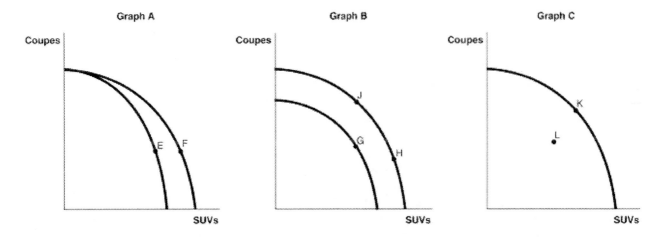

German auto producer, BMW currently produces two types of automobiles sports utility vehicles (SUVs) and coupes in its US plant. Since it opened in 1994, the company had made and continues to make several strategic production decisions. Figure 2–6 shows changes to its production possibilities frontier in response to some of these production strategies.

46. *Refer to Figure 2–6.* Between 1995 and 2003, worker productivity increased so that the total number of vehicles produced increased as the company added more machinery, workers and changed the layout of the factory. This is best represented by the
    A) movement from *E* to *F* in Graph A.
    B) movement from *G* to *H* in Graph B.
    C) movement from *G* to *H* in Graph C.
    D) Movement from *J* to *H* in Graph B.
Answer: B
Diff: 2   Type: MC   Page Ref: 58/58
Topic: Production Possibilities Frontier and Opportunity Costs
Skill: Conceptual
Objective: LO 1: Use a production possibilities frontier to analyze opportunity costs and trade–offs
AACSB Coding: Reflective Thinking
Special Feature: An Inside Look: BMW Managers Change Production Strategy

47. ***Refer to Figure 2-6.*** In response to changing consumer demands, BMW has cut back on the production of coupes and increased its production of SUVs. This strategy is best represented by
    A) movement from *E* to *F* in Graph A.
    B) movement from *G* to *H* in Graph B.
    C) movement from *K* to *L* in Graph C.
    D) Movement from *J* to *H* in Graph B.
    Answer: D
    Diff: 2   Type: MC   Page Ref: 58/58
    Topic: Production Possibilities Frontier and Opportunity Costs
    Skill: Conceptual
    Objective: LO 1: Use a production possibilities frontier to analyze opportunity costs and trade–offs
    AACSB Coding: Reflective Thinking
    Special Feature: An Inside Look: BMW Managers Change Production Strategy

48. ***Refer to Figure 2-6.*** In 2005, the company had to shut down a portion of its facility as it worked on remodeling the facility to merge two of its separate assembly lines in preparation for the production of a new model. The production decision to shut down temporarily will result in a
    A) movement from *E* to *F* in Graph A.
    B) movement from *G* to *H* in Graph B.
    C) movement from *K* to *L* in Graph C.
    D) Movement from *J* to *H* in Graph B.
    Answer: C
    Diff: 2   Type: MC   Page Ref: 58/58
    Topic: Production Possibilities Frontier and Opportunity Costs
    Skill: Conceptual
    Objective: LO 1: Use a production possibilities frontier to analyze opportunity costs and trade–offs
    AACSB Coding: Reflective Thinking
    Special Feature: An Inside Look: BMW Managers Change Production Strategy

49. Hurricane Katrina which hit the Gulf Coast region in August 2005, resulted in massive flooding which destroyed large sections of New Orleans. Suppose prior to this event, New Orleans was producing an output combination given by a point on its production possibilities frontier. How did the hurricane affect its production possibilities frontier?
    A) New Orleans' output combination moved from a point on the frontier to a point given by one of the intercepts.
    B) The production possibilities frontier does not shift but there is a movement from a point on the frontier to a point inside the frontier.
    C) The production possibilities frontier shifts inwards.
    D) The production possibilities frontier no longer exists.
    Answer: C
    Diff: 1   Type: MC   Page Ref: 41/41
    Topic: Production Possibilities Frontier and Opportunity Costs
    Skill: Conceptual
    Objective: LO 1: Use a production possibilities frontier to analyze opportunity costs and trade–offs
    AACSB Coding: Reflective Thinking
    Special Feature: Making the Connection: Trade-offs: Hurricane Katrina, Tsunami Relief, and Charitable Giving

50. An increase in the unemployment rate may be represented as a movement from a point on the production possibilities frontier to a point inside the frontier.
    Answer: ◉ True   False
    Diff: 2   Type: TF   Page Ref: 43/43
    Topic: Production Possibilities Frontier and Opportunity Costs
    Skill: Conceptual
    Objective: LO 1: Use a production possibilities frontier to analyze opportunity costs and trade-offs
    AACSB Coding: Reflective Thinking
    Special Feature: None

51. If a country is producing efficiently and is on the production possibilities frontier, the only way to produce more of one good is to produce less of the other.
    Answer: ◉ True   False
    Diff: 1   Type: TF   Page Ref: 43/43
    Topic: Production Possibilities Frontier and Opportunity Costs
    Skill: Analytical
    Objective: LO 1: Use a production possibilities frontier to analyze opportunity costs and trade-offs
    AACSB Coding: Reflective Thinking
    Special Feature: None

52. Consider a country that produces only two goods: pineapples and tractors. Suppose, it is possible for this country to increase its production of pineapples without producing fewer tractors, then its current output combination is inefficient.
    Answer: ◉ True   False
    Diff: 2   Type: TF   Page Ref: 39/39
    Topic: Production Possibilities Frontier and Opportunity Costs
    Skill: Analytical
    Objective: LO 1: Use a production possibilities frontier to analyze opportunity costs and trade-offs
    AACSB Coding: Reflective Thinking
    Special Feature: None

53. Any output combination outside a production possibility frontier is associated with unused or underutilized resources.
    Answer: ◉ True   False
    Diff: 1   Type: TF   Page Ref: 39/39
    Topic: Production Possibilities Frontier and Opportunity Costs
    Skill: Conceptual
    Objective: LO 1: Use a production possibilities frontier to analyze opportunity costs and trade-offs
    AACSB Coding: Reflective Thinking
    Special Feature: None

54. An increase in population shifts the production possibility frontier inwards over time.
    Answer: True   ◉ False
    Diff: 1   Type: TF   Page Ref: 43/43
    Topic: Production Possibilities Frontier and Opportunity Costs
    Skill: Conceptual
    Objective: LO 1: Use a production possibilities frontier to analyze opportunity costs and trade-offs
    AACSB Coding: Reflective Thinking
    Special Feature: None

55. If additional units of a good could be produced at a constant opportunity cost, the production possibility frontier would be bowed outward (concave).
Answer: True   ○ False
Diff: 2   Type: TF   Page Ref: 42/42
Topic: Production Possibilities Frontier and Opportunity Costs
Skill: Conceptual
Objective: LO 1: Use a production possibilities frontier to analyze opportunity costs and trade-offs
AACSB Coding: Reflective Thinking
Special Feature: None

56. On a diagram of a production possibility frontier, opportunity cost is represented by the slope of the production possibility frontier
Answer: ○ True   False
Diff: 2   Type: TF   Page Ref: 39/39
Topic: Production Possibilities Frontier and Opportunity Costs
Skill: Conceptual
Objective: LO 1: Use a production possibilities frontier to analyze opportunity costs and trade-offs
AACSB Coding: Reflective Thinking
Special Feature: None

57. To increase gas mileage, automobile manufacturers make cars small and light. Large cars absorb more of the impact of an accident than small cars but yield lower gas mileage These facts suggest that there exists a negative relationship between safety and gas mileage.
Answer: ○ True   False
Diff: 2   Type: TF   Page Ref: 37/37
Topic: Production Possibilities Frontier and Opportunity Costs
Skill: Analytical
Objective: LO 1: Use a production possibilities frontier to analyze opportunity costs and trade-offs
AACSB Coding: Analytic Skills
Special Feature: Economics in YOUR Life!: The Trade-off When You Buy a New Car

58. a.   Draw a production possibilities frontier for a country that produces two goods, wine and cheese. Assume that resources are not equally suited to both tasks.
    b.   Define opportunity costs.
    c.   Use your production possibilities frontier graph to demonstrate the principle of opportunity costs.

Answer: a.   The PPF is concave (bowed away from the origin) to reflect the fact that resources are not equally suited to both tasks.

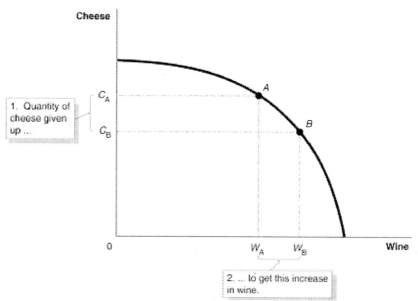

    b.   Opportunity cost is defined as the highest valued alternative that must be forgone by taking an action.
    c.   In the PPF graph in part (a), suppose the country is currently producing at point A and wishes to move to point B so that it can produce more wine. The only way it can obtain more wine is to give up some amount of cheese.

Diff: 2   Type: SA   Page Ref: 42/42
Topic: Production Possibilities Frontier and Opportunity Costs
Skill: Conceptual
Objective: LO 1: Use a production possibilities frontier to analyze opportunity costs and trade–offs
AACSB Coding: Analytic Skills
Special Feature: None

59.   *Table 2–1*

Possible Output Combinations	Apples (thousands of pounds)	Pear (thousands of pounds)
A	70	0
B	60	20
C	50	36
D	40	48
E	30	56
F	20	60
G	10	63
H	0	65

Refer to Table 2–1. The Fruit Farm produces only apples and pears. The table above shows the maximum possible output combinations of the two fruits using all resources and currently available technology.

a.   Graph The Fruit Farm's production possibilities frontier. Put apples on the horizontal axis and pears on the vertical axis. Be sure to identify the output combination points on your diagram.

b.   Suppose The Fruit farm is currently producing at point *D*. What is the opportunity cost of producing an additional 8,000 pounds of pears?

c.   Suppose The Fruit farm is currently producing at point *D*. What happens to the opportunity cost of producing more and more pears? Does it increase, decrease or remain constant? Explain your answer.

d.   Suppose The Fruit farm is currently producing at point G. What happens to the opportunity cost of producing more and more apples? Does it increase, decrease or remain constant? Explain your answer.

e.   Suppose Fruit farm is plagued by the apple maggot infestation which destroys apple trees but not pears. Show in a graph what happens to its PPF.

Answer: a.

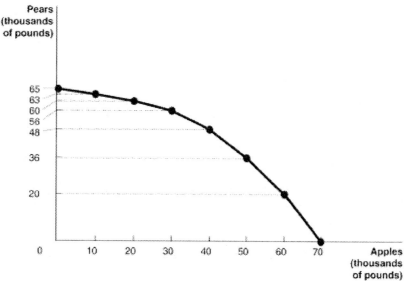

b.   10 pounds of apples
c.   It increases. For example to move to E, the Fruit Farm has to give up 10,000 pounds of apples to produce an additional 8,000 pounds of pears. For each additional 10,000 pounds of apples foregone, the payoff in terms of pears gets progressively smaller.
d.   It increases. Each time it wants to produce an additional 10,000 of apples, more and more pears must be given up.
e.

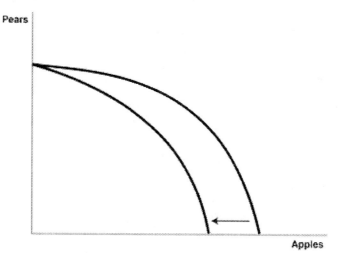

Diff: 3   Type: ES   Page Ref: 40/40
Topic: Production Possibilities Frontier and Opportunity Costs
Skill: Analytical
Objective: LO 1: Use a production possibilities frontier to analyze opportunity costs and trade–offs
AACSB Coding: Analytic Skills
Special Feature: Solved Problem: Drawing a Production Possibilities Frontier for Rosie's Boston Bakery

2.2   Comparative Advantage and Trade

1. You have an absolute advantage whenever you
   A) are better educated than someone else.
   B) can produce more of something than others with the same resources.
   C) prefer to do one particular activity.
   D) can produce something at a lower opportunity cost than others.
   Answer: B
   Diff: 1   Type: MC   Page Ref: 46/46
   Topic: Comparative Advantage and Trade
   Skill: Definition
   Objective: LO 2: Understand comparative advantage and explain how it is the basis for trade
   AACSB Coding: Reflective Thinking
   Special Feature: None

Table 2–2

	George	Jack
Lawns Mowed	10	6
Gardens Cultivated	5	4

Table 2–2 shows the output per day of two gardeners, George and Jack. They can either devote their time to mowing lawns or cultivating gardens.

2. *Refer to Table 2–2.* Which of the following statements is true?
   A) Jack has an absolute advantage in both tasks.
   B) George has an absolute advantage in both tasks.
   C) Jack has an absolute advantage in lawn mowing and George in garden cultivating.
   D) Jack has an absolute advantage in garden cultivating and George in lawn mowing.
   Answer: B
   Diff: 1   Type: MC   Page Ref: 45/45
   Topic: Comparative Advantage and Trade
   Skill: Conceptual
   Objective: LO 2: Understand comparative advantage and explain how it is the basis for trade
   AACSB Coding: Reflective Thinking
   Special Feature: None

3. *Refer to Table 2–2.* What is Jack's opportunity cost of mowing a lawn?
   A) half a garden cultivated.
   B) two lawns mowed.
   C) two-thirds of a garden cultivated.
   D) one and a half lawns mowed.
   Answer: C
   Diff: 2   Type: MC   Page Ref: 45/45
   Topic: Comparative Advantage and Trade
   Skill: Conceptual
   Objective: LO 2: Understand comparative advantage and explain how it is the basis for trade
   AACSB Coding: Analytic Skills
   Special Feature: None

4. *Refer to Table 2-2.* What is Jack's opportunity cost of cultivating a garden?
    A) half a garden cultivated
    B) two lawns mowed
    C) two-thirds of a garden cultivated.
    D) one and a half lawns mowed
   Answer: D
   Diff: 2   Type: MC   Page Ref: 45/45
   Topic: Comparative Advantage and Trade
   Skill: Conceptual
   Objective: LO 2: Understand comparative advantage and explain how it is the basis for trade
   AACSB Coding: Analytic Skills
   Special Feature: None

5. *Refer to Table 2-2.* What is George's opportunity cost of mowing a lawn?
    A) half a garden cultivated
    B) two lawns mowed
    C) two-thirds of a garden cultivated.
    D) one and a half lawns mowed
   Answer: A
   Diff: 2   Type: MC   Page Ref: 45/45
   Topic: Comparative Advantage and Trade
   Skill: Conceptual
   Objective: LO 2: Understand comparative advantage and explain how it is the basis for trade
   AACSB Coding: Analytic Skills
   Special Feature: None

6. *Refer to Table 2-2.* What is George's opportunity cost of cultivating a garden?
    A) half a garden cultivated
    B) two lawns mowed
    C) two-thirds of a garden cultivated
    D) one and a half lawns mowed
   Answer: B
   Diff: 2   Type: MC   Page Ref: 45/45
   Topic: Comparative Advantage and Trade
   Skill: Conceptual
   Objective: LO 2: Understand comparative advantage and explain how it is the basis for trade
   AACSB Coding: Analytic Skills
   Special Feature: None

7. ***Refer to Table 2–2.*** Which of the following statements is true?
    A) Jack has a comparative advantage in both tasks.
    B) George has a comparative advantage in both tasks.
    C) Jack has a comparative advantage in lawn mowing and George in garden cultivating.
    D) Jack has a comparative advantage in garden cultivating and George in lawn mowing.
    Answer: D
    Diff: 3   Type: MC   Page Ref: 45/45
    Topic: Comparative Advantage and Trade
    Skill: Analytical
    Objective: LO 2: Understand comparative advantage and explain how it is the basis for trade
    AACSB Coding: Analytic Skills
    Special Feature: None

8. Comparative advantage means
    A) the ability to produce more of a product with the same amount of resources than any other producer.
    B) the ability to produce a good or service at a lower opportunity cost than any other producer.
    C) the ability to produce a good or service at a higher opportunity cost than any other producer.
    D) compared to others you are better at producing a product.
    Answer: B
    Diff: 1   Type: MC   Page Ref: 47/47
    Topic: Comparative Advantage and Trade
    Skill: Definition
    Objective: LO 2: Understand comparative advantage and explain how it is the basis for trade
    AACSB Coding: Reflective Thinking
    Special Feature: None

9. Specializing in the production of a good or service in which one has a comparative advantage enables a country to do all of the following except
    A) engage in mutually beneficial trade with other nations.
    B) increase the variety of products that it can consume with no increase in resources.
    C) consume a combination of goods that lie outside its own production possibilities frontier.
    D) produce a combination of goods that lie outside its own production possibilities frontier.
    Answer: D
    Diff: 3   Type: MC   Page Ref: 47/47
    Topic: Comparative Advantage and Trade
    Skill: Conceptual
    Objective: LO 2: Understand comparative advantage and explain how it is the basis for trade
    AACSB Coding: Reflective Thinking
    Special Feature: None

10. For each watch that Switzerland produces, it gives up the opportunity to make 50 pounds of chocolate. Germany can produce 1 watch for every 100 pounds of chocolate it produces. Which of the following is true about the comparative advantage between the two countries?
    A) Switzerland has the comparative advantage in chocolate.
    B) Switzerland has the comparative advantage in watches.
    C) Germany has the comparative advantage in watches and chocolate.
    D) Germany has the comparative advantage in watches.
Answer: B
Diff: 2   Type: MC   Page Ref: 47/47
Topic: Comparative Advantage and Trade
Skill: Conceptual
Objective: LO 2: Understand comparative advantage and explain how it is the basis for trade
AACSB Coding: Analytic Skills
Special Feature: None

Figure 2-7

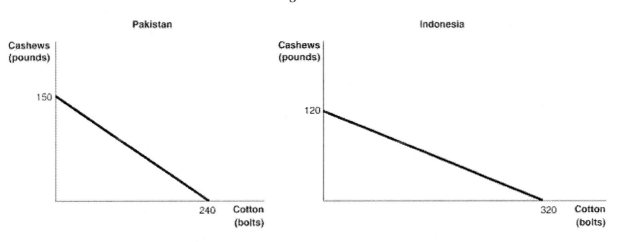

Figure 2-7 shows the production possibilities frontiers for Pakistan and Indonesia. Each country produces two goods, cotton and cashews.

12. *Refer to Figure 2-7.* What is the opportunity cost of producing 1 bolt of cloth in Pakistan?
    A) 5/8 pounds of cashews
    B) 3/8 pounds of cashews
    C) 1 3/5 pounds of cashews
    D) 150 pounds of cashews
Answer: A
Diff: 2   Type: MC   Page Ref: 46-7/46-7
Topic: Comparative Advantage and Trade
Skill: Conceptual
Objective: LO 2: Understand comparative advantage and explain how it is the basis for trade
AACSB Coding: Reflective Thinking
Special Feature: None

13. *Refer to Figure 2–7.* What is the opportunity cost of producing 1 bolt of cloth in Indonesia?
    A) 5/8 pounds of cashews
    B) 3/8 pounds of cashews
    C) 2 2/3 pounds of cashews
    D) 120 pounds of cashews
    Answer: B
    Diff: 2   Type: MC   Page Ref: 46–7/46–7
    Topic: Comparative Advantage and Trade
    Skill: Conceptual
    Objective: LO 2: Understand comparative advantage and explain how it is the basis for trade
    AACSB Coding: Analytic Skills
    Special Feature: None

14. *Refer to Figure 2–7.* What is the opportunity cost of producing 1 pound of cashews in Pakistan?
    A) 5/8 bolts of cotton
    B) 3/8 bolts of cotton
    C) 1 3/5 bolts of cotton
    D) 240 bolts of cotton
    Answer: C
    Diff: 2   Type: MC   Page Ref: 46–7/46–7
    Topic: Comparative Advantage and Trade
    Skill: Conceptual
    Objective: LO 2: Understand comparative advantage and explain how it is the basis for trade
    AACSB Coding: Analytic Skills
    Special Feature: None

15. *Refer to Figure 2–7.* What is the opportunity cost of producing 1 pound of cashews in Indonesia?
    A) 5/8 bolts of cotton
    B) 3/8 bolts of cotton
    C) 320 bolts of cotton
    D) 2 2/3 bolts of cotton
    Answer: D
    Diff: 2   Type: MC   Page Ref: 46–7/46–7
    Topic: Comparative Advantage and Trade
    Skill: Conceptual
    Objective: LO 2: Understand comparative advantage and explain how it is the basis for trade
    AACSB Coding: Analytic Skills
    Special Feature: None

16. ***Refer to Figure 2–7.*** Which country has a comparative advantage in the production of cotton?

    A) Indonesia

    B) They have equal productive abilities.

    C) Pakistan

    D) neither country

    Answer: A

    Diff: 2   Type: MC   Page Ref: 46–7/46–7

    Topic: Comparative Advantage and Trade

    Skill: Conceptual

    Objective: LO 2: Understand comparative advantage and explain how it is the basis for trade

    AACSB Coding: Analytic Skills

    Special Feature: None

17. ***Refer to Figure 2–7.*** Which country has a comparative advantage in the production of cashews?

    A) Indonesia

    B) They have equal productive abilities.

    C) Pakistan

    D) neither country

    Answer: C

    Diff: 2   Type: MC   Page Ref: 46–7/46–7

    Topic: Comparative Advantage and Trade

    Skill: Conceptual

    Objective: LO 2: Understand comparative advantage and explain how it is the basis for trade

    AACSB Coding: Analytic Skills

    Special Feature: None

18. ***Refer to Figure 2–7.*** If the two countries have the same amount of resources and the same technological knowledge, which country has an absolute advantage in the production of cotton?

    A) Indonesia

    B) They have the same advantage.

    C) Pakistan

    D) cannot be determined.

    Answer: A

    Diff: 2   Type: MC   Page Ref: 46–7/46–7

    Topic: Comparative Advantage and Trade

    Skill: Conceptual

    Objective: LO 2: Understand comparative advantage and explain how it is the basis for trade

    AACSB Coding: Analytic Skills

    Special Feature: None

19. Individuals who have never been the best at doing anything
    A) cannot have a comparative advantage in producing any product.
    B) can still have a comparative advantage in producing some product.
    C) perform all tasks at a higher opportunity cost than others.
    D) must have an absolute advantage in at least ones task.
    Answer: B
    Diff: 2   Type: MC   Page Ref: 46–7/46–7
    Topic: Comparative Advantage and Trade
    Skill: Conceptual
    Objective: LO 2: Understand comparative advantage and explain how it is the basis for trade
    AACSB Coding: Reflective Thinking
    Special Feature: None

Table 2–3

	One Digital Camera	*Wheat (per pound)*
China	100 hours	4 hours
South Korea	60 hours	3 hours

Table 2–3 shows the number of labor hours required to produce a digital camera and a pound of wheat in China and South Korea.

20. *Refer to Table 2–3.* Does either China or South Korea have an absolute advantage and if so, in what product?
    A) South Korea has an absolute advantage in wheat.
    B) China has an absolute advantage in wheat.
    C) South Korea has an absolute advantage in both products.
    D) China has an absolute advantage in digital cameras.
    Answer: C
    Diff: 1   Type: MC   Page Ref: 48/48
    Topic: Comparative Advantage and Trade
    Skill: Conceptual
    Objective: LO 2: Understand comparative advantage and explain how it is the basis for trade
    AACSB Coding: Analytic Skills
    Special Feature: Solved Problem: Comparative Advantage and the Gains from Trade

21. *Refer to Table 2–3.* What is China's opportunity cost of producing one digital camera?
    A) 25 pounds of wheat
    B) 40 pounds of wheat
    C) 0.04 pounds of wheat
    D) 4 pounds of wheat
    Answer: A
    Diff: 2   Type: MC   Page Ref: 48/48
    Topic: Comparative Advantage and Trade
    Skill: Conceptual
    Objective: LO 2: Understand comparative advantage and explain how it is the basis for trade
    AACSB Coding: Analytic Skills
    Special Feature: Solved Problem: Comparative Advantage and the Gains from Trade

22. *Refer to Table 2–3.* What is South Korea's opportunity cost of producing one digital camera?
    A) 25 pounds of wheat
    B) 20 pounds of wheat
    C) 60 pounds of wheat
    D) 0.05 pounds of wheat
    Answer: B
    Diff: 2   Type: MC   Page Ref: 48/48
    Topic: Comparative Advantage and Trade
    Skill: Conceptual
    Objective: LO 2: Understand comparative advantage and explain how it is the basis for trade
    AACSB Coding: Analytic Skills
    Special Feature: Solved Problem: Comparative Advantage and the Gains from Trade

23. *Refer to Table 2–3.* What is China's opportunity cost of producing one pound of wheat?
    A) 0.04 units of a digital camera
    B) 40 digital cameras
    C) 25 digital cameras
    D) 4 digital cameras
    Answer: A
    Diff: 2   Type: MC   Page Ref: 48/48
    Topic: Comparative Advantage and Trade
    Skill: Conceptual
    Objective: LO 2: Understand comparative advantage and explain how it is the basis for trade
    AACSB Coding: Analytic Skills
    Special Feature: Solved Problem: Comparative Advantage and the Gains from Trade

24. *Refer to Table 2–3.* What is South Korea's opportunity cost of producing one pound of wheat?
    A) 5 digital cameras
    B) 60 digital cameras
    C) 20 digital cameras
    D) 0.05 units of a digital camera
    Answer: D
    Diff: 2   Type: MC   Page Ref: 48/48
    Topic: Comparative Advantage and Trade
    Skill: Conceptual
    Objective: LO 2: Understand comparative advantage and explain how it is the basis for trade
    AACSB Coding: Analytic Skills
    Special Feature: Solved Problem: Comparative Advantage and the Gains from Trade

25. *Refer to Table 2–3.* China has a comparative advantage in
    A) both products.
    B) wheat production.
    C) digital camera production.
    D) neither product.
    Answer: B
    Diff: 2   Type: MC   Page Ref: 48/48
    Topic: Comparative Advantage and Trade
    Skill: Conceptual
    Objective: LO 2: Understand comparative advantage and explain how it is the basis for trade
    AACSB Coding: Analytic Skills
    Special Feature: Solved Problem: Comparative Advantage and the Gains from Trade

26. *Refer to Table 2–3.* South Korea has a comparative advantage in
    A) both products.
    B) wheat production.
    C) digital camera production.
    D) neither product.
    Answer: C
    Diff: 2   Type: MC   Page Ref: 48/48
    Topic: Comparative Advantage and Trade
    Skill: Conceptual
    Objective: LO 2: Understand comparative advantage and explain how it is the basis for trade
    AACSB Coding: Analytic Skills
    Special Feature: Solved Problem: Comparative Advantage and the Gains from Trade

27. *Refer to Table 2–3.* If the two countries specialize and trade, who should export wheat?
    A) There is no basis for trade between the two countries.
    B) China
    C) South Korea
    D) They should both be exporting wheat.
    Answer: B
    Diff: 1   Type: MC   Page Ref: 48/48
    Topic: Comparative Advantage and Trade
    Skill: Conceptual
    Objective: LO 2: Understand comparative advantage and explain how it is the basis for trade
    AACSB Coding: Analytic Skills
    Special Feature: Solved Problem: Comparative Advantage and the Gains from Trade

28. **Refer to Table 2–3.** If the two countries specialize and trade, who should export digital cameras?

    A) There is no basis for trade between the two countries.

    B) China

    C) South Korea

    D) They should both be importing digital cameras.

    Answer: C

    Diff: 1   Type: MC   Page Ref: 48/48

    Topic: Comparative Advantage and Trade

    Skill: Conceptual

    Objective: LO 2: Understand comparative advantage and explain how it is the basis for trade

    AACSB Coding: Analytic Skills

    Special Feature: Solved Problem: Comparative Advantage and the Gains from Trade

29. If the best lawyer in town is also the best at operating a word processor, then according to economic reasoning, this person should

    A) split her time evenly between being a lawyer and a word processor.

    B) specialize in being a lawyer because its opportunity cost is lower.

    C) should pursue the activity she enjoys more.

    D) specialize in being a work processor because it is more capital–intensive.

    Answer: B

    Diff: 1   Type: MC   Page Ref: 46–7/46–7

    Topic: Comparative Advantage and Trade

    Skill: Conceptual

    Objective: LO 2: Understand comparative advantage and explain how it is the basis for trade

    AACSB Coding: Reflective Thinking

    Special Feature: None

30. Rayburn Reed is a highly talented photographer. He has chosen to specialize in photography because of all of the following except

    A) he obviously has a comparative advantage in photography.

    B) his opportunity cost of pursuing another career is very low.

    C) for him, this is the most lucrative way to purchase the products that he wants to consume.

    D) his photographs are highly esteemed by art lovers who are willing to pay very high prices.

    Answer: B

    Diff: 3   Type: MC   Page Ref: 46–7/46–7

    Topic: Comparative Advantage and Trade

    Skill: Analytical

    Objective: LO 2: Understand comparative advantage and explain how it is the basis for trade

    AACSB Coding: Reflective Thinking

    Special Feature: None

31. If Blake can pick more cherries in one hour than Cody, then Blake has a comparative advantage in cherry picking.
    Answer: True   ⊙ False
    Diff: 2   Type: TF   Page Ref: 46/46
    Topic: Comparative Advantage and Trade
    Skill: Conceptual
    Objective: LO 2: Understand comparative advantage and explain how it is the basis for trade
    AACSB Coding: Reflective Thinking
    Special Feature: None

32. The basis for trade is comparative advantage, not absolute advantage.
    Answer: ⊙ True   False
    Diff: 2   Type: TF   Page Ref: 47/47
    Topic: Comparative Advantage and Trade
    Skill: Conceptual
    Objective: LO 2: Understand comparative advantage and explain how it is the basis for trade
    AACSB Coding: Reflective Thinking
    Special Feature: None

33. Suppose a country produces only two goods, then it is not possible to have a comparative advantage in the production of both those goods.
    Answer: ⊙ True   False
    Diff: 2   Type: TF   Page Ref: 47/47
    Topic: Comparative Advantage and Trade
    Skill: Conceptual
    Objective: LO 2: Understand comparative advantage and explain how it is the basis for trade
    AACSB Coding: Reflective Thinking
    Special Feature: None

34. In a two-good, two country world, if one country has an absolute advantage in the production of both goods, it cannot benefit by trading with the other country.
    Answer: True   ⊙ False
    Diff: 2   Type: TF   Page Ref: 47/47
    Topic: Comparative Advantage and Trade
    Skill: Conceptual
    Objective: LO 2: Understand comparative advantage and explain how it is the basis for trade
    AACSB Coding: Reflective Thinking
    Special Feature: None

35. If the opportunity cost of producing more of one good increases as more of that good is produced, then the production method is inefficient.
    Answer: True   ⊙ False
    Diff: 2   Type: TF   Page Ref: 47/47
    Topic: Comparative Advantage and Trade
    Skill: Conceptual
    Objective: LO 2: Understand comparative advantage and explain how it is the basis for trade
    AACSB Coding: Reflective Thinking
    Special Feature: None

36. It is possible to have a comparative advantage in producing a good or service without having an absolute advantage.
Answer: ◌ True   False
Diff: 2   Type: TF   Page Ref: 48/48
Topic: Comparative Advantage and Trade
Skill: Conceptual
Objective: LO 2: Understand comparative advantage and explain how it is the basis for trade
AACSB Coding: Reflective Thinking
Special Feature: Don't Let This Happen to YOU!: Don't Confuse Absolute Advantage and Comparative Advantage

37.

Table 2–4

	Digital Camera	*Wheat (bushels)*
China	100 hours	5 hours
South Korea	90 hours	3 hours

Refer to Table 2–4. This table shows the number of labor hours required to produce a digital cameras and a bushel of wheat in China and South Korea.

a.   Which country has an absolute advantage in the production of digital cameras?
b.   Which country has an absolute advantage in the production of wheat?
c.   What is China's opportunity cost of producing one digital camera?
d.   What is South Korea's opportunity cost of producing one digital camera?
e.   What is China's opportunity cost of producing one pound of wheat?
f.   What is South Korea's opportunity cost of producing one pound of what?
g.   If each country specializes in the production of the product in which it has a comparative advantage, who should produce digital cameras?
h.   If each country specializes in the production of the product in which it has a comparative advantage, who should produce wheat?
Answer: a.   South Korea has an absolute advantage in the production of digital cameras.
        b.   South Korea has an absolute advantage in wheat production.
        c.   China's the opportunity cost of producing one digital camera is 20 bushels of wheat.
        d.   South Korea's opportunity cost of producing one digital camera is 30 bushels of wheat
        e.   China's the opportunity cost of one bushel of wheat is 0.05 units of a digital camera.
        f.   South Korea's the opportunity cost of one bushel of wheat is 0.03 units of a digital camera.
        g.   China should specialize in producing digital cameras.
        h.   South Korea should specialize in producing wheat.
Diff: 3   Type: SA   Page Ref: 45/45
Topic: Comparative Advantage and Trade
Skill: Analytical
Objective: LO 2: Understand comparative advantage and explain how it is the basis for trade
AACSB Coding: Analytic Skills
Special Feature: None

38.   *Table 2-5*

	Digital Camera	*Wheat (bushels)*
China	100 hours	5 hours
South Korea	90 hours	3 hours

Refer to Table 2-5. This table shows the number of labor hours required to produce a digital camera and a bushel of wheat in China and South Korea.

a.   If each country has a total of 9,000 labor hours to devote to the production of the two goods, draw the production possibilities frontier for each country. Put "Digital Camera" on the horizontal axis and "Wheat" on the vertical axis. Be sure to identify the intercept values on your graphs.

b.   Suppose each country allocates 60% its labor hours to wheat production and 40% to the production of digital cameras. Complete Table 2-6 below to show each country's output of the two products.

Table 2-6: Production and Consumption with no Trade

	Digital Camera Output	*Wheat Output (bushels)*
China		
South Korea		
Total		

c.   If the two countries do not trade and consume whatever they produce, identify the current production and consumption point for each country on their respective production possibilities frontiers. Label China's consumption point "C" and South Korea's consumption point, "K".

d.   Suppose the two countries specialize and trade. Who should produce digital cameras and who should produce wheat? Explain your answer.

e.   Complete Table 2-7 below to show each country's output with specialization.

Table 2-7: Output with Specialization

	Digital Camera Output	*Wheat Output (bushels)*
China		
South Korea		
Total		

f.   Did specialization increase the combined output for the two countries without any increase in resources? If so, by how much?

g.   Suppose China and South Korea agree to trade so that in exchange for 1,200 bushels of wheat, the exporter of wheat receives 48 digital cameras. Complete Table 2.8 below to show each country's consumption bundle after trade.

h. Show the consumption points after trade on each country's production possibilities frontier. Label these points "B" for China and "J" for Korea.

i. Has trade made the two countries better off? Explain your answer.

Table 2-8: Consumption with Trade

	Digital Camera	*Wheat (bushels)*
China	42	1,200
South Korea	48	1,800

Answer:

a.

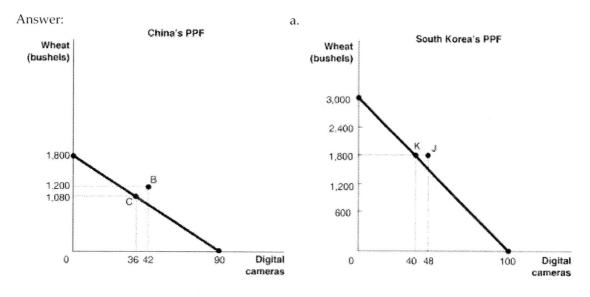

b.

Table 2–6: Production and Consumption with no Trade

	Digital Camera Output	*Wheat Output (bushels)*
China	36	1,080
South Korea	40	1,800
Total	76	2,800

c. See graph in part (a)

d. China should specialize in producing digital cameras because it has a lower opportunity cost: 20 bushels of wheat as opposed to South Korea's 30 bushels of wheat. South Korea should specialize in producing wheat because it has a lower opportunity cost: 0.03 units of a digital camera as opposed to China's 0.05 units of a digital camera.

e.

Table 2–7: Output with Specialization

	Digital Camera Output	Wheat Output (bushels)
China	90	0
South Korea	0	8,000
Total	90	8,000

f. Yes, digital camera output increased by 14 units from 76 to 90 units and wheat output increased by 120 bushels.

g.

Table 2–8: Consumption with Trade

	Digital Camera	Wheat (bushels)
China	42	1,200
South Korea	48	1,800

h. See graph in part (a)

i. Yes, trade has enabled the two countries to consume outside their PPFs.

Diff: 3   Type: ES   Page Ref: 48/48
Topic: Comparative Advantage and Trade
Skill: Analytical
Objective: LO 2: Understand comparative advantage and explain how it is the basis for trade
AACSB Coding: Analytic Skills
Special Feature: Solved Problem: Comparative Advantage and the Gains from Trade

39. Suppose in the United States, the opportunity cost of producing a motor engine is 4 auto bodies. In Canada, the opportunity cost of producing a motor engine is 2 auto bodies.
    a. What is the opportunity cost of producing an auto body for the United States?
    b. What is the opportunity cost of producing an auto body for Canada?
    c. Which country has a comparative advantage in the production of auto bodies?
    d. Which country has a comparative advantage in the production of motor engines?
    Answer: a. For the United States, the opportunity cost of producing an auto body is 1/4 of a motor engine.
    b. For Canada, the opportunity cost of producing an auto body is 1/2 of a motor engine.
    c. The United States has a comparative advantage in the production of auto bodies.
    d. Canada has a comparative advantage in the production of motor engines.

Diff: 3   Type: SA   Page Ref: 46–47
Topic: Comparative Advantage and Trade
Skill: Analytical
Objective: LO 2: Understand comparative advantage and explain how it is the basis for trade
AACSB Coding: Analytic Skills
Special Feature: None

2.3 The Market System

1. Which of the following is not a factor of production?
    A) an acre of farmland
    B) a drill press in a machine shop
    C) the manager of the local tire shop
    D) $1,000 in cash
    Answer: D
    Diff: 2   Type: MC   Page Ref: 50/50
    Topic: The Market System
    Skill: Conceptual
    Objective: LO 3: Explain the basic idea of how a market system works
    AACSB Coding: Reflective Thinking
    Special Feature: None

2. An example of a factor of production is
    A) a car produced by an auto manufacturer.
    B) a worker hired by an auto manufacturer.
    C) a loan granted to an auto manufacturer.
    D) the automobiles exported by an auto manufacturer.
    Answer: B
    Diff: 2   Type: MC   Page Ref: 50/50
    Topic: The Market System
    Skill: Conceptual
    Objective: LO 3: Explain the basic idea of how a market system works
    AACSB Coding: Reflective Thinking
    Special Feature: None

3. If a commercial dairy farm wants to raise funds to purchase feeding troughs, it does so in the
    A) output market.
    B) product market.
    C) factor market.
    D) dairy products market.
    Answer: C
    Diff: 1   Type: MC   Page Ref: 50/50
    Topic: The Market System
    Skill: Conceptual
    Objective: LO 3: Explain the basic idea of how a market system works
    AACSB Coding: Reflective Thinking
    Special Feature: None

4. A worker is hired in a
    A) goods and services market.
    B) product market.
    C) government market.
    D) factor market.
    Answer: D
    Diff: 1   Type: MC   Page Ref: 50/50
    Topic: The Market System
    Skill: Conceptual
    Objective: LO 3: Explain the basic idea of how a market system works
    AACSB Coding: Reflective Thinking
    Special Feature: None

5. When you purchase a new pair of jeans you do so in the
    A) factor market.
    B) input market
    C) product market
    D) resource market
    Answer: C
    Diff: 1   Type: MC   Page Ref: 50/50
    Topic: The Market System
    Skill: Conceptual
    Objective: LO 3: Explain the basic idea of how a market system works
    AACSB Coding: Reflective Thinking
    Special Feature: None

6. The resource income earned by those who supply labor services is called
    A) wages and salaries.
    B) stock options.
    C) profit.
    D) bonus.
    Answer: A
    Diff: 1   Type: MC   Page Ref: 50/50
    Topic: The Market System
    Skill: Conceptual
    Objective: LO 3: Explain the basic idea of how a market system works
    AACSB Coding: Reflective Thinking
    Special Feature: None

7. Which of the following statements is false about an entrepreneur?

    A) organizes the other factors of production into a working unit.

    B) develops the vision for the firm and funds the producing unit.

    C) sells his entrepreneurial services in the output market.

    D) risks the personal funds provided.

    Answer: C

    Diff: 2   Type: MC   Page Ref: 50/50
    Topic: The Market System
    Skill: Conceptual
    Objective: LO 3: Explain the basic idea of how a market system works
    AACSB Coding: Reflective Thinking
    Special Feature: None

8. The circular flow model demonstrates

    A) the role of the government in overseeing the market system.

    B) the roles played by households and firms in the market system.

    C) how shortages and surpluses are eliminated in a market.

    D) how demand and supply for goods and services are brought into equilibrium.

    Answer: B

    Diff: 2   Type: MC   Page Ref: 50–1/50–1
    Topic: The Market System
    Skill: Conceptual
    Objective: LO 3: Explain the basic idea of how a market system works
    AACSB Coding: Reflective Thinking
    Special Feature: None

9. Households

    A) have no influence on the circular flow in a market economy.

    B) purchase resources in the factor market.

    C) sell goods in the product market.

    D) sell resources in the factor market.

    Answer: D

    Diff: 1   Type: MC   Page Ref: 50–1/50–1
    Topic: The Market System
    Skill: Conceptual
    Objective: LO 3: Explain the basic idea of how a market system works
    AACSB Coding: Reflective Thinking
    Special Feature: None

10. Households
    A) purchase final goods and services in the factor market.
    B) purchase final goods and services in the product market.
    C) purchase resources in the product market.
    D) purchase resources in the factor market.
    Answer: B
    Diff: 1   Type: MC   Page Ref: 50–1/50–1
    Topic: The Market System
    Skill: Conceptual
    Objective: LO 3: Explain the basic idea of how a market system works
    AACSB Coding: Reflective Thinking
    Special Feature: None

11. In the circular flow model, producers
    A) sell goods and services in the input market.
    B) households spend earnings from resource sales on goods and services in the factor market.
    C) hire resources sold by households in the factor market.
    D) spend earnings from resource sales on goods and services in the product market.
    Answer: C
    Diff: 1   Type: MC   Page Ref: 50–1/50–1
    Topic: The Market System
    Skill: Conceptual
    Objective: LO 3: Explain the basic idea of how a market system works
    AACSB Coding: Reflective Thinking
    Special Feature: None

12. Which of the following is not a flow in the circular flow model?
    A) the flow of goods and services and the flow of resources to produce goods and services
    B) the flow of profit and the flow of revenue
    C) the flow of income earned by households and the flow of expenditures incurred by households
    D) the flow of revenue received by producers and the flow of payments to resource owners
    Answer: B
    Diff: 2   Type: MC   Page Ref: 50–1/50–1
    Topic: The Market System
    Skill: Conceptual
    Objective: LO 3: Explain the basic idea of how a market system works
    AACSB Coding: Reflective Thinking
    Special Feature: None

Figure 2-8

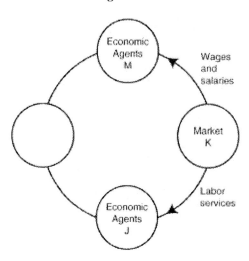

13. *Refer to Figure 2-8.* The segment of the circular flow diagram in the Figure shows the flow of labor services from market *K* to economic agents *J*. What is market *K* and who are economic agents *J*?

 A) *K* = factor markets; *J* = households
 B) *K* = product markets; *J* = households
 C) *K* = factor markets; *J* = firms
 D) *K* = product markets; *J* = firms
 Answer: C
 Diff: 2   Type: MC   Page Ref: 50-1/50-1
 Topic: The Market System
 Skill: Conceptual
 Objective: LO 3: Explain the basic idea of how a market system works
 AACSB Coding: Reflective Thinking
 Special Feature: None

14. *Refer to Figure 2-8.* The segment of the circular flow diagram in the Figure shows the flow of wages and salaries from market *K* to economic agents M. What is market *K* and who are economic agents *M*?

 A) *K* = factor markets; *M* = households
 B) *K* = product markets; *M* = households
 C) *K* = factor markets; *M* = firms
 D) *K* = product markets; *M* = firms
 Answer: A
 Diff: 2   Type: MC   Page Ref: 50-1/50-1
 Topic: The Market System
 Skill: Conceptual
 Objective: LO 3: Explain the basic idea of how a market system works
 AACSB Coding: Reflective Thinking
 Special Feature: None

15. Which of the following are flows in the circular flow model?
    A) the flow of goods and the flow of services
    B) the flow of costs and the flow of revenue
    C) the flow of income earned from the sale of resources and the flow of expenditures on goods and services.
    D) the flow of income received by households and the flow of tax revenues paid by households
    Answer: C
    Diff: 2   Type: MC   Page Ref: 50–1/50–1
    Topic: The Market System
    Skill: Conceptual
    Objective: LO 3: Explain the basic idea of how a market system works
    AACSB Coding: Reflective Thinking
    Special Feature: None

16. Which of the following statements is true about a simple circular flow model?
    A) Producers are neither buyers nor sellers in the product market.
    B) Households are neither buyers nor sellers in the input market.
    C) Producers are buyers in the factors market.
    D) Households are sellers in the product market.
    Answer: C
    Diff: 2   Type: MC   Page Ref: 50–1/50–1
    Topic: The Market System
    Skill: Conceptual
    Objective: LO 3: Explain the basic idea of how a market system works
    AACSB Coding: Reflective Thinking
    Special Feature: None

Figure 2–9

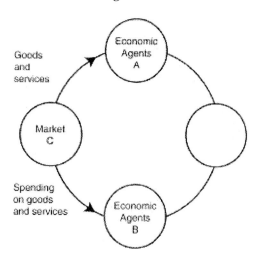

17. ***Refer to Figure 2–9.*** The segment of the circular flow diagram in the Figure shows the flow of goods and services from market C to economic agents A. What is market C and who are economic agents *A*?

    A) *C* = factor markets; *A* = households

    B) *C* = product markets; *A* = households

    C) *C* = factor markets; *A* = firms

    D) *C* = product markets; *A* = firms

Answer: B

Diff: 2   Type: MC   Page Ref: 50–1/50–1
Topic: The Market System
Skill: Conceptual
Objective: LO 3: Explain the basic idea of how a market system works
AACSB Coding: Reflective Thinking
Special Feature: None

Figure 2-10

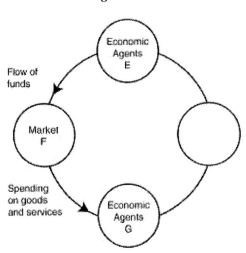

18. *Refer to Figure 2-10.* The segment of the circular flow diagram in the Figure shows the flow of funds from market *F* to economic agents G. The funds represent spending on goods and services. What is market *K* and who are economic agents *G*?

    A) *F* = factor markets; *G* = households
    B) *F* = product markets; *G* = households
    C) *F* = factor markets; *G* = firms
    D) *F* = product markets; *G* = firms

Answer: D

Diff: 2   Type: MC   Page Ref: 50-1/50-1
Topic: The Market System
Skill: Conceptual
Objective: LO 3: Explain the basic idea of how a market system works
AACSB Coding: Reflective Thinking
Special Feature: None

19. All of the following are examples of spending on factors of production in the circular flow model except

    A) Bima hires two students to work at his ice-cream store.
    B) "Get Fit Together'" purchases 3 new treadmills for its gym.
    C) Iris buys a dozen roses for her mother's birthday.
    D) The Banyan Tree rents a much larger property so that it can add a restaurant to its facilities.

Answer: C

Diff: 2   Type: MC   Page Ref: 50-1/50-1
Topic: The Market System
Skill: Conceptual
Objective: LO 3: Explain the basic idea of how a market system works
AACSB Coding: Reflective Thinking
Special Feature: None

20. All of the following are examples of spending on goods and services in the circular flow model except
    A) Amanda purchases a new electric guitar to pursue her hobby seriously.
    B) Chaitanya buys a new spa pedicure chair for her expanding nail salon business.
    C) Hernan buys a pizza at Papa C's.
    D) Lenny buys a new digital camera to take pictures at his son's graduation.
    Answer: B
    Diff: 2   Type: MC   Page Ref: 50–1/50–1
    Topic: The Market System
    Skill: Conceptual
    Objective: LO 3: Explain the basic idea of how a market system works
    AACSB Coding: Reflective Thinking
    Special Feature: None

21. "An Inquiry into the Nature and Causes of the Wealth of Nations" published in 1776 was written by?
    A) John Maynard Keynes
    B) Karl Marx
    C) Alfred Marshall
    D) Adam Smith
    Answer: D
    Diff: 1   Type: MC   Page Ref: 52/52
    Topic: The Market System
    Skill: Factual
    Objective: LO 3: Explain the basic idea of how a market system works
    AACSB Coding: Reflective Thinking
    Special Feature: None

Figure 2–11

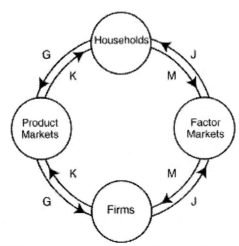

22. *Refer to Figure 2–11.* Which two arrows in the diagram depict the following transaction: Stanley purchases the novel, "Night of Sorrows" for his summer reading pleasure.
    A) *J* and *M*
    B) *J* and *G*
    C) *K* and *M*
    D) *K* and *G*
    Answer: D
    Diff: 2   Type: MC   Page Ref: 50–1/50–1
    Topic: The Market System
    Skill: Conceptual
    Objective: LO 3: Explain the basic idea of how a market system works
    AACSB Coding: Reflective Thinking
    Special Feature: None

23. *Refer to Figure 2–11.* Which two arrows in the diagram depict the following transaction: Lizzie Haxem hires "The Paint Pros," a professional painting company, to paint her home.
    A) *J* and *M*
    B) *K* and *G*
    C) *K* and *M*
    D) *J* and *G*
    Answer: B
    Diff: 2   Type: MC   Page Ref: 50–1/50–1
    Topic: The Market System
    Skill: Conceptual
    Objective: LO 3: Explain the basic idea of how a market system works
    AACSB Coding: Reflective Thinking
    Special Feature: None

24. ***Refer to Figure 2–11.*** Which two arrows in the diagram depict the following transaction: Carter earns a $400 commission for selling men's designer shoes at Brooks Brothers.
    A) *J* and *M*
    B) *K* and *G*
    C) *K* and *M*
    D) *J* and *G*
    Answer: A
    Diff: 2   Type: MC   Page Ref: 50–1/50–1
    Topic: The Market System
    Skill: Conceptual
    Objective: LO 3: Explain the basic idea of how a market system works
    AACSB Coding: Reflective Thinking
    Special Feature: None

25. Adam Smith's behavioral assumption about humans was that people
    A) typically act irrationally.
    B) usually act in a rational, self–interested way.
    C) are consistently greedy.
    D) typically act randomly.
    Answer: B
    Diff: 1   Type: MC   Page Ref: 52/52
    Topic: The Market System
    Skill: Conceptual
    Objective: LO 3: Explain the basic idea of how a market system works
    AACSB Coding: Reflective Thinking
    Special Feature: None

26. Which of the following countries does not come close to the free market benchmark?
    A) The United States
    B) Japan
    C) Cuba
    D) France
    Answer: C
    Diff: 1   Type: MC   Page Ref: 52/52
    Topic: The Market System
    Skill: Factual
    Objective: LO 3: Explain the basic idea of how a market system works
    AACSB Coding: Reflective Thinking
    Special Feature: None

27. Adam Smith's invisible hand refers to
    A) the government's unobtrusive role in ensuring that the economy functions efficiently.
    B) property ownership laws and the rule of the court system.
    C) the process by which individuals acting in their own self-interest bring about a market outcome that benefits society as a whole.
    D) the laws of nature that influence economics decisions.

    Answer: C
    Diff: 2   Type: MC   Page Ref: 52/52
    Topic: The Market System
    Skill: Conceptual
    Objective: LO 3: Explain the basic idea of how a market system works
    AACSB Coding: Reflective Thinking
    Special Feature: None

28. A critical function of the government in facilitating the operation of a market economy is
    A) producing goods and services for low income households.
    B) setting up and enforcing private property rights.
    C) ensuring an equal distribution of income to all citizens.
    D) controlling the market prices of food items.

    Answer: B
    Diff: 2   Type: MC   Page Ref: 54/54
    Topic: The Market System
    Skill: Conceptual
    Objective: LO 3: Explain the basic idea of how a market system works
    AACSB Coding: Reflective Thinking
    Special Feature: None

29. The term "property rights" refers to
    A) the physical possession of a house or any other property which the owner legally purchased.
    B) the ability to exercise control over one's own resources within the confines of the law.
    C) the government's right to appropriate land from wealthy land owners to redistribute to peasants
    D) the right of a business not to have its assets confiscated by the government in the event that the business is accused of committing fraud.

    Answer: B
    Diff: 1   Type: MC   Page Ref: 54/54
    Topic: The Market System
    Skill: Definition
    Objective: LO 3: Explain the basic idea of how a market system works
    AACSB Coding: Reflective Thinking
    Special Feature: None

30. The primary purpose of patents and copyrights is to
    A) provide owners with large profit forever.
    B) protect firms from being taken advantage of by competing firms.
    C) protect domestic firms from foreign competition.
    D) encourage the expenditure of funds on research and development to create new products.
    Answer: D
    Diff: 1   Type: MC   Page Ref: 54/54
    Topic: The Market System
    Skill: Conceptual
    Objective: LO 3: Explain the basic idea of how a market system works
    AACSB Coding: Reflective Thinking
    Special Feature: None

31. A major factor contributing to the slow growth rate of less developed economies is
    A) the lack of well-defined and enforceable property rights.
    B) the lack of natural resources.
    C) the lack of workers.
    D) the high rate of illiteracy.
    Answer: A
    Diff: 2   Type: MC   Page Ref: 54/54
    Topic: The Market System
    Skill: Factual
    Objective: LO 3: Explain the basic idea of how a market system works
    AACSB Coding: Reflective Thinking
    Special Feature: None

32. A successful market economy requires well defined property rights and
    A) balanced supplies of all factors of production.
    B) an independent court system to adjudicate disputes based on the law.
    C) detailed government regulations.
    D) a safety net to ensure that those who cannot participate in the market economy can earn an income.
    Answer: B
    Diff: 2   Type: MC   Page Ref: 54/54
    Topic: The Market System
    Skill: Conceptual
    Objective: LO 3: Explain the basic idea of how a market system works
    AACSB Coding: Reflective Thinking
    Special Feature: None

33. Consider the following items:
    a.   the novel "The DaVinci Code" by Dan Brown
    b.   the "The Spirited Shipper", an innovative wine shipping box
    c.   a Swiss chef's award–winning recipe
    d.   an original fabric design for example, the fabric used for "Coach" bags and luggage.

    Which of the items listed is an example of intellectual property?
      A) a and b only
      B) a, b, and c
      C) a and d only
      D) all of the items listed
    Answer: D
    Diff: 2   Type: MC   Page Ref: 54/54
    Topic: The Market System
    Skill: Conceptual
    Objective: LO 3: Explain the basic idea of how a market system works
    AACSB Coding: Reflective Thinking
    Special Feature: None

34. A guild is
      A) a group of independent producers competing with each other.
      B) an organization of producers that limits the amount of a good produced.
      C) a group of nations who agree not to compete with each other.
      D) a nation that is a free market benchmark.
    Answer: B
    Diff: 1   Type: MC   Page Ref: 54/54
    Topic: The Market System
    Skill: Definition
    Objective: LO 3: Explain the basic idea of how a market system works
    AACSB Coding: Reflective Thinking
    Special Feature: None

35. In 18th century Europe, governments gave guilds legal authority to limit production of goods. Did this authority obstruct or improve the market mechanism and how?
    A) It improved the market mechanism by making it more efficient because the guilds were able to quickly identify and rectify any market shortages and surpluses.
    B) It improved the market mechanism because the government's actions provided the correct set of signals to the market so that producers can adjust their output to better meet the needs of consumers.
    C) It obstructed the market mechanism because the guild's actions prevented the forces of demand and supply from coordinating the self-interested decisions of producers and consumers.
    D) It obstructed the market mechanism because with one more party having to coordinate activities (the guilds) there were delays in getting the products to consumers.
    Answer: C
    Diff: 2   Type: MC   Page Ref: 54/54
    Topic: The Market System
    Skill: Conceptual
    Objective: LO 3: Explain the basic idea of how a market system works
    AACSB Coding: Reflective Thinking
    Special Feature: None

36. The payment received by suppliers of entrepreneurial skills is called profit.
    Answer: True   False
    Diff: 1   Type: TF   Page Ref: 50/50
    Topic: The Market System
    Skill: Conceptual
    Objective: LO 3: Explain the basic idea of how a market system works
    AACSB Coding: Reflective Thinking
    Special Feature: None

134. In the circular flow model, households supply resources such as labor services in the product market.
    Answer: True   False
    Diff: 1   Type: TF   Page Ref: 51/51
    Topic: The Market System
    Skill: Conceptual
    Objective: LO 3: Explain the basic idea of how a market system works
    AACSB Coding: Reflective Thinking
    Special Feature: None

37. In economics, the term "free market" refers to a market where no sales tax is imposed on products sold.
    Answer: True   False
    Diff: 1   Type: TF   Page Ref: 52/52
    Topic: The Market System
    Skill: Conceptual
    Objective: LO 3: Explain the basic idea of how a market system works
    AACSB Coding: Reflective Thinking
    Special Feature: None

38. In a free market there are virtually no restrictions, or at best few restrictions on how factors of production can be employed.
    Answer: ○ True   False
    Diff: 1   Type: TF   Page Ref: 52/52
    Topic: The Market System
    Skill: Conceptual
    Objective: LO 3: Explain the basic idea of how a market system works
    AACSB Coding: Reflective Thinking
    Special Feature: None

39. A stand of redwood trees is not an example of a factor of production but the harvested and processed redwood is a factor of production.
    Answer: True   ○ False
    Diff: 2   Type: TF   Page Ref: 50/50
    Topic: The Market System
    Skill: Conceptual
    Objective: LO 3: Explain the basic idea of how a market system works
    AACSB Coding: Reflective Thinking
    Special Feature: None

40. Each person goes about her daily business seeking to maximize her own self interests. In doing so, she contributes to the welfare of society at large. This is the idea underlying Adam Smith's "invisible hand".
    Answer: ○ True   False
    Diff: 2   Type: TF   Page Ref: 52/52
    Topic: The Market System
    Skill: Conceptual
    Objective: LO 3: Explain the basic idea of how a market system works
    AACSB Coding: Reflective Thinking
    Special Feature: None

41. Define the term "property rights". Explain why the lack of well defined and enforceable property rights is detrimental to the smooth functioning of a market system.
    Answer: The term "property rights" refers to the rights that individuals or firms have to the exclusive use of their resources, within the confines of the law. Well defined and enforceable property rights provide the incentive for people and firms to invest resources and undertake risks. This encourages the production of a wide range of goods and services. Without property rights and the means to enforce these rights, no person would want to undertake such a risk.
    Diff: 2   Type: SA   Page Ref: 54/54
    Topic: The Market System
    Skill: Analytical
    Objective: LO 3: Explain the basic idea of how a market system works
    AACSB Coding: Reflective Thinking
    Special Feature: None

42. When videos on YouTube contained material from television shows or movies, YouTube had to obtain permission from several people who held rights to the television show or movie, which could be a time consuming process. YouTube's vice president for business development was quoted as saying, "It's almost like technology has pushed far beyond the business practices and the law, and now everything needs to kind of catch up." What do you think he meant by that statement?

Answer: His statement alludes to the fact that the nature of internet technology requires society to change the legal understanding or status of copyright as it stands and to re-examine the payment mechanism.

Diff: 3   Type: SA   Page Ref: 55/55
Topic: The Market System
Skill: Analytical
Objective: LO 3: Explain the basic idea of how a market system works
AACSB Coding: Analytic Skills
Special Feature: Making the Connection: Property Rights in Cyberspace: YouTube and MySpace

43. Adam Smith, the father of modern economics wrote in his book, *An Inquiry into the Nature and Causes of the Wealth of Nations*, "It is not from the benevolence of the butcher, the brewer, or the baker, that we expect our dinner but from their regard to their own interest." Explain what he meant by that statement and how such behavior promotes the wealth of a nation.

Answer: The statements refer to the fact that people act in their own self interest. For example, the butcher who sells meat and the baker who bakes bread carry out these activities because these tasks contributed to their livelihood, not because they were concerned about the diner. Nevertheless, their actions benefited the diner. This is precisely one of the virtues of a market: people do not have to act virtuously to produce worthwhile outcomes. Producing goods and services that consumers value increases the wealth of a nation.

Diff: 3   Type: SA   Page Ref: 53/53
Topic: The Market System
Skill: Analytical
Objective: LO 3: Explain the basic idea of how a market system works
AACSB Coding: Analytic Skills
Special Feature: Making the Connection: A Story of the Marketing System in Action: How do You Make an iPod?

Chapter 3   Where Prices Come From: The Interaction of Demand and Supply

3.1   The Demand Side of the Market

1. Although it is a popular product, Apple makes little profit from each song downloaded through iTunes. Why does Apple charge only $0.99 to download a song?
   - A) Although Apple makes a small amount of profit per song, total profit is large because the quantity sold is large.
   - B) Apple cannot raise the price above $0.99 per song because consumers can download songs at even lower prices from Apple's competitors.
   - C) The low price makes it more likely that consumers will buy iPods, which are relatively expensive.
   - D) Apple plans to increase the price of downloading songs after it sells a large enough number of iPods.

   Answer: C
   Diff: 2   Type: MC   Page Ref: 66/66
   Topic: Demand and supply
   Skill: Analytical
   Objective: LO1: Discuss the variables that influence demand.
   AACSB Coding: Analytic Skills
   Special Feature: Chapter Opener: Apple and the Demand for iPods

2. To compete with the iPod from Apple, Microsoft began marketing its own digital music player, called Zune. The textbook mentioned one strategy Microsoft could use to overcome the advantages Apple has from selling the most popular brand of music player. What was this strategy?
   - A) Microsoft could advertise Zune by sending emails to the many consumers who use the company's software.
   - B) Microsoft could spend some of its large advertising budget to run television and magazine ads for Zune.
   - C) Microsoft is considering suing Apple for copyright infringement; Microsoft was the first company to develop the technology used to produce digital music players.
   - D) Microsoft could try to sell Zune or downloaded songs at prices lower than those charged by Apple.

   Answer: D
   Diff: 1   Type: MC   Page Ref: 67/67
   Topic: Complements and substitutes
   Skill: Fact
   Objective: LO1: Discuss the variables that influence demand.
   AACSB Coding: Analytic Skills
   Special Feature: Economics in YOUR Life!: Will You Buy an iPod or a Zune?

3. What is the difference between an "increase in demand" and an "increase in quantity demanded"?
    A) There is no difference between the two terms; they both refer to a shift of the demand curve.
    B) An "increase in demand" is represented by a rightward shift of the demand curve while an "increase in quantity demanded" is represented by a movement along a given demand curve.
    C) There is no difference between the two terms; they both refer to a movement downward along a given demand curve.
    D) An "increase in demand" is represented by a movement along a given demand curve, while an "increase in quantity demanded" is represented by a rightward shift of the demand curve.
Answer: B
Diff: 1   Type: MC   Page Ref: 73/73
Topic: Demand
Skill: Definition
Objective: LO1: Discuss the variables that influence demand.
AACSB Coding: Reflective Thinking
Special Feature: None

4. A demand curve shows the relationship between
    A) the price of a product and the quantity of the product demanded.
    B) the amount of a product sellers are willing to sell at a particular price and the amount consumers are willing to buy at that price.
    C) the quantity that consumers are willing and able to buy and the quantity that sellers are willing and able to offer.
    D) the price of a produce and the demand for the product.
Answer: A
Diff: 1   Type: MC   Page Ref: 68/68
Topic: Demand
Skill: Definition
Objective: LO1: Discuss the variables that influence demand.
AACSB Coding: Reflective Thinking
Special Feature: None

5. If, in response to an increase in the price of chocolate, the quantity demanded of chocolate decreases economists would describe this as
    A) a decrease in demand.
    B) a decrease in quantity demanded.
    C) a change in consumer income.
    D) a decrease in consumers' taste for chocolate.
Answer: B
Diff: 2   Type: MC   Page Ref: 69/69
Topic: Quantity demanded
Skill: Definition
Objective: LO1: Discuss the variables that influence demand.
AACSB Coding: Analytic Skills
Special Feature: None

6. By drawing a demand curve with price on the vertical axis and quantity on the horizontal axis, economists assume that the most important determinant of the demand for a good is
    A) consumer income.
    B) consumer tastes and preferences.
    C) the price of the good.
    D) the quality of the good.
    Answer: C
    Diff: 1   Type: MC   Page Ref: 70/70
    Topic: Demand
    Skill: Analytical
    Objective: LO1: Discuss the variables that influence demand.
    AACSB Coding: Reflective Thinking
    Special Feature: None

7. The law of demand implies, holding everything else constant, that
    A) as the price of bagels increases, the quantity of bagels demanded will decrease.
    B) as the price of bagels increases, the demand for bagels will decrease.
    C) as the price of bagels increases, the quantity of bagels demanded will increase.
    D) as the price for bagels increases, the demand of bagels will increase.
    Answer: A
    Diff: 1   Type: MC   Page Ref: 69/69
    Topic: Law of demand
    Skill: Analytical
    Objective: LO1: Discuss the variables that influence demand.
    AACSB Coding: Analytic Skills
    Special Feature: None

8. The phrase "demand has increased" means that
    A) a demand curve has shifted to the left.
    B) there has been an upward movement along a demand curve.
    C) there has been a downward movement along a demand curve.
    D) a demand curve has shifted to the right.
    Answer: D
    Diff: 1   Type: MC   Page Ref: 69/69
    Topic: Demand
    Skill: Conceptual
    Objective: LO1: Discuss the variables that influence demand.
    AACSB Coding: Reflective Thinking
    Special Feature: None

9. Holding everything else constant, an increase in the price of MP3 players will result in
   A) a decrease in the quantity of MP3 players supplied.
   B) a decrease in the demand for MP3 players.
   C) an increase in the supply of MP3 players.
   D) a decrease in the quantity of MP3 players demanded.
   Answer: D
   Diff: 2   Type: MC   Page Ref: 70/70
   Topic: Law of demand
   Skill: Analytical
   Objective: LO1: Discuss the variables that influence demand.
   AACSB Coding: Analytic Skills
   Special Feature: None

10. A change in which variable will change the market demand for a product?
    A) The price of the product.
    B) Expected future prices.
    C) The number of firms in the market.
    D) The quantity supplied of the product.
    Answer: B
    Diff: 1   Type: MC   Page Ref: 73/73
    Topic: Variables that influence demand
    Skill: Conceptual
    Objective: LO1: Discuss the variables that influence demand.
    AACSB Coding: Reflective Thinking
    Special Feature: None

11.
Table 3-1

Loose leaf Tea Price per lb. (dollars)	Sunil's Quantity Demanded (lbs)	Mia's Quantity Demanded (lbs)	Rest of Market Quantity Demanded (lbs)	Market Quantity demanded (lbs)
$8	4	0	30	
6	7	2	40	
5	9	3	51	
4	12	5	64	
3	15	8	90	

Refer to Table 3-1. The table above shows the demand schedules for loose-leaf tea of two individuals (Sunil and Mia) and the rest of the market. At a price of $5, the quantity demanded in the market would be

    A) 51 lbs.
    B) 76 lbs.
    C) 63 lbs
    D) 146 lbs.
Answer: C
Diff: 2   Type: MC   Page Ref: 73/73
Topic: Market demand
Skill: Analytical
Objective: LO1: Discuss the variables that influence demand.
AACSB Coding: Analytic Skills
Special Feature: None

12. *Refer to Table 3-1*. The table above shows the demand schedules for loose-leaf tee of two individuals (Sunil and Mia) and the rest of the market. If the price of loose-tea raises from $3 to $4 the market quantity demanded would

    A) decrease by 32 pounds.
    B) increase by 64 pounds.
    C) increase by 32 pounds.
    D) decrease by 64 pounds.
Answer: A
Diff: 2   Type: MC   Page Ref: 73/73
Topic: Market demand
Skill: Analytical
Objective: LO1: Discuss the variables that influence demand.
AACSB Coding: Analytic Skills
Special Feature: None

13. The income effect of a price change refers to the impact of a change in
    A) income on the price of a good.
    B) demand when income changes.
    C) the quantity demanded when income changes.
    D) the price of a good on a consumer's purchasing power.
    Answer: D
    Diff: 3   Type: MC   Page Ref: 69/69
    Topic: The income effect of a price change
    Skill: Conceptual
    Objective: LO1: Discuss the variables that influence demand.
    AACSB Coding: Reflective Thinking
    Special Feature: None

14. Which of the following will *not* shift the demand curve for a good?
    A) An increase in population.
    B) An increase in the price of the good.
    C) A decrease in the price of a substitute good.
    D) An increase in consumer incomes.
    Answer: B
    Diff: 1   Type: MC   Page Ref: 70/70
    Topic: Change in demand
    Skill: Conceptual
    Objective: LO1: Discuss the variables that influence demand.
    AACSB Coding: Reflective Thinking
    Special Feature: None

15. A movement along the demand curve for toothpaste would be caused by
    A) a change in the price of toothbrushes.
    B) a change in consumer income.
    C) a change in the price of toothpaste.
    D) a change in population.
    Answer: C
    Diff: 1   Type: MC   Page Ref: 70/70
    Topic: Quantity demanded
    Skill: Conceptual
    Objective: LO1: Discuss the variables that influence demand.
    AACSB Coding: Reflective Thinking
    Special Feature: None

16. The substitution effect of a price change refers to
    A) the change in quantity demanded that results from a change in price making a good more or less expensive relative to other goods that are substitutes.
    B) the shift of a demand curve when the price of a substitute good changes.
    C) the movement along the demand curve due to a change in purchasing power brought about by the price change.
    D) the shift in the demand curve due to a change in purchasing power brought about by the price change.
    Answer: A
    Diff: 3   Type: MC   Page Ref: 69/69
    Topic: The substitution effect of a price change
    Skill: Definition
    Objective: LO1: Discuss the variables that influence demand.
    AACSB Coding: Reflective Thinking
    Special Feature: None

17. If the price of grapefruit rises, the substitution effect due to the price change will cause
    A) a decrease in the demand for grapefruit.
    B) a decrease in the demand for oranges, a substitute for grapefruit.
    C) a decrease in the quantity demanded of grapefruit.
    D) a decrease in the quantity supplied of grapefruit.
    Answer: C
    Diff: 3   Type: MC   Page Ref: 70/70
    Topic: The substitution effect of a price change
    Skill: Conceptual
    Objective: LO1: Discuss the variables that influence demand.
    AACSB Coding: Reflective Thinking
    Special Feature: None

18. The income effect of a price change results in a
    A) shift of the demand curve when income changes.
    B) movement along the demand curve due to a change in relative prices.
    C) shift of the demand curve due to a change in purchasing power brought about by the price change.
    D) movement along the demand curve due to a change in purchasing power brought about by the price change.
    Answer: D
    Diff: 2   Type: MC   Page Ref: 69/69
    Topic: The income effect of a price change
    Skill: Definition
    Objective: LO1: Discuss the variables that influence demand.
    AACSB Coding: Reflective Thinking
    Special Feature: None

19. If an increase in income leads to in an increase in the demand for peanut butter, then peanut butter is
    A) a neutral good.
    B) a normal good.
    C) a necessity.
    D) a complement.
    Answer: B
    Diff: 1   Type: MC   Page Ref: 69/69
    Topic: Normal goods
    Skill: Conceptual
    Objective: LO1: Discuss the variables that influence demand.
    AACSB Coding: Analytic Skills
    Special Feature: None

20. If a decrease in income leads to an increase in the demand for macaroni, then macaroni is
    A) an inferior good.
    B) a neutral good.
    C) a necessity.
    D) a normal good.
    Answer: A
    Diff: 2   Type: MC   Page Ref: 69/69
    Topic: Inferior good
    Skill: Analytical
    Objective: LO1: Discuss the variables that influence demand.
    AACSB Coding: Analytic Skills
    Special Feature: None

21. The Internet has created a new category in the book selling market, namely, the "barely used" book. How does the availability of barely used books affect the market for new books?
    A) the demand curve for new books shifts to the right.
    B) the demand curve for new books shifts to the left.
    C) the supply curve for new books shifts to the right.
    D) the supply curve for new books shifts to the left.
    Answer: B
    Diff: 2   Type: MC   Page Ref: 74/74
    Topic: Substitutes
    Skill: Analytical
    Objective: LO1: Discuss the variables that influence demand.
    AACSB Coding: Analytic Skills
    Special Feature: None

22. According to a recent study, "Stricter college alcohol policies, such as raising the price of alcohol, or banning alcohol on campus, decrease the number of students who use marijuana." On the basis of this information, how would you describe alcohol and marijuana?
    A) The two goods are substitutes in consumption.
    B) There is no relationship between the two goods.
    C) The two goods are complements in consumption.
    D) They are both luxury goods.
    Answer: C
    Diff: 3   Type: MC   Page Ref: 71/71
    Topic: Complements and substitutes
    Skill: Analytical
    Objective: LO1: Discuss the variables that influence demand.
    AACSB Coding: Analytic Skills
    Special Feature: None

23. If the price of automobiles were to increase, then
    A) the demand for gasoline would decrease.
    B) the demand for gasoline would increase.
    C) the supply of gasoline would increase.
    D) the quantity demanded of gasoline would decrease.
    Answer: A
    Diff: 2   Type: MC   Page Ref: 71/71
    Topic: Complements and substitutes
    Skill: Analytical
    Objective: LO1: Discuss the variables that influence demand.
    AACSB Coding: Analytic Skills
    Special Feature: None

24. Suppose that when the price of hamburgers increases, the Ruiz family increases their purchases of hot dogs. To the Ruiz family,
    A) hamburgers and hot dogs are complements.
    B) hamburgers and hot dogs are inferior goods.
    C) hamburgers and hot dogs are normal goods.
    D) hamburgers and hot dogs are substitutes.
    Answer: D
    Diff: 2   Type: MC   Page Ref: 71/71
    Topic: Complements and substitutes
    Skill: Analytical
    Objective: LO1: Discuss the variables that influence demand.
    AACSB Coding: Analytic Skills
    Special Feature: None

25. Suppose that when the price of hamburgers decreases, the Ruiz family increase their purchases of ketchup.
    A) hamburgers and ketchup are complements.
    B) hamburgers and ketchup and substitutes.
    C) hamburgers and ketchup are normal goods.
    D) hamburgers are normal goods and hot dogs are inferior goods.

Answer: A
Diff: 2   Type: MC   Page Ref: 71/71
Topic: Complements and substitutes
Skill: Analytical
Objective: LO1: Discuss the variables that influence demand.
AACSB Coding: Analytic Skills
Special Feature: None

26. Several studies have shown promising links between green tea consumption and cancer prevention. How does this affect the market for green tea?
    A) The green tea supply curve shifts to the right because of a change in tastes in favor of green tea.
    B) The green tea demand curve shifts to the right because of a change in tastes in favor of green tea.
    C) The green tea demand curve shifts to the left because this new information will increase the price of green tea.
    D) The green tea supply curve shifts to the left because this new information will increase the price of green tea.

Answer: B
Diff: 2   Type: MC   Page Ref: 74/74
Topic: Variables that influence demand
Skill: Analytical
Objective: LO1: Discuss the variables that influence demand.
AACSB Coding: Analytic Skills
Special Feature: None

27. Technological advances have resulted in lower prices for digital cameras. What is the impact of this on the market for traditional (non–digital) cameras?
    A) The demand curve for traditional cameras shifts to the right.
    B) The supply curve for traditional cameras shifts to the right.
    C) The demand curve for traditional cameras shifts to the left.
    D) The supply curve for traditional cameras shifts to the left.

Answer: C
Diff: 2   Type: MC   Page Ref: 74/74
Topic: Variables that influence demand
Skill: Analytical
Objective: LO1: Discuss the variables that influence demand.
AACSB Coding: Analytic Skills
Special Feature: None

28. How does the increasing use of digital cameras affect the market for traditional camera film?
    A) The demand curve for traditional camera film shifts to the right.
    B) The supply curve for traditional camera film shifts to the left.
    C) The supply curve for traditional camera film shifts to the right.
    D) The demand curve for traditional camera film shifts to the left.
    Answer: D
    Diff: 2   Type: MC   Page Ref: 74/74
    Topic: Variables that influence demand
    Skill: Analytical
    Objective: LO1: Discuss the variables that influence demand.
    AACSB Coding: Analytic Skills
    Special Feature: None

29. Technological advancements have led to lower prices and an increase in the sale of digital cameras. How does this affect the digital photo printing paper market?
    A) The demand curve for digital photo printing paper shifts to the right.
    B) The demand curve for digital photo printing paper shifts to the left.
    C) The supply curve for digital photo printing paper shifts to the right.
    D) The supply curve for digital photo printing paper shifts to the left.
    Answer: A
    Diff: 2   Type: MC   Page Ref: 74/74
    Topic: Change in demand, complements
    Skill: Analytical
    Objective: LO1: Discuss the variables that influence demand.
    AACSB Coding: Analytic Skills
    Special Feature: None

30. Buyers scrambled to secure stocks of Australian wool following a forecast of an 11 percent decline in wool production. What happens in the Australian wool market as a result of this announcement?
    A) The demand curve for Australian wool shifts to the left in anticipation of higher prices in the future.
    B) The demand curve for Australian wool shifts to the right in anticipation of higher prices in the future.
    C) The supply curve for Australian wool shifts to the right in anticipation of higher prices in the future.
    D) The supply curve for Australian wool shifts to the left in anticipation of lower quantities in the future.
    Answer: B
    Diff: 2   Type: MC   Page Ref: 74/74
    Topic: Variables that influence demand
    Skill: Analytical
    Objective: LO1: Discuss the variables that influence demand.
    AACSB Coding: Analytic Skills
    Special Feature: None

31. Tom Searchinger, a senior attorney at the Environmental Defense fund, observed that generous farm subsidies have encouraged farmers to produce more corn and more wheat. How does this affect the market for fertilizer?
    A) The supply of fertilizer increases.
    B) The supply of fertilizer decreases
    C) The demand for fertilizer increases.
    D) The demand for fertilizer decreases.
    Answer: C
    Diff: 2   Type: MC   Page Ref: 74/74
    Topic: Change in demand, complements
    Skill: Analytical
    Objective: LO1: Discuss the variables that influence demand.
    AACSB Coding: Analytic Skills
    Special Feature: None

32. In January, buyers of gold expect that the price of gold will fall in February. What happens in the gold market in January, holding everything else constant?
    A) The demand curve shifts to the right.
    B) The quantity demanded increases.
    C) The quantity demanded decreases
    D) The demand curve shifts to the left.
    Answer: D
    Diff: 2   Type: MC   Page Ref: 74/74
    Topic: Variables that influence demand
    Skill: Analytical
    Objective: LO1: Discuss the variables that influence demand.
    AACSB Coding: Analytic Skills
    Special Feature: None

33. In January, buyers of gold expect that the price of gold will rise in February. What happens in the gold market in January, holding all else constant?
    A) The supply curve shifts to the right.
    B) The demand curve shifts to the left.
    C) The demand curve shifts to the right.
    D) The quantity demanded increases.
    Answer: C
    Diff: 2   Type: MC   Page Ref: 74/74
    Topic: Change in demand
    Skill: Analytical
    Objective: LO1: Discuss the variables that influence demand.
    AACSB Coding: Analytic Skills
    Special Feature: None

34. Christopher Tang has argued that supermarkets should not necessarily remove goods from their shelves even if they are not selling well. Which of the following explains Tang's reasoning?
    A) A profit can be made from a slow-selling good if it sells at a high price.
    B) If a slow-selling product is a complement of another product, removing the slow-seller would reduce sales of both products.
    C) If a slow-selling product is a new product it may become a best-seller in the future.
    D) Removing slow-selling products will force consumers to buy these products at other stores.
    Answer: B
    Diff: 2   Type: MC   Page Ref: 71/71
    Topic: Complements and substitutes
    Skill: Conceptual
    Objective: LO1: Discuss the variables that influence demand.
    AACSB Coding: Reflective Thinking
    Special Feature: Making the Connection: Why Supermarkets Need to Understand Substitutes and Complements

35. Research by Christopher Tang suggests that supermarkets should consider which of the following when deciding whether to remove slow-selling goods from their shelves?
    A) Whether the goods removed are substitutes or complements with the remaining goods.
    B) Whether the goods removed have high profit margins.
    C) Whether the goods removed are popular with affluent consumers.
    D) Whether the goods removed are likely to be subject to shortages in the future.
    Answer: A
    Diff: 1   Type: MC   Page Ref: 73/73
    Topic: Complements and substitutes
    Skill: Conceptual
    Objective: LO1: Discuss the variables that influence demand.
    AACSB Coding: Reflective Thinking
    Special Feature: Making the Connection: Why Supermarkets Need to Understand Substitutes and Complements

36. In 2007 Apple announced it would sell a 90-minute video of Super Bowl highlights through its iTunes store.   Apple also announced that it would make available a special version of the highlights. Which of the following describes this special version?
    A) The special version was made to appeal to Europeans. The NFL is trying to build a greater audience for American football in Europe.
    B) The special version was made for fans of the teams that played in the Super Bowl, since these fans are most likely to buy the highlights.
    C) A special High Definition version was made available.
    D) The special version was made available in Spanish.
    Answer: D
    Diff: 1   Type: MC   Page Ref: 72/72
    Topic: Variables that influence demand
    Skill: Fact
    Objective: LO1: Discuss the variables that influence demand.
    AACSB Coding: Reflective Thinking
    Special Feature: Making the Connection: Companies Respond to a Growing Hispanic Population

37. In 2002 Apple decided not to develop and sell a "tablet PC" – a laptop with a special screen that can convert handwriting into text. Which of the following is one reason why Apple chose not to develop a tablet PC?
    A) The technology was considered to complex for the average computer user.
    B) Apple would not be able to produce enough tablet PC units to meet the demand for them.
    C) The price of the tablet PC would have been too high to sell many units.
    D) Microsoft had a patent on the technology used to make tablet PCs and was not willing to sell the rights to this technology to Apple.
    Answer: A
    Diff: 1   Type: MC   Page Ref: 75/75
    Topic: Variables that influence demand
    Skill: Fact
    Objective: LO1: Discuss the variables that influence demand.
    AACSB Coding: Reflective Thinking
    Special Feature: Making the Connection: Apple Forecasts the Demand for iPhones and Other Consumer Electronics

38. In 2002 Apple decided not to develop and sell a "tablet PC" – a laptop with a special screen that can convert handwriting into text. According to one Apple executive, the tablet PC project was not consistent with Apple's theory for success. What is this theory?
    A) Apple markets only products that it has patented. This prevents other companies from competing with Apple.
    B) Apple markets products that it can sell for high prices. The tablet PC would have sold for a low price.
    C) Apple believes its success will come from selling many inexpensive items rather than relatively few expensive items.
    D) Apple only sells items that it can build a successful advertising campaign around.
    Answer: C
    Diff: 1   Type: MC   Page Ref: 75/75
    Topic: Quantity demanded
    Skill: Fact
    Objective: LO1: Discuss the variables that influence demand.
    AACSB Coding: Reflective Thinking
    Special Feature: Making the Connection: Apple Forecasts the Demand for iPhones and Other Consumer Electronics

39. The supply curve for watches
    A) shows the supply of watches consumers are willing and able to buy at any given price.
    B) is downward sloping.
    C) shows the relationship between the quantity of watches firms are willing and able to supply and the quantity of watches consumers are willing and able to purchase.
    D) shows the relationship between the price of watches and the quantity supplied of watches.
    Answer: D
    Diff: 2   Type: MC   Page Ref: 76/76
    Topic: Supply
    Skill: Definition
    Objective: LO1: Discuss the variables that influence demand.
    AACSB Coding: Reflective Thinking
    Special Feature: None

40. An increase in the price of MP3 players will result in
    A) a smaller quantity of MP3 players supplied.
    B) a larger quantity of MP3 players supplied.
    C) a decrease in the demand for MP3 players.
    D) an increase in the supply of MP3 players.
    Answer: B
    Diff: 1   Type: MC   Page Ref: 77/77
    Topic: Quantity supplied
    Skill: Conceptual
    Objective: LO1: Discuss the variables that influence demand.
    AACSB Coding: Reflective Thinking
    Special Feature: None

41. The income effect of a price change refers to the change in the quantity demanded of a good that results from a change in purchasing power as a result of the price change.
    Answer: True   False
    Diff: 2   Type: TF   Page Ref: 69/69
    Topic: The income effect of a price change
    Skill: Definition
    Objective: LO1: Discuss the variables that influence demand.
    AACSB Coding: Reflective Thinking
    Special Feature: None

42. If the price of peaches, a substitute for plums, increases the demand for plums will decrease.
    Answer: True   False
    Diff: 1   Type: TF   Page Ref: 69/69
    Topic: Complements and substitutes
    Skill: Analytical
    Objective: LO1: Discuss the variables that influence demand.
    AACSB Coding: Analytic Skills
    Special Feature: None

43. A normal good is a good for which the quantity demanded increases as the price decreases, holding everything else constant.
    Answer: True   ○ False
    Diff: 1   Type: TF   Page Ref: 71/71
    Topic: Normal goods
    Skill: Definition
    Objective: LO1: Discuss the variables that influence demand.
    AACSB Coding: Reflective Thinking
    Special Feature: None

44. The substitution effect explains why there is an inverse relationship between the price of a product and the quantity of the product demanded.
    Answer: ○ True   False
    Diff: 1   Type: TF   Page Ref: 69/69
    Topic: Demand
    Skill: Conceptual
    Objective: LO1: Discuss the variables that influence demand.
    AACSB Coding: Reflective Thinking
    Special Feature: None

45. If consumers believe the price of MP3 players will increase in the future this will cause the demand for MP3 players to increase now.
    Answer: ○ True   False
    Diff: 1   Type: TF   Page Ref: 73/73
    Topic: Demand determinants
    Skill: Analytical
    Objective: LO1: Discuss the variables that influence demand.
    AACSB Coding: Analytic Skills
    Special Feature: None

46. What is the difference between a "change in demand" and a "change in quantity demanded"?
    Answer: A "change in demand" means the demand curve has shifted. This is caused by a change in any variable other than price that can influence the market demand of the good in question. A "change in quantity demanded" refers to a movement along the demand curve and this is caused by a change in the price of the good in question.
    Diff: 1   Type: ES   Page Ref: 73/73
    Topic: Demand
    Skill: Analytical
    Objective: LO1: Discuss the variables that influence demand.
    AACSB Coding: Analytic Skills
    Special Feature: None

47. What are the two effects that explain the Law of Demand? Briefly explain each effect.

Answer: The two effects that explain the Law of Demand are the income effect and the substitution effect. The income effect is the change in quantity demanded of a good that results from a change in purchasing power due to a change in the good's price. The substitution effect is the change in quantity demanded of a good that results from the effect of a change in the good's price making the good more or less expensive relative to other goods that are substitutes.

Diff: 3   Type: ES   Page Ref: 69
Topic: Law of demand
Skill: Fact
Objective: LO1: Discuss the variables that influence demand.
AACSB Coding: Reflective Thinking
Special Feature: None

48. Cole was discussing the market for cocoa beans with his friend John Schmidt. Cole said, "Ever since Venezuela announced that its cocoa harvest was its lowest ever in fifteen years, the price of cocoa beans has been rising and rising and people are buying more and more. I think the demand for cocoa beans must be upward sloping." Is Cole right? Briefly explain why or why not.

Answer: Cole has confused a change in demand as s result of a change in the expected future price of cocoa beans with a change in price. Following the announcement of the poor harvest buyers expected that the price of cocoa beans would rise. In anticipation of higher prices in the future, demand increased; this led to a higher equilibrium price. As long as buyers believe that the price of cocoa beans will rise in the future they will increase their demand today.

Diff: 2   Type: ES   Page Ref: 73/73
Topic: Change in Demand, Expected future Prices
Skill: Analytical
Objective: LO1: Discuss the variables that influence demand.
AACSB Coding: Analytic Skills
Special Feature: None

49. For each of the following pairs of products state which are complements, which are substitutes, and which are unrelated.
    a. Digital camera and memory stick
    b. 7Up and Mountain Dew
    c. Swimsuits and flip–flops
    d. Tylenol and cat food
    e. Photocopier and paper
    Answer: a.   Complements
             b.   Substitutes
             c.   Complements
             d.   Unrelated
             e.   Complements
    Diff: 1   Type: ES   Page Ref: 71/71
    Topic: Substitutes and complements
    Skill: Conceptual
    Objective: LO1: Discuss the variables that influence demand.
    AACSB Coding: Reflective Thinking
    Special Feature: None

3.2   The Supply Side of the Market

1. A supply schedule
    A) is a table that shows the relationship between the price of a product and the quantity of the product supplied.
    B) is a curve that shows the relationship between the price of a product and the quantity of the product supplied.
    C) is the relationship between the supply of a good and the cost of producing the good.
    D) is a table that shows the relationship between the price of a product and the quantity of the product that producers and consumers are willing to exchange.
    Answer: A
    Diff: 1   Type: MC   Page Ref: 76/76
    Topic: Supply
    Skill: Definition
    Objective: LO2: Discuss the variables that influence supply.
    AACSB Coding: Reflective Thinking
    Special Feature: None

2. If in the market for apples the supply has decreased then
    A) the supply curve for apples has shifted to the right.
    B) there has been a movement upwards along the supply curve for apples.
    C) the supply curve for apples has shifted to the left.
    D) there has been a movement downwards along the supply curve for apples.
    Answer: C
    Diff: 1   Type: MC   Page Ref: 78/78
    Topic: Change in supply
    Skill: Analytical
    Objective: LO2: Discuss the variables that influence supply.
    AACSB Coding: Analytic Skills
    Special Feature: None

3. If in the market for oranges the supply has increased then
    A) the supply curve for oranges has shifted to the right.
    B) the supply curve for oranges has shifted to the left.
    C) there has been a movement upwards along the supply curve for oranges.
    D) there has been a movement downwards along the supply curve for oranges.
    Answer: A
    Diff: 1   Type: MC   Page Ref: 78/78
    Topic: Change in supply
    Skill: Definition
    Objective: LO2: Discuss the variables that influence supply.
    AACSB Coding: Reflective Thinking
    Special Feature: None

4. Last month, the Tecumseh Corporation supplied 400 units of three-ring binders at $6 per unit. This month, the company supplied the same quantity of binders at $4 per unit. Based on this evidence, Tecumseh has experienced
    A) a decrease in supply.
    B) an increase in supply.
    C) an increase in the quantity supplied.
    D) a decrease in the quantity supplied.
    Answer: B
    Diff: 2   Type: MC   Page Ref: 76/76
    Topic: Change in supply
    Skill: Analytical
    Objective: LO2: Discuss the variables that influence supply.
    AACSB Coding: Analytic Skills
    Special Feature: None

5. What is the difference between an "increase in supply" and an "increase in quantity supplied"?
    A) There is no difference between the two terms; they both refer to a shift of the supply curve.
    B) There is no difference between the two terms; they both refer to a movement along a given supply curve
    C) An "increase in supply" means the supply curve has shifted to the right while an "increase in quantity supplied" means at any given price supply has increased.
    D) An "increase in supply" means the supply curve has shifted to the right while an "increase in quantity supplied" refers to a movement along a given supply curve in response to an increase in price.
    Answer: D
    Diff: 1   Type: MC   Page Ref: 79/79
    Topic: Supply
    Skill: Conceptual
    Objective: LO2: Discuss the variables that influence supply.
    AACSB Coding: Reflective Thinking
    Special Feature: None

6. One would speak of a movement along a supply curve for a good, rather than a change in supply, if
    A) the cost of producing the good changes.
    B) supplier expectations about future prices change.
    C) the price of the good changes
    D) prices of substitutes in production change.
    Answer: C
    Diff: 1   Type: MC   Page Ref: 77/77
    Topic: Quantity supplied
    Skill: Conceptual
    Objective: LO2: Discuss the variables that influence supply.
    AACSB Coding: Reflective Thinking
    Special Feature: None

7. Which of the following would cause a decrease in the supply of milk?
    A) An increase in the price of cookies (assuming that milk and cookies are complements).
    B) A decrease in the price of milk
    C) An increase the price of a product that producers sell instead of milk.
    D) An increase in the number of firms that produce milk.
    Answer: C
    Diff: 2   Type: MC   Page Ref: 77/77
    Topic: Change in supply
    Skill: Analytical
    Objective: LO2: Discuss the variables that influence supply.
    AACSB Coding: Analytic Skills
    Special Feature: None

8. In July, market analysts predict that the price of gold will rise in August. What happens in the gold market in July, holding everything else constant?
    A) The supply curve shifts to the right.
    B) The supply curve shifts to the left.
    C) The quantity demanded and the quantity supplied of gold increase.
    D) The demand curve shifts to the left.
    Answer: B
    Diff: 2   Type: MC   Page Ref: 78/78
    Topic: Variables that influence supply
    Skill: Conceptual
    Objective: LO2: Discuss the variables that influence supply.
    AACSB Coding: Reflective Thinking
    Special Feature: None

9. In October 2005, the U.S. Fish and Wildlife Service banned the importation of beluga caviar, the most prized of caviars, from the Caspian Sea. What happened in the market for caviar in the U. S.?
    A) The supply curve shifted to the left.
    B) The supply curve shifted to the right.
    C) The demand curve shifted to the right.
    D) The demand curve shifted to the left.
Answer: A
Diff: 2   Type: MC   Page Ref: 78/78
Topic: Change in supply
Skill: Analytical
Objective: LO2: Discuss the variables that influence supply.
AACSB Coding: Analytic Skills
Special Feature: None

10. George Gnat subscribes to a monthly pest control service for his home. Last week the owner of the service informed George that he will have to raise his monthly service fee because of increases in the price of gasoline used by his workers on their service trips. How is the market for pest control services affected by this?
    A) There is an increase in the supply of pest control services.
    B) There is a decrease in the demand for pest control services.
    C) There is a decrease in the quantity supplied of pest control services.
    D) There is a decrease in the supply of pest control services.
Answer: D
Diff: 2   Type: MC   Page Ref: 78/78
Topic: Change in Supply
Skill: Analytical
Objective: LO2: Discuss the variables that influence supply.
AACSB Coding: Analytic Skills
Special Feature: None

11. The popularity of digital cameras has enticed large discount stores like Wal-Mart and Costco to offer digital photo printing services. How does this affect the digital photo printing market?
    A) The demand curve for digital photo printing services shifts to the right.
    B) The demand curve for digital photo printing services shifts to the left.
    C) The supply curve for digital photo printing services shifts to the right.
    D) The supply curve for digital photo printing services shifts to the left.
Answer: C
Diff: 2   Type: MC   Page Ref: 77/77
Topic: Change in supply
Skill: Analytical
Objective: LO2: Discuss the variables that influence supply.
AACSB Coding: Analytic Skills
Special Feature: None

12. Farmers can plant either corn or soybeans in their fields. Which of the following would cause the supply of soybeans to increase?
    A) An increase in the price of soybeans.
    B) A decrease in the price of corn.
    C) An increase in the demand for corn.
    D) An increase in the price of soybean seeds.
    Answer: B
    Diff: 2   Type: MC   Page Ref: 77/77
    Topic: Change in supply
    Skill: Analytical
    Objective: LO2: Discuss the variables that influence supply.
    AACSB Coding: Analytic Skills
    Special Feature: None

13. Which of the following would shift the supply curve for MP3 players to the right?
    A) An increase in the price of a substitute in production.
    B) An increase in consumer income (assuming that all MP3 players are normal goods).
    C) a decrease in the number of firms that produce MP3 players.
    D) A decrease in the price of an input used to produce MP3 players.
    Answer: D
    Diff: 3   Type: MC   Page Ref: 77/77
    Topic: Change in supply
    Skill: Conceptual
    Objective: LO2: Discuss the variables that influence supply.
    AACSB Coding: Reflective Thinking
    Special Feature: None

14. If a firm expects that the price of its product will be lower in the future than it is today
    A) the firm has an incentive to increase supply now and decrease supply in the future.
    B) the firm has an incentive to decrease supply now and increase supply in the future.
    C) the firm has an incentive to increase quantity supplied now and decrease quantity supplied in the future.
    D) the firm will not change supply until it knows for certain what will happen to its price.
    Answer: A
    Diff: 3   Type: MC   Page Ref: 78/78
    Topic: Change in supply
    Skill: Conceptual
    Objective: LO2: Discuss the variables that influence supply.
    AACSB Coding: Reflective Thinking
    Special Feature: None

17. If a firm expects that the price of its product to be higher in the future than it is today
    A) the firm will go out of business.
    B) the firm has an incentive to increase supply now and decrease supply in the future.
    C) the firm has an incentive to decrease quantity supplied now and increase quantity supplied in the future.
    D) the firm has an incentive to decrease supply now and increase supply in the future.
    Answer: D
    Diff: 2   Type: MC   Page Ref: 78/78
    Topic: Change in supply
    Skill: Analytical
    Objective: LO2: Discuss the variables that influence supply.
    AACSB Coding: Analytic Skills
    Special Feature: None

16. A positive technological change will cause the quantity supplied of a good to increase.
    Answer: True   ⊘ False
    Diff: 1   Type: TF   Page Ref: 77/77
    Topic: Variables that influence supply
    Skill: Conceptual
    Objective: LO2: Discuss the variables that influence supply.
    AACSB Coding: Analytic Skills
    Special Feature: None

17. What is the law of supply? What does this law imply about the shape of the supply curve?
    Answer: The law of supply states that, holding everything else constant, an increase in price causes an increase in quantity supplied. The positive relationship between price and quantity supplied gives rise to an upward–sloping supply curve.
    Diff: 1   Type: ES   Page Ref: 76/76
    Topic: Law of supply
    Skill: Definition
    Objective: LO2: Discuss the variables that influence supply.
    AACSB Coding: Reflective Thinking
    Special Feature: None

18. Would a change in the price of in–line skates cause a change in the supply of in–line skates? Why or why not?
    Answer: No, a change in the price of in–line skates would not cause a change in the supply of in–line skates. Rather, it would cause change in quantity supplied. Supply changes only when there is a change in any variable other than price that would affect the supply of the good in question.
    Diff: 2   Type: ES   Page Ref: 78/78
    Topic: Supply
    Skill: Conceptual
    Objective: LO2: Discuss the variables that influence supply.
    AACSB Coding: Analytic Skills
    Special Feature: None

3.3   Market Equilibrium: Putting Demand and Supply Together

1. Which of the following is the correct way to describe equilibrium in a market?
   A) At equilibrium, demand equals supply.
   B) At equilibrium, quantity demanded equals quantity supplied.
   C) At equilibrium, market forces no longer apply.
   D) At equilibrium, scarcity is eliminated.
   Answer: B
   Diff: 1   Type: MC   Page Ref: 80/80
   Topic: Market equilibrium
   Skill: Definition
   Objective: LO3: Use a graph to illustrate market equilibrium.
   AACSB Coding: Reflective Thinking
   Special Feature: None

2. At a product's equilibrium price
   A) anyone who needs the product will be able to buy the product, regardless of ability to pay.
   B) the federal government will provide the product to anyone who cannot afford it.
   C) not all sellers who are willing to accept the price will find buyers for their products.
   D) any buyer who is willing and able to pay the price will find a seller for the product.
   Answer: D
   Diff: 1   Type: MC   Page Ref: 80/80
   Topic: Market equilibrium
   Skill: Conceptual
   Objective: LO3: Use a graph to illustrate market equilibrium.
   AACSB Coding: Reflective Thinking
   Special Feature: None

Figure 3-1

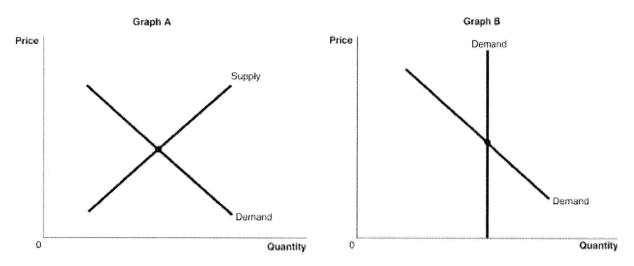

3. *Refer to Figure 3–1.* The figure above shows the supply and demand curves for two markets: the market for original Picasso paintings, and the market for designer jeans. Which graph most likely represents which market?

    A) Graph B represents the market for original Picasso paintings and Graph A represents the market for designer jeans.

    B) Graph A represents the market for original Picasso paintings and Graph B represents the market for designer jeans.

    C) Graph A represents both the market for original Picasso paintings and designer jeans.

    D) Graph B represents both the market for original Picasso paintings and designer jeans.

Answer: A

Diff: 2   Type: MC   Page Ref: 80/80
Topic: Demand and supply
Skill: Conceptual
Objective: LO3: Use a graph to illustrate market equilibrium.
AACSB Coding: Reflective Thinking
Special Feature: None

4. Hurricane Katrina damaged a large portion of refining and pipeline capacity when it swept through the Gulf coast states in August 2005. As a result of this, many gasoline distributors were not able to maintain normal deliveries. At the pre–hurricane equilibrium price (i.e., at the initial equilibrium price), we would expect to see

    A) a surplus of gasoline.

    B) the quantity demanded equal to the quantity supplied.

    C) a shortage of gasoline.

    D) an increase in the demand for gasoline.

Answer: C

Diff: 2   Type: MC   Page Ref: 80/80
Topic: Shortage
Skill: Analytical
Objective: LO3: Use a graph to illustrate market equilibrium.
AACSB Coding: Analytic Skills
Special Feature: None

Figure 3-2

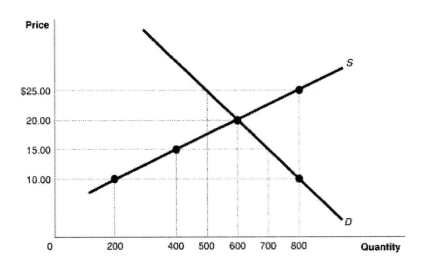

5. *Refer to Figure 3-2.* If the price is $25,
    A) there would be a surplus of 300 units.
    B) there would be a shortage of 300 units
    C) there would be a surplus of 200 units.
    D) there would be a shortage of 200 units.
Answer: A
Diff: 2   Type: MC   Page Ref: 80/80
Topic: Surplus
Skill: Conceptual
Objective: LO3: Use a graph to illustrate market equilibrium.
AACSB Coding: Reflective Thinking
Special Feature: None

6. *Refer to Figure 3-2.* At a price of $25, how many units will be sold?
    A) 400
    B) 500
    C) 600
    D) 800
Answer: B
Diff: 2   Type: MC   Page Ref: 80/80
Topic: Surplus
Skill: Conceptual
Objective: LO3: Use a graph to illustrate market equilibrium.
AACSB Coding: Analytic Skills
Special Feature: None

7. *Refer to Figure 3-2.* If the current market price is $25, the market will achieve equilibrium by
    A) a price increase, increasing the supply and decreasing the demand.
    B) a price decrease, decreasing the supply and increasing the demand.
    C) a price decrease, decreasing the quantity supplied and increasing the quantity demanded.
    D) a price increase, increasing the quantity supplied and decreasing the quantity demanded.
Answer: C
Diff: 2   Type: MC   Page Ref: 80/80
Topic: Market equilibrium
Skill: Analytical
Objective: LO3: Use a graph to illustrate market equilibrium.
AACSB Coding: Analytic Skills
Special Feature: None

Figure 3-3

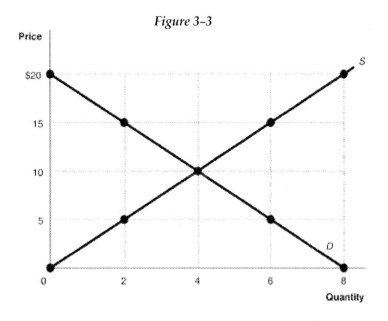

8. *Refer to Figure 3-3.* At a price of $5,
    A) there would be a surplus of 4 units.
    B) there would be a scarcity of 4 units.
    C) there would be a shortage of 6 units.
    D) there would be a shortage of 4 units.
Answer: D
Diff: 2   Type: MC   Page Ref: 80/80
Topic: Shortage, surplus
Skill: Analytical
Objective: LO3: Use a graph to illustrate market equilibrium.
AACSB Coding: Reflective Thinking
Special Feature: None

9. ***Refer to Figure 3-3.*** At a price of $15, the quantity sold
   A) is 2 units.
   B) is 4 units.
   C) is 6 units.
   D) cannot be determined.
   Answer: A
   Diff: 2   Type: MC   Page Ref: 80/80
   Topic: Shortage, surplus
   Skill: Analytical
   Objective: LO3: Use a graph to illustrate market equilibrium.
   AACSB Coding: Reflective Thinking
   Special Feature: None

10. ***Refer to Figure 3-3.*** In a free market such as that depicted above, a shortage is eliminated by
    A) a price increase, increasing the supply and decreasing the demand.
    B) a price decrease, decreasing the supply and increasing the demand.
    C) a price decrease, decreasing the quantity supplied and increasing the quantity demanded.
    D) a price increase, increasing the quantity supplied and decreasing the quantity demanded.
    Answer: D
    Diff: 2   Type: MC   Page Ref: 80/80
    Topic: Shortage
    Skill: Analytical
    Objective: LO3: Use a graph to illustrate market equilibrium.
    AACSB Coding: Analytic Skills
    Special Feature: None

11. Assume there is a shortage in the market for digital music players. Which of the following statements correctly describes this situation?
    A) The demand for digital music players is greater than the supply of digital music players.
    B) Some consumers will be unable to obtain digital music players at the market price and will have an incentive to offer to buy the product at a higher price.
    C) The price of digital music players will rise in response to the shortage; as the price rises the quantity demanded will increase and the quantity supplied will decrease.
    D) the shortage will cause an increase in the equilibrium price of digital music players.
    Answer: B
    Diff: 2   Type: MC   Page Ref: 80/80
    Topic: Shortage
    Skill: Conceptual
    Objective: LO3: Use a graph to illustrate market equilibrium.
    AACSB Coding: Analytic Skills
    Special Feature: None

12. Which of the following describes a characteristic of a perfectly competitive market?
    A) There are many buyers but few sellers.
    B) There are many sellers but few buyers.
    C) There are many buyers and sellers.
    D) Equilibrium is achieved when demand for the product sold in the market equals the
        supply.
    Answer: C
    Diff: 1   Type: MC   Page Ref: 80/80
    Topic: Perfectly competitive market
    Skill: Conceptual
    Objective: LO3: Use a graph to illustrate market equilibrium.
    AACSB Coding: Reflective Thinking
    Special Feature: None

Figure 3–4

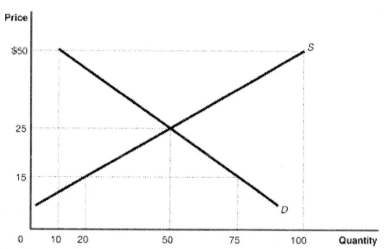

13. ***Refer to Figure 3–4.*** The figure above represents the market for canvas tote bags. Assume
    that the market price is $35. Which of the following statement is true?
    A) There is a surplus that will cause the price to decrease; quantity demanded will then
        increase and quantity supplied will decrease until the price equals $25.
    B) There is a surplus that will cause the price to decrease; quantity supplied will then
        increase and quantity demanded will decrease until the price equals $25.
    C) There will be a surplus that will cause the price to decrease; demand will then increase
        and supply will decrease until the price equals $25.
    D) There is a surplus that will cause the price to increase; quantity demanded will then
        decrease and quantity supplied will increase until the price equals $25.
    Answer: A
    Diff: 2   Type: MC   Page Ref: 80/80
    Topic: How markets eliminate surpluses
    Skill: Analytical
    Objective: LO3: Use a graph to illustrate market equilibrium.
    AACSB Coding: Analytic Skills
    Special Feature: None

14. ***Refer to Figure 3–4.*** The figure above represents the market for canvas tote bags. Assume that the price of tote bags is $15. At this price:
    A) the quantity demanded exceeds the quantity supplied of tote bags by 75. The price will eventually rise to $25 where quantity demanded will equal quantity supplied.
    B) the demand exceeds the supply of tote bags by 55. Some consumers will have an incentive to offer to buy tote bags at a higher price.
    C) there is a shortage, equal to 55 tote bags, that will be eliminated when the price rises to $25.
    D) there is a shortage, equal to 55 tote bags; the price of tote bags will rise until demand is equal to supply.
    Answer: C
    Diff: 3   Type: MC   Page Ref: 80/80
    Topic: How markets eliminate shortages
    Skill: Analytical
    Objective: LO3: Use a graph to illustrate market equilibrium.
    AACSB Coding: Analytic Skills
    Special Feature: None

15. ***Refer to Figure 3–4.*** The figure above represents the market for canvas tote bags. Compare the conditions in the market when the price is $50 and when the price is $35. Which of the following describes how the market differs at these prices?
    A) At each price there is a surplus; the surplus is greater at $35 than at $50.
    B) The difference between quantity supplied and quantity demanded is greater at $50 than at $35.
    C) At each price there is a surplus; firms will lower the equilibrium price in order to eliminate the surplus.
    D) At each price the supply of tote bags exceeds that demand for tote bags.
    Answer: B
    Diff: 3   Type: MC   Page Ref: 80/80
    Topic: Surplus
    Skill: Analytical
    Objective: LO3: Use a graph to illustrate market equilibrium.
    AACSB Coding: Reflective Thinking
    Special Feature: None

16. If the quantity demanded for a product exceeds the quantity supplied the market price will rise until
    A) the quantity demanded equals the quantity supplied. The product will then no longer be scarce.
    B) quantity demanded equals quantity supplied. The equilibrium price will then be greater than the market price.
    C) only wealthy consumers will be able to afford the product.
    D) quantity demanded equals quantity supplied. The market price will then equal the equilibrium price.
    Answer: D
    Diff: 2   Type: MC   Page Ref: 80/80
    Topic: How markets eliminate shortages
    Skill: Conceptual
    Objective: LO3: Use a graph to illustrate market equilibrium.
    AACSB Coding: Reflective Thinking
    Special Feature: None

17. Which of the following is evidence of a surplus of bananas?
    A) Firms raise the price of bananas.
    B) The price of bananas is lowered in order to increase sales.
    C) The equilibrium price of bananas rises due to an increase in demand.
    D) The quantity demanded of bananas is greater than the quantity supplied.
    Answer: B
    Diff: 2   Type: MC   Page Ref: 80/80
    Topic: How markets eliminate surpluses
    Skill: Analytical
    Objective: LO3: Use a graph to illustrate market equilibrium.
    AACSB Coding: Analytic Skills
    Special Feature: None

18. Even when the demand for one good is high, the price of the good is also affected by supply. The textbook illustrates this by comparing the price of two items that were auctioned on the same day. Which of the following describes the results of the auction?
    A) A letter written by Abraham Lincoln sold for a higher price than a letter written by John Wilkes Booth.
    B) A letter written by Abraham Lincoln was sold for a higher price than a letter written by Adam Smith.
    C) A letter written by John Wilkes Booth sold for a higher price than a letter written by Lee Harvey Oswald.
    D) A letter written by John Wilkes Booth sold for a higher price than a letter written by Abraham Lincoln.
    Answer: D
    Diff: 1   Type: MC   Page Ref: 81/81
    Topic: Demand and supply
    Skill: Analytical
    Objective: LO3: Use a graph to illustrate market equilibrium.
    AACSB Coding: Reflective Thinking
    Special Feature: Solved Problem: Demand and Supply Both Count: A Tale of Two Letters

19. Auctions in recent years have resulted in higher prices paid for letters written by John Wilkes Booth than those written by Abraham Lincoln. What is a reason for this difference in price?
    A) There is a surplus of letters written by Booth and a shortage of letters written by Lincoln.
    B) Many people are more fascinated by villains and anti-heroes than by heroic figures.
    C) There are more letters written by Lincoln available for collectors to buy than there are letters written by Booth.
    D) Booth was a well-known actor; the demand for his letters rose as wealthy actors attempted to buy them.
    Answer: C
    Diff: 1   Type: MC   Page Ref: 81/81
    Topic: Demand and supply
    Skill: Analytical
    Objective: LO3: Use a graph to illustrate market equilibrium.
    AACSB Coding: Reflective Thinking
    Special Feature: Solved Problem: Demand and Supply Both Count: A Tale of Two Letters

20. In response to a shortage the market price of a good will rise; as the price rises, the demand will decrease and supply will increase until equilibrium is reached.
    Answer: True   ○ False
    Diff: 2   Type: TF   Page Ref: 80/80
    Topic: How markets eliminate shortages
    Skill: Conceptual
    Objective: LO3: Use a graph to illustrate market equilibrium.
    AACSB Coding: Reflective Thinking
    Special Feature: None

21. Scarcity is defined as the situation that exists when the quantity demanded for a good is greater than the quantity supplied.
    Answer: True   ○ False
    Diff: 1   Type: TF   Page Ref: 80/80
    Topic: Shortage
    Skill: Definition
    Objective: LO3: Use a graph to illustrate market equilibrium.
    AACSB Coding: None
    Special Feature: None

22. Consider the collectors' market for first editions of two popular children's books, *Harry Potter and the Order of the Phoenix* by J. K. Rowling and *Ruby in the Smoke* by Philip Pullman. Sales of the Harry Potter novel are much greater than sales of *Ruby in the Smoke* yet the price of the Harry Potter novel is much lower than the price of Pullman's novel.

    a.   On one large diagram, draw a demand and supply graph for first editions of *Harry Potter and the Order of the Phoenix* and another demand and supply graph for first editions of *Ruby in the Smoke*.

    b.   Show how it is possible for the price of the Harry Potter novel to be much lower than the price of Pullman's novel, even though the demand for the Harry Potter novel is much greater than the demand for *Ruby in the Smoke*.

    c.   Provide a written explanation to accompany your graphical illustration.

Answer: a. and b. See the figure below.

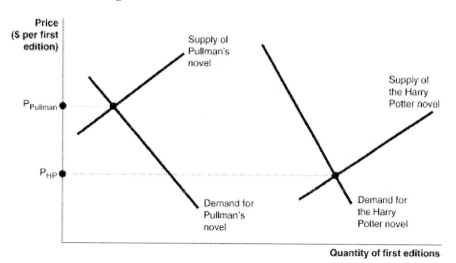

    c.   The demand for the Harry Potter novel is much greater than the demand for Pullman novel. Yet, the latter commands a higher price. The only way this can be true is if the supply of the Harry Potter book is much greater than the supply of the Pullman novel. Indeed this is true. Following the success of the earlier Harry Potter novels, the publisher increased the quantity of the first edition of J. K. Rowling's later book, *Harry Potter and the Order of the Phoenix*. Pullman's novels, on the other hand, have enjoyed only modest success.

Diff: 3   *Type: ES*   *Page Ref: 80/80*
Topic: Demand and supply
Skill: Analytical
Objective: LO3: Use a graph to illustrate market equilibrium.
AACSB Coding: Analytic Skills
Special Feature: None

23. Nearly a quarter of China's 1.3 billion people are under the age of 15. How will this affect high school enrollment over the next fifteen years? The labor market over the next fifteen years?

   Answer: The demand for high school education will increase. The supply of labor over the next 15 years will increase.

   Diff: 1   Type: ES   Page Ref: 81/81
   Topic: Demand and supply
   Skill: Conceptual
   Objective: LO3: Use a graph to illustrate market equilibrium.
   AACSB Coding: Reflective Thinking
   Special Feature: None

24. Shrimp is an increasingly popular part of the American diet. Louisiana shrimpers who represent the bulk of the U.S. industry were almost all put out of business by Hurricane Katrina. How did this affect the equilibrium price and quantity of shrimp?

   Answer: The supply of shrimp curve shifted to the left resulting in a higher equilibrium price and lower equilibrium quantity.

   Diff: 2   Type: ES   Page Ref: 80/80
   Topic: Changes in equilibrium, supply shift
   Skill: Conceptual
   Objective: LO3: Use a graph to illustrate market equilibrium.
   AACSB Coding: Reflective Thinking
   Special Feature: None

25. If the price of a product is below equilibrium, what forces it up?

   Answer: When the price is below equilibrium, a shortage occurs. Some consumers who are unable to obtain the product will have an incentive to offer to buy the product at a higher price. A higher price will simultaneously increase the quantity supplied and decrease the quantity demanded. This upward pressure on price continues until the shortage is eliminated and equilibrium is achieved.

   Diff: 2   Type: ES   Page Ref: 80/80
   Topic: How markets eliminate shortages
   Skill: Conceptual
   Objective: LO3: Use a graph to illustrate market equilibrium.
   AACSB Coding: Reflective Thinking
   Special Feature: None

26.

Table 3–2

Price per bushel	Quantity Demanded (bushels)	Quantity Supplied (bushels)
$2	40,000	0
4	36,000	4,000
6	30,000	8,000
8	24,000	16,000
10	20,000	20,000
12	18,000	28,000
14	12,000	36,000
16	6,000	40,000

Refer to Table 3–2. The table contains information about the sorghum market. Use the table to answer the following questions.

a. What are the equilibrium price and quantity of sorghum?
b. Suppose the prevailing price is $6 per bushel. Is there a shortage or a surplus in the market?
c. What is the quantity of the shortage or surplus?
d. How many bushels will be sold if the market price is $6 per bushel?
e. If the market price is $6 per bushel, what must happen to restore equilibrium in the market?
f. At what price will suppliers be able to sell 36,000 bushels of sorghum?
g. Suppose the market price is $14 per bushel. Is there a shortage or a surplus in the market?
h. What is the quantity of the shortage or surplus?
i. How many bushels will be sold if the market price is $14 per bushel?
j. If the market price is $14 per bushel, what must happen to restore equilibrium in the market?

Answer: a. Equilibrium price = $10; Equilibrium quantity = 20,000 bushels.
      b. There is a shortage.
      c. Shortage = 30,000–8,000 = 22,000 bushels.
      d. Quantity sold = 8,000 bushels.
      e. Price must rise.
      f. At $4 per bushel.
      g. There is a surplus.
      h. Surplus = 36,000–12,000 = 24,000 bushels.
      i. Quantity sold = 12,000 bushels.
      j. Price must fall.

Diff: 2   Type: ES   Page Ref: 80/80
Topic: Demand and supply
Skill: Analytical
Objective: LO3: Use a graph to illustrate market equilibrium.
AACSB Coding: Analytic Skills
Special Feature: None

3.4 The Effect of Demand and Supply Shifts on Equilibrium

1. Let D= demand, S = supply P = equilibrium price, Q= equilibrium quantity. What happens in the market for tropical hardwood trees if the governments restrict the amount of forest lands that can be logged?
   A) D decreases, S no change, P and Q decrease.
   B) S decreases, D no change, P increases, Q decreases.
   C) D and S decrease, P and Q increase.
   D) D no change, S decreases, P increases, Q increases.
   Answer: B
   Diff: 2   Type: MC   Page Ref: 83/83
   Topic: Changes in equilibrium, supply shift
   Skill: Analytical
   Objective: LO4: Use demand and supply graphs to predict changes in prices and quantities
   AACSB Coding: Analytic Skills
   Special Feature: None

2. Hurricane Katrina damaged a large portion of oil refining and pipeline capacity in the Gulf coast states. In the market for gasoline,
   A) the supply curve shifted to the left resulting in an increase in the equilibrium price.
   B) the supply curve shifted to the right resulting in an increase in the equilibrium price.
   C) the demand curve shifted to the left resulting in a decrease in the equilibrium price.
   D) the demand curve shifted to the right resulting in an increase in the equilibrium price
   Answer: A
   Diff: 2   Type: MC   Page Ref: 83/83
   Topic: Changes in equilibrium, supply shift
   Skill: Conceptual
   Objective: LO4: Use demand and supply graphs to predict changes in prices and quantities
   AACSB Coding: Analytic Skills
   Special Feature: None

3. Olive oil producers want to sell more olive oil at a higher price. Which of the following events would have this effect?
   A) An increase in the price of olive oil presses.
   B) A decrease in the cost of transporting olive oil to markets.
   C) An increase in the price of land used to plant olives.
   D) Research finds that consumption of olive oil reduces the risk of heart disease.
   Answer: D
   Diff: 3   Type: MC   Page Ref: 84/84
   Topic: Changes in equilibrium, demand shift
   Skill: Analytical
   Objective: LO4: Use demand and supply graphs to predict changes in prices and quantities
   AACSB Coding: Analytic Skills
   Special Feature: None

4. Which of the following would cause both the equilibrium price and equilibrium quantity of barley (assume that barley is an inferior good) to increase?
    A) An increase in consumer income.
    B) A drought that sharply reduces barley output.
    C) A decrease in consumer income.
    D) Unusually good weather that results in a bumper crop of barley.
    Answer: C
    Diff: 3   Type: MC   Page Ref: 84/84
    Topic: Changes in equilibrium, demand shift
    Skill: Analytical
    Objective: LO4: Use demand and supply graphs to predict changes in prices and quantities
    AACSB Coding: Analytic Skills
    Special Feature: None

5. Which of the following would cause the equilibrium price to decrease and the equilibrium quantity of white bread to increase?
    A) A decrease in the price of flour.
    B) An increase in the price of flour.
    C) An increase in the price of rye bread, a substitute for white bread.
    D) An increase in the price of butter, a complement for white bread.
    Answer: A
    Diff: 3   Type: MC   Page Ref: 84/84
    Topic: Changes in equilibrium, supply shift
    Skill: Analytical
    Objective: LO4: Use demand and supply graphs to predict changes in prices and quantities
    AACSB Coding: Analytic Skills
    Special Feature: None

6. Assume that the hourly price for the services of personal trainers has risen and sales of these services have also risen. One can conclude that
    A) the law of demand has been violated.
    B) the number of personal trainers has increased.
    C) the demand for personal trainers has increased.
    D) personal trainers are deliberately charging high prices because they provide services for wealthy clients.
    Answer: C
    Diff: 2   Type: MC   Page Ref: 84/84
    Topic: Changes in equilibrium, demand shift
    Skill: Analytical
    Objective: LO4: Use demand and supply graphs to predict changes in prices and quantities
    AACSB Coding: Analytic Skills
    Special Feature: None

7. Prices of California Merlot wine (assume that this is a normal good) have risen steadily in recent years. Over this same period, prices for French oak barrels used for wine storage have dropped and consumer incomes have risen. Which of the following best explains the rising prices of California Merlots?
    A) The supply curve for Merlot has shifted to the right while the demand curve for Merlot has shifted to the left.
    B) The demand curve for Merlot has shifted to the right faster than the supply curve has shifted to the right.
    C) The demand curve and the supply curve for Merlot have both shifted to the left.
    D) The supply curve for Merlot has shifted to the right faster than the demand curve has shifted to the right.
    Answer: B
    Diff: 3   Type: MC   Page Ref: 85/85
    Topic: The effect of shifts in demand and supply over time.
    Skill: Analytical
    Objective: LO4: Use demand and supply graphs to predict changes in prices and quantities
    AACSB Coding: Analytic Skills
    Special Feature: None

8. In recent years the cost of producing wines in the U.S. has increased largely due to rising rents for vineyards. At the same time, more and more Americans prefer wine over beer. Which of the following best explains the effect of these events in the wine market?
    A) The supply curve has shifted to the left and the demand curve has shifted to the right. As a result there has been an increase in the equilibrium quantity and an uncertain effect on the equilibrium price.
    B) Both the supply and demand curves have shifted to the right. As a result, there has been an increase in the equilibrium price and an uncertain effect on the equilibrium quantity.
    C) Both the supply and demand curves have shifted to the right. As a result, there has been an increase in both the equilibrium price and the equilibrium quantity.
    D) The supply curve has shifted to the left and the demand curve has shifted to the right. As a result, there has been an increase in the equilibrium price and an uncertain effect on the equilibrium quantity.
    Answer: D
    Diff: 3   Type: MC   Page Ref: 85/85
    Topic: Changes in equilibrium, demand and supply shift
    Skill: Analytical
    Objective: LO4: Use demand and supply graphs to predict changes in prices and quantities
    AACSB Coding: Analytic Skills
    Special Feature: None

9. An article in the *Wall Street Journal* in early 2001 noted two developments in the market for laser eye surgery. The first development concerned side effects from the surgery, including blurred vision. The second development was that the companies renting eye-surgery machinery to doctors had reduced their charges. In the market for laser eye surgeries, these two developments
   A) decreased demand and decreased supply, resulting in a decrease in the equilibrium quantity and an increase in the equilibrium price of laser eye surgeries.
   B) decreased demand and increased supply resulting in an increase in both the equilibrium quantity and the equilibrium price of laser eye surgeries.
   C) decreased demand and increased supply, resulting in a decrease in the equilibrium price and an uncertain effect on the equilibrium quantity of laser eye surgeries.
   D) decreased demand and increased supply, resulting in a decrease in both the equilibrium price and the equilibrium quantity of laser eye surgeries.
   Answer: C
   Diff: 3   Type: MC   Page Ref: 85/85
   Topic: Changes in equilibrium, demand and supply shift
   Skill: Analytical
   Objective: LO4: Use demand and supply graphs to predict changes in prices and quantities
   AACSB Coding: Analytic Skills
   Special Feature: None

10. A decrease in the demand for eggs due to changes in consumer tastes, accompanied by a decrease in the supply of eggs as a result of an outbreak of Avian flu, will result in
    A) a decrease in the equilibrium quantity of eggs and no change in the equilibrium price.
    B) a decrease in the equilibrium price of eggs and no change in the equilibrium quantity.
    C) a decrease in the equilibrium price of egg; the equilibrium quantity may increase or decrease.
    D) a decrease in the equilibrium quantity of eggs; the equilibrium price may increase or decrease.
    Answer: D
    Diff: 3   Type: MC   Page Ref: 85/85
    Topic: Changes in equilibrium, demand and supply shift
    Skill: Analytical
    Objective: LO4: Use demand and supply graphs to predict changes in prices and quantities
    AACSB Coding: Analytic Skills
    Special Feature: None

Figure 3-5

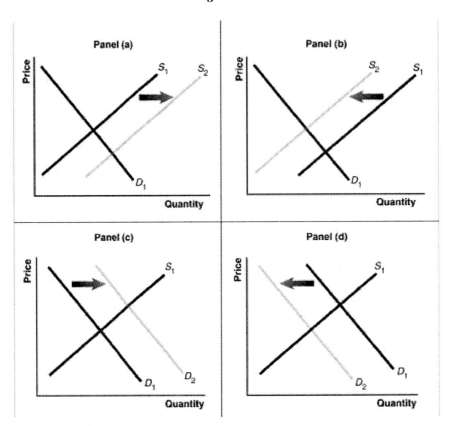

11. **Refer to Figure 3–5.** Assume that the graphs in this figure represent the demand and supply curves for bicycle helmets. Which panel best describes what happens in this market if there is a substantial increase in the price of bicycles?

    A) Panel (a)

    B) Panel (b)

    C) Panel (c)

    D) Panel (d)

Answer: D

Diff: 2   Type: MC   Page Ref: 85/85

Topic: Changes in equilibrium, demand shift

Skill: Conceptual

Objective: LO4: Use demand and supply graphs to predict changes in prices and quantities

AACSB Coding: Reflective Thinking

Special Feature: None

12. ***Refer to Figure 3–5.*** Assume that the graphs in this figure represent the demand and supply curves for women's clothing. Which panel best describes what happens in this market when the wages of seamstresses rise?
    A) Panel (a)
    B) Panel (b)
    C) Panel (c)
    D) Panel (d)
    Answer: B
    Diff: 2   Type: MC   Page Ref: 83/83
    Topic: Changes in equilibrium, supply shift
    Skill: Conceptual
    Objective: LO4: Use demand and supply graphs to predict changes in prices and quantities
    AACSB Coding: Reflective Thinking
    Special Feature: None

13. ***Refer to Figure 3–5.*** Assume that the graphs in this figure represent the demand and supply curves for almonds. Which panel best describes what happens in this market when there is an increase in the productivity of almond harvesters?
    A) Panel (a)
    B) Panel (b)
    C) Panel (c)
    D) Panel (d)
    Answer: A
    Diff: 2   Type: MC   Page Ref: 83/83
    Topic: Changes in equilibrium, supply shift
    Skill: Conceptual
    Objective: LO4: Use demand and supply graphs to predict changes in prices and quantities
    AACSB Coding: Reflective Thinking
    Special Feature: None

14. ***Refer to Figure 3–5.*** Assume that the graphs in this figure represent the demand and supply curves for Fruitopia, a soft drink. Which panel describes what happens in the market for Fruitopia when the price of Snapple, a substitute product, decreases?
    A) Panel (a)
    B) Panel (b)
    C) Panel (c)
    D) Panel (d)
    Answer: D
    Diff: 2   Type: MC   Page Ref: 84/84
    Topic: Changes in equilibrium, demand shift
    Skill: Conceptual
    Objective: LO4: Use demand and supply graphs to predict changes in prices and quantities
    AACSB Coding: Reflective Thinking
    Special Feature: None

15. *Refer to Figure 3–5.* Assume that the graphs in this figure represent the demand and supply curves for potatoes and that steak and potatoes are complements. What panel describes what happens in this market when the price of steak rises?
   A) Panel (a)
   B) Panel (b)
   C) Panel (c)
   D) Panel (d)
   Answer: D
   Diff: 2   Type: MC   Page Ref: 84/84
   Topic: Changes in equilibrium, demand shift
   Skill: Conceptual
   Objective: LO4: Use demand and supply graphs to predict changes in prices and quantities
   AACSB Coding: Reflective Thinking
   Special Feature: None

16. *Refer to Figure 3–5.* Assume that the graphs in this figure represent the demand and supply curves for rice. What happens in this market if buyers expect the price of rice to fall?
   A) Panel (a)
   B) Panel (b)
   C) Panel (c)
   D) Panel (d)
   Answer: D
   Diff: 2   Type: MC   Page Ref: 83/83
   Topic: Changes in equilibrium, demand shift
   Skill: Conceptual
   Objective: LO4: Use demand and supply graphs to predict changes in prices and quantities
   AACSB Coding: Reflective Thinking
   Special Feature: None

17. *Refer to Figure 3–5.* Assume that the graphs in this figure represent the demand and supply curves for used clothing, an inferior good. Which panel describes what happens in this market as a result of a decrease in income?
   A) Panel (a)
   B) Panel (b)
   C) Panel (c)
   D) Panel (d)
   Answer: C
   Diff: 2   Type: MC   Page Ref: 83/83
   Topic: Changes in equilibrium, demand shift
   Skill: Conceptual
   Objective: LO4: Use demand and supply graphs to predict changes in prices and quantities
   AACSB Coding: Reflective Thinking
   Special Feature: None

18. During the 1990s positive technological change in the production of chicken caused the price of chicken to fall. Holding everything else constant, how would this affect the market for pork (a substitute for chicken)?
    A) The supply of pork would increase and the equilibrium price of pork would decrease.
    B) The demand for pork would decrease and the equilibrium price of pork would decrease.
    C) The demand for pork would increase because consumers could afford to buy more chicken and pork.
    D) The demand for pork would decrease and the equilibrium price of pork would increase.

    Answer: B
    Diff: 2   Type: MC   Page Ref: 84/84
    Topic: Changes in equilibrium, demand shift
    Skill: Analytical
    Objective: LO4: Use demand and supply graphs to predict changes in prices and quantities
    AACSB Coding: Analytic Skills
    Special Feature: None

19. Assume that both the demand curve and the supply curve for MP3 players shift to the right but the demand curve shifts more than the supply curve. As a result
    A) both the equilibrium price and quantity of MP3 players will increase.
    B) the equilibrium price of MP3 players will increase; the equilibrium quantity may increase or decrease.
    C) the equilibrium price of MP3 players may increase or decrease; the equilibrium quantity will increase.
    D) the equilibrium price of MP3 players will decrease; the equilibrium quantity may increase or decrease.

    Answer: A
    Diff: 3   Type: MC   Page Ref: 85/85
    Topic: The effect of shifts in demand and supply over time.
    Skill: Analytical
    Objective: LO4: Use demand and supply graphs to predict changes in prices and quantities
    AACSB Coding: Analytic Skills
    Special Feature: None

20. "The price of digital cameras fell because of improvements in production technology. As a result, the demand for non-digital cameras decreased. This caused the price of non-digital cameras to fall; as the price of non-digital cameras fell the demand for non-digital cameras decreased even further." Evaluate this statement.

    A) The statement is false because the demand for non-digital cameras would increase as the price of digital cameras fell.

    B) The statement is false. A decrease in the price of digital cameras would decrease the demand for non-digital cameras, but a decrease in the price of non-digital cameras would not cause the demand for non-digital cameras to decrease.

    C) The statement is false because it confuses the law of demand with the law of supply.

    D) The statement is false because digital camera producers would not reduce their prices as a result of improvements in technology; doing so would reduce their profits.

Answer: B

Diff: 2   Type: MC   Page Ref: 84/84
Topic: The effect of a demand shift on equilibrium
Skill: Analytical
Objective: LO4: Use demand and supply graphs to predict changes in prices and quantities
AACSB Coding: Analytic Skills
Special Feature: None

Figure 3-6

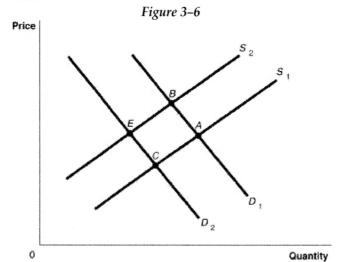

21. *Refer to Figure 3-6.* The graph in this figure illustrates an initial competitive equilibrium in the market for apples at the intersection of D_1 and S_1 (point A). If the price of oranges, a substitute for apples, decreases and the wages of apple workers increase how will the equilibrium point change?

    A) The equilibrium point will move from A to E.

    B) The equilibrium point will move from A to B.

    C) The equilibrium point will move from A to C.

    D) The equilibrium will first move from A to B, then return to A.

Answer: A

Diff: 3   Type: MC   Page Ref: 83/83
Topic: Changes in equilibrium, demand and supply shift
Skill: Analytical
Objective: LO4: Use demand and supply graphs to predict changes in prices and quantities
AACSB Coding: Analytic Skills
Special Feature: None

22. ***Refer to Figure 3-6.*** The graph in this figure illustrates an initial competitive equilibrium in the market for apples at the intersection of D_1 and S_1 (point A). If there is a shortage of apples how will the equilibrium point change?
    A) The equilibrium point will move from A to B.
    B) The equilibrium point will move from A to C.
    C) There will be no change in the equilibrium point.
    D) The equilibrium point will move from A to E.
    Answer: C
    Diff: 2   Type: MC   Page Ref: 84/84
    Topic: Shortage
    Skill: Analytical
    Objective: LO4: Use demand and supply graphs to predict changes in prices and quantities
    AACSB Coding: Analytic Skills
    Special Feature: None

23. ***Refer to Figure 3-6.*** The graph in this figure illustrates an initial competitive equilibrium in the market for apples at the intersection of D_2 and S_2 (point E). Which of the following changes would cause the equilibrium to change to point A?
    A) A positive change in the technology used to produce apples and decrease in the price of oranges, a substitute for apples.
    B) An increase in the wages of apple workers and a decrease in the price of oranges, a substitute for apples.
    C) An increase in the number of apple producers and a decrease in the number of apple trees as a result of disease.
    D) A decrease in the wages of apple workers and an increase in the price of oranges, a substitute for apples.
    Answer: D
    Diff: 3   Type: MC   Page Ref: 85/85
    Topic: How shifts in demand and supply affect equilibrium
    Skill: Analytical
    Objective: LO4: Use demand and supply graphs to predict changes in prices and quantities
    AACSB Coding: Analytic Skills
    Special Feature: None

24. **Refer to Figure 3-6**. The graph in this figure illustrates an initial competitive equilibrium in the market for apples at the intersection of D_1 and S_1 (point A). If there is an increase in the wages of apple workers and an increase in the price of oranges, a substitute for apples, the equilibrium could move to which point?

   A) B
   B) C
   C) E
   D) None of the points shown.

   Answer: D

   Diff: 3   Type: MC   Page Ref: 85/85
   Topic: How shifts in demand and supply affect equilibrium
   Skill: Analytical
   Objective: LO4: Use demand and supply graphs to predict changes in prices and quantities
   AACSB Coding: Analytic Skills
   Special Feature: None

25. Which of the following statements is true?

   A) An increase in demand causes a change in equilibrium price; the change in price does not cause a further change in demand or supply.
   B) A decrease in supply causes equilibrium price to rise; the increase in price then results in a decrease in demand.
   C) If both demand and supply increase there must be an increase in equilibrium price; equilibrium quantity may either increase or decrease.
   D) If demand decreases and supply increases one cannot determine if equilibrium price will increase or decrease without knowing which change is greater.

   Answer: A

   Diff: 3   Type: MC   Page Ref: 85/85
   Topic: How shifts in demand and supply affect equilibrium
   Skill: Conceptual
   Objective: LO4: Use demand and supply graphs to predict changes in prices and quantities
   AACSB Coding: Analytic Skills
   Special Feature: None

26. An increase in the equilibrium price for a product will result:

   A) when the quantity demanded for the product exceeds the quantity supplied.
   B) when there is a decrease in supply and an increase in demand for the product.
   C) when there is a decrease in supply and a decrease in demand for the product.
   D) when there is an increase in demand and an increase in the number of firms producing the product.

   Answer: B

   Diff: 2   Type: MC   Page Ref: 85/85
   Topic: How shifts in demand and supply affect equilibrium
   Skill: Analytical
   Objective: LO4: Use demand and supply graphs to predict changes in prices and quantities
   AACSB Coding: Analytic Skills
   Special Feature: None

27. The following appeared in a Florida newspaper a week after a hurricane hit the state. "Floridians are relieved that the storm produced no fatalities but homeowners face weeks, if not months, of rebuilding. Matters are made worse by the soaring prices of plywood and other building materials that always follow in a hurricane's path. Complaints of profiteering and price gouging have not deterred firms from raising their prices by over 100 percent." Which of the following offers the best explanation for the price increases referred to in the article?
    A) The hurricane reduced the number of suppliers of building materials.
    B) The hurricane created an artificial shortage of building materials.
    C) The hurricane caused an increase in the demand for building materials.
    D) There was a reduction in supply as firms shipped plywood and other materials to locations not affected by the storm.

Answer: C

Diff: 2   Type: MC   Page Ref: 85/85
Topic: How shifts in demand and supply affect equilibrium
Skill: Analytical
Objective: LO4: Use demand and supply graphs to predict changes in prices and quantities
AACSB Coding: Analytic Skills
Special Feature: None

28. Which of the following would cause an increase in the equilibrium price and decrease in the equilibrium quantity of watermelon?
    A) A decrease in demand and an increase in supply.
    B) A decrease in supply.
    C) An increase in demand and an increase in supply greater than the increase in demand.
    D) An increase in demand and an increase in supply.

Answer: B

Diff: 2   Type: MC   Page Ref: 85/85
Topic: How shifts in demand and supply affect equilibrium
Skill: Analytical
Objective: LO4: Use demand and supply graphs to predict changes in prices and quantities
AACSB Coding: Analytic Skills
Special Feature: None

29. Select the phrase that correctly completed the following statement. "A positive change in technology caused an increase in the supply of flat-screen televisions. As a result
    A) the price of flat-screen televisions decreased and the demand for flat-screen televisions increased."
    B) the equilibrium quantity of flat-screen televisions decreased."
    C) the price of flat-screen televisions decreased and the quantity demanded of flat-screen televisions increased."
    D) the price of flat-screen televisions decreased. The lower price caused the supply of flat-screen televisions to decrease."
    Answer: C
    Diff: 2   Type: MC   Page Ref: 85/85
    Topic: How shifts in demand and supply affect equilibrium
    Skill: Analytical
    Objective: LO4: Use demand and supply graphs to predict changes in prices and quantities
    AACSB Coding: Analytic Skills
    Special Feature: None

30. Starting in the 1960s researchers predicted that flat-screen televisions produced with liquid display crystal displays (LCD) would be sold to the public. But technical problems delayed the manufacture and sale of LCD televisions until the late 1990s. What was this technical problem?
    A) Until the 1990s only very small screens could be economically produced. These screens were not popular with consumers. New technology resulted in larger screens.
    B) Until the 1990s relatively few channels were available for consumers to watch. After cable and satellite television became popular consumers were able to watch many more stations; this led to an increase in the demand for LCD televisions.
    C) It was not until the 1990s that satellite television signals enabled consumers to watch programming from many countries. This led to a large increase in demand and made the sale of LCD televisions profitable.
    D) There was no way to make very thin, clean television screens until 1999 when Corning, Inc. finally developed a process to do this.
    Answer: D
    Diff: 1   Type: MC   Page Ref: 83/83
    Topic: Changes in equilibrium, supply shift
    Skill: Fact
    Objective: LO2: Discuss the variables that influence supply.
    AACSB Coding: Reflective Thinking
    Special Feature: Making the Connection: The Falling Price of LCD Televisions

31. New technology developed in 1999 resulted in a reduction in the cost of manufacturing flat-screen televisions that used liquid crystal displays (LCD). How did this change in technology affect the market for flat-screen televisions?
    A) The new technology caused an increase in the supply of flat-screen televisions and a decrease in price of flat-screen televisions.
    B) The new technology caused an increase in the supply of flat-screen televisions and an increase in price of flat-screen televisions.
    C) The new technology caused an increase in the demand for flat-screen televisions.
    D) The new technology caused an increase in the quantity of flat-screen televisions supplied.
    Answer: A
    Diff: 2   Type: MC   Page Ref: 83/83
    Topic: Change in supply
    Skill: Conceptual
    Objective: LO4: Use demand and supply graphs to predict changes in prices and quantities
    AACSB Coding: Reflective Thinking
    Special Feature: Making the Connection: The Falling Price of LCD Televisions

32. The price of lobster is typically lower in the summer than in the spring. Which of the following explanations for this difference is given in the textbook?
    A) Hot, humid weather usually reduces the demand for lobster.
    B) People who usually eat lobster in other seasons substitute less expensive fish when they go on vacation; this drives down the demand for lobster.
    C) The supply of lobster is greater in the summer than in the spring.
    D) Import restrictions are eased in the summer; as more lobsters are imported the price of lobster falls.
    Answer: C
    Diff: 1   Type: MC   Page Ref: 86/86
    Topic: The effect of shifts in demand and supply over time.
    Skill: Conceptual
    Objective: LO4: Use demand and supply graphs to predict changes in prices and quantities
    AACSB Coding: Reflective Thinking
    Special Feature: Solved Problem: High Demand and Low Prices in the Lobster Market?

33. "Because apples and oranges are substitutes, an increase in the price of oranges will cause the demand for apples to increase. This initial shift in demand for apples results in a higher price for apples; this higher price will cause the demand curve for apples to shift to the right." Which of the following correctly comments on this statement?
    A) The statement will be true, if consumer tastes for apples and oranges do not change.
    B) The statement is false because a change in the price of apples would not change the demand for apples.
    C) The statement is false because oranges are inferior goods; apples are normal goods.
    D) The statement is false because one cannot assume that apples and oranges are substitutes for all consumers.
    Answer: B
    Diff: 2   Type: MC   Page Ref: 88/88
    Topic: Change in demand
    Skill: Conceptual
    Objective: LO4: Use demand and supply graphs to predict changes in prices and quantities
    AACSB Coding: Reflective Thinking
    Special Feature: Don't Let This Happen to YOU!: Remember: A Change in a Good's Price Does Not Cause the Demand or Supply Curve to Shift.

34. The demand for lobster is lower in the spring than in the summer. If the price of lobster is higher in spring than in summer then:
    A) The supply of lobster is greater in summer than in spring.
    B) Consumers' tastes for lobster are greater in spring than in summer.
    C) There is a shortage of lobster in spring and a surplus of lobster in summer.
    D) There are more substitutes for lobster in summer than there are in spring.
    Answer: A
    Diff: 2   Type: MC   Page Ref: 86/86
    Topic: The effect of shifts in demand and supply over time.
    Skill: Analytical
    Objective: LO4: Use demand and supply graphs to predict changes in prices and quantities
    AACSB Coding: Analytic Skills
    Special Feature: Solved Problem: High Demand and Low Prices in the Lobster Market?

35. In 2007, Apple Inc. began selling iPhones, a combination cell phone and digital music player. Apple also sells iPods, a digital music player. If consumers consider iPhones and iPods substitutes, how will sales of iPhones affect the market for iPods?
    A) The demand for iPods will shift to the right, decreasing the equilibrium price and increasing the equilibrium quantity.
    B) The supply of iPods will increase, decreasing the equilibrium price and increasing the equilibrium quantity.
    C) There will be no effect on the market for iPods because few consumers who buy iPhones will also buy iPods.
    D) The demand for iPods will decrease, decreasing both the equilibrium price and quantity of iPods.
    Answer: A
    Diff: 2   Type: MC   Page Ref: 91/91
    Topic: The effect of a demand shift on equilibrium
    Skill: Analytical
    Objective: LO4: Use demand and supply graphs to predict changes in prices and quantities
    AACSB Coding: Analytic Skills
    Special Feature: An Inside Look: How Does the iPhone Help Apple and AT&T?

36. If the demand for a product increases and the supply of the same product decreases, the equilibrium price will increase.
    Answer: ◦ True   False
    Diff: 3   Type: TF   Page Ref: 85/85
    Topic: The effect of shifts in demand and supply over time.
    Skill: Analytical
    Objective: LO4: Use demand and supply graphs to predict changes in prices and quantities
    AACSB Coding: Analytic Skills
    Special Feature: None

37. As the number of firms in a market decreases, the supply curve will shift to the left and the equilibrium price will rise.
    Answer: ◦ True   False
    Diff: 2   Type: TF   Page Ref: 85/85
    Topic: Changes in equilibrium, supply shift
    Skill: Analytical
    Objective: LO4: Use demand and supply graphs to predict changes in prices and quantities
    AACSB Coding: Analytic Skills
    Special Feature: None

38. Discuss the correct and incorrect economic analysis in the following statements.

"If a disease kills a large number of turkeys, the supply of turkeys will decrease. This will result in a price increase, which will then cause the supply of turkeys to increase."
Answer: The supply of turkeys will decrease resulting in a higher equilibrium price and a lower equilibrium quantity but the higher price will not shift the supply curve for turkeys.
Diff: 2   Type: ES   Page Ref: 85/85
Topic: How shifts in demand and supply affect equilibrium
Skill: Analytical
Objective: LO4: Use demand and supply graphs to predict changes in prices and quantities
AACSB Coding: Analytic Skills
Special Feature: None

39. Discuss the correct and incorrect economic analysis in the following statements.

"The United Auto Workers Union has successfully negotiated a 9 percent increase in wages for its workers. This increase in the wage rate causes an increase in demand for automobiles, since many consumers now have greater incomes, and also a decrease in the supply of automobiles because the cost of production has increased. These effects cancel each other out resulting in no change in equilibrium price and quantity in the automobile market."
Answer: The wage rate is a determinant of the supply of automobiles, but not a determinant of the demand for automobiles. The increase in the wage rate will shift the automobile supply curve to the left along a given demand curve. This will result in a higher equilibrium price and a lower equilibrium quantity in the market for automobiles.
Diff: 3   Type: ES   Page Ref: 85/85
Topic: Changes in equilibrium, supply shift
Skill: Analytical
Objective: LO4: Use demand and supply graphs to predict changes in prices and quantities
AACSB Coding: Analytic Skills
Special Feature: None

40. According to the Australian Wool Innovation, severe drought conditions in Australia contributed to the lowest level of wool production in 50 years. This record low production has driven up prices sharply in Australian wool markets. Meanwhile, the price of raw cotton increased significantly for the first time in many years.

a. Illustrate this observation with one demand and supply graph for the market for Australian wool and another demand and supply graph for raw cotton.
b. Make sure that your graphs clearly show (1) the initial equilibrium before the decrease in the supply of Australian wool and (2) the final equilibrium.
c. Use arrows to indicate any shifts in the demand and supply curves for each market.
d. Label your graphs fully and write an explanation of your work.

Answer: a, b and c. See the figure below.

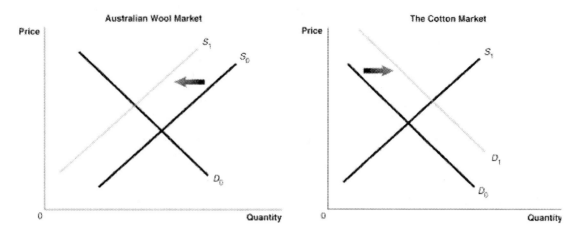

d. In the Australian wool market, the supply curve shifts to the left as a result of the drought. This leads to an increase in the equilibrium price of wool and a decrease in the equilibrium quantity. The higher price of wool causes buyers to substitute cotton for wool, thereby increasing the demand for cotton. In the cotton market, the demand curve for cotton moves to the right along a given supply curve resulting in a higher equilibrium price and higher equilibrium quantity of cotton.

Diff: 3   Type: ES   Page Ref: 83/83
Topic: Demand and supply
Skill: Analytical
Objective: LO4: Use demand and supply graphs to predict changes in prices and quantities
AACSB Coding: Analytic Skills
Special Feature: None

Chapter 4   Economic Efficiency, Government Price Setting, and Taxes

4.1   Consumer Surplus and Producer Surplus

1. The difference between the highest price a consumer is willing to pay for a good and the price the consumer actually pays is called
    A) producer surplus.
     B) the substitution effect.
    C) the income effect.
    D) consumer surplus.
   Answer: D
   Diff: 1   Type: MC   Page Ref: 100/100
   Topic: Consumer surplus
   Skill: Definition
   Objective: LO1: Distinguish between the concepts of consumer surplus and producer surplus.
   AACSB Coding: Reflective Thinking
   Special Feature: None

2. New York City has about two million apartments. Of this number
    A) all are subject to rent control.
     B) about one-half are subject to rent control.
    C) all are subject to price floors.
    D) about 10 percent are subject to rent control.
   Answer: B
   Diff: 1   Type: MC   Page Ref: 98/98
   Topic: Rent control
   Skill: Fact
   Objective: LO1: Distinguish between the concepts of consumer surplus and producer surplus.
   AACSB Coding: Reflective Thinking
   Special Feature: Chapter Opener: Should the Government Control Apartment Rents?

3. In 2004 New York City mayor Michael Bloomberg made a proposal concerning rent control in his city. What was Mayor Bloomberg's proposal?
    A) He proposed that rent control be abolished over a 20 year period.
    B) He proposed that rent control be extended to all New York City apartments over a 20 year period.
    C) He proposed that rent control be maintained on apartments that had been scheduled to be free from rent control.
    D) He proposed that rents be increased by 50 percent on all apartments subject to rent control.
    Answer: C
    Diff: 2   Type: MC   Page Ref: 98/98
    Topic: Rent control
    Skill: Fact
    Objective: LO1: Distinguish between the concepts of consumer surplus and producer surplus.
    AACSB Coding: Reflective Thinking
    Special Feature: Chapter Opener: Should the Government Control Apartment Rents?

4. Suppose there are two cities that have rent controlled apartments. In one city (Albany) all apartments are subject to rent control; in the other city (Halftrack) one–half of the apartments are rent controlled. Which of the following is most likely to be true?
    A) It will be difficult to find a rent–controlled apartment in Albany or Halftrack; rents for the Halftrack apartments not subject to controls will be higher than they would be without rent control.
    B) It will be easier to find an affordable apartment in Albany since rents will be low across the board.
    C) It will be easier to find an affordable apartment in Halftrack, either a rent–controlled apartment or another apartment, at a reasonable price.
    D) It will be impossible to rent an apartment in either city at any price.
    Answer: A
    Diff: 2   Type: MC   Page Ref: 99/99
    Topic: The economic effect of price ceilings and price floors
    Skill: Fact
    Objective: LO1: Distinguish between the concepts of consumer surplus and producer surplus.
    AACSB Coding: Reflective Thinking
    Special Feature: Economics in YOUR Life!: Does Rent Control Make It Easier to Find an Affordable Apartment?

5. Paul goes to Sportsmart to buy a new tennis racquet. He is willing to pay $200 for a new racquet, but buys one on sale for $125. Paul's consumer surplus from the purchase is
    A) $325
    B) $200
    C) $125
    D) $75
    Answer: D
    Diff: 1   Type: MC   Page Ref: 101/101
    Topic: Consumer surplus
    Skill: Conceptual
    Objective: LO1: Distinguish between the concepts of consumer surplus and producer surplus.
    AACSB Coding: Reflective Thinking
    Special Feature: None

6. Brett buys a new cell phone for $100. He receives consumer surplus of $80 from the purchase. How much does Brett value his cell phone?
    A) $180
    B) $100
    C) $80
    D) $20
    Answer: A
    Diff: 1   Type: MC   Page Ref: 101/101
    Topic: Consumer surplus
    Skill: Conceptual
    Objective: LO1: Distinguish between the concepts of consumer surplus and producer surplus.
    AACSB Coding: Reflective Thinking
    Special Feature: None

7. Willingness to pay measures
    A) the maximum price a buyer is willing to pay for a product minus the amount the buyer actually pays for it.
    B) the amount a seller actually receives for a good minus the minimum amount the seller is willing to accept for the good.
    C) the maximum price that a buyer is willing to pay for a good.
    D) the maximum price a buyer is willing to pay minus the minimum price a seller is willing to accept.
    Answer: C
    Diff: 1   Type: MC   Page Ref: 100/100
    Topic: Willingness to pay
    Skill: Definition
    Objective: LO1: Distinguish between the concepts of consumer surplus and producer surplus.
    AACSB Coding: Reflective Thinking
    Special Feature: None

8. A consumer is willing to purchase a product up to the point where
    A) he spends all of his income.
    B) the marginal benefit is equal to the price of the product.
    C) the quantity demanded is equal to the quantity supplied.
    D) he is indifferent between consuming and saving.
    Answer: B
    Diff: 1   Type: MC   Page Ref: 100/100
    Topic: Marginal benefit
    Skill: Conceptual
    Objective: LO1: Distinguish between the concepts of consumer surplus and producer surplus.
    AACSB Coding: Reflective Thinking
    Special Feature: None

9. Consumers are willing to purchase a product up to the point where
    A) the marginal benefit of consuming the product is equal to the marginal cost of consuming it.
    B) the consumer surplus is equal to the producer surplus.
    C) the marginal benefit of consuming the product equals the area below the supply curve and above the market price.
    D) the marginal benefit of consuming a product is equal to its price.
    Answer: D
    Diff: 1   Type: MC   Page Ref: 100/100
    Topic: Marginal benefit
    Skill: Conceptual
    Objective: LO1: Distinguish between the concepts of consumer surplus and producer surplus.
    AACSB Coding: Reflective Thinking
    Special Feature: None

10. The additional benefit to a consumer from consuming one more unit of a good or service
    A) is equal to consumer surplus.
    B) is equal to the opportunity cost of consuming the good or service.
    C) is equal to marginal benefit.
    D) is equal to economic surplus.
    Answer: C
    Diff: 1   Type: MC   Page Ref: 100/100
    Topic: Marginal benefit
    Skill: Definition
    Objective: LO1: Distinguish between the concepts of consumer surplus and producer surplus.
    AACSB Coding: Reflective Thinking
    Special Feature: None

11. Which of the following statements best describes the concept of consumer surplus?
    A) "Safeway was having a sale on Dreyers ice cream so I bought 3 quarts."
    B) "I was all ready to pay $300 for a new leather jacket that I had seen in Macy's but I ended up paying only $180 for the same jacket."
    C) "I paid $130 for a printer last week. This week the same store is selling the same printer for $110."
    D) "I sold my video tape copy of *Ben-Hur* for $18 at a garage sale even though I was willing to sell it for $10."
    Answer: B
    Diff: 1   Type: MC   Page Ref: 101/101
    Topic: Consumer Surplus
    Skill: Conceptual
    Objective: LO1: Distinguish between the concepts of consumer surplus and producer surplus.
    AACSB Coding: Reflective Thinking
    Special Feature: None

12. Each point on a demand curve shows
    A) the willingness of consumers to purchase a product at different prices.
    B) the consumer surplus received from purchasing a given quantity of a product.
    C) the economic surplus received from purchasing a given quantity of a product.
    D) the legally determined maximum price that sellers may charge for a given quantity of a product.
    Answer: A
    Diff: 2   Type: MC   Page Ref: 101–2/101–2
    Topic: Willingness to pay
    Skill: Conceptual
    Objective: LO1: Distinguish between the concepts of consumer surplus and producer surplus.
    AACSB Coding: Reflective Thinking
    Special Feature: None

Table 4–1

Consumer	Willingness to Pay
Tom	$40
Dick	$30
Harriet	$25

13. *Refer to Table 4–1.* The table above lists the highest prices three consumers, Tom, Dick and Harriet, are willing to pay for a short–sleeved polo shirt. If the price of one of the shirts is $28 dollars
    A) Tom will buy two shirts, Dick will buy one shirt and Harriet will buy no shirts.
    B) Tom will receive $12 of consumer surplus from buying one shirt.
    C) Tom and Dick receive a total of $70 of consumer surplus from buying one shirt each. Harriet will buy no shirts.
    D) Harriet will receive $25 of consumer surplus since she will buy no shirts.
    Answer: B
    Diff: 2   Type: MC   Page Ref: 101/101
    Topic: Consumer surplus
    Skill: Analytical
    Objective: LO1: Distinguish between the concepts of consumer surplus and producer surplus.
    AACSB Coding: Analytic Skills
    Special Feature: None

14. *Refer to Table 4–1.* The table above lists the highest prices three consumers, Tom, Dick and Harriet, are willing to pay for a short–sleeved polo shirt. If the price of the shirts falls from $28 to $20
    A) consumer surplus increases from $14 to $35.
    B) Tom will buy two shirts; Dick and Harriet will each buy one shirt.
    C) consumer surplus will increase from $70 to $95.
    D) Harriet will receive more consumer surplus than Tom or Dick.
    Answer: A
    Diff: 2   Type: MC   Page Ref: 101/101
    Topic: Consumer surplus
    Skill: Analytical
    Objective: LO1: Distinguish between the concepts of consumer surplus and producer surplus.
    AACSB Coding: Analytic Skills
    Special Feature: None

15. Marginal cost is
    A) the total cost of producing one unit of a good or service.
    B) the average cost of producing a good or service.
    C) the difference between the lowest price a firm would have been willing to accept and the price it actually receives.
    D) the additional cost to a firm of producing one more unit of a good or service.
    Answer: D
    Diff: 1   Type: MC   Page Ref: 103/103
    Topic: Marginal cost
    Skill: Definition
    Objective: LO1: Distinguish between the concepts of consumer surplus and producer surplus.
    AACSB Coding: Reflective Thinking
    Special Feature: None

Table 4-2

Marko's Polos	Marginal Cost (Dollars)
1st shirt	$7
2nd shirt	10
3rd shirt	15
4th shirt	20

16. ***Refer to Table 4-2.*** The table above lists the marginal cost of polo shirts by Marko's, a firm that specializes in producing men's clothing. If the market price of Marko's polo shirts is $18
    A) Marko's will produce four shirts.
    B) producer surplus from the first shirt is $18.
    C) producer surplus will equal $22.
    D) there will be a surplus; as a result, the price will fall to $7.
    Answer: C
    Diff: 3   Type: MC   Page Ref: 103-4/103-4
    Topic: Producer surplus
    Skill: Analytical
    Objective: LO1: Distinguish between the concepts of consumer surplus and producer surplus.
    AACSB Coding: Analytic Skills
    Special Feature: None

17. *Refer to Table 4-2.* The table above lists the marginal cost of polo shirts by Marko's, a firm that specializes in producing men's clothing. If the price of polo shirts increases from $15 to $20
    A) consumers will buy no polo shirts.
    B) the marginal cost of producing the third polo shirt will increase to $20.
    C) producer surplus will rise from $13 to $28.
    D) there will be a surplus of polo shirts.
    Answer: C
    Diff: 3   Type: MC   Page Ref: 103–4/103–4
    Topic: Producer surplus
    Skill: Analytical
    Objective: LO1: Distinguish between the concepts of consumer surplus and producer surplus.
    AACSB Coding: Analytic Skills
    Special Feature: None

18. The area above the market supply curve and below the market price
    A) is equal to the total amount of producer surplus in a market.
    B) is equal to the marginal cost of the last unit produced.
    C) is equal to the total amount of economic surplus in a market.
    D) is equal to the total cost of production.
    Answer: A
    Diff: 1   Type: MC   Page Ref: 104/104
    Topic: Producer surplus
    Skill: Definition
    Objective: LO1: Distinguish between the concepts of consumer surplus and producer surplus.
    AACSB Coding: Reflective Thinking
    Special Feature: None

19. The total amount of producer surplus in a market is equal to
    A) the difference between quantity supplied and quantity demanded.
    B) the area above the market supply curve and below the market price.
    C) the area above the market supply curve.
    D) the area between the demand curve and the supply curve below the market price.
    Answer: B
    Diff: 2   Type: MC   Page Ref: 104/104
    Topic: Producer surplus
    Skill: Definition
    Objective: LO1: Distinguish between the concepts of consumer surplus and producer surplus.
    AACSB Coding: Reflective Thinking
    Special Feature: None

20. Consumer surplus in a market for a product would be equal to the area under the demand curve if
    A) producer surplus was equal to zero.
    B) marginal cost was equal to the market price.
    C) the product was produced in a perfectly competitive market.
    D) the market price was zero.
    Answer: D
    Diff: 2   Type: MC   Page Ref: 105/105
    Topic: Consumer Surplus
    Skill: Conceptual
    Objective: LO1: Distinguish between the concepts of consumer surplus and producer surplus.
    AACSB Coding: Reflective Thinking
    Special Feature: None

21. Which of the following statements is true?
    A) Consumer surplus measures the total benefit from participating in a market.
    B) When a market is in equilibrium consumer surplus equals producer surplus.
    C) Consumer surplus measures the net benefit from participating in a market.
    D) Producer surplus measures the total benefit received by producers from participating in a market.
    Answer: C
    Diff: 2   Type: MC   Page Ref: 100/100
    Topic: What consumer surplus and producer surplus measure
    Skill: Analytical
    Objective: LO1: Distinguish between the concepts of consumer surplus and producer surplus.
    AACSB Coding: Analytic Skills
    Special Feature: None

22. A supply curve shows
    A) the quantities sold at different prices.
    B) the marginal cost of producing one more unit of a good or service.
    C) the marginal benefit from buying one more unit of a good or service.
    D) the total cost of producing different quantities of a good or service.
    Answer: B
    Diff: 1   Type: MC   Page Ref: 104/104
    Topic: Marginal cost
    Skill: Conceptual
    Objective: LO1: Distinguish between the concepts of consumer surplus and producer surplus.
    AACSB Coding: Reflective Thinking
    Special Feature: None

23. A demand curve shows
    A) the willingness of consumers to buy a product at different prices.
    B) the willingness of consumers to substitute one product for another product.
    C) the relationship between the price of a product and the demand for the product.
    D) the relationship between the price of a product and the total benefit consumers receive
       from the product.
Answer: A
Diff: 1   Type: MC   Page Ref: 100/100
Topic: Willingness to pay
Skill: Conceptual
Objective: LO1: Distinguish between the concepts of consumer surplus and producer surplus.
AACSB Coding: Reflective Thinking
Special Feature: None

Figure 4–1

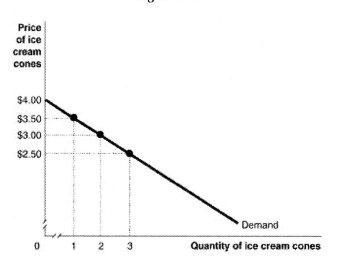

Figure 4-1 shows Kendra's demand for ice-cream cones curve.

24. *Refer to Figure 4–1.* Kendra's marginal benefit from consuming the second ice cream cone is
    A) $6.50
    B) $6.00
    C) $2.25
    D) $3.00
Answer: D
Diff: 1   Type: MC   Page Ref: 100–1/100–1
Topic: Marginal benefit
Skill: Analytical
Objective: LO1: Distinguish between the concepts of consumer surplus and producer surplus.
AACSB Coding: Analytic Skills
Special Feature: None

25. *Refer to Figure 4-1.* If the market price is $2.50, what is the consumer surplus on the second ice cream cone?

    A) $0.50
    B) $1.50
    C) $3.00
    D) $10.50

Answer: A
Diff: 1   Type: MC   Page Ref: 100–1/100–1
Topic: Consumer surplus
Skill: Analytical
Objective: LO1: Distinguish between the concepts of consumer surplus and producer surplus.
AACSB Coding: Analytic Skills
Special Feature: None

26. *Refer to Figure 4-1.* If the market price is $2.50, what is Kendra's consumer surplus?

    A) $9.00
    B) $7.50
    C) $1.50
    D) $0

Answer: C
Diff: 2   Type: MC   Page Ref: 100–1/100–1
Topic: Consumer surplus
Skill: Analytical
Objective: LO1: Distinguish between the concepts of consumer surplus and producer surplus.
AACSB Coding: Analytic Skills
Special Feature: None

27. *Refer to Figure 4-1.* What is the total amount that Kendra is willing to pay for 3 ice cream cones?

    A) $7.50
    B) $9.00
    C) $2.50
    D) $13.50

Answer: B
Diff: 2   Type: MC   Page Ref: 100–1/100–1
Topic: Willingness to pay
Skill: Analytical
Objective: LO1: Distinguish between the concepts of consumer surplus and producer surplus.
AACSB Coding: Analytic Skills
Special Feature: None

28. *Refer to Figure 4-1.* If the market price is $2.50, what is the maximum number of ice cream cones that Kendra will buy?
    A) 1
    B) 2
    C) 4
    D) 3
Answer: D
Diff: 1   Type: MC   Page Ref: 100–1/100–1
Topic: Consumer surplus and demand
Skill: Analytical
Objective: LO1: Distinguish between the concepts of consumer surplus and producer surplus.
AACSB Coding: Analytic Skills
Special Feature: None

29. Suppliers will be willing to supply a product only if
    A) the price received is less than the additional cost of producing the product.
    B) the price received is at least equal to the additional cost of producing the product.
    C) the price is higher than the average cost of producing the product.
    D) the price received is at least double the additional cost of producing the product.
Answer: B
Diff: 1   Type: MC   Page Ref: 105/105
Topic: Marginal cost
Skill: Conceptual
Objective: LO1: Distinguish between the concepts of consumer surplus and producer surplus.
AACSB Coding: Reflective Thinking
Special Feature: None

30. The difference between the lowest price a firm would have been willing to accept and the price it actually receives from the sale of a product is called
    A) producer surplus.
    B) profit.
    C) marginal revenue.
    D) price differential.
Answer: A
Diff: 1   Type: MC   Page Ref: 104/104
Topic: Producer surplus
Skill: Definition
Objective: LO1: Distinguish between the concepts of consumer surplus and producer surplus.
AACSB Coding: Reflective Thinking
Special Feature: None

Figure 4–2

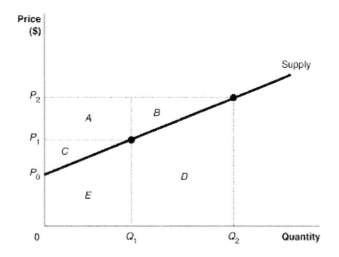

31. *Refer to Figure 4–2.* What area represents producer surplus at a price of P_2?

    A) $A + B$
    B) $B + D$
    C) $A + B + C$
    D) $A + B + C + D + E$
    Answer: C
    Diff: 1   Type: MC   Page Ref: 104/104
    Topic: Producer surplus
    Skill: Analytical
    Objective: LO1: Distinguish between the concepts of consumer surplus and producer surplus.
    AACSB Coding: Reflective Thinking
    Special Feature: None

32. *Refer to Figure 4–2.* What area represents the increase in producer surplus when the market price rises from P_1 to P_2?

    A) $B + D$
    B) $A + C + E$
    C) $C + E$
    D) $A + B$
    Answer: D
    Diff: 2   Type: MC   Page Ref: 104/104
    Topic: Producer surplus
    Skill: Analytical
    Objective: LO1: Distinguish between the concepts of consumer surplus and producer surplus.
    AACSB Coding: Analytic Skills
    Special Feature: None

33. Two economists from the University of Chicago estimated the benefit households received from subscribing to satellite television. The economists found that
    A) the consumer surplus from cable television exceeded the consumer surplus from satellite television.
    B) the average consumer of satellite television received a marginal benefit equal to $81.
    C) most consumers of satellite television were not willing to pay more than $81 per month.
    D) one year's benefit to consumers who subscribe to satellite television is about $2 billion.
    Answer: D
    Diff: 2   Type: MC   Page Ref: 102/102
    Topic: Consumer surplus
    Skill: Fact
    Objective: LO1: Distinguish between the concepts of consumer surplus and producer surplus.
    AACSB Coding: Reflective Thinking
    Special Feature: Making the Connection: The Consumer Surplus from Satellite Television

34. Producer surplus is the difference between the highest price someone is willing to pay and the price he actually pays.
    Answer: True   ⊚ False
    Diff: 1   Type: TF   Page Ref: 100/100
    Topic: What consumer surplus and producer surplus measure
    Skill: Conceptual
    Objective: LO1: Distinguish between the concepts of consumer surplus and producer surplus.
    AACSB Coding: Reflective Thinking
    Special Feature: None

35. The total amount of consumer surplus in a market is equal to the area below the demand curve.
    Answer: True   ⊚ False
    Diff: 1   Type: TF   Page Ref: 102/102
    Topic: Consumer surplus
    Skill: Conceptual
    Objective: LO1: Distinguish between the concepts of consumer surplus and producer surplus.
    AACSB Coding: Reflective Thinking
    Special Feature: None

36. The additional cost to a firm of producing one more unit of a good or service is equal to producer surplus.
    Answer: True   ⊚ False
    Diff: 1   Type: TF   Page Ref: 103/103
    Topic: Marginal cost
    Skill: Conceptual
    Objective: LO1: Distinguish between the concepts of consumer surplus and producer surplus.
    AACSB Coding: Reflective Thinking
    Special Feature: None

Figure 4–3

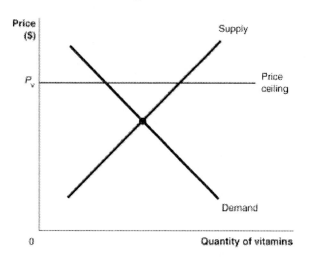

37. *Refer to Figure 4–3* which shows the market for vitamins. Suppose the government imposes a price ceiling of P_V. How will the price ceiling affect the quantity supplied, quantity demanded and quantity exchanged?

    Answer: The price ceiling will have no effect on the market outcome. An effective price ceiling must lie below the free market equilibrium. Thus, in this case the market outcome will be determined by forces of demand and supply.

    Diff: 3   Type: ES   Page Ref: 100/100
    Topic: Price ceiling
    Skill: Conceptual
    Objective: LO1: Distinguish between the concepts of consumer surplus and producer surplus.
    AACSB Coding: Reflective Thinking
    Special Feature: None

38. What is consumer surplus? Why would policy makers be interested in consumer surplus?

    Answer: Consumer surplus is the difference between what a consumer is willing to pay for a product and what she actually pays for the product. Since consumer surplus measures the benefit that consumers receive from a good as they themselves perceive it, it serves as a good measure of economic well–being. Thus, if policy makers care about consumer preferences, they could use this measure to make normative judgments about market outcomes.

    Diff: 3   Type: ES   Page Ref: 100/100
    Topic: Consumer surplus
    Skill: Conceptual
    Objective: LO1: Distinguish between the concepts of consumer surplus and producer surplus.
    AACSB Coding: Reflective Thinking
    Special Feature: None

4.2 The Efficiency of Competitive Markets

1. In a competitive market equilibrium
    A) total consumer surplus equals total producer surplus.
    B) marginal benefit and marginal cost are maximized.
    C) consumers and producers benefit equally.
    D) the marginal benefit equals the marginal cost of the last unit sold.
    Answer: D
    Diff: 1   Type: MC   Page Ref: 106/106
    Topic: Economic efficiency
    Skill: Conceptual
    Objective: LO2: Understand the concept of economic efficiency.
    AACSB Coding: Reflective Thinking
    Special Feature: None

2. When the marginal benefit equals the marginal cost of the last unit sold in a competitive market
    A) the net benefit of consumers is equal to the net benefit of producers.
    B) an economically efficient level of output is produced.
    C) producer surplus is equal to consumer surplus.
    D) total benefit is equal to total cost.
    Answer: B
    Diff: 1   Type: MC   Page Ref: 106/106
    Topic: Economic efficiency
    Skill: Conceptual
    Objective: LO2: Understand the concept of economic efficiency.
    AACSB Coding: Reflective Thinking
    Special Feature: None

3. Economic efficiency in a competitive market is achieved when
    A) economic surplus is equal to consumer surplus.
    B) consumers and producers are satisfied.
    C) the marginal benefit equals the marginal cost from the last unit sold.
    D) producer surplus equals the total amount firms receive from consumers minus the cost of production.
    Answer: C
    Diff: 1   Type: MC   Page Ref: 105–6/105–6
    Topic: Economic efficiency
    Skill: Definition
    Objective: LO2: Understand the concept of economic efficiency.
    AACSB Coding: Reflective Thinking
    Special Feature: None

Figure 4-4

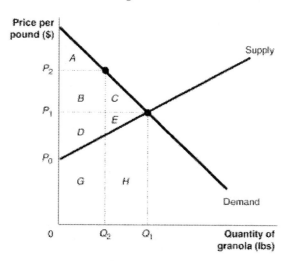

Figure 4-4 shows the market for granola. The market is initially in equilibrium at a price of P₁ and a quantity of Q₁. Now suppose producers decide to cut output to Q₂ in order to raise the price to P₂.

4. *Refer to Figure 4-4.* What area represents consumer surplus at P_2?

    A) *A*

    B) *A + B*

    C) *B + C*

    D) *A + B + D + F*

Answer: A

Diff: 1   Type: MC   Page Ref: 106-7/106-7

Topic: Consumer Surplus

Skill: Analytical

Objective: LO2: Understand the concept of economic efficiency.

AACSB Coding: Analytic Skills

Special Feature: None

5. *Refer to Figure 4-4.* What area represents producer surplus at P_2?

    A) *A + B + D*

    B) *B + D*

    C) *B + D + G*

    D) *B + C + D + E*

Answer: B

Diff: 1   Type: MC   Page Ref: 106-7/106-7

Topic: Producer surplus

Skill: Analytical

Objective: LO2: Understand the concept of economic efficiency.

AACSB Coding: Analytic Skills

Special Feature: None

6. *Refer to Figure 4-4.* What area represents the deadweight loss at P_2?
   A) $C + E + H$
   B) $G + H$
   C) $C + E$
   D) $B + C$
   Answer: C
   Diff: 1   Type: MC   Page Ref: 107/107
   Topic: Deadweight Loss
   Skill: Analytical
   Objective: LO2: Understand the concept of economic efficiency.
   AACSB Coding: Analytic Skills
   Special Feature: None

7. *Refer to Figure 4-4.* At the price P_2 consumers are willing to buy the Q_2 pounds of granola. Is this an economically efficient quantity?
   A) No, the marginal benefit of the last unit (Q_2) exceeds the marginal cost of that last unit.
   B) Yes, otherwise consumers would not buy Q_2 units.
   C) Yes, because the price P_2 shows what consumers are willing to pay for the product.
   D) No, the marginal cost of the last unit (Q_2) exceeds the marginal benefit of the last unit.
   Answer: A
   Diff: 1   Type: MC   Page Ref: 107/107
   Topic: Economic efficiency
   Skill: Analytical
   Objective: LO2: Understand the concept of economic efficiency.
   AACSB Coding: Analytic Skills
   Special Feature: None

8. Deadweight loss refers to
   A) the opportunity cost to firms from producing the equilibrium quantity in a competitive market.
   B) the sum of consumer and producer surplus.
   C) the loss of economic surplus when the marginal benefit equals the marginal cost of the last unit produced.
   D) the reduction in economic surplus resulting from not being in competitive equilibrium.
   Answer: D
   Diff: 1   Type: MC   Page Ref: 106/106
   Topic: Deadweight loss
   Skill: Definition
   Objective: LO2: Understand the concept of economic efficiency.
   AACSB Coding: Reflective Thinking
   Special Feature: None

9. Economic surplus
    A) does not exist when a competitive market is in equilibrium.
    B) is equal to the sum of consumer surplus and producer surplus.
    C) is the difference between quantity demanded and quantity supplied when the market price for a product is greater than the equilibrium price.
    D) is equal to the difference between consumer surplus and producer surplus.
Answer: B
Diff: 1   Type: MC   Page Ref: 106/106
Topic: Economic surplus
Skill: Definition
Objective: LO2: Understand the concept of economic efficiency.
AACSB Coding: Reflective Thinking
Special Feature: None

10. Economic surplus is maximized in a competitive market when
    A) demand is equal to supply.
    B) the deadweight loss equals the sum of consumer surplus and producer surplus.
    C) marginal benefit equals marginal cost.
    D) producers sell the quantity that consumers are willing to buy.
Answer: C
Diff: 2   Type: MC   Page Ref: 107/107
Topic: Economic surplus
Skill: Conceptual
Objective: LO2: Understand the concept of economic efficiency.
AACSB Coding: Reflective Thinking
Special Feature: None

11. Economic efficiency is defined as a market outcome in which the marginal benefit to consumers of the last unit produced is equal to the marginal cost of production, and in which
    A) the sum of consumer surplus and producer surplus is at a maximum.
    B) economic surplus is minimized.
    C) the sum of the benefits to firms is equal to the sum of the benefits to consumers.
    D) the sum of consumer surplus and producer surplus is minimized.
Answer: A
Diff: 2   Type: MC   Page Ref: 107/107
Topic: Economic efficiency
Skill: Definition
Objective: LO2: Understand the concept of economic efficiency.
AACSB Coding: Reflective Thinking
Special Feature: None

12. If, in a competitive market, marginal benefit is greater than marginal cost
    A) the net benefit to consumers from participating in the market is greater than the net benefit to producers.
    B) the government must force producers to lower price in order to achieve economic efficiency.
    C) the quantity sold is greater than the equilibrium quantity.
    D) the quantity sold is less than the equilibrium quantity.
    Answer: D
    Diff: 3   Type: MC   Page Ref: 107/107
    Topic: Economic efficiency
    Skill: Conceptual
    Objective: LO2: Understand the concept of economic efficiency.
    AACSB Coding: Reflective Thinking
    Special Feature: None

13. In a competitive market the demand curve shows the _____ received by consumers and the supply curve shows the _____.
    A) utility; average cost.
    B) marginal benefit; marginal cost
    C) economic surplus; opportunity cost
    D) net benefit; net cost
    Answer: B
    Diff: 1   Type: MC   Page Ref: 107/107
    Topic: Economic efficiency
    Skill: Conceptual
    Objective: LO2: Understand the concept of economic efficiency.
    AACSB Coding: Reflective Thinking
    Special Feature: None

Figure 4–5

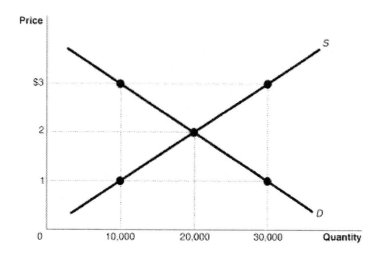

14. *Refer to Figure 4–5.* The figure above represents the market for iced tea. Assume that this is a competitive market. At a price of $3
    A) the marginal cost of iced tea is greater than the marginal benefit; therefore, output is inefficiently low.
    B) producers should lower the price to $1 in order to sell the quantity demanded of 10,000.
    C) the marginal benefit of iced tea is greater than the marginal cost; therefore, output is inefficiently low.
    D) the marginal benefit of iced tea is greater than the marginal cost; therefore, output is inefficiently high.
    Answer: C
    Diff: 2   Type: MC   Page Ref: 106/106
    Topic: Economic efficiency
    Skill: Analytical
    Objective: LO2: Understand the concept of economic efficiency.
    AACSB Coding: Analytic Skills
    Special Feature: None

15. *Refer to Figure 4–5.* The figure above represents the market for iced tea. Assume that this is a competitive market. If the price of iced tea is $1
    A) the quantity supplied is less than the economically efficient quantity.
    B) the quantity supplied is economically efficient but the quantity demanded is economically inefficient.
    C) economic surplus is maximized.
    D) not enough consumers want to buy iced tea.
    Answer: A
    Diff: 1   Type: MC   Page Ref: 106/106
    Topic: Economic efficiency
    Skill: Analytical
    Objective: LO2: Understand the concept of economic efficiency.
    AACSB Coding: Analytic Skills
    Special Feature: None

16. *Refer to Figure 4-5.* The figure above represents the market for iced tea. Assume that this is a competitive market. If the price of iced tea is $3, what changes in the market would result in an economically efficient output?
    A) The price would decrease, the quantity supplied would increase, and the quantity demanded would decrease.
    B) The quantity supplied would decrease, the quantity demanded would increase and the equilibrium price would decrease.
    C) The price would decrease, the demand would increase and the supply would decrease.
    D) The price would decrease, quantity demanded would increase and quantity supplied would decrease.

    Answer: D
    Diff: 1   Type: MC   Page Ref: 106/106
    Topic: Economic efficiency
    Skill: Analytical
    Objective: LO2: Understand the concept of economic efficiency.
    AACSB Coding: Reflective Thinking
    Special Feature: None

17. *Refer to Figure 4-5.* The figure above represents the market for iced tea. Assume that this is a competitive market. If 20,000 units of iced tea are sold
    A) the deadweight loss is equal to economic surplus.
    B) producer surplus equals consumer surplus.
    C) the marginal benefit of each of the 20,000 units of iced tea equals $3.
    D) marginal benefit is equal to marginal cost.

    Answer: D
    Diff: 1   Type: MC   Page Ref: 106/106
    Topic: Economic efficiency
    Skill: Analytical
    Objective: LO2: Understand the concept of economic efficiency.
    AACSB Coding: Reflective Thinking
    Special Feature: None

18. *Refer to Figure 4-5.* The figure above represents the market for iced tea. Assume that this is a competitive market. Which of the following is true?
    A) If the price of iced tea is $3 the output will be economically efficient but there will be a deadweight loss.
    B) If the price of iced tea is $3 consumers will purchase more than the economically efficient output.
    C) Both 10,000 and 30,000 are economically inefficient rates of output.
    D) If the price of iced tea is $3 producers will sell 30,000 units of iced tea but this output will be economically inefficient.

    Answer: C
    Diff: 1   Type: MC   Page Ref: 106/106
    Topic: Economic efficiency
    Skill: Analytical
    Objective: LO2: Understand the concept of economic efficiency.
    AACSB Coding: Reflective Thinking
    Special Feature: None

19. If equilibrium is achieved in a competitive market
    A) there will is no deadweight loss.
    B) the deadweight loss will be maximized.
    C) the deadweight loss will equal the sum of consumer surplus and producer surplus.
    D) the deadweight loss will be the same as the opportunity cost of the last unit of output sold.
    Answer: A
    Diff: 1   Type: MC   Page Ref: 106/106
    Topic: Deadweight loss
    Skill: Conceptual
    Objective: LO2: Understand the concept of economic efficiency.
    AACSB Coding: Reflective Thinking
    Special Feature: None

20. Economic efficiency is achieved when there is a market outcome in which the marginal benefit to consumers of the last unit produced is equal to its marginal cost of production and
    A) economic surplus plus consumer surplus equals producer surplus.
    B) consumer surplus plus producer surplus is maximized.
    C) economic surplus is minimized.
    D) the difference between consumer surplus and producer surplus is maximized.
    Answer: B
    Diff: 2   Type: MC   Page Ref: 107/107
    Topic: Economic efficiency
    Skill: Definition
    Objective: LO2: Understand the concept of economic efficiency.
    AACSB Coding: Reflective Thinking
    Special Feature: None

21. Economic efficiency is a market outcome in which the marginal benefit of consumers is equal to the marginal cost of production and the sum of consumer surplus and producer surplus is maximized.
    Answer: ○ True   False
    Diff: 1   Type: TF   Page Ref: 107/107
    Topic: Economic efficiency
    Skill: Definition
    Objective: LO2: Understand the concept of economic efficiency.
    AACSB Coding: Reflective Thinking
    Special Feature: None

22. The difference between consumer surplus and producer surplus in a market is equal to the deadweight loss.
    Answer: True   ○ False
    Diff: 1   Type: TF   Page Ref: 106–7/106–7
    Topic: Deadweight loss
    Skill: Analytical
    Objective: LO1: Distinguish between the concepts of consumer surplus and producer surplus.
    AACSB Coding: Reflective Thinking
    Special Feature: None

23. Will equilibrium in a market always result in an outcome that is economically efficient? Explain.

Answer: An economically efficient outcome means that at the equilibrium price the marginal benefit of the last unit of output sold is equal to its marginal cost. This will occur only in markets that are competitive (many buyers and many sellers) and there are no price controls.

Diff: 1   Type: ES   Page Ref: 107/107
Topic: Economic efficiency
Skill: Conceptual
Objective: LO2: Understand the concept of economic efficiency.
AACSB Coding: Analytic Skills
Special Feature: None

4.3   Government Intervention in the Market: Price Floors and Price Ceilings

1. When a competitive equilibrium is achieved in a market
    A) all individuals are better off than they would be if a price ceiling or price floor were imposed by government.
    B) the total net benefit to society is maximized.
    C) the total benefits to consumers are equal to the total benefits to producers.
    D) economic surplus equals the deadweight loss.

Answer: B

Diff: 1   Type: MC   Page Ref: 107/107
Topic: Economic efficiency
Skill: Conceptual
Objective: LO3: Explain the economic effect of government-imposed price ceilings and price floors.
AACSB Coding: Reflective Thinking
Special Feature: None

Table 4-3

Hourly Wage (Dollars)	Quantity of Labor Supplied	Quantity of Labor Demanded
$6.00	350,000	390,000
6.50	360,000	380,000
7.00	370,000	370,000
7.50	380,000	360,000
8.00	390,000	350,000
8.50	400,000	340,000

Table 4-3 shows the demand and supply schedules for the low-skilled labor market in the city of Westover.

2. *Refer to Table 4-3.* What is the equilibrium hourly wage (W*) and the equilibrium quantity of labor (Q*)?
   A) W* = $7.00; Q* = 370,000
   B) W* = $6.50; Q* = 380,000
   C) W* = $6.50; Q* = 360,000
   D) W* = $7.00; Q* = 740,000
   Answer: A
   Diff: 1   Type: MC   Page Ref: 108/108
   Topic: Economic efficiency
   Skill: Analytical
   Objective: LO3: Explain the economic effect of government-imposed price ceilings and price floors.
   AACSB Coding: Analytic Skills
   Special Feature: None

3. *Refer to Table 4-3.* If a minimum wage of $7.50 an hour is mandated, what is the quantity of labor demanded?
   A) 380,000
   B) 370,000
   C) 360,000
   D) 10,000
   Answer: C
   Diff: 1   Type: MC   Page Ref: 110/110
   Topic: Price floor
   Skill: Analytical
   Objective: LO3: Explain the economic effect of government-imposed price ceilings and price floors.
   AACSB Coding: Analytic Skills
   Special Feature: None

4. ***Refer to Table 4–3.*** If a minimum wage of $7.50 an hour is mandated, what is the quantity of labor supplied?
    A) 390,000
    B) 370,000
    C) 340,000
    D) 380,000
Answer: D
Diff: 1   Type: MC   Page Ref: 110/110
Topic: Price floor
Skill: Analytical
Objective: LO3: Explain the economic effect of government-imposed price ceilings and price floors.
AACSB Coding: Analytic Skills
Special Feature: None

5. ***Refer to Table 4–3.*** If a minimum wage of $7.50 is mandated there will be a
    A) shortage of 10,000 units of labor.
    B) surplus of 10,000 units of labor.
    C) shortage of 20,000 units of labor.
    D) surplus of 20,000 units of labor.
Answer: D
Diff: 1   Type: MC   Page Ref: 110/110
Topic: Price floor
Skill: Analytical
Objective: LO3: Explain the economic effect of government-imposed price ceilings and price floors.
AACSB Coding: Analytic Skills
Special Feature: None

6. ***Refer to Table 4–3.*** Suppose that the quantity of labor demanded increases by 40,000 at each wage level. What are the new free market equilibrium hourly wage and the new equilibrium quantity of labor?
    A) W = $8.00; Q = 390,000
    B) W = $7.50; Q = 380,000
    C) W = $6.50; Q = 380,000
    D) W = $6.00; Q = 390,000
Answer: A
Diff: 2   Type: MC   Page Ref: 110/110
Topic: Economic efficiency
Skill: Analytical
Objective: LO3: Explain the economic effect of government-imposed price ceilings and price floors.
AACSB Coding: Analytic Skills
Special Feature: None

7. Which of the following is not a consequence of minimum wage laws?
   A) Low skilled workers are hurt because it reduces the number of jobs providing low skilled
      workers with training.
   B) Employers will be reluctant to offer low–skill workers jobs with training.
   C) Producers have an incentive to offer workers non–wage benefits such as healthcare
      benefits and convenient working hours rather than a higher wage.
   D) Some workers benefit when the minimum wage is increased.

   Answer: C

   Diff: 1   Type: MC   Page Ref: 109–10/109–10
   Topic: Minimum wage
   Skill: Conceptual
   Objective: LO3: Explain the economic effect of government-imposed price ceilings and price floors.
   AACSB Coding: Reflective Thinking
   Special Feature: None

8. The minimum wage is an example of
   A) a subsidy for low–skilled workers.
   B) a price floor.
   C) a price ceiling.
   D) a black market.

   Answer: B

   Diff: 1   Type: MC   Page Ref: 109/109
   Topic: Minimum wage
   Skill: Definition
   Objective: LO3: Explain the economic effect of government-imposed price ceilings and price floors.
   AACSB Coding: Reflective Thinking
   Special Feature: None

9. To affect the market outcome a price ceiling
   A) must be set below the black market price.
   B) must be set below the legal price.
   C) must be set below the price floor.
   D) must be set below the equilibrium price.

   Answer: D

   Diff: 1   Type: MC   Page Ref: 110/110
   Topic: Price ceiling
   Skill: Conceptual
   Objective: LO3: Explain the economic effect of government-imposed price ceilings and price floors.
   AACSB Coding: Reflective Thinking
   Special Feature: None

10. Government intervention is agricultural markets in the U.S. began
    A) during World War II to ensure that enough food was available for domestic consumption.
    B) after World War I in order to assist farmers to adjust from a war-time economy to a peace-time economy.
    C) during the Great Depression.
    D) during the Korean War.
    Answer: C
    Diff: 1   Type: MC   Page Ref: 108/108
    Topic: Government intervention in the market
    Skill: Fact
    Objective: LO3: Explain the economic effect of government-imposed price ceilings and price floors.
    AACSB Coding: Reflective Thinking
    Special Feature: None

11. Economists refer a to a market where buying and selling take place at prices that violate government price regulations as
    A) a black market.
    B) an outlaw market.
    C) a noncompetitive market.
    D) a restricted market.
    Answer: A
    Diff: 1   Type: MC   Page Ref: 112/112
    Topic: Black market
    Skill: Definition
    Objective: LO3: Explain the economic effect of government-imposed price ceilings and price floors.
    AACSB Coding: Reflective Thinking
    Special Feature: None

Figure 4-6

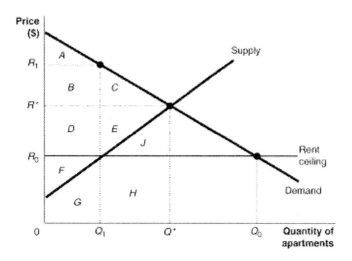

Figure 4–6 shows the market for apartments in Bay City. Recently, the government imposed a rent ceiling at R_0.

12. **Refer to Figure 4-6.** With rent control, the quantity supplied is Q_1. Suppose apartment owners ignore the law and rent this quantity for the highest rent they can get. What is the highest rent they can get?

 A) R^*
 B) R_1
 C) R_0
 D) more than R_1.

Answer: B
Diff: 2 Type: MC Page Ref: 110–1/110–1
Topic: Price ceiling
Skill: Analytical
Objective: LO3: Explain the economic effect of government–imposed price ceilings and price floors.
AACSB Coding: Analytic Skills
Special Feature: None

13. **Refer to Figure 4-6.** What is the area that represents consumer surplus after the imposition of the ceiling?

 A) $A + B + D$
 B) $A + B + C$
 C) $A + B + D + F$
 D) $A + B + D + F + G$

Answer: A
Diff: 2 Type: MC Page Ref: 111/111
Topic: Price ceiling
Skill: Analytical
Objective: LO3: Explain the economic effect of government–imposed price ceilings and price floors.
AACSB Coding: Reflective Thinking
Special Feature: None

14. ***Refer to Figure 4–6.*** What is the area that represents the producer surplus after the imposition of the ceiling?
- A) *F + G*
- B) *F*
- C) *D + F + G*
- D) *A + B + D + F + G*

Answer: B

Diff: 2   Type: MC   Page Ref: 111/111
Topic: Price ceiling
Skill: Analytical
Objective: LO3: Explain the economic effect of government–imposed price ceilings and price floors.
AACSB Coding: Reflective Thinking
Special Feature: None

15. ***Refer to Figure 4–6.*** What is the area that represents the portion of producer surplus transferred to consumers as a result of the rent ceiling?
- A) *D + E*
- B) *D + F*
- C) *D*
- D) *F*

Answer: C

Diff: 3   Type: MC   Page Ref: 111/111
Topic: Price ceiling
Skill: Analytical
Objective: LO3: Explain the economic effect of government–imposed price ceilings and price floors.
AACSB Coding: Reflective Thinking
Special Feature: None

16. ***Refer to Figure 4–6.*** What area represents the deadweight loss after the imposition of the ceiling?
- A) *G + H*
- B) *J + H*
- C) *C + E + J + H*
- D) *C + E*

Answer: D

Diff: 2   Type: MC   Page Ref: 111/111
Topic: Price ceiling
Skill: Analytical
Objective: LO3: Explain the economic effect of government–imposed price ceilings and price floors.
AACSB Coding: Reflective Thinking
Special Feature: None

17. Which term refers to a legally established minimum price that firms may charge?
    A) A price ceiling.
    B) A subsidy.
    C) A price floor.
    D) A tariff.
    Answer: C
    Diff: 1   Type: MC   Page Ref: 108/108
    Topic: Price floor
    Skill: Definition
    Objective: LO3: Explain the economic effect of government-imposed price ceilings and price floors.
    AACSB Coding: Reflective Thinking
    Special Feature: None

18. In order to be binding a price floor
    A) must lie above the free market equilibrium price.
    B) must lie below the free market equilibrium price.
    C) must coincide with the free market equilibrium price.
    D) must be high enough for firms to earn a profit.
    Answer: A
    Diff: 2   Type: MC   Page Ref: 108/108
    Topic: Price floor
    Skill: Conceptual
    Objective: LO3: Explain the economic effect of government-imposed price ceilings and price floors.
    AACSB Coding: Reflective Thinking
    Special Feature: None

19. A minimum wage law dictates
    A) the minimum quantity of labor that a firm must employ.
    B) the lowest wage that firms may pay for labor.
    C) the highest wage that firms must pay for labor.
    D) the minimum qualifications for labor.
    Answer: B
    Diff: 1   Type: MC   Page Ref: 109/109
    Topic: Minimum wage
    Skill: Definition
    Objective: LO3: Explain the economic effect of government-imposed price ceilings and price floors.
    AACSB Coding: Reflective Thinking
    Special Feature: None

Figure 4-7

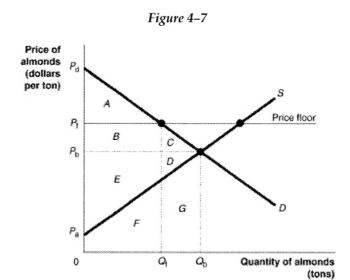

Figure 4-7 shows the demand and supply curves for the almond market. The government believes that the equilibrium price is too low and tries to help almond growers by setting a price floor at P_f.

20. **Refer to Figure 4-7.** What area represents consumer surplus after the imposition of the price floor?
   A) $A + B + E$
   B) $A + B$
   C) $A + B + E + F$
   D) A
   Answer: D
   Diff: 2   Type: MC   Page Ref: 108/108
   Topic: Price floor
   Skill: Analytical
   Objective: LO3: Explain the economic effect of government-imposed price ceilings and price floors.
   AACSB Coding: Analytic Skills
   Special Feature: None

21. **Refer to Figure 4-7.** What is the area that represents producer surplus after the imposition of the price floor?
   A) $A + B + E$
   B) $B + E$
   C) $B + E + F$
   D) $B + C + D + E$
   Answer: B
   Diff: 2   Type: MC   Page Ref: 108/108
   Topic: Price floor
   Skill: Analytical
   Objective: LO3: Explain the economic effect of government-imposed price ceilings and price floors.
   AACSB Coding: Analytic Skills
   Special Feature: None

22. *Refer to Figure 4–7.* What area represents the portion of consumer surplus that has been transferred to producer surplus as a result of the price floor?

    A) *B*

    B) *B + C*

    C) *B + E*

    D) *E*

Answer: A

Diff: 2   *Type: MC*   *Page Ref: 108/108*

Topic: Price floor

Skill: Analytical

Objective: LO3: Explain the economic effect of government-imposed price ceilings and price floors.

AACSB Coding: Analytic Skills

Special Feature: None

23. *Refer to Figure 4–7.* What area represents the deadweight loss after the imposition of the price floor?

    A) *C + D + G*

    B) *F + G*

    C) *C + D*

    D) *C + D + F + G*

Answer: C

Diff: 2   *Type: MC*   *Page Ref: 108/108*

Topic: Price floor

Skill: Analytical

Objective: LO3: Explain the economic effect of government-imposed price ceilings and price floors.

AACSB Coding: Analytic Skills

Special Feature: None

24. Congress passed the Freedom to Farm Act in 1996. What was the purpose of this Act?

    A) To encourage more people to become farmers.

    B) To grant free land to farmers in order to produce crops that were particularly scarce.

    C) To phase out the use of price ceilings in agricultural markets.

    D) To phase out price floors and return to a free market in agriculture.

Answer: D

Diff: 1   *Type: MC*   *Page Ref: 109/109*

Topic: Government intervention in the market

Skill: Fact

Objective: LO3: Explain the economic effect of government-imposed price ceilings and price floors.

AACSB Coding: Reflective Thinking

Special Feature: None

25. David Card and Alan Kruger conducted a study of fast-food restaurants in New Jersey and Pennsylvania. The study found that
    A) there was a large reduction in employment of low-skilled workers when the minimum wage was raised in these states.
    B) the earned income tax credit is more effective in raising the incomes of low-skilled workers than increases in the minimum wage.
    C) increases in the minimum wage had a very small impact on employment.
    D) increases in the prices of food have a greater effect on wage increases in New Jersey than in Pennsylvania.

    Answer: C
    Diff: 1   Type: MC   Page Ref: 110/110
    Topic: Minimum wage
    Skill: Fact
    Objective: LO3: Explain the economic effect of government-imposed price ceilings and price floors.
    AACSB Coding: Reflective Thinking
    Special Feature: Making the Connection: Price Floors in Labor Markets: The Debate over Minimum Wage Policy

26. Increases in the minimum wage are intended to raise the incomes of low-income workers. Many economists favor a different policy to achieve this goal, a policy that avoids the deadweight losses that result from the minimum wage. What is this policy?
    A) Distribution of food stamps to low-income consumers.
    B) Distribution of vouchers that can be used for rent or mortgage payments.
    C) The Alternative Minimum Tax.
    D) The earned income tax credit.

    Answer: D
    Diff: 2   Type: MC   Page Ref: 110/110
    Topic: Minimum wage
    Skill: Fact
    Objective: LO3: Explain the economic effect of government-imposed price ceilings and price floors.
    AACSB Coding: Reflective Thinking
    Special Feature: Making the Connection: Price Floors in Labor Markets: The Debate over Minimum Wage Policy

27. Which of the follow is *not* a result of imposing a rent ceiling?
    A) Some consumer surplus is converted to producer surplus.
    B) A reduction in the quantity supplied of apartments.
    C) An increase in the quantity demanded of apartments.
    D) The marginal benefit of the last apartment rented is greater than the marginal cost of supplying it.

    Answer: A
    Diff: 2   Type: MC   Page Ref: 111/111
    Topic: Price ceiling
    Skill: Conceptual
    Objective: LO3: Explain the economic effect of government-imposed price ceilings and price floors.
    AACSB Coding: Reflective Thinking
    Special Feature: None

28. Which of the following describes the difference between "scarcity" and "shortage"?
    A) There is no difference; either word can be used to describe the situation that exists when there is less of a good or service available than people want.
    B) In the economic sense, almost everything is scarce. A shortage of a good or service occurs when the quantity demanded is greater than the quantity supplied at the current market price.
    C) There is a shortage of almost everything. Scarcity occurs only if the quantity demanded of a good or service is greater than the quantity supplied at the current market price.
    D) In the economic sense, almost everything is scarce. A shortage of a good or service occurs when the quantity demanded is greater than the quantity supplied at the equilibrium price.

Answer: B
Diff: 2   Type: MC   Page Ref: 111/111
Topic: The economic effect of price ceilings and price floors
Skill: Analytical
Objective: LO3: Explain the economic effect of government-imposed price ceilings and price floors.
AACSB Coding: Analytic Skills
Special Feature: Don't Let This Happen to YOU!: Don't Confuse "Scarcity" with a "Shortage."

29. In cities with rent controls, the actual rents paid can be higher than the legal maximum. One explanation for this is
    A) rent control laws are so complicated that landlords and tenants may not be aware of what the legal price is.
    B) landlords are allowed to charge more than the legal maximum on some apartments so long as they charge less on others.
    C) because there is a shortage of apartments, tenants often are willing to pay rents higher than the law allows.
    D) the legal penalty landlords face for charging more than the legal maximum rent is less than the revenue earned by charging their tenants more than the maximum rent.

Answer: C
Diff: 2   Type: MC   Page Ref: 112-3/112-3
Topic: Rent control
Skill: Analytical
Objective: LO3: Explain the economic effect of government-imposed price ceilings and price floors.
AACSB Coding: Analytic Skills
Special Feature: Solved Problem: What's the Economic Effect of a "Black Market" for Apartments?

30. Some economists believe that giving Christmas gifts results in deadweight losses for gift recipients. Which of the following helps to explain this belief?
    A) Many people resent receiving cash for presents rather than gifts.
    B) In many cases people would have chosen different gifts for themselves than the ones they received.
    C) Many people who give gifts do so because they feel they have to, not because they want to.
    D) Economists have found that deadweight losses occur when people receive the same gifts from different people.
    Answer: B
    Diff: 2   Type: MC   Page Ref: 113/113
    Topic: Deadweight loss
    Skill: Conceptual
    Objective: LO3: Explain the economic effect of government-imposed price ceilings and price floors.
    AACSB Coding: Reflective Thinking
    Special Feature: Making the Connection: Does Holiday Gift Giving Have a Deadweight Loss?

31. John List and Jason Shogren conducted a study that tried to explain why people continue to give presents rather than cash for birthdays and holidays. Their study found that
    A) the deadweight loss from giving cash was twice as great as the deadweight loss from giving presents.
    B) on average, families and friends paid much more for presents than the recipients were willing to pay for them.
    C) government restrictions are responsible for most of the deadweight losses associated with gift giving.
    D) as much as half the value of a gift to a recipient was its sentimental value.
    Answer: D
    Diff: 2   Type: MC   Page Ref: 113/113
    Topic: Deadweight loss
    Skill: Conceptual
    Objective: LO3: Explain the economic effect of government-imposed price ceilings and price floors.
    AACSB Coding: Reflective Thinking
    Special Feature: Making the Connection: Does Holiday Gift Giving Have a Deadweight Loss?

32. Which of the following is a result of government price controls?
    A) Some people win and some people lose.
    B) Price controls benefit poor consumers but harm producers and wealthy consumers.
    C) Price controls increase economic efficiency
    D) The deadweight loss from price ceilings is greater than the deadweight loss from price floors.
    Answer: A
    Diff: 2   Type: MC   Page Ref: 114/114
    Topic: The economic effect of price ceilings and price floors
    Skill: Conceptual
    Objective: LO3: Explain the economic effect of government-imposed price ceilings and price floors.
    AACSB Coding: Reflective Thinking
    Special Feature: None

33. Economists are reluctant to state that price controls are desirable or undesirable because
    A) it is impossible to evaluate the impact on quantity demanded and quantity supplied as a result of price controls.
    B) whether the gains from the winners exceed the losses from the losers is not strictly an economic question.
    C) sometimes price controls result in increases in economic efficiency and sometimes they result in decreases in economic efficiency.
    D) economists are reluctant to conduct positive analysis of price controls.
    Answer: B
    Diff: 2   Type: MC   Page Ref: 114/114
    Topic: The economic effect of price ceilings and price floors
    Skill: Conceptual
    Objective: LO3: Explain the economic effect of government-imposed price ceilings and price floors.
    AACSB Coding: Reflective Thinking
    Special Feature: None

34. Government intervention in agriculture began in the Untied States in the 1930s.
    Answer: True   ⊘ False
    Diff: 1   Type: TF   Page Ref: 108
    Topic: Government intervention in the market
    Skill: Fact
    Objective: LO3: Explain the economic effect of government-imposed price ceilings and price floors.
    AACSB Coding: Reflective Thinking
    Special Feature: Making the Connection: Apple Forecasts the Demand for iPhones and Other Consumer Electronics

35. Shortage means the same thing as scarcity.
    Answer: True   ⊘ False
    Diff: 1   Type: TF   Page Ref: 111
    Topic: The economic effect of price ceilings and price floors
    Skill: Conceptual
    Objective: LO3: Explain the economic effect of government-imposed price ceilings and price floors.
    AACSB Coding: Reflective Thinking
    Special Feature: Don't Let This Happen to YOU!: Don't Confuse "Scarcity" with a "Shortage."

36. All renters benefit from rent control and all landlords lose.
    Answer: True   ⊘ False
    Diff: 1   Type: TF   Page Ref: 110–2/110–2
    Topic: Rent control
    Skill: Analytical
    Objective: LO3: Explain the economic effect of government-imposed price ceilings and price floors.
    AACSB Coding: Analytic Skills
    Special Feature: None

Table 4-4

37.

Price Per Bushel (Dollars)	Quantity Demanded (Bushels)	Quantity Supplied (Bushels)
$2	40,000	0
4	34,000	4,000
6	28,000	8,000
8	24,000	16,000
10	20,000	20,000
12	18,000	28,000
14	12,000	36,000
16	6,000	40,000

Table 4-4 above contains information about the corn market. Answer the following questions based on this table.

Refer to Table 4-4. An agricultural price floor is a price that the government guarantees farmers will receive for a particular crop. Suppose the federal government sets a price floor for corn at $12 per bushel.
a. What is the amount of shortage or surplus in the corn market as result of the price floor?
b. If the government agrees to purchase any surplus output at $12, how much will it cost the government?
c. If the government buys all of the farmers' output at the floor price, how many bushels of corn will it have to purchase and how much will it cost the government?
d. Suppose the government buys up all of the farmers' output at the floor price and then sells the output to consumers at whatever price it can get. Under this scheme, what is the price at which the government will be able to sell off all of the output it had purchased from farmers? What is the revenue received from the government's sale?
e. In this problem we have considered two government schemes: (1) a price floor is established and the government purchases any excess output and (2) the government buys all the farmers' output at the floor price and resells at whatever price it can get. Which scheme will taxpayers prefer?
f. Consider again the two schemes. Which scheme will the farmers prefer?
g. Consider again the two schemes. Which scheme will corn buyers prefer?
Answer: a. 10,000 surplus.
   b. $12 x 10,000 = $120,000.
   c. 28,000 bushels × $12 = $336,000.
   d. $6 per bushel and government receives $6 × 28,000 = $168,000.
   e. Taxpayers prefer scheme (1).
   f. In terms of revenue, farmers are indifferent between the two schemes.
   g. Corn buyers prefer scheme (2).
Diff: 3   Type: ES   Page Ref: 108/108
Topic: Price floor
Skill: Analytical
Objective: LO3: Explain the economic effect of government-imposed price ceilings and price floors.
AACSB Coding: Analytic Skills
Special Feature: None

Figure 4–8

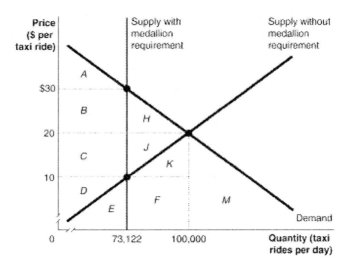

Figure 4–8 shows the market for cigarettes. The government plans to impose a unit tax in this market. The following question(s) are based on this figure.

38. **Refer to Figure 4–8.** To legally drive a taxicab in New York City, you must have a medallion issued by the city government. Assume that only 12,187 medallions have been issued. Let's also assume this puts an absolute limit on the number of taxi rides that can be supplied in New York City on any day, because no one breaks the law by driving a taxi without a medallion. Assume as well that each taxi provides 6 trips per day. In that case, the quantity supplied of taxi rides is 73,122 (or 6 rides per taxi × 12,187 taxis). This is shown in the diagram with a vertical line at this quantity. Assume that there are no government controls on the prices that drivers can charge for rides.

   a.   What would the equilibrium price and quantity be in this market if there were no medallion requirement?

   b.   If there were no medallion requirement, indicate the area that represents consumer surplus.

   c.   If there were no medallion requirement, indicate the area that represents producer surplus.

   d.   If there were no medallion requirement, indicate the area that represents economic surplus.

   e.   What are the price and quantity with the medallion requirement?

   f.   With a medallion requirement in place, what area represents consumer surplus?

   g.   With a medallion requirement in place, what area represents producer surplus?

   h.   With a medallion requirement in place, what area represents the deadweight loss?

   i.   Based on your answers to parts (c) and (g) are taxicab drivers better off with the medallion requirement for taxicabs than without?

   j.   Are consumers better off with or without the medallion requirement for taxicabs?

Answer: a.   P =$20, Q = 100,000 rides.
   b.   Consumer Surplus = A+ B+ H.
   c.   Producer Surplus = C + D + J.
   d.   Economic Surplus = A + B + C + D + H + J.
   e.   P = $30, Q = 73,122.
   f.   CS with medallion = A.
   g.   PS with medallion = B + C + D.
   h.   Deadweight loss = H + J.
   i.   Taxi drivers are better off with the requirement because producer surplus is greater by the area   by B–J.
   j.   Consumers are worse off.

Diff: 3   Type: ES   Page Ref: 108–9/108–9
Topic: Economic efficiency
Skill: Analytical
Objective: LO3: Explain the economic effect of government–imposed price ceilings and price floors.
AACSB Coding: Analytic Skills
Special Feature: None

39. The cities of Francistown and Nalady are five miles apart. Francistown enacts a rent control law that puts a ceiling on rents well below their equilibrium market value. Predict the impact of this law on the competitive equilibrium rent in Nalady, which does not have a rent control law.
   a.   Illustrate your answer with one demand and supply graph for the apartment market in Francistown and another demand and supply graph for the apartment marketing Nalady.
   b.   Make sure that your graphs clearly show (1) the initial equilibrium before the rent control
        in both markets and (2) what happens after the imposition of rent control.
   c.   Clearly show any shifts in the demand or supply curves, and the movement along the curves for each market.
   d.   Label your graphs fully and provide written explanation for your graphs.

Answer: See the figure below. The rent ceiling in Francistown creates a shortage of apartments. Renters will move to Nalady, causing the demand for apartments curve in Nalady to shift to the right. The price and quantity of apartments in Nalady increase.

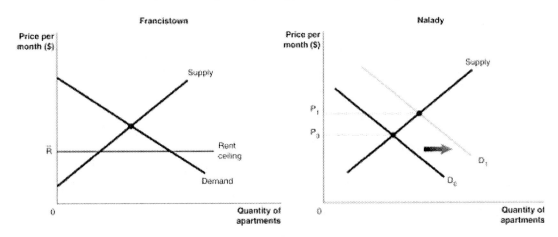

Diff: 3   Type: ES   Page Ref: 122/122
Topic: Rent control
Skill: Analytical
Objective: LO3: Explain the economic effect of government-imposed price ceilings and price floors.
AACSB Coding: Analytic Skills
Special Feature: An Inside Look on Policy: Is Rent Control a Lifeline or Stranglehold?

4.4   The Economic Impact of Taxes

1. The actual division of the burden of a tax between buyers and sellers in a market is called
   A) tax incidence.
   B) tax liability.
   C) tax bearer.
   D) tax parity.
   Answer: A
   Diff: 1   Type: MC   Page Ref: 116/116
   Topic: Tax incidence
   Skill: Definition
   Objective: LO4: Analyze the economic impact of taxes
   AACSB Coding: Reflective Thinking
   Special Feature: None

Figure 4-9

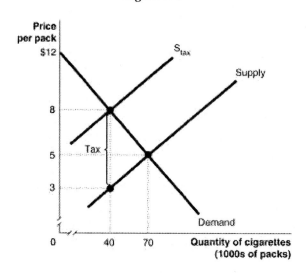

Figure 4-9 shows the market for cigarettes. The government plans to impose a unit tax in this market.

2. *Refer to Figure 4-9.* What is the size of the unit tax?
   A) $8
   B) $5
   C) $3
   D) Cannot be determined from the figure.
   Answer: B
   Diff: 1   Type: MC   Page Ref: 115-6/115-6
   Topic: Economic impact of taxes
   Skill: Analytical
   Objective: LO4: Analyze the economic impact of taxes
   AACSB Coding: Analytic Skills
   Special Feature: None

3. *Refer to Figure 4-9.* How much of the tax is paid by buyers?
   A) $8
   B) $5
   C) $4
   D) $3
   Answer: D
   Diff: 2   Type: MC   Page Ref: 116-7/116-7
   Topic: Economic impact of taxes
   Skill: Analytical
   Objective: LO4: Analyze the economic impact of taxes
   AACSB Coding: Analytic Skills
   Special Feature: None

4. *Refer to Figure 4-9.* The price buyers pay after the tax is
   A) $12
   B) $8
   C) $5
   D) $3
   Answer: B
   Diff: 1   Type: MC   Page Ref: 116-7/116-7
   Topic: Economic impact of taxes
   Skill: Analytical
   Objective: LO4: Analyze the economic impact of taxes
   AACSB Coding: Analytic Skills
   Special Feature: None

5. *Refer to Figure 4-9.* For each unit sold, the price sellers receive after the tax (net of tax) is
   A) $12
   B) $8
   C) $4.40
   D) $3
   Answer: D
   Diff: 1   Type: MC   Page Ref: 116-7/116-7
   Topic: Economic impact of taxes
   Skill: Analytical
   Objective: LO4: Analyze the economic impact of taxes
   AACSB Coding: Analytic Skills
   Special Feature: None

6. *Refer to Figure 4-9.* How much of the tax is paid by producers?
   A) $8
   B) $45
   C) $3
   D) $2
   Answer: D
   Diff: 2   Type: MC   Page Ref: 116-7/116-7
   Topic: Economic impact of taxes
   Skill: Analytical
   Objective: LO4: Analyze the economic impact of taxes
   AACSB Coding: Analytic Skills
   Special Feature: None

7. *Refer to Figure 4-9.* As a result of the tax, is there a loss in producer surplus?
    A) Yes, because producers are not selling as many units now.
    B) No, because the consumer pays the tax.
    C) No, because the market reaches a new equilibrium
    D) No, because producers are able to raise the price to cover their tax burden.
    Answer: A
    Diff: 2   Type: MC   Page Ref: 116-7/116-7
    Topic: Economic impact of taxes
    Skill: Analytical
    Objective: LO4: Analyze the economic impact of taxes
    AACSB Coding: Analytic Skills
    Special Feature: None

8. The government proposes a tax on halogen light bulbs. Sellers will bear the entire burden of the tax if the
    A) supply curve of halogen bulbs is horizontal.
    B) demand curve for halogen bulbs is vertical.
    C) demand curve for halogen bulbs is horizontal.
    D) demand curve is downward sloping and the supply curve is upward sloping.
    Answer: C
    Diff: 3   Type: MC   Page Ref: 116/116
    Topic: Economic impact of taxes
    Skill: Analytical
    Objective: LO4: Analyze the economic impact of taxes
    AACSB Coding: Analytic Skills
    Special Feature: None

9. Suppose the demand curve for a product is vertical and the supply curve is upward sloping. If a unit tax is imposed in the market for this product,
    A) sellers bear the entire burden of the tax.
    B) buyers bear the entire burden of the tax.
    C) the tax burden will be shared equally between buyers and sellers.
    D) buyers share the burden of the tax with government.
    Answer: B
    Diff: 2   Type: MC   Page Ref: 118/118
    Topic: Economic impact of taxes
    Skill: Analytical
    Objective: LO4: Analyze the economic impact of taxes
    AACSB Coding: Analytic Skills
    Special Feature: None

10. Suppose the demand curve for a product is downward sloping and the supply curve is upward sloping. If a unit tax is imposed in the market for this product,
    A) sellers bear the entire burden of the tax.
    B) the tax burden will be shared among the government, buyers and sellers.
    C) buyers bear the entire burden of the tax.
    D) the tax burden will be shared by buyers and sellers.
    Answer: D
    Diff: 2   Type: MC   Page Ref: 118/118
    Topic: Economic impact of taxes
    Skill: Analytical
    Objective: LO4: Analyze the economic impact of taxes
    AACSB Coding: Analytic Skills
    Special Feature: None

11.   *Figure 4–10*

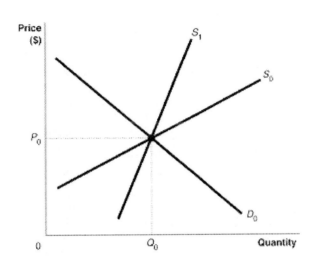

Refer to Figure 4–10. Suppose the market is initially in equilibrium at price P_0 and now the government imposes a tax on every unit sold. Which of the following statements best describes the impact of the tax? For demand curve D_0
    A) the producer bears a greater share of the tax burden if the supply curve is S_1.
    B) the producer bears a greater share of the tax burden if the supply curve is S_0.
    C) the producer's share of the tax burden is the same whether the supply curve is S_0 or S_1.
    D) the producer bears the entire burden of the tax if the supply curve is S_0 and the consumer bears the entire burden of the tax if the supply curve is S_1.

    Answer: A
    Diff: 3   Type: MC   Page Ref: 116–8/116–8
    Topic: Economic impact of taxes
    Skill: Analytical
    Objective: LO4: Analyze the economic impact of taxes
    AACSB Coding: Analytic Skills
    Special Feature: None

Figure 4-11

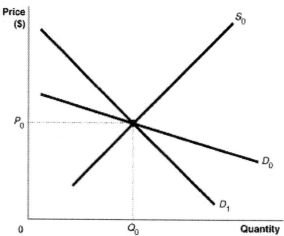

12. *Refer to Figure 4-11.* Suppose the market is initially in equilibrium at price P_0 and then the government imposes a tax on every unit sold. Which of the following statements best describes the impact of the tax?
    A) The consumer will bear a greater share of the tax burden if the demand curve is D_0.
    B) The consumer's share of the tax burden is the same whether the demand curve is D_0 or D_1.
    C) The consumer will bear a greater share of the tax burden if the demand curve is D_1.
    D) The consumer will bear the entire burden of the tax if the demand curve is D_0 and the producer will bear the entire burden of the tax if the demand curve is D_1.
    Answer: C
    Diff: 2   Type: MC   Page Ref: 116-8/116-8
    Topic: Economic impact of taxes
    Skill: Analytical
    Objective: LO4: Analyze the economic impact of taxes
    AACSB Coding: Analytic Skills
    Special Feature: None

13. Suppose an excise tax of $1 is imposed on every case of beer sold and sellers are responsible for paying this tax. How would the imposition of the tax be illustrated in a graph?
    A) The supply curve for cases of beer would shift to the right by $1.
    B) The supply curve for cases of beer would shift to the left by more than $1.
    C) The supply curve for cases of beer would shift to the left by less than $1.
    D) The supply curve for cases of beer shifts to the left by $1.
    Answer: D
    Diff: 1   Type: MC   Page Ref: 116-8/116-8
    Topic: Economic impact of taxes
    Skill: Analytical
    Objective: LO4: Analyze the economic impact of taxes
    AACSB Coding: Analytic Skills
    Special Feature: None

14. In Singapore the government places a $5,000 tax on the buyers of new automobiles. After the purchase of a new car, a buyer must pay the government $5,000. How would the imposition of the tax on buyers be illustrated in a graph?
    A) The tax will shift the demand curve to the right by $5,000.
    B) The tax will shift the demand curve to the left by $5,000.
    C) The tax will shift both the demand and supply curve to the right by $5,000.
    D) The tax will shift the supply curve to the left by $5,000.
    Answer: B
    Diff: 2   Type: MC   Page Ref: 116–8/116–8
    Topic: Economic impact of taxes
    Skill: Analytical
    Objective: LO4: Analyze the economic impact of taxes
    AACSB Coding: Analytic Skills
    Special Feature: None

15. When Congress passed a law that imposed a tax designed to fund its Social Security and Medicare programs it wanted employers and workers to share the burden of the tax equally. Most economists who have studied the incidence of the tax have concluded
    A) the tax is not high enough to cover the future costs of Social Security and Medicare.
    B) the tax on employers is too high because it reduces the employment of low–skilled workers.
    C) the burden of the tax falls almost entirely on workers.
    D) the tax rate should be greater for high income workers than for low income workers.
    Answer: C
    Diff: 2   Type: MC   Page Ref: 119/119
    Topic: Tax incidence
    Skill: Fact
    Objective: LO4: Analyze the economic impact of taxes
    AACSB Coding: Reflective Thinking
    Special Feature: Making the Connection: Is the Burden of a Social Security Tax Really Shared Equally between Workers and Firms?

16. A tax is imposed on employers and workers that are used to fund Social Security and Medicare. This tax is sometimes referred to as
    A) the Income Security Tax.
    B) the federal income tax.
    C) the ACIF.
    D) the payroll tax.
    Answer: D
    Diff: 2   Type: MC   Page Ref: 119/119
    Topic: Economic impact of taxes
    Skill: Fact
    Objective: LO4: Analyze the economic impact of taxes
    AACSB Coding: Reflective Thinking
    Special Feature: Making the Connection: Is the Burden of a Social Security Tax Really Shared Equally between Workers and Firms?

17. FICA is a payroll tax imposed on employers and workers that is used to fund Social Security and Medicare. Which of the following statements regarding the tax is true?
    A) Employers are required to pay a greater share of the tax than workers but most economists believe the burden of the tax is shared equally.
    B) Congress wanted the burden of the tax to be greater for employers than for workers.
    C) Most economists believe the burden of the tax falls almost entirely on workers.
    D) Most economists believe the burden of the tax falls mostly on employers.
    Answer: C
    Diff: 1   Type: MC   Page Ref: 119/119
    Topic: Tax incidence
    Skill: Fact
    Objective: LO4: Analyze the economic impact of taxes
    AACSB Coding: Reflective Thinking
    Special Feature: Making the Connection: Is the Burden of a Social Security Tax Really Shared Equally between Workers and Firms?

18. "Taxes are what we pay for a civilized society." This statement was made by
    A) Adam Smith
    B) Oliver Wendell Holmes.
    C) Herbert Hoover.
    D) Franklin Roosevelt
    Answer: B
    Diff: 1   Type: MC   Page Ref: 115/115
    Topic: Economic impact of taxes
    Skill: Fact
    Objective: LO4: Analyze the economic impact of taxes
    AACSB Coding: Reflective Thinking
    Special Feature: None

19. Economists have shown that the burden of a tax is the same whether the tax is collected from the buyer or the seller. Why, then, are gasoline and cigarette taxes imposed on sellers?
    A) Sellers are more honest than buyers.
    B) The demand for both gasoline and cigarettes is very elastic.
    C) The Equal Protection Clause of the U.S. Constitution prohibits the government from imposing taxes like these on buyers.
    D) It is more difficult for buyers to keep track of their purchases, and for the government to verify that the right of amount of tax revenue is collected.
    Answer: D
    Diff: 1   Type: MC   Page Ref: 115–6/115–6
    Topic: Economic impact of taxes
    Skill: Conceptual
    Objective: LO4: Analyze the economic impact of taxes
    AACSB Coding: Reflective Thinking
    Special Feature: None

20. An efficient tax is
    A) a tax that imposes an equal tax burden on buyers and sellers.
    B) a tax that raises a maximum amount of revenue.
    C) a tax that imposes a small excess burden relative to the tax revenue that it raises.
    D) a tax that is used to fund research and development of new technology.
    Answer: C
    Diff: 1   Type: MC   Page Ref: 116/116
    Topic: Economic impact of taxes
    Skill: Definition
    Objective: LO4: Analyze the economic impact of taxes
    AACSB Coding: Reflective Thinking
    Special Feature: None

21. The division of the burden of a tax between buyers and sellers in a market is called tax allocation.
    Answer: True   ○ False
    Diff: 1   Type: TF   Page Ref: 116/116
    Topic: Tax incidence
    Skill: Definition
    Objective: LO4: Analyze the economic impact of taxes
    AACSB Coding: Reflective Thinking
    Special Feature: None

22. A tax is efficient if it imposes a small excess burden relative to the tax revenue it raises.
    Answer: True   ○ False
    Diff: 1   Type: TF   Page Ref: 116/116
    Topic: Economic impact of taxes
    Skill: Conceptual
    Objective: LO4: Analyze the economic impact of taxes
    AACSB Coding: Reflective Thinking
    Special Feature: None

Figure 4–12

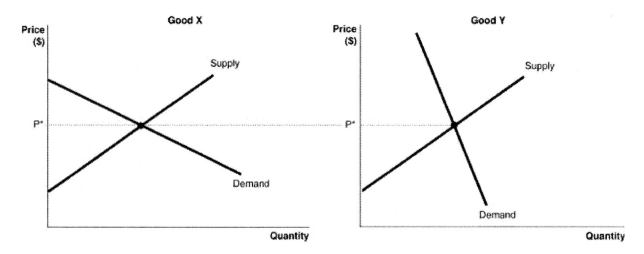

23. *Refer to Figure 4–12.* The figure above illustrates the markets for two goods, Good X and Good Y. Suppose an identical dollar tax is imposed in each market.
   a. Compare the consumer burden and producer burden in each market. Illustrate your answer graphically.
   b. If the goal of the government is to raise revenue with minimum impact to quantity consumed, in which market should the tax be imposed?
   c. If the goal of the government is to discourage consumption, in which market should the tax be imposed?
   Answer: a.   See the Figure below

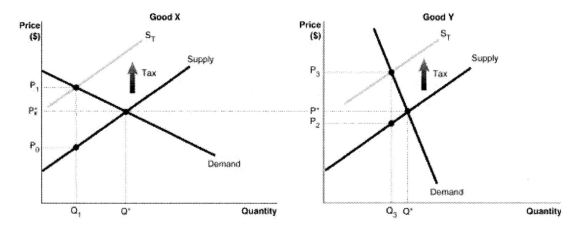

   b.   Market for Good Y
   c.   Market for Good X.
Diff: 3   Type: ES   Page Ref: 116–7/116–7
Topic: Economic impact of taxes
Skill: Analytical
Objective: LO4: Analyze the economic impact of taxes
AACSB Coding: Analytic Skills
Special Feature: None

Figure 4-13

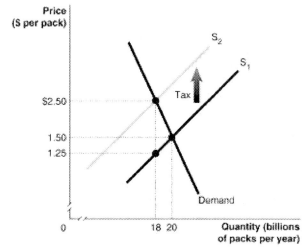

24. *Refer to Figure 4-13.* The figure above represents demand and supply in the market for cigarettes. Use the diagram to answer the following questions.
    a. How much is the government tax on each pack of cigarettes?
    b. What portion of the unit tax is paid by consumers?
    c. What portion of the unit tax is paid by producers?
    d. What is the quantity sold after the imposition of the tax?
    e. What is the after-tax revenue per pack received by producers?
    f. What is the total tax revenue collected by the government?
    g. What is the value of the excess burden of the tax?
    h. Is this cigarette tax efficient?

    Answer: a. $1.25
            b. Consumer burden =$1.00
            c. Producer burden = $0.25
            d. Quantity traded = 18 billion
            e. Net Price to seller = $1.25
            f. Tax Revenue = $22.5 billion
            g. Excess burden (deadweight loss) = $1.25 billion
            h. Yes, a tax is efficient if it imposes a small excess burden relative to the tax revenue it raises.

Diff: 2   Type: ES   Page Ref: 116-7/116-7
Topic: Economic impact of taxes
Skill: Analytical
Objective: LO4: Analyze the economic impact of taxes
AACSB Coding: Analytic Skills
Special Feature: None

4.5 Appendix: Quantitative Demand and Supply Analysis

1. The following equations represent the demand and supply for silver pendants.

$Q_D = 50 - 2P$

$Q_S = -10 + 2P$

What is the equilibrium price (P) and quantity of (Q – in thousands) of pendants?
  A) P = $15; Q = 20 thousand
  B) P = $50; Q = 10 thousand
  C) P = $20; Q = 15 thousand
  D) P = $10; Q = 30 thousand
Answer: A
Diff: 3   Type: MC   Page Ref: 131–4/131–4
Topic: Quantitative demand and supply analysis
Skill: Analytical
Objective: Appendix: Use quantitative demand and supply
AACSB Coding: Analytic Skills
Special Feature: None

2.

Table 4–5

Demand	Supply
$P = 50 - Q_D$	$P = 10 + 1/3 \, Q_S$
$Q_D = 50 - P$	$Q_S = 3P - 30$

Refer to Table 4–5. The equations above describe the demand and supply for Aunt Maud's Premium Hand Lotion. What are the equilibrium price and quantity (in thousands) for Aunt Maud's Lotion?
  A) $20 and 30 thousand
  B) $30 and 20 thousand
  C) $60 and 30 thousand
  D) $20 and 60 thousand
Answer: A
Diff: 3   Type: MC   Page Ref: 131–4/131–4
Topic: Quantitative demand and supply analysis
Skill: Analytical
Objective: Appendix: Use quantitative demand and supply
AACSB Coding: Analytic Skills
Special Feature: None

3. ***Refer to Table 4–5.*** The equations above describe the demand and supply for Aunt Maud's Premium Hand Lotion. The equilibrium price and quantity for Aunt Maud's lotion are $20 and 30 thousand units. What is the value of consumer surplus?
    A) $900 thousand
    B) $450 thousand
    C) $1,500 thousand
    D) $300 thousand
Answer: B
Diff: 3   Type: MC   Page Ref: 131–4/131–4
Topic: Quantitative demand and supply analysis
Skill: Analytical
Objective: Appendix: Use quantitative demand and supply
AACSB Coding: Analytic Skills
Special Feature: None

4. ***Refer to Table 4–5.*** The equations above describe the demand and supply for Aunt Maud's Premium Hand Lotion. The equilibrium price and quantity for Aunt Maud's lotion are $20 and 30 thousand units. What is the value of producer surplus?
    A) $600 thousand
    B) $150 thousand
    C) $300 thousand
    D) $30 thousand
Answer: B
Diff: 3   Type: MC   Page Ref: 131–4/131–4
Topic: Quantitative demand and supply analysis
Skill: Analytical
Objective: Appendix: Use quantitative demand and supply
AACSB Coding: Analytic Skills
Special Feature: None

5. ***Refer to Table 4–5.*** The equations above describe the demand and supply for Aunt Maud's Premium Hand Lotion. The equilibrium price and quantity for Aunt Maud's lotion are $20 and 30 thousand units. What is the value of economic surplus in this market?
    A) $1,500 thousand
    B) $600 thousand
    C) $2,100 thousand
    D) $1,050 thousand
Answer: B
Diff: 3   Type: MC   Page Ref: 131–4/131–4
Topic: Quantitative demand and supply analysis
Skill: Analytical
Objective: Appendix: Use quantitative demand and supply
AACSB Coding: Analytic Skills
Special Feature: None

6. You are given the following market data for Venus automobiles in Saturnia.
   Demand: P = 35,000 − 0.5Q
   Supply: P = 8,000 + 0.25Q
   where P = Price and Q = Quantity.

   a. Calculate the equilibrium price and quantity.
   b. Calculate the consumer surplus in this market.
   c. Calculate the producer surplus in this market.
   Answer: a. Price = $17,000; Quantity = 36,000
   　　　　　b. Consumer surplus = $324 million
   　　　　　c. Producer Surplus = $162 million.
   Diff: 3　　　Type: SA　　　Page Ref: 100–4/100–4
   Topic: Economic surplus
   Skill: Analytical
   Objective: Appendix: Use quantitative demand and supply
   AACSB Coding: Analytic Skills
   Special Feature: None

7. The demand and supply equations for the apple market are:
   Demand: P = 12 − 0.01Q (1)
   Supply: P = 0.02Q   (2)
   where P= price per bushel, and Q=quantity.

   a. Calculate the equilibrium price and quantity.
   b. Suppose the government guaranteed producers a price of $10 per bushel. What would be the effect on quantity supplied? Provide a numerical value.
   c. By how much would the $10 price change the quantity demanded of apples? Provide a numerical value.
   d. Would there be a shortage or surplus of apples?
   e. What is the size of this shortage or surplus? Provide a numerical value.
   Answer: a.　Q = 400 bushels, P = $8.
   　　　　　b. Quantity supplied would increase to 500 bushels.
   　　　　　c. Quantity demanded would fall to 200 bushels.
   　　　　　d. There would be a surplus.
   　　　　　e. Surplus = 300 bushels.
   Diff: 2　　　Type: ES　　　Page Ref: 108/108
   Topic: The economic effect of price ceilings and price floors
   Skill: Analytical
   Objective: Appendix: Use quantitative demand and supply
   AACSB Coding: Analytic Skills
   Special Feature: None

Chapter 5 Externalities, Environmental Policy, and Public Goods

5.1   Externalities and Economic Efficiency

1. An externality
   A) is a benefit or cost that affects someone who is not directly involved in the production or consumption of a good or service.
   B) enhances market efficiency.
   C) is a private cost or benefit that results from the production or consumption of a good or service that is external to a market.
   D) refers to production or consumption that occurs outdoors.
   Answer: A
   Diff: 1   Type: MC   Page Ref: 138/138
   Topic: Externalities
   Skill: Definition
   Objective: LO 1: Identify examples of positive and negative externalities and use graphs to show how externalities affect economic efficiency.
   AACSB Coding: Reflective Thinking
   Special Feature: None

2. Pollution is an example of a
   A) public good.
   B) positive externality.
   C) private cost.
   D) negative externality
   Answer: D
   Diff: 1   Type: MC   Page Ref: 138/138
   Topic: Negative externality
   Skill: Conceptual
   Objective: LO 1: Identify examples of positive and negative externalities and use graphs to show how externalities affect economic efficiency.
   AACSB Coding: Reflective Thinking
   Special Feature: None

3. Emissions of sulfur dioxide cause pollution that damages trees, crops and buildings. This type of pollution is know as
    A) a greenhouse gas.
    B) acid rain.
    C) fossil fuel pollution.
    D) ozone depleting pollution.
    Answer: B
    Diff: 1   Type: MC   Page Ref: 136/136
    Topic: Negative externality
    Skill: Fact
    Objective: LO 1: Identify examples of positive and negative externalities and use graphs to show how externalities affect economic efficiency.
    AACSB Coding: Reflective Thinking
    Special Feature: Chapter Opener: Economic Policy and the Environment

4. Which of the following would result in a positive externality?
    A) A local government establishes a price ceiling on rental apartments.
    B) An electric utility burns coal that causes acid rain. .
    C) Medical research results in a cure for malaria.
    D) McDonald's adds new fat-free items to its menu.
    Answer: C
    Diff: 1   Type: MC   Page Ref: 138/138
    Topic: Positive externality
    Skill: Conceptual
    Objective: LO 1: Identify examples of positive and negative externalities and use graphs to show how externalities affect economic efficiency.
    AACSB Coding: Reflective Thinking
    Special Feature: None

5. In the past the federal government often employed what is called a "command and control" approach to the reduction of pollution emissions. Many economists are critical of this approach because
    A) it does not lead to significant reductions in pollution.
    B) they believe a market-based approach will reduce emissions more efficiently.
    C) the "command and control" approach is designed to help firms at the expense of
        consumers.
    D) the "command and control" approach leads to negative externalities.
    Answer: B
    Diff: 1   Type: MC   Page Ref: 136/136
    Topic: Command and control approach
    Skill: Fact
    Objective: LO 1: Identify examples of positive and negative externalities and use graphs to show how externalities affect economic efficiency.
    AACSB Coding: Reflective Thinking
    Special Feature: Chapter Opener: Economic Policy and the Environment

6. A positive externality results when
    A) economists are sure that a good or service provides benefits to consumers.
    B) someone pays for a good or service even though she is not directly affected by the production or   consumption of it.
    C) when people who live in one country benefit from the production of a good or service that occurs in another country.
    D) people who are not directly involved in producing or paying for a good or service benefit from it.
Answer: D
Diff: 2   Type: MC   Page Ref: 138/138
Topic: Positive externality
Skill: Conceptual
Objective: LO 1: Identify examples of positive and negative externalities and use graphs to show how externalities affect economic efficiency.
AACSB Coding: Reflective Thinking
Special Feature: None

7. Which of the following describes how negative externality affects a competitive market?
    A) The externality causes a difference between the private cost of production and the social cost.
    B) The externality causes a difference between the private cost of production and the private benefit from consumption.
    C) The externality causes consumer surplus to exceed producer surplus.
    D) The externality causes a difference between the private cost of production and the equilibrium price.
Answer: A
Diff: 2   Type: MC   Page Ref: 138/138
Topic: Negative externality
Skill: Conceptual
Objective: LO 1: Identify examples of positive and negative externalities and use graphs to show how externalities affect economic efficiency.
AACSB Coding: Reflective Thinking
Special Feature: None

8. Alternative approaches for reducing carbon dioxide emissions are
    A) carbon taxes and carbon scrubbing.
    B) carbon trading and carbon subsidies.
    C) carbon taxes and carbon trading.
    D) burning low carbon coal and deforestation.
Answer: C
Diff: 2   Type: MC   Page Ref: 137/137
Topic: Government policies for externalities
Skill: Fact
Objective: LO 1: Identify examples of positive and negative externalities and use graphs to show how externalities affect economic efficiency.
AACSB Coding: Reflective Thinking
Special Feature: Economics in YOUR Life!: What's the "Best" Level of Pollution

9. Which of the following describes how a positive externality affects a competitive market?
   A) The externality causes a difference between the private benefit from consumption and the social benefit.
   B) The externality causes a difference between the private benefit from production and the social cost of production.
   C) The externality causes quantity demanded to exceed quantity supplied.
   D) The externality causes a difference between the social cost of production and the social cost of consumption.

Answer: A

Diff: 2   Type: MC   Page Ref: 138/138
Topic: Positive externality
Skill: Conceptual
Objective: LO 1: Identify examples of positive and negative externalities and use graphs to show how externalities affect economic efficiency.
AACSB Coding: Reflective Thinking
Special Feature: None

10. "A competitive market achieves economic efficiency by maximizing the sum of consumer surplus and producer surplus." This statement
    A) is true only if there are positive externalities in production in the market.
    B) is true only if there are no negative externalities in the market.
    C) is true only if there are no positive or negative externalities in the market.
    D) is true in theory, but economic efficiency cannot be achieved in a real market.

Answer: C

Diff: 2   Type: MC   Page Ref: 138/138
Topic: Economic efficiency
Skill: Conceptual
Objective: LO 1: Identify examples of positive and negative externalities and use graphs to show how externalities affect economic efficiency.
AACSB Coding: Reflective Thinking
Special Feature: None

11. If there are no externalities a competitive market achieves economic efficiency. If there is a negative externality, economic efficiency will not be achieved because
    A) too little of the good will be produced.
    B) too much of the good will be produced.
    C) a deadweight loss will occur that is equal to the area under the demand curve for the good.
    D) economic surplus is maximized.

Answer: B

Diff: 2   Type: MC   Page Ref: 139/139
Topic: Negative externality
Skill: Conceptual
Objective: LO 1: Identify examples of positive and negative externalities and use graphs to show how externalities affect economic efficiency.
AACSB Coding: Reflective Thinking
Special Feature: None

12. When there is a negative externality, the private cost of production _____ the social cost of production.
    A) is greater than
    B) is equal to
    C) eliminates
    D) is less than
    Answer: D
    Diff: 1   Type: MC   Page Ref: 139/139
    Topic: Negative externality
    Skill: Conceptual
    Objective: LO 1: Identify examples of positive and negative externalities and use graphs to show how externalities affect economic efficiency.
    AACSB Coding: Reflective Thinking
    Special Feature: None

13. When there is a positive externality
    A) the private benefit received by consumers is greater than the external benefit.
    B) the social benefit received by consumers is greater than the private benefit.
    C) the private benefit received by consumers is greater than the private cost.
    D) the private benefit received by consumers is greater than the social benefit.
    Answer: B
    Diff: 2   Type: MC   Page Ref: 140/140
    Topic: Positive externality
    Skill: Conceptual
    Objective: LO 1: Identify examples of positive and negative externalities and use graphs to show how externalities affect economic efficiency.
    AACSB Coding: Reflective Thinking
    Special Feature: None

14. When production generates a negative externality, the true cost of production is the
    A) private cost of production.
    B) private cost of production.
    C) social cost of production.
    D) average cost of production.
    Answer: C
    Diff: 1   Type: MC   Page Ref: 138-9/138-9
    Topic: Negative externality
    Skill: Conceptual
    Objective: LO 1: Identify examples of positive and negative externalities and use graphs to show how externalities affect economic efficiency.
    AACSB Coding: Reflective Thinking
    Special Feature: None

15. If the social cost of producing a good or service exceeds the private cost,
    A) a positive externality exists.
    B) the sum of consumer surplus and producer surplus is maximized.
    C) the market achieves economic efficiency.
    D) a negative externality exists.
    Answer: D
    Diff: 1   Type: MC   Page Ref: 139/139
    Topic: Negative externality
    Skill: Conceptual
    Objective: LO 1: Identify examples of positive and negative externalities and use graphs to show how externalities affect economic efficiency.
    AACSB Coding: Reflective Thinking
    Special Feature: None

16. The cost borne by a producer in the production of a good or service is called
    A) private cost.
    B) public cost.
    C) social cost.
    D) internal cost.
    Answer: A
    Diff: 1   Type: MC   Page Ref: 138/138
    Topic: Private cost
    Skill: Definition
    Objective: LO 1: Identify examples of positive and negative externalities and use graphs to show how externalities affect economic efficiency.
    AACSB Coding: Reflective Thinking
    Special Feature: None

17. If the social benefit of consuming a good or a service exceeds the private benefit
    A) a negative externality exists.
    B) the market achieves economic efficiency.
    C) a positive externality exists.
    D) the sum of consumer surplus and producer surplus is maximized.
    Answer: C
    Diff: 1   Type: MC   Page Ref: 140/140
    Topic: Positive externality
    Skill: Conceptual
    Objective: LO 1: Identify examples of positive and negative externalities and use graphs to show how externalities affect economic efficiency.
    AACSB Coding: Reflective Thinking
    Special Feature: None

18. When there is an externality in a market
    A) the externality will move the market to an economically efficient equilibrium.
    B) the externality will cause the market price to be less than or greater than the equilibrium price.
    C) the government should use price controls to enable the market to reach equilibrium.
    D) government intervention may increase economic efficiency.
    Answer: D
    Diff: 2   Type: MC   Page Ref: 138/138
    Topic: Externalities
    Skill: Conceptual
    Objective: LO 1: Identify examples of positive and negative externalities and use graphs to show how externalities affect economic efficiency.
    AACSB Coding: Reflective Thinking
    Special Feature: None

19. Assume that emissions from electric utilities contribute to pollution in the form of acid rain. Which of the following describes how this affects the market for electricity?
    A) The equilibrium in the market is not efficient; the marginal benefit from electricity is greater than the marginal social cost.
    B) A deadweight loss occurs; at equilibrium the additional social cost of production is greater than the additional benefit to consumers.
    C) The equilibrium in the market is not efficient; because of the cost of the acid rain, economic efficiency would be greater if more electricity were produced.
    D) The equilibrium in the market is not efficient; consumer surplus is equal to producer surplus.
    Answer: B
    Diff: 2   Type: MC   Page Ref: 138/138
    Topic: The effect of pollution on economic efficiency
    Skill: Conceptual
    Objective: LO 1: Identify examples of positive and negative externalities and use graphs to show how externalities affect economic efficiency.
    AACSB Coding: Reflective Thinking
    Special Feature: None

20. Medical research that ends in a cure for a serious disease produces positive externalities. What is the impact of this positive externality on economic efficiency?
    A) At equilibrium, less than the economically efficient quantity of medical research is produced.
    B) A deadweight loss occurs because at equilibrium the marginal social cost of medical research is greater than the marginal social benefit.
    C) At equilibrium, more than the economically efficient quantity of medical research is produced.
    D) A deadweight loss occurs because at equilibrium the marginal social cost equals the marginal social benefit.

Answer: A
Diff: 2   Type: MC   Page Ref: 140/140
Topic: Positive externality
Skill: Conceptual
Objective: LO 1: Identify examples of positive and negative externalities and use graphs to show how externalities affect economic efficiency.
AACSB Coding: Reflective Thinking
Special Feature: None

Figure 5-1

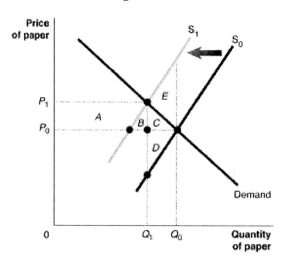

Suppose there are several paper mills producing paper for a market. These mills, located upstream from a fishing village, discharge a large amount of wastewater into the river. The waste material affects the number of fish in the river, and the use of the river for recreation and as a public water supply source. Figure 5-1 shows the paper market. Use this Figure to answer the following question(s).

21. *Refer to Figure 5-1.* What does S_0 represent?
    A) The market supply curve that reflects social cost
    B) The market supply curve that reflects only external cost.
    C) The market supply curve that reflects only private benefit.
    D) The market supply curve that reflects private cost.
    Answer: D
    Diff: 1   Type: MC   Page Ref: 140-1/140-1
    Topic: Negative externality
    Skill: Conceptual
    Objective: LO 1: Identify examples of positive and negative externalities and use graphs to show how externalities affect economic efficiency.
    AACSB Coding: Reflective Thinking
    Special Feature: None

22. *Refer to Figure 5-1.* What does S_1 represent?
    A) The market supply curve that reflects social cost.
    B) The market supply curve that reflect private cost.
    C) The market supply curve that reflects external cost.
    D) The market supply curve that reflects social benefit.
    Answer: A
    Diff: 1   Type: MC   Page Ref: 140-1/140-1
    Topic: Negative externality
    Skill: Conceptual
    Objective: LO 1: Identify examples of positive and negative externalities and use graphs to show how externalities affect economic efficiency.
    AACSB Coding: Reflective Thinking
    Special Feature: None

23. *Refer to Figure 5-1.* What is the economically efficient output level?
    A) Q_0.
    B) Q_1 minus Q_0.
    C) Q_1.
    D) Q_0 plus Q_1.
    Answer: C
    Diff: 1   Type: MC   Page Ref: 140-1/140-1
    Topic: Negative externality
    Skill: Conceptual
    Objective: LO 1: Identify examples of positive and negative externalities and use graphs to show how externalities affect economic efficiency.
    AACSB Coding: Reflective Thinking
    Special Feature: None

24. ***Refer to Figure 5–1.*** What is the deadweight loss from producing at the market equilibrium?
    A) Area C.
    B) Area E.
    C) Area D.
    D) Area F.
    Answer: B
    Diff: 2   Type: MC   Page Ref: 140–1/140–1
    Topic: Negative externality
    Skill: Conceptual
    Objective: LO 1: Identify examples of positive and negative externalities and use graphs to show how externalities affect economic efficiency.
    AACSB Coding: Reflective Thinking
    Special Feature: None

25. ***Refer to Figure 5–1.*** Why is there a deadweight loss?
    A) Because the marginal social cost of producing each additional unit in excess of Q_1 exceeds the marginal benefit
    B) Because the marginal private cost of producing each additional unit in excess of Q_1 exceeds the marginal benefit
    C) Because the marginal social benefit of producing each additional unit in excess of Q_1 exceeds the private cost
    D) Because the marginal private benefit of producing each additional unit in excess of Q_1 exceeds the social cost
    Answer: A
    Diff: 3   Type: MC   Page Ref: 140–1/140–1
    Topic: Economic efficiency
    Skill: Conceptual
    Objective: LO 1: Identify examples of positive and negative externalities and use graphs to show how externalities affect economic efficiency.
    AACSB Coding: Reflective Thinking
    Special Feature: None

Figure 5-2

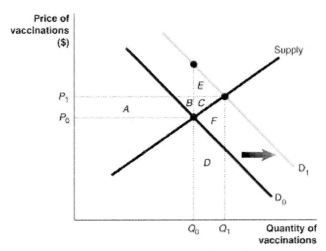

Figure 5-2 shows the market for measles vaccinations, a product whose use generates positive externalities. The following question(s) are based on Figure 5-2.

26. **Refer to Figure 5-2.** What does D_0 represent?
    A) The demand curve reflecting social benefit.
    B) The positive externalities curve.
    C) The demand curve reflecting private benefit.
    D) The social welfare curve.
    Answer: C
    Diff: 1   Type: MC   Page Ref: 141/141
    Topic: Positive externality
    Skill: Conceptual
    Objective: LO 1: Identify examples of positive and negative externalities and use graphs to show how externalities affect economic efficiency.
    AACSB Coding: Reflective Thinking
    Special Feature: None

27. **Refer to Figure 5-2.** What is the economically efficient output level?
    A) Q_0
    B) $Q_0 + Q_1$
    C) $Q_1 - Q_0$
    D) Q_1
    Answer: D
    Diff: 1   Type: MC   Page Ref: 141/141
    Topic: Positive externality
    Skill: Conceptual
    Objective: LO 1: Identify examples of positive and negative externalities and use graphs to show how externalities affect economic efficiency.
    AACSB Coding: Reflective Thinking
    Special Feature: None

28. *Refer to Figure 5–2.* What does D_1 represent?
    A) The social welfare curve
    B) The demand curve reflecting social benefit
    C) The demand curve reflecting private benefit
    D) The positive externalities curve
    Answer: B
    Diff: 1   Type: MC   Page Ref: 141/141
    Topic: Positive externality
    Skill: Conceptual
    Objective: LO 1: Identify examples of positive and negative externalities and use graphs to show how externalities affect economic efficiency.
    AACSB Coding: Reflective Thinking
    Special Feature: None

29. *Refer to Figure 5–2.* What is the market equilibrium output level?
    A) Q_0
    B) Q_1
    C) $Q_0 + Q_1$
    D) $Q_1 - Q_0$
    Answer: A
    Diff: 1   Type: MC   Page Ref: 141/141
    Topic: Positive externality
    Skill: Conceptual
    Objective: LO 1: Identify examples of positive and negative externalities and use graphs to show how externalities affect economic efficiency.
    AACSB Coding: Reflective Thinking
    Special Feature: None

30. *Refer to Figure 5–2.* What is the deadweight loss resulting from producing at the market equilibrium?
    A) B + C
    B) E + C
    C) F
    D) C
    Answer: B
    Diff: 2   Type: MC   Page Ref: 141/141
    Topic: Positive externality
    Skill: Conceptual
    Objective: LO 1: Identify examples of positive and negative externalities and use graphs to show how externalities affect economic efficiency.
    AACSB Coding: Reflective Thinking
    Special Feature: None

31. **Refer to Figure 5-2.** Why is there a deadweight loss?
     A) Because the marginal private benefit for each additional unit between Q_0 and Q_1 exceeds the marginal cost
     B) Because the marginal private cost for each additional unit between Q_0 and Q_1 exceeds the marginal private benefit
     C) Because the marginal social cost for each additional unit between Q_0 and Q_1 exceeds the marginal social benefit
     D) Because the marginal social benefit for each additional unit between Q_0 and Q_1 exceeds the marginal cost
     Answer: D
     Diff: 3   Type: MC   Page Ref: 141/141
     Topic: Positive externality
     Skill: Conceptual
     Objective: LO 1: Identify examples of positive and negative externalities and use graphs to show how externalities affect economic efficiency.
     AACSB Coding: Reflective Thinking
     Special Feature: None

32. The social cost of a good or service is the cost borne by the producer.
     Answer: True   ○ False
     Diff: 2   Type: TF   Page Ref: 138/138
     Topic: Social cost
     Skill: Definition
     Objective: LO 1: Identify examples of positive and negative externalities and use graphs to show how externalities affect economic efficiency.
     AACSB Coding: Reflective Thinking
     Special Feature: None

32. An externality is an example of a market failure.
     Answer: ○ True   False
     Diff: 1   Type: TF   Page Ref: 140/140
     Topic: Externalities
     Skill: Conceptual
     Objective: LO 1: Identify examples of positive and negative externalities and use graphs to show how externalities affect economic efficiency.
     AACSB Coding: Reflective Thinking
     Special Feature: None

33. When negative externalities exist, the competitive market supply curve does not include all of the costs borne by members of society.
     Answer: ○ True   False
     Diff: 1   Type: TF   Page Ref: 139/139
     Topic: Negative externality
     Skill: Conceptual
     Objective: LO 1: Identify examples of positive and negative externalities and use graphs to show how externalities affect economic efficiency.
     AACSB Coding: Reflective Thinking
     Special Feature: None

34.   *Figure 5-3*

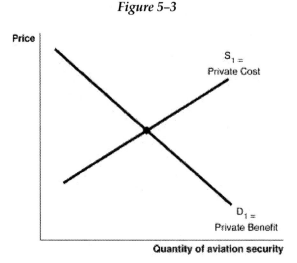

Figure 5-3 shows the market for aviation security. Aviation security generates a positive externality because people who are not airline passengers benefit from aviation security. Use the diagram to answer the following questions.

a. In the absence of any government intervention what is the equilibrium level of security that airlines will supply? Denote this level, Q*. Briefly explain why this quantity is not the economically efficient level of aviation security.

b. In the diagram, illustrate the presence of positive externalities in the aviation security market. Label any new curve that you draw.

c. On your diagram identify the economically efficient level of aviation security. Denote this level Qe.

d. Explain how a government subsidy for the airlines can bring about the economically efficient aviation security level. Be sure to identify the size of the subsidy.

Answer:

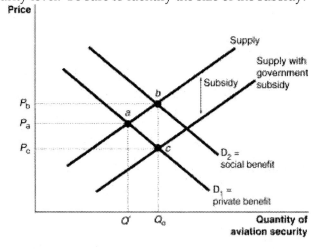

a. See the figure above. Q* is not the optimal level because aviation security creates positive externalities. As a result the social benefit exceeds the private benefit for any quantity. Since airlines do not factor in the external benefits they will offer less than the economically efficient level of aviation security.

b. See the figure above.

     c.   See the figure above.

     d.   To induce airlines to offer a higher level of security the government can subsidize the airlines. The size of the subsidy required to internalize the positive externality is

     equal to the external benefit at the economically efficient output level.

Diff: 3   Type: ES   Page Ref: 139/139
Topic: Positive externality
Skill: Analytical
Objective: LO 1: Identify examples of positive and negative externalities and use graphs to show how externalities affect economic efficiency.
AACSB Coding: Analytic Skills
Special Feature: None

35. A negative externality is an example of market failure. The root of the problem lies in the definition and enforcement of property rights. Explain.

    Answer: If harmed parties do not have rights or have rights that are not enforced or weakly enforced, producers can make choices that impose costs on others and do not have to bear the full cost of their actions. This creates a discrepancy between the private cost of production and the social cost of production, the true cost of production being the social cost. Since, the private cost is less than the social cost, firms will produce more than the economically efficient output level resulting in a market failure. (Students can also explain using positive externalities.)

Diff: 3   Type: ES   Page Ref: 140/140
Topic: Negative externality
Skill: Conceptual
Objective: LO 1: Identify examples of positive and negative externalities and use graphs to show how externalities affect economic efficiency.
AACSB Coding: Reflective Thinking
Special Feature: None

5.2   Private Solutions to Externalities: The Coase Theorem

1. Ronald Coase was awarded the 1991 Nobel Prize in Economics primarily for addressing problems related to externalities. Which of the following describes Coase's work?
    A) Coase argued that government intervention is necessary to achieve economic efficiency in markets that are affected by externalities.
    B) Coase proved that economic efficiency cannot be achieved in a market that is affected by positive or negative externalities.
    C) Coase argued that under some circumstances private solutions to the problems of externalities will occur.
    D) Coase proved that a competitive market achieved a greater degree of economic efficiency than a non-competitive market when externalities occur.
    Answer: C
    Diff: 2   Type: MC   Page Ref: 141/141
    Topic: The Coase Theorem
    Skill: Conceptual
    Objective: LO 2: Discuss the Coase Theorem and explain how private bargaining can lead to economic efficiency in a market with an externality.
    AACSB Coding: Reflective Thinking
    Special Feature: None

2. Which of the following statements describes the Coase Theorem?
    A) It is not possible to completely eliminate an externality.
    B) Under some circumstances private solutions to the problems that result from externalities can be found.
    C) Completely eliminating an eternality is not economically efficient.
    D) A negative externality occurs when the marginal social cost of production exceeds the social benefit.
    Answer: B
    Diff: 1   Type: MC   Page Ref: 141/141
    Topic: The Coase Theorem
    Skill: Conceptual
    Objective: LO 2: Discuss the Coase Theorem and explain how private bargaining can lead to economic efficiency in a market with an externality.
    AACSB Coding: Reflective Thinking
    Special Feature: None

3. Congress passed the Clean Air Act in 1970. Since this act was passed, emissions of the six main air pollutants
   A) have fallen by more than one-half.
   B) have increased significantly due to the growth of the U.S. economy.
   C) cannot be measured since Congress failed to appropriate money to monitor the level of emissions.
   D) have remained essentially constant, even though significant economic growth has occurred in the U.S. since 1970.

   Answer: A
   Diff: 1   Type: MC   Page Ref: 142/142
   Topic: Government policies for externalities
   Skill: Fact
   Objective: LO 2: Discuss the Coase Theorem and explain how private bargaining can lead to economic efficiency in a market with an externality.
   AACSB Coding: Reflective Thinking
   Special Feature: Making the Connection: The Clean Air Act: How a Government Policy Reduced Infant Mortality

4. Kenneth Chay and Michael Greenstone examined the impact of reductions in air pollution since the passage of the Clean Air Act of 1970. Which of the following statements summarizes their findings?
   A) The marginal benefit of reductions in air pollution was less than the marginal cost.
   B) The marginal cost of reducing emissions of sulfur dioxide has increased over time as the marginal benefit of the reductions has increased.
   C) The benefits of reducing the six main air pollutants in the two years following the Act greatly exceeded the costs.
   D) In the two years following passage of the Act fewer infants died than would have died if the Act had not been passed.

   Answer: D
   Diff: 2   Type: MC   Page Ref: 142/142
   Topic: Government policies for externalities
   Skill: Fact
   Objective: LO 2: Discuss the Coase Theorem and explain how private bargaining can lead to economic efficiency in a market with an externality.
   AACSB Coding: Reflective Thinking
   Special Feature: Making the Connection: The Clean Air Act: How a Government Policy Reduced Infant Mortality

5. If electric utilities continually reduce their emissions of sulfur dioxide
   A) the utilities will eventually be forced to go out of business.
   B) the marginal benefit of additional emissions will rise.
   C) the marginal cost of further emissions will rise.
   D) the total benefit of sulfur dioxide emissions will fall.
   Answer: C
   Diff: 2   Type: MC   Page Ref: 142/142
   Topic: Marginal benefit and marginal cost of pollution reduction
   Skill: Analytical
   Objective: LO 2: Discuss the Coase Theorem and explain how private bargaining can lead to economic efficiency in a market with an externality.
   AACSB Coding: Reflective Thinking
   Special Feature: None

6. If the marginal benefit of reducing emissions of some air pollutant is greater than the marginal cost
   A) further reductions will make society better off.
   B) the marginal benefit will rise and the marginal cost will fall as further reductions are made.
   C) economic efficiency will be achieved when emissions are reduced to zero.
   D) private businesses, rather the consumers, should be made to pay for the cost of further reductions.
   Answer: A
   Diff: 2   Type: MC   Page Ref: 145/145
   Topic: Marginal benefit and marginal cost of pollution reduction
   Skill: Analytical
   Objective: LO 2: Discuss the Coase Theorem and explain how private bargaining can lead to economic efficiency in a market with an externality.
   AACSB Coding: Reflective Thinking
   Special Feature: None

7. If the marginal benefit of reducing emissions of some air pollutant is less than the marginal cost
   A) further reductions will make society better off.
   B) further reduction will make society worse off.
   C) pollution taxes should be imposed on producers to pay for further reductions.
   D) economic efficiency will be increased if further reductions are made.
   Answer: B
   Diff: 2   Type: MC   Page Ref: 145/145
   Topic: Marginal benefit and marginal cost of pollution reduction
   Skill: Analytical
   Objective: LO 2: Discuss the Coase Theorem and explain how private bargaining can lead to economic efficiency in a market with an externality.
   AACSB Coding: Reflective Thinking
   Special Feature: None

8. James Meade, who won the Nobel Prize in Economics in 1977, argued that positive externalities resulted from
    A) reducing emissions of sulfur dioxide.
    B) producing automobiles and automobile tires.
    C) home owners in the Northeast moving to the South and Southwest United States.
    D) apple growing and beekeeping.
   Answer: D
   Diff: 1   Type: MC   Page Ref: 146/146
   Topic: Positive externality
   Skill: Fact
   Objective: LO 2: Discuss the Coase Theorem and explain how private bargaining can lead to economic efficiency in a market with an externality.
   AACSB Coding: Reflective Thinking
   Special Feature: Making the Connection: The Fable of Bees

9. According to Steven Cheung: "Pollination contracts usually include stipulations regarding the number and strength of ...[bee] colonies, the rental fee per hive, the time of delivery...the protection of bees from pesticides, and the strategic placing of hives." Cheung cites this as evidence that
    A) the high costs of writing and enforcing complicated written agreements between owners of beehives and apple orchards prevents economic efficiency from being achieved in these markets.
    B) government intervention is not always necessary to bring about an economically efficient number of apple trees and beehives.
    C) government regulation of contracts between owners of beehives and apple orchards is necessary to bring about an economically efficient number of apple trees and beehives.
    D) the beekeeping and apple growing businesses have become more complicated and costly over time due to the legal costs involved.
   Answer: B
   Diff: 2   Type: MC   Page Ref: 146/146
   Topic: The Coase Theorem
   Skill: Fact
   Objective: LO 2: Discuss the Coase Theorem and explain how private bargaining can lead to economic efficiency in a market with an externality.
   AACSB Coding: Reflective Thinking
   Special Feature: Making the Connection: The Fable of Bees

10. Steven Cheung examined the relationship between beekeepers and apple growers. Cheung noted that: "Pollination contracts usually include stipulations regarding the number and strength of ... [bee] colonies, the rental fee per hive, the time of delivery...the protection of bees from pesticides, and the strategic placing of hives." Cheung's suggests that the relationship between beekeepers and apple growers is an example of
    A) the Coase Theorem.
    B) how excessive legal costs can prevent economic efficiency from being achieved.
    C) negative externalities.
    D) government intervention improving economic efficiency.
Answer: A
Diff: 3   Type: MC   Page Ref: 146/146
Topic: The Coase Theorem
Skill: Analytical
Objective: LO 2: Discuss the Coase Theorem and explain how private bargaining can lead to economic efficiency in a market with an externality.
AACSB Coding: Reflective Thinking
Special Feature: Making the Connection: The Fable of Bees

11. Which of the following statements about the economically efficient level of air pollution is correct?
    A) The economically efficient level of pollution is zero.
    B) The economically efficient level of pollution occurs where all social costs equal all social benefits.
    C) The economically efficient level of pollution occurs where the marginal cost of pollution reduction equals the marginal social benefit of reduction.
    D) The economically efficient level of pollution occurs where total benefits of pollution reduction are maximized.
Answer: C
Diff: 2   Type: MC   Page Ref: 143/143
Topic: Economic efficiency
Skill: Conceptual
Objective: LO 2: Discuss the Coase Theorem and explain how private bargaining can lead to economic efficiency in a market with an externality.
AACSB Coding: Reflective Thinking
Special Feature: None

12. The costs in time and other resources that parties incur in the process of facilitating an exchange of goods and services are called
    A) enforcement costs.
    B) implicit costs.
    C) explicit costs.
    D) transaction costs.
Answer: D
Diff: 1   Type: MC   Page Ref: 147/147
Topic: Transactions costs
Skill: Definition
Objective: LO 2: Discuss the Coase Theorem and explain how private bargaining can lead to economic efficiency in a market with an externality.
AACSB Coding: Reflective Thinking
Special Feature: None

13. Private solutions to the problem of externalities are most likely when
    A) government actively encourages these solutions.
    B) transaction costs are low and the number of bargaining parties is small.
    C) transaction costs are low and the number of bargaining parties is large.
    D) transaction costs are low and the monetary damages to third parties is high.
    Answer: B
    Diff: 2   Type: MC   Page Ref: 147/147
    Topic: The Coase Theorem
    Skill: Conceptual
    Objective: LO 2: Discuss the Coase Theorem and explain how private bargaining can lead to economic efficiency in a market with an externality.
    AACSB Coding: Reflective Thinking
    Special Feature: None

14. Assume that air pollution from a copper smelter imposes external costs of people who live near the smelter. If the victims of the pollution could not legally enforce the right of their property not to be damaged, the amount of pollution reduction
    A) would be significantly less than if the owners of the smelter were legally liable for damages.
    B) would be less than the amount at which the marginal benefit of pollution reduction equaled the marginal cost.
    C) would be the same as if it would be if the owners of the smelter were legally liable.
    D) would be too small; the government would have to intervene to bring about an efficient outcome.
    Answer: C
    Diff: 3   Type: MC   Page Ref: 146/146
    Topic: The Coase Theorem
    Skill: Analytical
    Objective: LO 2: Discuss the Coase Theorem and explain how private bargaining can lead to economic efficiency in a market with an externality.
    AACSB Coding: Reflective Thinking
    Special Feature: None

15. Compare two situations. (A) A firm is not legally responsible for damages that result from air pollution caused by its production of steel. (B) A firm *is* legally responsible for damages that result from its production of steel. Ronald Coase argued that
    A) bargaining between the firm and the victims of the air pollution caused by the firm will result in little reduction of pollution in either situation (A) or (B) because the firm has greater economic and political power than the victims.
    B) bargaining between the firm and the victims of the air pollution caused by the firm would lead to a greater reduction in pollution in situation (A) than situation (B).
    C) bargaining between the firm and the victims of the air pollution caused by the firm would lead to a smaller reduction in pollution in situation (A) than situation (B).
    D) bargaining between the firm and the victims of the air pollution caused by the firm would lead to an equal reduction in pollution in situation (A) and situation (B).
    Answer: D
    Diff: 3   Type: MC   Page Ref: 146–7/146–7
    Topic: The Coase Theorem
    Skill: Conceptual

Objective: LO 2: Discuss the Coase Theorem and explain how private bargaining can lead to economic efficiency in a market with an externality.
AACSB Coding: Reflective Thinking
Special Feature: None

Figure 5-4

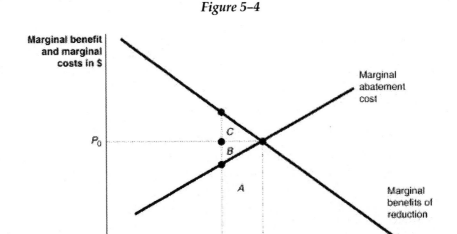

Consider a chemical plant that discharges toxic fumes over a nearby community. To reduce the emissions of toxic fumes the firm can install pollution abatement devices. Figure 5-4 shows the marginal benefit and the marginal cost from reducing the toxic fumes emissions.

16. *Refer to Figure 5-4.* What is the economically efficient level of pollution reduction?
    A) 9 million tons
    B) 8 million tons
    C) 12.5 million tons
    D) 0 tons
Answer: A
Diff: 1   Type: MC   Page Ref: 142-5/142-5
Topic: Marginal benefit and marginal cost of pollution reduction
Skill: Conceptual
Objective: LO 2: Discuss the Coase Theorem and explain how private bargaining can lead to economic efficiency in a market with an externality.
AACSB Coding: Reflective Thinking
Special Feature: None

17. *Refer to Figure 5–4.* Suppose the emissions reduction target is currently established at 8 million tons. What is the area that represents the cost of eliminating an additional 1 million tons?

    A) A
    B) B + C
    C) A + B
    D) A + B + C

    Answer: A
    Diff: 2   Type: MC   Page Ref: 145/145
    Topic: Marginal benefit and marginal cost of pollution reduction
    Skill: Analytical
    Objective: LO 2: Discuss the Coase Theorem and explain how private bargaining can lead to economic efficiency in a market with an externality.
    AACSB Coding: Analytic Skills
    Special Feature: None

18. *Refer to Figure 5–4.* Suppose the emissions reduction target is currently established at 8 million tons. Should society undertake to reduce an additional 1 million tons so that the total reduction is 9 million tons?

    A) No, because there is a net cost represented by the area B + C.
    B) Yes, because the marginal benefit exceeds the marginal costs.
    C) Yes, because toxic fumes are dangerous and must be eliminated at any cost.
    D) No, because the firms will pass the additional cost on to consumers.

    Answer: B
    Diff: 2   Type: MC   Page Ref: 145/145
    Topic: Marginal benefit and marginal cost of pollution reduction
    Skill: Analytical
    Objective: LO 2: Discuss the Coase Theorem and explain how private bargaining can lead to economic efficiency in a market with an externality.
    AACSB Coding: Analytic Skills
    Special Feature: None

19. Suppose a negative externality exists in a market. If transactions costs are low and parties are willing to bargain then, according to the Coase theorem,

    A) an efficient solution can be reached only if property rights are assigned to the victims of the pollution.
    B) an efficient solution can be reached only if property rights are assigned to the polluters.
    C) an efficient solution can be reached regardless of the initial assignment of property rights.
    D) government intervention is critical to reach an efficient solution.

    Answer: C
    Diff: 2   Type: MC   Page Ref: 147/147
    Topic: The Coase Theorem
    Skill: Conceptual
    Objective: LO 2: Discuss the Coase Theorem and explain how private bargaining can lead to economic efficiency in a market with an externality.
    AACSB Coding: Reflective Thinking
    Special Feature: None

20. Congressman Murphy made the following proposal: "We should establish policies that completely eliminate air pollution. This is the only way to ensure that none of our citizens suffers the negative effects of air pollution." If Congressman Murphy's proposal were adopted and all forms of air pollution were eliminated which of the following would be true?

    A) The total cost of pollution reductions would equal the total benefit to society.

    B) Economic efficiency would be maximized

    C) The total benefit to society from reductions in air pollution would be maximized.

    D) The marginal cost from pollution reductions would exceed the marginal benefit.

Answer: D

Diff: 2   Type: MC   Page Ref: 144/144
Topic: Marginal benefit and marginal cost of pollution reduction
Skill: Conceptual
Objective: LO 2: Discuss the Coase Theorem and explain how private bargaining can lead to economic efficiency in a market with an externality.
AACSB Coding: Reflective Thinking
Special Feature: Don't Let This Happen to YOU!: Remember That It's the Net Benefit That Counts

21. The Coase Theorem asserts that government intervention is a prerequisite for addressing externality problems.

Answer: True   False

Diff: 1   Type: TF   Page Ref: 147/147
Topic: The Coase Theorem
Skill: Conceptual
Objective: LO 2: Discuss the Coase Theorem and explain how private bargaining can lead to economic efficiency in a market with an externality.
AACSB Coding: Reflective Thinking
Special Feature: None

22. If transactions costs are low private bargaining will always result in an efficient solution to the problem of externalities.

Answer: True   False

Diff: 2   Type: TF   Page Ref: 147/147
Topic: The Coase Theorem
Skill: Conceptual
Objective: LO 2: Discuss the Coase Theorem and explain how private bargaining can lead to economic efficiency in a market with an externality.
AACSB Coding: Reflective Thinking
Special Feature: None

23. State the Coase theorem. What are some of the limitations of the Coase theorem in practice?

    Answer: The Coase theorem states the following: If transactions costs are low, private bargaining will result in an efficient solution to the problem of externalities. Some limitations of the theorem are as follows. First, the Coase theorem works only if the transaction costs are low, which is unlikely if there are many bargaining parties. Second, private solutions to the problem of externalities will occur only if all parties to the agreement have full information about the costs and benefits associated with the externality. In reality, this may not be likely or may be difficult to ensure. Third, all parties must be willing to accept a reasonable agreement. For example, if those suffering from the effects of pollution do not have information on the costs of reducing pollution it is unlikely that parties can reach an agreement. Unreasonable demands can hinder an agreement.

    Diff: 2   *Type: ES*   *Page Ref: 147/147*
    Topic: The Coase Theorem
    Skill: Analytical
    Objective: LO 2: Discuss the Coase Theorem and explain how private bargaining can lead to economic efficiency in a market with an externality.
    AACSB Coding: Analytic Skills
    Special Feature: None

24. Ronald Coase is famous for the Coase Theorem, which is based on the premise that there is an economically efficient level of pollution reduction. Many economists believe that the tradable emissions allowance program that has been used to deal with the problem of acid rain has been successful in reducing emissions of sulfur dioxide in an economically efficient manner. Why isn't this program an example of the Coase Theorem?

    Answer: The Coase Theorem states that if transactions costs are low private bargaining will result in an efficient solution to the problem of externalities. Tradable emissions allowance programs are one type of market–based solution to the problem of negative externalities, but these programs are initiated by government, not private parties.

    Diff: 3   *Type: ES*   *Page Ref: 147/147*
    Topic: The Coase Theorem
    Skill: Analytical
    Objective: LO 2: Discuss the Coase Theorem and explain how private bargaining can lead to economic efficiency in a market with an externality.
    AACSB Coding: Analytic Skills
    Special Feature: None

5.3   Government Policies to Deal with Externalities

1. The first economist to systematically analyze market failure was
    A) Adam Smith.
    B) Ronald Coase.
    C) A. C. Pigou.
    D) J. E. Meade.
   Answer: C
   Diff: 1   Type: MC   Page Ref: 147/147
   Topic: Market failure
   Skill: Fact
   Objective: LO 3: Analyze government policies to achieve economic efficiency in a market with an externality.
   AACSB Coding: Reflective Thinking
   Special Feature: None

2. Assume that production from an electric utility caused acid rain. If the government imposed
   a tax on the utility equal to the cost of the acid rain, the government's action would
    A) externalize the externality.
    B) result in a marginal social benefit greater than the marginal cost of the electricity.
    C) be an example of supply side economic policy.
    D) internalize the externality.
   Answer: D
   Diff: 2   Type: MC   Page Ref: 147/147
   Topic: Pigovian taxes and subsidies
   Skill: Conceptual
   Objective: LO 3: Analyze government policies to achieve economic efficiency in a market with an externality.
   AACSB Coding: Reflective Thinking
   Special Feature: None

3. Assume that production from an electric utility caused acid rain and that the government
   imposed a tax on the utility equal to the cost of the acid rain. This is an example of
    A) a transaction cost.
    B) a Pigovian tax.
    C) a Pigovian subsidy.
    D) the Coase Theorem.
   Answer: B
   Diff: 2   Type: MC   Page Ref: 147/147
   Topic: Pigovian taxes and subsidies
   Skill: Conceptual
   Objective: LO 3: Analyze government policies to achieve economic efficiency in a market with an externality.
   AACSB Coding: Reflective Thinking
   Special Feature: None

Figure 5-5

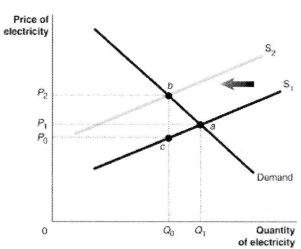

Coal burning utilities release sulfur dioxide and nitric acid which react with water to produce acid rain. Acid rain damages trees and crops and kills fish. Because the utilities do not bear the cost of the acid rain they overproduce the quantity of electricity. This is illustrated in Figure 5-5.

4. *Refer to Figure 5-5.* S_1 represents the supply curve that reflect the private cost of production and S_2 represents the supply curve that reflects the social cost of production. One way to internalize the external cost generated by utilities cost is to impose a Pigovian tax on the production of electricity. What is the size of the Pigovian tax that will internalize the cost of the externality?

    A) P_0

    B) P_2-P_0

    C) P_1-P_0

    D) P_2-P_1

Answer: B
Diff: 3   *Type: MC*   *Page Ref: 148–9/148–9*
Topic: Pigovian taxes and subsidies
Skill: Analytical
Objective: LO 3: Analyze government policies to achieve economic efficiency in a market with an externality.
AACSB Coding: Analytic Skills
Special Feature: None

5. Policies that mandate the installation of specific pollution control devices are called
    A) command and control policies.
    B) benefit policies.
    C) welfare policies.
    D) incentive policies.
Answer: A
Diff: 1   Type: MC   Page Ref: 150/150
Topic: Command and control approach
Skill: Definition
Objective: LO 3: Analyze government policies to achieve economic efficiency in a market with an externality.
AACSB Coding: Reflective Thinking
Special Feature: None

6. Economic incentives are designed to make individual self-interest coincide with social interest. According to economists, which of the following methods of pollution control best uses economic incentives to reduce pollution?
    A) Rewarding environmental groups for monitoring the activities of private firms that produce products which generate pollution.
    B) Imposing quantitative limits on the amount of pollution and imposing a penalty for non-compliance with these limits.
    C) Requiring the installation of specific pollution control devices.
    D) Instituting a system of tradable emissions allowances.
Answer: D
Diff: 3   Type: MC   Page Ref: 150/150
Topic: Government policies for externalities
Skill: Conceptual
Objective: LO 3: Analyze government policies to achieve economic efficiency in a market with an externality.
AACSB Coding: Reflective Thinking
Special Feature: None

Figure 5-6

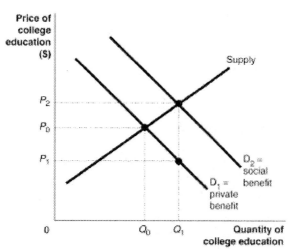

College education benefits society by producing a more employable workforce, reducing crime and creating a better informed citizenry. Thus, the social benefits of college education exceed the private benefits for any level of college education. This is illustrated in Figure 5-6.

7. *Refer to Figure 5-6.* One way to obtain the economically efficient amount of college education is for governments to subsidize college education. What is the size of the per-student Pigovian subsidy that the government must provide to internalize the external benefits? (Note that the subsidy can be granted to the education institutions or, to the students directly or indirectly; for example, through low-interest student loans.)
   A) P2-P0
   B) P2-P1
   C) P0-P1
   D) P1
   Answer: B
   Diff: 2   Type: MC   Page Ref: 149/149
   Topic: Pigovian taxes and subsidies
   Skill: Analytical
   Objective: LO 3: Analyze government policies to achieve economic efficiency in a market with an externality.
   AACSB Coding: Analytic Skills
   Special Feature: None

8. State and local governments subsidize college students with grants and low-interest loans. The loans and subsidies are examples of
    A) positive externalities.
    B) Coase subsidies.
    C) Pigovian subsidies.
    D) emission allowances.
    Answer: C
    Diff: 2   Type: MC   Page Ref: 150/150
    Topic: Pigovian taxes and subsidies
    Skill: Fact
    Objective: LO 3: Analyze government policies to achieve economic efficiency in a market with an externality.
    AACSB Coding: Reflective Thinking
    Special Feature: None

9. Which of the following is an example of a Pigovian tax?
    A) Payments by utilities to obtain tradable emissions allowances.
    B) A payroll tax.
    C) Payments for licenses to pollute.
    D) A tax imposed on a utility that internalizes the cost of externalities caused by the utility.
    Answer: D
    Diff: 2   Type: MC   Page Ref: 150/150
    Topic: Pigovian taxes and subsidies
    Skill: Definition
    Objective: LO 3: Analyze government policies to achieve economic efficiency in a market with an externality.
    AACSB Coding: Reflective Thinking
    Special Feature: None

10. The efficient level of paper production will occur where the
    A) marginal private benefit from consuming paper is equal to the marginal social cost of production.
    B) marginal social benefit from consuming paper is equal to the marginal social cost of production.
    C) the economically efficient level of the output of paper is equal to the economically efficient level of inputs.
    D) production of paper no longer produces negative externalities.
    Answer: A
    Diff: 1   Type: MC   Page Ref: 148/148
    Topic: Marginal benefit and marginal cost of pollution reduction
    Skill: Conceptual
    Objective: LO 3: Analyze government policies to achieve economic efficiency in a market with an externality.
    AACSB Coding: Reflective Thinking
    Special Feature: Solved Problem: Using a Tax to Deal with a Negative Externality

11. Which of the following describes a positive externality?
    A) John Henry paints the outside of his house in order to increase its market value just before he puts the house up for sale.
    B) People who do not attend college still benefit from others who receive a college education.
    C) The government imposes a tax on cigarettes in order to discourage smoking among teenagers.
    D) Mary volunteers to drive her neighbor's children to soccer practice.
    Answer: B
    Diff: 2   Type: MC   Page Ref: 149/149
    Topic: Positive externality
    Skill: Conceptual
    Objective: LO 3: Analyze government policies to achieve economic efficiency in a market with an externality.
    AACSB Coding: Reflective Thinking
    Special Feature: None

12. The U.S. government has frequently used a "command and control" approach in dealing with pollution. Which of the following describes this approach?
    A) The government uses taxes in order to internalize the externalities caused by pollution.
    B) The government uses subsidies to encourage firms to use new technology that reduces pollution.
    C) The government imposes quantitative limits on the amount of pollution firms are allowed to generate.
    D) The government distributes information to consumers and producers on how to reduce pollution.
    Answer: C
    Diff: 2   Type: MC   Page Ref: 150/150
    Topic: Command and control approach
    Skill: Definition
    Objective: LO 3: Analyze government policies to achieve economic efficiency in a market with an externality.
    AACSB Coding: Reflective Thinking
    Special Feature: None

13. Which of the following is an example of the U.S. government's use of a "command and control" approach to reducing pollution?
    A) In 1990 Congress approved measures designed to reduce sulfur dioxide emissions to 8.5 million tons annually by 2010.
    B) The U.S. government imposed a tax on electric utilities to reduce damages from acid rain.
    C) The government issued electric utilities tradable emissions allowances in other to reduce emissions of nitrogen oxide.
    D) In 1983 the U.S. government required the installation of catalytic converters to reduce emissions from all new automobiles.

Answer: D
Diff: 2   Type: MC   Page Ref: 150/150
Topic: Command and control approach
Skill: Fact
Objective: LO 3: Analyze government policies to achieve economic efficiency in a market with an externality.
AACSB Coding: Reflective Thinking
Special Feature: None

14. Economists generally favor the use of tradable emissions allowances to reduce pollution. However, the use of these allowances has been criticized by some environmentalists. Which of the following describes this criticism?
    A) Some environmentalists believe the allowances give firms a license to pollute.
    B) Some environmentalists believe that the price of allowances is often too high for consumers to afford.
    C) Some environmentalists believe that Pigovian taxes are a more efficient way to reduce pollution.
    D) Some environmentalists oppose allowances on legal grounds; they believe the use of allowances is unconstitutional.

Answer: A
Diff: 2   Type: MC   Page Ref: 150/150
Topic: Tradable emissions allowances
Skill: Conceptual
Objective: LO 3: Analyze government policies to achieve economic efficiency in a market with an externality.
AACSB Coding: Reflective Thinking
Special Feature: None

15. President George W. Bush opposed the 1997 Kyoto Treaty that was designed to reduce emissions of greenhouse gases that many people believe contribute to global warming. Which of the following did President Bush used to explain his opposition to the Kyoto Treaty?
    A) Poor nations had agreed to sign on the treaty, but no other wealthy nations had. Therefore, the treaty would be ineffective.
    B) The president accepted the recommendation of the European Union to reject the treaty because it would be too difficult to monitor.
    C) The president was not willing to commit to the treaty because he believed the cost of doing so would be too high.
    D) The president did not want to antagonize leaders from China and Russian who had opposed the treaty.
    Answer: C
    Diff: 2   Type: MC   Page Ref: 152/152
    Topic: Government policies for externalities
    Skill: Fact
    Objective: LO 3: Analyze government policies to achieve economic efficiency in a market with an externality.
    AACSB Coding: Reflective Thinking
    Special Feature: Making the Connection: Can Tradable Permits Reduce Global Warming?

16. The Kyoto Treaty of 1997 was designed to commit nations to reduce emissions of carbon dioxide and other greenhouse gases that contribute to global warming. Which of the following describes how the position of the United States regarding the Treaty differed from the position taken by most European nations?
    A) European nations favored using a global system of tradable emissions allowances for reducing emissions of carbon dioxide. The United States wanted more evidence that this type of system could be effective on a global scale.
    B) The United States favored using a global system of tradable emissions allowances for reducing emissions of carbon dioxide. European nations favored requiring each country to reduce emissions by specific amounts.
    C) The United States objected to asking China and India to sign on to the treaty because the costs of doing so would be too high. European nations insisted that China and India be included.
    D) The United States wanted a command and control approach to reducing emissions of greenhouse gases. European nations wanted to use a market–based system to reduce greenhouse gas emissions.
    Answer: B
    Diff: 3   Type: MC   Page Ref: 152/152
    Topic: Government policies for externalities
    Skill: Fact
    Objective: LO 3: Analyze government policies to achieve economic efficiency in a market with an externality.
    AACSB Coding: Reflective Thinking
    Special Feature: Making the Connection: Can Tradable Permits Reduce Global Warming?

17. In 1990 the U.S. Congress decided on an approach to deal with the problem of acid rain. This objective of this approach is to reduce sulfur dioxide emissions to 8.5 million tons per year by 2010. Which of the following describes the approach that was used to reach this goal?
    A) Electric utilities are required to reduce their emissions of sulfur dioxide by the same percentage.
    B) Electric utilities are required to reduce their emissions of sulfur dioxide by the same number of tons.
    C) Electric utilities are required to use the same technology to reduce their emissions of sulfur dioxide.
    D) Electric utilities were given allowances equal to the total amount of sulfur dioxide emissions; the utilities are allowed to buy and sell these allowances.
    Answer: D
    Diff: 2   Type: MC   Page Ref: 150/150
    Topic: Tradable emissions allowances
    Skill: Fact
    Objective: LO 3: Analyze government policies to achieve economic efficiency in a market with an externality.
    AACSB Coding: Reflective Thinking
    Special Feature: None

18. Congress used a market–based approach to reduce emissions of sulfur dioxide. Why is this approach considered market–based?
    A) Utilities are allowed to buy electricity from other utilities in open markets.
    B) Electric utilities are free to buy and sell allowances; the allowances equal the total amount of sulfur dioxide the utilities can emit.
    C) Electric utilities are free to buy and sell allowances; the allowances limit the number of new plants utilities can build.
    D) Electric utilities are free to buy and sell allowances; each allowance allows one utility to buy a plant from another utility.
    Answer: B
    Diff: 2   Type: MC   Page Ref: 150/150
    Topic: Tradable emissions allowances
    Skill: Fact
    Objective: LO 3: Analyze government policies to achieve economic efficiency in a market with an externality.
    AACSB Coding: Reflective Thinking
    Special Feature: None

19. In 1990 the U.S. Congress decided to use a market–based approach to reduce emissions of sulfur dioxide. The goal is to reduce emissions of sulfur dioxide to 8.5 million tons annually by 2010. How has this approached worked so far?
     A) The market–based approach cannot be evaluated until 2010.
     B) The market–based approach has been successful in reducing sulfur dioxide emissions, but the cost of the program is greater than what was expected in 1990.
     C) The market–based approach has been successful in reducing sulfur dioxide emissions at a cost lower than was expected in 1990.
     D) The market–based approach has been successful in reducing sulfur dioxide emissions but not enough was budgeted for the program in 1990 to enable the program to reach its goals.

     Answer: C
     Diff: 2   Type: MC   Page Ref: 150/150
     Topic: Tradable emissions allowances
     Skill: Fact
     Objective: LO 3: Analyze government policies to achieve economic efficiency in a market with an externality.
     AACSB Coding: Reflective Thinking
     Special Feature: None

20. In 1990 the U.S. Congress decided to use a market–based approach to reduce emissions of sulfur dioxide. Just before this program was enacted the Edison Electric Company estimated that is would cost utilities over $7 billion annually to comply with the program. How has the actual cost compared to this estimate?
     A) The actual costs were much lower than Edison estimated.
     B) Edison's estimates were remarkably close the actual figures.
     C) Edison's estimates were less than the actual figures, mostly because of unanticipated inflation.
     D) The actual costs were greater than Edison had estimated in the 1990s, but since then annual costs have fallen.

     Answer: A
     Diff: 2   Type: MC   Page Ref: 150/150
     Topic: Tradable emissions allowances
     Skill: Fact
     Objective: LO 3: Analyze government policies to achieve economic efficiency in a market with an externality.
     AACSB Coding: Reflective Thinking
     Special Feature: None

21. When the government imposes a tax equal to the external cost of producing of a product that causes pollution the government is said to externalize the externality.
     Answer: True   ◌ False
     Diff: 1   Type: TF   Page Ref: 147/147
     Topic: Negative externality
     Skill: Conceptual
     Objective: LO 3: Analyze government policies to achieve economic efficiency in a market with an externality.
     AACSB Coding: Reflective Thinking
     Special Feature: None

22. A.C. Pigou argued that the government can deal with a positive externality in consumption by giving consumers a subsidy equal to the value of the externality.
Answer: ◉ True ⃝ False
Diff: 1 Type: TF Page Ref: 147/147
Topic: Pigovian taxes and subsidies
Skill: Fact
Objective: LO 3: Analyze government policies to achieve economic efficiency in a market with an externality.
AACSB Coding: Reflective Thinking
Special Feature: None

23. Some environmentalists have criticized tradable emissions allowances on the grounds that they give permit holders a license to pollute. Furthermore, environmentalists argue that those who sell their permits receive a monetary benefit from their contribution to polluting the environment. Use economic reasoning to evaluate this criticism.
Answer: The criticism ignores one of the central lessons of economics: resources are scarce and tradeoffs exist. Resources spent reducing one type of pollution are not available for other uses. Furthermore, the opportunity cost of polluting (using the permit) is the price of the permit. In other words, firms are forced to face the cost of polluting. So although firms receive a monetary benefit from the sale of permits, the scheme gives them the incentive to find the cheapest way to reduce pollution.
Diff: 3 Type: ES Page Ref: 150/150
Topic: Tradable emissions allowances
Skill: Analytical
Objective: LO 3: Analyze government policies to achieve economic efficiency in a market with an externality.
AACSB Coding: Analytic Skills
Special Feature: None

24. The U.S. government established a tradable emissions allowance program to deal with the acid rain problem. Power plants are issued allowances to emit sulfur dioxide based on their past emission levels. The power plants are free to buy and sell these allowances. However, each plant must present the Environmental Protection Agency with enough allowances to cover its own emissions. An alternative to issuing tradable allowances is to require all power plants to install pollution abatement equipment. Explain how the tradable emissions allowance program made it possible to meet the government's emission goals at a much lower cost than the alternative.
Answer: This program recognizes that the marginal social cost of abatement is not equal across all producers. For example, older utilities that find it costly to reduce emissions by installing expensive pollution control devices (high marginal cost of pollution reduction) can lower their costs by buying allowances to discharge specified amounts of sulfur dioxide. On the other hand, firms with a low marginal cost of reduction can sell their permits to the high marginal cost firms. Firms have an incentive to discover the least costly way to reduce their emissions. By giving firms the option of either purchasing allowances or installing pollution control devices to reduce their own emissions the program achieves the government's emission goals in a cost-effective way. Requiring all power plants to install abatement equipment would result in higher costs since firms would not be able to select the most cost-effective means to reduce their emissions.

Diff: 3   Type: ES   Page Ref: 150/150
Topic: Tradable emissions allowances
Skill: Analytical
Objective: LO 3: Analyze government policies to achieve economic efficiency in a market with an externality.
AACSB Coding: Analytic Skills
Special Feature: None

5.4   Four Categories of Goods

1. Public goods are distinguished by two primary characteristics. What are they?
    A) Nonrivalry and nonexcludability.
    B) Government intervention and low prices.
    C) Market failure and high prices.
    D) Rivalry and exclusivity.
    Answer: A
    Diff: 1   Type: MC   Page Ref: 153/153
    Topic: Public goods
    Skill: Definition
    Objective: LO 4: Explain how goods can be categorized on the basis of whether they are rival or excludable, and use graphs to illustrate the efficient quantities of public goods and common resources.
    AACSB Coding: Reflective Thinking
    Special Feature: None

2. Goods can be classified on the basis of whether their consumption is
    A) internal and excludable.
    B) rival and competitive.
    C) includable and cooperative.
    D) rival and excludable.
    Answer: D
    Diff: 1   Type: MC   Page Ref: 152/152
    Topic: Categories of goods
    Skill: Conceptual
    Objective: LO 4: Explain how goods can be categorized on the basis of whether they are rival or excludable, and use graphs to illustrate the efficient quantities of public goods and common resources.
    AACSB Coding: Reflective Thinking
    Special Feature: None

3. Classifying a good as excludable means
   A) that someone can be barred from consuming the good based on race, creed or some other irrelevant characteristic.
   B) that anyone who does not pay for the good cannot consume it.
   C) that consumption of the good causes no externalities.
   D) that a producer with patent or copyright protection can exclude any other producer from selling his product.
   Answer: B
   Diff: 1   Type: MC   Page Ref: 152/152
   Topic: Excludability
   Skill: Definition
   Objective: LO 4: Explain how goods can be categorized on the basis of whether they are rival or excludable, and use graphs to illustrate the efficient quantities of public goods and common resources.
   AACSB Coding: Reflective Thinking
   Special Feature: None

4. Classifying a good as rival means
   A) that the good is produced in a competitive market.
   B) that there is a shortage of the good.
   C) that when one person consumes a unit of the good no one else can consume it.
   D) anyone who does not pay for the good cannot consume it.
   Answer: C
   Diff: 1   Type: MC   Page Ref: 152/152
   Topic: Rivalry
   Skill: Definition
   Objective: LO 4: Explain how goods can be categorized on the basis of whether they are rival or excludable, and use graphs to illustrate the efficient quantities of public goods and common resources.
   AACSB Coding: Reflective Thinking
   Special Feature: None

5. A private good is
   A) a good that is rivalrous and nonexcludable.
   B) a good that is nonrivalrous and nonexcludable.
   C) a good that is rivalrous and excludable.
   D) a good that is nonrivalrous and excludable.
   Answer: C
   Diff: 1   Type: MC   Page Ref: 153/153
   Topic: Categories of goods
   Skill: Definition
   Objective: LO 4: Explain how goods can be categorized on the basis of whether they are rival or excludable, and use graphs to illustrate the efficient quantities of public goods and common resources.
   AACSB Coding: Reflective Thinking
   Special Feature: None

6. A public good is
    A) a good that is rivalrous and excludable.
    B) good that is nonrivalrous and nonexcludable.
    C) a good that is nonrivalrous and excludable.
    D) a good that is rivalrous and nonexcludable.
    Answer: B
    Diff: 1   Type: MC   Page Ref: 153/153
    Topic: Categories of goods
    Skill: Definition
    Objective: LO 4: Explain how goods can be categorized on the basis of whether they are rival or excludable, and use graphs to illustrate the efficient quantities of public goods and common resources.
    AACSB Coding: Reflective Thinking
    Special Feature: None

7. Goods that are excludable but not rival are
    A) public goods.
    B) semi-private goods.
    C) common resources.
    D) quasi-public goods.
    Answer: D
    Diff: 2   Type: MC   Page Ref: 153/153
    Topic: Categories of goods
    Skill: Definition
    Objective: LO 4: Explain how goods can be categorized on the basis of whether they are rival or excludable, and use graphs to illustrate the efficient quantities of public goods and common resources.
    AACSB Coding: Reflective Thinking
    Special Feature: None

8. A good that is rival but not excludable is a
    A) common resource.
    B) public good.
    C) quasi-public good.
    D) quasi-private good.
    Answer: A
    Diff: 2   Type: MC   Page Ref: 153/153
    Topic: Categories of goods
    Skill: Definition
    Objective: LO 4: Explain how goods can be categorized on the basis of whether they are rival or excludable, and use graphs to illustrate the efficient quantities of public goods and common resources.
    AACSB Coding: Reflective Thinking
    Special Feature: None

9. In the United States over 80 percent of individuals
    A) do not have health insurance.
    B) have health insurance provided by their state government or the federal government.
    C) who have health insurance receive it from their employers.
    D) receive health insurance from the Veterans Administration or Medicare.
    Answer: C
    Diff: 2   Type: MC   Page Ref: 154/154
    Topic: Health care
    Skill: Fact
    Objective: LO 4: Explain how goods can be categorized on the basis of whether they are rival or excludable, and use graphs to illustrate the efficient quantities of public goods and common resources.
    AACSB Coding: Reflective Thinking
    Special Feature: Making the Connection: Should the Government Run the Health Care System?

10. In Canada, Japan and most European countries health care
    A) is provided privately; individuals are responsible for paying for their own medical insurance.
    B) is either provided directly by the government or the government reimburses its citizens' health care expenses.
    C) in provided exclusively through hospitals and clinics that are owned by employers.
    D) is paid for by insurance provided as part of a benefits package from employers.
    Answer: B
    Diff: 2   Type: MC   Page Ref: 153/153
    Topic: Health care
    Skill: Fact
    Objective: LO 4: Explain how goods can be categorized on the basis of whether they are rival or excludable, and use graphs to illustrate the efficient quantities of public goods and common resources.
    AACSB Coding: Reflective Thinking
    Special Feature: Making the Connection: Should the Government Run the Health Care System?

11. The free rider problem refers to a situation in which
    A) people consume a pure public good without payment, even though the good may not be produced if no one chooses to pay.
    B) the marginal cost of allowing additional consumers to consume a public good is zero.
    C) high income individuals subsidize the production of goods, such as education, that make society better off.
    D) markets fail to allocate resources efficiently when benefits outweigh costs.
    Answer: A
    Diff: 1   Type: MC   Page Ref: 153/153
    Topic: Free riding
    Skill: Definition
    Objective: LO 4: Explain how goods can be categorized on the basis of whether they are rival or excludable, and use graphs to illustrate the efficient quantities of public goods and common resources.
    AACSB Coding: Reflective Thinking
    Special Feature: None

12. Which of the following best illustrates the free-rider problem?
    A) Since no one owns elephants and elephants are valued for their hide, meat and ivory, elephants can be hunted to extinction
    B) For every purchase of a $30 fare card, you are entitled to five free bus rides.
    C) If your neighbors professionally landscape their front yards, it is likely that the market value of your property will increase.
    D) All three homeowners in a quiet cul-de-sac have expressed the desirability of security lighting in the common parking area. One of the homeowners installs the lighting and asks you to contribute toward the cost. You choose not to contribute.
    Answer: D
    Diff: 2   Type: MC   Page Ref: 153/153
    Topic: Free riding
    Skill: Conceptual
    Objective: LO 4: Explain how goods can be categorized on the basis of whether they are rival or excludable, and use graphs to illustrate the efficient quantities of public goods and common resources.
    AACSB Coding: Reflective Thinking
    Special Feature: None

13. "Free riding" is a characteristic of which type of good?
    A) A private good.
    B) A common resource.
    C) A public good.
    D) A good that is both rival and excludable.
    Answer: C
    Diff: 2   Type: MC   Page Ref: 153/153
    Topic: Free riding
    Skill: Conceptual
    Objective: LO 4: Explain how goods can be categorized on the basis of whether they are rival or excludable, and use graphs to illustrate the efficient quantities of public goods and common resources.
    AACSB Coding: Reflective Thinking
    Special Feature: None

14. Some economists have argued that certain characteristics of the delivery of health care justify government intervention. One of these characteristics is
    A) health care is a public good.
    B) health care is nonrivalrous and nonexcludable.
    C) health care generates negative externalities.
    D) health care generates positive externalities.
    Answer: D
    Diff: 3   Type: MC   Page Ref: 154/154
    Topic: Health care
    Skill: Conceptual
    Objective: LO 4: Explain how goods can be categorized on the basis of whether they are rival or excludable, and use graphs to illustrate the efficient quantities of public goods and common resources.
    AACSB Coding: Reflective Thinking
    Special Feature: Making the Connection: Should the Government Run the Health Care System?

15. Consumers usually pay less than the total cost of medical treatment because
    A) a third party, usually an insurance company, often pays most of the bill.
    B) the federal government pays for most medical procedures.
    C) competition forces doctors and hospitals to charge prices that do not cover their costs.
    D) a third party, usually an employer, often pays most of the bill.
    Answer: A
    Diff: 2   Type: MC   Page Ref: 155/155
    Topic: Health care
    Skill: Conceptual
    Objective: LO 4: Explain how goods can be categorized on the basis of whether they are rival or excludable, and use graphs to illustrate the efficient quantities of public goods and common resources.
    AACSB Coding: Reflective Thinking
    Special Feature: Making the Connection: Should the Government Run the Health Care System?

16. Under current tax law individuals do not pay taxes on health insurance benefits they receive from their employers. As a result
    A) the federal government spends more than it receives in tax revenue.
    B) individuals are encouraged to want generous health coverage that reduces their incentives to cut costs.
    C) the quality of health care provided is less than it would be if benefits were taxed.
    D) politicians are encouraged to raise income and payroll taxes.
    Answer: B
    Diff: 2   Type: MC   Page Ref: 155/155
    Topic: Health care
    Skill: Conceptual
    Objective: LO 4: Explain how goods can be categorized on the basis of whether they are rival or excludable, and use graphs to illustrate the efficient quantities of public goods and common resources.
    AACSB Coding: Reflective Thinking
    Special Feature: Making the Connection: Should the Government Run the Health Care System?

17. Which of the following describes the difference between the market demand curve for a private good and the demand curve for a public good?
    A) The market demand curve for a private good is derived by adding vertically the quantities that consumers demand at each price. The demand curve for a public good is derived by adding horizontally the quantities that consumers demand at each price.
    B) The market demand curve for a private good is derived by adding horizontally the quantity of the good demanded at each price by each consumer. The demand curve for a public good is derived by adding up the price each consumer is willing to pay for each quantity of the good.
    C) The market demand curve for a private good will always is downward sloping. The demand curve for a public good will always is upward sloping.
    D) The market demand curve is drawn holding everything other than the price of the good constant; the demand curve for a public good is drawn by allowing all variables that affect demand to change.
    Answer: B
    Diff: 3   Type: MC   Page Ref: 156/156
    Topic: Public goods
    Skill: Conceptual
    Objective: LO 4: Explain how goods can be categorized on the basis of whether they are rival or

excludable, and use graphs to illustrate the efficient quantities of public goods and common resources.
AACSB Coding: Analytic Skills
Special Feature: None

18. To derive a demand curve for a public good, we
    A) add the price that each consumer is willing to pay for each quantity of the public good.
    B) add the quantities that each consumer is willing to purchase at each price of the public good.
    C) multiply the quantity demanded at each price by the number of the consumers.
    D) multiply the price by the quantity for each consumer and add up across all consumers.
    Answer: A
    Diff: 2   Type: MC   Page Ref: 156/156
    Topic: Public goods
    Skill: Conceptual
    Objective: LO 4: Explain how goods can be categorized on the basis of whether they are rival or excludable, and use graphs to illustrate the efficient quantities of public goods and common resources.
    AACSB Coding: Reflective Thinking
    Special Feature: Solved Problem: Determining the Optimal Level of Public Goods

19. It is difficult for a private market to provide the economically efficient quantity of a public good because
    A) by law governments cannot use cost–benefit analysis to determine this quantity.
    B) public goods produce positive and negative externalities.
    C) individual preferences are not revealed in the market for the good.
    D) it is too expensive to produce the necessary amount of the good.
    Answer: C
    Diff: 2   Type: MC   Page Ref: 157/157
    Topic: Public goods
    Skill: Conceptual
    Objective: LO 4: Explain how goods can be categorized on the basis of whether they are rival or excludable, and use graphs to illustrate the efficient quantities of public goods and common resources.
    AACSB Coding: Reflective Thinking
    Special Feature: None

Figure 5-7

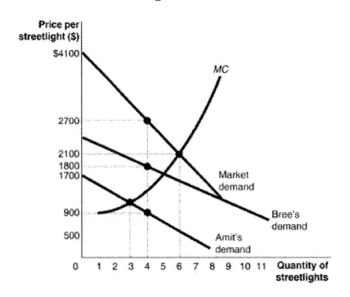

Amit and Bree are the only two homeowners on an isolated private road. Both agree that installing street lights along the road would be beneficial and want to do so. Figure 5-7 shows their willingness to pay for different quantities of street lights, the market demand for street lights and the marginal cost of installing the street lights.

20. **Refer to Figure 5-7.** How much is Amit willing to pay to have 4 street lights installed?
    A) $1,800
    B) $2,700
    C) $3,600
    D) $900
    Answer: D
    Diff: 1   Type: MC   Page Ref: 156-7/156-7
    Topic: Public goods
    Skill: Conceptual
    Objective: LO 4: Explain how goods can be categorized on the basis of whether they are rival or excludable, and use graphs to illustrate the efficient quantities of public goods and common resources.
    AACSB Coding: Reflective Thinking
    Special Feature: None

21. *Refer to Figure 5–7.* How much is Bree willing to pay to have 4 street lights installed?
    A) $2,700
    B) $1,500
    C) $1,800
    D) $7,200
    Answer: C
    Diff: 1   Type: MC   Page Ref: 156–7/156–7
    Topic: Public goods
    Skill: Conceptual
    Objective: LO 4: Explain how goods can be categorized on the basis of whether they are rival or excludable, and use graphs to illustrate the efficient quantities of public goods and common resources.
    AACSB Coding: Reflective Thinking
    Special Feature: None

22. *Refer to Figure 5–7.* What is the optimal quantity of street lights to install?
    A) 3
    B) 9
    C) 4
    D) 6
    Answer: D
    Diff: 3   Type: MC   Page Ref: 156–7/156–7
    Topic: Public goods
    Skill: Conceptual
    Objective: LO 4: Explain how goods can be categorized on the basis of whether they are rival or excludable, and use graphs to illustrate the efficient quantities of public goods and common resources.
    AACSB Coding: Reflective Thinking
    Special Feature: None

23. *Refer to Figure 5–7.* Suppose Amit and Bree know each other's preferences so that it is not possible for one to deceive the other. Which of the following statements best describes the circumstances under which the optimal quantity of street lights could be achieved?
    A) The optimal quantity will be installed only if the two parties agree to pay according to their willingness to pay as indicated by their respective demand curves.
    B) Because there are only two consumers, it is likely that private bargaining will result in the optimal quantity being installed.
    C) The optimal quantity will be installed only if the two parties split the cost of installation equally.
    D) The optimal quantity will be installed only if Bree pays for the entire installation cost.
    Answer: B
    Diff: 3   Type: MC   Page Ref: 156–7/156–7
    Topic: Public goods
    Skill: Conceptual
    Objective: LO 4: Explain how goods can be categorized on the basis of whether they are rival or excludable, and use graphs to illustrate the efficient quantities of public goods and common resources.
    AACSB Coding: Reflective Thinking
    Special Feature: None

24. Which of the following is an example of a common resource?
    A) Elephants in the wild.
    B) Lions in a zoo.
    C) A college education.
    D) Public transportation.
    Answer: A
    Diff: 1   Type: MC   Page Ref: 160/160
    Topic: Common resources
    Skill: Conceptual
    Objective: LO 4: Explain how goods can be categorized on the basis of whether they are rival or excludable, and use graphs to illustrate the efficient quantities of public goods and common resources.
    AACSB Coding: Reflective Thinking
    Special Feature: None

25. An important difference between the demand for a private good and the demand for a public good is that
    A) individuals reveal their preferences for a public good but they do not have to reveal their preferences a private good.
    B) the resources used to provide public goods are common resources or government owned; the resources used to produce private goods are all privately owned.
    C) individuals reveal their preferences for a private good but they do not have to reveal their preferences for a public good.
    D) the demand for a private good produces consumption externalities; the demand for a public good produces production externalities.
    Answer: C
    Diff: 3   Type: MC   Page Ref: 157/157
    Topic: Demand for a public good
    Skill: Conceptual
    Objective: LO 4: Explain how goods can be categorized on the basis of whether they are rival or excludable, and use graphs to illustrate the efficient quantities of public goods and common resources.
    AACSB Coding: Reflective Thinking
    Special Feature: None

26. In order to determine what quantity of a public good should be supplied governments sometimes use
    A) quantitative analysis.
    B) economic forecasting.
    C) econometrics.
    D) cost–benefit analysis.
    Answer: D
    Diff: 1   Type: MC   Page Ref: 158/158
    Topic: Public goods
    Skill: Conceptual
    Objective: LO 4: Explain how goods can be categorized on the basis of whether they are rival or excludable, and use graphs to illustrate the efficient quantities of public goods and common resources.
    AACSB Coding: Reflective Thinking
    Special Feature: None

27. The "tragedy of the commons" is a term that refers to
    A) tragic events such as forest fires and hurricanes that cause more damage than they should because of the failure of government to develop a common approach to handling disasters.
    B) the tendency for a common resource to be overused.
    C) the failure of Britain's House of Commons to respond quickly to tragedies such as the Great Plague.
    D) free riding that causes too little of a public good to be produced.
    Answer: B
    Diff: 1   *Type: MC*   *Page Ref: 160/160*
    Topic: The Tragedy of the Commons
    Skill: Definition
    Objective: LO 4: Explain how goods can be categorized on the basis of whether they are rival or excludable, and use graphs to illustrate the efficient quantities of public goods and common resources.
    AACSB Coding: Reflective Thinking
    Special Feature: None

28. In England during the Middle Ages each village had an area of pasture on which any family in the village was allowed to graze its cows and sheep without charge. Eventually, the grass in the pasture would be depleted and no family's cow or sheep would get enough to eat. The reason the grass was depleted was
    A) the area of pasture was nonexcludable and the consumption of the grass was rival.
    B) self-interest motives led livestock owners to raise too many cows and sheep.
    C) due to a policy of neglect on the part of the English government.
    D) it did not get enough rainfall.
    Answer: A
    Diff: 2   *Type: MC*   *Page Ref: 160/160*
    Topic: The Tragedy of the Commons
    Skill: Conceptual
    Objective: LO 4: Explain how goods can be categorized on the basis of whether they are rival or excludable, and use graphs to illustrate the efficient quantities of public goods and common resources.
    AACSB Coding: Reflective Thinking
    Special Feature: None

29. Haiti was once a heavily forested country. Today, 80 percent of Haiti's forests have been cut down, primarily to be burned to create charcoal. The reduction in the number of trees has lead to devastating floods when it rains heavily. This is an example of
    A) tragic externalities.
    B) the Tragedy of the Commons.
    C) human greed.
    D) the consequences of not having a market economic system.
    Answer: B
    Diff: 1   *Type: MC*   *Page Ref: 160/160*
    Topic: The Tragedy of the Commons
    Skill: Conceptual
    Objective: LO 4: Explain how goods can be categorized on the basis of whether they are rival or excludable, and use graphs to illustrate the efficient quantities of public goods and common resources.
    AACSB Coding: Reflective Thinking
    Special Feature: None

30. Negative externalities and the tragedy of the commons are problems that have a common source. What is this common source?
    A) Self-interest motives of producers and consumers.
    B) A lack of concern for human rights.
    C) A lack of competition.
    D) A lack of clearly defined and enforced property rights.
    Answer: D
    Diff: 1   Type: MC   Page Ref: 161/161
    Topic: Market failure
    Skill: Conceptual
    Objective: LO 4: Explain how goods can be categorized on the basis of whether they are rival or excludable, and use graphs to illustrate the efficient quantities of public goods and common resources.
    AACSB Coding: Reflective Thinking
    Special Feature: None

31. Which of the following is a possible solution when a scarce resource is subject to the tragedy of the commons?
    A) Access to the commons can be restricted through community norms and laws.
    B) Offer subsidies to consumers.
    C) Force people to move away from the commons.
    D) Persuade people to use less of the scarce resource through an advertising campaign.
    Answer: A
    Diff: 2   Type: MC   Page Ref: 162/162
    Topic: The Tragedy of the Commons
    Skill: Analytical
    Objective: LO 4: Explain how goods can be categorized on the basis of whether they are rival or excludable, and use graphs to illustrate the efficient quantities of public goods and common resources.
    AACSB Coding: Analytic Skills
    Special Feature: None

31. A public good that is a good that is both rival and excludable.
    Answer: True   ⦾ False
    Diff: 1   Type: TF   Page Ref: 153/153
    Topic: Public goods
    Skill: Definition
    Objective: LO 4: Explain how goods can be categorized on the basis of whether they are rival or excludable, and use graphs to illustrate the efficient quantities of public goods and common resources.
    AACSB Coding: Reflective Thinking
    Special Feature: None

32. Under current U.S. tax laws individuals do not pay taxes on health insurance benefits they receive from their employers.
    Answer: ⦾ True   False
    Diff: 2   Type: TF   Page Ref: 155/155
    Topic: Health care
    Skill: Conceptual
    Objective: LO 4: Explain how goods can be categorized on the basis of whether they are rival or excludable, and use graphs to illustrate the efficient quantities of public goods and common resources.
    AACSB Coding: Reflective Thinking
    Special Feature: Making the Connection: Should the Government Run the Health Care System?

33. The social benefit of a given level of a public good is the vertical sum of all private benefits for that level.

    Answer: ⊙ True   False
    Diff: 1   Type: TF   Page Ref: 156/156
    Topic: Public goods
    Skill: Conceptual
    Objective: LO 4: Explain how goods can be categorized on the basis of whether they are rival or excludable, and use graphs to illustrate the efficient quantities of public goods and common resources.
    AACSB Coding: Reflective Thinking
    Special Feature: None

34. A modern example of the tragedy of the commons is the forests in many poor countries.

    Answer: ⊙ True   False
    Diff: 1   Type: TF   Page Ref: 160/160
    Topic: The Tragedy of the Commons
    Skill: Fact
    Objective: LO 4: Explain how goods can be categorized on the basis of whether they are rival or excludable, and use graphs to illustrate the efficient quantities of public goods and common resources.
    AACSB Coding: Reflective Thinking
    Special Feature: None

35. State whether each of the following goods and services is nonrival, nonexcludable or both.
    a.   A toll road
    b.   A public park
    c.   A lighthouse
    d.   An art museum
    e.   A radio broadcast of A Prairie Home Companion
    Answer: a.   Nonrival, although rivalry could exist during traffic congestion.
    b.   Both, although rivalry could exist under some circumstances, such as when there is a sporting event or a private party.
    c.   Both
    d.   Nonrival and excludable if admission requires the purchase of a ticket.
    e.   Both
    Diff: 2   Type: ES   Page Ref: 152-3/152-3
    Topic: Public Goods
    Skill: Conceptual
    Objective: LO 4: Explain how goods can be categorized on the basis of whether they are rival or excludable, and use graphs to illustrate the efficient quantities of public goods and common resources.
    AACSB Coding: Reflective Thinking
    Special Feature: None

36. How does a public good differ from a quasi-public good? In your answer give an example
    of each type of good.

    Answer: A pubic good is: (a) nonrivalrous - one person's consumption of the good does not
            prevent anyone else from consuming it; (b) nonexcludable - anyone can consume the
            good without paying for it. An example of a public good is national defense. A
            quasi-public good is excludable, but nonrival. This means that people who do not
            pay for the good do not consume it, but one's person's consumption does not affect
            the consumption of anyone else. An example of a quasi-public good is a toll road.

    Diff: 2   Type: ES   Page Ref: 153/153
    Topic: Categories of goods
    Skill: Conceptual
    Objective: LO 4: Explain how goods can be categorized on the basis of whether they are rival or
    excludable, and use graphs to illustrate the efficient quantities of public goods and common resources.
    AACSB Coding: Reflective Thinking
    Special Feature: None

37. "When it comes to public goods, individuals do not reveal their true preferences because it is
    not in their self interest to do so." Evaluate this statement.

    Answer: The statement is true. For example, in the case of a private good such as a hamburger,
            a consumer either reveals her willingness to pay by purchasing the good at the market
            price or goes without it. This is not the case with a public good. Once produced,
            individuals cannot be excluded from consuming the good even if they have not paid
            for the good. Therefore, it is in a consumer's interest not to reveal her true preferences
            for the good.

    Diff: 3   Type: ES   Page Ref: 157/157
    Topic: Public goods
    Skill: Analytical
    Objective: LO 4: Explain how goods can be categorized on the basis of whether they are rival or
    excludable, and use graphs to illustrate the efficient quantities of public goods and common resources.
    AACSB Coding: Analytic Skills
    Special Feature: None

38. Define the tragedy of the commons. Give three examples of common resources. Briefly
    explain why common property resources are subject to overuse.

    Answer: The tragedy of the commons refers to situations where common resources are subject
            to overuse and pollution. Examples include forest land, pasture land, fish in the ocean,
            lions in the wild, shrimp population in the gulf states, a public library, and space on a
            public beach. Common resources are subject to overuse because each individual
            captures the private benefit fully but only bears part of the cost of using the resource.
            As a result, each individual has no incentive to maintain the quality or purity of the
            resource.

    Diff: 2   Type: ES   Page Ref: 160/160
    Topic: The Tragedy of the Commons
    Skill: Analytical
    Objective: LO 4: Explain how goods can be categorized on the basis of whether they are rival or
    excludable, and use graphs to illustrate the efficient quantities of public goods and common resources.
    AACSB Coding: Analytic Skills
    Special Feature: None

Chapter 6: Elasticity: The Responsiveness of Demand and Supply

6.1   The Price Elasticity of Demand and Its Measurement

1. Economists use the concept of _____ to measure how one economic variable, such as quantity, responds to a change in another economic variable, such as price.
    A) slope
    B) efficiency
    C) relativity
    D) elasticity
Answer: D
Diff: 1   Type: MC   Page Ref: 174/174
Topic: Elasticity
Skill: Conceptual
Objective: LO1: Define the price elasticity of demand and understand how to measure it.
AACSB Coding: Reflective Thinking
Special Feature: None

2. The _____ measures the responsiveness of quantity demanded to a change in price.
    A) law of demand
    B) price elasticity of demand
    C) substitution effect
    D) income effect
Answer: B
Diff: 1   Type: MC   Page Ref: 174/174
Topic: Price elasticity of demand
Skill: Definition
Objective: LO1: Define the price elasticity of demand and understand how to measure it.
AACSB Coding: Reflective Thinking
Special Feature: None

3. Unlike most retail firms book publishers face a unique problem. What is this problem?
    A) They sell two different versions – hard cover and paperback – of the same product.
    B) They have competition from libraries where people can borrow books instead of buying them.
    C) Bookstores have the right to return unsold books.
    D) Books are more durable than food or other perishable items sold by other retail firms.
Answer: C
Diff: 1   Type: MC   Page Ref: 172/172
Topic: Elasticity and economic issues
Skill: Fact
Objective: LO1: Define the price elasticity of demand and understand how to measure it.
AACSB Coding: Reflective Thinking
Special Feature: Chapter Opener: Do People Care about the Price of Books?

4. To calculate the price elasticity of demand we divide
     A) the percentage change in quantity demanded by the percentage change in price.
     B) the percentage change in price by the percentage change in quantity demanded.
     C) rise by the run.
     D) the average price by the average quantity demanded.
   Answer: A
   Diff: 1   Type: MC   Page Ref: 175/175
   Topic: Price elasticity of demand
   Skill: Definition
   Objective: LO1: Define the price elasticity of demand and understand how to measure it.
   AACSB Coding: Reflective Thinking
   Special Feature: None

5. The slope of a demand curve is not used to measure the price elasticity of demand because
     A) the slope of a linear demand curve is not constant.
     B) the slope of a line cannot have a negative value.
     C) the measurement of slope is sensitive to the units chosen for price and quantity.
     D) the slope of the demand curve does not tell us how much quantity changes as price
        changes.
   Answer: C
   Diff: 1   Type: MC   Page Ref: 174/174
   Topic: Price elasticity and the slope of a demand curve
   Skill: Conceptual
   Objective: LO1: Define the price elasticity of demand and understand how to measure it.
   AACSB Coding: Reflective Thinking
   Special Feature: None

6. If the slope of a demand curve is equal to –0.1 then
     A) demand is inelastic.
     B) we don't know whether the demand is elastic or inelastic.
     C) the demand is elastic at low prices and inelastic at high prices.
     D) as price increases by 10 percent quantity demanded decreases by 1 percent.
   Answer: B
   Diff: 2   Type: MC   Page Ref: 174/174
   Topic: Price elasticity and the slope of a demand curve
   Skill: Conceptual
   Objective: LO1: Define the price elasticity of demand and understand how to measure it.
   AACSB Coding: Reflective Thinking
   Special Feature: None

7. The price elasticity of demand for beef is estimated to be 0.60 (in absolute value). This means that a 20 percent increase in the price of beef, holding every thing else constant, will cause the quantity of beef demanded to
    A) decrease by 12 percent.
    B) decrease by 60 percent.
    C) decrease by 32 percent.
    D) decrease by 26 percent.
Answer: A
Diff: 2   Type: MC   Page Ref: 175/175
Topic: Price elasticity of demand
Skill: Analytical
Objective: LO1: Define the price elasticity of demand and understand how to measure it.
AACSB Coding: Analytic Skills
Special Feature: None

8. If the absolute value of the price elasticity of demand for pizza equals 2.5 then
    A) pizza is a normal good.
    B) the demand for pizza is inelastic.
    C) pizza has few substitutes.
    D) the demand for pizza is elastic.
Answer: D
Diff: 1   Type: MC   Page Ref: 175–6/175–6
Topic: Elastic and inelastic demand
Skill: Conceptual
Objective: LO1: Define the price elasticity of demand and understand how to measure it.
AACSB Coding: Reflective Thinking
Special Feature: None

9. When the price of tortilla chips rose by 10 percent, the quantity of tortilla chips sold fell 4 percent. This indicates that the demand for tortilla chips is
    A) inelastic.
    B) elastic.
    C) unit–elastic
    D) perfectly inelastic.
Answer: A
Diff: 2   Type: MC   Page Ref: 175–6/175–6
Topic: Elastic and inelastic demand
Skill: Analytical
Objective: LO1: Define the price elasticity of demand and understand how to measure it.
AACSB Coding: Analytic Skills
Special Feature: None

10. A linear downward sloping demand curve has price elasticities (in absolute values) that
    A) increase as price decreases.
    B) remain constant along the demand curve.
    C) decrease as price decreases.
    D) greater than or equal to 1.
    Answer: C
    Diff: 1   Type: MC   Page Ref: 178/178
    Topic: Price elasticity of demand
    Skill: Conceptual
    Objective: LO1: Define the price elasticity of demand and understand how to measure it.
    AACSB Coding: Reflective Thinking
    Special Feature: None

11. Carrie Bradshaw claims that when it comes to buying shoes, "price is no object." If this is
    true, then her demand for shoes is
    A) perfectly elastic
    B) perfectly inelastic.
    C) unit-elastic.
    D) horizontal.
    Answer: B
    Diff: 1   Type: MC   Page Ref: 178/178
    Topic: Perfectly inelastic demand
    Skill: Conceptual
    Objective: LO1: Define the price elasticity of demand and understand how to measure it.
    AACSB Coding: Reflective Thinking
    Special Feature: None

12. If the price elasticity of demand for insulin is equal to zero then the demand curve for
    insulin is
    A) horizontal.
    B) downward sloping.
    C) curvilinear.
    D) vertical.
    Answer: D
    Diff: 1   Type: MC   Page Ref: 178/178
    Topic: Perfectly inelastic demand
    Skill: Conceptual
    Objective: LO1: Define the price elasticity of demand and understand how to measure it.
    AACSB Coding: Reflective Thinking
    Special Feature: None

13. If the demand for iPods is price elastic, then
    A) the percentage change in quantity demanded is greater than the percentage change in price (in absolute value).
    B) the percentage change in quantity demanded is less than the percentage change in price (in absolute value).
    C) the percentage change in quantity demanded is equal to the percentage change in price.
    D) quantity demanded is not responsive to changes in price.
    Answer: A
    Diff: 1   Type: MC   Page Ref: 175/175
    Topic: Elastic and inelastic demand
    Skill: Definition
    Objective: LO1: Define the price elasticity of demand and understand how to measure it.
    AACSB Coding: Reflective Thinking
    Special Feature: None

14. If the demand for a steak is unit-elastic, then
    A) the percentage change in quantity demanded is 1 percent greater than the percentage change in price.
    B) the percentage change in quantity demanded is equal to the percentage change in price.
    C) the percentage change in quantity demanded is 100 percent greater than the percentage change in price (in absolute value).
    D) quantity demanded does not respond to changes in price.
    Answer: B
    Diff: 2   Type: MC   Page Ref: 175/175
    Topic: Unit-elastic demand
    Skill: Definition
    Objective: LO1: Define the price elasticity of demand and understand how to measure it.
    AACSB Coding: Reflective Thinking
    Special Feature: None

15. If the demand for cell phone service is inelastic, then
    A) the percentage change in quantity demanded is greater than the percentage change in price (in absolute value).
    B) the percentage change in quantity demanded is equal to the percentage change in price.
    C) the quantity demanded does not change in response to changes in price.
    D) the percentage change in quantity demanded is less than the percentage change in price (in absolute value).
    Answer: D
    Diff: 1   Type: MC   Page Ref: 175/175
    Topic: Elastic and inelastic demand
    Skill: Definition
    Objective: LO1: Define the price elasticity of demand and understand how to measure it.
    AACSB Coding: Reflective Thinking
    Special Feature: None

16.

Figure 6-1

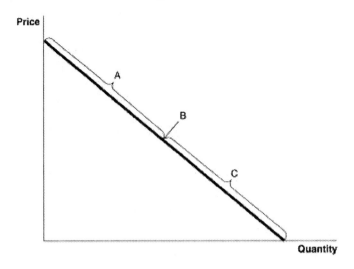

Refer to Figure 6-1. The section of the demand curve labeled "A" represents
   A) the inelastic section of the demand curve.
   B) the unit-elastic section of the demand curve.
   C) the elastic section of the demand curve.
   D) the perfectly elastic section of the demand curve.
Answer: C
Diff: 1   Type: MC   Page Ref: 178-9/178-9
Topic: Elastic and inelastic demand
Skill: Conceptual
Objective: LO1: Define the price elasticity of demand and understand how to measure it.
AACSB Coding: Reflective Thinking
Special Feature: None

Figure 6-2

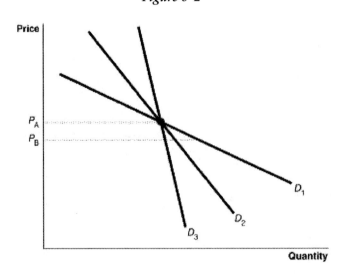

17. *Refer to Figure 6-2.* As price falls from P_A to P_B, the quantity demanded increases most along D_1; therefore,

    A) D_1 is unit elastic.

    B) D_1 is more inelastic than D_2 or D_3.

    C) D_1 is more elastic than D_2 or D_3

    D) D_1 is elastic at P_A but inelastic at P_B.

Answer: C

Diff: 2   *Type: MC*   *Page Ref: 179/179*
Topic: Price elasticity and the slope of a demand curve
Skill: Conceptual
Objective: LO1: Define the price elasticity of demand and understand how to measure it.
AACSB Coding: Reflective Thinking
Special Feature: None

18. The midpoint formula is used to measure the elasticity of demand between two points on a demand curve

    A) when demand is elastic.

    B) in special cases when the percentage change in the quantity demanded is equal to the percentage change in price.

    C) to ensure that the elasticity has a negative value.

    D) to ensure that we have only one value of the price elasticity of demand between two points on a demand curve.

Answer: D

Diff: 1   *Type: MC*   *Page Ref: 176/176*
Topic: The midpoint formula
Skill: Conceptual
Objective: LO1: Define the price elasticity of demand and understand how to measure it.
AACSB Coding: Reflective Thinking
Special Feature: None

19. When the price of peaches is $2.80 per lb. the quantity demanded is 100 lbs. When the price of peaches is $2.00 per lb. the quantity demanded is 140 lbs. When the midpoint formula is used to measure the price elasticity of demand we can say that the demand for peaches is

    A) relatively, but not perfectly, elastic.

    B) unit-elastic.

    C) completely inelastic.

    D) relatively, but not perfectly, inelastic.

Answer: B

Diff: 3   *Type: MC*   *Page Ref: 176/176*
Topic: The midpoint formula
Skill: Analytical
Objective: LO1: Define the price elasticity of demand and understand how to measure it.
AACSB Coding: Analytic Skills
Special Feature: None

20. Assume that when the price of cantaloupes is $2.50 the demand for cantaloupes is unit-elastic, and that the demand curve for cantaloupes is linear and downward sloping. If firms lower the price of cantaloupes to $2.00 which of the following statements can be made regarding the price elasticity of demand for cantaloupes?
    A) The demand for cantaloupes at $2.00 must be inelastic.
    B) We cannot determine whether the demand for cantaloupes is elastic or inelastic without knowing what the quantity demanded is at each price.
    C) The demand for cantaloupes at $2.00 must be elastic.
    D) The demand for cantaloupes at $2.00 must be unit-elastic.
    Answer: A
    Diff: 2   Type: MC   Page Ref: 178/178
    Topic: Elastic and inelastic demand
    Skill: Analytical
    Objective: LO1: Define the price elasticity of demand and understand how to measure it.
    AACSB Coding: Analytic Skills
    Special Feature: None

21. Assume that the demand curve for sunblock is linear and downward sloping. Which of the following statements about the slope of the demand curve for sunblock and the price elasticity of demand for sunblock are true?
    A) The slope and the price elasticity of demand are constant at all points along the demand curve for sunblock.
    B) The slope is constant, but the price elasticity of demand is not constant at all points along the demand curve for sunblock.
    C) The slope is not constant, but the price elasticity of demand is constant at all points along the demand curve for sunblock.
    D) The slope of the demand curve for sunblock is constant and equal to zero; demand is perfectly inelastic.
    Answer: B
    Diff: 2   Type: MC   Page Ref: 179/179
    Topic: Price elasticity and the slope of a demand curve
    Skill: Conceptual
    Objective: LO1: Define the price elasticity of demand and understand how to measure it.
    AACSB Coding: Reflective Thinking
    Special Feature: None

22. If the percentage change in the quantity demanded of beach towels is less than the percentage change in the price of beach towels then
    A) the price elasticity of demand for beach towels is greater than 1 in absolute value.
    B) the demand for beach towels is unit–elastic.
    C) the price elasticity of demand for beach towels is equal to zero.
    D) the price elasticity of demand for beach towels is less than 1 in absolute value.
    Answer: D
    Diff: 2   Type: MC   Page Ref: 175/175
    Topic: Price elasticity of demand
    Skill: Definition
    Objective: LO1: Define the price elasticity of demand and understand how to measure it.
    AACSB Coding: Reflective Thinking
    Special Feature: None

23. We should never assume that an inelastic demand curve is a perfectly inelastic demand curve because
    A) there has never been evidence of a perfectly inelastic demand curve.
    B) an inelastic demand curve may be perfectly inelastic at some times but not others.
    C) perfectly inelastic demand curves are rare.
    D) an inelastic demand curve may be elastic at high prices.
    Answer: C
    Diff: 1   Type: MC   Page Ref: 178/178
    Topic: Perfectly inelastic demand
    Skill: Fact
    Objective: LO1: Define the price elasticity of demand and understand how to measure it.
    AACSB Coding: Reflective Thinking
    Special Feature: Don't Let This Happen to YOU!: Don't Confuse Inelastic with Perfectly Inelastic

24.   *Table 6–1*

Price	Quantity
$35	40
$25	50

Refer to Table 6–1. Suppose you own a bookstore. You believe that you can sell 40 copies per day of the latest Harry Potter novel when the price is $35. You consider lowering the price to $25 and believe this will increase the quantity sold to 50 books per day. Compute the price elasticity of demand using the mid–point formula and these data. Select the correct implication from your work.
    A) The demand for the Harry Potter book is inelastic. Revenue will fall if the price is lowered.
    B) The demand for the Harry Potter book is elastic. Revenue will rise if the price is lowered.
    C) The demand for the Harry Potter book is inelastic. Revenue will rise if the price is lowered.
    D) The demand for the Harry Potter book is elastic. Revenue will fall if the price is lowered.
    Answer: A

Diff: 3   Type: MC   Page Ref: 177/177
Topic: Price elasticity of demand and total revenue
Skill: Analytical
Objective: LO1: Define the price elasticity of demand and understand how to measure it.
AACSB Coding: Analytic Skills
Special Feature: Solved Problem: Calculating the Price Elasticity of Demand

25. Of the following, which is the best example of good with a perfectly inelastic demand?
    A) The demand for tickets in New York City when the Mets or Yankees are in the World Series.
    B) The demand for gasoline.
    C) A diabetic's demand for insulin.
    D) The demand for a college education by a student who has a full scholarship to an Ivy League school.
    Answer: C
    Diff: 1   Type: MC   Page Ref: 178/178
    Topic: Perfectly inelastic demand
    Skill: Conceptual
    Objective: LO1: Define the price elasticity of demand and understand how to measure it.
    AACSB Coding: Reflective Thinking
    Special Feature: None

26. A perfectly elastic demand curve is
    A) vertical.
    B) horizontal.
    C) curvilinear.
    D) upward sloping.
    Answer: B
    Diff: 1   Type: MC   Page Ref: 178/178
    Topic: Price elasticity of demand
    Skill: Conceptual
    Objective: LO1: Define the price elasticity of demand and understand how to measure it.
    AACSB Coding: Reflective Thinking
    Special Feature: None

27. A newspaper story on the effect of higher milk prices on the market for ice cream contained the following:

    "As a result [of the increase in milk prices], retail prices for ice cream are up 4 percent from last year. . . . And ice cream consumption is down 3 percent."
    Source: John Curran, "Ice Cream, They Scream: Milk Fat Costs Drive Up Ice Cream Prices," Associated Press, July 23, 2001.

    Based on the information given, what is the price elasticity of demand for ice cream?
    A) 0.75 (in absolute value)
    B) 1.33 (in absolute value)
    C) 12%
    D) We do not have enough information to calculate the elasticity.
    Answer: A
    Diff: 2   Type: MC   Page Ref: 175–6/175–6
    Topic: Price elasticity of demand
    Skill: Analytical
    Objective: LO1: Define the price elasticity of demand and understand how to measure it.
    AACSB Coding: Analytic Skills
    Special Feature: None

28. Suppose that when the price per case of Bullmoose beer rises from $14 to $16, the quantity demanded falls from 300 to 200 cases per week. Using the midpoint formula, what is the price elasticity of demand (in absolute value) over this range?
    A) 0.33
    B) 0.032
    C) 2
    D) 3
    Answer: D
    Diff: 3   Type: MC   Page Ref: 176/176
    Topic: The midpoint formula
    Skill: Analytical
    Objective: LO1: Define the price elasticity of demand and understand how to measure it.
    AACSB Coding: Analytic Skills
    Special Feature: None

29. If the units in which quantity demanded is measured are changed, say from gallons to quarts, then both the value of the slope and the value of price elasticity of demand curve will change.
    Answer: True   ◌ False
    Diff: 1   Type: TF   Page Ref: 178/178
    Topic: The midpoint formula
    Skill: Conceptual
    Objective: LO1: Define the price elasticity of demand and understand how to measure it.
    AACSB Coding: Reflective Thinking
    Special Feature: None

30. When quantity demanded is infinitely responsive to changes in price demand is perfectly elastic.
    Answer: ○ True   False
    Diff: 1   *Type: TF*   *Page Ref: 174/174*
    Topic: Perfectly elastic demand
    Skill: Conceptual
    Objective: LO1: Define the price elasticity of demand and understand how to measure it.
    AACSB Coding: Reflective Thinking
    Special Feature: None

31. The current price of canvas messenger bags is $36 each and sales of the bags equal 400 per week. If the price elasticity of demand is – 2.5 and the price changes to $44, how many messenger bags will be sold per week? Use the midpoint formula.
    Answer: 240 bags.
    Diff: 3   *Type: ES*   *Page Ref: 176/176*
    Topic: Price elasticity of demand
    Skill: Analytical
    Objective: LO1: Define the price elasticity of demand and understand how to measure it.
    AACSB Coding: Analytic Skills
    Special Feature: None

32. The U.S. government's focus on supply reduction efforts in its "war on drugs" has been relatively unsuccessful at addressing illegal drug use. Some economists believe that a successful anti-drug program must concentrate on reducing demand; for example, through drug education and voluntary treatment programs for addicts.
    a. Suppose the price elasticity of demand for cocaine is –0.5. What will happen to the equilibrium price, quantity and total revenue from cocaine sales if the government succeeds in its efforts to reduce demand? What is likely to happen to the incentive to sell cocaine?
    b. Suppose the government continues to concentrate its efforts on supply reduction and is able to reduce the supply of cocaine. As a result of the reduction in supply the price of cocaine increases by 25 percent. If the price elasticity of demand is –0.5, what is likely to happen to the incentive to sell cocaine?
    c. Based on your answers, explain why one approach might be preferred over the other.
    Answer: a. Since the demand is inelastic, a decrease in demand will lead to a decrease in price, quantity and total revenue. Reduced revenue is likely to deter drug trafficking.
    b. The increase in price increases revenue when demand is inelastic; this will increase the incentive to sell cocaine.
    c. If people respond to incentives, the government will have more success is reducing cocaine consumption if it uses anti-drug programs that concentrate on reducing demand rather than programs that concentrate on reducing supply.
    Diff: 3   *Type: ES*   *Page Ref: 175-9/175-9*
    Topic: Price elasticity of demand
    Skill: Analytical
    Objective: LO1: Define the price elasticity of demand and understand how to measure it.
    AACSB Coding: Reflective Thinking, Analytic Skills
    Special Feature: None

6.2 The Determinants of the Price Elasticity of Demand

1. The larger the share of a good in a consumer's budget, holding everything else constant, the
   A) more price elastic is a consumer's demand.
   B) more vertical is a consumer's demand curve.
   C) more price inelastic is a consumer's demand.
   D) more unit–elastic is a consumer's demand.
   Answer: A
   Diff: 2   Type: MC   Page Ref: 182/182
   Topic: Determinants of the price elasticity of demand
   Skill: Conceptual
   Objective: LO2: Understand the determinants of the price elasticity of demand.
   AACSB Coding: Reflective Thinking
   Special Feature: None

2. The most important determinant of the price elasticity of demand for a good is
   A) the definition of the market for a good.
   B) the availability of substitutes for the good.
   C) the share of the good in the consumer's budget.
   D) whether the good is a necessity or a luxury.
   Answer: B
   Diff: 2   Type: MC   Page Ref: 180/180
   Topic: Determinants of the price elasticity of demand
   Skill: Fact
   Objective: LO2: Understand the determinants of the price elasticity of demand.
   AACSB Coding: Reflective Thinking
   Special Feature: None

3. Which of the following statements is true?
   A) In general, if a product has few substitutes it will have an elastic demand.
   B) The more time that passes the more inelastic the demand for a product becomes.
   C) The demand curve for a necessity is more elastic than the demand curve for a luxury.
   D) The more narrowly we define a market, the more elastic the demand for a product will
      be.
   Answer: D
   Diff: 2   Type: MC   Page Ref: 182/182
   Topic: Determinants of the price elasticity of demand
   Skill: Conceptual
   Objective: LO2: Understand the determinants of the price elasticity of demand.
   AACSB Coding: Reflective Thinking
   Special Feature: None

4. Which of the following is not a determinant of a good's price elasticity of demand?
   A) The slope of the demand curve.
   B) The share of the good in the consumer's total budget.
   C) Whether the good is a luxury or a necessity.
   D) The passage of time.
   Answer: A
   Diff: 2   Type: MC   Page Ref: 181/181
   Topic: Determinants of the price elasticity of demand
   Skill: Conceptual
   Objective: LO2: Understand the determinants of the price elasticity of demand.
   AACSB Coding: Reflective Thinking
   Special Feature: None

5. If the absolute value of the price elasticity of demand for DVD movies is 0.8 then the elasticity of demand for the DVD for the Bruce Willis movie "The Sixth Sense" should be
   A) less then 0.8 in absolute value.
   B) greater than 0.8 in absolute value.
   C) equal to 1 in absolute value.
   D) equal to zero because the DVD of this movie has been out for several years.
   Answer: B
   Diff: 2   Type: MC   Page Ref: 181/181
   Topic: Determinants of the price elasticity of demand
   Skill: Conceptual
   Objective: LO2: Understand the determinants of the price elasticity of demand.
   AACSB Coding: Reflective Thinking
   Special Feature: None

6. The larger the share of a good in a consumer's budget, holding everything else constant, the
   A) more vertical is the consumer's demand curve.
   B) more price elastic is the consumer's demand curve.
   C) more price inelastic is the consumer's demand curve.
   D) more unit–price elastic is the consumer's demand curve.
   Answer: B
   Diff: 1   Type: MC   Page Ref: 182/182
   Topic: Determinants of the price elasticity of demand
   Skill: Conceptual
   Objective: LO2: Understand the determinants of the price elasticity of demand.
   AACSB Coding: Reflective Thinking
   Special Feature: None

7. Holding everything else constant, the demand for a good tends to be more elastic
    A) the more substitutes there are for the good.
    B) the shorter the time period involved.
    C) the more consumers perceive the good to be a necessity.
    D) the less important the product is in consumers' budgets.
    Answer: A
    Diff: 2   Type: MC   Page Ref: 180/180
    Topic: Determinants of the price elasticity of demand
    Skill: Conceptual
    Objective: LO2: Understand the determinants of the price elasticity of demand.
    AACSB Coding: Reflective Thinking
    Special Feature: None

8. Holding everything else constant, the absolute value of the price elasticity of demand for Saucony tennis shoes is _____ the price elasticity of demand for tennis shoes.
    A) less than
    B) equal to
    C) twice as great as
    D) greater than
    Answer: D
    Diff: 2   Type: MC   Page Ref: 182/182
    Topic: Determinants of the price elasticity of demand
    Skill: Conceptual
    Objective: LO2: Understand the determinants of the price elasticity of demand.
    AACSB Coding: Reflective Thinking
    Special Feature: None

9. Which of the following could explain why the demand for table salt is inelastic?
    A) Salt is a luxury good.
    B) Salt is a rare commodity.
    C) Households devote a very small portion of their income to salt purchases.
    D) Salt is a luxury for high income consumers but a necessity for low income consumers.
    Answer: C
    Diff: 1   Type: MC   Page Ref: 182/182
    Topic: Determinants of the price elasticity of demand
    Skill: Conceptual
    Objective: LO2: Understand the determinants of the price elasticity of demand.
    AACSB Coding: Reflective Thinking
    Special Feature: None

10. Economist Jerry Hausman estimated the price elasticity of demand for breakfast cereal. He found that
    A) the price elasticity for a particular brand of raisin bran was the same as the elasticity of demand for all family cereals.
    B) the price elasticity of demand for Post Raisin Bran is less than the price elasticity of demand for Kellogg's Raisin Bran.
    C) the price elasticity of all family breakfast cereals is greater than the price elasticity of demand for Post Rains Bran or Kellogg's Resin Bran.
    D) the price elasticity of demand for a particular brand of raisin bran was larger in absolute value than the elasticity for all family cereals.
    Answer: D
    Diff: 2   Type: MC   Page Ref: 181/181
    Topic: Determinants of the price elasticity of demand
    Skill: Fact
    Objective: LO2: Understand the determinants of the price elasticity of demand.
    AACSB Coding: Reflective Thinking
    Special Feature: Making the Connection: The Price Elasticity of Demand for Breakfast Cereal

11. Economist Jerry Hausman estimated the price elasticity of demand for "Post Resin Bran" and "All types of breakfast cereals." He found that the price elasticity of demand for Post Resin Bran was –2.5 and the price elasticity of demand for "All types of breakfast cereals" was –0.9. Which of the following can be implied from Hausman's estimates?
    A) The demand for "All types of breakfast cereals" is elastic.
    B) A 1 percent increase in the price of Post Resin Bran will lead to a 25 percent decrease in the quantity demanded of Post Resin Bran.
    C) The demand for Post Resin Bran is more elastic than the demand for "All types of breakfast cereals."
    D) A 1 percent decrease in the price of breakfast cereals will lead to a 2.5 percent increase in the quantity demanded of Post Resin Bran.
    Answer: C
    Diff: 2   Type: MC   Page Ref: 181/181
    Topic: Determinants of the price elasticity of demand
    Skill: Conceptual
    Objective: LO2: Understand the determinants of the price elasticity of demand.
    AACSB Coding: Reflective Thinking
    Special Feature: Making the Connection: The Price Elasticity of Demand for Breakfast Cereal

12. Most people buy salt infrequently and in small quantities. Even a doubling of the price of salt is likely to result in a small decline in the quantity of salt demanded. Therefore,
    A) the demand for salt will be perfectly inelastic.
    B) salt is a normal good.
    C) the demand for salt is relatively inelastic.
    D) the price elasticity of demand for salt is greater than 1 (in absolute value).
    Answer: C
    Diff: 1   Type: MC   Page Ref: 182/182
    Topic: Determinants of the price elasticity of demand
    Skill: Conceptual
    Objective: LO2: Understand the determinants of the price elasticity of demand.
    AACSB Coding: Reflective Thinking
    Special Feature: None

13.   *Table 6–2*

	Estimated Price Elasticity of Demand
Coca–Cola	–3.0
All carbonated soft drinks	–1.5
All soft drinks	–0.8

Refer to Table 6–2. Assume that an economist has estimated the price elasticity of demand values in the table below. Use the data in the table to select the correct statement.
    A) The demand for Coca–Cola is inelastic.
    B) The elasticity for "All soft drinks" is less than the elasticity for Coca–Cola because Coca–Cola is more of a luxury than a necessity; "All soft drinks" represent goods that are more necessity than luxury.
    C) The difference in elasticity values is explained by the fact that the more narrowly we define a market the more elastic the demand will be.
    D) There are fewer substitutes for "All carbonated soft drinks" than there are for "All soft drinks."
    Answer: C
    Diff: 2   Type: MC   Page Ref: 180–2/180–2
    Topic: Determinants of the price elasticity of demand
    Skill: Conceptual
    Objective: LO2: Understand the determinants of the price elasticity of demand.
    AACSB Coding: Reflective Thinking
    Special Feature: None

14. In general a "big ticket item" such as a house or new car will
    A) tend to have a more elastic demand than a lower priced good.
    B) tend to have an inelastic demand because spending on the item takes up a large share of the average consumer's budget.
    C) tend to have an inelastic demand because it has many substitutes.
    D) tend to have a more inelastic demand the more time that passes.
    Answer: A
    Diff: 2   Type: MC   Page Ref: 182/182
    Topic: Determinants of the price elasticity of demand
    Skill: Conceptual
    Objective: LO2: Understand the determinants of the price elasticity of demand.
    AACSB Coding: Reflective Thinking
    Special Feature: None

15. Jill Borts believes that the price elasticity of demand for her economics textbook is relatively inelastic. She argues "I was told I had to purchase a book written by Hubbard and O'Brien that is required by my instructor. If I wanted to buy a mystery novel I would have many authors to choose from. Therefore, the demand for mystery novels is more elastic than the demand for my textbook." Is Jill correct?
    A) The demand for the textbook is more inelastic, but Jill's reasoning is incorrect. The reason the textbook has an inelastic demand is that it is more expensive than any novel.
    B) She is correct.
    C) She is confused. She should have concluded that the textbook has a more elastic demand than a novel.
    D) She is correct that the textbook has a more inelastic demand, but that is because most students pay for their textbooks with credit or debit cards. Most people pay for novels and other books with cash or by check.
    Answer: B
    Diff: 2   Type: MC   Page Ref: 182/182
    Topic: Determinants of the price elasticity of demand
    Skill: Analytical
    Objective: LO2: Understand the determinants of the price elasticity of demand.
    AACSB Coding: Reflective Thinking
    Special Feature: None

16. The demand for The Federalist Papers is likely to be more elastic than the demand for a best-selling mystery novel.
    Answer: True   ○ False
    Diff: 2   Type: TF   Page Ref: 182/182
    Topic: Determinants of the price elasticity of demand
    Skill: Analytical
    Objective: LO2: Understand the determinants of the price elasticity of demand.
    AACSB Coding: Reflective Thinking
    Special Feature: None

17. The price elasticity of demand for Kellogg's Raisin Bran is larger in absolute value than the price elasticity for all breakfast cereals.
    Answer: ◌ True   False
    Diff: 1   Type: TF   Page Ref: 181/181
    Topic: Determinants of the price elasticity of demand
    Skill: Conceptual
    Objective: LO2: Understand the determinants of the price elasticity of demand.
    AACSB Coding: Reflective Thinking
    Special Feature: None

18. For each pair of items below determine which product would have the higher price elasticity of demand (in absolute value).
    a.   Blood pressure medicine for someone who has high blood pressure and the purchase of Clairol hair coloring product.
    b.   A new Ford Escort or a tank of gas for your current car.
    c.   A Seiko watch or watches in general.
    Answer: a.   The demand for the hair product is more price elastic (its elasticity has a higher absolute value) than the demand for blood pressure medicine. The latter is more necessity than luxury and has virtually no substitutes. There are substitutes for the Clairol hair coloring product and it is not a necessity.
        b.   The demand for a new car is more price elastic than the demand for a tank of gas for your current car. The Ford Escort: (a) has many substitutes (b) will consume a relatively large portion of your budget and (c) has a substitute – your current car. Gasoline for the car you own is more necessity than luxury.
        c.   The demand for Seiko watches is more price elastic than demand for watches in general. Narrowly defined markets (such as the Seiko watch market) have many substitutes.
    Diff: 2   Type: ES   Page Ref: 180–2/180–2
    Topic: Determinants of the price elasticity of demand
    Skill: Conceptual
    Objective: LO2: Understand the determinants of the price elasticity of demand.
    AACSB Coding: Reflective Thinking
    Special Feature: None

6.3   The Relationship between Price Elasticity of Demand and Total Revenue

1. Total revenue is equal to
    A) the amount of funds earned by a firm minus its costs of production.
    B) the total quantity sold of a product over a given period of time.
    C) the price of a product multiplied by the number of units of the product sold.
    D) the monetary value of the capital (for example, plant and equipment) a firm owns.
    Answer: C
    Diff: 1   Type: MC   Page Ref: 182/182
    Topic: Price elasticity of demand and total revenue
    Skill: Definition
    Objective: LO3: Understand the relationship between the price elasticity of demand and total revenue.
    AACSB Coding: Reflective Thinking
    Special Feature: None

2. Which of the following statements is true?
    A) Whenever a firm raises its price its total revenue will increase.
    B) When a firm lowers its price its total revenue may either increase or decrease.
    C) Whenever a firm increases its quantity sold its revenue will increase.
    D) Total revenue will equal zero when the demand for a product is unit–elastic.
Answer: B
Diff: 2   Type: MC   Page Ref: 182/182
Topic: Price elasticity of demand and total revenue
Skill: Conceptual
Objective: LO3: Understand the relationship between the price elasticity of demand and total revenue.
AACSB Coding: Reflective Thinking
Special Feature: None

3.   *Table 6–3*

Hourly Rental Rate ($)	Quantity Demanded (hours)
$60	40
75	32
80	30
100	24

Refer to Table 6–3. Katie Graham owns a kayak rental service in Santa Barbara. Table 6.3 below shows her estimated demand schedule for kayak rentals per week. She would like to increase her sales revenue by changing the price she charges for rentals. At present she charges $75. Based on the information in the table, Katie
    A) is not able to increase her revenue by changing her price because the demand for kayak rentals is unit–elastic.
    B) should lower her price to $60 to increase her revenue because the demand for kayak rentals is price elastic.
    C) should raise her price to $80 to increase her revenue because the demand for kayak rentals is price inelastic.
    D) should raise her price to earn the most revenue.
Answer: A
Diff: 3   Type: MC   Page Ref: 183–4/183–4
Topic: Price elasticity of demand and total revenue
Skill: Analytical
Objective: LO3: Understand the relationship between the price elasticity of demand and total revenue.
AACSB Coding: Analytic Skills
Special Feature: None

4. Which of the following explains why a firm would be interested in the knowing the price elasticity of demand for a good it sells?
    A) The price elasticity of demand can be used to determine the impact of changes in income on quantity sold.
    B) Knowing the price elasticity of demand allows the firm to determine how the cost of producing additional units of the good will change.
    C) Knowing the price elasticity of demand allows the firm to calculate how changes in the price of the good will affect the firm's total profit.
    D) The price elasticity of demand allows the firm to calculate how changes in the price of the good will affect the firm's total revenue.
    Answer: D
    Diff: 2   Type: MC   Page Ref: 182/182
    Topic: Price elasticity of demand and total revenue
    Skill: Conceptual
    Objective: LO3: Understand the relationship between the price elasticity of demand and total revenue.
    AACSB Coding: Reflective Thinking
    Special Feature: None

5. Opera Estate Girls' School is considering increasing its tuition to raise revenue. If the school believes that raising tuition will increase revenue
    A) it is assuming that the demand for attending the school is inelastic.
    B) it is assuming that the demand for attending the school is elastic.
    C) it is assuming that the demand for attending the school is unit–elastic.
    D) it is assuming that the demand for attending the school is perfectly elastic.
    Answer: A
    Diff: 2   Type: MC   Page Ref: 183–4/183–4
    Topic: Price elasticity of demand and total revenue
    Skill: Conceptual
    Objective: LO3: Understand the relationship between the price elasticity of demand and total revenue.
    AACSB Coding: Reflective Thinking
    Special Feature: None

6.   *Figure 6–3*

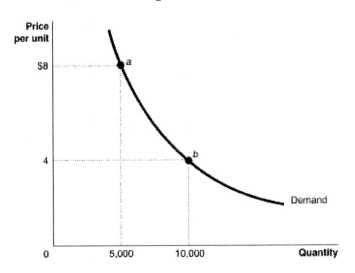

Refer to Figure 6–3. Between points a and b on the demand curve, demand is
   A) perfectly inelastic.
   B) unit–elastic.
   C) perfectly elastic.
   D) elastic.
Answer: B
Diff: 1   Type: MC   Page Ref: 185/185
Topic: Price elasticity of demand and total revenue
Skill: Conceptual
Objective: LO3: Understand the relationship between the price elasticity of demand and total revenue.
AACSB Coding: Analytic Skills
Special Feature: None

7. Assume that the market for barley is in equilibrium and the demand for barley is inelastic.
   Predict what happens to the revenue of barley farmers if a prolonged drought reduces the
   supply of barley. The drought will cause farm revenue to
   A) rise because there will be a shortage of barley.
   B) rise because the percentage decrease in quantity sold is less than the percentage
      increase in price.
   C) rise because the percentage increase in quantity sold is greater than the percentage
      increase in price.
   D) fall because of the decrease in the quantity of barley sold.
Answer: B
Diff: 3   Type: MC   Page Ref: 184/184
Topic: Price elasticity of demand and total revenue
Skill: Conceptual
Objective: LO3: Understand the relationship between the price elasticity of demand and total revenue.
AACSB Coding: Reflective Thinking
Special Feature: None

8. Assume that you own a small boutique hotel. In an attempt to raise revenue you reduce your rates by 20 percent. However, your revenue falls. What does this indicate about the demand for your boutique hotel rooms?
   A) Boutique hotel rooms are inferior goods.
   B) Demand is inelastic.
   C) The demand curve for your hotel rooms is vertical.
   D) Demand is elastic.
   Answer: D
   Diff: 2   Type: MC   Page Ref: 184–5/184/5
   Topic: Price elasticity of demand and total revenue
   Skill: Analytical
   Objective: LO3: Understand the relationship between the price elasticity of demand and total revenue.
   AACSB Coding: Reflective Thinking
   Special Feature: None

9. Which of the following statements is true?
   A) If the price of a good is lowered and total revenue decreases, demand is elastic.
   B) If the price of a good is raised and total revenue does not change, demand is perfectly elastic.
   C) If the price of a good is raised and total revenue increases, demand is inelastic.
   D) If the price of a good is lowered and total revenue increases, demand is inelastic.
   Answer: C
   Diff: 2   Type: MC   Page Ref: 184/184
   Topic: Price elasticity of demand and total revenue
   Skill: Conceptual
   Objective: LO3: Understand the relationship between the price elasticity of demand and total revenue.
   AACSB Coding: Reflective Thinking
   Special Feature: None

10. Which of the following correctly comments on the following statement? "The only way to increase the revenue from selling a product is to increase the product's price."
   A) It is not true. Revenue will increase as the price of the product increases only if demand is elastic.
   B) This statement is not true. Revenue will increase as the price of the product increases only if demand is inelastic.
   C) The statement is true.
   D) This statement is not true. Revenue will decrease as the price of the product increases because quantity demanded will fall.
   Answer: B
   Diff: 3   Type: MC   Page Ref: 184/184
   Topic: Solved Problem
   Skill: Conceptual
   Objective: LO3: Understand the relationship between the price elasticity of demand and total revenue.
   AACSB Coding: Reflective Thinking
   Special Feature: Solved Problem: Price and Revenue Don't Always Move in the Same Direction

11. In 2001 the prices of VHS movie tapes were practically identical while DVD prices for different movie titles varied considerably. What explanation can be given for this?
    A) in 2001 VHS tapes were inferior goods while DVDs were luxuries.
    B) In 2001 most VHS tapes were sold by discount retailers such as Wal–Mart; most DVDs were sold online.
    C) In 2001 the price elasticity demand for VHS tapes was inelastic; for DVDs the price elasticity of demand was elastic.
    D) In 2001 movie studies had determined their pricing strategies for VHS tapes but were unsure of the price elasticities of DVDs.
    Answer: D
    Diff: 2   Type: MC   Page Ref: 185/185
    Topic: Elasticity and economic issues
    Skill: Fact
    Objective: LO3: Understand the relationship between the price elasticity of demand and total revenue.
    AACSB Coding: Reflective Thinking
    Special Feature: Making the Connection: Determining the Price Elasticity of Demand for DVD's by Market Experiment

12. If the price elasticity of demand is unit–elastic, a 10 percent increase in price will result in a 10 percent increase in revenue.
    Answer: True   ⊙ False
    Diff: 1   Type: TF   Page Ref: 184/184
    Topic: Price elasticity of demand and total revenue
    Skill: Conceptual
    Objective: LO3: Understand the relationship between the price elasticity of demand and total revenue.
    AACSB Coding: Reflective Thinking
    Special Feature: None

13. If demand for a product is perfectly inelastic a change in price will not change total revenue.
    Answer: True   ⊙ False
    Diff: 1   Type: TF   Page Ref: 184/184
    Topic: Price elasticity of demand and total revenue
    Skill: Conceptual
    Objective: LO3: Understand the relationship between the price elasticity of demand and total revenue.
    AACSB Coding: Reflective Thinking
    Special Feature: None

14. Suppose the absolute value of the price elasticity of demand for basketball game tickets on your campus is greater than 1. Increasing ticket prices will increase the total revenue from ticket sales.
    Answer: True   ⊙ False
    Diff: 1   Type: TF   Page Ref: 184/184
    Topic: Price elasticity of demand and total revenue
    Skill: Conceptual
    Objective: LO3: Understand the relationship between the price elasticity of demand and total revenue.
    AACSB Coding: Reflective Thinking
    Special Feature: None

15. The Mass Rapid Transit (MRT) System in Hong Kong has been running significant losses. Transport Ministry officials have argued over whether to raise fares to combat the losses. One argument against a fare increase is that it will aggravate traffic congestion on the streets during peak commuter hours. Suppose that the current fare is $4 and the government is considering raising it to $6. Officials estimate that this reduces the number of rides purchased from 10,000 to 8,000 per day.

    a.   What is the estimated elasticity of demand for MRT rides?

    b.   What does this elasticity of demand suggest to you about what will happen to total revenue earned by the transit system?

    c.   Last year, the MRT system incurred a loss of $50,000 per day. Do you think the fare increase will resolve the deficit problem as well as Ministry officials anticipate? Explain.

    Answer: a.   Price elasticity = – 0.56.

            b.   Total Revenue will increase.

            c.   The expected increase in revenue is $8,000 per day. It is unlikely that the fare increase alone will resolve the problem.

Diff: 2   *Type: ES*   *Page Ref: 184–6/184–6*
Topic: Elasticity and economic issues
Skill: Analytical
Objective: LO3: Understand the relationship between the price elasticity of demand and total revenue.
AACSB Coding: Analytic Skills
Special Feature: None

16. Ali's Gyros operates near a college campus. Ali has been selling 120 gyros a day at $4.50 each and is considering a price cut. He estimates that he would be able to sell 200 gyros per day at $3.50 each.

    a.   Calculate the price elasticity of demand using the midpoint formula.

    b.   Calculate the change in revenue as a result of the price cut.

    Answer: a.   Price elasticity of demand = –2

            b.   Change in revenue = $700–$540 = $160

Diff: 2   *Type: ES*   *Page Ref: 184–6/184–6*
Topic: Elasticity and economic issues
Skill: Analytical
Objective: LO3: Understand the relationship between the price elasticity of demand and total revenue.
AACSB Coding: Analytic Skills
Special Feature: None

17. You are the manager of a theater. At present the theater charges the same admission price of $8 to all customers, regardless of age. You propose a two-tier pricing scheme: $5 for children under the age of 12 and $10 for adults. You tell your supervisor that your proposal is likely to increase revenues. What must be true about the price elasticity of demand if your proposal is to achieve its goal of raising revenue? Explain your answer.

Answer: You believe that the price elasticity of demand for theatre tickets for children is elastic. Hence, a decrease in price will increase revenue. The demand for tickets for adults is inelastic; therefore, increasing price for this group will increase revenue.

Diff: 2   Type: ES   Page Ref: 184–6/184–6
Topic: Price elasticity of demand and total revenue
Skill: Conceptual
Objective: LO3: Understand the relationship between the price elasticity of demand and total revenue.
AACSB Coding: Reflective Thinking
Special Feature: None

6.4   Other Demand Elasticities

1. The income elasticity of demand measures
   A) the responsiveness of quantity demanded to changes in income.
   B) how a consumer's purchasing power is affected by a change in the price of a product.
   C) the percentage change in the price of a product divided by the percentage change in consumer income.
   D) the income effect of a change in price.
   Answer: A
   Diff: 1   Type: MC   Page Ref: 187/187
   Topic: Income elasticity of demand
   Skill: Definition
   Objective: LO4: Define the cross–price elasticity of demand and the income elasticity of demand, and understand their determinants and how they are measured.
   AACSB Coding: Reflective Thinking
   Special Feature: None

2. If a 5 percent increase in income leads to a 10 percent increase in quantity demanded for a product this product is
   A) a necessity.
   B) a substitute for another good.
   C) a luxury.
   D) an inferior good.
   Answer: C
   Diff: 1   Type: MC   Page Ref: 187/187
   Topic: Income elasticity of demand
   Skill: Conceptual
   Objective: LO4: Define the cross–price elasticity of demand and the income elasticity of demand, and understand their determinants and how they are measured.
   AACSB Coding: Reflective Thinking
   Special Feature: None

3. If a 6 percent increase in income leads to a 4 percent increase in quantity demanded for audio books the income elasticity of demand is
   A) –0.66
   B) 1.5
   C) 2
   D) 0.66
   Answer: D
   Diff: 2   Type: MC   Page Ref: 187/187
   Topic: Income elasticity of demand
   Skill: Conceptual
   Objective: LO4: Define the cross–price elasticity of demand and the income elasticity of demand, and understand their determinants and how they are measured.
   AACSB Coding: Reflective Thinking
   Special Feature: None

4. If a 5 percent increase in income leads to a 10 percent decrease in quantity demanded for a product this product is
   A) an income elastic good
   B) an inferior good.
   C) a necessity.
   D) a luxury good.
   Answer: B
   Diff: 1   Type: MC   Page Ref: 188/188
   Topic: Income elasticity of demand
   Skill: Conceptual
   Objective: LO4: Define the cross–price elasticity of demand and the income elasticity of demand, and understand their determinants and how they are measured.
   AACSB Coding: Reflective Thinking
   Special Feature: None

5. If the quantity demanded for a good rises as income rises then the income elasticity of demand for this good is _____ than 0, and the good is _____ good.
   A) greater; an inferior
   B) less; a normal
   C) less; an inferior
   D) greater; a normal
   Answer: D
   Diff: 1   Type: MC   Page Ref: 187/187
   Topic: Income elasticity of demand
   Skill: Conceptual
   Objective: LO4: Define the cross–price elasticity of demand and the income elasticity of demand, and understand their determinants and how they are measured.
   AACSB Coding: Reflective Thinking
   Special Feature: None

6. Last year, Joan bought 50 pounds of hamburger when her household income was $40,000. This year, her household income was only $30,000 and Joan bought 60 pounds of hamburger. Holding everything else constant, Joan's income elasticity of demand for hamburger is

    A) positive, so Joan considers hamburger to be an inferior good.
    B) negative, so Joan considers hamburger to be an inferior good.
    C) positive, so Joan considers hamburger to be a normal good and a necessity.
    D) negative, so Joan considers hamburger to be a normal good.

Answer: B
Diff: 1   Type: MC   Page Ref: 188/188
Topic: Income elasticity of demand
Skill: Conceptual
Objective: LO4: Define the cross–price elasticity of demand and the income elasticity of demand, and understand their determinants and how they are measured.
AACSB Coding: Reflective Thinking
Special Feature: None

7. Which of the following items is likely to have the highest income elasticity of demand?

    A) A luxury cruise to several European countries
    B) Water
    C) Breakfast cereal
    D) A hamburger

Answer: A
Diff: 1   Type: MC   Page Ref: 187/187
Topic: Income elasticity of demand
Skill: Conceptual
Objective: LO4: Define the cross–price elasticity of demand and the income elasticity of demand, and understand their determinants and how they are measured.
AACSB Coding: Reflective Thinking
Special Feature: None

8. Suppose you are considering buying stock in the stock market, and your objective is to maximize your net worth. Furthermore, your study of the market reveals that the economy will be slowing down over the next several months. Under these conditions, it would be best to purchase stock in companies that produce

    A) normal goods.
    B) luxury goods.
    C) inferior goods.
    D) price elastic goods.

Answer: C
Diff: 3   Type: MC   Page Ref: 188/188
Topic: Income elasticity of demand
Skill: Conceptual
Objective: LO4: Define the cross–price elasticity of demand and the income elasticity of demand, and understand their determinants and how they are measured.
AACSB Coding: Reflective Thinking
Special Feature: None

9. The cross-price elasticity of demand measures the
   A) absolute change in the quantity demanded of one good divided by the absolute change in the price of another good.
   B) percentage change in the quantity demanded of one good divided by the percentage change in the price of another good.
   C) percentage change in the price of one good divided by the percentage change in the quantity demanded of another good.
   D) percentage change in the quantity demanded of one good in one location divided by the price of the same good in another location.
   Answer: B
   Diff: 2   *Type: MC*   *Page Ref: 186/186*
   Topic: Cross-price elasticity of demand
   Skill: Definition
   Objective: LO4: Define the cross-price elasticity of demand and the income elasticity of demand, and understand their determinants and how they are measured.
   AACSB Coding: Reflective Thinking
   Special Feature: None

10. The cross-price elasticity of demand between Coca-Cola and Pepsi-Cola is calculated by dividing
    A) the percentage change in quantity demanded of Coca-Cola by the percentage change in the quantity demanded of Pepsi-Cola.
    B) the percentage change in the price of Pepsi-Cola by the percentage change in quantity demanded of Coca-Cola.
    C) the percentage change in the price of Coca-Cola by the percentage change in the price of Pepsi-Cola.
    D) the percentage change in the quantity demanded of Coca-Cola by the percentage change in the price of Pepsi-Cola.
    Answer: D
    Diff: 1   *Type: MC*   *Page Ref: 186/186*
    Topic: Cross-price elasticity of demand
    Skill: Conceptual
    Objective: LO4: Define the cross-price elasticity of demand and the income elasticity of demand, and understand their determinants and how they are measured.
    AACSB Coding: Reflective Thinking
    Special Feature: None

11. In order to prove that Motrin and Ibuprofen are substitutes, one should measure the
_____ and get a _____.
    A) cross-price elasticity; positive number
    B) cross-price elasticity; negative number
    C) price elasticity of demand; number greater than1 (in absolute value)
    D) price elasticity of demand; number less than 1 (in absolute value)
    Answer: A
    Diff: 2   Type: MC   Page Ref: 186-7/186-7
    Topic: Cross-price elasticity of demand
    Skill: Conceptual
    Objective: LO4: Define the cross-price elasticity of demand and the income elasticity of demand, and understand their determinants and how they are measured.
    AACSB Coding: Reflective Thinking
    Special Feature: None

12. If the cross-price elasticity of demand between beer and wine is 0.31, then beer and wine are
    A) complements.
    B) price inelastic goods.
    C) substitutes.
    D) necessities.
    Answer: C
    Diff: 2   Type: MC   Page Ref: 187-8/187-8
    Topic: Cross-price elasticity of demand
    Skill: Conceptual
    Objective: LO4: Define the cross-price elasticity of demand and the income elasticity of demand, and understand their determinants and how they are measured.
    AACSB Coding: Reflective Thinking
    Special Feature: None

13. Which of the following pairs of good is likely to have a negative cross-price elasticity of demand?
    A) Pancakes and syrup.
    B) Hot dogs and hamburgers.
    C) Orange juice and grapefruit juice.
    D) Peanuts and cat food.
    Answer: A
    Diff: 2   Type: MC   Page Ref: 187/187
    Topic: Cross-price elasticity of demand
    Skill: Conceptual
    Objective: LO4: Define the cross-price elasticity of demand and the income elasticity of demand, and understand their determinants and how they are measured.
    AACSB Coding: Reflective Thinking
    Special Feature: None

14. When the price of tortilla chips rose by 10 percent, the quantity of tortilla chips sold fell 4 percent, and the sale of dips (like salsa and bean dip) also fell 8 percent. This set of facts indicates that
    A) the cross–price elasticity between tortilla chips and dips is 0.8, so the two are substitutes.
    B) the cross–price elasticity between tortilla chips and dips is - 0.4, so the two are complements.
    C) the cross–price elasticity between tortilla chips and dips is - 0.8, so the two are complements.
    D) the cross–price elasticity between tortilla chips and dips is 0.4, so the two are substitutes.
    Answer: C
    Diff: 2   Type: MC   Page Ref: 187/187
    Topic: Cross–price elasticity of demand
    Skill: Analytical
    Objective: LO4: Define the cross–price elasticity of demand and the income elasticity of demand, and understand their determinants and how they are measured.
    AACSB Coding: Analytic Skills
    Special Feature: None

15. Suppose the cross–price elasticity of demand between DVDs at Amazon.com and DVDs at Buy.com is 3.5. Based on this information, predict what happens when Amazon.com lowers its DVD prices by 10 percent.
    A) The quantity of DVDs demanded on Amazon.com will increase by 35 percent.
    B) The quantity of DVDs demanded on Buy.com will increase by 35 percent.
    C) The quantity of DVDs demanded on Amazon.com will decrease by 35 percent.
    D) The quantity of DVDs demanded on Buy.com will decrease by 35 percent.
    Answer: D
    Diff: 2   Type: MC   Page Ref: 187/187
    Topic: Cross–price elasticity of demand
    Skill: Conceptual
    Objective: LO4: Define the cross–price elasticity of demand and the income elasticity of demand, and understand their determinants and how they are measured.
    AACSB Coding: Reflective Thinking
    Special Feature: None

16. During an economic expansion as consumer incomes rise, holding everything else constant,
    A) the demand for most goods, except luxuries, will rise.
    B) the demand for luxuries will rise while the demand for inferior goods will fall.
    C) the demand for luxuries and inferior goods will rise.
    D) the prices of luxuries will fall while the prices of inferior goods will rise.
    Answer: B
    Diff: 1   Type: MC   Page Ref: 187/187
    Topic: Income elasticity of demand
    Skill: Conceptual
    Objective: LO4: Define the cross–price elasticity of demand and the income elasticity of demand, and understand their determinants and how they are measured.
    AACSB Coding: Reflective Thinking
    Special Feature: None

17. Studies show that the income elasticity of demand for wine is 5.03 and the income elasticity of demand for spirits is 1.21. This indicates that
    A) wine and spirits are luxury goods.
    B) wine is a luxury good and spirits are inferior goods.
    C) wine and spirits are highly price elastic.
    D) wine is a luxury good and spirits are necessities.
    Answer: A
    Diff: 2   Type: MC   Page Ref: 188/188
    Topic: Income elasticity of demand
    Skill: Conceptual
    Objective: LO4: Define the cross–price elasticity of demand and the income elasticity of demand, and understand their determinants and how they are measured.
    AACSB Coding: Reflective Thinking
    Special Feature: Making the Connection: Price Elasticity, Cross-Price Elasticity, and Income Elasticity in the Market for Alcoholic Beverages

18. Economists estimated that the cross–price elasticity of demand for beer and wine is 0.31 and the income elasticity of wine is 5.03. This means that
    A) beer and wine are substitutes and wine is an inferior good.
    B) beer and wine are complements and wine is a luxury good.
    C) beer and wine are substitutes and wine is a luxury good.
    D) beer and wine are complements and wine is an inferior good.
    Answer: C
    Diff: 2   Type: MC   Page Ref: 188/188
    Topic: Cross–price and income elasticities of demand
    Skill: Analytical
    Objective: LO4: Define the cross–price elasticity of demand and the income elasticity of demand, and understand their determinants and how they are measured.
    AACSB Coding: Analytic Skills
    Special Feature: Making the Connection: Price Elasticity, Cross-Price Elasticity, and Income Elasticity in the Market for Alcoholic Beverages

19. Economists estimated that the price elasticity of beer is −0.23 and the income elasticity of beer is −0.09. This means that

    A) an increase in the price of beer will increase the quantity demanded of beer and beer is a normal good.

    B) an increase in the price of beer will lead to an increase in revenue for beer sellers and beer is an inferior good.

    C) a decrease in the price of beer will lead to an increase in revenue for beer sellers and beer is an inferior good.

    D) an increase in the price of beer will lead to a decrease in the quantity demanded of beer and beer is a necessity.

Answer: B

Diff: 3   Type: MC   Page Ref: 188/188
Topic: Price and income elasticities of demand
Skill: Analytical
Objective: LO4: Define the cross-price elasticity of demand and the income elasticity of demand, and understand their determinants and how they are measured.
AACSB Coding: Analytic Skills
Special Feature: Making the Connection: Price Elasticity, Cross-Price Elasticity, and Income Elasticity in the Market for Alcoholic Beverages

20. Economists have estimated that the cross-price elasticity of demand between beer and spirits is 0.15, the income elasticity for spirits is 1.21 and the income elasticity for wine is 5.03. These elasticities mean that

    A) beer and spirits are complements, spirits and wine are luxuries.

    B) beer and spirits are normal goods, spirits and wine are luxuries.

    C) beer and spirits are complements, spirits are substitutes.

    D) beer and spirits are substitutes, spirits and wine are luxuries.

Answer: D

Diff: 2   Type: MC   Page Ref: 188/188
Topic: Cross-price and income elasticities of demand
Skill: Analytical
Objective: LO4: Define the cross-price elasticity of demand and the income elasticity of demand, and understand their determinants and how they are measured.
AACSB Coding: Analytic Skills
Special Feature: Making the Connection: Price Elasticity, Cross-Price Elasticity, and Income Elasticity in the Market for Alcoholic Beverages

21. The absolute value of the price elasticity of demand for telescopes is 1.5. Therefore, telescopes can be classified as a luxury.

Answer: True   False

Diff: 2   Type: TF   Page Ref: 187/187
Topic: Income elasticity of demand
Skill: Conceptual
Objective: LO4: Define the cross-price elasticity of demand and the income elasticity of demand, and understand their determinants and how they are measured.
AACSB Coding: Reflective Thinking
Special Feature: None

22. A recent study indicated that "Stricter college alcohol policies such as raising the price of alcohol, or banning alcohol on campus, decreases the number of students who use marijuana." This indicates that the cross price elasticity between alcohol and marijuana is positive.
    Answer: True   ⊘ False
    Diff: 2   Type: TF   Page Ref: 187/187
    Topic: Cross–price elasticity of demand
    Skill: Conceptual
    Objective: LO4: Define the cross–price elasticity of demand and the income elasticity of demand, and understand their determinants and how they are measured.
    AACSB Coding: Reflective Thinking
    Special Feature: None

23.   *Table 6–4*

Income	Prices	Quantities Purchased Good X	Quantities Purchased Good Y
$30,000	Px = $6, Py = $3	2	20
$50,000	Px = $6, Py = $4	5	10

a. Using the information below, calculate the income elasticity of demand for good X and characterize the good. Use the midpoint formula.
b. Can you calculate the income elasticity of demand for good Y? If you can, show your calculation and characterize the good. If you cannot, explain why.

Answer: a.   The income elasticity of demand for good X = 1.71. X is both a normal good and a luxury.

b.   Since both income and P_y change, you cannot calculate the income elasticity for good Y. The income elasticity can be measured if a change in income causes the quantity of Y purchased to change, holding everything else constant.

Diff: 3   Type: ES   Page Ref: 187–8/187–8
Topic: Income elasticity of demand
Skill: Analytical
Objective: LO4: Define the cross–price elasticity of demand and the income elasticity of demand, and understand their determinants and how they are measured.
AACSB Coding: Analytic Skills
Special Feature: None

24. When the price of Starbucks coffee increased by 8 percent, the quantity demanded of Peets coffee increased by 10 percent. Calculate the cross price elasticity of demand between Starbucks coffee and Peets coffee. What is the relationship between the two products?
    Answer: The cross price elasticity = 1.25. The two products are substitutes.
    Diff: 2   Type: ES   Page Ref: 186–7/186–7
    Topic: Cross-price elasticity of demand
    Skill: Analytical
    Objective: LO4: Define the cross-price elasticity of demand and the income elasticity of demand, and understand their determinants and how they are measured.
    AACSB Coding: Analytic Skills
    Special Feature: None

25. Suppose a 4 percent increase in income results in a 2 percent decrease in the quantity demanded of a good. Calculate the income elasticity of demand for the good and determine what type of good it is.
    Answer: Income elasticity of demand = – 0.5. The good is inferior.
    Diff: 2   Type: ES   Page Ref: 187/187
    Topic: Income elasticity of demand
    Skill: Conceptual
    Objective: LO4: Define the cross-price elasticity of demand and the income elasticity of demand, and understand their determinants and how they are measured.
    AACSB Coding: Analytic Skills
    Special Feature: None

6.5   Use Elasticity to Analyze the Disappearing Family Unit

1. From 1950 to 2006 the number of people who live on farms has fallen from 23 million to fewer than 3 million? Which of the following factors have contributed to this trend?
    A) Increases in the cost of farming and a desire for young adults to move to urban areas.
    B) Rapid growth in farm production and low income and price elasticities for food products.
    C) Slow growth in agricultural productivity and low income elasticites for food products.
    D) Government policies that have increased the cost of living and working on farms.
    Answer: B
    Diff: 2   Type: MC   Page Ref: 189/189
    Topic: Elasticity and economic issues
    Skill: Analytical
    Objective: LO5: Use price elasticity and income elasticity to analyze economic issues.
    AACSB Coding: Reflective Thinking
    Special Feature: None

2. Between 1950 and 2006 the number of acres devoted to wheat production in the U.S. has
   _____ and the price of wheat has _____.
   A) declined; decreased.
   B) more than doubled; increased by about 50 percent.
   C) declined; more than doubled.
   D) increased; more than doubled.
   Answer: A
   Diff: 2   Type: MC   Page Ref: 189/189
   Topic: Elasticity and economic issues
   Skill: Fact
   Objective: LO5: Use price elasticity and income elasticity to analyze economic issues.
   AACSB Coding: Reflective Thinking
   Special Feature: None

3. Between 1950 and 2006 the productivity of wheat farmers in the U.S. has more than doubled.
   This means that
   A) the amount of land and other resources devoted to wheat production has more than
      doubled.
   B) the incomes of wheat farmers have more than doubled.
   C) the total amount of wheat produced has more than doubled.
   D) the amount of wheat produced by the average farmer has more than doubled.
   Answer: D
   Diff: 2   Type: MC   Page Ref: 189/189
   Topic: Elasticity and economic issues
   Skill: Conceptual
   Objective: LO5: Use price elasticity and income elasticity to analyze economic issues.
   AACSB Coding: Reflective Thinking
   Special Feature: None

4. The paradox of American farming is
   A) the demand for imported luxury food products has risen as the demand for domestic
      food products has fallen.
   B) the demand for food has risen as the number of people who pursue farming as a career
      has fallen.
   C) food has become cheaper and more abundant as the number of farms has decreased.
   D) the amount of food produced has increased as the average farm size has fallen.
   Answer: C
   Diff: 1   Type: MC   Page Ref: 190/190
   Topic: Elasticity and economic issues
   Skill: Fact
   Objective: LO5: Use price elasticity and income elasticity to analyze economic issues.
   AACSB Coding: Reflective Thinking
   Special Feature: None

5. Since 1950 there has been a substantial increase in wheat production. The increase in production has led to a decrease in the price of wheat because of which of the following factors?
    A) The absolute value of the price elasticity of demand for wheat is less than 1 and the income elasticity of demand for wheat is greater than 1.
    B) The absolute value of the price elasticity of demand for wheat is greater than 1 and wheat is a close substitute for other food products.
    C) The absolute value of the price elasticity of demand for wheat is less than 1 and the income elasticity of demand for wheat is low.
    D) The income elasticity of demand for wheat is high and wheat is an inferior good.
    Answer: C
Diff: 3   Type: MC   Page Ref: 189/189
Topic: Elasticity and economic issues
Skill: Analytical
Objective: LO5: Use price elasticity and income elasticity to analyze economic issues.
AACSB Coding: Reflective Thinking
Special Feature: None

6. The price of wheat has fallen since 1950. Which of the following explains this price decline?
    A) The price elasticity of demand is less than 1 (in absolute value) and the income elasticity of demand for wheat is low.
    B) The price elasticity of demand is greater than 1 (in absolute value) and the income elasticity of demand for wheat is low.
    C) The price elasticity of demand is less than 1 (in absolute value) and wheat is an inferior good.
    D) The price elasticity of demand is greater than 1 (in absolute value) and the income elasticity of demand for wheat is greater than 1.
    Answer: A
Diff: 2   Type: MC   Page Ref: 189–90/189–90
Topic: Elasticity and economic issues
Skill: Conceptual
Objective: LO5: Use price elasticity and income elasticity to analyze economic issues.
AACSB Coding: Reflective Thinking
Special Feature: None

7. Assume that the price elasticity of demand for cocaine is –2.0. If legalization causes the price of cocaine to fall by 95 percent what will be the increase in the quantity of cocaine demanded?
    A) 19 percent.
    B) 1.9 percent.
    C) 0.9 percent.
    D) 190 percent
    Answer: D
Diff: 2   Type: MC   Page Ref: 190/190
Topic: Price elasticity of demand
Skill: Analytical
Objective: LO5: Use price elasticity and income elasticity to analyze economic issues.
AACSB Coding: Reflective Thinking
Special Feature: Solved Problem: Using Price Elasticity to Analyze Policy toward Illegal Drugs

8. Assume that the price elasticity of demand for cocaine is –0.02. If legalization causes the price of cocaine to fall by 95 percent what will be the increase in the quantity of cocaine demanded?
   A) 19 percent.
   B) 1.9 percent.
   C) 9 percent.
   D) 190 percent.
   Answer: B
   Diff: 2   Type: MC   Page Ref: 190/190
   Topic: Price elasticity of demand
   Skill: Analytical
   Objective: LO5: Use price elasticity and income elasticity to analyze economic issues.
   AACSB Coding: Analytic Skills
   Special Feature: Solved Problem: Using Price Elasticity to Analyze Policy toward Illegal Drugs

9. Assume that legalization of cocaine use led to a large decrease in its price and only a small increase in the quantity of cocaine demanded. Economic analysis would lead one to conclude that
   A) cocaine should be legalized because the benefits of legalization would exceed the costs.
   B) cocaine should not be legalized because the benefits are uncertain.
   C) cocaine should not be legalized on moral grounds since moral benefits and costs can't be measured.
   D) legalization is a normative issue. Economic analysis can be used to contribute to discussion of this issue but cannot decide it.
   Answer: D
   Diff: 1   Type: MC   Page Ref: 190/190
   Topic: Elasticity and economic issues
   Skill: Conceptual
   Objective: LO5: Use price elasticity and income elasticity to analyze economic issues.
   AACSB Coding: Reflective Thinking
   Special Feature: Solved Problem: Using Price Elasticity to Analyze Policy toward Illegal Drugs

10. A study of the effects of the minimum wage on employment of low–skilled workers estimated the price elasticity of demand for low–skilled workers is –0.75. Suppose that the government is considering raising the minimum wage from $6.00 per hour to $6.50 per hour. Based on this information, calculate the percentage change in the employment of low skilled workers. Use the midpoint formula.
    Answer: percent change in quantity demanded = – 6 percent.
    Diff: 3   Type: ES   Page Ref: 190/190
    Topic: Price elasticity of demand
    Skill: Analytical
    Objective: LO5: Use price elasticity and income elasticity to analyze economic issues.
    AACSB Coding: Analytic Skills
    Special Feature: None

11. The government of Bassaland is looking for new revenue sources. It is considering imposing an excise tax on two goods: palm wine and diapers. If the price elasticity of demand for the goods are –0.47 and –1.89 respectively, which good should it tax if the goal is to raise revenue? If the government wants to tax only one good, which good should it tax if the goal is to discourage consumption? Explain your answer.

    Answer: If the goal is to raise revenue, it should tax palm wine. The demand for palm wine is inelastic, so an increase in its price will result in an increase in revenue. If the goal is to discourage consumption it should tax diapers since the demand for diapers is elastic, while the demand for palm wine is inelastic.

Diff: 2   Type: ES   Page Ref: 190/190
Topic: Elasticity and economic issues
Skill: Conceptual
Objective: LO5: Use price elasticity and income elasticity to analyze economic issues.
AACSB Coding: Reflective Thinking
Special Feature: None

6.6   The Price Elasticity of Supply and Its Measurements

1. The price elasticity of supply measures
    A) the responsiveness of quantity supplied to changes in input prices.
    B) the responsiveness of quantity supplied to changes in technology.
    C) the responsiveness of quantity supplied to changes in price.
    D) a supplier's ability to produce a good in the face of scarcity.
    Answer: C
Diff: 1   Type: MC   Page Ref: 191/191
Topic: Price elasticity of supply
Skill: Definition
Objective: LO6: Define the price elasticity of supply, and understand its main determinants and how it is measured.
AACSB Coding: Reflective Thinking
Special Feature: None

2. To calculate the price elasticity of supply we divide
    A) the percentage change in price by the percentage change in quantity supplied.
    B) the percentage change in quantity supplied by the percentage change in price.
    C) rise by the run
    D) the average price by the average quantity supplied.
    Answer: B
Diff: 1   Type: MC   Page Ref: 191/191
Topic: Price elasticity of supply
Skill: Definition
Objective: LO6: Define the price elasticity of supply, and understand its main determinants and how it is measured.
AACSB Coding: Reflective Thinking
Special Feature: None

3. Suppose the supply of bicycles is price elastic. This means that
   A) consumers will respond significantly to an increase in the quantity supplied of bicycles.
   B) suppliers will increase the quantity supplied of bicycles, but not immediately.
   C) suppliers face many substitutes for bicycles.
   D) suppliers will respond significantly to changes in the price of bicycles.
   Answer: D
   Diff: 1   Type: MC   Page Ref: 192/192
   Topic: Price elasticity of supply
   Skill: Conceptual
   Objective: LO6: Define the price elasticity of supply, and understand its main determinants and how it is measured.
   AACSB Coding: Reflective Thinking
   Special Feature: None

4. If the quantity supplied of walkie-talkies increases by 5 percent when prices increase by 12 percent, then
   A) the supply of walkie-talkies is inelastic.
   B) the supply of walkie-talkies is elastic.
   C) the walkie-talkie supply curve will shift to the right.
   D) the walkie-talkie supply curve will shift to the left.
   Answer: A
   Diff: 2   Type: MC   Page Ref: 191/191
   Topic: Price elasticity of supply
   Skill: Conceptual
   Objective: LO6: Define the price elasticity of supply, and understand its main determinants and how it is measured.
   AACSB Coding: Reflective Thinking
   Special Feature: None

5. Suppose when the price of jean-jackets increased by 10 percent, the quantity supplied increased by 16 percent. Based on this information the price elasticity of supply of jean-jackets is
   A) 0.625.
   B) 6%.
   C) 1.6.
   D) 1.6%.
   Answer: C
   Diff: 2   Type: MC   Page Ref: 191/191
   Topic: Price elasticity of supply
   Skill: Analytical
   Objective: LO6: Define the price elasticity of supply, and understand its main determinants and how it is measured.
   AACSB Coding: Analytic Skills
   Special Feature: None

6. If an 8 percent decrease in the price of lobster leads to a 15 percent decrease in the quantity supplied of lobster, then the supply of lobster is
   A) unit–elastic.
   B) unitarily elastic.
   C) elastic.
   D) perfectly inelastic.
   Answer: C
   Diff: 1   Type: MC   Page Ref: 194/194
   Topic: Price elasticity of supply
   Skill: Conceptual
   Objective: LO6: Define the price elasticity of supply, and understand its main determinants and how it is measured.
   AACSB Coding: Reflective Thinking
   Special Feature: None

7. If a supply curve is a horizontal line, supply is said to be
   A) perfectly inelastic.
   B) unit–elastic.
   C) inelastic.
   D) perfectly elastic.
   Answer: D
   Diff: 1   Type: MC   Page Ref: 195/195
   Topic: Price elasticity of supply
   Skill: Conceptual
   Objective: LO6: Define the price elasticity of supply, and understand its main determinants and how it is measured.
   AACSB Coding: Reflective Thinking
   Special Feature: None

8. A supply curve that is vertical
   A) is perfectly elastic.
   B) is perfectly inelastic
   C) is impossible.
   D) has an elasticity equal to 1.
   Answer: B
   Diff: 1   Type: MC   Page Ref: 195/195
   Topic: Price elasticity of supply
   Skill: Conceptual
   Objective: LO6: Define the price elasticity of supply, and understand its main determinants and how it is measured.
   AACSB Coding: Reflective Thinking
   Special Feature: None

Table 6–5

Price ($)	Quantity demanded	Quantity supplied
$6	5,000	2,000
7	4,000	2,000
8	3,000	2,000
9	2,000	2,000
10	1,000	2,000

The town of Bloomfield is well known for its basketball team. The price of basketball game tickets is determined by market forces. Table 6–5 above shows the demand and supply schedules for basketball games tickets.

9. *Refer to Table 6–5.* What is the most distinctive feature of the supply curve?
    A) The supply curve is perfectly inelastic.
    B) The supply curve is horizontal.
    C) The supply curve is upward sloping.
    D) The supply curve is perfectly elastic.
    Answer: A
    Diff: 2   Type: MC   Page Ref: 194–5/194–5
    Topic: Price elasticity of supply
    Skill: Conceptual
    Objective: LO6: Define the price elasticity of supply, and understand its main determinants and how it is measured.
    AACSB Coding: Reflective Thinking
    Special Feature: None

10. *Refer to Table 6–5.* What is the numerical value of the price elasticity of supply?
    A) 1
    B) greater than 0 but less than 1
    C) 0
    D) greater than 1
    Answer: C
    Diff: 2   Type: MC   Page Ref: 191–3/191–3
    Topic: Price elasticity of supply
    Skill: Conceptual
    Objective: LO6: Define the price elasticity of supply, and understand its main determinants and how it is measured.
    AACSB Coding: Reflective Thinking
    Special Feature: None

11. The price elasticity of supply is usually a positive number because
    A) quantity supplied increases in response to income increases.
    B) quantity supplied increases in response to price increases.
    C) the quantity demanded usually rises when price falls and therefore suppliers would want to capitalize on this increase in demand.
    D) price rises when supply increases.

    Answer: B
    Diff: 1   Type: MC   Page Ref: 191/191
    Topic: Price elasticity of supply
    Skill: Conceptual
    Objective: LO6: Define the price elasticity of supply, and understand its main determinants and how it is measured.
    AACSB Coding: Reflective Thinking
    Special Feature: None

12. The price elasticity of supply of hot dog buns is estimated to be 1.5. Holding everything else constant, this means that a 10 percent decrease in the price of hot dog buns will cause the quantity of hot dog buns supplied to decrease by
    A) 1.5 percent.
    B) 15 percent.
    C) approximately 25 percent.
    D) approximately 5 percent.

    Answer: B
    Diff: 2   Type: MC   Page Ref: 191–3/191–3
    Topic: Price elasticity of supply
    Skill: Analytical
    Objective: LO6: Define the price elasticity of supply, and understand its main determinants and how it is measured.
    AACSB Coding: Analytic Skills
    Special Feature: None

13. Which of the following is a key determinant of the price elasticity of supply?
    A) The slope of the supply curve.
    B) The availability of substitutes in production.
    C) The available technology.
    D) The time it takes to change output in response to a change in price.

    Answer: D
    Diff: 2   Type: MC   Page Ref: 192/192
    Topic: Determinants of supply elasticity
    Skill: Conceptual
    Objective: LO6: Define the price elasticity of supply, and understand its main determinants and how it is measured.
    AACSB Coding: Reflective Thinking
    Special Feature: None

Figure 6–4

14. **Refer to Figure 6–4.** Suppose the diagram shows the supply curves for a product in the short run and in the long run. Which supply curve represents supply in the short run and which curve represents supply in the long run?

    A) S_B represents supply in the short run and S_A represents supply in the long run.

    B) Either S_A or S_B could represent supply in the short run; in the long run the supply curve must be a vertical line.

    C) Either S_A or S_B could represent supply in the long run; in the short run the supply curve must be a horizontal line.

    D) S_A represents supply in the short run and S_B represents supply in the long run.

Answer: D

Diff: 2   *Type: MC*   *Page Ref: 193/193*

Topic: Determinants of supply elasticity

Skill: Analytical

Objective: LO6: Define the price elasticity of supply, and understand its main determinants and how it is measured.

AACSB Coding: Analytic Skills

Special Feature: None

15. ***Refer to Figure 6–4.*** The diagram shows two supply curves, S_A and S_B. As price rises from P_0 to P_1, which supply curve is more elastic?

    A) S_A

    B) S_B

    C) They are equally inelastic.

    D) They are equally elastic.

    Answer: B

    Diff: 1   Type: MC   Page Ref: 193/193
    Topic: Price elasticity of supply
    Skill: Conceptual
    Objective: LO6: Define the price elasticity of supply, and understand its main determinants and how it is measured.
    AACSB Coding: Reflective Thinking
    Special Feature: None

16. Suppose the demand curve for a product is represented by a typical downward–sloping curve. Now suppose the demand for this product increases. Which of the following statements accurately predicts the resulting increase in price?

    A) The more elastic the supply curve, the greater the price increase.

    B) The more elastic the supply curve, the smaller the price increase.

    C) The increase in price is not affected by the elasticity of the supply curve.

    D) There will be no increase in price if the supply curve is perfectly inelastic.

    Answer: B

    Diff: 3   Type: MC   Page Ref: 194/194
    Topic: Price elasticity of supply
    Skill: Analytical
    Objective: LO6: Define the price elasticity of supply, and understand its main determinants and how it is measured.
    AACSB Coding: Analytic Skills
    Special Feature: None

17. The process involved in bringing oil to world markets can take years. Substitutes for oil–based products such as gasoline are limited. As a result

    A) the supply of oil is very elastic and the demand for oil is very elastic over short periods of time.

    B) the supply of oil is very inelastic and the demand for gasoline is inelastic over short periods of time.

    C) the supply of oil and the demand for oil shift to the right over short periods of time.

    D) the supply of oil and the demand for oil are both perfectly elastic over short periods of time.

    Answer: B

    Diff: 2   Type: MC   Page Ref: 192/192
    Topic: Elasticity and economic issues
    Skill: Conceptual
    Objective: LO6: Define the price elasticity of supply, and understand its main determinants and how it is measured.
    AACSB Coding: Reflective Thinking
    Special Feature: Making the Connection: Why Are Oil Prices So Unstable?

18. Shifts in the supply of oil have caused large changes in price since the 1970s because
    A) the supply of oil is very inelastic while the demand for oil is very elastic over short
       periods of time.
    B) the supply of oil is very elastic while the demand for oil is inelastic over short periods
       of time.
    C) both the supply of oil and the demand for oil are inelastic over short periods of time.
    D) the supply of oil and the demand for oil are perfectly elastic over short periods of time.
    Answer: C
    Diff: 2   Type: MC   Page Ref: 192/192
    Topic: Elasticity and economic issues
    Skill: Conceptual
    *Objective: LO6: Define the price elasticity of supply, and understand its main determinants and how it is
    measured.*
    AACSB Coding: Reflective Thinking
    Special Feature: Making the Connection: Why Are Oil Prices So Unstable?

19. Which of the following statements is true?
    A) The supply of oil is very elastic over short time periods but becomes perfectly inelastic
       over time. A given shift in supply results in a greater increase in the price of oil when
       the supply of oil is perfectly inelastic.
    B) The supply of oil is very inelastic over short time periods but becomes more elastic
       over time. A given shift in supply results in a smaller increase in the price of oil when
       the supply is more elastic.
    C) The supply of oil is perfectly inelastic; therefore, as the demand for oil increases over
       time the price of oil increases significantly.
    D) Over short periods of time increases in the demand for oil are greater than increases in
       the supply of oil. Over the long run increases in the demand and the supply of oil are
       about equal. As a result, the price of oil increases greatly in the short run but is stable
       in the long run.
    Answer: B
    Diff: 2   Type: MC   Page Ref: 192/192
    Topic: Elasticity and economic issues
    Skill: Conceptual
    *Objective: LO6: Define the price elasticity of supply, and understand its main determinants and how it is
    measured.*
    AACSB Coding: Reflective Thinking
    Special Feature: Making the Connection: Why Are Oil Prices So Unstable?

20. Borders Group Inc., a large book retailer, discontinued its Holiday Savings Rewards program in 2007. The program offered customers who spent at least $200 at Borders stores by mid-November a discount on future purchases through the Christmas season. Why did Borders discontinue this program?

   A) The demand for books purchased during the Christmas season was inelastic.
   B) In recent years people have bought fewer books as Christmas presents. This decline in demand reduced the appeal of Holiday Savings Program and made it unprofitable for Borders.
   C) Discount programs offered by competitors, such as Amazon.com, can be used year-round. Borders decided to offer its own year-round discount program.
   D) The supply of books during the Christmas season is inelastic; as a result, Borders had difficulty keeping popular books in stock when customers wanted to take advantage of the Holiday Savings Rewards program.

   Answer: A
   Diff: 3   Type: MC   Page Ref: 198/198
   Topic: Price elasticity of demand and total revenue
   Skill: Analytical
   Objective: LO3: Understand the relationship between the price elasticity of demand and total revenue.
   AACSB Coding: Reflective Thinking, Analytic Skills
   Special Feature: An Inside Look: Borders Slashes Buyer Rewards, Cuts Discounts

21. Barry Mays placed an order for *Harry Potter and the Deathly Hallows* with Amazon.com before the book's publication date. Barry read all of the previous Harry Potter books and was anxious to read *Deathly Hallows* as soon as he could. Margaret Shoner read all of the Harry Potter books too, but was willing to wait until she could buy a paperback edition of *Deathly Hallows*. From this information we can say that Barry's demand for *Deathly Hallows*

   A) was more elastic than Margaret's.
   B) was perfectly inelastic, while Margaret's demand for the book was perfectly elastic.
   C) was more inelastic than Margaret's. Therefore, we can say that the book was a necessity for Barry and a luxury for Margaret.
   D) was more inelastic than Margaret's.

   Answer: D
   Diff: 3   Type: MC   Page Ref: 196/196
   Topic: Price elasticity of demand
   Skill: Analytical
   Objective: LO2: Understand the determinants of the price elasticity of demand.
   AACSB Coding: Reflective Thinking, Analytic Skills
   Special Feature: Economics in YOUR Life!: How Much Do Book Prices Matter to You?

22. There are a limited number of original Picasso paintings. This means that the supply of original Picasso paintings is perfectly inelastic.
   Answer: ◉ True   False
   Diff: 1   Type: TF   Page Ref: 194/194
   Topic: Price elasticity of supply
   Skill: Conceptual
   Objective: LO6: Define the price elasticity of supply, and understand its main determinants and how it is measured.
   AACSB Coding: Reflective Thinking
   Special Feature: None

23. For a given demand curve, will there be a greater loss of economic efficiency from a binding price floor when supply is elastic or inelastic? Illustrate your answer with a demand and supply graph. In your graph you must show two supply curves, one elastic and the other inelastic.

Answer:

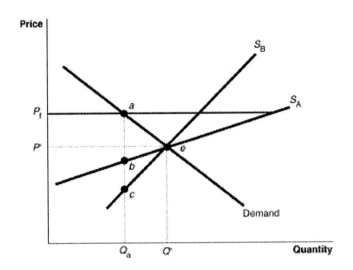

See the figure above. S_A is the elastic supply curve, and S_B the inelastic supply curve. For a given demand curve, a binding price floor at P_f creates a greater loss of economic efficiency when supply is inelastic rather than elastic. This can be seen from the diagram: When the supply curve is S_A (elastic) the loss in economic efficiency is represented by the area *abe* while the loss in economic efficiency is represented by the area *ace* when the supply curve is S_A (inelastic).

Diff: 3   Type: ES   Page Ref: 194/194
Topic: Price elasticity of supply
Skill: Analytical
Objective: LO6: Define the price elasticity of supply, and understand its main determinants and how it is measured.
AACSB Coding: Analytic Skills
Special Feature: None

24. Suppose the current price of oil is $60 a barrel and the quantity supplied is 800 million barrels per day. If the price elasticity of the supply of oil in the short run is estimated at 0.5, use the midpoint formula to calculate the percentage change in quantity supplied when the price of oil rises to $68 a barrel.

Answer: The percentage change in quantity supplied = 6.25 percent.

Diff: 3   Type: ES   Page Ref: 194/194
Topic: Price elasticity of supply
Skill: Analytical
Objective: LO6: Define the price elasticity of supply, and understand its main determinants and how it is measured.
AACSB Coding: Analytic Skills
Special Feature: None

Chapter 7 Firms, the Stock Market, and Corporate Governance

7.1 Types of Firms

1. Which of the following must a firm in a market economy do today to succeed?
    A) Produce the goods and services that consumers want at a lower cost than consumers themselves can produce.
    B) Organize the factors of production into a functioning, efficient unit.
    C) Have access to sufficient funds.
    D) Market firms today must do all of these things.
    Answer: D
    Diff: 1   Type: MC   Page Ref: 210/210
    Topic: Firms
    Skill: Conceptual
    Objective: LO1: Categorize the major types of firms in the United States
    AACSB Coding: Reflective Thinking
    Special Feature: None

2. How has organizing a successful firm in a market economy changed over the last century?
    A) It has become easier as more and more firms discover how to do it.
    B) As government intervention has decreased, firms now have more freedom.
    C) There has been no change one way or the other over the last century.
    D) It has become more difficult to organize an efficient and successful firm.
    Answer: D
    Diff: 1   Type: MC   Page Ref: 210/210
    Topic: Firms
    Skill: Conceptual
    Objective: LO1: Categorize the major types of firms in the United States
    AACSB Coding: Reflective Thinking
    Special Feature: None

3. Larry Page and Sergey Brin sold shares of ownership in Google to the public in 2004. The price of shares of stock in Google's initial public offering was determined by
    A) an automated online auction.
    B) the Federal Reserve.
    C) Google's board of directors.
    D) the president of the New York Stock Exchange.
    Answer: A
    Diff: 1   Type: MC   Page Ref: 208/208
    Topic: Corporations
    Skill: Factual
    Objective: LO1: Categorize the major types of firms in the United States
    AACSB Coding: Reflective Thinking
    Special Feature: Chapter Opener: Google: From Dorm Room to Wall Street

4. What type of business is the easiest to set up?
   A) sole proprietorship
   B) partnership
   C) corporation
   D) There is no difference in the ease of establishment.
   Answer: A
   Diff: 2   Type: MC   Page Ref: 210/210
   Topic: Types of firms
   Skill: Conceptual
   Objective: LO1: Categorize the major types of firms in the United States
   AACSB Coding: Reflective Thinking
   Special Feature: None

5. Which type of business is the most difficult to set up?
   A) sole proprietorship
   B) partnership
   C) corporation
   D) There is no difference in the difficulty of establishment.
   Answer: C
   Diff: 2   Type: MC   Page Ref: 210/210
   Topic: Types of firms
   Skill: Conceptual
   Objective: LO1: Categorize the major types of firms in the United States
   AACSB Coding: Reflective Thinking
   Special Feature: None

6. Which type of business has the most government rules and regulations affecting it?
   A) sole proprietorship
   B) partnership
   C) corporation
   D) They all have the same set of rules and regulations affecting them.
   Answer: C
   Diff: 1   Type: MC   Page Ref: 210/210
   Topic: Types of firms
   Skill: Factual
   Objective: LO1: Categorize the major types of firms in the United States
   AACSB Coding: Reflective Thinking
   Special Feature: None

7. Which type of business has the least government rules and regulations affecting it?
    A) sole proprietorship
    B) partnership
    C) corporation
    D) They all have the same set of rules and regulations affecting them.
    Answer: A
    Diff: 1   Type: MC   Page Ref: 210/210
    Topic: Types of firms
    Skill: Factual
    Objective: LO1: Categorize the major types of firms in the United States
    AACSB Coding: Reflective Thinking
    Special Feature: None

8. What is the primary difference between a sole proprietorship and a partnership?
    A) Proprietorships have unlimited liability while partnerships have limited liability.
    B) Partnerships can issue stocks and bonds while proprietorships cannot.
    C) Partnerships have more owners than do proprietorships.
    D) There is no real difference between the two types of firms.
    Answer: C
    Diff: 1   Type: MC   Page Ref: 210/210
    Topic: Types of firms
    Skill: Definition
    Objective: LO1: Categorize the major types of firms in the United States
    AACSB Coding: Reflective Thinking
    Special Feature: None

9. How do a sole proprietorship and a corporation differ?
    A) Proprietorships have unlimited liability while corporations have limited liability.
    B) Corporations can issue stocks and bonds, while proprietorships cannot.
    C) Corporations face more taxes than do proprietorships.
    D) All of these are differences between the two types of businesses.
    Answer: D
    Diff: 1   Type: MC   Page Ref: 210/210
    Topic: Types of firms
    Skill: Definition
    Objective: LO1: Categorize the major types of firms in the United States
    AACSB Coding: Reflective Thinking
    Special Feature: None

10. Assume you set up a sole proprietorship and your lawyer tells you that as the owner you will face unlimited liability. What does that mean?
    A) You are liable for organizing the business.
    B) You could stand to lose your personal wealth if the business goes bankrupt.
    C) There is no legal responsibility of the business in case a customer sues, as the business is legally untouchable.
    D) None of these explain what unlimited liability means.
    Answer: B
    Diff: 1   Type: MC   Page Ref: 210/210
    Topic: Liability
    Skill: Definition
    Objective: LO1: Categorize the major types of firms in the United States
    AACSB Coding: Reflective Thinking
    Special Feature: None

11. Who controls a sole proprietorship?
    A) stockholders
    B) bondholders
    C) the owner
    D) all of these
    Answer: C
    Diff: 1   Type: MC   Page Ref: 210/210
    Topic: Proprietorship
    Skill: Conceptual
    Objective: LO1: Categorize the major types of firms in the United States
    AACSB Coding: Reflective Thinking
    Special Feature: None

12. Who owns a corporation?
    A) the board of directors
    B) the stockholders
    C) the employees
    D) the CEO
    Answer: B
    Diff: 1   Type: MC   Page Ref: 210/210
    Topic: Corporations
    Skill: Conceptual
    Objective: LO1: Categorize the major types of firms in the United States
    AACSB Coding: Reflective Thinking
    Special Feature: None

13. How does the owner of a sole proprietorship relate to the business?
    A) The owner and the business are separate legal entities.
    B) The owner and the business are not separate legal entities.
    C) The assets of the owner are considered separate from the asset of the business.
    D) None of these describe the legal relationship of the owner to the business.
    Answer: B
    Diff: 1   Type: MC   Page Ref: 210/210
    Topic: Types of business
    Skill: Conceptual
    Objective: LO1: Categorize the major types of firms in the United States
    AACSB Coding: Reflective Thinking
    Special Feature: None

14. The world-famous insurance company, Lloyd's of London, is an example of a company that is set up as a(n)
    A) partnership.
    B) corporation.
    C) sole proprietorship.
    D) individually owned business.
    Answer: A
    Diff: 2   Type: MC   Page Ref: 211/211
    Topic: Proprietorship and partnership
    Skill: Factual
    Objective: LO1: Categorize the major types of firms in the United States
    AACSB Coding: Reflective Thinking
    Special Feature: Making the Connection: What's in a "Name"? Lloyds of London Learns about Unlimited Liability the Hard Way

15. Because the company Lloyd's of London was set up as a partnership, owners of the company face
    A) limited liability.
    B) unlimited liability.
    C) stockholder remorse.
    D) negative economic profits.
    Answer: B
    Diff: 1   Type: MC   Page Ref: 211/211
    Topic: Liability
    Skill: Conceptual
    Objective: LO1: Categorize the major types of firms in the United States
    AACSB Coding: Reflective Thinking
    Special Feature: Making the Connection: What's in a "Name"? Lloyds of London Learns about Unlimited Liability the Hard Way

16. How does the owner of a corporation relate to the business?
    A) The owners of the business have a separate legal distinction from the business.
    B) The owners of the business have no separate legal distinction from the business.
    C) The personal assets are part of the corporation's assets.
    D) None of these describe the legal relationship of corporate owners to the business.
    Answer: A
    Diff: 2   Type: MC   Page Ref: 211/211
    Topic: Corporations
    Skill: Conceptual
    Objective: LO1: Categorize the major types of firms in the United States
    AACSB Coding: Reflective Thinking
    Special Feature: None

17. What does limited liability mean?
    A) The owners of the business are personally responsible for paying expenses incurred by the business.
    B) Only employees can have a claim on the assets of the business.
    C) The personal assets of the owners cannot be claimed if the business is bankrupt.
    D) Anybody with a liability against a firm can claim only what their liability refers to.
    Answer: C
    Diff: 1   Type: MC   Page Ref: 210/210
    Topic: Limited liability
    Skill: Definition
    Objective: LO1: Categorize the major types of firms in the United States
    AACSB Coding: Reflective Thinking
    Special Feature: None

18. Which of the following is not an advantage of starting a new business as a proprietorship?
    A) The owner has complete control over the business.
    B) Few government rules and regulations to comply with.
    C) Business profits are only taxed once, not twice.
    D) Ease of attaining additional funding.
    Answer: D
    Diff: 2   Type: MC   Page Ref: 210/210
    Topic: Business types
    Skill: Conceptual
    Objective: LO1: Categorize the major types of firms in the United States
    AACSB Coding: Reflective Thinking
    Special Feature: None

19. Jeremy is thinking of starting up a small business selling NASCAR memorabilia. He is considering setting up his business as a sole proprietorship. What is one advantage to Jeremy of setting up his business as a sole proprietorship?
    A) As a sole proprietor, Jeremy would face limited liability.
    B) As a sole proprietor, Jeremy would have the ability to share risk with shareholders.
    C) As a sole proprietor, Jeremy would have both ownership and control over the business.
    D) All of the above would be advantages of setting up his business as a sole proprietorship.

    Answer: C
    Diff: 2   Type: MC   Page Ref: 210/210
    Topic: Business types
    Skill: Conceptual
    Objective: LO1: Categorize the major types of firms in the United States
    AACSB Coding: Reflective Thinking
    Special Feature: None

20. Jeremy is thinking of starting up a small business selling NASCAR memorabilia. He asks his friend, Carmen, if she'd like to join him in setting up a partnership to start the business. What is one disadvantage in joining the partnership that Carmen should consider?
    A) Carmen should realize that profits in the partnership will be reduced by dividend payments to shareholders.
    B) Carmen should realize that, as an owner of the business, she will be personally responsible for the business' debts.
    C) Carmen should realize that the profits of the business will also be taxed as dividend income, so she faces the potential for double taxation of that business income.
    D) Carmen should realize that the Jeremy will have complete control over the business because it was his idea.

    Answer: B
    Diff: 2   Type: MC   Page Ref: 210/210
    Topic: Business types
    Skill: Conceptual
    Objective: LO1: Categorize the major types of firms in the United States
    AACSB Coding: Reflective Thinking
    Special Feature: None

21. Which of the following is not an advantage of starting a new business as a corporation?
    A) Separation of ownership and business liability.
    B) Enhanced ability to raise funds.
    C) Ability to share risks.
    D) Possibility of double taxation.

    Answer: D
    Diff: 2   Type: MC   Page Ref: 211/211
    Topic: Business types
    Skill: Conceptual
    Objective: LO1: Categorize the major types of firms in the United States
    AACSB Coding: Reflective Thinking
    Special Feature: None

22. Which of the following is an advantage of starting a new business as a corporation?
    A) Double taxation
    B) Ease in setting up.
    C) Low expenses of legally organizing.
    D) Greater ability to raise funds.
    Answer: D
    Diff: 2   Type: MC   Page Ref: 211/211
    Topic: Corporations
    Skill: Conceptual
    Objective: LO1: Categorize the major types of firms in the United States
    AACSB Coding: Reflective Thinking
    Special Feature: None

23. How are corporate profits taxed in the United States?
    A) Earnings are taxed first by state sales taxes and then as corporate profits at the Federal level.
    B) Earnings are taxed first as personal income then as corporate profits at the Federal level.
    C) Earnings are taxed first as corporate profits then as personal income after dividends are paid.
    D) Corporate profits are not taxed at all.
    Answer: C
    Diff: 2   Type: MC   Page Ref: 211/211
    Topic: Corporate taxes
    Skill: Factual
    Objective: LO1: Categorize the major types of firms in the United States
    AACSB Coding: Reflective Thinking
    Special Feature: None

24. What is the most common type of business?
    A) corporations
    B) partnerships
    C) sole proprietorships
    D) They are equally represented because of Federal laws.
    Answer: C
    Diff: 1   Type: MC   Page Ref: 210/210
    Topic: Types of business
    Skill: Factual
    Objective: LO1: Categorize the major types of firms in the United States
    AACSB Coding: Reflective Thinking
    Special Feature: None

25. Which is the least common type of business?
    A) corporations
    B) partnerships
    C) sole proprietorships
    D) Impossible to determine without further information.
    Answer: B
    Diff: 2   Type: MC   Page Ref: 210/210
    Topic: Types of business
    Skill: Factual
    Objective: LO1: Categorize the major types of firms in the United States
    AACSB Coding: Reflective Thinking
    Special Feature: None

26. Which type of businesses earns the majority of revenues in the United States?
    A) corporations
    B) partnerships
    C) sole proprietorships
    D) none of these
    Answer: A
    Diff: 2   Type: MC   Page Ref: 211/211
    Topic: Types of business
    Skill: Factual
    Objective: LO1: Categorize the major types of firms in the United States
    AACSB Coding: Reflective Thinking
    Special Feature: None

27. Which type of businesses earns the majority of profits in the United States?
    A) corporations
    B) partnerships
    C) sole proprietorships
    D) none of these
    Answer: A
    Diff: 2   Type: MC   Page Ref: 212/212
    Topic: Business types
    Skill: Factual
    Objective: LO1: Categorize the major types of firms in the United States
    AACSB Coding: Reflective Thinking
    Special Feature: None

28. Who controls a sole proprietorship?
    A) owner
    B) stockholders
    C) bondholders
    D) employees
    Answer: A
    Diff: 1   Type: MC   Page Ref: 210/210
    Topic: Business types
    Skill: Definition
    Objective: LO1: Categorize the major types of firms in the United States
    AACSB Coding: Reflective Thinking
    Special Feature: None

29. When a business is set up as a sole proprietorship, the owner of the business faces limited liability.
    Answer: True   ◎ False
    Diff: 1   Type: TF   Page Ref: 210/210
    Topic: Business types
    Skill: Factual
    Objective: LO1: Categorize the major types of firms in the United States
    AACSB Coding: Reflective Thinking
    Special Feature: None

30. The only type of business that faces unlimited liability is a sole proprietorship.
    Answer: True   ◎ False
    Diff: 2   Type: TF   Page Ref: 210/210
    Topic: Business types
    Skill: Factual
    Objective: LO1: Categorize the major types of firms in the United States
    AACSB Coding: Reflective Thinking
    Special Feature: None

31. In the United States, corporate profits are taxed at the corporate level and then are taxed again as personal income in the form of dividend payments.
    Answer: ◎ True   False
    Diff: 1   Type: TF   Page Ref: 211/211
    Topic: Business types
    Skill: Factual
    Objective: LO1: Categorize the major types of firms in the United States
    AACSB Coding: Reflective Thinking
    Special Feature: None

32. Define a sole proprietorship.
    Answer: A firm owned by one person.
    Diff: 1   Type: SA   Page Ref: 210/210
    Topic: Proprietorship
    Skill: Definition
    Objective: LO1: Categorize the major types of firms in the United States
    AACSB Coding: Reflective Thinking
    Special Feature: None

33. How do unlimited and limited liability differ?
    Answer: Unlimited liability means that if a firm is bankrupt, lenders can take the owner's personal wealth. Limited liability means that the owner can lose only what is invested in the firm.
    Diff: 1   Type: SA   Page Ref: 210/210
    Topic: Liability
    Skill: Definition
    Objective: LO1: Categorize the major types of firms in the United States
    AACSB Coding: Reflective Thinking
    Special Feature: None

34. What are the advantages of setting up a proprietorship or partnership as opposed to a corporation?
    Answer: Ease of formation and owners have control.
    Diff: 2   Type: SA   Page Ref: 211/211
    Topic: Proprietorship and partnership
    Skill: Conceptual
    Objective: LO1: Categorize the major types of firms in the United States
    AACSB Coding: Reflective Thinking
    Special Feature: None

35. What type of business has the potential for double taxation of profits and why?
    Answer: Corporations earn profits that are taxed at the corporate level and, after dividends are paid to stockholders, then are taxed as personal income.
    Diff: 2   Type: SA   Page Ref: 211/211
    Topic: Corporations
    Skill: Conceptual
    Objective: LO1: Categorize the major types of firms in the United States
    AACSB Coding: Reflective Thinking
    Special Feature: None

7.2   The Structure of Corporations and the Principle-Agent Problem

1. What is an inside director?
    A) A movie director who also appears in the movie.
    B) Member of a corporate board of directors that is also a manager of the business.
    C) The CEO that is selected by the corporation's board of directors.
    D) A board of director chair who has been in the job for at least three years.
    Answer: B
    Diff: 2   Type: MC   Page Ref: 213/213
    Topic: Corporate control
    Skill: Definition
    Objective: LO2: Describe the typical management structure of corporations and understand the concepts of separation of ownership from control and the principal–agent problem.
    AACSB Coding: Reflective Thinking
    Special Feature: None

2. The way in which a corporation is structured and the impact a corporation's structure has on the firm's behavior is referred to as

    A) corporate taxation

    B) structure composition theory

    C) structural behavior

    D) corporate governance

Answer: D

Diff: 1   Type: MC   Page Ref: 212/212
Topic: Corporations
Skill: Definition
Objective: LO2: Describe the typical management structure of corporations and understand the concepts of separation of ownership from control and the principal-agent problem.
AACSB Coding: Reflective Thinking
Special Feature: None

3. Who operates and controls a corporation in its day–to–day activities?

    A) board of directors

    B) stockholders

    C) employees

    D) management

Answer: D

Diff: 2   Type: MC   Page Ref: 213/213
Topic: Corporations
Skill: Conceptual
Objective: LO2: Describe the typical management structure of corporations and understand the concepts of separation of ownership from control and the principal-agent problem.
AACSB Coding: Reflective Thinking
Special Feature: None

4. Who hires the managers of a corporation?

    A) board of directors

    B) stockholders

    C) managers

    D) employees

Answer: A

Diff: 2   Type: MC   Page Ref: 213/213
Topic: Corporations
Skill: Factual
Objective: LO2: Describe the typical management structure of corporations and understand the concepts of separation of ownership from control and the principal-agent problem.
AACSB Coding: Reflective Thinking
Special Feature: None

5. Who owns a corporation?
    A) board of directors
    B) stockholders
    C) hired managers
    D) none of these
    Answer: B
    Diff: 1   Type: MC   Page Ref: 213/213
    Topic: Corporations
    Skill: Factual
    Objective: LO2: Describe the typical management structure of corporations and understand the concepts
    of separation of ownership from control and the principal–agent problem.
    AACSB Coding: Reflective Thinking
    Special Feature: None

6. Who selects the board of directors of a corporation?
    A) The state where the corporation is chartered.
    B) employees
    C) stockholders
    D) managers
    Answer: C
    Diff: 2   Type: MC   Page Ref: 213/213
    Topic: Corporate control
    Skill: Factual
    Objective: LO2: Describe the typical management structure of corporations and understand the concepts
    of separation of ownership from control and the principal–agent problem.
    AACSB Coding: Reflective Thinking
    Special Feature: None

7. What do economists call the situation where a hired manager does not have the same
   interests as the owners of the business?
    A) conquest and control
    B) financial problem
    C) principal–agent problem
    D) financial intermediary problem
    Answer: C
    Diff: 1   Type: MC   Page Ref: 213/213
    Topic: Corporate control
    Skill: Definition
    Objective: LO2: Describe the typical management structure of corporations and understand the concepts
    of separation of ownership from control and the principal–agent problem.
    AACSB Coding: Reflective Thinking
    Special Feature: None

8. In many corporations, there is "separation of ownership from control." What does this mean?
    A) The shareholders control the corporation, although the board of directors owns the corporation.
    B) The managers of the corporation run the corporation, although the shareholders own the corporation.
    C) The board of directors controls corporate operations, although the managers of the corporation own the corporation.
    D) Top corporate managers only make decisions that have been approved unanimously by shareholders.
    Answer: B
    Diff: 1   Type: MC   Page Ref: 213/213
    Topic: Corporate control
    Skill: Definition
    Objective: LO2: Describe the typical management structure of corporations and understand the concepts of separation of ownership from control and the principal–agent problem.
    AACSB Coding: Reflective Thinking
    Special Feature: None

9. By tying the salaries of top corporate managers to the price of the corporation's stock, corporations hope to avoid
    A) corporate governance.
    B) conflict between the CFO and the CEO.
    C) the principal–agent problem.
    D) paying high salaries to their managers.
    Answer: C
    Diff: 2   Type: MC   Page Ref: 213/213
    Topic: Principal–agent
    Skill: Conceptual
    Objective: LO2: Describe the typical management structure of corporations and understand the concepts of separation of ownership from control and the principal–agent problem.
    AACSB Coding: Reflective Thinking
    Special Feature: None

10. What can be done to deal with the principal–agent problem?
    A) Threaten to liquidate the firm.
    B) Link top manager salaries to the profits of the firm or the price of the firm's stock.
    C) Have the CEO be a rotating position.
    D) Forbid managers from owning any company stock.
    Answer: B
    Diff: 2   Type: MC   Page Ref: 213/213
    Topic: Corporate control
    Skill: Conceptual
    Objective: LO2: Describe the typical management structure of corporations and understand the concepts of separation of ownership from control and the principal–agent problem.
    AACSB Coding: Reflective Thinking
    Special Feature: None

11. The existence of the principal-agent problem
    A) increases the risk of buying stock in a corporation.
    B) increases the risk of becoming the sole proprietor of a business.
    C) implies that managers that have the same incentives as the board of directors.
    D) does all of the above.
    Answer: A
    Diff: 2   Type: MC   Page Ref: 225/225
    Topic: Principal-agent
    Skill: Conceptual
    Objective: LO2: Describe the typical management structure of corporations and understand the concepts
    of separation of ownership from control and the principal-agent problem.
    AACSB Coding: Reflective Thinking
    Special Feature: Economics in YOUR Life!: Is It Risky to Own Stock?

12. Corporate managers and shareholders always have the same goals.
    Answer: True   ○ False
    Diff: 1   Type: TF   Page Ref: 213/213
    Topic: Principal-agent
    Skill: Conceptual
    Objective: LO2: Describe the typical management structure of corporations and understand the concepts
    of separation of ownership from control and the principal-agent problem.
    AACSB Coding: Reflective Thinking
    Special Feature: None

13. The principal-agent problem that exists between shareholders and managers also exists
    between managers and workers.
    Answer: ○ True   False
    Diff: 1   Type: TF   Page Ref: 213/213
    Topic: Principal-agent
    Skill: Conceptual
    Objective: LO2: Describe the typical management structure of corporations and understand the concepts
    of separation of ownership from control and the principal-agent problem.
    AACSB Coding: Reflective Thinking
    Special Feature: Solved Problem: Does the Principles-Agent Problem Apply to the Relationship Between
    Managers and Workers?

14. Who decides who controls a corporation?
    Answer: Stockholders elect a board of directors that controls the corporation.
    Diff: 2   Type: SA   Page Ref: 213/213
    Topic: Corporations
    Skill: Factual
    Objective: LO1: Categorize the major types of firms in the United States
    AACSB Coding: Reflective Thinking
    Special Feature: None

15. Explain what potential conflict exists between shareholders in a corporation and the corporation's managers.

    Answer: The "principal-agent problem" exists anytime an agent pursues his or her own interests instead of the interests of the principal who hired them. In the context of corporations, this can occur if hired managers might not have the same set of goals that corporate owners have.

    Diff: 2   Type: SA   Page Ref: 213/213
    Topic: Principal–agent
    Skill: Definition
    Objective: LO2: Describe the typical management structure of corporations and understand the concepts of separation of ownership from control and the principal–agent problem.
    AACSB Coding: Reflective Thinking
    Special Feature: None

16. How does the principal-agent problem extend to managers and employees?

    Answer: Just as corporate shareholders (owners) cannot consistently monitor managers, managers cannot always monitor employees of the corporation. As a result, corporate employees may not have the same goals as their managers.

    Diff: 2   Type: SA   Page Ref: 213/213
    Topic: Principal–agent
    Skill: Conceptual
    Objective: LO2: Describe the typical management structure of corporations and understand the concepts of separation of ownership from control and the principal–agent problem.
    AACSB Coding: Reflective Thinking
    Special Feature: Solved Problem: Does the Principles-Agent Problem Apply to the Relationship Between Managers and Workers?

17. Scott is a manager at a pool cleaning business. He has hired 10 workers to clean pools for him and is considering what type of payment scheme he should set up for his workers. He can pay each of his workers each $10 per hour to clean pools, or he can pay his workers $20 for each pool a worker cleans. (It takes 2 hours, on average, for an employee to clean a pool thoroughly.)   If Scott wants to maximize the number of pools his workers clean in one day, which payment scheme should he use? Explain.

    Answer: If Scott wants to maximize the number of pools his workers clean in one day, he should pay them $20 for each pool so that workers also will have an incentive to clean as many pools as possible. However, if the workers are rushing through cleaning pools, it is likely that the pools will not be cleaned as thoroughly.

    Diff: 2   Type: SA   Page Ref: 213/213
    Topic: Principal–agent
    Skill: Analytical
    Objective: LO2: Describe the typical management structure of corporations and understand the concepts of separation of ownership from control and the principal–agent problem.
    AACSB Coding: Analytic Skills
    Special Feature: Solved Problem: Does the Principles-Agent Problem Apply to the Relationship Between Managers and Workers?

7.3   How Firms Raise Funds

1. How can a proprietorship or partnership raise funds for expansion?
    A) Borrow from someone or an institution willing to lend the funds.
    B) Reinvest profit back into the business.
    C) Take on a partner or more partners.
    D) Any of these would generate funds for expansion.
    Answer: D
    Diff: 2   Type: MC   Page Ref: 214/214
    Topic: Fund raising
    Skill: Conceptual
    Objective: LO3: Explain how firms obtain the funds they need to operate and expand.
    AACSB Coding: Reflective Thinking
    Special Feature: None

2. What is the central role of financial intermediaries in a market economy?
    A) The creation and printing of money.
    B) Keeping the price level stable.
    C) Bringing together savers and borrowers.
    D) Providing safe deposit boxes for people and businesses.
    Answer: C
    Diff: 2   Type: MC   Page Ref: 215/215
    Topic: Financial intermediaries
    Skill: Definition
    Objective: LO3: Explain how firms obtain the funds they need to operate and expand.
    AACSB Coding: Reflective Thinking
    Special Feature: None

3. What takes place in the indirect finance market?
    A) Part ownership of corporations is sold in the form of stocks.
    B) Corporate and government bonds are sold to savers.
    C) Deposits of savers are accepted and loans made to borrowers.
    D) Government purchases of buildings and equipment are sold to the highest bidder.
    Answer: C
    Diff: 2   Type: MC   Page Ref: 215/215
    Topic: Financial intermediaries
    Skill: Definition
    Objective: LO3: Explain how firms obtain the funds they need to operate and expand.
    AACSB Coding: Reflective Thinking
    Special Feature: None

4. Which of the following does not take place in the direct finance market?
    A) Ownership in corporations is sold in the form of common stock.
    B) Deposits from savers are accumulated and loans made to borrowers.
    C) Ownership in corporations is sold in the form of preferred stock.
    D) Corporate bonds are sold to savers.
Answer: B
Diff: 2   Type: MC   Page Ref: 215/215
Topic: Finance market
Skill: Conceptual
Objective: LO3: Explain how firms obtain the funds they need to operate and expand.
AACSB Coding: Reflective Thinking
Special Feature: None

5. If Abercrombie & Fitch borrows $8 million from a bank to finance the construction of a new store, this is an example of
    A) a stock market transaction
    B) direct finance
    C) a bond market transaction
    D) indirect finance
Answer: D
Diff: 2   Type: MC   Page Ref: 217/217
Topic: Financial markets
Skill: Conceptual
Objective: LO3: Explain how firms obtain the funds they need to operate and expand.
AACSB Coding: Analytic Skills
Special Feature: None

6. If Abercrombie & Fitch wants to raise $8 million to finance the construction of a new store, and the company wishes to raise the funds through direct finance. Which of the following methods could it use?
    A) It could sell $8 million in bonds.
    B) It could borrow $8 million from a bank.
    C) It could issue $8 million in stocks.
    D) It could choose either A or C.
Answer: D
Diff: 2   Type: MC   Page Ref: 215/215
Topic: Financial markets
Skill: Conceptual
Objective: LO3: Explain how firms obtain the funds they need to operate and expand.
AACSB Coding: Analytic Skills
Special Feature: None

7. What is different about buying stocks and buying bonds?
    A) A stock can possibly pay dividends forever, but bonds have a fixed number of payments.
    B) Differences of opinion about a stock's future may vary considerably but there is less difference about a bond's future.
    C) The future growth of a stock is more uncertain than the payments of a bond.
    D) All these are differences between stocks and bonds.
Answer: D
Diff: 2   Type: MC   Page Ref: 215/215
Topic: Stocks vs. bonds
Skill: Conceptual
Objective: LO3: Explain how firms obtain the funds they need to operate and expand.
AACSB Coding: Reflective Thinking
Special Feature: None

8. Which of the following is a characteristic of a bond?
    A) A promise to repay a fixed amount of funds.
    B) The face value or principal plus interest is repaid at a specified period of time.
    C) The length of coupon payments is fixed by the stated maturity period.
    D) All of these are characteristic of bonds.
Answer: D
Diff: 2   Type: MC   Page Ref: 215/215
Topic: Bonds
Skill: Conceptual
Objective: LO3: Explain how firms obtain the funds they need to operate and expand.
AACSB Coding: Reflective Thinking
Special Feature: None

9. If a corporate bond with face value of $1,000 has an interest rate of eight percent paid once a year for a term of 30 years, what is the size of the coupon payment?
    A) $1,000
    B) $300
    C) $80
    D) $8
Answer: C
Diff: 2   Type: MC   Page Ref: 215/215
Topic: Bonds
Skill: Analytical
Objective: LO3: Explain how firms obtain the funds they need to operate and expand.
AACSB Coding: Analytic Skills
Special Feature: None

10. If a corporate bond with a face value of $2,000 pays coupon payments yearly of $50, what is the coupon rate?
    A) 4%
    B) 2.5%
    C) 25%
    D) 40%
    Answer: A
    Diff: 2   *Type: MC*   *Page Ref: 215/215*
    Topic: Bonds
    Skill: Analytical
    Objective: LO3: Explain how firms obtain the funds they need to operate and expand.
    AACSB Coding: Analytic Skills
    Special Feature: None

11. When an investor buys a corporate bond,
    A) the investor becomes part owner of the corporation.
    B) the principal of the bond is a loan to the corporation.
    C) the interest made on the bond represents the bondholder's limited liability in the company.
    D) the face value of the bond is equal to what the investor paid for the bond.
    Answer: B
    Diff: 2   *Type: MC*   *Page Ref: 215/215*
    Topic: Bonds
    Skill: Conceptual
    Objective: LO3: Explain how firms obtain the funds they need to operate and expand.
    AACSB Coding: Reflective Thinking
    Special Feature: None

12. The coupon rate of a bond is equal to
    A) the coupon payment.
    B) the interest payment.
    C) the interest rate.
    D) the face value.
    Answer: B
    Diff: 2   *Type: MC*   *Page Ref: 215/215*
    Topic: Bonds
    Skill: Analytical
    Objective: LO3: Explain how firms obtain the funds they need to operate and expand.
    AACSB Coding: Reflective Thinking
    Special Feature: None

13. If a corporation earns a profit, how do owners of the firm share in the profit?
    A) Coupon payments on that firm's bonds.
    B) Dividend payments on shares of that firm's stock.
    C) By selling any bonds or stocks owned and realizing a capital gain.
    D) By raising the interest rate on bonds.
    Answer: B
    Diff: 2   Type: MC   Page Ref: 215/215
    Topic: Stocks
    Skill: Conceptual
    Objective: LO3: Explain how firms obtain the funds they need to operate and expand.
    AACSB Coding: Reflective Thinking
    Special Feature: None

14. If a corporation retains all its profits and distributes none of the profit to owners, how can owners benefit?
    A) If the retained earnings are expected to create future profits, the market price of the firm's stock will increase and create a capital gain for stockholders if the stock is sold.
    B) Shares of stock can be converted into bonds so stockholders will be able to earn coupon payments.
    C) Owners will only benefit if some profits are paid out in the form of dividends.
    D) By changing the board of directors.
    Answer: A
    Diff: 2   Type: MC   Page Ref: 215/215
    Topic: Fund raising
    Skill: Conceptual
    Objective: LO3: Explain how firms obtain the funds they need to operate and expand.
    AACSB Coding: Reflective Thinking
    Special Feature: None

15. If a corporation goes bankrupt, which of the following has first claim on the firm's assets?
    A) stockholders
    B) the state where chartered
    C) employees
    D) bondholders
    Answer: D
    Diff: 2   Type: MC   Page Ref: 215/215
    Topic: Corporations
    Skill: Factual
    Objective: LO3: Explain how firms obtain the funds they need to operate and expand.
    AACSB Coding: Reflective Thinking
    Special Feature: None

16. What is a primary market?
    A) Where primary inputs like steel are sold.
    B) A market where you can sell any bonds you own as a private investor.
    C) Where a newly issued claims are sold to initial buyers by the borrowing firm.
    D) Where you can sell any stocks you own as a private investor.

Answer: C
Diff: 2   Type: MC   Page Ref: 216/216
Topic: Primary market
Skill: Definition
Objective: LO3: Explain how firms obtain the funds they need to operate and expand.
AACSB Coding: Reflective Thinking
Special Feature: None

17. What happens in the secondary market?
    A) Secondary inputs like electricity are sold.
    B) A corporate financial manager will raise funds for expansion of the firm.
    C) Newly issued claims are sold by the borrowing firm to the initial buyer.
    D) Already issued claims are sold from one investor to another.

Answer: D
Diff: 1   Type: MC   Page Ref: 216/216
Topic: Secondary market
Skill: Conceptual
Objective: LO3: Explain how firms obtain the funds they need to operate and expand.
AACSB Coding: Reflective Thinking
Special Feature: None

18. When you buy previously–issued shares of Google stock, this transaction takes place in the
    A) primary market
    B) bond market
    C) secondary market
    D) bear market

Answer: C
Diff: 1   Type: MC   Page Ref: 216/216
Topic: Secondary market
Skill: Conceptual
Objective: LO3: Explain how firms obtain the funds they need to operate and expand.
AACSB Coding: Reflective Thinking
Special Feature: Don't Let This Happen to YOU!: When Google Shares Change hands, Google Doesn't Get the Money

19. Which of the following is part of the secondary market?
    A) New York Stock Exchange
    B) the over–the–counter market
    C) NASDAQ
    D) all of these
    Answer: D
    Diff: 2   Type: MC   Page Ref: 216/216
    Topic: Secondary market
    Skill: Conceptual
    Objective: LO3: Explain how firms obtain the funds they need to operate and expand.
    AACSB Coding: Reflective Thinking
    Special Feature: None

20. When the coupon rate on newly issued bonds increases relative to older, outstanding bonds, what happens?
    A) The market price of the older bond falls in the secondary market.
    B) The market price of the older bond rises in the secondary market.
    C) Older bonds can still be sold at their face value.
    D) Older bonds will sell for less than their face value.
    Answer: A
    Diff: 2   Type: MC   Page Ref: 215/215
    Topic: Market price
    Skill: Conceptual
    Objective: LO3: Explain how firms obtain the funds they need to operate and expand.
    AACSB Coding: Reflective Thinking
    Special Feature: None

21. You have a bond that pays $60 per year in coupon payments. Which of the following would result in an increase in the price of your bond?
    A) Coupon payments on newly–issued bonds rise to $80 per year.
    B) The likelihood that the firm issuing your bond will default on debt increases.
    C) The price of a share of stock in the company falls.
    D) Coupon payments on newly–issued bonds fall to $50 per year.
    Answer: D
    Diff: 2   Type: MC   Page Ref: 215/215
    Topic: Bond market pricing
    Skill: Conceptual
    Objective: LO3: Explain how firms obtain the funds they need to operate and expand.
    AACSB Coding: Reflective Thinking
    Special Feature: None

22. A stock's dividend yield is determined by
    A) dividing the dividend payment by the stock's initial price.
    B) dividing the dividend payment by the stock's closing market price.
    C) dividing the stock's closing market price by the dividend payment.
    D) subtracting the stock's initial purchase price from the stocks' closing market price on a given day.

    Answer: B
    Diff: 2   Type: MC   Page Ref: 215/215
    Topic: Dividend yield
    Skill: Analytical
    Objective: LO3: Explain how firms obtain the funds they need to operate and expand.
    AACSB Coding: Reflective Thinking
    Special Feature: None

23. What do the highest stock price and the lowest stock price over the previous year indicate?
    A) Add them together and divide by two to get the stock's current market price.
    B) What the stock's price–earnings ratio is.
    C) How volatile the stock's market price has been.
    D) They generate the dividend yield

    Answer: C
    Diff: 2   Type: MC   Page Ref: 217/217
    Topic: Stocks
    Skill: Conceptual
    Objective: LO3: Explain how firms obtain the funds they need to operate and expand.
    AACSB Coding: Reflective Thinking
    Special Feature: None

24. How is a stock's price–earnings ratio found?
    A) by dividing the dividend by the closing price of the stock.
    B) by dividing the dividend by the firm's earnings per share.
    C) by dividing current market price of the stock by the firm's earnings per share.
    D) by subtracting the firm's earnings per share from the closing price of the stock.

    Answer: C
    Diff: 2   Type: MC   Page Ref: 217/217
    Topic: Stock quote
    Skill: Analytical
    Objective: LO3: Explain how firms obtain the funds they need to operate and expand.
    AACSB Coding: Reflective Thinking
    Special Feature: None

25. In June 2007 General Motors (GM) posted a price–earnings ratio of 9.84. If the price of the stock at that time was $36 per share, which of the following must have been true?
    A) GM's revenues that month were $366 million.
    B) GM's earnings per share was 3.66
    C) GM's coupon payment was $35 per year.
    D) GM's dividend yield for the year was 26%.
    Answer: B
    Diff: 2   Type: MC   Page Ref: 217/217
    Topic: Earnings per share
    Skill: Analytical
    Objective: LO3: Explain how firms obtain the funds they need to operate and expand.
    AACSB Coding: Analytic Skills
    Special Feature: None

26. What are earnings per share equal to?
    A) The last dividend payment made.
    B) Total dividend payments plus retained earnings divided by outstanding stock shares.
    C) The amount by which the stock's market price has increased in the last year.
    D) Revenues divided by the number of stockholders.
    Answer: B
    Diff: 2   Type: MC   Page Ref: 217/217
    Topic: Earnings per share
    Skill: Definition
    Objective: LO3: Explain how firms obtain the funds they need to operate and expand.
    AACSB Coding: Reflective Thinking
    Special Feature: None

27. What is current yield?
    A) The dividend of the stock divided by its closing market price.
    B) A bond's coupon payment divided by the bond's current price.
    C) The size of the capital gain on either a stock or bond.
    D) A warning to be cautious when investing in a particular stock or bond.
    Answer: B
    Diff: 1   Type: MC   Page Ref: 217/217
    Topic: Current yield
    Skill: Definition
    Objective: LO3: Explain how firms obtain the funds they need to operate and expand.
    AACSB Coding: Reflective Thinking
    Special Feature: None

28. In 2007, the dividend yield on General Motors (GM) stock fell from 8.6% to 4.4%. Which of the following would have generated that result?

   A) The closing price of GM stock fell.

   B) GM announced a decrease in the dividend it would pay per share.

   C) The price–earnings ratio rose.

   D) GM issued bonds with a coupon rate equal to 8%.

   Answer: B

   Diff: 3   Type: MC   Page Ref: 217/217
   Topic: Dividend yield
   Skill: Analytical
   Objective: LO3: Explain how firms obtain the funds they need to operate and expand.
   AACSB Coding: Reflective Thinking
   Special Feature: Making the Connection: Following Abercrombie & Fitch's Stock Price in the Financial Pages

29. How can a corporation raise funds needed for expansion?

   A) by selling bonds

   B) by issuing stock

   C) by borrowing from financial institutions

   D) All of the above allow corporations to raise funds needed for firm expansion.

   Answer: D

   Diff: 1   Type: MC   Page Ref: 214/214
   Topic: Fund raising
   Skill: Conceptual
   Objective: LO3: Explain how firms obtain the funds they need to operate and expand.
   AACSB Coding: Reflective Thinking
   Special Feature: None

30. If you purchase a share of stock from your friend who initially purchased the stock three years ago, your purchase of the stock represents a transaction in the primary financial market

   Answer: True   ◉ False

   Diff: 1   Type: TF   Page Ref: 216/216
   Topic: Secondary market
   Skill: Conceptual
   Objective: LO2: Describe the typical management structure of corporations and understand the concepts of separation of ownership from control and the principal–agent problem.
   AACSB Coding: Reflective Thinking
   Special Feature: None

31. Direct finance includes the sale by a corporation of stocks or bonds, but does not include borrowing money from a bank.

   Answer: ◉ True   False

   Diff: 2   Type: TF   Page Ref: 215/215
   Topic: Fund raising
   Skill: Conceptual
   Objective: LO3: Explain how firms obtain the funds they need to operate and expand.
   AACSB Coding: Reflective Thinking
   Special Feature: None

32. How can a sole proprietorship raise funds needed for firm expansion?
    Answer: By retaining earnings, taking on partners, or borrowing from relatives, friends, or a
        bank.
    Diff: 1   Type: SA   Page Ref: 214/214
    Topic: Proprietorship
    Skill: Conceptual
    Objective: LO3: Explain how firms obtain the funds they need to operate and expand.
    AACSB Coding: Reflective Thinking
    Special Feature: None

33. What is a corporate bond and what does it specify?
    Answer: A bond is a promise to repay a fixed amount of funds with the coupon interest rate,
        the face value of the bond, and the maturity period specified.
    Diff: 2   Type: SA   Page Ref: 215/215
    Topic: Bonds
    Skill: Definition
    Objective: LO3: Explain how firms obtain the funds they need to operate and expand.
    AACSB Coding: Reflective Thinking
    Special Feature: None

34. Who is the seller in a primary market and who is the seller in a secondary market?
    Answer: The corporation issuing a bond or a stock is the seller in a primary market, while
        anyone who holds a stock or bond can sell in the secondary market.
    Diff: 2   Type: SA   Page Ref: 216/216
    Topic: Financial markets
    Skill: Conceptual
    Objective: LO3: Explain how firms obtain the funds they need to operate and expand.
    AACSB Coding: Reflective Thinking
    Special Feature: None

35. If you own a bond with a seven percent coupon rate and new bonds are paying five percent,
    what will happen to your bond's market price?
    Answer: It will go up.
    Diff: 3   Type: SA   Page Ref: 215/215143
    Topic: Bonds
    Skill: Conceptual
    Objective: LO3: Explain how firms obtain the funds they need to operate and expand.
    AACSB Coding: Analytic Skills
    Special Feature: None

36. What role do well functioning financial markets play in a market economy?
    Answer: They allocate saved funds to the best use of these funds.
    Diff: 2   Type: SA   Page Ref: 215/215
    Topic: Financial markets
    Skill: Conceptual
    Objective: LO3: Explain how firms obtain the funds they need to operate and expand.
    AACSB Coding: Reflective Thinking
    Special Feature: None

7.4   Using Financial Statements to Evaluate a Corporation

1. What are liabilities?
    A) Anything of value owned by a person or a business.
    B) Anything a person or a business owes to entities outside the business.
    C) The total cost of labor for a firm.
    D) Only those unpaid expenses for which a business or person is making interest
        payments
    Answer: B
    Diff: 1   Type: MC   Page Ref: 220/220
    Topic: Liabilities
    Skill: Definition
    Objective: LO4: Understand the information provided in corporations' financial statements.
    AACSB Coding: Reflective Thinking
    Special Feature: None

2. Although China's savings rate is much higher than most other nations, the country's
    financial system is in trouble because
    A) banks are not regulated by the Chinese government.
    B) the percentage of nonperforming loans granted by the financial system has decreased
        over time.
    C) loans are sometimes made for political reasons, not based on profit expectations.
    D) the costs of government regulations that require accounting transparency have
        prohibited banks from making profits on loans.
    Answer: C
    Diff: 2   Type: MC   Page Ref: 219/219
    Topic: Financial markets
    Skill: Conceptual
    Objective: LO4: Understand the information provided in corporations' financial statements.
    AACSB Coding: Multicultural and Diversity
    Special Feature: Making the Connection: A Bull in China's Financial Shop

3. Which of the following is an example of an implicit cost a firm might incur?
    A) The out-of-pocket expense to hire resources.
    B) Taxes owed to the state and Federal governments.
    C) The rental value of the office space the company owns and uses for itself.
    D) The revenue a firm generates in using its resources.
    Answer: C
    Diff: 2   Type: MC   Page Ref: 220/220
    Topic: Costs
    Skill: Conceptual
    Objective: LO4: Understand the information provided in corporations' financial statements.
    AACSB Coding: Reflective Thinking
    Special Feature: None

4. What is economic profit?
    A) Gross revenue minus explicit costs.
    B) Gross revenue minus implicit costs.
    C) Gross revenue minus explicit and implicit costs.
    D) The same as accounting profit.
Answer: C
Diff: 1   Type: MC   Page Ref: 221/221
Topic: Economic profit
Skill: Definition
Objective: LO4: Understand the information provided in corporations' financial statements.
AACSB Coding: Reflective Thinking
Special Feature: None

5. Which of the following would explain why accounting profit might be greater than economic profit?
    A) A firm has implicit costs as well as explicit costs.
    B) A firm has only explicit costs.
    C) A firm's net income is greater than its accounting profit.
    D) A firm's net income is less than its accounting profit.
Answer: A
Diff: 2   Type: MC   Page Ref: 221/221
Topic: Economic profit
Skill: Conceptual
Objective: LO4: Understand the information provided in corporations' financial statements.
AACSB Coding: Reflective Thinking
Special Feature: None

6. The minimum amount that investors must earn on the funds they invest in a firm, expressed as a percentage of the amount invested, is referred to as
    A) the explicit costs of production
    B) net worth
    C) net income
    D) a normal rate of return
Answer: D
Diff: 2   Type: MC   Page Ref: 221/221
Topic: Profit
Skill: Definition
Objective: LO4: Understand the information provided in corporations' financial statements.
AACSB Coding: Reflective Thinking
Special Feature: None

7. Laura's Pizza Place incurs $800,000 per year in explicit costs and $100,000 in implicit costs. The restaurant earns $1.3 million in revenues and has $5 million in net worth. Based on this information, what is economic profit for Laura's Pizza Place?
    A) $200,000
    B) $500,000
    C) $400,000
    D) $2.8 million
Answer: C
Diff: 2   Type: MC   Page Ref: 221/221
Topic: Economic profit
Skill: Analytical
Objective: LO4: Understand the information provided in corporations' financial statements.
AACSB Coding: Analytic Skills
Special Feature: None

8. Laura's Pizza Place incurs $800,000 per year in explicit costs and $100,000 in implicit costs. The restaurant earns $1.3 million in revenues. Based on this information, what is accounting profit for Laura's Pizza Place?
    A) $200,000
    B) $500,000
    C) $400,000
    D) $900,000
Answer: B
Diff: 2   Type: MC   Page Ref: 220/220
Topic: Profit
Skill: Analytical
Objective: LO4: Understand the information provided in corporations' financial statements.
AACSB Coding: Analytic Skills
Special Feature: None

9. Jake sells Star Wars memorabilia on eBay. His annual revenue is $42,000 per year, and the explicit costs of his business are $10,000. What is his accounting profit?
    A) $10,000
    B) $42,000
    C) $32,000
    D) $22,000
Answer: C
Diff: 1   Type: MC   Page Ref: 220/220
Topic: Profit
Skill: Analytical
Objective: LO4: Understand the information provided in corporations' financial statements.
AACSB Coding: Analytic Skills
Special Feature: None

10. Jake sells Star Wars memorabilia on eBay. His annual revenue is $42,000 per year, the explicit costs of his business are $10,000, and the opportunity costs of his business are $18,000 per year. What are the implicit costs of his business?

    A) $32,000

    B) $8,000

    C) $18,000

    D) $24,000

    Answer: C

    Diff: 3   Type: MC   Page Ref: 220/220

    Topic: Costs

    Skill: Analytical

    Objective: LO4: Understand the information provided in corporations' financial statements.

    AACSB Coding: Analytic Skills

    Special Feature: None

11. Jake sells Star Wars memorabilia on eBay. His annual revenue is $42,000 per year, the explicit costs of his business are $10,000, and the economic costs of his business are $18,000 per year. What is his economic profit?

    A) $24,000

    B) $32,000

    C) $34,000

    D) $14,000

    Answer: A

    Diff: 3   Type: MC   Page Ref: 221/221

    Topic: Profit

    Skill: Analytical

    Objective: LO4: Understand the information provided in corporations' financial statements.

    AACSB Coding: Analytic Skills

    Special Feature: None

12. A firm's accounting profit is also its

    A) economic profit

    B) income statement

    C) net income

    D) statement of liabilities

    Answer: C

    Diff: 1   Type: MC   Page Ref: 220/220

    Topic: Profit

    Skill: Conceptual

    Objective: LO4: Understand the information provided in corporations' financial statements.

    AACSB Coding: Reflective Thinking

    Special Feature: None

13. A nonmonetary opportunity cost is called a(n) _____, while a cost that involves spending money is called a(n) _____.
    A) accounting cost; explicit cost
    B) implicit cost; explicit cost
    C) accounting profit; economic profit
    D) normal rate of return; asset
    Answer: B
    Diff: 1   Type: MC   Page Ref: 220/220
    Topic: Costs
    Skill: Definition
    Objective: LO4: Understand the information provided in corporations' financial statements.
    AACSB Coding: Reflective Thinking
    Special Feature: None

14. Which of the following would be considered an implicit cost of operating a business?
    A) advertising expenses
    B) wages paid to workers
    C) a normal rate of return for investors
    D) any explicit cost
    Answer: C
    Diff: 3   Type: MC   Page Ref: 221/221
    Topic: Costs
    Skill: Definition
    Objective: LO4: Understand the information provided in corporations' financial statements.
    AACSB Coding: Reflective Thinking
    Special Feature: None

15. What is shown on a firm's income statement?
    A) costs
    B) profits
    C) revenues
    D) All of these are shown on a firm's income statement.
    Answer: D
    Diff: 1   Type: MC   Page Ref: 220/220
    Topic: Income statement
    Skill: Definition
    Objective: LO4: Understand the information provided in corporations' financial statements.
    AACSB Coding: Reflective Thinking
    Special Feature: None

16. A firm's net worth is calculated as
    A) the difference between a firm's revenues and explicit costs
    B) the difference between a firm's revenues and implicit costs
    C) the difference between a firm's assets and liabilities
    D) the difference between a firm's liabilities and outstanding equities
    Answer: C
    Diff: 1   Type: MC   Page Ref: 220/220
    Topic: Balance sheet
    Skill: Definition
    Objective: LO4: Understand the information provided in corporations' financial statements.
    AACSB Coding: Reflective Thinking
    Special Feature: None

17. Accounting profit is the difference between a firm's revenue and its opportunity costs.
    Answer: True   ◌ False
    Diff: 1   Type: TF   Page Ref: 220/220
    Topic: Profit
    Skill: Definition
    Objective: LO4: Understand the information provided in corporations' financial statements.
    AACSB Coding: Reflective Thinking
    Special Feature: None

18. An increase in liabilities will reduce a firm's net worth.
    Answer: ◌ True   False
    Diff: 1   Type: TF   Page Ref: 220/220
    Topic: Liabilities
    Skill: Conceptual
    Objective: LO4: Understand the information provided in corporations' financial statements.
    AACSB Coding: Reflective Thinking
    Special Feature: None

19. What is the difference between explicit and implicit costs?
    Answer: Explicit costs are out-of-pocket expenditures for resources hired from outside the
            firm while implicit costs are opportunity costs for using firm-owned resources.
    Diff: 2   Type: SA   Page Ref: 220/220
    Topic: Costs
    Skill: Conceptual
    Objective: LO3: Explain how firms obtain the funds they need to operate and expand.
    AACSB Coding: Reflective Thinking
    Special Feature: None

20. How is economic profit found?
    Answer: Economic profits equals total revenues minus explicit and implicit costs.
    Diff: 2   Type: SA   Page Ref: 221/221
    Topic: Profit
    Skill: Definition
    Objective: LO4: Understand the information provided in corporations' financial statements.
    AACSB Coding: Reflective Thinking
    Special Feature: None

7.5   Corporate Governance Policy

1. Why do corporations want to keep the price of their stock high?
    A) A higher stock price increases the funds the firm can raise when it sells a given amount of stock
    B) Corporations can pay their managers lower salaries and avoid principal–agent problems when stock prices are higher.
    C) Higher stock prices are correlated with lower expected profitability.
    D) All of the above provide incentive for corporations to keep the price of their stock high.
    Answer: A
    Diff: 2   Type: MC   Page Ref: 222/222
    Topic: Corporate control
    Skill: Conceptual
    Objective: LO5: Understand the role of government in corporate governance.
    AACSB Coding: Reflective Thinking
    Special Feature: None

2. The financial statements of firms generally are audited by
    A) employees of the firm being audited.
    B) employees of private accounting firms.
    C) employees of the federal government.
    D) the board of directors of the corporation being audited.
    Answer: B
    Diff: 2   Type: MC   Page Ref: 222/222
    Topic: Financial statements
    Skill: Conceptual
    Objective: LO5: Understand the role of government in corporate governance.
    AACSB Coding: Reflective Thinking
    Special Feature: None

3. In 2002, the Enron corporation was accused of falsifying information regarding liabilities on Enron's balance sheets, thereby
    A) increasing Enron's assets on the balance sheet.
    B) reducing Enron's profit on the balance sheet.
    C) increasing Enron's net worth on the balance sheet.
    D) reducing Enron's net income on the income statement.
    Answer: C
    Diff: 2   Type: MC   Page Ref: 222/222
    Topic: Financial statements
    Skill: Factual
    Objective: LO5: Understand the role of government in corporate governance.
    AACSB Coding: Analytic Skills
    Special Feature: None

4. David Myers, former controller for WorldCom, pleaded guilty to falsely reported costs for WorldCom that were _____ than they actually were, resulting in reported accounting profits for WorldCom that were _____ than their actual level.
   A) higher; higher
   B) lower; higher
   C) lower; lower
   D) higher; lower
   Answer: B
   Diff: 1   Type: MC   Page Ref: 222/222
   Topic: Financial statements
   Skill: Factual
   Objective: LO5: Understand the role of government in corporate governance.
   AACSB Coding: Reflective Thinking
   Special Feature: None

5. In response to accounting scandals in 2002, the federal government passed what legislation requiring that corporate directors have a certain level of expertise with financial information and mandating that chief executive officers personally certify the accuracy of financial statements?
   A) The Accountant Reliability Act
   B) the 24th amendment to the Constitution
   C) Kennedy–Lott Act
   D) Sarbanes–Oxley Act
   Answer: D
   Diff: 1   Type: MC   Page Ref: 222/222
   Topic: Financial statements
   Skill: Factual
   Objective: LO5: Understand the role of government in corporate governance.
   AACSB Coding: Reflective Thinking
   Special Feature: None

6. The Sarbanes–Oxley Act of 2002 was passed in response to what event?
   A) a series of accounting scandals
   B) unexpected increases in dividend payments to stockholders at various corporations
   C) volatility in NASDAQ indexes
   D) historically low bond prices
   Answer: A
   Diff: 1   Type: MC   Page Ref: 222/222
   Topic: Financial statements
   Skill: Factual
   Objective: LO5: Understand the role of government in corporate governance.
   AACSB Coding: Reflective Thinking
   Special Feature: None

7. In addition to requiring that CEO's personally certify the accuracy of financial statements, the Sarbanes–Oxley Act of 2002 also requires that
    A) CEO's conduct audits of their corporations themselves.
    B) firms raise funds for expansion through the sale of bonds only, not stocks.
    C) auditors disclose any potential conflicts of interest.
    D) corporations issue financial statements monthly rather than quarterly.
    Answer: C
    Diff: 1   Type: MC   Page Ref: 222/222
    Topic: Financial statements
    Skill: Factual
    Objective: LO5: Understand the role of government in corporate governance.
    AACSB Coding: Reflective Thinking
    Special Feature: None

8. Google CEO, Eric Schmidt, was paid $1 in annual salary during 2006. The bulk of his compensation came from increases the value of Google stock he owned. As a result, Schmidt's incentive was to
    A) take actions that increased Google's stock price.
    B) reduce the number of shares of Google stock he owned.
    C) reduce Google's profits.
    D) undertake all of the above actions.
    Answer: A
    Diff: 1   Type: MC   Page Ref: 226/226
    Topic: Principal–agent
    Skill: Conceptual
    Objective: LO5: Understand the role of government in corporate governance.
    AACSB Coding: Reflective Thinking
    Special Feature: An Inside Look: Executive Compensation at Google

9. The Sarbanes–Oxley Act of 2002 requires that firms maintain effective controls over financial reporting. This requirement has increased costs for many corporations, and some economists believe that this increased cost has resulted in
    A) an increase in the likelihood that firms will issue stock to raise finances.
    B) a decrease in the proportion of new stock listings in the United States relative to new stock listings in foreign countries.
    C) an increase in the benefits of uncovering dishonest accounting irregularities.
    D) a decrease in the number of stocks listed on the New York Stock Exchange relative to NASDAQ.
    Answer: B
    Diff: 1   Type: MC   Page Ref: 223/223
    Topic: Costs
    Skill: Conceptual
    Objective: LO5: Understand the role of government in corporate governance.
    AACSB Coding: Reflective Thinking
    Special Feature: None

10. The Sarbanes–Oxley Act of 2002 requires that each member of the board of directors personally certify the accuracy of financial reports.
Answer: True   ○ False
Diff: 2   Type: TF   Page Ref: 222/222
Topic: Financial statements
Skill: Conceptual
Objective: LO5: Understand the role of government in corporate governance.
AACSB Coding: Reflective Thinking
Special Feature: None

11. What is the best mix of inside and outside members on a corporate board of directors?
Answer: Some inside directors are needed on a board to provide the board with information that only top managers would have access to, but there should not be some many inside directors that they can control the board's actions.
Diff: 3   Type: SA   Page Ref: 223/223
Topic: Directors
Skill: Analytical
Objective: LO5: Understand the role of government in corporate governance.
AACSB Coding: Reflective Thinking
Special Feature: Solved Problem: What Makes a Good Board of Directors?

12. Why might it be good for members of a corporation's board of directors to own the firm's stock?
Answer: When directors own the firm's stock, then they will share with other stockholders the desire for the firm to maximize profit. The directors will be more likely to insist that top managers take actions to increase profits rather than to pursue other objectives that may be in the interests of the managers but not the stockholders.
Diff: 2   Type: SA   Page Ref: 222/222
Topic: Directors
Skill: Conceptual
Objective: LO5: Understand the role of government in corporate governance.
AACSB Coding: Reflective Thinking
Special Feature: None

7.6   Appendix: Tools to Measure a Firm's Financial Information

1. Which of the following is operating income?
    A) explicit plus implicit costs
    B) stockholders' equity
    C) revenue minus operating expenses
    D) net profit
Answer: C
Diff: 1   Type: MC   Page Ref: 238/238
Topic: Operating income
Skill: Definition
Objective: Appendix: Understand the concept of present value and the information contained on a firm's income statement and balance sheet
AACSB Coding: Reflective Thinking
Special Feature: None

2. Why is a dollar today more valuable than a dollar a year from now?
    A) The dollar today can be immediately used to buy something.
    B) A dollar a year from now will likely have less purchasing power because of inflation.
    C) The unknown future is riskier than the known present.
    D) All of these.
Answer: D
Diff: 1   Type: MC   Page Ref: 233/233
Topic: Present value
Skill: Conceptual
Objective: Appendix: Understand the concept of present value and the information contained on a firm's income statement and balance sheet
AACSB Coding: Reflective Thinking
Special Feature: None

3. If you put $100 into a bank account that earns five percent interest per year what is the formula you should use to determine the account's future value in one year?
    A) Future value equals the present value divided by the rate of interest.
    B) Future value equals the present value multiplied by the rate of interest.
    C) Future value equals the present value multiplied by one plus the rate of interest in decimals.
    D) All these yield the same answer.
Answer: C
Diff: 2   Type: MC   Page Ref: 233/233
Topic: Future value
Skill: Analytical
Objective: Appendix: Understand the concept of present value and the information contained on a firm's income statement and balance sheet
AACSB Coding: Reflective Thinking
Special Feature: None

4. If you want to know the present value of a future payment received in one year, what formula can you use?
    A) Present value equals future payment times the current market rate of interest.
    B) Present value equals future payment divided by one plus the rate of interest.
    C) Present value equals one plus the rate of interest in decimals divided by future payment.
    D) Present value equals future payments times one plus the rate of interest.
Answer: B
Diff: 2   Type: MC   Page Ref: 234/234
Topic: Present value
Skill: Definition
Objective: Appendix: Understand the concept of present value and the information contained on a firm's income statement and balance sheet
AACSB Coding: Reflective Thinking
Special Feature: None

5. The present value of $300 received 5 years in the future would be calculated as which of the following when the interest rate is 5%?
    A) $300/(1.5)^5$
    B) $300/(1.05)^5$
    C) 300 x 1.5 x 5
    D) 5.05/300
Answer: A, B
Diff: 2   Type: MC   Page Ref: 234/234
Topic: Present value
Skill: Analytical
Objective: Appendix: Understand the concept of present value and the information contained on a firm's income statement and balance sheet
AACSB Coding: Analytic Skills
Special Feature: None

6. What is the present value of $888 in a one year if the current rate of interest is five percent?
    A) $4,440
    B) $845.71
    C) $177.60
    D) none of these
Answer: B
Diff: 2   Type: MC   Page Ref: 234/234
Topic: Present value
Skill: Analytical
Objective: Appendix: Understand the concept of present value and the information contained on a firm's income statement and balance sheet
AACSB Coding: Analytic Skills
Special Feature: None

7. If you own a $1,000 face value bond with one year remaining to maturity and a five percent coupon rate and new bonds are paying 12 percent, what is the most you can get for your old bond?
    A) $1,120
    B) $1,000
    C) $937.50
    D) Impossible to determine without additional information.
Answer: C
Diff: 2   Type: MC   Page Ref: 236/236
Topic: Present value
Skill: Analytical
Objective: Appendix: Understand the concept of present value and the information contained on a firm's income statement and balance sheet
AACSB Coding: Analytic Skills
Special Feature: None

8. If a stock's dividend is expected to grow at a constant rate of eight percent in the future and it has just paid a dividend of $1.25 a share and you have an alternative investment of equal risk that will earn a 12 percent rate of return, what would you be willing to pay per share for this stock?
    A) $1.25
    B) $31.25
    C) $1.12
    D) $1.40
Answer: B
Diff: 3   Type: MC   Page Ref: 237/237
Topic: Stock price
Skill: Analytical
Objective: Appendix: Understand the concept of present value and the information contained on a firm's income statement and balance sheet
AACSB Coding: Analytic Skills
Special Feature: None

9. What must balance on a balance sheet?
    A) Total assets must equal total liabilities plus equity.
    B) Revenues must equal costs.
    C) Retained earnings plus dividends paid must equal earnings per share.
    D) All of these must balance.
Answer: A
Diff: 2   Type: MC   Page Ref: 239/239
Topic: Balance sheet
Skill: Conceptual
Objective: Appendix: Understand the concept of present value and the information contained on a firm's income statement and balance sheet
AACSB Coding: Reflective Thinking
Special Feature: None

10. The price of a financial asset should be equal to
    A) the face value of the asset.
    B) the present value of the sum of the coupon payments and the interest rate.
    C) the face value of the asset divided by the interest rate.
    D) the present value of payments to be received from owning that asset.
Answer: D
Diff: 2   Type: MC   Page Ref: 235/235
Topic: Present value
Skill: Conceptual
Objective: Appendix: Understand the concept of present value and the information contained on a firm's income statement and balance sheet
AACSB Coding: Reflective Thinking
Special Feature: None

11. How much is a bond that pays $50 in coupon payments for 3 years and $1,000 at the end of the third year worth if the interest rate is 10%?

   A) $876
   B) $1,150
   C) $1,045
   D) $952

   Answer: A
   Diff: 2   Type: MC   Page Ref: 235/235
   Topic: Present value
   Skill: Analytical
   Objective: Appendix: Understand the concept of present value and the information contained on a firm's income statement and balance sheet
   AACSB Coding: Analytic Skills
   Special Feature: None

12. Seth's grandmother gave him a $50 savings bond for his birthday. The bond pays $50 at maturity, which is in five years. If the interest rate is 5%, the bond has a present value of $43.19.

   Answer: True   ⊚ False
   Diff: 2   Type: TF   Page Ref: 235/235
   Topic: Present value
   Skill: Analytical
   Objective: Appendix: Understand the concept of present value and the information contained on a firm's income statement and balance sheet
   AACSB Coding: Analytic Skills
   Special Feature: None

13. Net worth and stockholders' equity are both equal to the difference between assets and liabilities.

   Answer: ⊚ True   False
   Diff: 2   Type: TF   Page Ref: 239/239
   Topic: Financial statements
   Skill: Definition
   Objective: Appendix: Understand the concept of present value and the information contained on a firm's income statement and balance sheet
   AACSB Coding: Reflective Thinking
   Special Feature: None

14. With state and multistate lotteries, winners are typically given the choice between a lump sum payment today or a 20 year series of annuities. How should a winner decide which is better?

   Answer: By determining the present value of the multiyear annuity payout and comparing it to the lump sum payment. Which ever has the largest present value is the best choice.
   Diff: 2   Type: SA   Page Ref: 235/163
   Topic: Present value
   Skill: Analytical
   Objective: Appendix: Understand the concept of present value and the information contained on a firm's income statement and balance sheet
   AACSB Coding: Reflective Thinking
   Special Feature: Solved Problem: How to Receive Your Contest Winnings

Chapter 8   Comparative Advantage and the Gains from International Trade

8.1   The United States in the International Economy

1. Ethanol is made from corn or sugar and can be used as a substitute for gasoline as a fuel in automobiles. Brazil makes ethanol from sugar at about one-half the cost of ethanol produced in the Unites States from corn. Which of the following statements is true?
   A) The U.S. imports ethanol from Brazil and thereby reduces its dependence on imports of petroleum from the Middle East.
   B) For political reasons, Brazil has refused to export ethanol to the U.S.
   C) Brazil exports ethanol to the U.S. but has placed a limit on the amount it exports.
   D) The U.S. government imposed a tariff on imports of ethanol, effectively pricing Brazilian ethanol out of the market.
   Answer: D
   Diff: 1   Type: MC   Page Ref: 242-3/242-3
   Topic: Trade restrictions
   Skill: Fact
   Objective: LO1: Discuss the role of international trade in the U.S. economy
   AACSB Coding: Reflective Thinking
   Special Feature: Chapter Opener: Comparative Advantage and the Gains from International Trade

2. Workers in industries protected by tariffs and quotas are likely to support these trade restrictions because
   A) they do not want to offend their employers who want them.
   B) politicians lobby to convince workers the restrictions will make them better off.
   C) they believe the restrictions will protect their jobs.
   D) they don't understand that the restrictions will threaten their jobs.
   Answer: C
   Diff: 1   Type: MC   Page Ref: 243/243
   Topic: Trade restrictions
   Skill: Fact
   Objective: LO1: Discuss the role of international trade in the U.S. economy
   AACSB Coding: Reflective Thinking
   Special Feature: Economics in YOUR Life!: Why Haven't You Heard of the Sugar Quota?

3. The United States Congress has enacted a quota on the importation of sugar. As a result
    A) U.S. companies are able to sell sugar domestically at a price about three times as high as the world price.
    B) many firms that use sugar to make candy are able to keep producing their products in the U.S. Among these are the firms that produce Life Savers and Cherry Balls.
    C) U.S. consumers enjoy a greater variety of products that are made with a lot of sugar (for example, candy bars and chocolate).
    D) sugar producers in other countries benefit since they don't face as much international competition.

Answer: A
Diff: 1   Type: MC   Page Ref: 242–3/242–3
Topic: Trade restrictions
Skill: Fact
Objective: LO1: Discuss the role of international trade in the U.S. economy
AACSB Coding: Reflective Thinking
Special Feature: Chapter Opener: Comparative Advantage and the Gains from International Trade

4. Over the past several decades there has been a rapid growth in international trade. This growth has been due to all except one of the following factors. Which factor has not contributed to the growth of international trade?
    A) The spread of reliable communications.
    B) A change in the tariffs charged on many goods.
    C) A reduction in shipping costs.
    D) Favorable changes in government policies.

Answer: B
Diff: 1   Type: MC   Page Ref: 244/244
Topic: The importance of international trade
Skill: Fact
Objective: LO1: Discuss the role of international trade in the U.S. economy
AACSB Coding: Reflective Thinking
Special Feature: None

5. Trade that is within a country or between countries is based on the principle of
    A) absolute advantage.
    B) scarcity.
    C) competition.
    D) comparative advantage.

Answer: D
Diff: 1   Type: MC   Page Ref: 245/245
Topic: Comparative advantage
Skill: Fact
Objective: LO1: Discuss the role of international trade in the U.S. economy
AACSB Coding: Reflective Thinking
Special Feature: None

6. A tax imposed by a government on imports of a good into a country is called
    A) an import levy.
    B) an import fine.
    C) a tariff.
    D) an import quota.
    Answer: C
    Diff: 1   Type: MC   Page Ref: 244/244
    Topic: Tariffs
    Skill: Definition
    Objective: LO1: Discuss the role of international trade in the U.S. economy
    AACSB Coding: Reflective Thinking
    Special Feature: None

7. Goods and services bought domestically but produced in other countries are referred to as
    A) exports.
    B) imports.
    C) transfer payments.
    D) foreign consumption.
    Answer: B
    Diff: 1   Type: MC   Page Ref: 244/244
    Topic: Imports
    Skill: Definition
    Objective: LO1: Discuss the role of international trade in the U.S. economy
    AACSB Coding: Reflective Thinking
    Special Feature: None

8. Domestically produced goods and services sold to other countries are referred to as
    A) exports.
    B) imports.
    C) transfer payments.
    D) capital outflow.
    Answer: A
    Diff: 1   Type: MC   Page Ref: 244/244
    Topic: Exports
    Skill: Definition
    Objective: LO1: Discuss the role of international trade in the U.S. economy
    AACSB Coding: Reflective Thinking
    Special Feature: None

9. When Roxanne, a U.S. citizen, purchases a designer dress from Barneys of New York that was made in Milan the purchase is
    A) both a U.S. and an Italian import.
    B) a U.S. import and an Italian export.
    C) a U.S. export and an Italian import.
    D) neither an export nor an import for either country.
Answer: B
Diff: 1   Type: MC   Page Ref: 244/244
Topic: Imports
Skill: Definition
Objective: LO1: Discuss the role of international trade in the U.S. economy
AACSB Coding: Reflective Thinking
Special Feature: None

10. Which of the following statements about the importance of trade to the U.S. economy is false?
    A) Since 1950, both exports and imports have steadily increased as a fraction of U.S. gross domestic product.
    B) Overall, about 20 percent of U.S. manufacturing jobs depend directly or indirectly on exports.
    C) The United States is the largest exporter in the world.
    D) The U.S. economy is highly dependent on international trade for growth in its gross domestic product.
Answer: D
Diff: 1   Type: MC   Page Ref: 245-6/245-6
Topic: The importance of international trade
Skill: Fact
Objective: LO1: Discuss the role of international trade in the U.S. economy
AACSB Coding: Reflective Thinking
Special Feature: None

11. Boeing's 747 jumbo jets experienced declining sales in the 1990s. Since then the 747 has experienced a resurgence in popularity. Which of the following is one reason for the comeback of the 747?
    A) The 747 has better safety records than competing planes.
    B) The 747 is able to travel at greater speeds than other jets.
    C) The 747 has a larger cargo capacity than other planes.
    D) The 747 is less expensive than comparable jets offered by Airbus, Boeing's main competitor.
Answer: C
Diff: 1   Type: MC   Page Ref: 246-7/246-7
Topic: Trade
Skill: Fact
Objective: LO1: Discuss the role of international trade in the U.S. economy
AACSB Coding: Reflective Thinking
Special Feature: Making the Connection: How Expanding International Trade Has Helped Boeing

12. Despite the decline in passenger travel after September 11, 2001, air freight shipments have grown rapidly. This has increased the demand for
    A) Boeing 747 jumbo jets.
    B) flight attendants.
    C) airport terminals.
    D) air traffic controllers.
    Answer: A
    Diff: 1   Type: MC   Page Ref: 246-7/246-7
    Topic: Trade
    Skill: Fact
    Objective: LO1: Discuss the role of international trade in the U.S. economy
    AACSB Coding: Reflective Thinking
    Special Feature: Making the Connection: How Expanding International Trade Has Helped Boeing

13. Which of the following statements is true?
    A) Japan is more dependent on foreign trade than is the United States.
    B) Imports and exports account for over one-half of the GDP of Belgium.
    C) France is the leading exporting country, accounting for 10 percent of total world exports.
    D) Because the cost of labor used on farms is so high, the United States exports very little of its wheat, rice and corn crops.
    Answer: B
    Diff: 1   Type: MC   Page Ref: 245-6/245-6
    Topic: The importance of international trade
    Skill: Fact
    Objective: LO1: Discuss the role of international trade in the U.S. economy
    AACSB Coding: Reflective Thinking
    Special Feature: None

14. Twenty-seven countries in Europe have formed the European Union (EU). After the EU was formed it
    A) eliminated all tariffs among its member countries.
    B) completed a trade treaty (NAFTA) that reduced tariff rates between the EU and North American countries.
    C) greatly decreased imports and exports among its member countries.
    D) barred imports of 747 jumbo jets by its member countries; all EU countries must now buy jets from Airbus, a European company.
    Answer: A
    Diff: 1   Type: MC   Page Ref: 244/244
    Topic: The importance of international trade
    Skill: Fact
    Objective: LO1: Discuss the role of international trade in the U.S. economy
    AACSB Coding: Reflective Thinking
    Special Feature: None

15. NAFTA refers to a 1994 agreement that eliminated most tariffs among which countries?
    A) Canada, the United Kingdom and Mexico.
    B) The United States, the United Kingdom and Mexico.
    C) The United States, Canada and Mexico.
    D) The United States, Mexico and Cuba.
    Answer: C
    Diff: 1   Type: MC   Page Ref: 244/244
    Topic: The importance of international trade
    Skill: Fact
    Objective: LO1: Discuss the role of international trade in the U.S. economy
    AACSB Coding: Reflective Thinking
    Special Feature: None

16. In the 1930s the United States charged an average tariff rate
    A) that was less than its average tariff rate in 2007.
    B) that cut its exports to other countries by 50 percent.
    C) was less than 2 percent.
    D) that exceeded 50 percent.
    Answer: D
    Diff: 1   Type: MC   Page Ref: 244/244
    Topic: Tariffs
    Skill: Fact
    Objective: LO1: Discuss the role of international trade in the U.S. economy
    AACSB Coding: Reflective Thinking
    Special Feature: None

17. Which of the following statements is true?
    A) Exports benefit trading countries because exports create jobs. Imports do not benefit trading countries because they result in a loss of jobs.
    B) Each year China exports about 50 percent of its wheat crop and 40 percent of its rice crop.
    C) Most of the leading exporting countries are large, high-income countries.
    D) All sectors of the U.S. economy are affected equally by international trade.
    Answer: C
    Diff: 1   Type: MC   Page Ref: 244-5/244-5
    Topic: The importance of international trade
    Skill: Fact
    Objective: LO1: Discuss the role of international trade in the U.S. economy
    AACSB Coding: Reflective Thinking
    Special Feature: None

18. Although the United States is the leading exporting country, international trade is less important to the U.S. than it is to most other countries.
    Answer: ◎ True   False
    Diff: 1   Type: TF   Page Ref: 245/245
    Topic: The importance of international trade
    Skill: Fact
    Objective: LO1: Discuss the role of international trade in the U.S. economy
    AACSB Coding: Reflective Thinking
    Special Feature: None

19. Since September 11, 2001 a slowdown in international trade has decreased the demand for the Boeing Company's 747 jumbo jets.

Answer: True   ◌ False

Diff: 1   Type: TF   Page Ref: 245-6/245-6
Topic: Trade
Skill: Fact
Objective: LO1: Discuss the role of international trade in the U.S. economy
AACSB Coding: Reflective Thinking
Special Feature: None

8.2   Comparative Advantage in International Trade

1. Absolute advantage is
    A) the ability to produce more of a good or service than competitors when using the same amount of resources.
    B) the ability to produce higher quality goods compared to one's competitors.
    C) the ability to produce a good or service at a higher opportunity cost than one's competitors.
    D) the ability to produce more of a good or service than competitors that have more resources.

Answer: A

Diff: 1   Type: MC   Page Ref: 248/248
Topic: Absolute advantage
Skill: Definition
Objective: LO2: Understand the difference between comparative advantage and absolute advantage in international trade
AACSB Coding: Reflective Thinking
Special Feature: None

Table 8–1

	Berries	*Fish*
Rob	20	80
Bill	30	60

Rob Crusoe and Bill Friday spent their week–long vacation on a desert island where they had to find and make their own food. Rob and Bill spent one day each fishing and picking berries. The following table lists the pounds of output Rob and Bill produced.

2. ***Refer to Table 8–1.*** Use the table above to select the statement that accurately interprets the data in the table.
    A) Rob has an absolute advantage in picking berries and Bill has an absolute advantage in catching fish.
    B) Bill has an absolute advantage in picking berries and Rob has an absolute advantage in catching fish.
    C) Bill has an absolute advantage in picking berries and catching fish.
    D) Rob has an absolute advantage in picking berries and catching fish.
    Answer: B
    Diff: 2   Type: MC   Page Ref: 247–8/247–8
    Topic: Absolute advantage
    Skill: Analytical
    Objective: LO2: Understand the difference between comparative advantage and absolute advantage in international trade
    AACSB Coding: Analytic Skills
    Special Feature: None

3. ***Refer to Table 8–1.*** Use the table above to select the statement that accurately interprets the data in the table.
    A) Bill has a greater opportunity cost than Rob for picking berries.
    B) Bill's opportunity cost for catching fish is less than Rob's.
    C) Rob has a greater opportunity cost than Bill for picking berries.
    D) Bill's opportunity cost for picking berries and catching fish are both greater than Rob's.
    Answer: C
    Diff: 3   Type: MC   Page Ref: 247–8/247–8
    Topic: Opportunity cost
    Skill: Analytical
    Objective: LO2: Understand the difference between comparative advantage and absolute advantage in international trade
    AACSB Coding: Analytic Skills
    Special Feature: None

4. *Refer to Table 8-1.* Use the table above to select the statement that accurately interprets the data in the table.
    A) Bill has a comparative advantage in catching fish.
    B) Rob has a comparative advantage in picking berries.
    C) Rob has a comparative advantage in catching fish and picking berries.
    D) Bill has a comparative advantage in picking berries.
    Answer: D
    Diff: 3   Type: MC   Page Ref: 247-8/247-8
    Topic: Comparative advantage
    Skill: Analytical
    Objective: LO2: Understand the difference between comparative advantage and absolute advantage in international trade
    AACSB Coding: Analytic Skills
    Special Feature: None

5. *Refer to Table 8-1.* Use the table above to select the statement that accurately interprets the data in the table.
    A) Rob has a comparative advantage in catching fish.
    B) Bill has an absolute advantage in catching fish.
    C) Bill has a comparative advantage in catching fish.
    D) Rob has a comparative advantage in picking berries and catching fish.
    Answer: A
    Diff: 3   Type: MC   Page Ref: 247-8/247-8
    Topic: Comparative advantage
    Skill: Analytical
    Objective: LO2: Understand the difference between comparative advantage and absolute advantage in international trade
    AACSB Coding: Analytic Skills
    Special Feature: None

6. An economic principle that explains why people pursue different occupations is
    A) absolute advantage.
    B) international trade.
    C) comparative advantage.
    D) NAFTA.
    Answer: C
    Diff: 1   Type: MC   Page Ref: 247/247
    Topic: Comparative advantage
    Skill: Conceptual
    Objective: LO2: Understand the difference between comparative advantage and absolute advantage in international trade
    AACSB Coding: Reflective Thinking
    Special Feature: None

7. Assume that Nation A has a comparative advantage in producing corn and exports corn to Nation B. We can conclude that
   A) Nation A also has an absolute advantage in producing corn relative to Nation B.
   B) Nation A has a lower opportunity cost of producing corn relative to Nation B.
   C) Nation B has an absolute disadvantage in producing corn relative to Nation B.
   D) Labor costs are higher for corn producers in Nation B than in Nation A.
   Answer: B
   Diff: 2   Type: MC   Page Ref: 247–8/247–8
   Topic: Comparative advantage
   Skill: Conceptual
   Objective: LO2: Understand the difference between comparative advantage and absolute advantage in international trade
   AACSB Coding: Reflective Thinking
   Special Feature: None

8. Whenever a buyer and a seller agree to trade both must believe they will be made better off
   A) unless the buyer resides in a different country than the seller resides in. International trade may make the buyer or seller worse off.
   B) unless one party is richer than the other.
   C) only if the buyer and seller live in countries with market economies.
   D) whether the buyer and seller live in the same city or different countries.
   Answer: D
   Diff: 1   Type: MC   Page Ref: 247–8/247–8
   Topic: Comparative advantage
   Skill: Analytical
   Objective: LO2: Understand the difference between comparative advantage and absolute advantage in international trade
   AACSB Coding: Reflective Thinking
   Special Feature: None

9. If Japanese workers are more productive than French workers then trade between Japan and France
   A) can take place only if France has an absolute advantage in producing a good or service Japanese buyers want.
   B) cannot take place because Japanese goods and services will be less expensive than French goods and services.
   C) cannot take place until French workers become more productive.
   D) will take place so long as each country has a comparative advantage in a good or service that buyers in the other country want.
   Answer: D
   Diff: 1   Type: MC   Page Ref: 247–8/247–8
   Topic: Comparative advantage
   Skill: Conceptual
   Objective: LO2: Understand the difference between comparative advantage and absolute advantage in international trade
   AACSB Coding: Reflective Thinking
   Special Feature: None

10. If the _____ cost of production for two goods is different between two countries then mutually beneficial trade is possible.
    A) marginal
    B) explicit
    C) opportunity
    D) implicit
    Answer: C
    Diff: 1   *Type: MC*   *Page Ref: 247–8/247–8*
    Topic: Opportunity cost
    Skill: Conceptual
    Objective: LO2: Understand the difference between comparative advantage and absolute advantage in international trade
    AACSB Coding: Reflective Thinking
    Special Feature: None

11. If Canada has a comparative advantage relative to Mexico in the production of timber then
    A) the explicit cost of production for timber is lower in Canada than in Mexico.
    B) the opportunity cost of production for timber is lower in Canada than in Mexico.
    C) the implicit costs of production for timber are lower in Canada than in Mexico.
    D) the average cost of production for timber is lower in Canada than in Mexico.
    Answer: B
    Diff: 1   *Type: MC*   *Page Ref: 247–8/247–8*
    Topic: Opportunity cost
    Skill: Conceptual
    Objective: LO2: Understand the difference between comparative advantage and absolute advantage in international trade
    AACSB Coding: Reflective Thinking
    Special Feature: None

12. If Sweden exports cell phones to Denmark and Denmark exports butter to Sweden, which of the following would explain this pattern of trade?
    A) Sweden has a lower opportunity cost of producing cell phones than Denmark and Denmark has a comparative advantage in producing butter.
    B) The opportunity cost of producing butter in Denmark is higher than the opportunity cost of producing butter in Sweden.
    C) Sweden must have an absolute advantage in producing cell phones and Denmark must have an absolute advantage in producing butter.
    D) Sweden has a higher opportunity cost of producing cell phones than Denmark, and Denmark has a higher opportunity cost of producing butter.
    Answer: A
    Diff: 2   *Type: MC*   *Page Ref: 247–8/247–8*
    Topic: Comparative advantage
    Skill: Conceptual
    Objective: LO2: Understand the difference between comparative advantage and absolute advantage in international trade
    AACSB Coding: Reflective Thinking
    Special Feature: None

13. The ability of a firm or country to produce a good or service at a lower opportunity cost than other producers is called absolute advantage.
Answer: True ○ False
Diff: 2   Type: TF   Page Ref: 247-8/247-8
Topic: Comparative advantage
Skill: Definition
Objective: LO2: Understand the difference between comparative advantage and absolute advantage in international trade
AACSB Coding: Reflective Thinking
Special Feature: None

14. If country A has an absolute advantage in the production of two goods compared to country B, country A can still benefit from trade with country B.
Answer: ○ True   False
Diff: 1   Type: TF   Page Ref: 248/248
Topic: Comparative advantage
Skill: Conceptual
Objective: LO2: Understand the difference between comparative advantage and absolute advantage in international trade
AACSB Coding: Reflective Thinking
Special Feature: None

8.3   How Countries Gain from International Trade

1. A situation in which a country does not trade with other countries is called
    A) autarky.
    B) self-actualization.
    C) autonomy.
    D) independence.
Answer: A
Diff: 1   Type: MC   Page Ref: 249/249
Topic: Trade
Skill: Definition
Objective: LO3: Explain how countries gain from international trade
AACSB Coding: Reflective Thinking
Special Feature: None

2. The terms of trade refers to
    A) the rules and regulations that countries must adhere to when trading.
    B) the ratio at which a country can trade its exports for imports from other countries.
    C) the role of the government in overseeing international trade.
    D) a legal document that specifies the terms of a trade agreed to by two countries.
Answer: B
Diff: 1   Type: MC   Page Ref: 249/249
Topic: Trade
Skill: Definition
Objective: LO3: Explain how countries gain from international trade
AACSB Coding: Reflective Thinking
Special Feature: None

3. Countries that engage in trade will tend to specialize in the production of goods and services in which they have _____ and will _____ these goods and services.
    A) a comparative advantage; import
    B) an absolute advantage; export
    C) a comparative advantage; export
    D) an absolute advantage; import
    Answer: C
    Diff: 1   Type: MC   Page Ref: 249/249
    Topic: Comparative advantage
    Skill: Conceptual
    Objective: LO3: Explain how countries gain from international trade
    AACSB Coding: Reflective Thinking
    Special Feature: None

4. The first discussion of comparative advantage appears in a book written by
    A) Adam Smith.
    B) Paul Samuelson.
    C) David Portugal.
    D) David Ricardo.
    Answer: D
    Diff: 1   Type: MC   Page Ref: 250–1/250–1
    Topic: Comparative advantage
    Skill: Fact
    Objective: LO3: Explain how countries gain from international trade
    AACSB Coding: Reflective Thinking
    Special Feature: Solved Problem: The Gains from Trade

5. The first example used to explain comparative advantage used two countries (England and Portugal) and two goods (wine and cloth) to show that
    A) each country would be better off from trade if it had an absolute advantage in producing one of the goods.
    B) each country would have a comparative advantage in the production of the good for which it had an absolute advantage.
    C) mutually beneficial trade was possible between two countries even if one had an absolute advantage in the production of both goods.
    D) mutually beneficial trade was possible between two countries even if one had a comparative advantage in the production of both goods.
    Answer: C
    Diff: 2   Type: MC   Page Ref: 250–1/250–1
    Topic: Comparative advantage
    Skill: Conceptual
    Objective: LO3: Explain how countries gain from international trade
    AACSB Coding: Reflective Thinking
    Special Feature: Solved Problem: The Gains from Trade

6. The first example of comparative advantage appeared in a book that was published in 1817. This example showed that mutually beneficial trade between two countries (England and Portugal) was possible. The example assumed that two goods (wine and cloth) could be produced by both countries. Which of the following describes the conclusion of this example?

    A) Portugal had a comparative advantage in wine and England had a comparative advantage in cloth.

    B) Portugal had a comparative advantage in both wine and cloth, but its advantage in cloth was greater.

    C) England had a comparative advantage in both wine and cloth, but its advantage in cloth was greater.

    D) England had an absolute advantage in both wine and cloth, but a comparative advantage in wine.

Answer: A

Diff: 1   Type: MC   Page Ref: 250–1/250–1
Topic: Comparative advantage
Skill: Fact
Objective: LO3: Explain how countries gain from international trade
AACSB Coding: Reflective Thinking
Special Feature: Solved Problem: The Gains from Trade

7. Examples of comparative advantage show how trade between two countries can make each better off. Compared to their pre-trade positions, trade makes both countries better off because in each country

    A) total employment is greater.

    B) total consumption of goods is greater.

    C) wages are higher.

    D) total welfare is greater.

Answer: B

Diff: 1   Type: MC   Page Ref: 249/249
Topic: How countries gain from trade
Skill: Conceptual
Objective: LO3: Explain how countries gain from international trade
AACSB Coding: Reflective Thinking
Special Feature: None

8. In the real world we don't observe countries completely specializing in the production of goods for which they have a comparative advantage. One reasons for this is

    A) comparative advantage works better in theory than in practice.

    B) some countries have more resources than other countries.

    C) tastes for many traded goods are similar in many countries because of globalization.

    D) production of most goods involves increasing opportunity costs.

Answer: D

Diff: 2   Type: MC   Page Ref: 252/252
Topic: Specialization in production
Skill: Conceptual
Objective: LO3: Explain how countries gain from international trade
AACSB Coding: Reflective Thinking
Special Feature: None

9. Automobiles and many other products are differentiated. As a result
    A) different countries may each have a comparative advantage in producing different types of automobiles.
    B) consumers of automobiles have difficulty deciding what type of imported automobile to buy.
    C) the quality of imported automobiles is less than it could be.
    D) we see countries specializing completely in the production of automobiles.
    Answer: A
    Diff: 2   Type: MC   Page Ref: 252/252
    Topic: Specialization in production
    Skill: Conceptual
    Objective: LO3: Explain how countries gain from international trade
    AACSB Coding: Reflective Thinking
    Special Feature: None

10. A consequence of increasing marginal costs of producing digital music players in Japan is
    A) Japan will not export digital music players.
    B) Japan will stop short of complete specialization in the production of digital music players.
    C) Japan will import cell phones from countries that don't experience increasing marginal costs.
    D) Japan will likely impose trade restrictions on imported digital music players.
    Answer: B
    Diff: 2   Type: MC   Page Ref: 252/252
    Topic: Specialization in production
    Skill: Conceptual
    Objective: LO3: Explain how countries gain from international trade
    AACSB Coding: Reflective Thinking
    Special Feature: None

11. Textbook examples of trade between two nations are simplified in order to show how two nations both benefit from trade. These examples are misleading because
    A) in the real world, rich countries can take advantage of poor countries.
    B) they do not account for the reduction in wages that occurs in both countries as a result of trade.
    C) some individuals in both countries may be made worse off because of trade.
    D) trade restrictions are likely to be imposed as trade grows over time.
    Answer: C
    Diff: 2   Type: MC   Page Ref: 252–3/252–3
    Topic: How countries gain from trade
    Skill: Conceptual
    Objective: LO3: Explain how countries gain from international trade
    AACSB Coding: Reflective Thinking
    Special Feature: None

12. Which of the following statements is true?
    A) All individuals in both countries are made better off as a result of international trade.
    B) Within each country, some individuals are made better off as a result of international trade, but one of the countries will be worse off overall.
    C) Although some individuals are made better off as a result of international trade, both countries may be made worse off overall.
    D) Each country as a whole is made better off as a result of international trade, but individuals within each country may be made worse off.
    Answer: D
    Diff: 2   Type: MC   Page Ref: 252-3/252-3
    Topic: How countries gain from trade
    Skill: Conceptual
    Objective: LO3: Explain how countries gain from international trade
    AACSB Coding: Reflective Thinking
    Special Feature: None

13. A Federal Reserve publication proclaimed that "Trade is a win–win situation for all countries that participate." This statement is
    A) false since it ignores the workers who lose their jobs as result of international trade.
    B) false since not all countries participate in international trade.
    C) true because it refers to countries; individuals may be losers as a result of international trade.
    D) true because all consumers and workers benefit from international trade.
    Answer: C
    Diff: 1   Type: MC   Page Ref: 252/252
    Topic: How countries gain from trade
    Skill: Conceptual
    Objective: LO3: Explain how countries gain from international trade
    AACSB Coding: Reflective Thinking
    Special Feature: None

14. Which of the following is not a source of comparative advantage?
    A) Relative abundance of labor and capital.
    B) Technology.
    C) Climate and natural resources.
    D) A strong foreign currency exchange rate.
    Answer: D
    Diff: 1   Type: MC   Page Ref: 253/253
    Topic: Sources of comparative advantage
    Skill: Fact
    Objective: LO3: Explain how countries gain from international trade
    AACSB Coding: Reflective Thinking
    Special Feature: None

15. The United States has developed a comparative advantage in digital computers, airliners and many prescription drugs. The source of its comparative advantage in these products is
    A) a favorable climate.
    B) technology.
    C) abundant supplies of natural resources.
    D) a strong central government.
    Answer: B
    Diff: 1   Type: MC   Page Ref: 253/253
    Topic: Sources of comparative advantage
    Skill: Fact
    Objective: LO3: Explain how countries gain from international trade
    AACSB Coding: Reflective Thinking
    Special Feature: None

16. Once an industry becomes established in a certain area firms that locate in that area gain advantages over firms located elsewhere, leading to lower costs of production. Economists refer to the lower costs that result form increases in the size of an industry in a certain area as
    A) external economies.
    B) positive externalities.
    C) strategic advantages.
    D) technological change.
    Answer: A
    Diff: 2   Type: MC   Page Ref: 253/253
    Topic: Sources of comparative advantage
    Skill: Definition
    Objective: LO3: Explain how countries gain from international trade
    AACSB Coding: Reflective Thinking
    Special Feature: None

17. China has developed a comparative advantage in the production of children's toys. The source of this comparative advantage is
    A) superior process technology.
    B) a large supply of unskilled workers and relatively little capital.
    C) investment in capital used to produce toys.
    D) a large supply of natural resources.
    Answer: B
    Diff: 2   Type: MC   Page Ref: 253/253
    Topic: Sources of comparative advantage
    Skill: Fact
    Objective: LO3: Explain how countries gain from international trade
    AACSB Coding: Reflective Thinking
    Special Feature: None

18. Dalton, Georgia has developed into a leading producer of carpets, despite its small size. What is the reason for Dalton's comparative advantage in carpet production?
    A) The development of superior process technology.
    B) An abundant supply of unskilled labor.
    C) Dalton is located near a railroad hub that it uses to transport carpet.
    D) External economies.
    Answer: D
    Diff: 2   Type: MC   Page Ref: 253–4/253–4
    Topic: Sources of comparative advantage
    Skill: Fact
    Objective: LO3: Explain how countries gain from international trade
    AACSB Coding: Reflective Thinking
    Special Feature: Making the Connection: Why is Dalton, Georgia, the Carpet–Making Capital of the World?

19. Costa Rica is a leading exporter of bananas. What explains the comparative advantage of this country in banana production?
    A) Climate and soil conditions in Costa Rica are well–suited for banana production.
    B) Investment by multinational firms such as Chiquita Brands International and the Dole Food Company.
    C) A large supply of unskilled labor.
    D) Positive externalities.
    Answer: A
    Diff: 1   Type: MC   Page Ref: 253/253
    Topic: Sources of comparative advantage
    Skill: Fact
    Objective: LO3: Explain how countries gain from international trade
    AACSB Coding: Reflective Thinking
    Special Feature: None

20. In the 1970s and 1980s the United States lost its comparative advantage in consumer electronics goods to Japan. What factor was most responsible for the development of Japan's comparative advantage in consumer electronics goods?
    A) Japanese firms benefited from external economies.
    B) Japan has abundant supplies of labor.
    C) Japanese firms excelled in process technology.
    D) Japan has abundant supplies of natural resources needed to produce electronics goods.
    Answer: C
    Diff: 2   Type: MC   Page Ref: 254–5/254–5
    Topic: Sources of comparative advantage
    Skill: Fact
    Objective: LO3: Explain how countries gain from international trade
    AACSB Coding: Reflective Thinking
    Special Feature: None

21. One reason a country does not specialize completely in production is that production of most goods involves increasing opportunity costs.
    Answer: ○ True   False
    Diff: 1   Type: TF   Page Ref: 252/252
    Topic: Specialization in production
    Skill: Conceptual
    Objective: LO3: Explain how countries gain from international trade
    AACSB Coding: Reflective Thinking
    Special Feature: None

22. One of main sources of comparative advantage is internal economies.
    Answer: True   ○ False
    Diff: 1   Type: TF   Page Ref: 253/253
    Topic: Sources of comparative advantage
    Skill: Conceptual
    Objective: LO3: Explain how countries gain from international trade
    AACSB Coding: Reflective Thinking
    Special Feature: None

23. Examples of comparative advantage often begin with two countries that each produce the same two goods. Each country is then shown to have a comparative advantage in producing the good it can produce at a lower opportunity cost, and specializes in the production of the good for which it has a comparative advantage. How do these examples prove that both nations are made better off as a result of trade than they would be without trade?
    Answer: To show that both countries are better off it is necessary to demonstrate that total consumption, not just production, of both goods is greater after than before trade. If a country specializes completely in producing one good – apples, for example – it has given up the opportunity to produce another good that consumers value; let's say this other good is plums. Apple lovers now have more of the good they like, but the country as a whole cannot be better off unless the change in production benefits plum lovers too. This can be done by trading some of the additional apples that are produced for some of the plums the other country has produced. Trade may benefit apple lovers more than plum lovers (or vice versa) but if after trade more of both goods can be consumed then trade has unambiguously made all consumers better off than they were previously.
    Diff: 2   Type: ES   Page Ref: 249–51/249–51
    Topic: How countries gain from trade
    Skill: Conceptual
    Objective: LO3: Explain how countries gain from international trade
    AACSB Coding: Reflective Thinking
    Special Feature: None

24. The simple trade model demonstrates that countries can expand consumption by specializing in the production of good and services in which they have a comparative advantage. In reality we do not see complete specialization in production. State three reasons why this is case.

Answer: Three reasons outlined in the text are:

1.   Not all goods and services are traded internationally.

2.   As more exported goods are produced, the opportunity cost of producing additional units   eventually increases.

3.   Since most products are differentiated some buyers prefer to purchase domestically produced products while others will prefer to buy similar products produced abroad. The automobile   industry is a good example of this.

Diff: 3   Type: ES   Page Ref: 252/252
Topic: Specialization in production
Skill: Conceptual
Objective: LO3: Explain how countries gain from international trade
AACSB Coding: Reflective Thinking
Special Feature: None

25. Suppose in Vietnam a worker can produce either 16 units of cloth or 2 bicycles while in China a worker can produce either 20 units of cloth or 5 bicycles.
    a.   Which country has an absolute advantage in cloth production? In bicycle production?
    b.   What is the opportunity cost of 1 unit of cloth in Vietnam? In China?
    c.   What is the opportunity cost of 1 bicycle in Vietnam? In China?
    d.   Which country has a comparative advantage in cloth production? In bicycle production?
    e.   Suppose each country has 1,000 workers. Currently, each country devotes 40 percent of its labor force to cloth production and 60 percent to bicycle production. What is the output of cloth and bicycle for each country and what is the total output of cloth and bicycles between the two countries?
    f.   Suppose each country specializes in the production of the good in which it has a comparative
         advantage. What is the total output of cloth and bicycles in the two countries?
    g.   Provide a numerical example to show how Vietnam and China can both gain from trade. Assume that the terms of trade are established at 6 units of cloth for 1 bicycle.

Answer: a.   China has an absolute advantage in the production of both goods.
    b.   In Vietnam, the opportunity cost of 1 unit of cloth = 1/8 bicycle. In China, the opportunity cost of 1 unit of cloth = 1/4 bicycle.
    c.   In Vietnam, the opportunity cost of 1 bicycle = 8 units of cloth. In China, the opportunity cost of 1 bicycle= 4 units of cloth.
    d.   Vietnam has a comparative advantage in cloth production and China in bicycle production.
    e.

	Cloth	*Bicycles*
Vietnam	400 × 16 = 6,400	600 × 2 = 1,200
China	400 × 20 = 8,000	600 × 5 = 3,000
Total	14,400	4,200

f. If each country specializes, output is:

	Cloth	*Bicycles*
Vietnam	1,000 × 16 = 16,000	
China		1,000 × 5 = 5,000
Total	16,000	5,000

g.

Vietnam	
Output	16,000 units of cloth
Exports	9,000 units of cloth
Consumes	7,000 units of cloth
Imports	1,500 bicycles

China	
Output	5,000 bicycles
Exports	1,500 bicycles
Consumes	3,500 bicycles
Imports	9,000 units of cloth

Diff: 3   Type: ES   Page Ref: 247–51/247–51
Topic: Gains from trade
Skill: Analytical
Objective: LO3: Explain how countries gain from international trade
AACSB Coding: Analytic Skills
Special Feature: None

26. What are the four main sources of comparative advantage? Briefly explain each source and provide examples.
    Answer: The 4 main sources cited are:

    1. climate and natural resources
    2. relatively abundant supplies of labor and capital
    3. technology
    4. external economies.

    Some examples of natural resource rich countries include Saudi Arabia (rich in oil), Malaysia (rich in palm oil), Indonesia (rich in tropical hardwoods), Kenya with its exotic wildlife (for tourism). Advantageous climate is also a source of comparative advantage. For example, the South of France and certain parts of Italy have a particular blend of climactic conditions and land that is particularly suited to the cultivation of truffles.

    Countries like the U.S. have many highly skilled workers and a huge stock of capital equipment compared to say, China and India which have more low–skilled workers and relatively little machinery. As a result, the U.S. has a comparative advantage in the production of goods that require skilled workers or sophisticated machinery (software, biotechnology) while China and India have a comparative advantage in the production of goods that require low skilled workers and small amounts of simple machinery (carpets, clothing items).

The text discusses the distinction between product technologies and process technologies and how they lead to specialization in different kinds of products. For example, the U.S. is undoubtedly the world leader in research and development leading to a comparative advantage in technology-intensive products and services. Examples include the development of new products in the field of medicine, telecommunications and bioengineering. Countries that are strong in process technologies are likely to concentrate on improving the process used to make existing products.

External economies occur outside of a firm, within an industry. Thus, when an industry's scope of operations expands due to, for example, the creation of a better transportation network, firms located in that network gain advantages over firms located outside the network.

Diff: 3   Type: ES   Page Ref: 253/253
Topic: Sources of comparative advantage
Skill: Conceptual
Objective: LO3: Explain how countries gain from international trade
AACSB Coding: Reflective Thinking
Special Feature: None

8.4   Government Policies That Restrict International Trade

1. Trade between countries that is without restrictions is called
   A) unobstructed commerce.
   B) unabated trade.
   C) free trade.
   D) unencumbered trade.
   Answer: C
   Diff: 1   Type: MC   Page Ref: 255/255
   Topic: Trade
   Skill: Definition
   Objective: LO4: Analyze the economic effects of government policies that restrict international trade
   AACSB Coding: Reflective Thinking
   Special Feature: None

Figure 8-1

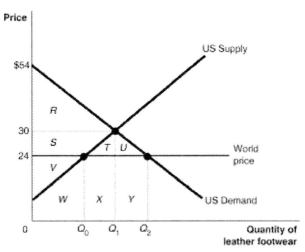

Figure 8-1 shows the U.S. demand and supply for leather footwear.

2. **Refer to Figure 8-1.** Under autarky, the equilibrium price is _____, the consumer surplus is _____ and the producer surplus is _____.
   A) $30; consumer surplus = area R; producer surplus = area S + V
   B) $30; consumer surplus = area R + S + V; producer surplus = area T + W+ X
   C) $24; consumer surplus = area R + S; producer surplus = area V
   D) $30; consumer surplus = area R; producer surplus = area S + T + V + W + X
   Answer: A
   Diff: 2   Type: MC   Page Ref: 255-6/255-6
   Topic: Gains from trade
   Skill: Analytical
   Objective: LO4: Analyze the economic effects of government policies that restrict international trade
   AACSB Coding: Analytic Skills
   Special Feature: None

3. **Refer to Figure 8-1.** Suppose the government allows imports of leather footwear into the U.S. What happens to the market price and what is the quantity of imports?
   A) The price equals $24 and imports equal Q_2 units.
   B) The price falls to $24 and imports equal $Q_2 - Q_1$ units.
   C) The price falls to $24 and imports equal $Q_1 - Q_0$ units.
   D) The price equals $24 and imports equals $Q_2 - Q_0$ units.
   Answer: D
   Diff: 2   Type: MC   Page Ref: 255-6/255-6
   Topic: Gains from trade
   Skill: Analytical
   Objective: LO4: Analyze the economic effects of government policies that restrict international trade
   AACSB Coding: Analytic Skills
   Special Feature: None

4. ***Refer to Figure 8-1.*** Suppose the government allows imports of leather footwear into the U.S. The market price falls to $24. What areas represent consumer surplus and domestic producer surplus?

    A) Consumer surplus = R + S; producer surplus = V.

    B) Consumer surplus = R + S + T + U; producer surplus = V.

    C) Consumer surplus = R + S + T + U; producer surplus = V + W + X + Y.

    D) Consumer surplus = R + S + T; producer surplus = W + X + Y.

Answer: B

Diff: 2   *Type: MC*   *Page Ref: 255-6/255-6*
Topic: Gains from trade
Skill: Analytical
Objective: LO4: Analyze the economic effects of government policies that restrict international trade
AACSB Coding: Analytic Skills
Special Feature: None

5. Which of the following is not an example of a trade restriction?

    A) Tariffs.

    B) Quotas and voluntary export restraints.

    C) Legislation requiring that cars sold in a country have a 50 percent domestic content.

    D) Consumer preferences for goods produced domestically.

Answer: D

Diff: 1   *Type: MC*   *Page Ref: 256-8/256-8*
Topic: Trade restrictions
Skill: Fact
Objective: LO4: Analyze the economic effects of government policies that restrict international trade
AACSB Coding: Reflective Thinking
Special Feature: None

6. International trade

    A) harms consumers but helps exporting firms.

    B) helps consumers but harms exporting firms and their workers.

    C) helps consumers but hurts firms that are less efficient than their foreign competitors.

    D) helps consumers and firms that compete with their foreign competitors.

Answer: C

Diff: 1   *Type: MC*   *Page Ref: 256/256*
Topic: Gains from trade
Skill: Conceptual
Objective: LO4: Analyze the economic effects of government policies that restrict international trade
AACSB Coding: Reflective Thinking
Special Feature: None

7. A tariff is
    A) a limit placed on the quantity of goods that can be imported into a country.
    B) a tax imposed by a government on goods imported into a country.
    C) a subsidy granted to importers of a vital input.
    D) a health and safety restriction imposed on an imported product.
    Answer: B
    Diff: 1   Type: MC   Page Ref: 256–7/256–7
    Topic: Tariff
    Skill: Definition
    Objective: LO4: Analyze the economic effects of government policies that restrict international trade
    AACSB Coding: Reflective Thinking
    Special Feature: None

8. A tax imposed by a government on imports of a good into a country is called a
    A) tariff.
    B) quota.
    C) value added tax.
    D) sales tax.
    Answer: A
    Diff: 1   Type: MC   Page Ref: 256–7/256–7
    Topic: Tariff
    Skill: Definition
    Objective: LO4: Analyze the economic effects of government policies that restrict international trade
    AACSB Coding: Reflective Thinking
    Special Feature: None

9. Which of the following is the best example of a tariff?
    A) A subsidy from the U.S. government to domestic manufacturers of residential air
       conditioners to enable them to compete more effectively with foreign producers.
    B) A limit on the quantity of residential air conditioners that can be imported from a
       foreign country.
    C) A $150 fee imposed on all imported residential air conditioners.
    D) A tax placed on all residential air conditioners sold in the domestic market to help
       offset the impact of emissions on the environment.
    Answer: C
    Diff: 1   Type: MC   Page Ref: 256–7/256–7
    Topic: Tariff
    Skill: Conceptual
    Objective: LO4: Analyze the economic effects of government policies that restrict international trade
    AACSB Coding: Reflective Thinking
    Special Feature: None

10. A tariff
   A) makes domestic consumers better off.
   B) makes both domestic producers and consumers better off.
   C) makes everyone worse off.
   D) makes domestic producers better off.
   Answer: D
   Diff: 1   Type: MC   Page Ref: 257/257
   Topic: Tariff
   Skill: Conceptual
   Objective: LO4: Analyze the economic effects of government policies that restrict international trade
   AACSB Coding: Reflective Thinking
   Special Feature: None

Figure 8–2

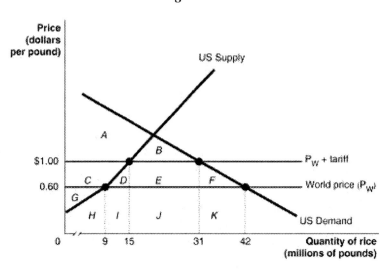

Suppose the U.S. government imposes a $0.40 per pound tariff on rice imports. Figure 8–2 shows the impact of this tariff.

11. *Refer to Figure 8–2.* The tariff revenue collected by the government equals the area
   A) D + E + F.
   B) E.
   C) B + D + E + F.
   D) C + D + E + F.
   Answer: B
   Diff: 2   Type: MC   Page Ref: 256-7/256-7
   Topic: Tariff
   Skill: Analytical
   Objective: LO4: Analyze the economic effects of government policies that restrict international trade
   AACSB Coding: Analytic Skills
   Special Feature: None

12. *Refer to Figure 8-2.* With the tariff in place, the U.S.
    A) imports 16 million pounds of rice.
    B) imports 9 million pounds of rice.
    C) imports 15 million pounds of rice.
    D) exports 31 million pounds of rice.
    Answer: A
    Diff: 2   Type: MC   Page Ref: 256-7/256-7
    Topic: Tariff
    Skill: Analytical
    Objective: LO4: Analyze the economic effects of government policies that restrict international trade
    AACSB Coding: Analytic Skills
    Special Feature: None

13. *Refer to Figure 8-2.* As a result of the tariff, domestic producers increase their quantity supplied by
    A) 15 million pounds of rice.
    B) 22 million pounds of rice.
    C) 31 million pounds or rice.
    D) 6 million pounds of rice.
    Answer: D
    Diff: 2   Type: MC   Page Ref: 256-7/256-7
    Topic: Tariff
    Skill: Analytical
    Objective: LO4: Analyze the economic effects of government policies that restrict international trade
    AACSB Coding: Analytic Skills
    Special Feature: None

14. *Refer to Figure 8-2.* The increase in domestic producer surplus as a result of the tariff is equal to the area
    A) C.
    B) C + G.
    C) A + C + G.
    D) C + D + G + G + I.
    Answer: A
    Diff: 2   Type: MC   Page Ref: 256-7/256-7
    Topic: Tariff
    Skill: Analytical
    Objective: LO4: Analyze the economic effects of government policies that restrict international trade
    AACSB Coding: Analytic Skills
    Special Feature: None

15. **Refer to Figure 8-2.** The tariff causes domestic consumption of rice
    A) to fall by 27 million pounds.
    B) to fall by 11 million pounds.
    C) to rise by 6 million pounds.
    D) to rise by 16 million pounds.
    Answer: B
    Diff: 2   Type: MC   Page Ref: 256-7/256-7
    Topic: Tariff
    Skill: Analytical
    Objective: LO4: Analyze the economic effects of government policies that restrict international trade
    AACSB Coding: Analytic Skills
    Special Feature: None

16. **Refer to Figure 8-2.** The loss in domestic consumer surplus as a result of the tariff is equal to
    the area
    A) B + D + E + F.
    B) D + E + F.
    C) C + D + E + F.
    D) B.
    Answer: C
    Diff: 2   Type: MC   Page Ref: 256-7/256-7
    Topic: Tariff
    Skill: Analytical
    Objective: LO4: Analyze the economic effects of government policies that restrict international trade
    AACSB Coding: Analytic Skills
    Special Feature: None

17. An agreement negotiated by two countries that places a numerical limit on the quantity of a
    good that can be imported by one country from another country is called
    A) a non-tariff trade barrier.
    B) an export quota.
    C) an import quota.
    D) a voluntary export restraint.
    Answer: D
    Diff: 1   Type: MC   Page Ref: 257-8/257-8
    Topic: Trade restrictions
    Skill: Definition
    Objective: LO4: Analyze the economic effects of government policies that restrict international trade
    AACSB Coding: Reflective Thinking
    Special Feature: None

18. In the 1980s Japan agreed to limit the quantity of automobiles it would export to the United States. Why did the Japanese government agree to this trade restriction?
    A) Japanese automobile producers lobbied for the restrictions in order to increase the price of their exports to the U.S.
    B) The Japanese government wanted to limit sales to the United States in order to make more automobiles available for Japanese consumers.
    C) The Japanese government feared that the alternative would be a tariff or quota on imports of Japanese automobiles imposed by the U.S. government.
    D) The Japanese government wanted more automobiles to be available for export to countries other than the United States.
    Answer: C
    Diff: 1   Type: MC   Page Ref: 257–8/257–8
    Topic: Trade restrictions
    Skill: Fact
    Objective: LO4: Analyze the economic effects of government policies that restrict international trade
    AACSB Coding: Reflective Thinking
    Special Feature: None

19. Which of the following is the best example of a quota?
    A) A limit imposed on the number of sports utility vehicles that the U.S. can import from Japan.
    B) A subsidy granted by the U.S. government to domestic garment manufacturers so they can compete more effectively with foreign garment manufacturers.
    C) A tax placed on all sports utility vehicles sold in the domestic market.
    D) A $5000 per–car fee imposed on all sports utility vehicles imported into the U.S.
    Answer: A
    Diff: 1   Type: MC   Page Ref: 257–8/257–8
    Topic: Quota
    Skill: Conceptual
    Objective: LO4: Analyze the economic effects of government policies that restrict international trade
    AACSB Coding: Reflective Thinking
    Special Feature: None

20. In order to avoid the imposition of other types of trade barriers, foreign producers will sometimes agree to limit their exports to a country. What are these types of agreements called?
    A) Involuntary export restraints.
    B) Voluntary export restraints.
    C) Implicit quotas.
    D) Sanctions.
    Answer: B
    Diff: 1   Type: MC   Page Ref: 257–8/257–8
    Topic: Non–tariff barriers
    Skill: Definition
    Objective: LO4: Analyze the economic effects of government policies that restrict international trade
    AACSB Coding: Reflective Thinking
    Special Feature: None

Figure 8–3

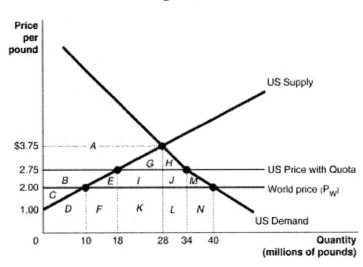

Since 1953 the U.S. has imposed a quota to limit the imports of peanuts. Figure 8–3 illustrates the impact of the quota.

21. *Refer to Figure 8–3.* Without the quota, the domestic price of peanuts equals the world price which is $2.00 per pound. What is the quantity of peanuts supplied by domestic producers in the absence of a quota?
    A) 28 million pounds
    B) 10 million pounds
    C) 40 million pounds
    D) 30 million pounds
Answer: B
Diff: 2   Type: MC   Page Ref: 259–60/259–60
Topic: Quota
Skill: Analytical
Objective: LO4: Analyze the economic effects of government policies that restrict international trade
AACSB Coding: Analytic Skills
Special Feature: Solved Problem: Measuring the Economic Effect of a Quota

22. *Refer to Figure 8–3.* If there was no quota, how many pounds of peanuts would domestic consumers purchase and what quantity would be imported?
    A) 28 million pounds of which 18 million pounds would be imported.
    B) 40 million pounds of which 12 million pounds would be imported.
    C) 40 million pounds of which 30 million pounds would be imported.
    D) 40 million pounds all of which would be imported.
Answer: C
Diff: 2   Type: MC   Page Ref: 259–60/259–60
Topic: Quota
Skill: Analytical
Objective: LO4: Analyze the economic effects of government policies that restrict international trade
AACSB Coding: Analytic Skills
Special Feature: Solved Problem: Measuring the Economic Effect of a Quota

23. *Refer to Figure 8–3.* What is the area of domestic producer surplus without a quota?
    A) C
    B) C + B
    C) A + B + C
    D) A + B + C + D
    Answer: A
    Diff: 2   Type: MC   Page Ref: 259–60/259–60
    Topic: Quota
    Skill: Analytical
    Objective: LO4: Analyze the economic effects of government policies that restrict international trade
    AACSB Coding: Analytic Skills
    Special Feature: Solved Problem: Measuring the Economic Effect of a Quota

24. *Refer to Figure 8–3.* With a quota in place, what is the quantity consumed in the domestic market and what portion of this is supplied by domestic producers?
    A) Domestic consumption equals 28 million pounds of which 18 million pounds is produced by domestic producers.
    B) Domestic consumption equals 40 million pounds of which 22 million pounds is produced by domestic producers.
    C) Domestic consumption equals 34 million pounds of which 16 million pounds is produced by domestic producers.
    D) Domestic consumption equals 34 million pounds of which 18 million pounds is produced by domestic producers.
    Answer: D
    Diff: 2   Type: MC   Page Ref: 259–60/259–60
    Topic: Quota
    Skill: Analytical
    Objective: LO4: Analyze the economic effects of government policies that restrict international trade
    AACSB Coding: Analytic Skills
    Special Feature: Solved Problem: Measuring the Economic Effect of a Quota

25. *Refer to Figure 8–3.* What is the area of consumer surplus after the imposition of the quota?
    A) A + G + H
    B) G + H + E + I+ J + M
    C) G + H
    D) A
    Answer: A
    Diff: 1   Type: MC   Page Ref: 259–60/259–60
    Topic: Quota
    Skill: Analytical
    Objective: LO4: Analyze the economic effects of government policies that restrict international trade
    AACSB Coding: Analytic Skills
    Special Feature: Solved Problem: Measuring the Economic Effect of a Quota

26. *Refer to Figure 8-3.* What is the area of domestic producer surplus after the imposition of a quota?
    A) B
    B) B + C
    C) B + E + I + J + M
    D) E + I + J + M
    Answer: B
    Diff: 2   Type: MC   Page Ref: 259–60/259–60
    Topic: Quota
    Skill: Analytical
    Objective: LO4: Analyze the economic effects of government policies that restrict international trade
    AACSB Coding: Analytic Skills
    Special Feature: Solved Problem: Measuring the Economic Effect of a Quota

27. *Refer to Figure 8-3.* What is the area that represents revenue to foreign producers who are granted permission to sell in the U.S. market when there is a quota?
    A) I + J
    B) E + I + J + M
    C) I + J + K + L
    D) G + H + I + J
    Answer: C
    Diff: 2   Type: MC   Page Ref: 258–9/258–9
    Topic: Quota
    Skill: Analytical
    Objective: LO4: Analyze the economic effects of government policies that restrict international trade
    AACSB Coding: Analytic Skills
    Special Feature: None

28. *Refer to Figure 8-3.* What is the area that represents the deadweight loss as a result of the quota?
    A) G + H
    B) G + H + I + J
    C) E + I + J + M
    D) E + M
    Answer: D
    Diff: 2   Type: MC   Page Ref: 259–60/259–60
    Topic: Quota
    Skill: Analytical
    Objective: LO4: Analyze the economic effects of government policies that restrict international trade
    AACSB Coding: Analytic Skills
    Special Feature: Solved Problem: Measuring the Economic Effect of a Quota

29. Which of the following is common to both tariffs and quotas?
    A) Tariffs and quotas are both used as a means to increase government revenue.
    B) Tariffs and quotas both increase economic efficiency.
    C) Tariffs and quotas are both designed to reduce foreign competition faced by domestic firms.
    D) Tariffs and quotas are both examples of voluntary export restraints.
    Answer: C
    Diff: 1   Type: MC   Page Ref: 260/260
    Topic: Trade restrictions
    Skill: Conceptual
    Objective: LO4: Analyze the economic effects of government policies that restrict international trade
    AACSB Coding: Reflective Thinking
    Special Feature: None

30. Trade restrictions are often motivated by a desire to save domestic jobs threatened by competition from imports. Which of the following counter-arguments is made by economists who oppose trade restrictions?
    A) Statistics show that trade restrictions actually do not save jobs.
    B) Consumers pay a high cost for jobs saved through trade restrictions.
    C) Trade restrictions have a limited impact because most Americans prefer domestic goods over imports.
    D) Trade restrictions benefit consumers in the short run but not in the long run.
    Answer: B
    Diff: 2   Type: MC   Page Ref: 260-1/260-1
    Topic: Trade restrictions
    Skill: Conceptual
    Objective: LO4: Analyze the economic effects of government policies that restrict international trade
    AACSB Coding: Reflective Thinking
    Special Feature: None

31. Which of the following statements is true?
    A) Economic efficiency would be increased if the U.S. eliminated all of its trade restrictions, but only if all other countries eliminated their trade restrictions too.
    B) The U. S. economy would gain from the elimination of its tariffs but not from the elimination of its quotas.
    C) Eliminating its tariffs and quotas unilaterally would not benefit the U.S. because this would remove the leverage it would have to persuade other countries to eliminate their trade restrictions.
    D) The U.S. economy would gain from the elimination of tariffs and quotas even if other countries do not reduce their tariffs and quotas.
    Answer: D
    Diff: 1   Type: MC   Page Ref: 261/261
    Topic: How countries gain from trade
    Skill: Conceptual
    Objective: LO4: Analyze the economic effects of government policies that restrict international trade
    AACSB Coding: Reflective Thinking
    Special Feature: None

32. Governments sometimes erect barriers to trade other than tariffs and quotas. Which of the following is not an example of this type of trade barrier?
    A) A requirement that the employees of domestic firms that engage in foreign trade pay income taxes.
    B) A requirement that imports meet health and safety requirements.
    C) Restrictions on imports for national security reasons.
    D) A requirement that the U.S. government buy military uniforms only from U.S. manufacturers.
    Answer: A
    Diff: 1   Type: MC   Page Ref: 261-2/261-2
    Topic: Trade restrictions
    Skill: Conceptual
    Objective: LO4: Analyze the economic effects of government policies that restrict international trade
    AACSB Coding: Reflective Thinking
    Special Feature: None

33. A tariff is a numerical limit on the quantity of a good that can be imported.
    Answer: True   ⊘ False
    Diff: 2   Type: TF   Page Ref: 256-7/256-7
    Topic: Tariff
    Skill: Definition
    Objective: LO4: Analyze the economic effects of government policies that restrict international trade
    AACSB Coding: Reflective Thinking
    Special Feature: None

34. The U. S. would gain from the elimination of tariffs and quotas even if other countries do not reduce their tariffs and quotas.
    Answer: ⊘ True   False
    Diff: 1   Type: TF   Page Ref: 261/261
    Topic: Barriers to trade
    Skill: Conceptual
    Objective: LO4: Analyze the economic effects of government policies that restrict international trade
    AACSB Coding: Reflective Thinking
    Special Feature: None

35.

Figure 8–4

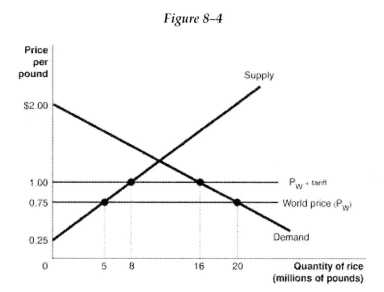

Refer to Figure 8–4. Suppose the U.S. government imposes a $0.25 per pound tariff on rice imports. Figure 8–4 shows the demand and supply curves for rice and the impact of this tariff. Use the figure to answer questions a–i.

a. Following the imposition of the tariff, what is the price that domestic consumers must now pay and   what is the quantity purchased?

b. Calculate the value of consumer surplus with the tariff in place.

c. What is the quantity supplied by domestic rice growers with the tariff in place?

d. Calculate the value of producer surplus received by U.S. rice growers with the tariff in place.

e. What is the quantity of rice imported with the tariff in place?

f. What is the amount of tariff revenue collected by the government?

g. The tariff has reduced consumer surplus. Calculate the loss in consumer surplus due to the tariff.

h. What portion of the consumer surplus loss is redistributed to domestic producers? To the government?

i. Calculate the deadweight loss due to the tariff.

Answer: a. Price = $1.00 per pound; Quantity purchased = 16 million pounds

   b. Consumer surplus = 1/2 x 16 million x $1 = $8 million

   c. Quantity supplied by domestic producers = 8 million pounds

   d. Producer surplus to rice growers = 1/2 x 8 million x $0.75 = $3 million

   e. Quantity imported = 8 million pounds

   f. Tariff revenue collected by the government = $0.25 x 8 million = $2 million

   g. Loss in consumer surplus due to the tariff = 16 million x $0.25 + 1/2 x 4 million x $0.25 = $4.5 million

   h. Amount redistributed to domestic producers = 5 million x $0.25 + 1/2 x 3 million x $0.25 = $1.625 million. Amount redistributed to the government = 8 million x $0.25 = $2 million

   i. Deadweight loss due to the tariff = 1/2 x 4 million x $0.25 + 1/2 x 3 million x $0.25 = $875,000

Diff: 3   Type: ES   Page Ref: 256-7/256-7
Topic: Tariff
Skill: Analytical
Objective: LO4: Analyze the economic effects of government policies that restrict international trade
AACSB Coding: Analytic Skills
Special Feature: None

36.   *Figure 8-5*

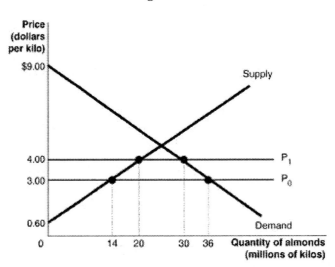

Refer to Figure 8-5. Bragabong currently both produces and imports almonds. The government of Bragabong decides to restrict international trade in almonds by imposing a quota that allows imports of only 10 million kilos each year. Figure 8-5 shows the estimated demand and supply curves for almonds in Bragabong and the results of imposing the quota. Answer questions a-j using the figure.

a.   If there is no quota what is the domestic price of almonds and what is the quantity of almonds demanded by consumers?

b.   If there is no quota how many kilos of almonds would domestic producers supply and what quantity would be imported?

c.   If there is no quota what is the dollar value of consumer surplus?

d.   If there is no quota what is the dollar value of producer surplus received by producers in Bragabong?

e.   If there is no quota what is the revenue received by foreign producers who supply almonds to Bragabong?

f.   With a quota in place what is the price that consumers of Bragabong must now pay and what is the quantity demanded?

g.   With a quota in place what is the dollar value of consumer surplus? Are consumers better off?

h.   With a quota in place what is the dollar value of producer surplus received by producers in Bragabong? Are domestic producers better off?

i.   Calculate the revenue to foreign producers who are granted permission to sell in Bragabong after the imposition of the quota.

j.   Calculate the deadweight loss as a result of the quota.

Answer: a. Price without a quota = $3 per kilo; quantity demanded = 36 million kilos
  b. Quantity supplied by domestic producers when there is no quota = 14 million kilos; quantity imported = 22 million kilos
  c. Consumer surplus without a quota = 1/2 x $6 x 36 million = $108 million
  d. Domestic producer surplus without a quota = 1/2 x 14 million x $2.40 = $16.8 million
  e. Revenue received by foreign producers when there is no quota =22 million x $3 = $66 million
  f. Price with a quota = $4.00 per kilo; quantity demanded = 30 million kilos
  g. Consumer surplus with a quota = 1/2 x $5 x 30 million = $75 million. No, consumers are worse off.
  h. Domestic producer surplus with a quota = 1/2 x $3.40 x 20 million = $34 million. Yes, domestic producers are better off.
  i. With a quota revenue to foreign producers = $4 x 10 million = $40 million
  j. Deadweight loss = 1/2 x $1 x 6 million + 1/2 x $1 x 6 million = $6 million

Diff: 3   Type: ES   Page Ref: 258–60/258–60
Topic: Quota
Skill: Analytical
Objective: LO4: Analyze the economic effects of government policies that restrict international trade
AACSB Coding: Analytic Skills
Special Feature: None

3. a. Distinguish between a tariff and a quota.
  b. In what ways are tariffs and quotas similar?
  c. In what ways are tariffs and quotas different?
  d. Why might a foreign producer prefer a quota rather than a tariff?
  Answer: a. A tariff is a tax imposed by a government on imports while a quota is a numerical limit imposed by the government on the quantity of a good that can be imported into a country.
    b. Compared to unrestricted trade, both a tariff and a quota result in: (1) a higher domestic price for the protected good; (2) a lower quantity consumed; (3) a decrease in consumer surplus; (4) an increase in producer surplus; (5) an inefficient allocation of resources (a deadweight loss).
    c. One important difference between a tariff and a quota is that a tariff generates revenue for the government. Part of the decrease in consumer surplus is redistributed to the government in the form of tariff revenue. A quota generates no revenue for the government. Part of the decrease in consumer surplus is redistributed to the foreign producers who are allowed to sell the good in the domestic market.
    d. A foreign producer might prefer a quota to a tariff because the producer is able to sell the product at a higher price and also to capture part of the decrease in consumer surplus.

Diff: 3   Type: ES   Page Ref: 256–60/256–60
Topic: Trade restrictions
Skill: Conceptual
Objective: LO4: Analyze the economic effects of government policies that restrict international trade
AACSB Coding: Reflective Thinking
Special Feature: None

8.5 The Arguments over Trade Policy and Globalization

1. Disagreements about whether the U.S. government should regulate international trade
    A) began during the Great Depression.
    B) began after World War I when government officials no longer believed in isolationism.
    C) date back to the beginning of the country.
    D) did not occur until the end of the Mexican War in 1848.
    Answer: C
    Diff: 1   Type: MC   Page Ref: 262/262
    Topic: Trade policies and globalization
    Skill: Fact
    Objective: LO5: Evaluate the arguments over trade policy and globalization
    AACSB Coding: Reflective Thinking
    Special Feature: None

2. The Smoot–Hawley Tariff
    A) lowered U.S. tariffs by 50 percent following World War II.
    B) was passed by the U.S. Congress following the Civil War as a means of increasing government revenue.
    C) was passed by the U.S. Congress upon a recommendation made by the General Agreement on Tariffs and Trade (GATT) in 1948.
    D) raised average tariff rates by over 50 percent in the U.S. in 1930.
    Answer: D
    Diff: 1   Type: MC   Page Ref: 262/262
    Topic: Protectionism
    Skill: Fact
    Objective: LO5: Evaluate the arguments over trade policy and globalization
    AACSB Coding: Reflective Thinking
    Special Feature: None

3. In 1930 the U.S. government attempted to help domestic firms that were harmed by the Great Depression by
    A) establishing the General Agreement on Tariffs and Trade (GATT).
    B) passing the Smoot–Hawley Tariff.
    C) establishing the World Trade Organization (WTO).
    D) passing the North American Free Trade Agreement (NAFTA).
    Answer: B
    Diff: 1   Type: MC   Page Ref: 262/262
    Topic: Protectionism
    Skill: Fact
    Objective: LO5: Evaluate the arguments over trade policy and globalization
    AACSB Coding: Reflective Thinking
    Special Feature: None

4. In 1995 the General Agreement on Tariffs and Trade (GATT), which was established in 1948, was replaced by the World Trade Organization (WTO). Why did members of the GATT push for the establishment of the WTO?
   A) The GATT agreement covered only trade in goods. The WTO was created to cover trade in goods, services and intellectual property.
   B) The charter of the GATT had run out and a new organization was needed to promote international trade.
   C) The creation of the European Union (EU) made the GATT obsolete. The WTO was formed to regulate trade between the EU and other nations.
   D) By 1995 tariffs had been eliminated. The WTO was created to reduce non-tariff trade barriers.

Answer: A

Diff: 2   Type: MC   Page Ref: 262/262
Topic: Trade policies and globalization
Skill: Fact
Objective: LO5: Evaluate the arguments over trade policy and globalization
AACSB Coding: Reflective Thinking
Special Feature: None

5. The World Trade Organization (WTO) promotes foreign trade and investment, or globalization. In recent years opposition to globalization has led to violent protests at meetings of the WTO. One reason for these anti-globalization protests is
   A) foreign trade and investment are examples of zero-sum games.
   B) protesters believe that globalization will result in a return to communism in developing countries.
   C) protesters believe that free trade destroys the distinctive cultures of many countries.
   D) protesters object to the loss of intellectual property (such as software programs and movies) that results from foreign trade and investment.

Answer: C

Diff: 2   Type: MC   Page Ref: 263/263
Topic: Trade policies and globalization
Skill: Fact
Objective: LO5: Evaluate the arguments over trade policy and globalization
AACSB Coding: Reflective Thinking
Special Feature: None

6. Prior to the 1998 World Cup, France banned the use of all soccer balls made by child workers. Several economists criticized the ban. Which of the following is an argument these economists used to justify the use of child labor in some countries?
   A) Soccer balls are easy to carry and workers were given soccer balls to play with.
   B) Child workers were allowed to attend school during the periods they worked.
   C) Child workers were given gloves to protect their hands while they stitched soccer balls.
   D) Some of the alternatives to stitching soccer balls include begging and prostitution

Answer: D
Diff: 1   Type: MC   Page Ref: 263–4/263–4
Topic: Trade policies and globalization
Skill: Fact
Objective: LO5: Evaluate the arguments over trade policy and globalization
AACSB Coding: Reflective Thinking
Special Feature: Making the Connection: The Unintended Consequences of Banning Goods Made with Child Labor

7. Protectionism
   A) is the use of cheap labor to protect firms from paying high wages.
   B) is the use of trade barriers to protect domestic firms from foreign competition.
   C) refers to reductions in tariffs and other barriers that protect consumers from paying high prices.
   D) refers to the use of copyright and trademark laws to protect inventors and artists from losing the rights to their creative efforts.

Answer: B
Diff: 1   Type: MC   Page Ref: 264/264
Topic: Protectionism
Skill: Definition
Objective: LO5: Evaluate the arguments over trade policy and globalization
AACSB Coding: Reflective Thinking
Special Feature: None

8. Your roommate Hansen argues that American producers cannot compete with foreign producers because wages are lower in foreign countries than in the U.S. Hansen
   A) is incorrect. Free trade raises living standards by increasing economic efficiency.
   B) is right in asserting the need to protect high wages if the U.S. wishes to maintain its high standard of living.
   C) is correct in arguing that the high wages of U.S. workers make it impossible to compete with workers in low–wage countries. .
   D) is advancing the anti–dumping argument for protectionism.

Answer: A
Diff: 2   Type: MC   Page Ref: 264–5/264–5
Topic: Trade policies and globalization
Skill: Conceptual
Objective: LO5: Evaluate the arguments over trade policy and globalization
AACSB Coding: Reflective Thinking
Special Feature: None

9. Many economists criticize protectionism because it causes losses to consumers and eliminates jobs in domestic industries that use protected products. Why, then, do some people support protectionism?
    A) The criticisms of economists are based on theory. In fact, protectionism increases consumer and producer surplus as well as employment.
    B) Supporters of protectionism in high-income countries believe that wages will fall as a result of competition with firms from developing countries.
    C) Supporters of protectionism believe free trade will cause their countries to lose their comparative advantage.
    D) Supporters of protectionism believe that free trade will lead to inflation.
    Answer: B
    Diff: 2   Type: MC   Page Ref: 264–5/264–5
    Topic: Protectionism
    Skill: Fact
    Objective: LO5: Evaluate the arguments over trade policy and globalization
    AACSB Coding: Reflective Thinking
    Special Feature: None

10. All but one of the following statements is used to justify protectionism. Which statement is *not* used to justify protectionism?
    A) Free trade leads to higher prices for imported goods.
    B) Free trade reduces employment by driving domestic firms out of business.
    C) A country should not rely on other countries for goods that are critical to its national defense.
    D) Trade restrictions are necessary to protect new firms until they can gain experience and become more productive.
    Answer: A
    Diff: 2   Type: MC   Page Ref: 264–5/264–5
    Topic: Protectionism
    Skill: Conceptual
    Objective: LO5: Evaluate the arguments over trade policy and globalization
    AACSB Coding: Reflective Thinking
    Special Feature: None

11. Which of the following describes the infant industry argument for protectionism?
    A) An industry must be protected in its early stages of development so that firms can compete with government-subsidized foreign competition.
    B) Some strategic industries must be protected to ensure adequate supplies of resources needed for national defense in emergencies.
    C) Domestic producers in high-wage countries must be protected from foreign producers in low-wage countries to produce a level playing field.
    D) Domestic producers require time to gain experience and lower their unit costs; this will allow these producers to compete successfully in international markets.

Answer: D
Diff: 2   Type: MC   Page Ref: 265/265
Topic: Protectionism
Skill: Definition
Objective: LO5: Evaluate the arguments over trade policy and globalization
AACSB Coding: Reflective Thinking
Special Feature: None

12. Which of the following describes the national security argument for protectionism?
    A) Nearly all industries can make some claim to strategic importance so such trade restrictions can get out of hand.
    B) Increases in economic surplus outweigh the decreases in consumer surplus that result from protectionism.
    C) Some goods should be insulated from foreign competition to ensure an adequate supply of these goods in the event of an international conflict.
    D) Private companies (for example, Coca-Cola) should not be forced to reveal their trade secrets to foreign companies.

Answer: C
Diff: 2   Type: MC   Page Ref: 265/265
Topic: Protectionism
Skill: Conceptual
Objective: LO5: Evaluate the arguments over trade policy and globalization
AACSB Coding: Reflective Thinking
Special Feature: None

13. Economists believe the most persuasive argument for protectionism is to protect infant industries. But the argument has a drawback. What is this drawback?
    A) Governments always make the level of protection for infant industries too high.
    B) Governments are usually too impatient and do not allow protection to remain in place long enough to allow industries to be competitive in international markets.
    C) Governments usually use tariffs, rather than quotas, to protect infant industries in order to collect tariff revenue. (Quotas do not result in government revenue).
    D) Protection lessens the need for firms to become productive enough to compete with foreign firms; this often results in infant industries never "growing up."
    Answer: D
    Diff: 2   Type: MC   Page Ref: 265/265
    Topic: Protectionism
    Skill: Conceptual
    Objective: LO5: Evaluate the arguments over trade policy and globalization
    AACSB Coding: Reflective Thinking
    Special Feature: None

14. The North American Free Trade Agreement (NAFTA) went into effect in 1994. NAFTA reduced trade barriers among the United States, Mexico and Canada. Many people in the United States opposed the agreement for fear that it would result in a loss of jobs and lower wages. Most economists have concluded that
    A) although consumers have benefited from lower prices, the opposition was correct.
    B) in fact, no workers lost their jobs as a result of NAFTA and wages of U.S. workers have not fallen.
    C) although some workers lost their jobs NAFTA helped the U.S. economy become more efficient and expanded consumption.
    D) although some jobs were created in the U.S. there has been a net loss of U.S. jobs to Mexico and Canada.
    Answer: C
    Diff: 2   Type: MC   Page Ref: 265-6/265-6
    Topic: Trade policies and globalization
    Skill: Fact
    Objective: LO5: Evaluate the arguments over trade policy and globalization
    AACSB Coding: Reflective Thinking
    Special Feature: Making the Connection: Has NAFTA Helped or Hurt the Economy?

15. The selling of a product for a price below its cost of production is called
    A) fair competition.
    B) dumping.
    C) unfair competition.
    D) operating at a loss.
    Answer: B
    Diff: 1   Type: MC   Page Ref: 266/266
    Topic: Dumping
    Skill: Definition
    Objective: LO5: Evaluate the arguments over trade policy and globalization
    AACSB Coding: Reflective Thinking
    Special Feature: None

16. It is difficult to determine if foreign companies are selling their products for prices below their costs of production because
    A) the true costs of production are difficult to calculate.
    B) the firms have no legal obligation to reveal this information.
    C) costs are calculated in the firms' local currencies.
    D) domestic taxes increase the firms' costs but it is difficult to determine the incidence of these taxes.

Answer: A
Diff: 1   Type: MC   Page Ref: 266
Topic: Dumping
Skill: Conceptual
Objective: LO5: Evaluate the arguments over trade policy and globalization
AACSB Coding: Reflective Thinking
Special Feature: None

17. Measuring the impact of a quota or tariff on the U.S. economy is an example of _____. Stating that a quota or tariff should be eliminated is an example of _____.
    A) statistical analysis; economic analysis
    B) positive analysis; normative analysis
    C) econometric analysis; protectionism
    D) trade analysis; an opinion

Answer: B
Diff: 1   Type: MC   Page Ref: 266-7/266-7
Topic: Gains from trade
Skill: Fact
Objective: LO5: Evaluate the arguments over trade policy and globalization
AACSB Coding: Reflective Thinking
Special Feature: None

18. One reason for the success that firms have in getting the government to erect barriers to foreign competition is that jobs lost to foreign competition are easy to identify but jobs created by foreign trade are often hard to identify. Which of the following is a second reason?
    A) The costs that tariffs and quotas impose on consumers are large in total but relatively small per person.
    B) People who benefit from foreign trade tend not to vote in elections; people who are harmed by foreign trade are much more likely to vote.
    C) Firms that benefit from trade barriers have more money than firms that are harmed to lobby government officials to support the barriers.
    D) The benefits from free trade are less than the costs.

Answer: A
Diff: 1   Type: MC   Page Ref: 267/267
Topic: Economics in Your Life
Skill: Conceptual
Objective: LO5: Evaluate the arguments over trade policy and globalization
AACSB Coding: Reflective Thinking
Special Feature: Economics in YOUR Life!: Why Haven't You Heard of the Sugar Quota?

19. The quota on imported sugar costs U.S. consumers more than $2 billion annually and protects very few jobs. Why does Congress maintain a sugar quota that protects only a few thousand workers while forcing millions of people to pay higher prices for sugar products?
    A) Most U.S. citizens do not buy sugar products and want to help workers in the sugar industry.
    B) Voters fear that if they oppose the sugar lobby, the lobby may oppose issues that they want Congress to support.
    C) Citizens are not as involved in social and political issues as they used to be.
    D) The per person cost of the sugar quota is too small for many people to lobby Congress to make their views known.
    Answer: D
    Diff: 1   Type: MC   Page Ref: 267/267
    Topic: Trade restrictions
    Skill: Conceptual
    Objective: LO5: Evaluate the arguments over trade policy and globalization
    AACSB Coding: Reflective Thinking
    Special Feature: Economics in YOUR Life!: Why Haven't You Heard of the Sugar Quota?

20. One result of a bilateral trade agreement reached between the United States and South Korea in 2007 was the phasing out of a 40 percent tariff on beef imposed by the South Korean government. Which of the following is the most likely result from the elimination of this tariff?
    A) The price of beef in South Korea will rise.
    B) There will be an increase in the incomes of workers in South Korea's beef industry.
    C) The South Korean economy will benefit but some workers and firms in the beef industry will suffer losses.
    D) The supply of beef produced by South Korean firms will increase.
    Answer: C
    Diff: 2   Type: MC   Page Ref: 268-9/268-9
    Topic: Trade policies and globalization
    Skill: Conceptual
    Objective: LO5: Evaluate the arguments over trade policy and globalization
    AACSB Coding: Reflective Thinking
    Special Feature: An Inside Look: The United States and South Korea Reach a Trade Deal

21. In 2007 South Korea and the United States signed a bilateral trade agreement that lowered tariffs imposed by both countries' governments. An article in the *New York Times* declared that "Consumers in both countries are the deal's big winners." But the article also noted that news of the agreement resulted in protests from many South Koreans. Why did Korean citizens protest an agreement that would benefit their economy?
    A) Many South Koreans used the trade agreement as an excuse to protest United States policy toward North Korea.
    B) The protests were the result of false news reports in South Korea that the agreement would result in higher prices of beef. The protests ended after the press correctly reported that beef prices would be lowered.
    C) Political opponents of the South Korean government organized the protests. These opponents protested all of the government's policies because 2007 was an election year in South Korea.
    D) Although the trade agreement will benefit the entire South Korean economy, certain groups will suffer losses. These groups protested the agreement.
    Answer: D
    Diff: 2   Type: MC   Page Ref: 268-9/268-9
    Topic: Trade policies and globalization
    Skill: Analytical
    Objective: LO5: Evaluate the arguments over trade policy and globalization
    AACSB Coding: Analytic Skills
    Special Feature: An Inside Look: The United States and South Korea Reach a Trade Deal

22. The General Agreement on Tariffs and Trade (GATT) was formed to replace the World Trade Organization (WTO) because the WTO was empowered only to reduce barriers to trade in goods. The GATT is an agreement to reduce barriers to trade in goods, services and intellectual property.
    Answer: ⊙ True   False
    Diff: 2   Type: TF   Page Ref: 262/262
    Topic: Barriers to trade
    Skill: Fact
    Objective: LO5: Evaluate the arguments over trade policy and globalization
    AACSB Coding: Reflective Thinking
    Special Feature: None

23. Protectionism refers to the use of trade barriers to shield domestic firms from foreign competition.
    Answer: ⊙ True   False
    Diff: 1   Type: TF   Page Ref: 264/264
    Topic: Protectionism
    Skill: Definition
    Objective: LO5: Evaluate the arguments over trade policy and globalization
    AACSB Coding: Reflective Thinking
    Special Feature: None

24. a.   Define the term "globalization".
    b.   Describe the benefits of globalization.
    c.   Who is likely to oppose globalization and why?
    Answer: a.   Globalization refers to the process of countries becoming more open to foreign trade and investment.
    b.   The benefits of globalization include: (1) consumers have access to a wider array of goods and services at lower prices than under autarky; (2) trade permits a far more efficient allocation of resources than is possible under autarky; (3) specialization in production leads to productivity gains which raise a nation's standard of living.
    c.   Opposition to globalization comes from three sources: (1) firms and workers harmed by globalization. The revenues and profits of domestic firms that produce the same goods and services that are imported will fall and some workers may lose their jobs; (2) those who fear that low-income countries are at risk of losing their cultural identity as multinational corporations sell western goods in the markets of these countries; (3) those who are concerned that multinational corporations will relocate factories in low income countries to take advantage of low-cost labor while disregarding the interests of these countries (e.g., noncompliance with environmental standards) and its citizens (e.g. hiring child labor).

Diff: 3   Type: ES   Page Ref: 262-7/262-7
Topic: Globalization
Skill: Conceptual
Objective: LO5: Evaluate the arguments over trade policy and globalization
AACSB Coding: Reflective Thinking
Special Feature: None

25. Some government officials argue that the success achieved by firms in Dalton, Georgia in developing a comparative advantage in carpet making because of external economies can be used to justify trade barriers as a means to protect an "infant industry." After an infant industry gains experience it can compete in international markets and the trade barriers can be removed. What objections do economists make to this argument in favor of trade barriers?
    Answer: Many economists believe that this is the most persuasive argument for protection but experience teaches us that tariffs and quotas can stifle the incentive firms have to become more efficient producers, which is the reason for imposing trade restrictions in the first place. Few firms volunteer to have trade restrictions removed once they have been established.

Diff: 2   Type: ES   Page Ref: 265/265
Topic: Protectionism
Skill: Conceptual
Objective: LO5: Evaluate the arguments over trade policy and globalization
AACSB Coding: Reflective Thinking
Special Feature: None

26. The textbook referred to the following quotation from a Federal Reserve publication: "Trade is a win-win situation for all countries that participate." But many firms and workers oppose free trade policies and protests against globalization have become a regular occurrence at meetings of the World Trade Organization. If trade is a "win-win" situation why is there strong opposition to free trade and globalization?

Answer: Free trade between any two countries can be shown to make both countries better off by increasing the amount of goods and services available to consumers. Free trade gives incentives to countries to produce goods and services for which they have a comparative advantage. This allows for an efficient allocation of scarce resources. But devoting more resources to the production of one product means fewer resources are devoted to producing another product. Firms that produce these products experience a loss in revenue and profits and some workers are likely to lose their jobs. Even if other opportunities are available for workers they often require acquiring new skills and movement to another area of the country. There are *net* gains from free trade – gains exceed losses – but it is not surprising that those who are harmed oppose free trade policies.

Diff: 2   Type: ES   Page Ref: 262-7/262-7
Topic: How countries gain from trade
Skill: Conceptual
Objective: LO5: Evaluate the arguments over trade policy and globalization
AACSB Coding: Reflective Thinking
Special Feature: None

8.6   Appendix: Multinational Firms

1. Which of the following completes the following statement? Multinational enterprises
   A) date from the end of World War II where improvements in communication and transportation technology allowed firms to conduct operations in more than one country.
   B) are firms that operate in at least six countries.
   C) were relatively rare until the 20th century, although a number of multinational firms were established before the Middle Ages.
   D) were first started in the United States in the 19th century Multinational firms are now headquartered in many countries.

Answer: C
Diff: 1   Type: MC   Page Ref: 277/277
Topic: Multinational enterprises
Skill: Fact
Objective: Appendix: Understand why firms operate in more than one country
AACSB Coding: Reflective Thinking
Special Feature: None

2. Two key technological innovations made it possible for some U.S. corporations to begin operating in several continents beginning in the late 19th century. One of these innovations was the completion of the transatlantic cable. What was the second innovation?
  A) The completion of rail systems that made transportation by train over long distances feasible.
  B) The completion of the Erie Canal.
  C) The development of electric power plants that operated on alternating current.
  D) The development of more efficient steam engines.
  Answer: D
  Diff: 1   Type: MC   Page Ref: 277/277
  Topic: Multinational enterprises
  Skill: Fact
  Objective: Appendix: Understand why firms operate in more than one country
  AACSB Coding: Reflective Thinking
  Special Feature: None

3. When firms build or buy facilities in foreign countries they are said to engage in
  A) foreign direct investment.
  B) foreign portfolio investment.
  C) foreign exploratory investment.
  D) foreign indirect investment.
  Answer: A
  Diff: 1   Type: MC   Page Ref: 277/277
  Topic: Multinational enterprises
  Skill: Definition
  Objective: Appendix: Understand why firms operate in more than one country
  AACSB Coding: Reflective Thinking
  Special Feature: None

4. U.S. corporations expand their operations outside of the United States when they expect to increase their profits from doing so. Which of the following is one reason why firms might expect to increase their profits from operating in another country?
  A) The firms believe that elasticity of demand for their products is greater in another country.
  B) The firms want to avoid paying tariffs.
  C) The firms believe that operating in another country will increase the demand for their products in the United States.
  D) The firms want to buy foreign currency at a more favorable exchange rate.
  Answer: B
  Diff: 1   Type: MC   Page Ref: 278-9/278-9
  Topic: Multinational enterprises
  Skill: Analytical
  Objective: Appendix: Understand why firms operate in more than one country
  AACSB Coding: Analytic Skills
  Special Feature: None

5. During the 1990s, some U.S. corporations relocated their manufacturing operations to poor countries where they paid workers lower wages than they paid their workers in the U.S. However, most economists do not believe that relocating jobs abroad has reduced total employment in the United States or reduced the average wage paid to U.S. workers. One reason for this belief is that
  A) so far, the number of jobs lost to poor countries is too small to affect either total employment or wages. It will take at least 10 more years of relocation to have this effect.
  B) the corporations that have relocated their operations have also increased employment of U.S. workers; many of these workers earn high wages so that neither employment nor average wages have changed in the U.S.
  C) in order for employment to increase, wages must fall.
  D) competition from lower-wage foreign workers has not reduced wages in the U.S. because wages are determined by the ability of workers to produce goods and services.

Answer: D
Diff: 2   Type: MC   Page Ref: 280/280
Topic: Multinational enterprises
Skill: Analytical
Objective: Appendix: Understand why firms operate in more than one country
AACSB Coding: Analytic Skills
Special Feature: Making the Connection: Have Multinational Corporations Reduced Employment and Lowered Wages in the United States?

Chapter 9   Consumer Choice and Behavioral Economics

9.1   Utility and Consumer Decision Making

1. Coca-Cola hired rapper Shawn "Jay-Z" Carter to appear in television commercials to endorse Cherry Coke. This is
    A) an attempt by Coca-Cola to distinguish Cherry Coke from similar products sold by rival firms.
    B) Coca-Cola's first attempt to use a celebrity to advertise one of its products.
    C) an attempt by Coca-Cola to shift the indifference curves of their customers.
    D) an attempt by Coca-Cola to change the elasticity of demand for Cherry Coke.
    Answer: A
    Diff: 1   Type: MC   Page Ref: 284-5/284-5
    Topic: Social influences on decision making
    Skill: Fact
    Objective: LO 1: Define utility and explain how consumers choose goods and services to maximize their utility.
    AACSB Coding: Reflective Thinking
    Special Feature: Chapter Opener: Can Jay-Z Get You to Drink Cherry Coke?

2. Economists usually assume that people act in a rational, self-interested way. In explaining how consumers make choices this means that economists believe
    A) consumers will always buy goods and services at the lowest possible prices.
    B) consumers spend their incomes to order to accumulate the most goods and services.
    C) consumers make choices that will leave them as satisfied as possible given their incomes, tastes and the prices of goods and services available to them.
    D) consumers will spend their incomes and time on activities that benefit themselves as much as possible, without regard to the welfare of others.
    Answer: C
    Diff: 1   Type: MC   Page Ref: 286/286
    Topic: Rational decision making
    Skill: Conceptual
    Objective: LO 1: Define utility and explain how consumers choose goods and services to maximize their utility.
    AACSB Coding: Reflective Thinking
    Special Feature: None

3. The satisfaction a person receives from consuming goods and services is called
    A) contentment.
    B) psychic income.
    C) wealth.
    D) utility.
Answer: D
Diff: 1   *Type: MC*   *Page Ref: 286/286*
Topic: Utility
Skill: Definition
Objective: LO 1: Define utility and explain how consumers choose goods and services to maximize their utility.
AACSB Coding: Reflective Thinking
Special Feature: None

4. The economic model of consumer behavior predicts that
    A) consumers will try to earn as much income as they can over their lifetimes.
    B) consumers will choose to buy the combination of goods and services that make them as well off as possible from those combinations that their budgets allow them to buy.
    C) consumers will try to accumulate as many goods and services as they can before they die.
    D) consumers divide their time between consumption and leisure activities in order to maximize social welfare.
Answer: B
Diff: 1   *Type: MC*   *Page Ref: 286/286*
Topic: Consumer behavior
Skill: Conceptual
Objective: LO 1: Define utility and explain how consumers choose goods and services to maximize their utility.
AACSB Coding: Reflective Thinking
Special Feature: None

5. An economist observes two consumers in a supermarket. One of the consumers buys a case of Coca-Cola and the other buys a case of Pepsi-Cola. Both colas sell for the same price and the ages and incomes of the consumers are also the same. Based on this information, how would the economist explain the consumers' choices?
    A) One of the consumers made the wrong choice, but it is impossible to say which one.
    B) Both consumers should have considered buying other colas that had lower prices.
    C) Both consumers should have purchased less than a case because they would be able to buy more later.
    D) Apparently, the consumers had different tastes.
Answer: D
Diff: 1   *Type: MC*   *Page Ref: 286/286*
Topic: Consumer behavior
Skill: Conceptual
Objective: LO 1: Define utility and explain how consumers choose goods and services to maximize their utility.
AACSB Coding: Reflective Thinking
Special Feature: None

6. The word "util" has been used by economists in the past as an objective measure of utility. Today economists believe that
    A) utility cannot be measured objectively.
    B) utility can be measured objectively because people can use prices of different goods to measure utility.
    C) all of the important conclusions of the economic model of consumer behavior depend on utility being measured objectively.
    D) the util is actually a subjective (or normative), rather than an objective, measure of utility.
    Answer: A
    Diff: 2   Type: MC   Page Ref: 286–7/286–7
    Topic: Utility
    Skill: Conceptual
    Objective: LO 1: Define utility and explain how consumers choose goods and services to maximize their utility.
    AACSB Coding: Reflective Thinking
    Special Feature: None

7. Suppose the marginal utilities for the first three cans of soda are 100, 80 and 60, respectively. The total utility received from consuming 2 cans is
    A) 20.
    B) 90.
    C) 180.
    D) 80.
    Answer: C
    Diff: 1   Type: MC   Page Ref: 287–8/287–8
    Topic: Utility
    Skill: Analytical
    Objective: LO 1: Define utility and explain how consumers choose goods and services to maximize their utility.
    AACSB Coding: Reflective Thinking
    Special Feature: None

8. The additional utility that George receives from consuming one more slice of pizza is called
    A) average utility.
    B) marginal utility.
    C) total utility.
    D) diminishing utility.
    Answer: B
    Diff: 1   Type: MC   Page Ref: 287/287
    Topic: Marginal utility
    Skill: Definition
    Objective: LO 1: Define utility and explain how consumers choose goods and services to maximize their utility.
    AACSB Coding: Reflective Thinking
    Special Feature: None

9. Marginal utility is
    A) the change in total utility divided by the price of the last unit of a good or service consumed.
    B) the change in total utility a person receives from consuming an additional unit of a good or service.
    C) the utility from consuming a given quantity of a good or service.
    D) the decrease in total utility from consuming more and more units of a good or service.
Answer: B
Diff: 1   Type: MC   Page Ref: 287/287
Topic: Marginal utility
Skill: Definition
Objective: LO 1: Define utility and explain how consumers choose goods and services to maximize their utility.
AACSB Coding: Reflective Thinking
Special Feature: None

10. If marginal utility of apples is diminishing and is a positive amount consuming one more apple will cause
    A) total utility to decrease.
    B) a consumer to get no satisfaction from consuming apples.
    C) a consumer's total utility to increase.
    D) a consumer to go beyond her optimal consumption of apples.
Answer: C
Diff: 2   Type: MC   Page Ref: 287-8/287-8
Topic: Utility
Skill: Conceptual
Objective: LO 1: Define utility and explain how consumers choose goods and services to maximize their utility.
AACSB Coding: Reflective Thinking
Special Feature: None

11. If Paul decides to buy a $60 ticket to a Cirque du Soleil show rather than a $45 ticket for a Blue Man Group performance we can conclude that
    A) the marginal utility per dollar spent on Cirque du Soleil is lower than the marginal utility per dollar spent on Blue Man Group.
    B) Paul's demand for a ticket to see Cirque du Soleil is more elastic than his demand for a ticket to see Blue Man Group.
    C) Paul is not making a rational choice.
    D) the marginal utility per dollar spent on Cirque du Soleil is higher than the marginal utility per dollar spent on Blue Man Group.
Answer: D
Diff: 2   Type: MC   Page Ref: 287-91/287-91
Topic: Marginal utility per dollar
Skill: Analytical
Objective: LO 1: Define utility and explain how consumers choose goods and services to maximize their utility.
AACSB Coding: Analytic Skills
Special Feature: None

12. If the marginal utility Ida Mae receives from eating chicken wings is negative then
    A) her total utility from eating chicken wings has fallen.
    B) her total utility from eating chicken wings is negative as well.
    C) Ida Mae does not like chicken wings.
    D) her total utility has risen, but by less from the last chicken wing than from the next to last chicken wing.
    Answer: A
    Diff: 2   Type: MC   Page Ref: 287–8/287–8
    Topic: Diminishing marginal utility
    Skill: Analytical
    Objective: LO 1: Define utility and explain how consumers choose goods and services to maximize their utility.
    AACSB Coding: Reflective Thinking
    Special Feature: None

13. If Joey Kobayashi experiences diminishing marginal utility from eating hot dogs then
    A) his total utility from eating hot dogs is negative.
    B) the marginal utility from the next hot dog Joey eats will be negative. .
    C) the additional satisfaction he receives from eating another hot dog will be less then the satisfaction he received from his eating his last hot dog.
    D) Joey is maximizing the marginal utility per dollar he receives from eating hot dogs.
    Answer: C
    Diff: 2   Type: MC   Page Ref: 287–8/287–8
    Topic: Diminishing marginal utility
    Skill: Conceptual
    Objective: LO 1: Define utility and explain how consumers choose goods and services to maximize their utility.
    AACSB Coding: Reflective Thinking
    Special Feature: None

14. Optimal decisions are made
    A) in the marketplace.
    B) if information about prices and marginal utilities is known.
    C) when marginal utility is minimized.
    D) at the margin.
    Answer: D
    Diff: 1   Type: MC   Page Ref: 287–91/287–91
    Topic: Rational decision making
    Skill: Fact
    Objective: LO 1: Define utility and explain how consumers choose goods and services to maximize their utility.
    AACSB Coding: Reflective Thinking
    Special Feature: None

15. Total utility is maximized in the consumption of two goods by
    A) equating the marginal utility for each good consumed.
    B) equating the marginal utility per dollar for each good consumed.
    C) equating the total utility of each good divided by its price.
    D) maximizing expenditure on each good.
Answer: B
Diff: 2   Type: MC   Page Ref: 287–91/287–91
Topic: Marginal utility per dollar
Skill: Conceptual
Objective: LO 1: Define utility and explain how consumers choose goods and services to maximize their utility.
AACSB Coding: Reflective Thinking
Special Feature: None

16. In making decisions about what to consume a person's goal is to
    A) allocate her limited income among all the products she wishes to buy so that she receives the highest total utility.
    B) buy low-priced goods rather than high-priced goods.
    C) maximize her marginal utility from the goods and services she wishes to buy using her limited income.
    D) consume as many necessities as possible and then, if there is money left over, to buy luxuries.
Answer: A
Diff: 2   Type: MC   Page Ref: 287–91/287–91
Topic: Rational decision making
Skill: Conceptual
Objective: LO 1: Define utility and explain how consumers choose goods and services to maximize their utility.
AACSB Coding: Reflective Thinking
Special Feature: None

17. The amount of income a consumer has to spend on goods and services is known as
    A) purchasing power.
    B) effective demand.
    C) a budget constraint.
    D) wealth.
Answer: C
Diff: 1   Type: MC   Page Ref: 289/289
Topic: Budget constraint
Skill: Definition
Objective: LO 1: Define utility and explain how consumers choose goods and services to maximize their utility.
AACSB Coding: Reflective Thinking
Special Feature: None

18. A budget constraint
   A) represents the bundles of consumption that make a consumer equally happy.
   B) refers to the limited amount of income available to consumers to spend on good and services.
   C) reflects the desire by consumers to increase their income.
   D) shows the prices that a consumer chooses to pay for products he consumes.
   Answer: B
   Diff: 1   Type: MC   Page Ref: 289/289
   Topic: Budget constraint
   Skill: Definition
   Objective: LO 1: Define utility and explain how consumers choose goods and services to maximize their utility.
   AACSB Coding: Reflective Thinking
   Special Feature: None

19. The restriction that a consumer's total expenditure on goods and services purchased cannot exceed the income available is referred to as
   A) maximizing behavior.
   B) economizing behavior.
   C) the price constraint.
   D) the budget constraint.
   Answer: D
   Diff: 1   Type: MC   Page Ref: 289/289
   Topic: Budget constraint
   Skill: Definition
   Objective: LO 1: Define utility and explain how consumers choose goods and services to maximize their utility.
   AACSB Coding: Reflective Thinking
   Special Feature: None

20. Which of the following is explained by the law of diminishing marginal utility?
   A) The marginal utility of Isabel's second bottle of Coca-Cola is greater than the marginal utility of her third bottle of Coca-Cola.
   B) The marginal utility of Isabel's second bottle of Coca-Cola is greater than the marginal utility of her third pretzel.
   C) The marginal utility of Isabel's second bottle of Coca-Cola is greater than the marginal utility of her friend Margie's third pretzel.
   D) The total utility of one bottle of Coca-Cola is greater than the total utility of two bottles of Coca-Cola.
   Answer: A
   Diff: 1   Type: MC   Page Ref: 287/287
   Topic: Diminishing marginal utility
   Skill: Conceptual
   Objective: LO 1: Define utility and explain how consumers choose goods and services to maximize their utility.
   AACSB Coding: Reflective Thinking
   Special Feature: None

21. Marv Pilson has $50 worth of groceries in a shopping cart at his local Shop 'n Save. Assume that the marginal utility per dollar of the liter bottles of soft drink in Marv's cart equals 50. The marginal utility per dollar of the boxes of cereal in Marv's cart equals 20. Marv has only $50 to spend, but has not yet paid for his groceries. How can Marv increase his total utility without spending more than $50?
    A) Marv should substitute his favorite soft drink or the cereal in his cart for generic brands that have lower prices.
    B) Marv should buy more boxes of cereal and fewer bottles of soft drink.
    C) Marv should buy fewer boxes of cereal and more bottles of soft drink.
    D) Marv should buy fewer boxes of cereal and fewer bottles of soft drink. He can then spend more on other items.
Answer: C
Diff: 2   Type: MC   Page Ref: 287–91/287–91
Topic: Utility and Consumer Decision Making
Skill: Analytical
Objective: LO 1: Define utility and explain how consumers choose goods and services to maximize their utility.
AACSB Coding: Analytic Skills
Special Feature: None

22.   *Table 9–1*

	Ice Cream Cones	Lime Fizz Soda
Quantity	MU/P	MU/P
1	15	40
2	12.5	35
3	10	26
4	7.5	18
5	5	15
6	2.5	7

Refer to Table 9–1. The table above show's Lee's marginal utility per dollar from consuming ice cream cones and cans of Lime Fizz Soda. The price of an ice cream cone is $2 and the price of Lime Fizz Soda is $1. Use this information to select the correct statement.
    A) We cannot determine how many ice cream cones and cans of Lime Fizz Soda Lee will consume without knowing what his income is.
    B) To maximize his utility Lee should consume 1 ice cream cone and 5 cans of Lime Fizz Soda.
    C) We cannot determine how many ice cream cones and cans of Lime Fizz Soda will maximize Lee's utility because we are given only the marginal utility per dollar values. We also need to know the marginal utility for each quantity.
    D) If Lee has an unlimited budget he will maximize his utility by buying only Lime Fizz Soda.
Answer: A

Diff: 2   Type: MC   Page Ref: 291–2/291–2
Topic: Rule of equal marginal utility per dollar
Skill: Analytical
Objective: LO 1: Define utility and explain how consumers choose goods and services to maximize their utility.
AACSB Coding: Analytic Skills
Special Feature: Solved Problem: Finding the Optimal Level of Consumption

23.   *Table 9–2*

	Ice Cream Cones	Lime Fizz Soda
Quantity	MU	MU
1	30	40
2	25	35
3	20	26
4	15	18
5	10	15
6	5	7

Refer to Table 9–2. The table above shows Lee's marginal utility from consuming ice cream cones and cans of Lime Fizz Soda. Select the phrase that completes the following statement. "We can determine the number of ice cream cones and cans of Lime Fizz Soda Lee should consume to maximize his utility

A) if we know what Lee's income is."

B) if we know what Lee's income is and the price of an ice cream cone and the price of a can Lime Fizz Soda."

C) by adding up the marginal utilities for ice cream cones and Lime Fizz Soda."

D) if we know the values of the marginal utility per dollar for ice cream cones and Lime Fizz Soda."

Answer: B

Diff: 2   Type: MC   Page Ref: 291–2/291–2
Topic: Rule of equal marginal utility per dollar
Skill: Analytical
Objective: LO 1: Define utility and explain how consumers choose goods and services to maximize their utility.
AACSB Coding: Analytic Skills
Special Feature: Solved Problem: Finding the Optimal Level of Consumption

24. During a study session for an economics exam with three other students Peter Daltry commented on an example of a consumer who had to decide the on number of slices of pizza and cups of Coca-Cola he would consume. Peter explained that "To maximize his utility this consumer must equate the marginal utility per dollar for pizza and Coca-Cola." Was Peter's analysis correct?
    A) Peter described one of the conditions necessary for utility maximization. The consumer also must equate the marginal utility of pizza and the marginal utility of cups of Coca-Cola.
    B) Peter's statement is correct.
    C) Peter's statement is correct but we must also assume that the consumer is rational.
    D) Peter describes one of the conditions necessary for utility maximization. The second condition is that total spending on both goods must equal the amount available to be spent.
Answer: D
Diff: 2   Type: MC   Page Ref: 287–91/287–91
Topic: Utility and decision making
Skill: Conceptual
Objective: LO 1: Define utility and explain how consumers choose goods and services to maximize their utility.
AACSB Coding: Reflective Thinking
Special Feature: None

Table 9–3

Quantity	Steak & Cheese MU	Steak & Cheese MU/P	Grilled Chicken MU	Grilled Chicken MU/P
1	40	10	30	15
2	32	8	24	12
3	20	5	16	8
4	12	3	12	6
5	6	1.5	8	4
6	2	.5	4	2

25. *Refer to Table 9–3.* For steak and cheese and grilled chicken sandwiches the table contains the values of the marginal utility (MU) and marginal utility per dollar (MU/P) for Mabel Jarvis. Mabel has $14 to spend on steak and cheese and grilled chicken sandwiches. Which of the following statements is false?
    A) The price of steak and cheese sandwiches is $4. The price of grilled chicken sandwiches is $2.
    B) If Mabel maximizes her utility she will buy three grilled chicken sandwiches.
    C) If Mable maximizes her utility she will buy two steak and cheese sandwiches.
    D) We do not have enough information to determine how many sandwiches Mabel will buy to maximize her utility.
Answer: D

Diff: 2   Type: MC   Page Ref: 287–91/287–91
Topic: Rule of equal marginal utility per dollar
Skill: Analytical
Objective: LO 1: Define utility and explain how consumers choose goods and services to maximize their utility.
AACSB Coding: Analytic Skills
Special Feature: None

26. ***Refer to Table 9–3.*** For steak and cheese and grilled chicken sandwiches the table contains the values of the marginal utility (MU) and marginal utility per dollar (MU/P) for Mabel Jarvis. Mabel has $14 to spend on steak and cheese and grilled chicken sandwiches. Which of the following statements is true?
     A) If Mabel maximizes her utility she will buy three steak and cheese sandwiches and two grilled chicken sandwiches.
     B) If Mabel was maximizing her utility and then received an additional $4 her next purchase would be another grilled chicken sandwich.
     C) Mabel will first buy two steak and cheese sandwiches; then with her remaining $6 she will buy three grilled chicken sandwiches.
     D) To maximize her utility, Mabel will need a total of $36, the income needed to buy 6 steak and cheese sandwiches and 6 grilled chicken sandwiches.
   Answer: B
   Diff: 3   Type: MC   Page Ref: 287–291/287–291
   Topic: Rule of equal marginal utility per dollar
   Skill: Analytical
   Objective: LO 1: Define utility and explain how consumers choose goods and services to maximize their utility.
   AACSB Coding: Analytic Skills
   Special Feature: None

27. The marginal utility per dollar that Harold Stratton receives from oranges is greater than the marginal utility per dollar Harold receives from pears. To maximize his utility, what should Harold do?
     A) He should acquire more income so that he can afford to buy more oranges and pears.
     B) He should reduce his consumption of both oranges and pears so that he can buy a greater variety of goods.
     C) He should buy fewer pears and more oranges.
     D) He should buy fewer oranges and more pears.
   Answer: C
   Diff: 1   Type: MC   Page Ref: 287–91/287–91
   Topic: Rule of equal marginal utility per dollar
   Skill: Analytical
   Objective: LO 1: Define utility and explain how consumers choose goods and services to maximize their utility.
   AACSB Coding: Reflective Thinking
   Special Feature: None

28. There are two conditions necessary for a consumer to maximize her utility. One is that the marginal utilities per dollar spent on each good and service consumed are equal. What is the other condition?
    A) Total spending on all goods and services must equal the amount available to be spent.
    B) The consumer must be satisfied with the choices she makes.
    C) The total spent on each good and service is the same.
    D) The prices of each good and service consumed must not be too high.
    Answer: A
    Diff: 1   Type: MC   Page Ref: 287–91/287–91
    Topic: Rule of equal marginal utility per dollar
    Skill: Conceptual
    Objective: LO 1: Define utility and explain how consumers choose goods and services to maximize their utility.
    AACSB Coding: Reflective Thinking
    Special Feature: None

Table 9–4

Quantity	Italian Sub MU	Italian Sub MU/$4	Chicken Taco MU	Taco MU/$2	Taco MU/$1
1	40	10	30	15	30
2	32	8	24	12	24
3	20	5	16	8	16
4	12	3	12	6	12
5	6	1.5	8	4	8
6	2	.5	4	2	4

29. *Refer to Table 9–4,* which lists the values of Harry Taber's marginal utility and marginal utility per dollar for Italian submarine (sub) sandwiches and tacos. Assume that the price of the sub sandwiches is $4 and the price of tacos is $2. When Harry's income is $14 he buys two Italian sub sandwiches and three tacos. The last column lists the values of the marginal utility per dollar for tacos when the price of tacos decreases to $1. Complete this statement: As a result of the change in price
    A) Harry's purchasing power has increased. He will reduce his consumption of tacos so he can buy one more sub. This is an example of the substitution effect of a price change.
    B) Harry's purchasing power has increased. If tacos are a normal good for Harry he will buy fewer tacos. This is an example of the income effect of a price change.
    C) Harry's purchasing power has increased. If tacos are a normal good for Harry he will buy more tacos. This is an example of the income effect of a price change.
    D) Harry's purchasing power has increased. Harry buys fewer tacos. This is an example of the substitution effect of a price change
    Answer: C
    Diff: 3   Type: MC   Page Ref: 294–5/294–5
    Topic: Income and substitution effect of a price change
    Skill: Analytical
    Objective: LO 1: Define utility and explain how consumers choose goods and services to maximize their utility.
    AACSB Coding: Analytic Skills
    Special Feature: None

30. **Refer to Table 9-4,** which lists the values of Harry Taber's marginal utility and marginal utility per dollar for Italian submarine (sub) sandwiches and tacos. Assume that the price of the sub sandwiches is $4 and the price of tacos is $2. When Harry's income is $14 he buys two Italian sub sandwiches and three tacos. The last column lists the values of the marginal utility per dollar for tacos when the price of tacos decreases to $1. Complete this statement: As a result of the change in price the marginal utility of each taco Harry consumes increases and

    A) the substitution effect of the price change will cause Harry to buy more tacos and fewer subs.

    B) the substitution effect of the price change will cause Harry to buy more tacos if they are a normal good, and fewer tacos if they are an inferior good.

    C) the substitution effect will cause Harry to buy another sub because his purchasing power has increased.

    D) the substitution effect will cause Harry to buy fewer tacos.

Answer: A

Diff: 3   Type: MC   Page Ref: 294–5/294–5
Topic: Income and substitution effect of a price change
Skill: Analytical
Objective: LO 1: Define utility and explain how consumers choose goods and services to maximize their utility.
AACSB Coding: Analytic Skills
Special Feature: None

31. Marge buys 5 CDs and 7 DVDs. The marginal utility of the 5th CD and the marginal utility of the 7th DVD are both equal to 30 utils. Can we say that this is the optimal combination of CDs and DVDs for Marge?

    A) No. We need to know her preferences for CDs and DVDs.

    B) Yes.

    C) No. We need to know the prices of the CDs and DVDs.

    D) No. If this was the optimal combination, the marginal utility per dollar of the 5th CD and the 7th DVD would be equal.

Answer: D

Diff: 3   Type: MC   Page Ref: 293/293
Topic: Rule of equal marginal utility per dollar
Skill: Analytical
Objective: LO 1: Define utility and explain how consumers choose goods and services to maximize their utility.
AACSB Coding: Analytic Skills
Special Feature: Don't let This Happen to YOU!: Equalize Marginal Utilities Per Dollar

Table 9–5

Quantity of Burgers	Marginal Utility	Quantity of Pepsi	Marginal Utility
1	20	1	30
2	14	2	10
3	10	3	7
4	3	4	5
5	1	5	1
6	–5	6	0
7	–10	7	–4

Table 9–5 lists Jay's marginal utilities for burgers and Pepsi. Jay has $7 to spend on these two goods. The price of a burger is $2 and the price of a can of Pepsi is $1.

32. *Refer to Table 9–5.* What is Jay's optimal consumption bundle?
    A) 1 burger and 2 Pepsis
    B) 2 burgers and 3 Pepsis
    C) 3 burgers and 1 Pepsi
    D) 3 burgers and 2 Pepsis
Answer: B
Diff: 3   Type: MC   Page Ref: 287–93/287–93
Topic: Rule of Marginal Utility Per Dollar
Skill: Analytical
Objective: LO 1: Define utility and explain how consumers choose goods and services to maximize their utility.
AACSB Coding: Analytic Skills
Special Feature: None

33. *Refer to Table 9–5.* If Jay can eat all the burgers he wants for free, how many burgers will he consume?
    A) 7 burgers
    B) 6 burgers
    C) 5 burgers
    D) 3 burgers
Answer: C
Diff: 2   Type: MC   Page Ref: 287–93/287–93
Topic: Rule of equal marginal utility per dollar
Skill: Analytical
Objective: LO 1: Define utility and explain how consumers choose goods and services to maximize their utility.
AACSB Coding: Analytic Skills
Special Feature: None

34. Suppose Barry is maximizing his utility from consuming used paperback novels and audio books. The price of a used novel = $4 and the price of an audio book = $8. If the marginal utility of the last novel was 32 units of utility (utils) what was the marginal utility of the last audio book purchased?
    A) 2 utils.
    B) 12 utils.
    C) 16 utils.
    D) 64 utils.
    Answer: D
    Diff: 3   Type: MC   Page Ref: 287–93/287–93
    Topic: Rule of equal marginal utility per dollar
    Skill: Analytical
    Objective: LO 1: Define utility and explain how consumers choose goods and services to maximize their utility.
    AACSB Coding: Analytic Skills
    Special Feature: None

35. Terence has $50 per week to spend on Subway sandwiches and milkshakes. The price of a Subway sandwich is $5 and the price of a milkshake is $4. He buys 6 sandwiches and 5 milkshakes. The marginal utility of the 6th sandwich = 25 and the marginal utility of the 5th milkshake = 24. Which of the following is true?
    A) He is not maximizing his utility and should buy more milkshakes.
    B) He is maximizing his utility.
    C) He is not maximizing his utility and should buy more Subway sandwiches.
    D) He is not maximizing his utility because he is not spending all of his income.
    Answer: A
    Diff: 2   Type: MC   Page Ref: 287–93/287–93
    Topic: Rule of equal marginal utility per dollar
    Skill: Conceptual
    Objective: LO 1: Define utility and explain how consumers choose goods and services to maximize their utility.
    AACSB Coding: Analytic Skills
    Special Feature: None

36. Suppose Renee can increase her total utility from consuming video rentals and books by buying one more book and one video rental fewer. Which of the following is true?
    A) The marginal utility of video rentals is negative.
    B) The marginal utility per dollar spent on books exceeds that of video rentals.
    C) The marginal utility of the last book consumed exceeds the marginal utility of the last video rental consumed.
    D) The marginal utility of the last video rental consumed exceeds the marginal utility of the last book consumed.
    Answer: B
    Diff: 2   Type: MC   Page Ref: 287–93/287–93
    Topic: Rule of equal marginal utility per dollar
    Skill: Conceptual
    Objective: LO 1: Define utility and explain how consumers choose goods and services to maximize their utility.
    AACSB Coding: Reflective Thinking
    Special Feature: None

Table 9–6

Quantity of Beer (glasses)	Total Utility	Quantity of Pizza (slices)	Total Utility
1	25	1	20
2	45	2	35
3	60	3	45
4	65	4	50
5	69	5	52
6	70	6	52

Table 9–6 shows Antonio's utility from beer and pizza.

37. *Refer to Table 9–6.* What is Antonio's marginal utility from consuming the fifth beer?
    A) 13.6 utils
    B) 4 utils
    C) 69 utils
    D) 134 utils
    Answer: B
    Diff: 1   Type: MC   Page Ref: 286–7/286–7
    Topic: Marginal utility
    Skill: Analytical
    Objective: LO 1: Define utility and explain how consumers choose goods and services to maximize their utility.
    AACSB Coding: Analytic Skills
    Special Feature: None

38. *Refer to Table 9–6.* Suppose Antonio has $10 to spend and the price of beer = $2 per glass and the price of pizza = $2 per slice. How many of each good will he consume when he maximizes his utility?
    A) 2 glasses of beer, 1 slice of pizza
    B) 2 glasses of beer, 3 slices of pizza
    C) 3 glasses of beer, 2 slices of pizza
    D) 4 glasses of beer, 5 slices of pizza
    Answer: C
    Diff: 2   Type: MC   Page Ref: 287–93/287–93
    Topic: Rule of equal marginal utility per dollar
    Skill: Analytical
    Objective: LO 1: Define utility and explain how consumers choose goods and services to maximize their utility.
    AACSB Coding: Reflective Thinking
    Special Feature: None

39. If Lisa spends her income on veggie burgers and pints of soy milk and the price of veggie burgers is three times the price of a pint of soy milk, then when Lisa maximizes her utility she will buy
    A) both goods until the marginal utility of veggie burgers is three times the marginal utility of soy milk.
    B) three times as many veggie burgers as pints of soy milk.
    C) three times as many pints of soy milk as veggie burgers.
    D) both goods until the marginal utility of a pint of soy milk is three times the marginal utility of veggie burgers.

Answer: A
Diff: 2   Type: MC   Page Ref: 287–96/287–93
Topic: Rule of equal marginal utility per dollar
Skill: Analytical
Objective: LO 1: Define utility and explain how consumers choose goods and services to maximize their utility.
AACSB Coding: Analytic Skills
Special Feature: None

40. The income effect of a price change refers to
    A) the change in demand that occurs when consumer income changes.
    B) the change in the quantity demanded that results from a change in price making the good more or less expensive relative to other goods, holding everything else constant.
    C) the change in demand that occurs when both income and price change.
    D) the change in the quantity demanded of a good that results from the effect of a change in price on consumer purchasing power, holding everything else constant.

Answer: D
Diff: 1   Type: MC   Page Ref: 294–5/294–5
Topic: Income and substitution effect of a price change
Skill: Conceptual
Objective: LO 1: Define utility and explain how consumers choose goods and services to maximize their utility.
AACSB Coding: Reflective Thinking
Special Feature: None

41. Which of the following describes the substitution effect of a price change?
    A) The change in demand that results from a change in price making the good more or less expensive relative to other goods, holding constant the effect of the price change on consumer purchasing power.
    B) The change in quantity demanded of a good that results from the effect of a change in price on consumer purchasing power, holding everything else constant.
    C) The change in quantity demanded of a good that results from the change in the price of a substitute for the good.
    D) The change in quantity demanded of a good that results from a change in price making the good more or less expensive relative to other goods, holding constant the effect of the price change on consumer purchasing power.

    Answer: D
    Diff: 2   Type: MC   Page Ref: 294–5/294–5
    Topic: Income and substitution effect of a price change
    Skill: Conceptual
    Objective: LO 1: Define utility and explain how consumers choose goods and services to maximize their utility.
    AACSB Coding: Reflective Thinking
    Special Feature: None

42. Which of the following correctly describes the result of a price increase for an inferior good?
    A) Both the substitution effect and the income effect cause the consumer to buy less of the good.
    B) The substitution effect causes the consumer to buy less of the good and the income effect causes the consumer to buy more of the good.
    C) The substitution effect causes the demand for the good to decrease; the income effect causes the demand for the good to increase.
    D) The substitution effect causes the demand for the good to increase; the income effect causes the demand for the good to decrease.

    Answer: B
    Diff: 2   Type: MC   Page Ref: 294–5/294–5
    Topic: Income and substitution effect of a price change
    Skill: Conceptual
    Objective: LO 1: Define utility and explain how consumers choose goods and services to maximize their utility.
    AACSB Coding: Reflective Thinking
    Special Feature: None

43. The substitution effect of a decrease in the price of movie tickets results in
    A) an increase in the quantity demanded of movie tickets.
    B) a decrease in the quantity demanded of movie tickets.
    C) an increase in the demand for movie tickets.
    D) a decrease in the demand for movie tickets.
    Answer: A
    Diff: 1   Type: MC   Page Ref: 294–5/294–5
    Topic: Income and substitution effect of a price change
    Skill: Conceptual
    Objective: LO 1: Define utility and explain how consumers choose goods and services to maximize their utility.
    AACSB Coding: Reflective Thinking
    Special Feature: None

44. The income effect of a decrease in the price of macaroni and cheese (assume this is an inferior good) results in
    A) a decrease in the demand for macaroni and cheese.
    B) an increase in the quantity demanded of macaroni and cheese.
    C) a decrease in the quantity demanded of macaroni and cheese.
    D) an increase in the demand for macaroni and cheese.
    Answer: C
    Diff: 2   Type: MC   Page Ref: 294–5/294–5
    Topic: Income Effect of Price Change
    Skill: Conceptual
    Objective: LO 1: Define utility and explain how consumers choose goods and services to maximize their utility.
    AACSB Coding: Reflective Thinking
    Special Feature: None

45. The income effect of an increase in the price of peaches is
    A) the change in the quantity demanded of peaches that results from the price increase making peaches more expensive than other fruit, holding constant the effect of the price change on consumer purchasing power.
    B) the change in the demand for peaches as a result of the change in the price of peaches, holding all other factors constant.
    C) the change in the quantity demanded of other fruit that results from the impact of the price change on purchasing power, holding all other factors constant.
    D) the change in the quantity demanded of peaches that results from the effect of the change in price on consumer purchasing power, holding all other factors constant.
    Answer: D
    Diff: 3   Type: MC   Page Ref: 294–5/294–5
    Topic: Income and substitution effect of a price change
    Skill: Conceptual
    Objective: LO 1: Define utility and explain how consumers choose goods and services to maximize their utility.
    AACSB Coding: Reflective Thinking
    Special Feature: None

46. The substitution effect of an increase in the price of peaches is
    A) the change in the quantity demanded that results from a change in the price of peaches making peaches more expensive relative to other goods, holding constant the effect of the price change on consumer purchasing power.
    B) the change in the demand for nectarines (a substitute good) that results when peaches become more expensive relative to nectarines, holding constant the effect of the price change on consumer purchasing power.
    C) the change in the quantity demanded of peaches that results from the effect of the change in the price of peaches on the consumer's purchasing power.
    D) the change in the demand for peaches that results when the price of peaches increases.
    Answer: A
    Diff: 2   Type: MC   Page Ref: 294–5/294–5
    Topic: Income and substitution effect of a price change
    Skill: Definition
    Objective: LO 1: Define utility and explain how consumers choose goods and services to maximize their utility.
    AACSB Coding: Reflective Thinking
    Special Feature: None

47. The French Bakery ran a special which decreased the price of its croissants from $1.50 to $1.00. Although her money income had not changed, Toni decided to buy 2 croissants instead of her usual 1 bagel and 1 croissant. Toni's actions are explained by which of the following?
    A) Income effect only or substitution effect only but not both effects.
    B) Income and substitution effects.
    C) Price effect.
    D) Consumption effect.
    Answer: B
    Diff: 2   Type: MC   Page Ref: 294–5/294–5
    Topic: Income and substitution effect of a price change
    Skill: Analytical
    Objective: LO 1: Define utility and explain how consumers choose goods and services to maximize their utility.
    AACSB Coding: Analytic Skills
    Special Feature: None

48. The income effect of a decrease in the price of legal services, a normal good, results in
    A) a decrease in the demand for legal services.
    B) a decrease in the quantity demanded of legal services.
    C) an increase in the quantity demanded of legal services.
    D) an increase in the demand for legal services.
    Answer: C
    Diff: 2   Type: MC   Page Ref: 294–5/294–5
    Topic: Income and substitution effect of a price change
    Skill: Conceptual
    Objective: LO 1: Define utility and explain how consumers choose goods and services to maximize their utility.
    AACSB Coding: Reflective Thinking
    Special Feature: None

49. A change in the price of a good has two effects on the quantity consumed. What are these effects?
    A) The income effect and the substitution effect.
    B) The utility effect and the budget effect.
    C) The total utility effect and marginal utility effect.
    D) The consumption effect and expenditure effect.
    Answer: A
    Diff: 1   Type: MC   Page Ref: 294–5/294–5
    Topic: Income and substitution effect of a price change
    Skill: Conceptual
    Objective: LO 1: Define utility and explain how consumers choose goods and services to maximize their utility.
    AACSB Coding: Reflective Thinking
    Special Feature: None

50. The substitution effect of a change in the price of cauliflower is the portion of the change in the quantity of cauliflower demanded that can be attributed to the change in the price of a substitute vegetable such as asparagus.
    Answer: True   False
    Diff: 2   Type: TF   Page Ref: 294–5/294–5
    Topic: Income and substitution effect of a price change
    Skill: Conceptual
    Objective: LO 1: Define utility and explain how consumers choose goods and services to maximize their utility.
    AACSB Coding: Reflective Thinking
    Special Feature: None

51. To maximize utility consumers should buy goods and services to the point where the marginal utility of each item consumed is equal.
    Answer: True   False
    Diff: 2   Type: TF   Page Ref: 287–91/287–91
    Topic: Marginal utility per dollar
    Skill: Conceptual
    Objective: LO 1: Define utility and explain how consumers choose goods and services to maximize their utility.
    AACSB Coding: Reflective Thinking
    Special Feature: None

52. In explaining consumer behavior economists explain how consumer tastes and preferences are formed.
    Answer: True   False
    Diff: 1   Type: TF   Page Ref: 286–7/286–7
    Topic: Utility and decision making
    Skill: Conceptual
    Objective: LO 1: Define utility and explain how consumers choose goods and services to maximize their utility.
    AACSB Coding: Reflective Thinking
    Special Feature: None

53. If by purchasing more apples and fewer oranges you increase your total utility, then apples must be cheaper than oranges.
    Answer: True ○ False
    Diff: 1   Type: TF   Page Ref: 287–91/287–91
    Topic: Rule of equal marginal utility per dollar
    Skill: Conceptual
    Objective: LO 1: Define utility and explain how consumers choose goods and services to maximize their utility.
    AACSB Coding: Reflective Thinking
    Special Feature: None

54. Economists assume people's tastes are identical.
    Answer: True ○ False
    Diff: 1   Type: TF   Page Ref: 286–7/286–7
    Topic: Utility and decision making
    Skill: Conceptual
    Objective: LO 1: Define utility and explain how consumers choose goods and services to maximize their utility.
    AACSB Coding: Reflective Thinking
    Special Feature: None

55. Economists do not think it is possible to compare the relative utility that two people get from consuming an additional unit of a particular good.
    Answer: ○ True   False
    Diff: 1   Type: TF   Page Ref: 286–7/286–7
    Topic: Utility and decision making
    Skill: Conceptual
    Objective: LO 1: Define utility and explain how consumers choose goods and services to maximize their utility.
    AACSB Coding: Reflective Thinking
    Special Feature: None

56. The Wong family consumes 3 pounds of fish and 5 pounds of chicken per month. The price of fish is $8 per pound and chicken is $4 per pound.
    a. What is the amount of income allocated to fish and chicken consumption?
    b. What is price ratio (price of fish relative to the price of chicken)?
    c. Explain the meaning of the price ratio you computed.
    d. If the Wongs maximize utility, what is the ratio of the marginal utility of fish to the marginal utility of chicken?
    e. If the price of chicken rises, will the Wong family consume more chicken, less chicken or the same amount of chicken? Explain your answer using the rule of equal marginal utility per dollar.
    Answer: a.   Income = $44
          b.   Price of fish/Price of chicken = $8/$4 = 2
          c.   To buy a pound of fish the family has to give up 2 pounds of chicken.
          d.   MUfish/MUchicken = Price of fish/Price of chicken = $8/$4 = 2
          e.   If the price of chicken rises, the marginal utilities per dollar will not be equal. Specifically, MUfish/Price fish > MU chicken/Price chicken. The family can raise its total utility by buying less chicken and more fish.

Diff: 3   Type: SA   Page Ref: 287–93/287–93
Topic: Rule of equal marginal utility per dollar
Skill: Analytical
Objective: LO 1: Define utility and explain how consumers choose goods and services to maximize their utility.
AACSB Coding: Analytic Skills
Special Feature: None

57. You participate in a taste test for a new protein supplement called "Boost." You are given five consecutive one ounce vials of the supplement and after consuming each vial you are asked to note your reaction. You consume the first vial and your response is: "Hmmm, quite good!" After the second, you say, "Not bad at all." After the third, you note, "It's alright." and after the fourth you wince, "No more, the after-taste is getting to me. I need water." What economic principle does this scenario illustrate? Define the principle.

Answer: It illustrates the law of diminishing marginal utility which states that consumers experience diminishing additional satisfaction as they consume more of a good or service during a given period of time.

Diff: 2   Type: SA   Page Ref: 287/287
Topic: Diminishing marginal utility
Skill: Conceptual
Objective: LO 1: Define utility and explain how consumers choose goods and services to maximize their utility.
AACSB Coding: Reflective Thinking
Special Feature: None

58. The increase in consumption of a good when its price falls is caused by two effects. What are these two effects? Explain the difference between these effects.

Answer: The two effects are the substitution and income effects. According to the substitution effect, more is consumed when the price of a good falls because the price of the good in question is now lower relative to the prices of other goods. In addition, the fall in price increases the consumer's purchasing power causing the quantity demanded to increase for a normal good and decrease for an inferior good. This is the income effect. For most goods, the income effect is small relative to the substitution effect which is why the overall effect of a price fall is an increase in quantity demanded.

Diff: 2   Type: SA   Page Ref: 294–5/294–5
Topic: Income and substitution effect of a price change
Skill: Conceptual
Objective: LO 1: Define utility and explain how consumers choose goods and services to maximize their utility.
AACSB Coding: Reflective Thinking
Special Feature: None

59. You wish to buy only one CD. Use the rule of equal marginal utility per dollar to determine which one to purchase: (a) Usher's latest CD for $15 which gives you 75 units of utility, or (b) Tom Petty and the Heartbreakers' Greatest Hits for $10 that gives you 100 units of utility?

    Answer: You should buy the Tom Petty CD because the MU per dollar is 10 while MU per dollar for the Usher CD is only 5.

    Diff: 1   Type: SA   Page Ref: 287–91/287–91
    Topic: Rule of equal marginal utility per dollar
    Skill: Conceptual
    Objective: LO 1: Define utility and explain how consumers choose goods and services to maximize their utility.
    AACSB Coding: Reflective Thinking
    Special Feature: None

60. Lilly Davis has $5 per week to spend on any combination of ice cream and candy. The price of an ice cream cone is $2 and the price of a candy bar is $1. The table below shows Lilly's utility values. Use the table to answer the questions that follow the table.

Quantity of ice cream cones	Total Utility	Marginal Utility	Marginal Utility per dollar	Quantity of candy	Total Utility	Marginal Utility
1	20			1	20	
2	38			2	38	
3	52			3	48	
4	62			4	54	

a. Complete the table by filling in the blank spaces.
b. Suppose Lilly purchases 2 ice cream cones and 1 candy bar. Is she consuming the optimal consumption bundle? If so, explain why. If not, what combination should she buy and why?

Answer: a.

Quantity of ice cream cones	Total Utility	Marginal Utility	Marginal Utility per dollar	Quantity of candy	Total Utility	Marginal Utility
1	20	20	10	1	20	20
2	38	18	9	2	38	18
3	52	14	7	3	48	10
4	62	10	5	4	54	6

b. If Lilly purchases 2 ice cream cones and 1 candy bar she is not maximizing her utility. The marginal utility per dollar spent on ice cream cones = 9 and marginal utility per dollar spent on candy bars = 20. Her total utility from this bundle is 58 utils. If she buys 1 ice cream cone and 3 candy bars, she will equate her marginal utilities per dollar and the total utility from this bundle = 68.

Diff: 2   Type: SA   Page Ref: 287–93/287–93
Topic: Rule of equal marginal utility per dollar
Skill: Analytical
Objective: LO 1: Define utility and explain how consumers choose goods and services to maximize their

utility.
AACSB Coding: Analytic Skills
Special Feature: None

9.2   Where Demand Curves Come From

1. We can derive the market demand curve for gold earrings
   A) only if the tastes of all gold earring consumers are similar.
   B) by adding horizontally the individual demand curves of each gold earring consumer.
   C) by adding vertically the quantity demanded of each gold earring consumed at each price.
   D) by adding the prices each gold earring consumer is willing to pay for each quantity.
   Answer: B
   Diff: 1   Type: MC   Page Ref: 295-6/295-6
   Topic: Market demand curve
   Skill: Conceptual
   Objective: LO 2: Use the concept of utility to explain the law of demand.
   AACSB Coding: Reflective Thinking
   Special Feature: None

2. The income effect due to a price decrease will result in an increase in the quantity demanded for
   A) a Giffen good.
   B) an inferior good.
   C) a public good.
   D) a normal good.
   Answer: D
   Diff: 2   Type: MC   Page Ref: 295-7/295-7
   Topic: Income and substitution effect of a price change
   Skill : Conceptual
   Objective: LO 2: Use the concept of utility to explain the law of demand.
   AACSB Coding: Reflective Thinking
   Special Feature: None

3. Which of the following is a characteristic of a Giffen good?
   A) It has an upward sloping demand curve.
   B) It is a special type of luxury good named after the economist who first described it.
   C) It is a normal good for low-income consumers and an inferior good for high-income consumers.
   D) It refers to a good that is no longer used by consumers.
   Answer: A
   Diff: 2   Type: MC   Page Ref: 295-7/295-7
   Topic: Giffen goods
   Skill: Conceptual
   Objective: LO 2: Use the concept of utility to explain the law of demand.
   AACSB Coding: Reflective Thinking
   Special Feature: None

4. Which of the following statements is true?
   A) Demand curves do not slope upward because the income effect of a price change is stronger than the substitution effect of a price change.
   B) The demand curves of normal goods are downward sloping; the demand curves of inferior goods are upward sloping.
   C) We can conceive of Giffen goods, but none has ever been discovered.
   D) The substitution effect for a Giffen good is stronger than the income effect.

Answer: C
Diff: 2   Type: MC   Page Ref: 295–7/295–7
Topic: Giffen goods
Skill: Conceptual
Objective: LO 2: Use the concept of utility to explain the law of demand.
AACSB Coding: Reflective Thinking
Special Feature: None

9.3   Social Influences on Decision Making

1. Traditionally, economists have considered culture, customs, and religion as
   A) very important influences on the choices consumers make.
   B) relatively unimportant factors in explaining the choices consumers make.
   C) important influences in explaining consumer choices in command economies but less important in market economies.
   D) subject to normative economic analysis rather than positive economic analysis.

Answer: B
Diff: 1   Type: MC   Page Ref: 298/298
Topic: Social influences on decision making
Skill: Fact
Objective: LO 3: Explain how social influences can affect consumption choices.
AACSB Coding: Reflective Thinking
Special Feature: None

2. Consider a good whose consumption takes place publicly. Your decision to buy that good depends on
   A) both on the characteristics of the product and on how many other people are buying the good.
   B) only on the characteristics of the good.
   C) only on how many other people buy the good.
   D) only on the price of the good.

Answer: A
Diff: 1   Type: MC   Page Ref: 298/298
Topic: Social Influences on Decision Making
Skill: Conceptual
Objective: LO 3: Explain how social influences can affect consumption choices.
AACSB Coding: Reflective Thinking
Special Feature: None

3. Which of the following statements describes economists' attitudes regarding the influence of social factors on the choices consumers make?
    A) Economists formerly believed they were very important but now they believe they are not important.
    B) Economists believe social factors affect consumer choice in markets for public goods but not in markets for private goods.
    C) Liberal economists believe social factors are very important; conservative economists do not believe social factors have any influence on consumers.
    D) Economists traditionally believed they were unimportant, but many economists now believe social factors are important.

Answer: D
Diff: 1   Type: MC   Page Ref: 298/298
Topic: Social influences on decision making
Skill: Conceptual
Objective: LO 3: Explain how social influences can affect consumption choices.
AACSB Coding: Reflective Thinking
Special Feature: None

4. Economists Gary Becker and Kevin Murphy are associated with which of the following?
    A) The discovery of the first example of a Giffen good.
    B) They have argued that social factors are not important in explaining the choices consumers make.
    C) Consumers appear to receive utility from consuming goods they believe are popular.
    D) They discovered that price changes have both income and substitution effects.

Answer: C
Diff: 1   Type: MC   Page Ref: 298/298
Topic: Social influences on decision making
Skill: Conceptual
Objective: LO 3: Explain how social influences can affect consumption choices.
AACSB Coding: Reflective Thinking
Special Feature: None

5. Which of the following is *not* a reason why companies such as Nike and Titleist pay Tiger Woods to endorse their products?
    A) Many consumers feel more fashionable if they use the same products that Tiger Woods uses.
    B) Some consumers will buy a product endorsed by Tiger Woods because they believe he is particularly knowledgeable about the product.
    C) Some consumers want to feel closer to a celebrity who endorses a product.
    D) Some consumers believe that Tiger Woods is more rational than the average consumer.

Answer: D
Diff: 2   Type: MC   Page Ref: 298-9/298-9
Topic: Social influences on decision making
Skill: Conceptual
Objective: LO 3: Explain how social influences can affect consumption choices.
AACSB Coding: Reflective Thinking
Special Feature: Making the Connection: Why Do Firms Pay Tiger Woods to Endorse Their Products?

6. Which of the following refers to the increase in the usefulness of a product as the number of consumers who use it increases?
    A) Positive externalities.
    B) Network externalities.
    C) External marginal utility.
    D) The impact of celebrity endorsements.
Answer: B
Diff: 2   Type: MC   Page Ref: 299/299
Topic: Network externalities
Skill: Definition
Objective: LO 3: Explain how social influences can affect consumption choices.
AACSB Coding: Reflective Thinking
Special Feature: None

7. Tiger Woods endorses Titleist golf equipment and Buick automobiles. One reason Titleist pays Tiger Woods for his endorsement is that consumers believe he is more knowledgeable about golf than they are.   Why would the makers of Buick automobiles pay Tiger Woods to endorse their products?
    A) Many consumers believe Tiger Woods is more knowledgeable about automobiles than they are.
    B) More people play golf than any other sport.
    C) Some consumers believe that buying products endorsed by Tiger Woods makes them appear to be more fashionable.
    D) Buick receives free publicity whenever Tiger Woods wins a tournament.
Answer: C
Diff: 1   Type: MC   Page Ref: 298–9/298/9
Topic: Social influences on decision making
Skill: Conceptual
Objective: LO 3: Explain how social influences can affect consumption choices.
AACSB Coding: Reflective Thinking
Special Feature: Making the Connection: Why Do Firms Pay Tiger Woods to Endorse Their Products?

8. Which of the following is used to explain why a consumer's willingness to buy a cell phone increases as the number of other people who own and use cell phones increases?
    A) Network externalities.
    B) Market failure.
    C) Diminishing marginal utility.
    D) The income effect of a price change.
Answer: A
Diff: 1   Type: MC   Page Ref: 299/299
Topic: Network externalities
Skill: Conceptual
Objective: LO 3: Explain how social influences can affect consumption choices.
AACSB Coding: Reflective Thinking
Special Feature: None

9. Once a product becomes established, network externalities may create _____ costs that make consumers reluctant to buy a new product with better technology.
    A) external
    B) implicit
    C) switching
    D) marginal
Answer: C
Diff: 1   Type: MC   Page Ref: 299/299
Topic: Network externalities
Skill: Conceptual
Objective: LO 3: Explain how social influences can affect consumption choices.
AACSB Coding: Reflective Thinking
Special Feature: None

10. The order of the letters along the rows of computer keyboards could be changed to allow users to type faster, but this would inconvenience the vast majority of people who learned to type with the current keyboard layout. The costs of switching to a new layout make this change unlikely. This is an example of
    A) path dependency.
    B) how social influences overwhelm the substitution effect of a price change.
    C) how the elasticity of demand for typewriters has been affected by externalities.
    D) how consumers sometimes do not behave rationally.
Answer: A
Diff: 1   Type: MC   Page Ref: 299/299
Topic: Social influences on decision making
Skill: Conceptual
Objective: LO 3: Explain how social influences can affect consumption choices.
AACSB Coding: Reflective Thinking
Special Feature: None

11. A standard which came to the market first, such as the QWERTY letter layout in typewriters, can become entrenched (this layout is still used in computer keyboards today). What is this phenomenon called?
    A) Network externalities.
    B) Path dependency.
    C) Sunk cost
    D) Comparative advantage.
Answer: B
Diff: 1   Type: MC   Page Ref: 299/299
Topic: Social influences on decision making
Skill: Conceptual
Objective: LO 3: Explain how social influences can affect consumption choices.
AACSB Coding: Reflective Thinking
Special Feature: None

12. An advantage of Microsoft windows is its compatibility with the widest range of hardware and software. The dominance of Windows is self–reinforcing: hardware and software manufacturers ensure that their products are compatible with Windows in order to have access to the large number of Windows users. Which principle best describes this scenario?
    A) Endowment effects.
    B) Endorsement effects.
    C) Economies of scale.
    D) Network externalities.
Answer: D
Diff: 1   Type: MC   Page Ref: 299/299
Topic: Social influences on decision making
Skill: Conceptual
Objective: LO 3: Explain how social influences can affect consumption choices.
AACSB Coding: Reflective Thinking
Special Feature: None

13. Some economists have argued that path dependence and switching costs can lead to market failure. Which of the following is an example of this argument?
    A) Costly celebrity endorsements lead many consumers to buy a product even though it is more expensive or less effective than a product that is not endorsed by a celebrity.
    B) A consumer who won a lottery for a Super Bowl ticket refuses to sell it for $3,000 even though he would not have paid $3,000 for a ticket if he had not won the lottery.
    C) While playing the *ultimate game*, an allocator decides to share $20 equally with a recipient rather than keep the $20 for herself.
    D) VHS video recorders became more popular with consumers than Sony Betamax recorders even though the Betamax recorders embodied a superior technology.
Answer: D
Diff: 2   Type: MC   Page Ref: 299–303/299–303
Topic: Network externalities
Skill: Conceptual
Objective: LO 3: Explain how social influences can affect consumption choices.
AACSB Coding: Reflective Thinking
Special Feature: None

14. Many economists do not believe that network externalities lock consumers into the use of products that have technology inferior to other, similar products. These economists believe that
    A) consumers are always rational.
    B) in practice, the gains from using a superior technology exceed the losses consumers incur from switching costs.
    C) there is no good evidence that switching costs exist.
    D) the government will prevent products with inferior technology from being sold to consumers.

Answer: B
Diff: 2   Type: MC   Page Ref: 299/299
Topic: Social influences on decision making
Skill: Conceptual
Objective: LO 3: Explain how social influences can affect consumption choices.
AACSB Coding: Reflective Thinking
Special Feature: None

15. All but one of the following have been suggested by some economists as possible consequences of path dependency and switching costs. Which of the following is not a possible consequence of path dependency and switching costs?
    A) Consumers may get locked into using products with inferior technology.
    B) Market failure.
    C) Diseconomies of scale.
    D) Government intervention may be necessary in affected markets in order to improve economic efficiency.

Answer: C
Diff: 2   Type: MC   Page Ref: 299/299
Topic: Network externalities
Skill: Conceptual
Objective: LO 3: Explain how social influences can affect consumption choices.
AACSB Coding: Reflective Thinking
Special Feature: None

16. Some economists have suggested that network externalities result in consumers being locked into the use of products with inferior technologies. Economists Stan Leibowitz and Stephen Margolis have studied cases that have been cited as examples of this and found
    A) there is no convincing evidence that the alternative technologies were superior.
    B) consumers sometimes do become locked into the use of products with inferior technologies.
    C) that in all of these cases network externalities resulted in market failure.
    D) that consumers use products with inferior technologies when their prices are lower than products with superior technologies.

Answer: A
Diff: 2   Type: MC   Page Ref: 299/299
Topic: Network externalities
Skill: Analytical
Objective: LO 3: Explain how social influences can affect consumption choices.
AACSB Coding: Reflective Thinking
Special Feature: None

17. Maurice Allais, Reinhard Selten and Vernon Smith all were awarded the Nobel Prize in Economics in part because
    A) of their work with experimental economics.
    B) they discovered the first example of a Giffen good.
    C) of their work on the substitution and effect effects of price changes.
    D) they proved that external economies would lead to market failure.
    Answer: A
    Diff: 2   Type: MC   Page Ref: 300/300
    Topic: Experimental economics
    Skill: Fact
    Objective: LO 3: Explain how social influences can affect consumption choices.
    AACSB Coding: Reflective Thinking
    Special Feature: None

18. Which of the following is an experiment that tests the significance of fairness in consumer decision making?
    A) The fairness challenge.
    B) Equity and consumer choice.
    C) The ultimate game.
    D) Are you rational?
    Answer: C
    Diff: 2   Type: MC   Page Ref: 300/300
    Topic: Experimental economics
    Skill: Fact
    Objective: LO 3: Explain how social influences can affect consumption choices.
    AACSB Coding: Reflective Thinking
    Special Feature: None

19. The quantity demanded of tickets to the Super Bowl is always greater than the than the quantity supplied. Which of the following in the best explanation why the National Football League does not raise the price of tickets to the level where the quantity demanded equals the quantity supplied?
    A) Raising the price would reduce the demand for tickets; there would then be a surplus and the game would not sell out.
    B) The cost of raising the price and printing new tickets would exceed the revenue the NFL would receive from higher ticket prices.
    C) The demand for Super Bowl tickets is elastic; raising the price would reduce total revenue.
    D) The NFL is concerned that raising ticket prices would be considered unfair.
    Answer: D
    Diff: 2   Type: MC   Page Ref: 300-3/300-3
    Topic: Business implications of fairness
    Skill: Analytical
    Objective: LO 3: Explain how social influences can affect consumption choices.
    AACSB Coding: Analytic Skills
    Special Feature: None

20. Economist Alan Krueger conducted a survey of people who attended the Super Bowl in 2001. What was the purpose of Krueger's survey?
    A) He wanted to know why people would pay a substantial amount to watch the Super Bowl in person rather than watch the game on television.
    B) He asked those who attended the game whether they believed it would be fair for the National Football League to raise the price of tickets to an amount less than they would be willing to pay.
    C) He compared the willingness to pay for Super Bowl tickets to the willingness to pay for tickets to other sporting events (the World Series, the World Cup and the Olympics).
    D) He compared the difference between the willingness to pay for tickets between (a) fans from the cities with teams that played in the Super Bowl, and (b) fans who receive utility from attending an event they believe is popular.
    Answer: B
    Diff: 2   *Type: MC*   *Page Ref: 302–3/302–3*
    Topic: Social influences on decision making
    Skill: Fact
    Objective: LO 3: Explain how social influences can affect consumption choices.
    AACSB Coding: Reflective Thinking
    Special Feature: Making the Connection: Professor Krueger Goes to the Super Bowl.

21. Economist Alan Krueger surveyed people who attended the 2001 Super Bowl in order to determine whether they believed it would be fair for the National Football League (NFL) to raise the price of tickets to a level that was less than the amount most fans would be willing to pay. What conclusion did Krueger come to based on his survey results?
    A) Whatever the NFL would gain from raising ticket prices in the short run, it would more than lose in the long run.
    B) The NFL should raise ticket prices so long as the price is less than the maximum fans would be willing to pay.
    C) The demand for Super Bowl tickets is elastic.
    D) The substitution effect from an increase in price is greater than the income effect.
    Answer: A
    Diff: 2   *Type: MC*   *Page Ref: 302–3/302–3*
    Topic: Social influences on decision making
    Skill: Fact
    Objective: LO 3: Explain how social influences can affect consumption choices.
    AACSB Coding: Reflective Thinking
    Special Feature: Making the Connection: Professor Krueger Goes to the Super Bowl.

22. During its run on Broadway the play *The Producers* regularly sold out all of available tickets at the St. James Theater. The theater could have raised ticket prices from $75 to $125 and still sold all available tickets but chose not to do so. The best explanation for this decision is
    A) theater owners are unaware of the elasticity of demand for Broadway shows.
    B) theater owners do not want to raise their tickets on weekends, when demand is high, and then have to lower prices during the week, when demand is lower.
    C) firms sometimes give up profits in the short run to keep their customers happy and increase their profits in the long run.
    D) theater owners are not motivated to maximize their profits.
    Answer: C
    Diff: 1   Type: MC   Page Ref: 301–2/301–2
    Topic: Business implications of fairness
    Skill: Conceptual
    Objective: LO 3: Explain how social influences can affect consumption choices.
    AACSB Coding: Reflective Thinking
    Special Feature: None

23. All but one of the following economists were awarded a Nobel prize for their contributions to experimental economics and their explorations of the influence fairness has on consumer decision–making. Which economist *did not* receive a Nobel Prize for this work?
    A) Vernon Smith
    B) Alan Krueger
    C) Daniel Kahneman
    D) Maurice Allais
    Answer: B
    Diff: 1   Type: MC   Page Ref: 300–3/300–3
    Topic: Social influences on decision making
    Skill: Fact
    Objective: LO 3: Explain how social influences can affect consumption choices.
    AACSB Coding: Reflective Thinking
    Special Feature: None

24. In an experiment that employed the *dictator game* economists at Cornell University gave student "allocators" the option of dividing $20 in only two ways (a) $18 for themselves and $2 to another student, or (b) $10 for themselves and $10 to another student. What was one result from this experiment?
    A) Most allocators chose to give themselves $18 and $2 to the other students.
    B) Most of the students who were not allocators did not like having someone else make decisions for them.
    C) A majority of the female allocators chose option (a); a majority of the male allocators chose option (b).
    D) Most of the allocators apparently valued acting fairly.
    Answer: D
    Diff: 2   Type: MC   Page Ref: 300–1/300–1
    Topic: Experimental economics
    Skill: Fact
    Objective: LO 3: Explain how social influences can affect consumption choices.
    AACSB Coding: Reflective Thinking
    Special Feature: None

25. Economists have used the ultimatum game and the dictator game in experiments designed to determine
    A) whether consumers care about fairness when they make decisions.
    B) whether consumers believe it is fair for producers to raise the price of a product for which there is excess demand.
    C) whether consumers understand the difference between implicit costs and explicit costs.
    D) whether consumers understand the rule of equal marginal utility per dollar spent.
    Answer: A
    Diff: 2   Type: MC   Page Ref: 300–1/300–1
    Topic: Experimental economics
    Skill: Fact
    Objective: LO 3: Explain how social influences can affect consumption choices.
    AACSB Coding: Reflective Thinking
    Special Feature: None

26. Many people leave their servers tips in restaurants, even when they are not likely to visit the restaurant again. This is evidence that
    A) people would rather pay for good service at an inexpensive restaurant than pay higher prices and receive poor service at an expensive restaurant.
    B) people enjoy eating at restaurants more than eating at home.
    C) people treat others fairly even if doing so makes them worse off financially.
    D) there has been an improvement in the service people receive in restaurants over time, partly because the restaurant industry has become more competitive.
    Answer: C
    Diff: 1   Type: MC   Page Ref: 300/300
    Topic: Social influences on decision making
    Skill: Conceptual
    Objective: LO 3: Explain how social influences can affect consumption choices.
    AACSB Coding: Reflective Thinking
    Special Feature: None

27. In their surveys of consumers Daniel Kaheman, Jack Knetsch and Richard Thaler found that
    A) most people considered it unfair for firms to raise their prices because of an increase in their costs, but fair to raise their prices after an increase in demand.
    B) most people considered any increase in price to be unfair as it led to an increase in profits.
    C) most people believed that low income people were hurt most by increases in prices.
    D) most people considered an increase in price by firms following an increase in their costs to be fair but believed it was unfair for firms to raise their prices because of an increase in demand.
    Answer: D
    Diff: 2   Type: MC   Page Ref: 302/302
    Topic: Social influences on decision making
    Skill: Fact
    Objective: LO 3: Explain how social influences can affect consumption choices.
    AACSB Coding: Reflective Thinking
    Special Feature: None

28. In a survey of consumers Daniel Kaheman, Jack Knetsch and Richard Thaler asked their opinion of a hardware store's decision to
    A) go out of business because a larger hardware store opened in the same city; 82 percent of those surveyed believed it was unfair for the larger store to compete with the smaller store.
    B) raise the price of snow shovels the day following a snowstorm; 82 percent of those surveyed believed this was unfair.
    C) sell tickets to sporting and cultural events at prices higher than prices paid at the ticket windows for the same events; 82 percent of those surveyed believed this was unfair.
    D) remain in business even though the store was not making an economic profit; 82 percent of those surveyed believed it would be unfair for the store to go out of business if there no other hardware stores in the same area.

    Answer: B
    Diff: 2   Type: MC   Page Ref: 302/302
    Topic: Social influences on decision making
    Skill: Fact
    Objective: LO 3: Explain how social influences can affect consumption choices.
    AACSB Coding: Reflective Thinking
    Special Feature: None

29. The ultimate game and the dictator game are used in economic experiments to test whether fairness is an important influence on consumer decision-making.

    Answer: ◉ True   False
    Diff: 1   Type: TF   Page Ref: 300–1/300–1
    Topic: Social influences on decision making
    Skill: Fact
    Objective: LO 3: Explain how social influences can affect consumption choices.
    AACSB Coding: Reflective Thinking
    Special Feature: None

30. A network externality causes firms to sacrifice profits in the short run in order to satisfy their customers and increase their long-run profits.

    Answer: True   ◉ False
    Diff: 1   Type: TF   Page Ref: 299–302/299–302
    Topic: Social influences on decision making
    Skill: Definition
    Objective: LO 3: Explain how social influences can affect consumption choices.
    AACSB Coding: Reflective Thinking
    Special Feature: None

31. Studies on consumer behavior have found that most people value fairness enough that they will refuse to participate in transactions they consider unfair, even if they are worse off as a result. How does this affect a firm's decision to raise prices in the event of a temporary increase in demand?

Answer: If the firm chooses to raise prices, consumers will consider this price increase unfair and might choose to buy elsewhere. This loss of consumer goodwill could lead to lower profits in the long run. It is rational for firms to forego raising prices in the short run to keep customers happy. This can lead to increased profits in the long run.

Diff: 2   Type: SA   Page Ref: 300–3/300–3
Topic: Behavioral economics
Skill: Conceptual
Objective: LO 3: Explain how social influences can affect consumption choices.
AACSB Coding: Reflective Thinking
Special Feature: None

32. Economists have noted that businesses of a certain type tend to congregate geographically, attracting workers with skills in those fields. This, in turn, lures more firms seeking employees with those skills. Some examples include commercial banking, software development, and the automobile industry. What mechanism is at work here? Briefly explain how the mechanism works to the advantage of employers and employees.

Answer: The mechanism at work is a network externality. Employers will have access to a larger pool of skilled employees. At the same time, the efficiency of the job search for employees will be enhanced. In addition, industries are likely to draw ancillary services which could yield further efficiency gains for producers.

Diff: 2   Type: SA   Page Ref: 299/299
Topic: Network externalities
Skill: Conceptual
Objective: LO 3: Explain how social influences can affect consumption choices.
AACSB Coding: Reflective Thinking
Special Feature: None

33. Music writer Anthony Kuzminski praised rock star Tom Petty in a 2007 article in the online *Unrated Magazine*. Kuzminski wrote: "Something Petty never can get enough credit for is his fan-friendly attitude. He kept ticket prices for [his concerts] at $50 when other acts this summer are charging upwards of $100 for stadium gigs. Petty could charge more, but he doesn't see the point. He has stated time and time again he still makes millions when he's on the road, regardless of his ticket prices. He is the last of the fan friendly rock stars out there." Use economic reasoning to write a rationale for Tom Petty's decision to charge prices for his band's ("Tom Petty and the Heartbreakers") concerts that are less than market clearing prices.
Source: Anthony Kuzminski, "Tom Petty & The Heartbreakers at the Vic Theater"
http://www.unratedmagazine.com/

Answer: Tickets to Tom Petty's concerts consistently sell at prices lower than tickets to concerts by other well-known rock bands. This means that he and the Heartbreakers earn lower profits in the short run but his actions ensure the loyalty of concert goers, and profits, in the long run.

Diff: 2   Type: SA   Page Ref: 301-2/301-2
Topic: Business implications of fairness
Skill: Analytical
Objective: LO 3: Explain how social influences can affect consumption choices.
AACSB Coding: Analytic Skills
Special Feature: None

9.4   Behavioral Economics: Do People Make Their Choices Rationally?

1. A new area of economics studies situations in which people appear to be making choices that do not appear to be economically rational. This area is called
    A) behavioral economics.
    B) irrational economics.
    C) social economics.
    D) new wave economics.

Answer: A

Diff: 1   Type: MC   Page Ref: 303/303
Topic: Behavioral economics
Skill: Definition
Objective: LO 4: Describe the behavioral economics approach to understanding decision making.
AACSB Coding: Reflective Thinking
Special Feature: None

2. Behavioral economics refers to the study of situations
   A) where consumers and firms appear to make choices that are appropriate to reach their goals.
   B) where consumers and firms appear to value fairness when they make choices.
   C) where consumers and firms disobey the laws of demand and supply.
   D) where consumers and firms do not appear to be making choices that are economically rational.
   Answer: D
   Diff: 1   Type: MC   Page Ref: 303/303
   Topic: Behavioral economics
   Skill: Definition
   Objective: LO 4: Describe the behavioral economics approach to understanding decision making.
   AACSB Coding: Reflective Thinking
   Special Feature: None

3. One reason that consumers and businesses might not act rationally is
   A) it is difficult to obtain enough information about the elasticities of demand and supply.
   B) they may not realize their actions are inconsistent with their goals.
   C) consumer tastes change constantly.
   D) they do not always value fairness when they make choices.
   Answer: B
   Diff: 1   Type: MC   Page Ref: 303/303
   Topic: Behavioral economics
   Skill: Conceptual
   Objective: LO 4: Describe the behavioral economics approach to understanding decision making.
   AACSB Coding: Reflective Thinking
   Special Feature: None

4. Which of the following is a common mistake consumers commit when they make decisions?
   A) They take into account nonmonetary opportunity costs but ignore monetary costs.
   B) They are overly pessimistic about their future behavior.
   C) They fail to ignore sunk costs.
   D) They sometimes value fairness too much.
   Answer: C
   Diff: 1   Type: MC   Page Ref: 303/303
   Topic: Behavioral economics
   Skill : Conceptual
   Objective: LO 4: Describe the behavioral economics approach to understanding decision making.
   AACSB Coding: Reflective Thinking
   Special Feature: None

5. The highest-valued alternative that must be given up to engage in an activity is the definition of
   A) utility.
   B) implicit cost.
   C) opportunity cost.
   D) economic sacrifice.

Answer: C

Diff: 1   Type: MC   Page Ref: 303/303
Topic: Opportunity cost
Skill: Definition
Objective: LO 4: Describe the behavioral economics approach to understanding decision making.
AACSB Coding: Reflective Thinking
Special Feature: None

6. Which of the following is *not* a common mistake made by consumers?
   A) The failure to take into account the implicit costs of an activity.
   B) The failure to ignore sunk costs.
   C) Being overly optimistic about their future behavior.
   D) Being overly pessimistic about their future behavior.

Answer: D

Diff: 1   Type: MC   Page Ref: 303/303
Topic: Behavioral economics
Skill: Conceptual
Objective: LO 4: Describe the behavioral economics approach to understanding decision making.
AACSB Coding: Reflective Thinking
Special Feature: None

7. Alan Krueger conducted a survey of fans at the 2001 Super Bowl who purchased tickets to the game for $325 or $400. Krueger found that (a) 94 percent of those surveyed would not have paid $3,000 for their tickets, and (b) 92 percent of those surveyed would not have sold their tickets for $3,000. These results are evidence of
   A) the high value fans place on watching the Super Bowl in person, rather than on television.
   B) the failure of consumers to take into account nonmonetary opportunity costs.
   C) the failure of consumers to ignore sunk costs.
   D) consumers being overly optimistic about their future behavior.

Answer: B

Diff: 2   Type: MC   Page Ref: 303-4/303-4
Topic: Behavioral economics
Skill: Conceptual
Objective: LO 4: Describe the behavioral economics approach to understanding decision making.
AACSB Coding: Reflective Thinking
Special Feature: None

8. Alan Krueger conducted a survey of fans at the 2001 Super Bowl who purchased tickets to the game for $325 or $400. Krueger found that (a) 94 percent of those surveyed would not have paid $3,000 for their tickets, and (b) 92 percent of those surveyed would not have sold their tickets for $3,000. These results are an example of
   A) the tendency of people to be unwilling to sell a good they already own even if they are offered a price that is greater than the price they would be willing to pay if they did not already own it.
   B) the tendency for consumers to account for monetary costs but to ignore sunk costs.
   C) consumers placing a high value on a product because it makes them appear to be fashionable.
   D) the law of demand.
Answer: A
Diff: 2   Type: MC   Page Ref: 303–4/303–4
Topic: Behavioral economics
Skill: Conceptual
Objective: LO 4: Describe the behavioral economics approach to understanding decision making.
AACSB Coding: Reflective Thinking
Special Feature: None

9. Alan Krueger conducted a survey of fans at the 2001 Super Bowl who purchased tickets to the game for $325 or $400. Krueger found that (a) 94 percent of those surveyed would not have paid $3,000 for their tickets, and (b) 92 percent of those surveyed would not have sold their tickets for $3,000. These results are an example of
   A) rational consumer behavior.
   B) the endowment effect.
   C) the fallacy of composition.
   D) the failure to ignore sunk costs.
Answer: B
Diff: 2   Type: MC   Page Ref: 303–4/303–4
Topic: Behavioral economics
Skill: Conceptual
Objective: LO 4: Describe the behavioral economics approach to understanding decision making.
AACSB Coding: Reflective Thinking
Special Feature: None

10. What is the endowment effect?
    A) The tendency of people to be unwilling to sell something they already own even if they are offered a price that is greater than what they would be willing to pay to buy the good if they did not already own it.
    B) The tendency of people to be unwilling to sell something they already own because of its sentimental value.
    C) The tendency of people to overstate the value of a good they already own even though similar items can be purchased at a lower price.
    D) The sum total of assets that a person has acquired over the years.

Answer: A
Diff: 1   Type: MC   Page Ref: 303–4/303–4
Topic: Behavioral economics
Skill: Definition
Objective: LO 4: Describe the behavioral economics approach to understanding decision making.
AACSB Coding: Reflective Thinking
Special Feature: None

11. Most film processing companies have a policy of printing every picture on a roll of film and allowing customers to request a refund for pictures that were not clearly developed. The companies do this knowing that most customers do not ask for refunds. This is an example of consumers
    A) failing to ignore sunk costs.
    B) being overly optimistic about their future behavior.
    C) not taking nonmonetary opportunity costs into account.
    D) not making themselves aware of the policy regarding refunds.

Answer: C
Diff: 2   Type: MC   Page Ref: 304/304
Topic: Behavioral economics
Skill: Analytical
Objective: LO 4: Describe the behavioral economics approach to understanding decision making.
AACSB Coding: Analytic Skills
Special Feature: None

12. Costs that have already been incurred, and which cannot be recovered, are known as
    A) short–run fixed costs.
    B) implicit costs.
    C) unavoidable costs.
    D) sunk costs.

Answer: D
Diff: 1   Type: MC   Page Ref: 305/305
Topic: Sunk cost
Skill: Definition
Objective: LO 4: Describe the behavioral economics approach to understanding decision making.
AACSB Coding: Reflective Thinking
Special Feature: None

13. A sunk cost is
    A) another term that means opportunity cost.
    B) a term used to describe the cost of capital that the owners of a firm sink into their business.
    C) the highest valued alternative that must be given up to engage in an activity.
    D) a cost that has already been paid and cannot be recovered.
    Answer: D
    Diff: 1   Type: MC   Page Ref: 305/305
    Topic: Sunk cost
    Skill: Definition
    Objective: LO 4: Describe the behavioral economics approach to understanding decision making.
    AACSB Coding: Reflective Thinking
    Special Feature: None

14. Suppose you pre-ordered a non-refundable movie ticket to "Harry Potter and the Goblet of Fire." On the day of the movie you decide that you would rather not go to the movie. According to economists, what is the rational thing to do?
    A) Since the cost of the movie ticket is a sunk cost, it should not influence your decision. Your decision should be based solely on whether you want to see the movie or not.
    B) You should not waste resources. Since you have paid for the ticket you should watch the movie.
    C) Your should go to the movie to minimize your loses.
    D) You should go to the movie to maximize your utility.
    Answer: A
    Diff: 1   Type: MC   Page Ref: 306-7/306-7
    Topic: Sunk cost
    Skill: Conceptual
    Objective: LO 4: Describe the behavioral economics approach to understanding decision making.
    AACSB Coding: Reflective Thinking
    Special Feature: None

15. Harvey Miller owns a baseball that was hit for a home run by Ted Williams. Harvey, a long-time Boston Red Sox fan, recently refused to sell his baseball for $75,000 even though he would not have paid someone more than $10,000 for the baseball if he did not already own it. Harvey explained his decision not to sell the baseball by noting that: "Ted Williams was my hero. This baseball has a great deal of sentimental value for me." Which of the following can explain Harvey's behavior?
    A) The difference between implicit and explicit costs.
    B) The scarcity of home run baseballs hit by Ted Williams.
    C) The endowment effect.
    D) How social influences can affect consumption choices.
    Answer: C
    Diff: 2   Type: MC   Page Ref: 303-4/303-4
    Topic: Behavioral economics
    Skill: Conceptual
    Objective: LO 4: Describe the behavioral economics approach to understanding decision making.
    AACSB Coding: Reflective Thinking
    Special Feature: None

16. Economists David Laibson and Xavier Gabaix examined the behavior of consumers when buying products that consist of a "base good" and "add-ons." Firms typically compete on the price of the base good (for example, a printer) rather than an add-on (for example, ink cartridges). They found that firms are often successful in hiding the prices of add-ons from consumers. What explanation do Laibson and Gabaix offer for why some firms do not offer lower-priced add-ons and advertise the higher prices of rival firms?
    A) Firms fear that an ad campaign could lead to competition that would force all firms to lower the prices of their add-ons.
    B) Using advertising to inform consumers who typically ignore the price of ad-ons is not a profitable strategy.
    C) Firms fear that competition for add-ons would force them to also lower the prices of their base goods.
    D) The demand for add-ons is very inelastic. Lowering the price of add-ons would reduce total revenue.
    Answer: B
    Diff: 2   Type: MC   Page Ref: 304-5/304-5
    Topic: Making the Connection
    Skill: Fact
    Objective: LO 4: Describe the behavioral economics approach to understanding decision making.
    AACSB Coding: Reflective Thinking
    Special Feature: Making the Connection: Why Do Hilton Hotels and Other Firms Hide Their Prices?

17. Economists David Laibson and Xavier Gabaix examined the behavior of consumers when buying products that consist of a "base good" and "add-ons." What is meant by these terms?
    A) A base good is a necessity; an add-on is a luxury.
    B) A base good is a normal good; an add-on is an inferior good.
    C) An add-on is a product that must be purchased (for example, an ink cartridge) in order to be able to use the base good (for example, a printer).
    D) A base good is a standardized product; an add-on is a differentiated product.
    Answer: C
    Diff: 1   Type: MC   Page Ref: 304-5/304-5
    Topic: Behavioral economics
    Skill: Fact
    Objective: LO 4: Describe the behavioral economics approach to understanding decision making.
    AACSB Coding: Reflective Thinking
    Special Feature: Making the Connection: Why Do Hilton Hotels and Other Firms Hide Their Prices?

18. Health Clubs typically experience an increase in one-year memberships in January, but many new customers cancel their memberships before the end of the year. Which of the following is the best explanation for this behavior?
    A) Some health club members suffer minor injuries that prevent them from working out.
    B) Some people are overly optimistic about their future behavior.
    C) Some people fail to treat their membership fees as sunk costs.
    D) Some members receive utility from activities they believe are popular.
    Answer: B
    Diff: 3   Type: MC   Page Ref: 306-7/306-7
    Topic: Behavioral economics
    Skill: Conceptual
    Objective: LO 4: Describe the behavioral economics approach to understanding decision making.
    AACSB Coding: Reflective Thinking
    Special Feature: None

19. Studies have shown that students who earn high grades in college will have earned much more over a 40 year period than students who receive low grades. Despite this, surveys show that many students fail to study enough hours outside of the classroom to earn high grades. Which of the following is the best explanation for this?
    A) Some students can earn high grades by studying fewer hours than other students.
    B) The surveys used to make this observation were based on a non-random sample of students.
    C) Because of new technology developed in the 1990s, students can make more efficient use of their study time today than students who attended college before the 1990s.
    D) Students overvalue the utility they receive from activities other than studying.
    Answer: D
    Diff: 1   Type: MC   Page Ref: 306-7/306-7
    Topic: Behavioral economics
    Skill: Conceptual
    Objective: LO 4: Describe the behavioral economics approach to understanding decision making.
    AACSB Coding: Reflective Thinking
    Special Feature: Making the Connection: Why Don't Students Study More?

20. Which of the following is an example of consumers being unrealistic about their future behavior?
    A) People forgo saving for retirement because they plan to save in the future when they expect to earn higher salaries.
    B) College students who can afford to attend a private university attend a public university in order to spend less on tuition.
    C) Parents contribute to a tuition fund for their children soon after they are born.
    D) A college student works part-time to earn income to pay for a used car even though she is a full-time student.
    Answer: A
    Diff: 2   Type: MC   Page Ref: 307-8/307-8
    Topic: Solved Problem
    Skill: Conceptual
    Objective: LO 4: Describe the behavioral economics approach to understanding decision making.
    AACSB Coding: Reflective Thinking
    Special Feature: Solved Problem: How Do You Get People to Save More of Their Income?

21. Wilbur Rickhiser, a financial advisor, recently told one of his clients: "The biggest mistake you can make is to hold onto a stock for too long in order to avoid a loss. Let's say you bought a stock for $50 per share but that six months later the price fell to $40 after a poor earnings report. Many of my clients in this situation will hold the stock, hoping the price will later rise above $50. In most cases like this the price does not rise and may even fall. You must know when to cut your losses." Which of the following is the best explanation for Rickhiser's advice?
    A) People sometimes buy stocks because other people are buying them or they want to appear to be fashionable.
    B) People sometimes make mistakes when they buy stocks because of the endowment effect.
    C) People sometimes make mistakes when they buy stocks or when they buy goods and services: they ignore the monetary opportunity costs of their choices.
    D) People often fail to ignore the sunk costs of their decisions. The cost of the stock bought at $50 per share is a sunk cost.
    Answer: D
    Diff: 3   Type: MC   Page Ref: 305–6/305–6
    Topic: Sunk cost
    Skill: Conceptual
    Objective: LO 4: Describe the behavioral economics approach to understanding decision making.
    AACSB Coding: Reflective Thinking
    Special Feature: None

22. Suppose Adam Einberg pays $100 for a ticket to a new Broadway play and $100 was the maximum price he was willing to pay. On the day of the performance of the play Adam refuses to sell the ticket for $150. How would behavioral economists explain Adam's refusal to sell his ticket?
    A) Adam's tastes had changed from the time he bought the ticket to the time of the performance of the play.
    B) When Adam bought the ticket he was being unrealistic about his future behavior.
    C) The endowment effect explains Adam's actions. People like Adam seem to value things that they have more than the things they do not have.
    D) Adam's income probably increased between the time he bought the ticket and the day of the play's performance.
    Answer: C
    Diff: 2   Type: MC   Page Ref: 303–4/303–4
    Topic: Consumer behavior
    Skill: Conceptual
    Objective: LO 4: Describe the behavioral economics approach to understanding decision making.
    AACSB Coding: Reflective Thinking
    Special Feature: None

23. Assume that you had a ticket for a basketball playoff game that you bought for $50, the maximum price you were willing to pay. If a friend of yours offers to buy the ticket for $100 and but you decide not to sell it, how can your decision be explained?
    A) You expect to receive greater utility from attending the playoff game than you received from buying the ticket.
    B) By the endowment effect.
    C) By the law of diminishing marginal utility.
    D) The income effect from the increase in the price of the ticket from $50 to $100 was greater than the substitution effect.
    Answer: B
    Diff: 2   Type: MC   Page Ref: 308/308
    Topic: Behavioral economics
    Skill: Analytical
    Objective: LO 4: Describe the behavioral economics approach to understanding decision making.
    AACSB Coding: Reflective Thinking
    Special Feature: Economics in YOUR Life!: Do You Make Consistent Decisions?

24. In 2007 Elizabeth Arden hired Mariah Carey to develop and market a line of fragrance products. Elizabeth Arden must believe
    A) that the demand for fragrance products is elastic.
    B) that the demand for the other fragrance products its sells – those not associated with Mariah Carey – have experienced diminishing marginal utility.
    C) fragrance products are luxury goods.
    D) Mariah Carey's association with Elizabeth Arden will lead to an increase in the demand for Carey's line of fragrance products.
    Answer: A
    Diff: 1   Type: MC   Page Ref: 310–1/310–1
    Topic: Social influences on decision making
    Skill: Conceptual
    Objective: LO 4: Describe the behavioral economics approach to understanding decision making.
    AACSB Coding: Reflective Thinking
    Special Feature: An Inside Look: Can Mariah Carey Get You to Buy Elizabeth Arden Perfume?

25. A common mistake made by consumers is the failure to take into account the monetary costs of their actions.
    Answer: True   False
    Diff: 1   Type: TF   Page Ref: 303–4/303–4
    Topic: Behavioral economics
    Skill: Conceptual
    Objective: LO 4: Describe the behavioral economics approach to understanding decision making.
    AACSB Coding: Reflective Thinking
    Special Feature: None

26. One reason college students do not study enough to get high grades is that they are unrealistic about their future behavior.
    Answer: ○ True   False
    Diff: 2   Type: TF   Page Ref: 306-7/306-7
    Topic: Behavioral economics
    Skill: Conceptual
    Objective: LO 4: Describe the behavioral economics approach to understanding decision making.
    AACSB Coding: Reflective Thinking
    Special Feature: None

27. A construction project in Congressman Foghorn's district is unfinished. Foghorn has asked that a new appropriations bill include funds to complete the project, despite a report by an independent agency that the project is a waste of taxpayer money. Foghorn's project is a bridge that crosses a river between two cities in his district. The press has criticized Foghorn and dubbed the project "a bridge too far" since another bridge, located closer to the same two cities Foghorn's bridge will connect, already exists and can accommodate all traffic between the two cities. Foghorn argues that if the bridge project is not completed, the $50 million already spent will have been wasted. Is Foghorn's argument economically rational? Explain your answer.
    Answer: Foghorn's argument is not rational. The $50 million that has been spent on bridge construction is a sunk cost that should be ignored when deciding whether to spend additional tax revenue on the bridge. Foghorn should argue that the additional, or marginal, cost of finishing the project is less than the additional benefits that would be provided by the second bridge. If the estimated additional benefits are less than the additional cost the bridge should not be finished.
    Diff: 3   Type: ES   Page Ref: 305-6/305-6
    Topic: Sunk cost
    Skill: Analytical
    Objective: LO 4: Describe the behavioral economics approach to understanding decision making.
    AACSB Coding: Analytic Skills
    Special Feature: None

28. Behavioral economists examine choices that consumers make that are not economically rational. Economists generally assume that people are rational; that is, they weigh the benefits and costs of an action and choose an action only if the benefits outweigh the costs. Why do consumers not act rationally when the result is that they make themselves worse off?

Answer: Most people who do not act rationally do not realize that their actions are inconsistent with their goals. Another way to explain this is that they do not weigh the benefits and costs of their decisions correctly. Three mistakes are commonly made. First, while people usually account for the monetary costs of their choices they often ignore the nonmonetary opportunity costs. Monetary costs are easier to recognize because they call for payments of money, but nonmonetary opportunity costs do not. Second, people fail to ignore sunk costs. Although people may regret spending money for an activity, if the money cannot be recovered it should not factor into making current or future decisions. Finally, people often overvalue the benefit or utility they receive from current choices (for example, smoking) and undervalue the utility they expect to receive in the future (for example, not contracting lung cancer).

Diff: 3   Type: ES   Page Ref: 303–9/303–9
Topic: Behavioral economics
Skill: Analytical
Objective: LO 4: Describe the behavioral economics approach to understanding decision making.
AACSB Coding: Reflective Thinking
Special Feature: None

9.5   Appendix: Using Indifference Curves and Budget Lines in Understanding Consumer Behavior

1. Which of the following statements about utility and preferences is false?
    A) If Sidra prefers tea to coffee and coffee to hot chocolate, then she must prefer tea to hot chocolate.
    B) Preferences can be ranked.
    C) If two individuals, Ingrid and Inez, each consume the same bundle of goods, then both Inez and Ingrid must receive the same utility from the bundle.
    D) Utility cannot be compared across consumers

Answer: C

Diff: 2   Type: MC   Page Ref: 317–8/317–8
Topic: Indifference curves
Skill: Conceptual
Objective: Appendix: Using indifference curves to explain consumer behavior.
AACSB Coding: Reflective Thinking
Special Feature: None

2. A curve that shows combinations of consumption bundles that give a consumer the same utility is called
    A) a utility curve.
    B) an indifference curve.
    C) a preference curve.
    D) a demand curve.
Answer: B
Diff: 1   Type: MC   Page Ref: 317/317
Topic: Indifference curves
Skill: Definition
Objective: Appendix: Using indifference curves to explain consumer behavior.
AACSB Coding: Reflective Thinking
Special Feature: None

3. The slope of the indifference curve is referred to as
    A) the marginal rate of substitution.
    B) the price ratio.
    C) the marginal rate of consumption.
    D) the marginal tradeoff rate.
Answer: A
Diff: 1   Type: MC   Page Ref: 318/318
Topic: Indifference curves
Skill: Conceptual
Objective: Appendix: Using indifference curves to explain consumer behavior.
AACSB Coding: Reflective Thinking
Special Feature: None

4. What does the marginal rate of substitution measure?
    A) It measures the rate at which a consumer must give up one good to purchase another good.
    B) It measures the rate at which a consumer will substitute one good for another when the price of one good changes.
    C) It measures the change in utility from consuming one additional unit of a good.
    D) It measures the rate at which a consumer is willing to trade off one product for another while keeping utility constant.
Answer: D
Diff: 2   Type: MC   Page Ref: 318/318
Topic: Marginal rate of substitution
Skill: Conceptual
Objective: Appendix: Using indifference curves to explain consumer behavior.
AACSB Coding: Reflective Thinking
Special Feature: None

5. Vinny consumes tacos and chicken wings. To keep his utility constant, he must be given more tacos if he consumes fewer chicken wings. This means that
    A) Vinny's indifference curve for tacos and chicken wings must have a negative slope.
    B) the prices Vinny pays for tacos and chicken wings are always the same.
    C) Vinny's marginal utility from each good must be constant along his convex indifference curves for tacos and chicken wings.
    D) Vinny's marginal rate of substitution must be constant along his indifference curves for tacos and chicken wings

Answer: A

Diff: 3   Type: MC   Page Ref: 318/318
Topic: Marginal rate of substitution
Skill: Analytical
Objective: Appendix: Using indifference curves to explain consumer behavior.
AACSB Coding: Reflective Thinking
Special Feature: None

6. Which of the following statements is false?
    A) There is an indifference curve associated with any combination of goods selected by a consumer.
    B) A consumer is indifferent among all consumption bundles along a given budget line.
    C) All consumption bundles along a given indifference curve are equally desirable.
    D) Consumption bundles that lie on higher indifference curves yield higher utility.

Answer: B

Diff: 2   Type: MC   Page Ref: 317-20/317-20
Topic: Indifference curves
Skill: Analytical
Objective: Appendix: Using indifference curves to explain consumer behavior.
AACSB Coding: Reflective Thinking
Special Feature: None

7. Which of the following is *not* a characteristic of indifference curves?
    A) Indifference curves cannot intersect.
    B) Indifference curves are usually bowed in, or convex.
    C) The slope of an indifference curve is negative.
    D) The closer to the origin, the greater the utility level.

Answer: D

Diff: 2   Type: MC   Page Ref: 317-9/317-9
Topic: Indifference curves
Skill: Conceptual
Objective: Appendix: Using indifference curves to explain consumer behavior.
AACSB Coding: Reflective Thinking
Special Feature: None

Figure 9–1

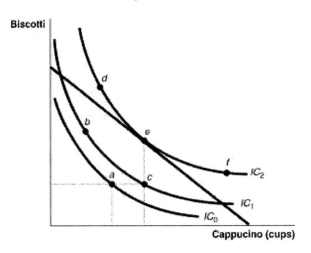

8. *Refer to Figure 9–1.* Given the budget constraint in the diagram, which of the following statements is false?
   A) The consumer receives the same level of utility from consumption bundles d, e and f.
   B) Consumption bundles b and c yield the same level of utility, which is higher than the utility represented by bundle a.
   C) Although the consumer receives the same level of utility from bundles d and e, she cannot afford to purchase bundle d.
   D) The consumer's optimal bundle could be bundle d, e or f.
   Answer: C
   Diff: 2   Type: MC   Page Ref: 320–1/320–1
   Topic: Optimal consumption
   Skill: Analytical
   Objective: Appendix: Using indifference curves to explain consumer behavior.
   AACSB Coding: Analytic Skills
   Special Feature: None

9. *Refer to Figure 9–1.* If the price of biscotti is $1.50 and the price of a cappuccino is $3.00, what is the slope of the budget constraint?
   A) –2
   B) –(3.00 – 1.50)/(3.00 + 1.50) = – 1/3
   C) – 1/2
   D) The slope cannot be determined without the value of income
   Answer: A
   Diff: 2   Type: MC   Page Ref: 319–20/319–20
   Topic: Budget constraint
   Skill: Analytical
   Objective: Appendix: Using indifference curves to explain consumer behavior.
   AACSB Coding: Analytic Skills
   Special Feature: None

10. Assume that Anne has $300 to spend on DVDs and CDs. Her optimal consumption of DVDs and CDs is illustrated by a tangency between a budget line and an indifference curve. Now assume that the price of CDs rises but the price of DVDs falls. How can you show that Anne is made better off by these price changes?

    A) Show that the price changes shift Anne's budget line outward; the budget line is tangent to a higher indifference curve.

    B) Show that the price changes move Anne along her budget line to a higher indifference curve.

    C) Show that Anne can afford to buy the optimal combination of DVDs and CDs at their original prices; then show that Anne can now reach a higher indifference curve.

    D) Show that Anne can now afford to buy more DVDs, which give her greater utility than CDs.

Answer: C

Diff: 2   Type: MC   Page Ref: 322-4/322-4
Topic: Solved Problem
Skill: Analytical
Objective: Appendix: Using indifference curves to explain consumer behavior.
AACSB Coding: Analytic Skills
Special Feature: Solved Problem: When Does a Price Change Make a Consumer Better Off?

11. Total utility is constant along a given indifference curve.

Answer: ○ True   False

Diff: 1   Type: TF   Page Ref: 317-8/317-8
Topic: Indifference curves
Skill: Conceptual
Objective: Appendix: Using indifference curves to explain consumer behavior.
AACSB Coding: Reflective Thinking
Special Feature: None

12. An increase in income results in an outward shift of an indifference curve.

Answer: True   ○ False

Diff: 1   Type: TF   Page Ref: 326-8/326-8
Topic: Indifference curves
Skill: Conceptual
Objective: Appendix: Using indifference curves to explain consumer behavior.
AACSB Coding: Reflective Thinking
Special Feature: None

Chapter 10   Technology, Production, and Costs

10.1   Technology: An Economic Definition

1. In 1955 the chairman of the Sony corporation offered to sell transistor radios through department stores in the U.S. If a store bought 5,000 radios Sony would sell them at $29.95 each. If the store ordered more than 5,000 radios Sony offered a different price. Which of the following describes Sony's offer?
   - A) For an order of over 5,000 Sony would charge a higher price because of diminishing returns in the production of radios.
   - B) Any order over 5,000 would qualify for a lower price; each additional 5,000 radios ordered qualified for additional discounts.
   - C) Sony offered a discounted price on orders for more than 10,000 radios and a higher price for orders greater than 30,000 radios.
   - D) The price of the radios was negotiated between Sony and individual stores for orders greater than 5,000 radios.

   Answer: C
   Diff: 1   Type: MC   Page Ref: 352–3/352–3
   Topic: Average total cost
   Skill: Fact
   Objective: LO 1: Define technology and give examples of technological change.
   AACSB Coding: Reflective Thinking
   Special Feature: Chapter Opener: Sony Uses a Cost Curve to Determine the Price of Radios

2. The basic activity of a firm is
   - A) to set the prices of its products as high as possible.
   - B) to compete with other firms that produce similar products.
   - C) to provide jobs for its employees.
   - D) to use inputs to produce outputs of goods and services.

   Answer: D
   Diff: 1   Type: MC   Page Ref: 334/334
   Topic: Technology
   Skill: Conceptual
   Objective: LO 1: Define technology and give examples of technological change.
   AACSB Coding: Reflective Thinking
   Special Feature: None

3. The processes a firm uses to turn inputs into outputs of goods and services is called
    A) technology.
    B) technological change.
    C) marginal analysis.
    D) positive economic analysis.
Answer: A
Diff: 1   Type: MC   Page Ref: 334/334
Topic: Technology
Skill: Definition
Objective: LO 1: Define technology and give examples of technological change.
AACSB Coding: Reflective Thinking
Special Feature: None

4. When a firm produces more output using the same inputs or the same output using fewer inputs we say that the firm
    A) experiences an increase in demand.
    B) experiences positive technological change.
    C) will hire more workers in order to produce more output.
    D) is operating in the short run.
Answer: B
Diff: 1   Type: MC   Page Ref: 334/334
Topic: Technology and technological change
Skill: Definition
Objective: LO 1: Define technology and give examples of technological change.
AACSB Coding: Reflective Thinking
Special Feature: None

5. A firm increased its production and sales because the firm's manager rearranged the layout of his factory floor. This is an example of
    A) investment in human capital.
    B) economies of scale.
    C) positive technological change.
    D) inspired management.
Answer: C
Diff: 1   Type: MC   Page Ref: 334/334
Topic: Technology and technological change
Skill: Conceptual
Objective: LO 1: Define technology and give examples of technological change.
AACSB Coding: Reflective Thinking
Special Feature: None

6. When a firm experiences a positive technological change
    A) the price of a share of the firm's stock rises.
    B) the firm is able to produce more output using the same inputs, or the same output using fewer inputs.
    C) the value of the firm's assets rises.
    D) the firm will hire additional workers in order to increase production.
    Answer: B
    Diff: 2   Type: MC   Page Ref: 334/334
    Topic: Technology and technological change
    Skill: Definition
    Objective: LO 1: Define technology and give examples of technological change.
    AACSB Coding: Reflective Thinking
    Special Feature: None

7. A "stockout" occurs when
    A) brokers run out of shares of stock to sell of a particular company.
    B) a disruption due to a power outage, etc., causes a temporary production shutdown.
    C) a company holds too many goods in inventories.
    D) a firm loses sales because goods consumers want are not available.
    Answer: D
    Diff: 1   Type: MC   Page Ref: 334–5/334–5
    Topic: Technology and technological change
    Skill: Fact
    Objective: LO 1: Define technology and give examples of technological change.
    AACSB Coding: Reflective Thinking
    Special Feature: Making the Connection: Improving Inventory Control at Wal-Mart

8. Technological change is a key reason why Wal-Mart has become one of the largest firms in the world. Which of the following is a change in technology implemented by Wal-Mart?
    A) Wal-Mart developed a supply chain that allows it to manage inventories efficiently.
    B) Instead of buying goods it sells from other companies Wal-Mart makes many of these goods in its own factories.
    C) Wal-Mart employs hundreds of scientists and engineers who develop new cost-saving techniques.
    D) Wal-Mart hires managers from many of the top business schools in the United States.
    Answer: A
    Diff: 1   Type: MC   Page Ref: 334–5/334–5
    Topic: Technology and technological change
    Skill: Fact
    Objective: LO 1: Define technology and give examples of technological change.
    AACSB Coding: Reflective Thinking
    Special Feature: Making the Connection: Improving Inventory Control at Wal-Mart

9. Which of the following statements correctly describes the distinction between technology and technological change?
   A) Technology refers to the processes used by a firm to transform inputs into output of goods and services while technological change is a change in a firm's ability to produce a given level of output with a given quantity of inputs.
   B) Technology refers to the ability of a firm to increase its maximum output from a given quantity of inputs and technological change is the process by which the firm achieves this productivity gain.
   C) Technology is product–centered; its refers to developing new products with limited resources while technological change is process–centered in that it focuses on developing new production techniques.
   D) Technology involves research and development while technological change involves the use of more efficient machinery.

Answer: A
Diff: 2   Type: MC   Page Ref: 334/334
Topic: Technology
Skill: Definition
Objective: LO 1: Define technology and give examples of technological change.
AACSB Coding: Reflective Thinking
Special Feature: None

10. Which of the following is an example of positive technological change?
    A) A firm offers workers a higher wage to work on weekends and at night. As a result, the firm is able to increase its weekly production of surf boards.
    B) A firm buys an additional machine that it uses to make surf boards. As a result, the firm is able to increase its weekly production of surf boards.
    C) A firm conducts a new advertising campaign. As a result, the demand for the firm's surf boards increases.
    D) A firm's workers participate in a training program designed to increase the number of surf boards they can produce per day.

Answer: D
Diff: 2   Type: MC   Page Ref: 334/334
Topic: Technology and technological change
Skill: Conceptual
Objective: LO 1: Define technology and give examples of technological change.
AACSB Coding: Reflective Thinking
Special Feature: None

11. When a firm experiences negative technological change it can produce the same output with fewer inputs.
    Answer: True   ⊘ False
    Diff: 1   Type: TF   Page Ref: 334-5/334-5
    Topic: Technology and technological change
    Skill: Definition
    Objective: LO 1: Define technology and give examples of technological change.
    AACSB Coding: Reflective Thinking
    Special Feature: None

12. Describe the difference between technology and positive technological change.

Answer: A firm's technology refers to the processes it uses to turn its land, labor, capital and entrepreneurial inputs into outputs of goods and services. When a firm experiences positive technological change it is able to produce more output using the same inputs or the same output using fewer inputs. Technological change can result from rearranging the layout of a store or manufacturing plant, the installation of faster or more durable equipment or other factors.

Diff: 2   Type: SA   Page Ref: 334-5/334-5
Topic: Technology and technological change
Skill: Definition
Objective: LO 1: Define technology and give examples of technological change.
AACSB Coding: Reflective Thinking
Special Feature: None

10.2   The Short Run and the Long Run in Economics

1. Which of the following statements best describes the economic short run?
    A) It is a period of one year or less.
    B) It is a period during which firms are free to vary all of their inputs.
    C) It is a period during which at least one of the firm's inputs is fixed.
    D) It is a period during which fixed inputs become variable inputs because of depreciation.

Answer: C

Diff: 1   Type: MC   Page Ref: 335/335
Topic: The short run
Skill: Definition
Objective: LO 2: Distinguish between the economic short run and the economic long run.
AACSB Coding: Reflective Thinking
Special Feature: None

2. When firms analyze the relationship between their level of production and their costs they separate the time period involved into
    A) morning and evening.
    B) 6 months or less; 6 months to 1 year; more than 1 year.
    C) a fixed period and a variable period.
    D) the short run and the long run.

Answer: D

Diff: 1   Type: MC   Page Ref: 335/335
Topic: The short run and the long run
Skill: Conceptual
Objective: LO 2: Distinguish between the economic short run and the economic long run.
AACSB Coding: Reflective Thinking
Special Feature: None

3. The long run refers to a time period
    A) during which a firm is able to purchase all of its inputs, including its plant and equipment.
    B) long enough for a firm to vary all of its inputs, to adopt new technology and change the size of its physical plant.
    C) long enough for a firm to pay all of its creditors in full.
    D) long enough for a firm to change the use of its variable inputs.
    Answer: B
    Diff: 1   Type: MC   Page Ref: 335/335
    Topic: The long run
    Skill: Definition
    Objective: LO 2: Distinguish between the economic short run and the economic long run.
    AACSB Coding: Reflective Thinking
    Special Feature: None

4. Which of the following can a firm do in the long run but not in the short run?
    A) Decrease the size of its physical plant.
    B) Reduce its rate of output by laying off workers.
    C) Increase its variable costs.
    D) Increase its use of raw materials.
    Answer: A
    Diff: 1   Type: MC   Page Ref: 335/335
    Topic: The short run and the long run
    Skill: Conceptual
    Objective: LO 2: Distinguish between the economic short run and the economic long run.
    AACSB Coding: Reflective Thinking
    Special Feature: None

5. Which of the following statements is *false*?
    A) An explicit cost is a nonmonetary opportunity cost.
    B) In the short run: Total Cost = Fixed Cost + Variable Cost
    C) Variable costs are costs that change as output changes.
    D) In the long run there are no fixed costs.
    Answer: A
    Diff: 2   Type: MC   Page Ref: 335-7/335-7
    Topic: Explicit and implicit costs
    Skill: Definition
    Objective: LO 2: Distinguish between the economic short run and the economic long run.
    AACSB Coding: Reflective Thinking
    Special Feature: None

6. In the long run which of the following is true?
    A) Total Cost = Fixed Cost + Variable Cost
    B) The size of a firm's physical plant can be changed but the firm cannot adopt new technology.
    C) There are no fixed costs.
    D) The firm can vary its explicit costs but not its implicit costs.
    Answer: C
    Diff: 2   Type: MC   Page Ref: 335-7/335-7
    Topic: The long run
    Skill: Conceptual
    Objective: LO 2: Distinguish between the economic short run and the economic long run.
    AACSB Coding: Reflective Thinking
    Special Feature: None

7. Which of the following are implicit costs for a typical firm?
    A) The cost of labor.
    B) The opportunity cost of capital owned and used by the firm.
    C) The cost of energy used in production.
    D) A business licensing fee.
    Answer: B
    Diff: 1   Type: MC   Page Ref: 336-7/336-7
    Topic: Implicit cost
    Skill: Conceptual
    Objective: LO 2: Distinguish between the economic short run and the economic long run.
    AACSB Coding: Reflective Thinking
    Special Feature: None

8. Which of the following is typically considered a fixed cost by academic book publishers but a variable cost by companies that print books?
    A) Postage and supplies
    B) Travel
    C) Rent
    D) Wages and salaries
    Answer: D
    Diff: 1   Type: MC   Page Ref: 336/336
    Topic: Fixed costs
    Skill: Fact
    Objective: LO 2: Distinguish between the economic short run and the economic long run.
    AACSB Coding: Reflective Thinking
    Special Feature: Making the Connection: Fixed Costs in the Publishing Industry

9. Which of the following statements is false?
    A) An implicit cost is a nonmonetary opportunity cost.
    B) Economic costs include both accounting costs and implicit costs.
    C) An explicit cost is a cost that involves spending money.
    D) Economists consider all costs to be implicit costs.
    Answer: D
    Diff: 2   Type: MC   Page Ref: 336–7/336–7
    Topic: Implicit costs and explicit costs
    Skill: Conceptual
    Objective: LO 2: Distinguish between the economic short run and the economic long run.
    AACSB Coding: Reflective Thinking
    Special Feature: None

10. An explicit cost is defined as
    A) a cost that does not change as output changes.
    B) a nonmonetary opportunity cost.
    C) a cost that involves spending money.
    D) a nonmonetary accounting cost.
    Answer: C
    Diff: 1   Type: MC   Page Ref: 336/336
    Topic: Explicit cost
    Skill: Definition
    Objective: LO 2: Distinguish between the economic short run and the economic long run.
    AACSB Coding: Reflective Thinking
    Special Feature: None

11. Which of the following statements is true?
    A) An explicit cost is an actual cost; an implicit cost is a theoretical cost.
    B) Opportunity costs may be explicit costs or implicit costs.
    C) An explicit cost is more important, dollar for dollar, than an implicit cost.
    D) Explicit costs are accounting costs, not economic costs; implicit costs are economic costs, not accounting costs.
    Answer: B
    Diff: 2   Type: MC   Page Ref: 336–7/336–7
    Topic: Explicit and implicit costs
    Skill: Conceptual
    Objective: LO 2: Distinguish between the economic short run and the economic long run.
    AACSB Coding: Reflective Thinking
    Special Feature: None

12. Jennifer Borts moves her office from the premises she rents at a local mall to her home. As a result of this move
    A) Jennifer's explicit costs fall and her implicit costs rise.
    B) Jennifer's total costs fall.
    C) Jennifer's implicit costs fall.
    D) Jennifer's opportunity costs fall.
    Answer: A
    Diff: 2   Type: MC   Page Ref: 336-7/336-7
    Topic: Implicit costs and explicit costs
    Skill: Conceptual
    Objective: LO 2: Distinguish between the economic short run and the economic long run.
    AACSB Coding: Reflective Thinking
    Special Feature: None

13. Manny Franks owns a small firm that makes plastic molds. At the beginning of 2002 Manny bought capital equipment to make molds for $500,000. At the end of 2002 the value of Manny's capital equipment was $450,000. The difference between these two capital values is
    A) considered a capital loss.
    B) a variable cost.
    C) an explicit cost of production.
    D) economic depreciation.
    Answer: D
    Diff: 1   Type: MC   Page Ref: 336-7/336-7
    Topic: Economic depreciation
    Skill: Definition
    Objective: LO 2: Distinguish between the economic short run and the economic long run.
    AACSB Coding: Reflective Thinking
    Special Feature: None

14. The relationship between the inputs employed by a firm and the maximum output that it can produce with those inputs is the firm's _____.
    A) production function.
    B) supply curve, or supply schedule.
    C) marginal product of labor.
    D) average product of labor.
    Answer: A
    Diff: 1   Type: MC   Page Ref: 337-8/337-8
    Topic: The production function
    Skill: Definition
    Objective: LO 2: Distinguish between the economic short run and the economic long run.
    AACSB Coding: Reflective Thinking
    Special Feature: None

15. The Santa Fe Spark Plug Company supplies spark plugs to automotive parts dealers. An increase in the demand for its product led Santa Fe to hire 150 new workers. Santa Fe also plans to expand the capacity of its plant but this project will take 2 years to complete. Which of the following statements is true?
    A) The wages and benefits paid to the new workers are implicit costs.
    B) The long run for Santa Fe is longer than 1 year.
    C) The short run for Santa Fe is 1 year.
    D) In the short run Santa Fe's variable costs increase but its fixed costs decrease.
    Answer: B
    Diff: 1   Type: MC   Page Ref: 335/335
    Topic: Short run and long run costs
    Skill: Conceptual
    Objective: LO 2: Distinguish between the economic short run and the economic long run.
    AACSB Coding: Reflective Thinking
    Special Feature: None

16. Which of the following statements is true?
    A) Opportunity cost = explicit cost – implicit cost
    B) Total cost = fixed cost + implicit cost
    C) Total cost = fixed cost + variable cost
    D) Variable cost = wages + salaries + benefits
    Answer: C
    Diff: 1   Type: MC   Page Ref: 335/335
    Topic: Implicit costs and explicit costs
    Skill: Conceptual
    Objective: LO 2: Distinguish between the economic short run and the economic long run.
    AACSB Coding: Reflective Thinking
    Special Feature: None

17. The rules of accounting generally require that _____ costs be used for purposes of keeping a company's financial records and for paying taxes. These costs are sometimes called _____ costs.
    A) economic; legal
    B) real; explicit
    C) total; economic
    D) explicit; accounting
    Answer: D
    Diff: 1   Type: MC   Page Ref: 337/337
    Topic: Explicit and implicit costs
    Skill: Fact
    Objective: LO 2: Distinguish between the economic short run and the economic long run.
    AACSB Coding: Reflective Thinking
    Special Feature: None

18. Stan owns a software design business. He does not have time to expand his office space or redesign the layout of his office. He can increase the amount of work he does by working more hours, asking his current employees to work more hours, or hiring more employees. The relationship between Stan's inputs and the maximum output his firm can produce is called his

    A) long-run production function.
    B) production possibilities frontier.
    C) short-run production function.
    D) cost function.

    Answer: C
    Diff: 1   Type: MC   Page Ref: 337-8/337-8
    Topic: Production function
    Skill: Conceptual
    Objective: LO 2: Distinguish between the economic short run and the economic long run.
    AACSB Coding: Reflective Thinking
    Special Feature: None

19. Stan owns a software design business. He obtained a bank loan to buy computer equipment for his business. He pays $1,000 per month for interest on the loan. He has 10 employees, each of whom is paid $4,000 per month. Because his business has been successful, next month he will increase employee wages to $5,000. If the revenue from his business remains at its current level, Stan is considering an addition to his office. Which of the following statements regarding Stan's business is false?

    A) The payments Stan makes to his employees are variable costs and explicit costs.
    B) The monthly payment Stan makes for his bank loan is an implicit cost.
    C) The monthly payment Stan makes for his bank loan is a fixed cost.
    D) The time and effort Stan spends on his software design business is an implicit cost.

    Answer: B
    Diff: 2   Type: MC   Page Ref: 336-7/336-7
    Topic: Short run and long run costs
    Skill: Analytical
    Objective: LO 2: Distinguish between the economic short run and the economic long run.
    AACSB Coding: Analytic Skills
    Special Feature: None

20. Average total cost is

    A) total cost divided by the quantity of output produced.
    B) total explicit costs divided by the quantity of output produced.
    C) variable cost divided by the quantity of output produced.
    D) the change in fixed plus variable cost divided by the quantity of output produced.

    Answer: A
    Diff: 1   Type: MC   Page Ref: 338/338
    Topic: Average total cost
    Skill: Definition
    Objective: LO 2: Distinguish between the economic short run and the economic long run.
    AACSB Coding: Reflective Thinking
    Special Feature: None

21. Bill owns "Bill's Home of Blues" a store that specializes in selling CDs and DVDs of blues musicians of the 1960s and 1970s. Bill took out a loan from his bank to pay for his store and its initial inventory. Bill pays the bank $900 per week for his loan. The $900 bank payment
    A) is a long-run implicit cost.
    B) is a fixed cost.
    C) is a short-run implicit cost.
    D) is a variable cost.
    Answer: B
    Diff: 1   Type: MC   Page Ref: 336-7/336-7
    Topic: Fixed costs
    Skill: Conceptual
    Objective: LO 2: Distinguish between the economic short run and the economic long run.
    AACSB Coding: Reflective Thinking
    Special Feature: None

22. In the short-run, changes in output can only be brought about by a change in the quantity of variable inputs.
    Answer: ⊚ True   False
    Diff: 1   Type: TF   Page Ref: 335/335
    Topic: Short run production and short run cost
    Skill: Conceptual
    Objective: LO 2: Distinguish between the economic short run and the economic long run.
    AACSB Coding: Reflective Thinking
    Special Feature: None

23. In the short run changes in marginal cost are independent of fixed cost.
    Answer: ⊚ True   False
    Diff: 1   Type: TF   Page Ref: 335/335
    Topic: Marginal cost
    Skill: Conceptual
    Objective: LO 2: Distinguish between the economic short run and the economic long run.
    AACSB Coding: Reflective Thinking
    Special Feature: None

24. Sally quit her job as an auto mechanic earning $50,000 per year to start her own business. To save money she operates her business out of a small building she owns which, until she started her own business, she had rented out for $10,000 per year. She also invested her $20,000 savings (which earned a market interest rate of 5% per year) in her business. You are given the following information about the first year of her operations.

Total Revenue	$120,000
Cost of labor	40,000
Cost of materials	15,000
Equipment rental	5,000

a. Calculate her economic costs.
b. Calculate her accounting costs.
c. Calculate her implicit costs.
d. Sally tells you that she would really like to move to a location closer to town but she decided against it because "right now I don't pay any rent and it will cost me $10,000 a year to rent near town." Do you agree with her reasoning?

Answer: a. $121,000 = 40,000 (labor) + 15,000 (materials) + 5,000 (equipment) + 10,000 (opportunity cost of building) + 1,000 (5% of 20,000, the opportunity cost of her savings) + 50,000 (opportunity cost of Sally's labor)

b. $60,000 = 40,000 (labor) + 15,000 (materials) + 5,000 (equipment)

c. $61,000 = 10,000 (opportunity cost of building) + 1,000 (5% of 20,000, the opportunity cost of her savings) + 50,000 (opportunity cost of Sally's labor)

d. No. Although she does not incur a monetary cost for her garage space now, it is an opportunity cost. and part of the economic cost of doing business. Sally could just as well rent her space out now, collect the rent and move closer to town.

Diff: 2   Type: ES   Page Ref: 335–7/335–7
Topic: Explicit and implicit costs
Skill: Analytical
Objective: LO 2: Distinguish between the economic short run and the economic long run.
AACSB Coding: Analytic Skills
Special Feature: None

10.3   The Marginal Product of Labor and the Average Product of Labor

1.   The marginal product of labor is defined as
    A) the change in total revenue that results when an additional unit of a labor is hired.
    B) the additional labor required to produce one more unit of output.
    C) the additional labor cost of producing one more unit of output.
    D) the change in output that a firm produces as a result of hiring one more worker.
    Answer: D
Diff: 1   Type: MC   Page Ref: 339/339
Topic: Marginal product of labor
Skill: Definition
Objective: LO 3: Understand the relationship between the marginal product of labor and the average product of labor.
AACSB Coding: Reflective Thinking
Special Feature: None

2. Diminishing marginal product of labor occurs when adding another unit of labor
    A) decreases output.
    B) changes output by an amount smaller than the output added by the previous unit of labor.
    C) increases output by an amount larger than the output added by the previous unit of labor.
    D) decreases output by an amount smaller than the output added by the previous unit of labor.
Answer: B
Diff: 2   Type: MC   Page Ref: 339–40/339–40
Topic: Marginal product of labor
Skill: Conceptual
Objective: LO 3: Understand the relationship between the marginal product of labor and the average product of labor.
AACSB Coding: Reflective Thinking
Special Feature: None

3. Increases in the marginal product of labor result from
    A) the use of new technology.
    B) hiring more efficient workers.
    C) the division of labor and specialization.
    D) increasing the usage of all inputs.
Answer: C
Diff: 1   Type: MC   Page Ref: 339–40/339–40
Topic: Marginal product of labor
Skill: Conceptual
Objective: LO 3: Understand the relationship between the marginal product of labor and the average product of labor.
AACSB Coding: Reflective Thinking
Special Feature: None

4. Gertrude Stork's Chocolate Shoppe normally employs 4 workers. When the Chocolate Shoppe hired a 5th worker the Shoppe's total output decreased. Therefore,
    A) The marginal product of the 5th worker is negative.
    B) the total output of Gertrude Stork's Chocolate Shoppe is negative.
    C) The average product of the 5th worker is negative.
    D) The 5th worker should be hired only if he is willing to accept a wage lower than the wage paid to the other 4 workers.
Answer: A
Diff: 2   Type: MC   Page Ref: 340/340
Topic: Marginal product of labor
Skill: Conceptual
Objective: LO 3: Understand the relationship between the marginal product of labor and the average product of labor.
AACSB Coding: Reflective Thinking
Special Feature: None

5. An avocado orchard employs five full-time workers. Currently, the average product of labor is 120 pounds of avocados per day. The orchard hires a 6th full-time worker and his marginal product is 150 pounds of avocados. The average product of the six workers will now be
    A) more than 120 pounds.
    B) less than 120 pounds.
    C) equal to 120 pounds.
    D) less than the marginal product of labor.
Answer: A
Diff: 2   Type: MC   Page Ref: 341-2/341-2
Topic: Average product of labor
Skill: Conceptual
Objective: LO 3: Understand the relationship between the marginal product of labor and the average product of labor.
AACSB Coding: Reflective Thinking
Special Feature: None

Figure 10-1

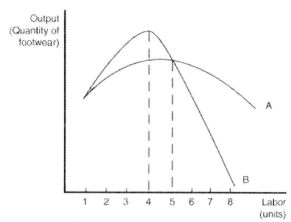

Fancy Footwear manufactures shoes. Figure 10-1 shows Fancy Footwear's marginal product of labor and average product of labor curves in the short run.

6. *Refer to Figure 10-1.* Which of the following statements correctly describes the curves in the figure?
    A) The marginal product of labor curve is represented by curve A and the average product of labor curve is represented by curve B.
    B) The marginal product of labor curve is represented by curve B and the average product of labor curve is represented by curve A.
    C) Curve A could represent either the average product curve or the marginal product and curve. Curve B represents the total product curve.
    D) Curve B could represent either the average product curve or the marginal product curve. Curve A represents the total product curve.
Answer: B

Diff: 1   Type: MC   Page Ref: 341–2/341–2
Topic: Marginal and average product of labor
Skill: Conceptual
Objective: LO 3: Understand the relationship between the marginal product of labor and the average product of labor.
AACSB Coding: Reflective Thinking
Special Feature: None

7. *Refer to Figure 10–1.* For what quantity of labor does production display diminishing returns?
   A) For more than 5 units of labor.
   B) For more than 1 unit of labor.
   C) For more than 8 units of labor.
   D) For more than 4 units of labor.
   Answer: D

Diff: 1   Type: MC   Page Ref: 339–42/339–42
Topic: Diminishing returns
Skill: Conceptual
Objective: LO 3: Understand the relationship between the marginal product of labor and the average product of labor.
AACSB Coding: Analytic Skills
Special Feature: None

8. In the short run, why does a production function eventually display diminishing returns to labor?
   A) As the number of workers increases it becomes difficult to monitor them.
   B) As a firm hires more workers the skills and the work ethic of the additional workers will eventually decline.
   C) As the number of workers increases eventually the gains from the division of labor and specialization are used up.
   D) The opportunity cost of hiring additional workers must eventually rise.
   Answer: C

Diff: 2   Type: MC   Page Ref: 339–40/339–40
Topic: Law of diminishing returns
Skill: Conceptual
Objective: LO 3: Understand the relationship between the marginal product of labor and the average product of labor.
AACSB Coding: Reflective Thinking
Special Feature: None

Table 10–1

Number of workers	Apples per day (bushels)
1	50
2	120
3	180
4	230
5	270
6	300

Table 10–1 summarizes production at the Crunchy Apple Orchard for the month of April 2005.

9. ***Refer to Table 10–1.*** What is the marginal product of the 4th worker?
   A) 230 bushels
   B) 50 bushels
   C) 57.4 bushels
   D) 12.4 bushels
   Answer: B
   Diff: 1   Type: MC   Page Ref: 339–40/339–40
   Topic: Marginal product of labor
   Skill: Conceptual
   Objective: LO 3: Understand the relationship between the marginal product of labor and the average product of labor.
   AACSB Coding: Analytic Skills
   Special Feature: None

10. ***Refer to Table 10–1.*** What is the average product of labor when the orchard employs 5 workers?
    A) 270 bushels
    B) 40 bushels
    C) 8 bushels
    D) 54 bushels
    Answer: D
    Diff: 1   Type: MC   Page Ref: 339–42/339–42
    Topic: Average product of labor
    Skill: Conceptual
    Objective: LO 3: Understand the relationship between the marginal product of labor and the average product of labor.
    AACSB Coding: Analytic Skills
    Special Feature: None

11. The division of labor and specialization explain
    A) why, when the marginal product of labor increases, so does the average product of labor.
    B) why the average product of labor falls when firms use more capital or change the layout of their business.
    C) why the marginal product of labor rises as a firm hires its first units of labor.
    D) why firms may find it profitable to use more workers when the marginal product of labor is negative.

Answer: C
Diff: 2   Type: MC   Page Ref: 339/339
Topic: Marginal product of labor
Skill: Conceptual
Objective: LO 3: Understand the relationship between the marginal product of labor and the average product of labor.
AACSB Coding: Reflective Thinking
Special Feature: None

12. Sam Lewis owns a firm in New York City's garment district. If Sam keeps adding workers to use the same number of sewing machines, eventually the workplace will become so crowded that workers will get in each other's way. At this point
    A) the marginal product of labor in Sam's business would be negative and his total output would decrease.
    B) Sam should encourage his workers to share their sewing machines.
    C) Sam's business will be in violation of safety rules that have been established by the New York City government.
    D) Sam should begin using a division of labor in his business.

Answer: A
Diff: 1   Type: MC   Page Ref: 339-40/339-40
Topic: Negative marginal product of labor
Skill: Conceptual
Objective: LO 3: Understand the relationship between the marginal product of labor and the average product of labor.
AACSB Coding: Reflective Thinking
Special Feature: None

13. In his book *The Wealth of Nations* Adam Smith employed the example of a pin factory in order to explain what economic concept?
    A) The relationship between the marginal and average product of labor.
    B) The law of diminishing returns.
    C) Why no firm would want to hire so many workers as to experience a negative marginal product of labor.
    D) The division of labor.
    Answer: D
    Diff: 1   Type: MC   Page Ref: 340/340
    Topic: Division of labor
    Skill: Fact
    Objective: LO 3: Understand the relationship between the marginal product of labor and the average product of labor.
    AACSB Coding: Reflective Thinking
    Special Feature: Making the Connection: Adam Smith's Famous Account of the Division of Labor in a Pin Factory

14. The total output produced by a firm divided by the quantity of workers employed by the firm is the definition of
    A) the marginal product of labor.
    B) the division of labor.
    C) the average product of labor.
    D) the average cost of production.
    Answer: C
    Diff: 1   Type: MC   Page Ref: 341/341
    Topic: Average product of labor
    Skill: Definition
    Objective: LO 3: Understand the relationship between the marginal product of labor and the average product of labor.
    AACSB Coding: Reflective Thinking
    Special Feature: None

15. After Suzie, owner of Suzie's Sweet Shop hires her 8th worker the average product of labor declines. Which of the following statements must be true?
    A) The marginal product of the 8th worker is negative.
    B) The marginal product of the 8th worker is less than the average product of labor before the 8th worker was hired.
    C) Suzie's profits would be greater if she did not hire the 8th worker.
    D) The average product of labor is negative.
    Answer: B
    Diff: 2   Type: MC   Page Ref: 341–42/341–42
    Topic: Marginal and average product of labor
    Skill: Conceptual
    Objective: LO 3: Understand the relationship between the marginal product of labor and the average product of labor.
    AACSB Coding: Reflective Thinking
    Special Feature: None

16. Which of the following statements is true?
    A) The average product of labor is at its maximum when the average product of labor equals the marginal product of labor.
    B) The average product of labor is at its minimum when the average product of labor equals the marginal product of labor.
    C) The average product of labor tells us how much output changes as the quantity of workers hired changes.
    D) Whenever the marginal product of labor is greater than the average product of labor the average product of labor must be decreasing.
    Answer: A
    Diff: 2   Type: MC   Page Ref: 341–42/341–42
    Topic: Average product of labor
    Skill: Conceptual
    Objective: LO 3: Understand the relationship between the marginal product of labor and the average product of labor.
    AACSB Coding: Reflective Thinking
    Special Feature: None

17. Which of the following describes how output changes in the short run? Because of specialization and the division of labor, as more workers are hired
    A) output will first increase at an increasing rate, then output will increase at a decreasing rate.
    B) output will first decrease at an increasing rate, then increase at a decreasing rate.
    C) the marginal product of labor will first decrease, then increase at a decreasing rate.
    D) the marginal product of labor will first be negative and then will be positive.
    Answer: A
    Diff: 2   Type: MC   Page Ref: 339–42/339–42
    Topic: Marginal product of labor
    Skill: Conceptual
    Objective: LO 3: Understand the relationship between the marginal product of labor and the average product of labor.
    AACSB Coding: Reflective Thinking
    Special Feature: None

18.

Table 10-2

Quantity of Workers	Quantity of Boxes	Marginal Product of Labor	Average Product of Labor
0	0	-----	-----
1	50		
2	200		
3	240		
4	264		
5	300		

Refer to Table 10-2. The table above refers to the relationship between the number of cardboard boxes produced per day by Manny's House of Boxes. The capital used to produce the boxes is fixed. Diminishing returns to labor are first observed in this example after Manny hires the _____ worker.

A) second
B) third
C) fourth
D) fifth

Answer: B

Diff: 1   Type: MC   Page Ref: 339–42/339–42
Topic: Marginal and average product of labor
Skill: Analytical
Objective: LO 3: Understand the relationship between the marginal product of labor and the average product of labor.
AACSB Coding: Analytic Skills
Special Feature: None

19. *Refer to Table 10-2.* The table above refers to the relationship between the number of cardboard boxes produced per day by Manny's House of Boxes. The capital used to produce the boxes is fixed. The highest value of the average product is labor is _____ when Manny hires _____ workers.

A) 80; 3
B) 100; 3
C) 100; 2
D) 80; 4

Answer: C

Diff: 2   Type: MC   Page Ref: 341–2/341–2
Topic: Marginal and average product of labor
Skill: Analytical
Objective: LO 3: Understand the relationship between the marginal product of labor and the average product of labor.
AACSB Coding: Analytic Skills
Special Feature: None

20. *Refer to Table 10–2.* The table above refers to the relationship between the number of cardboard boxes produced per day by Manny's House of Boxes. The capital used to produce the boxes is fixed. The average product of labor will equal 60 boxes when Manny hires
    A) the second worker.
    B) the third worker.
    C) the fourth worker.
    D) the fifth worker.
Answer: D
Diff: 1   Type: MC   Page Ref: 339–42/339–42
Topic: Average product of labor
Skill: Analytical
Objective: LO 3: Understand the relationship between the marginal product of labor and the average product of labor.
AACSB Coding: Analytic Skills
Special Feature: None

21. If a firm experiences diminishing returns its marginal product must be negative.
Answer: True   ◌ False
Diff: 1   Type: TF   Page Ref: 339–40/339–40
Topic: Diminishing returns
Skill: Conceptual
Objective: LO 3: Understand the relationship between the marginal product of labor and the average product of labor.
AACSB Coding: Reflective Thinking
Special Feature: None

22. The additional output a firm produces by hiring one more worker is called the marginal product of labor.
Answer: ◌ True   False
Diff: 1   Type: TF   Page Ref: 339/339
Topic: Marginal product of labor
Skill: Definition
Objective: LO 3: Understand the relationship between the marginal product of labor and the average product of labor.
AACSB Coding: Reflective Thinking
Special Feature: None

23.

Table 10-3

Labor (hours)	Quantity of fish (pounds)	Marginal Product (pounds)
1	10	
2	18	
3	24	
4	28	
5	30	
6	32	

Refer to Table 10–3. The table above shows the following relationship between hours spent fishing and the quantity of fish caught for Juan, a commercial fisherman.

a. Complete the Marginal Product column in Table 10-3.
b. Characterize the production function i.e. does the production function display increasing marginal returns, diminishing marginal returns, etc.
c. Using the data above, graph Juan's marginal product curve. Be sure to label the horizontal and vertical axes. Is your graph consistent with your answer to part (b)? Explain.
d. Juan uses the following inputs for fishing — a small wooden boat (B), a fishing pole (P) and of course, his labor (L). Treating the boat and the fishing pole as fixed inputs and using the data above, graph Juan's Total Product of Labor curve. Be sure to label the horizontal and vertical axes.
e. (Extra Credit) The opportunity cost of Juan's time is $8 per hour. Suppose Juan receives $2 per pound for his fish, what is the optimal number of hours he should spend fishing? Explain how you arrived at your answer. Hint: Recall marginal benefit and marginal cost analysis.

Answer: a.

Labor (hours)	Quantity of fish (pounds)	Marginal Product (pounds)
1	10	10
2	18	8
3	24	6
4	28	4
5	30	2
6	32	2

b. The production displays diminishing marginal returns and then constant marginal returns with the 5th labor hour.
c. See graph of "Marginal Product" below. Yes, the marginal curve slopes downwards and is horizontal for the 5th and 6th units of labor.

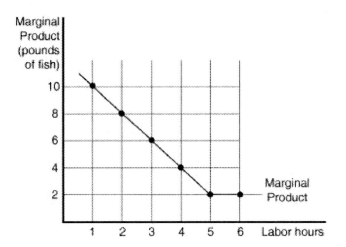

d.

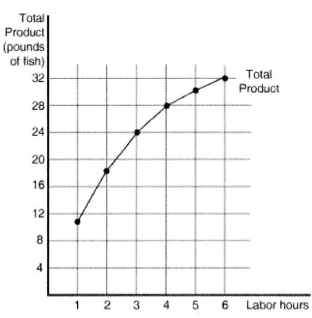

e. If Juan can sell his fish for $2 per pound, he should work for a total of 4 hours, up to the point where the marginal benefit from an additional unit of labor (i.e. marginal product x price per pound) equals the marginal cost of his time.

Diff: 2   Type: ES   Page Ref: 339–42/339–42
Topic: Production function
Skill: Analytical
Objective: LO 3: Understand the relationship between the marginal product of labor and the average product of labor.
AACSB Coding: Analytic Skills
Special Feature: None

10.4   The Relationship Between Short-Run Production and Short-Run Costs

1. The change in a firm's total cost from producing one more unit of a good or service is the firm's
    A) explicit cost of production.
    B) marginal cost of production.
    C) average cost of production.
    D) implicit cost of production.
Answer: B
Diff: 1   Type: MC   Page Ref: 343/343
Topic: Marginal cost
Skill: Definition
Objective: LO 4: Explain and illustrate the relationship between marginal cost and average total cost.
AACSB Coding: Reflective Thinking
Special Feature: None

2. Which of the following explains why the marginal cost curve has a U shape?
    A) Initially, the marginal product of labor falls, then rises.
    B) Initially, the average product of labor rises, then falls.
    C) Initially, the marginal product of labor rises, then falls.
    D) Initially, the average cost of production rises, then falls.
Answer: C
Diff: 2   Type: MC   Page Ref: 344-5/344-5
Topic: Short run production and short run cost
Skill: Conceptual
Objective: LO 4: Explain and illustrate the relationship between marginal cost and average total cost.
AACSB Coding: Reflective Thinking
Special Feature: None

3. The shape of the average total cost curve is determined by the shape of
    A) the marginal cost curve.
    B) the average fixed cost curve.
    C) the average product curve.
    D) the firm's production function.
Answer: A
Diff: 1   Type: MC   Page Ref: 344-5/344-5
Topic: Average total cost
Skill: Conceptual
Objective: LO 4: Explain and illustrate the relationship between marginal cost and average total cost.
AACSB Coding: Reflective Thinking
Special Feature: None

4. Jill Johnson owns a pizzeria. She currently produces 10,000 pizzas per month at a total cost of $500. If she produced one more pizza her total cost rises to $500.11. What does this tell us about Jill's marginal cost of producing pizzas?
    A) The marginal cost of producing pizzas is constant.
    B) The marginal cost of producing pizzas is falling.
    C) The marginal cost of producing pizzas cannot be determined without more information.
    D) The marginal cost of producing pizzas is rising.
Answer: D
Diff: 1   Type: MC   Page Ref: 345/345
Topic: Marginal cost and average total cost
Skill: Analytical
Objective: LO 4: Explain and illustrate the relationship between marginal cost and average total cost.
AACSB Coding: Analytic Skills
Special Feature: Solved Problem: The Relationship between Marginal Cost and Average Cost

5. Marginal cost is calculated for a particular increase in output by
    A) multiplying the total cost by the change in output.
    B) multiplying the change in total cost by the change in output.
    C) dividing the total cost by the change in output.
    D) dividing the change in total cost by the change in output.
Answer: D
Diff: 1   Type: MC   Page Ref: 343–4/343–4
Topic: Marginal cost
Skill: Definition
Objective: LO 4: Explain and illustrate the relationship between marginal cost and average total cost.
AACSB Coding: Reflective Thinking
Special Feature: None

6. When the marginal product of labor rises
    A) the marginal cost of production will exceed the average total cost.
    B) the marginal cost of production also rises.
    C) the marginal cost of production falls.
    D) the average total cost of production also rises.
Answer: C
Diff: 2   Type: MC   Page Ref: 342–4/342–4
Topic: Short run production and short run cost
Skill: Analytical
Objective: LO 4: Explain and illustrate the relationship between marginal cost and average total cost.
AACSB Coding: Reflective Thinking
Special Feature: None

7. Akio Morita, chairman of Sony, used a curve to determine the price of radios his company sold. This curve was
    A) a demand curve.
    B) an average total cost curve.
    C) a marginal cost curve.
    D) a production function.
Answer: B
Diff: 1   Type: MC   Page Ref: 343/343
Topic: Average total cost
Skill: Fact
Objective: LO 4: Explain and illustrate the relationship between marginal cost and average total cost.
AACSB Coding: Reflective Thinking
Special Feature: None

8. Which of the following statements is *false*?
    A) Marginal cost will equal average total cost when marginal cost is at its lowest point.
    B) When marginal cost is less than average total cost, average total cost will fall.
    C) When marginal cost is greater than average total cost, average total cost will rise.
    D) Marginal cost will equal average total cost when average total cost is at its lowest point.
Answer: A
Diff: 2   Type: MC   Page Ref: 344–5/344–5
Topic: Marginal cost and average total cost
Skill: Analytical
Objective: LO 4: Explain and illustrate the relationship between marginal cost and average total cost.
AACSB Coding: Reflective Thinking
Special Feature: None

9. The change in a firm's total cost from producing one more unit of a good or service is
    A) the result of economies of scale.
    B) the definition of marginal product
    C) the definition of marginal cost.
    D) impossible to observe in large firms with many manufacturing plants.
Answer: C
Diff: 1   Type: MC   Page Ref: 343/343
Topic: Marginal cost
Skill: Definition
Objective: LO 4: Explain and illustrate the relationship between marginal cost and average total cost.
AACSB Coding: Reflective Thinking
Special Feature: None

10. If average total cost is falling marginal cost must also be falling.
Answer: True   False
Diff: 2   Type: TF   Page Ref: 342–5/342–5
Topic: Marginal–average relationship
Skill: Analytical
Objective: LO 4: Explain and illustrate the relationship between marginal cost and average total cost.
AACSB Coding: Reflective Thinking
Special Feature: None

11.

Table 10-4

Number of workers	Output (boxes)	Marginal Product of Labor	Office Rent	Labor Cost	Total Cost
0	0	--			
1	220		$400	$200	
2		250			$800
3	680				
4		160			$1,200
5	940			$1,000	
6	980				$1,600

Refer to Table 10-4. Suzette's Fancy Packaging subcontracts with Sunshineland Pecans to box dried fruit and nuts for Suzette's mail order business. Suzette rents space for her factory for $400 a week in a nearby strip mall. She can hire temporary workers for $200 a week. Table 10-4 above shows her output and cost data. Use the table to answer questions a-e.

a. Complete the table.
b. In the last week of summer Suzette closes her business to go on a family vacation. What are her costs during that week?
c. In one week Suzette exactly breaks even. If her revenue for the week is $1,200 how many boxes of fruit and nut did she produce?
d. Judging from the marginal product of labor data, would you say that Suzette had to settle
   for increasingly unproductive workers? Explain your answer.
e. Suzette has received an order for 1,500 boxes of nuts per week for the next 3 months. If she expects the trend in the marginal product of labor will continue in the same direction, what do you think she should do? Should she not commit until she can move to a larger space or should she just hire more workers? Explain your answer.

Answer: a.

Number of workers	Output (boxes)	Marginal Product of Labor	Office Rent	Labor Cost	Total Cost
0	0	--	$400	0	$400
1	220	220	$400	$200	$600
2	470	250	$400	$400	$800
3	680	210	$400	$600	$1,000
4	840	160	$400	$800	$1,200
5	940	100	$400	$1,000	$1,400
6	980	40	$400	$1,200	$1,600

b. $400
c. 840 boxes
d. Diminishing marginal product of labor does not imply that the workers are unproductive. Rather, the marginal product declines because of the presence of a fixed factor, in this case the mall space. After hiring the 6th workers the other

begun to get in each other's way.

    e.   She should not commit to meeting the order until she can move to a larger space
workers have   and hire more workers.

Diff: 3   Type: ES   Page Ref: 342–5/342–5
Topic: Short run production and short run cost
Skill: Analytical
Objective: LO 4: Explain and illustrate the relationship between marginal cost and average total cost.
AACSB Coding: Analytic Skills
Special Feature: None

2. Explain why the marginal cost of production must increase if the marginal product of a
   variable resource is decreasing.

     Answer: Consider a variable input such as labor. If the marginal product of labor is decreasing
          it means that the output produced by each additional unit of labor hired is smaller
          than previous units of labor. If all workers are paid the same wage the marginal cost
          of additional output each worker produces depends on the worker's marginal
          product. If the marginal product falls then the marginal cost of that additional output
          must rise.

Diff: 2   Type: ES   Page Ref: 342–5/342–5
Topic: Short run production and short run cost
Skill: Conceptual
Objective: LO 4: Explain and illustrate the relationship between marginal cost and average total cost.
AACSB Coding: Reflective Thinking
Special Feature: None

10.5   Graphing Cost Curves

1. Which of the following equations is incorrect?
    A) ATC – AFC = AVC
    B) AVC + AFC = ATC
    C) AFC = ATC – AVC
    D) ATC = AVC – AFC

Answer: D

Diff: 1   Type: MC   Page Ref: 346/346
Topic: Cost curves
Skill: Conceptual
Objective: LO 5: Graph average total cost, average variable cost, average fixed cost, and marginal cost.
AACSB Coding: Reflective Thinking
Special Feature: None

2. Which of the following equations is correct?

    A) AVC – ATC = AFC

    B) AVC + ATC = AFC

    C) AFC + AVC = ATC

    D) ATC + AVC = AFC

Answer: C

Diff: 1   Type: MC   Page Ref: 346/346

Topic: Cost curves

Skill: Conceptual

Objective: LO 5: Graph average total cost, average variable cost, average fixed cost, and marginal cost.

AACSB Coding: Reflective Thinking

Special Feature: None

3. Average fixed cost is equal to

    A) the amount of total cost that does not change as output changes in the short run.

    B) fixed cost divided by the quantity of output produced.

    C) fixed cost multiplied by the quantity of output produced.

    D) average total cost plus average variable cost.

Answer: B

Diff: 1   Type: MC   Page Ref: 346/346

Topic: Average fixed cost

Skill: Definition

Objective: LO 5: Graph average total cost, average variable cost, average fixed cost, and marginal cost.

AACSB Coding: Reflective Thinking

Special Feature: None

4. Which of the following statements is true?

    A) As output increases average fixed cost becomes smaller and smaller.

    B) Average fixed cost does not change as output increases.

    C) The marginal cost curve intersects the average fixed cost curve from below at its minimum point.

    D) When marginal cost is greater than average fixed cost average fixed cost increases.

Answer: A

Diff: 1   Type: MC   Page Ref: 346/346

Topic: Average fixed cost

Skill: Conceptual

Objective: LO 5: Graph average total cost, average variable cost, average fixed cost, and marginal cost.

AACSB Coding: Reflective Thinking

Special Feature: None

5. As output increases
    A) average variable cost becomes smaller and smaller.
    B) the difference between average total cost and average variable cost decreases.
    C) marginal cost increases continuously.
    D) the difference between average total cost and average variable cost becomes greater and greater.
Answer: B
Diff: 2   Type: MC   Page Ref: 346/346
Topic: Cost curves
Skill: Conceptual
Objective: LO 5: Graph average total cost, average variable cost, average fixed cost, and marginal cost.
AACSB Coding: Reflective Thinking
Special Feature: None

6. Which of the following statements is false?
    A) When marginal cost equals average total cost, average total cost is at its highest value.
    B) The marginal cost curve intersects the average variable cost curve and the average total cost curves at their minimum points.
    C) The difference between average total cost and average fixed cost is average variable cost.
    D) Firms often refer to the process of lowering average fixed cost as "spreading the overhead."
Answer: A
Diff: 2   Type: MC   Page Ref: 346/346
Topic: Cost curves
Skill: Conceptual
Objective: LO 5: Graph average total cost, average variable cost, average fixed cost, and marginal cost.
AACSB Coding: Reflective Thinking
Special Feature: None

Figure 10–2

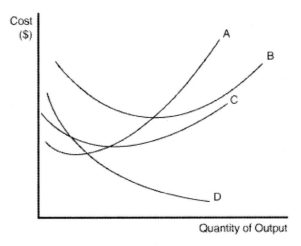

Figure 10–2 contains information about the short run cost structure of a firm.

7. *Refer to Figure 10–2.* In the figure above which letter represents the average variable cost curve?
   A) A
   B) B
   C) C
   D) D
   Answer: C
   Diff: 2   Type: MC   Page Ref: 346–7/346–7
   Topic: Cost curves
   Skill: Analytical
   Objective: LO 5: Graph average total cost, average variable cost, average fixed cost, and marginal cost.
   AACSB Coding: Analytic Skills
   Special Feature: None

8. *Refer to Figure 10–2.* In the figure above which letter represents the average fixed cost curve?
   A) A
   B) B
   C) C
   D) D
   Answer: D
   Diff: 2   Type: MC   Page Ref: 346–7/346–7
   Topic: Cost curves
   Skill: Analytical
   Objective: LO 5: Graph average total cost, average variable cost, average fixed cost, and marginal cost.
   AACSB Coding: Analytic Skills
   Special Feature: None

9. ***Refer to Figure 10–2.*** In the figure above which letter represents the average total cost curve?
   A) A
   B) B
   C) C
   D) D
   Answer: B
   Diff: 2   Type: MC   Page Ref: 346–7/346–7
   Topic: Cost curves
   Skill: Analytical
   Objective: LO 5: Graph average total cost, average variable cost, average fixed cost, and marginal cost.
   AACSB Coding: Analytic Skills
   Special Feature: None

10. ***Refer to Figure 10–2.*** In the figure above which letter represents the marginal cost curve?
    A) A
    B) B
    C) C
    D) D
    Answer: A
    Diff: 2   Type: MC   Page Ref: 346–7/346–7
    Topic: Cost curves
    Skill: Analytical
    Objective: LO 5: Graph average total cost, average variable cost, average fixed cost, and marginal cost.
    AACSB Coding: Analytic Skills
    Special Feature: None

Figure 10–4

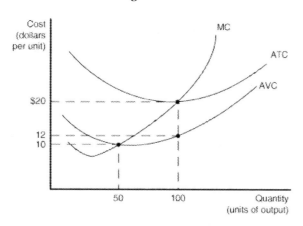

Figure 10–4 shows the cost structure for a firm.

11. ***Refer to Figure 10–3.*** When the output level is 100 units average fixed cost is
    A) $10.
    B) $5.
    C) $8.
    D) This cannot be determined from the diagram.
    Answer: C

Diff: 2 Type: MC Page Ref: 346-7/346-7
Topic: Cost curves
Skill: Conceptual
Objective: LO 5: Graph average total cost, average variable cost, average fixed cost, and marginal cost.
AACSB Coding: Analytic Skills
Special Feature: None

12. *Refer to Figure 10-3.* When output level is 100, what is the total cost of production?
    A) $20
    B) $1,000
    C) $1,200
    D) $2,000
Answer: D
Diff: 2 Type: MC Page Ref: 346-7/346-7
Topic: Cost curves
Skill: Conceptual
Objective: LO 5: Graph average total cost, average variable cost, average fixed cost, and marginal cost.
AACSB Coding: Analytic Skills
Special Feature: None

13. Which of the following is true at the output level where average total cost is at its minimum?
    A) Marginal cost equals average total cost.
    B) Average variable cost equals fixed cost.
    C) Marginal cost equals average variable cost.
    D) Average total cost equals average fixed cost.
Answer: A
Diff: 1 Type: MC Page Ref: 346-7/346-7
Topic: Cost curves
Skill: Conceptual
Objective: LO 5: Graph average total cost, average variable cost, average fixed cost, and marginal cost.
AACSB Coding: Reflective Thinking
Special Feature: None

14. All of the following cost curves are U-shaped except one. Which curve is not U-shaped?
    A) The marginal cost curve.
    B) The average fixed cost curve.
    C) The average total cost curve.
    D) The average variable cost curve.
Answer: B
Diff: 1 Type: MC Page Ref: 346-7/346-7
Topic: Cost curves
Skill: Conceptual
Objective: LO 5: Graph average total cost, average variable cost, average fixed cost, and marginal cost.
AACSB Coding: Reflective Thinking
Special Feature: None

Figure 10-4

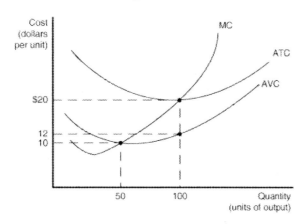

Figure 10-4 shows the cost structure for a firm.

15. Refer to Figure 10-4. If output is 100 units what is the fixed cost of production?
    A) $8
    B) $1,000
    C) $800
    D) This cannot be determined from the diagram.
    Answer: C
    Diff: 1   Type: MC   Page Ref: 346-7/346-7
    Topic: Cost curves
    Skill: Analytical
    Objective: LO 5: Graph average total cost, average variable cost, average fixed cost, and marginal cost.
    AACSB Coding: Analytic Skills
    Special Feature: None

16. A firm's short-run average total cost curve is parallel to its short-run average variable cost curve.
    Answer: True   ⊙ False
    Diff: 2   Type: TF   Page Ref: 346-7/346-7
    Topic: Cost curves
    Skill: Analytical
    Objective: LO 5: Graph average total cost, average variable cost, average fixed cost, and marginal cost.
    AACSB Coding: Reflective Thinking
    Special Feature: None

17.   *Figure 10-5*

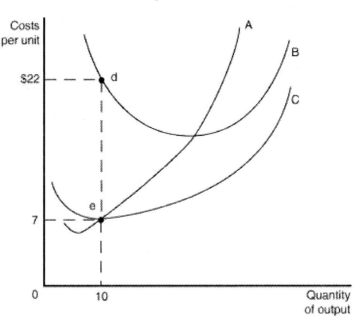

Refer to *Figure 10–5* above to answer the following questions.
a.   Identify the curves in the diagram.
         A _____
         B _____
         C _____
b.   What is the numerical value of fixed cost when the quantity of output=10?
c.   What is the numerical value of variable cost when the quantity of output=10?
d.   What is the numerical value of total cost when the quantity of output =10?
e.   What is the numerical value of average fixed cost when the quantity of output =10?
f.   What is the numerical value of average total cost when the quantity of output =10?
g.   On the graph identify the area that represents the total variable cost of production when the quantity of output =10.
h.   On the graph identify the area that represents the fixed cost of production when the quantity of output =10.
Answer: a.   A=Marginal cost curve; B = Average total cost curve; C = Average variable cost curve.
         b. $150
         c. $70
         d. $220
         e. $15
         f. $22
         g.   the area of the rectangle 0$7e10
         h.   the area of the rectangle $7$22de
Diff: 3   Type: ES   Page Ref: 346–7/346–7
Topic: Cost curves
Skill: Analytical
Objective: LO 5: Graph average total cost, average variable cost, average fixed cost, and marginal cost.
AACSB Coding: Analytic Skills
Special Feature: None

18. Use the general relationship between marginal and average values to explain why a marginal cost curve must intersect an average total cost curve and an average variable cost curve at their minimum points.

Answer: The relationship between marginal and average values can be stated as follows: if the marginal value is below the average value for a variable, it pulls the average value down and if the marginal value is above the he average value, it pulls the average value up. Applying this to cost curves, if average total cost is falling, marginal cost must lie below average total cost. If average total cost is rising, marginal cost must lie above average total cost. Therefore, the marginal cost curve must intersect the average total cost curve at its minimum point. The same principle applies to the average variable cost curve.

Diff: 2   Type: ES   Page Ref: 346–7/346–7
Topic: Marginal–average relationship
Skill: Conceptual
Objective: LO 5: Graph average total cost, average variable cost, average fixed cost, and marginal cost.
AACSB Coding: Reflective Thinking
Special Feature: None

19.   *Figure 10–6*

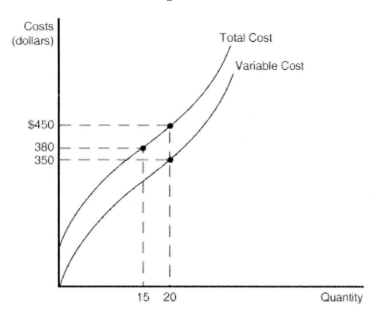

Refer to Figure 10–6 above to solve the following problems.
a. Calculate the fixed cost of production.
b. Calculate the average total cost of production when the firm produces 20 units of output.
c. Calculate the average variable cost of production when the firm produces 20 units of output.
d. Calculate the average fixed cost of production when the firm produces 20 units of output.
e. Calculate the average fixed cost of production when the firm produces 15 units of output.
f. If the firm increases output from 15 to 20 units what is the marginal cost of output?

Answer: a. $100

     b. $22.5

     c. $17.5

     d. $5

     e. $6.67

     f. $14

Diff: 3   Type: ES   Page Ref: 346–7/346–7
Topic: Cost curves
Skill: Analytical
Objective: LO 5: Graph average total cost, average variable cost, average fixed cost, and marginal cost.
AACSB Coding: Analytic Skills
Special Feature: None

10.6   Costs in the Long Run

1. In the long run
    A) the firm's fixed costs are greater than its fixed costs in the short run.
    B) all of the firm's costs are explicit costs; there are no implicit costs of production.
    C) the firm is more profitable than it is in the short run.
    D) all of the firm's costs are variable costs.
    Answer: D
    Diff: 1   Type: MC   Page Ref: 346–7/346–7
    Topic: The long run
    Skill: Conceptual
    Objective: LO 6: Understand how firms use the long-run average cost curve to plan.
    AACSB Coding: Reflective Thinking
    Special Feature: None

2. Which of the following statements regarding a firm's long run average total cost (LRATC) curve and its short–run average total cost (SRATC) curve is true?
    A) The shape of the LRATC is affected by the law of diminishing returns.
    B) The SRATC, but not the LRATC, can be used by a firm's managers for planning.
    C) The LRATC shows the lowest cost at which a firm is able to produce a given level of output when no inputs are fixed.
    D) The contribution of average fixed cost to LRATC is greater than its contribution to SRATC.
    Answer: C
    Diff: 2   Type: MC   Page Ref: 346–7/346–7
    Topic: Short run and long run costs
    Skill: Definition
    Objective: LO 6: Understand how firms use the long-run average cost curve to plan.
    AACSB Coding: Reflective Thinking
    Special Feature: None

3. If a firm's long run average total curve shows that it can produce 5,000 DVDs at an average cost of $2.00 and 15,000 DVDs at an average cost of $1.50 this is evidence of
    A) diminishing returns.
     B) economies of scale.
    C) diseconomies of scale.
    D) the law of supply.
  Answer: B
  Diff: 2   Type: MC   Page Ref: 347–8/347–8
  Topic: Economies of scale
  Skill: Conceptual
  Objective: LO 6: Understand how firms use the long-run average cost curve to plan.
  AACSB Coding: Reflective Thinking
  Special Feature: None

4. Economies of scale occur when
    A) a firm's long-run average total costs fall as it increases the quantity of output it produces.
     B) the marginal product of labor is greater than the average product of labor.
    C) short-run marginal cost falls.
    D) the demand for a firm's output increases.
  Answer: A
  Diff: 1   Type: MC   Page Ref: 347–8/347–8
  Topic: Economies of scale
  Skill: Definition
  Objective: LO 6: Understand how firms use the long-run average cost curve to plan.
  AACSB Coding: Reflective Thinking
  Special Feature: None

5. In 2002 Motorola and Siemens considered the following arrangement: Motorola would give Siemens its wireless infrastructure business in exchange for Siemens giving Motorola its mobile phone headsets business. What was the motive for this arrangement?
    A) Neither firm had enough labor to provide both wireless infrastructure and mobile phone headsets on their own.
     B) The firms wanted to take advantage of lower trade barriers that resulted from the formation of the European Union.
    C) The firms wanted to take advantage of economies of scale.
    D) The firms were preparing to cooperate in advance of their planned merger.
  Answer: C
  Diff: 1   Type: MC   Page Ref: 349–50/349–50
  Topic: Economies of scale
  Skill: Fact
  Objective: LO 6: Understand how firms use the long-run average cost curve to plan.
  AACSB Coding: Reflective Thinking
  Special Feature: Solved Problem: Using Long-Run Average Cost Curves to Understand Business Strategy

6. In 2002 Motorola and Siemens considered the following arrangement: Motorola would give Siemens its wireless infrastructure business in exchange for Siemens giving Motorola its mobile phone headset business. This arrangement would be successful if
    A) Motorola and Siemens produced at less than the minimum efficient scale in the wireless infrastructure and phone handset businesses.
    B) by cooperating, Motorola and Siemens could reduce the total number of workers they employed.
    C) the federal government ruled Motorola and Siemens had not violated antitrust laws.
    D) Motorola had an absolute advantage in the wireless infrastructure business and Siemens had an absolute advantage in the mobile phone headset business.
Answer: A
Diff: 2   Type: MC   Page Ref: 349–50/349–50
Topic: Economies of scale
Skill: Fact
Objective: LO 6: Understand how firms use the long–run average cost curve to plan.
AACSB Coding: Reflective Thinking
Special Feature: Solved Problem: Using Long–Run Average Cost Curves to Understand Business Strategy

7. Which of the following is *not* a reason why firms experience economies of scale?
    A) Technology can make it possible to increase production with a smaller increase in at least one input.
    B) Workers and managers can become more specialized, enabling them to be more productive.
    C) Larger firms may be able to purchase inputs at lower costs than smaller competitors.
    D) As output increases the managers can begin to have difficulty coordinating the operations of their firms.
Answer: D
Diff: 2   Type: MC   Page Ref: 348/348
Topic: Economies of scale
Skill: Conceptual
Objective: LO 6: Understand how firms use the long–run average cost curve to plan.
AACSB Coding: Reflective Thinking
Special Feature: None

8. Over the past twenty years, the number of small family farms has fallen significantly and in its place there are fewer, but larger, farms owned by corporations. Which of the following best explains this trend?
    A) Diseconomies of scale in farming.
    B) Economies of scale in farming.
    C) Diminishing returns to labor in farming.
    D) Declining productivity.
Answer: B
Diff: 1   Type: MC   Page Ref: 347–9/347–9
Topic: Economies of scale
Skill: Conceptual
Objective: LO 6: Understand how firms use the long–run average cost curve to plan.
AACSB Coding: Reflective Thinking
Special Feature: None

9. Diseconomies of scale occur when
   A) long-run average costs rise as a firm increases its output.
   B) long-run average cost fall as a firm expands its plant size.
   C) short-run average costs rise as a firm expands its plant size.
   D) long-run labor costs rise as a firm increases its output.
   Answer: A
   Diff: 1   Type: MC   Page Ref: 349/349
   Topic: Diseconomies of scale
   Skill: Definition
   Objective: LO 6: Understand how firms use the long-run average cost curve to plan.
   AACSB Coding: Reflective Thinking
   Special Feature: None

10. A curve showing the lowest cost at which a firm is able to produce a given level of output in the long run is
    A) a long-run production function.
    B) a long-run marginal cost curve.
    C) a minimum efficient scale curve.
    D) a long-run average total cost curve.
    Answer: D
    Diff: 1   Type: MC   Page Ref: 347-8/347-8
    Topic: Long run average cost
    Skill: Definition
    Objective: LO 6: Understand how firms use the long-run average cost curve to plan.
    AACSB Coding: Reflective Thinking
    Special Feature: None

11. The ABC Company manufactures routers that are used to provide high-speed Internet service. ABC sells an average of 1,000 routers each month. But to exhaust economies of scale in its industry ABC would have to sell 3,000 routers each month. Therefore,
    A) ABC is experiencing diseconomies of scale.
    B) ABC is experiencing diminishing returns.
    C) to reach minimum efficient scale ABC would have to sell at least 3,000 routers each month.
    D) ABC will soon go out of business.
    Answer: C
    Diff: 1   Type: MC   Page Ref: 347-8/347-8
    Topic: Minimum efficient scale
    Skill: Conceptual
    Objective: LO 6: Understand how firms use the long-run average cost curve to plan.
    AACSB Coding: Reflective Thinking
    Special Feature: None

12. The level of output at which all economies of scale have been exhausted is known as
    A) constant returns to scale.
    B) minimum efficient scale.
    C) the economically efficient output level.
    D) optimal economic size.
    Answer: B
    Diff: 1   Type: MC   Page Ref: 348-9/348-9
    Topic: Minimum efficient scale
    Skill: Definition
    Objective: LO 6: Understand how firms use the long-run average cost curve to plan.
    AACSB Coding: Reflective Thinking
    Special Feature: None

13. Minimum efficient scale is defined as the level of output at which
    A) all economies of scale are exhausted.
    B) diminishing returns affect average total cost.
    C) the firm's long-run average total cost starts falling.
    D) the maximum output is produced.
    Answer: A
    Diff: 1   Type: MC   Page Ref: 348-9/348-9
    Topic: Minimum efficient scale
    Skill: Definition
    Objective: LO 6: Understand how firms use the long-run average cost curve to plan.
    AACSB Coding: Reflective Thinking
    Special Feature: None

14. Which of the following is a reason why a firm would experience diseconomies of scale?
    A) To finance an increase in the size of its plant a firm must borrow more money or sell more shares of stock.
    B) As the size of the firm increases, it becomes more difficult to find markets where it doesn't already have operations.
    C) As the size of the firm increases it becomes more difficult to coordinate the operations of its manufacturing plants.
    D) As the size of the firm increases, it must operate in other countries where differences in language, customs and laws increase its average costs.
    Answer: C
    Diff: 1   Type: MC   Page Ref: 349-50/349-50
    Topic: Diseconomies of scale
    Skill: Conceptual
    Objective: LO 6: Understand how firms use the long-run average cost curve to plan.
    AACSB Coding: Reflective Thinking
    Special Feature: None

Figure 10–7

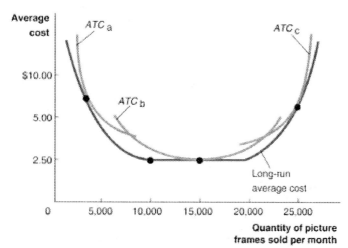

15. **Refer to Figure 10–7.** The figure above illustrates the long–run average cost curve for a firm that produces picture frames. The graph in Figure 10–7 also includes short–run average cost curves for three firm sizes: ATC_a, ATC_b and ATC_c. The minimum efficient scale of output is reached at what rate of output?
    A) 10,000 workers.
    B) 5,000 picture frames.
    C) 20,000 picture frames.
    D) 10,000 picture frames.
Answer: D
Diff: 1   Type: MC   Page Ref: 347–9/347–9
Topic: Minimum efficient scale
Skill: Analytical
Objective: LO 6: Understand how firms use the long–run average cost curve to plan.
AACSB Coding: Analytic Skills
Special Feature: None

16. **Refer to Figure 10–7.** The figure above illustrates the long–run average cost curve for a firm that produces picture frames. The graph in Figure 10–7 also includes short–run average cost curves for three firm sizes: ATC_a, ATC_b and ATC_c. For output rates greater than 20,000 picture frames per month
    A) the firm will not make a profit because the average cost of production will be too high.
    B) the firm will experience diseconomies of scale.
    C) the firm will experience diminishing returns.
    D) the short–run average total cost will equal the long–run average total cost of production.
Answer: B
Diff: 1   Type: MC   Page Ref: 347–9/347–9
Topic: Long run average cost
Skill: Analytical
Objective: LO 6: Understand how firms use the long–run average cost curve to plan.
AACSB Coding: Analytic Skills
Special Feature: None

17. *Refer to Figure 10-7.* The figure above illustrates the long-run average cost curve for a firm that produces picture frames. The graph in Figure 10-7 also includes short-run average cost curves for three firm sizes: ATC_a, ATC_b and ATC_c. Constant returns to scale

    A) occur for output rates greater than 5,000 picture frames.

    B) occur between 5,000 and 20,000 picture frames per month.

    C) occur between 10,000 and 20,000 pictures frames per month.

    D) will shift the long-run average cost curve downward.

Answer: C

Diff: 1   Type: MC   Page Ref: 347-9/347-9

Topic: Long run average cost

Skill: Analytical

Objective: LO 6: Understand how firms use the long-run average cost curve to plan.

AACSB Coding: Analytic Skills

Special Feature: None

18. *Refer to Figure 10-7.* The figure above illustrates the long-run average cost curve for a firm that produces picture frames. The graph in Figure 10-7 also includes short-run average cost curves for three firm sizes: ATC_a, ATC_b and ATC_c. In the short run if the firm sells fewer than 5,000 picture frames per month

    A) it should produce with the scale of operation associated with ATC_a.

    B) it should produce with the scale of operation associated with ATC_b.

    C) it should produce with the scale of operation associated with ATC_c.

    D) it will experience constant returns to scale.

Answer: A

Diff: 1   Type: MC   Page Ref: 347-9/347-9

Topic: Long run average cost

Skill: Analytical

Objective: LO 6: Understand how firms use the long-run average cost curve to plan.

AACSB Coding: Analytic Skills

Special Feature: None

19. *Refer to Figure 10-7.* The figure above illustrates the long-run average cost curve for a firm that produces picture frames. The graph in Figure 10-7 also includes short-run average cost curves for three firm sizes: ATC_a, ATC_b and ATC_c. If the firm chooses to produce and sell 25,000 frames per month by operating in the short run with a scale operation represented by ATC_c

    A) the firm will not be operating efficiently.

    B) the firm will be operating efficiently.

    C) the firm would lower its average costs by reducing its scale of operation.

    D) the firm will not be able to earn a profit.

Answer: B

Diff: 2   Type: MC   Page Ref: 347-9/347-9

Topic: Long run average cost

Skill: Analytical

Objective: LO 6: Understand how firms use the long-run average cost curve to plan.

AACSB Coding: Analytic Skills

Special Feature: None

Table 10–5

Quantity (sets)	Long Run Average Cost
100	$40
200	35
300	30
400	30
500	35

Elegant Settings manufactures stainless steel cutlery. Table 10–5 shows the company's cost data.

20. *Refer to Table 10–5.* Elegant Settings experiences
    A) economies of scale up to an output level of 400.
    B) diminishing returns up to an output level of 400.
    C) increasing returns beyond an output level of 400.
    D) economies of scale at an output of 300 or less and diseconomies of scale at an output level above 400.
    Answer: D
    Diff: 2   Type: MC   Page Ref: 347–50/347–50
    Topic: Long run average cost
    Skill: Analytical
    Objective: LO 6: Understand how firms use the long–run average cost curve to plan.
    AACSB Coding: Analytic Skills
    Special Feature: None

21. *Refer to Table 10–5.* What is the minimum efficient scale of production?
    A) 100 units
    B) 200 units
    C) 300 units
    D) 400 units
    Answer: C
    Diff: 1   Type: MC   Page Ref: 348–9/348–9
    Topic: Minimum efficient scale
    Skill: Conceptual
    Objective: LO 6: Understand how firms use the long–run average cost curve to plan.
    AACSB Coding: Reflective Thinking
    Special Feature: None

22. The River Rouge plant was built by the Ford Motor Company in the 1920s to produce the company's Model A car. Which of the following is evidence that the River Rouge plant suffered from diseconomies of scale?
    A) Despite an expensive advertising campaign the Model A did not earn the company a profit.
    B) Model A cars made at the River Rouge plant failed to earn Ford a profit. Ford eventually constructed smaller plants to make the Model A at a lower average cost.
    C) Model A cars made at the River Rouge plant failed to earn a profit. Ford reduced the average cost of the Model A by cutting its employees' wages.
    D) Model A cars made at the River Rouge plant failed to earn a profit because the price of steel used to manufacture the Model A rose when workers in the steel industry went on strike.
    Answer: B
    Diff: 1   Type: MC   Page Ref: 350–1/350–1
    Topic: Diseconomies of scale
    Skill: Conceptual
    Objective: LO 6: Understand how firms use the long–run average cost curve to plan.
    AACSB Coding: Reflective Thinking
    Special Feature: Making the Connection: The Colossal River Rouge: Diseconomies of Scale at Ford Motor Company

23. Which of the following statements explains the difference between diminishing returns and diseconomies of scale?
    A) Diminishing returns are the result of changes in explicit costs. Diseconomies of scale are the result of changes in explicit costs and implicit costs.
    B) Diminishing returns refer to production while diseconomies of scale refer to costs.
    C) Dimishing returns cause a firm's marginal cost curve to rise; diseconomies of scale cause a firm's marginal cost curve to fall.
    D) Diminishing returns apply only to the short run; diseconomies of scale apply only in the long run.
    Answer: D
    Diff: 1   Type: MC   Page Ref: 351/351
    Topic: Short run and long run costs
    Skill: Conceptual
    Objective: LO 6: Understand how firms use the long–run average cost curve to plan.
    AACSB Coding: Reflective Thinking
    Special Feature: Don't Let This Happen to YOU!: Don't Confuse Diminishing Returns with Diseconomies of Scale

24. Two stores – Lazy Guys and Ralph's Recliners – are located in the same city. Both stores buy recliner chairs from the same manufacturer at the same price and both stores are about the same size, so that the fixed costs of production for both stores are the same. But Ralph's Recliners sells more recliners per month and Ralph's has a lower average total cost of production. Which of the following can explain why the average total cost of production is lower for Ralph's Recliners?
    A) Because Ralph's Recliners sells more output its average fixed costs are lower than Lazy Guy's average fixed cost.
    B) The rent Lazy Guys pays for its building is greater than the rent paid by Ralph's Recliners.
    C) Ralph's explicit costs are less because Ralph owns the land on which his building is located. Lazy Guy must make lease payments for the land on which its store is located.
    D) The price of recliners charged by Ralph's is greater than the price charged by Lazy Guys.

Answer: A

Diff: 2   Type: MC   Page Ref: 352/352
Topic: Average fixed cost
Skill: Conceptual
Objective: LO 6: Understand how firms use the long-run average cost curve to plan.
AACSB Coding: Reflective Thinking
Special Feature: Economics in YOUR Life!: Using Cost Concepts in Your Own Business

25. Assume that you observe the long-run average cost curve of ACME Bookstores, a national chain. Starting from the point on the curve where output is zero and moving to the right which of the following lists the behavior of long-run average costs in the correct sequence (that is, which will be observed first, second, etc.)?
    A) Minimum efficient scale; economies of scale; constant returns to scale; diseconomies of scale.
    B) Economies of scale; constant returns to scale; diseconomies of scale; minimum efficient scale.
    C) Constant returns to scale; economies of scale; minimum efficient scale; diseconomies of scale.
    D) Economies of scale; minimum efficient scale; constant returns to scale; diseconomies of scale.

Answer: D

Diff: 2   Type: MC   Page Ref: 347-9/347-9
Topic: Long run average cost
Skill: Conceptual
Objective: LO 6: Understand how firms use the long-run average cost curve to plan.
AACSB Coding: Reflective Thinking
Special Feature: None

26. Sales of flat-panel televisions have increased rapidly in recent years in the United States, Japan and Europe. A key factor spurring sales of the thin, light-weight televisions has been a dramatic reduction in their prices. Which of the following is one reason for this price reduction?
    A) Tariffs on flat-panel televisions have been removed as the result of an agreement among the leaders of the governments of the United States, Japan and Europe.
    B) Sony, Samsung Electronics and other manufacturers of flat-panel televisions have increased their usage of cheap, unskilled labor by outsourcing production to developing nations.
    C) Increased production of flat-panel televisions has led to a lowering of their marginal and average costs of production.
    D) Governments have subsidized the production of flat-screen televisions in anticipation of a shift of broadcast systems to digital signals that will broaden the availability of HDTV content.
    Answer: C
    Diff: 2   Type: MC   Page Ref: 354-5/354-5
    Topic: Marginal cost and average total cost
    Skill: Conceptual
    Objective: LO 6: Understand how firms use the long-run average cost curve to plan.
    AACSB Coding: Reflective Thinking
    Special Feature: An Inside Look: Lower Manufacturing Costs Push Down the Price of Flat-Panel TVs

27. Minimum efficient scale is defined as the level of output at which the short-run average total cost stops decreasing.
    Answer: True   ⊚ False
    Diff: 1   Type: TF   Page Ref: 349/349
    Topic: Minimum efficient scale
    Skill: Definition
    Objective: LO 6: Understand how firms use the long-run average cost curve to plan.
    AACSB Coding: Reflective Thinking
    Special Feature: None

28. If a firm is experiencing diseconomies of scale, its long-run average cost curve is increasing.
    Answer: ⊚ True   False
    Diff: 1   Type: TF   Page Ref: 348-9/348-9
    Topic: Diseconomies of scale
    Skill: Definition
    Objective: LO 6: Understand how firms use the long-run average cost curve to plan.
    AACSB Coding: Reflective Thinking
    Special Feature: None

29. A U-shaped long run average cost curve implies that a firm experiences economies of scale at low levels of production and diseconomies of scale at high levels of production.
Answer: ◌ True　　　False
Diff: 1　　Type: TF　　Page Ref: 347-8/347-8
Topic: Long run average cost
Skill: Conceptual
Objective: LO 6: Understand how firms use the long-run average cost curve to plan.
AACSB Coding: Reflective Thinking
Special Feature: None

31.　　　　　　　　　　　　　*Table 10-6*

	Fixed Cost	Average Variable Cost
Small Plant	$10,000	$2.00
Medium Plant	15,000	1.30
Large plant	25,00	0.50

Refer to Table 10-6. Clock It To Me manufactures clock radios. The table below shows estimates of fixed cost per period and average variable cost for three possible plant sizes.

a. You are employed as the company's cost accountant and have been asked to prepare cost estimates for various output levels for each of the three possible plant sizes. Record your calculations in the table below.

	Average Cost of Production		
	5,000 clock radios	8,000 clock radios	20,000 clock radios
Small Plant			
Medium Plant			
Large Plant			

b. For each of the three output levels, which plant size will generate the lowest average total cost of production?
c. Suppose the firm currently sells 8,000 clocks per period (using the optimal plant size for this output level). Now, however, it has just secured a long-term contract to supply 20,000 clocks per period. In the short run, what is the average total cost of producing? 20,000 clocks. Provide a numerical value based on your answer in part a.
d. What happens to average total cost of production in the long run? Provide a numerical value based on your answer in part a.

Answer: a.

	Average Cost of Production		
	5,000 clock radios	8,000 clock radios	20,000 clock radios
Small Plant	$4.00	$3.25	$2.50
Medium Plant	4.30	3.18	2.05
Large Plant	5.50	3.63	1.75

b. For an output of 5,000 units, the lowest average cost is achieved with a small plant size. For an output of 8,000 units, the lowest average cost is achieved with a medium plant size and for output 20,000 units the lowest average cost is achieved with a large plant size.

c. The firm currently has a medium–sized plant. In the short run, average total cost of producing 20,000 units is $2.05.

d. In the long run, when it is able to build a larger plant, the average total cost will fall to $1.75.

Diff: 3   *Type: ES*   *Page Ref: 346–51/346–51*
Topic: Short run and long run costs
Skill: Analytical
Objective: LO 6: Understand how firms use the long–run average cost curve to plan.
AACSB Coding: Analytic Skills
Special Feature: None

32. State the law of diminishing returns. How do diminishing returns differ from diseconomies of scale? Be sure to define diseconomies of scale in your answer.

Answer: The law of diminishing returns states that at some point, adding more of a variable input to the same amount of a fixed input will eventually cause the marginal product of the variable input to decline. The law applies in the short run when there is at least one fixed factor of production. Diseconomies of scale applies in the long run when a firm is free to vary all of its inputs. Diseconomies of scale exist when a firm's long run average cost rises as it increases output.

Diff: 2   *Type: ES*   *Page Ref: 348–51/348–51*
Topic: The short run and the long run
Skill: Conceptual
Objective: LO 6: Understand how firms use the long–run average cost curve to plan.
AACSB Coding: Reflective Thinking
Special Feature: None

10.7 Using Isoquants and Isocosts to Understand Production and Cost

1. A curve that shows all the combinations of two inputs, such as labor and capital, that will produce the same level of output is called
    A) an isoquant.
    B) an isocost line
    C) a budget line.
    D) an optimal input combination curve.
Answer: A
Diff: 1   Type: MC   Page Ref: 364/364
Topic: Isoquant
Skill: Definition
Objective: Appendix: Use isoquants and isocosts to understand production and cost.
AACSB Coding: Reflective Thinking
Special Feature: None

2. The rate at which a firm is able to substitute one input for another while keeping the level of output constant is called the
    A) opportunity cost of inputs.
    B) marginal rate of technical substitution.
    C) input trade-off rate.
    D) isoquant substitution rate.
Answer: B
Diff: 1   Type: MC   Page Ref: 365/365
Topic: Isoquant
Skill: Definition
Objective: Appendix: Use isoquants and isocosts to understand production and cost.
AACSB Coding: Reflective Thinking
Special Feature: None

3. The slope of an isocost line _____ and equals the negative of _____.
    A) increases as we move down the line; the ratio of input prices
    B) decreases as we move down the line; the ratio of the marginal products
    C) is constant; the ratio of input prices
    D) is constant; the ratio of the marginal products
Answer: C
Diff: 2   Type: MC   Page Ref: 365-6/365-6
Topic: Isocost
Skill: Conceptual
Objective: Appendix: Use isoquants and isocosts to understand production and cost.
AACSB Coding: Reflective Thinking
Special Feature: None

4. As a firm moves to higher isocost lines,
   A) its profits increase.
   B) its revenue increases.
   C) its input price ratio increases.
   D) its total cost increases.
   Answer: D
   Diff: 1   Type: MC   Page Ref: 365-6/365-6
   Topic: Isocost
   Skill: Conceptual
   Objective: Appendix: Use isoquants and isocosts to understand production and cost.
   AACSB Coding: Reflective Thinking
   Special Feature: None

5. An isocost line shows
   A) combinations of two inputs that result in the same total cost for a firm.
   B) combinations of two inputs that result in the same total output for a firm.
   C) combinations of the two inputs that result in the same profit for a firm.
   D) the different levels of total cost that result from various combinations of two inputs.
   Answer: A
   Diff: 1   Type: MC   Page Ref: 365/365
   Topic: Isocost
   Skill: Conceptual
   Objective: Appendix: Use isoquants and isocosts to understand production and cost.
   AACSB Coding: Reflective Thinking
   Special Feature: None

Figure 10–8

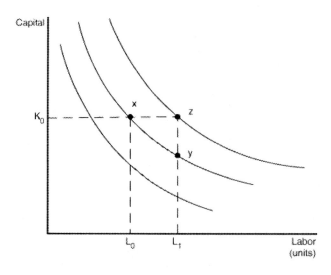

6. *Refer to Figure 10-8.* The figure above illustrates a series of isoquants. Which of the following statements is true?
   - A) Points x, z, and y all represent the same output.
   - B) Points z and y represent the same output; this output is produced with more capital at z than at y.
   - C) Point x and y represent the same output but the cost of production at y is greater than the cost of production at x.
   - D) Point z represents a greater output than point x or point y.

   Answer: D
   Diff: 2   Type: MC   Page Ref: 364–5/364–5
   Topic: Isoquant
   Skill: Conceptual
   Objective: Appendix: Use isoquants and isocosts to understand production and cost.
   AACSB Coding: Reflective Thinking
   Special Feature: None

7. A change in the slope of an isocost line is due to a change in
   - A) the output price.
   - B) the price of one or both inputs.
   - C) total cost.
   - D) quantity of output.

   Answer: B
   Diff: 1   Type: MC   Page Ref: 367–8/367–8
   Topic: Isocost
   Skill: Conceptual
   Objective: Appendix: Use isoquants and isocosts to understand production and cost.
   AACSB Coding: Reflective Thinking
   Special Feature: None

8. Consider a firm that uses two inputs, labor and capital, to produce its output. Assume labor is measured on the horizontal axis and capital on the vertical axis. Which of the following best explains why the marginal rate of technical substitution decreases in absolute value as we move down an isoquant?
   - A) The law of diminishing returns: for a given decline in capital, decreasing amounts of labor are required to produce the same level of output
   - B) The law of increasing marginal opportunity cost: if a firm uses less and less capital it must use more and more labor, which drives up the cost of labor.
   - C) The law of diminishing returns: for a given decline in capital, increasing amounts of labor are required to produce the same level of output
   - D) The law of imperfect substitutability: labor and capital are not perfect substitutes; therefore, a firm must replace decreases in capital with increases in labor.

   Answer: C
   Diff: 3   Type: MC   Page Ref: 364–5/364–5
   Topic: Isoquant
   Skill: Conceptual
   Objective: Appendix: Use isoquants and isocosts to understand production and cost.
   AACSB Coding: Reflective Thinking
   Special Feature: None

Figure 10-9

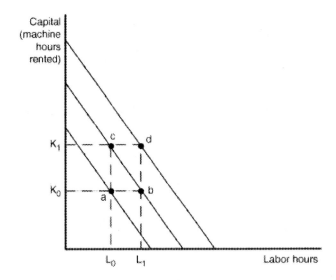

9. *Refer to Figure 10-9.* Assume that production isoquants are convex. Total cost and output produced must increase for each of the following movements except one. Which movement is the exception?

    A) Point a to point b.

    B) Point a to point c.

    C) Point b to point c.

    D) Point b to point d.

Answer: C

Diff: 2   *Type: MC*   *Page Ref: 365-7/365-7*

Topic: Isocost

Skill: Conceptual

Objective: Appendix: Use isoquants and isocosts to understand production and cost.

AACSB Coding: Reflective Thinking

Special Feature: None

10. A firm's expansion path

    A) is the same thing as its long-run average cost curve.

    B) is a curve that shows a firm's cost-minimizing combination of inputs for every level of output, holding input prices constant.

    C) shows the targeted growth rate in sales over the long run.

    D) is a curve that shows expected profits at various price levels.

Answer: B

Diff: 1   *Type: MC*   *Page Ref: 372-3/372-3*

Topic: Expansion path

Skill: Definition

Objective: Appendix: Use isoquants and isocosts to understand production and cost.

AACSB Coding: Reflective Thinking

Special Feature: None

Figure 10–10

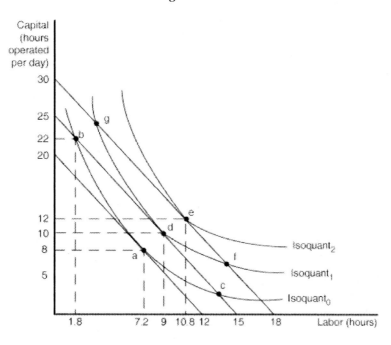

11. *Refer to Figure 10–10.* Starting from point d a movement along isoquant₁ to point f

   A) increases the total cost of production with no change in output.

   B) increases output but not the total cost of production.

   C) increases the total cost of production and decreases output.

   D) increases both the total cost of production and output.

   Answer: A

   Diff: 2   Type: MC   Page Ref: 367–8/367–8
   Topic: Isoquant
   Skill: Conceptual
   Objective: Appendix: Use isoquants and isocosts to understand production and cost.
   AACSB Coding: Reflective Thinking
   Special Feature: None

12. *Refer to Figure 10–10.* Starting from point e, a movement along the isocost to point f

   A) decreases the total cost of production but not output.

   B) increases the total cost of production and decreases output.

   C) decreases both the total cost of production and output.

   D) decreases output but not the total cost of production.

   Answer: D

   Diff: 2   Type: MC   Page Ref: 367–8/367–8
   Topic: Isocost
   Skill: Conceptual
   Objective: Appendix: Use isoquants and isocosts to understand production and cost.
   AACSB Coding: Reflective Thinking
   Special Feature: None

13. *Refer to Figure 10–10.* A curve that connects points a, d and e is called
    A) an input–output curve.
    B) a total cost line.
    C) an expansion path.
    D) an indifference line.
    Answer: C
    Diff: 1   Type: MC   Page Ref: 372–3/372–3
    Topic: Expansion path
    Skill: Definition
    Objective: Appendix: Use isoquants and isocosts to understand production and cost.
    AACSB Coding: Reflective Thinking
    Special Feature: None

14. The financial success of the movies *The Lion King* and *Toy Story* led to
    A) a decrease in the salaries of animators and an increase in the number of animators used to produce films.
    B) an increase in demand for actors to play roles in animated films.
    C) the Disney studio's attempt to buy Pixar Animation Studios.
    D) a reduction in the price of computers and software relative to the price of labor (animators) used to produce animated films.
    Answer: D
    Diff: 2   Type: MC   Page Ref: 368–9/368–9
    Topic: Changes in input prices
    Skill: Fact
    Objective: Appendix: Use isoquants and isocosts to understand production and cost.
    AACSB Coding: Reflective Thinking
    Special Feature: Making the Connection: The Changing Input Mix in Walt Disney Film Animation

15. Joan Jillson owns a coffee shop. Assume that the marginal product of the labor Joan employs (MP_L) equals 500 cups per week and the marginal product of her shop's capital (MP_K) equals 1,000. Assume also that the wage (w) Joan pays her workers equals \$250 per week and the rental price (r) of her capital – her coffee machines – equals \$500 per week. Which of the following correctly analyzes whether Joan is minimizing her costs?
    A) No, Joan is not minimizing her costs because MP_K is greater than MP_L and r is greater than w.
    B) Yes, Joan is minimizing her costs because MP_K/r equals MP_L/w.
    C) No, Joan is not minimizing her costs because MP_L x w is less than MP_K x r.
    D) Yes, Joan is minimizing her costs because the she is a price–taker in the markets for labor and capital.
    Answer: B
    Diff: 2   Type: MC   Page Ref: 371/371
    Topic: Cost minimization
    Skill: Analytical
    Objective: Appendix: Use isoquants and isocosts to understand production and cost.
    AACSB Coding: Analytic Skills
    Special Feature: Solved Problem: Determining the Optimal Combination of Inputs

16. Economists Cade Massey and Richard Thaler analyzed whether teams in the National Football League distributed salaries efficiently. Massey and Thaler found that
    A) the first few players selected in first round of the NFL draft are paid much higher salaries relative to their marginal products than players drafted later in the first round.
    B) rookies are paid salaries greater than their marginal products; veteran players are paid salaries less than their marginal products.
    C) veteran players who sign as free agents are paid more relative to their marginal products than rookie players selected in the first round of the draft.
    D) both rookie players and veteran players are paid less than the value of their marginal products because of the lack of competition among teams.
    Answer: A
    Diff: 2   Type: MC   Page Ref: 372/372
    Topic: Marginal product of labor
    Skill: Fact
    Objective: Appendix: Use isoquants and isocosts to understand production and cost.
    AACSB Coding: Reflective Thinking
    Special Feature: Making the Connection: Do National Football League Teams Behave Efficiently?

17. The slope of an isoquant is equal to the ratio of the price of the input on the horizontal axis divided by the price of the input on the vertical axis, multiplied by –1.
    Answer: True   ⊚ False
    Diff: 2   Type: TF   Page Ref: 364–5/364–5
    Topic: Isoquant
    Skill: Conceptual
    Objective: Appendix: Use isoquants and isocosts to understand production and cost.
    AACSB Coding: Reflective Thinking
    Special Feature: None

18. Firms in different countries that face different input prices may produce the same good using different combinations of inputs, even though they have access to the same technology.
    Answer: ⊚ True   False
    Diff: 2   Type: TF   Page Ref: 367–368/367–368
    Topic: Cost minimization
    Skill: Conceptual
    Objective: Appendix: Use isoquants and isocosts to understand production and cost.
    AACSB Coding: Reflective Thinking
    Special Feature: None

Chapter 11   Firms in Perfectly Competitive Markets

11.1   Perfectly Competitive Markets

1. Consider this quote, "Perfect Competition in the Market for Organic Apples": Between 1997 and 2001, many apple farmers switched from traditional to organic growing methods, increasing production of organically grown apples from 1.2 million boxes per year to more than 3 million boxes. If the market for organic apples is perfectly competitive, which of the following statements is inconsistent with the statement above?
    A) The price of organic apples is likely to rise over time as more and more farmers switch to organic methods of farming.
    B) It is relatively easy to enter the organic apples market.
    C) Organic apple farmers are earning short run economic profits.
    D) The market supply curve for organic apples shifts to the right.
Answer: A
Diff: 2   Type: MC   Page Ref: 376/376
Topic: Perfectly Competitive Markets
Skill: Analytical
Objective: LO 1: Define a perfectly competitive market, and explain why a perfect competitor faces a horizontal demand curve.
AACSB Coding: Reflective Thinking
Special Feature: Chapter Opener: Perfect Competition in the Market for Organic Apples

2. Between 1997 and 2001, the movement from traditional methods to organic growing methods in the apple market was prompted mainly by
    A) the U.S. Department of Agriculture.
    B) the U.S. Organic Producers Association.
    C) environmental groups who aggressively disseminate information on sustainable farming.
    D) the rising number of consumers who demand organic products.
Answer: D
Diff: 1   Type: MC   Page Ref: 376/376
Topic: Perfectly Competitive Markets
Skill: Conceptual
Objective: LO 1: Define a perfectly competitive market, and explain why a perfect competitor faces a horizontal demand curve.
AACSB Coding: Reflective Thinking
Special Feature: Chapter Opener: Perfect Competition in the Market for Organic Apples

3. Which of the following is not a characteristic of a perfectly competitive market structure?
   A) All firms sell identical products.
   B) There are no restrictions to entry by new firms.
   C) There are restrictions on exit of firms.
   D) There are a very large number of firms that are small compared to the market.
   Answer: C
   Diff: 1   Type: MC   Page Ref: 378/378
   Topic: Perfectly Competitive Markets
   Skill: Definition
   Objective: LO 1: Define a perfectly competitive market, and explain why a perfect competitor faces a horizontal demand curve.
   AACSB Coding: Reflective Thinking
   Special Feature: None

4. Which of the following is not a characteristic of a monopolistically competitive market structure?
   A) There are no barriers to entry of new firms.
   B) Each firm must react to actions of other firms.
   C) All sellers sell products that are differentiated.
   D) There is a large number of independently acting small sellers.
   Answer: B
   Diff: 1   Type: MC   Page Ref: 378/378
   Topic: Perfectly Competitive Markets
   Skill: Definition
   Objective: LO 1: Define a perfectly competitive market, and explain why a perfect competitor faces a horizontal demand curve.
   AACSB Coding: Reflective Thinking
   Special Feature: None

5. Which of the following is a characteristic of an oligopolistic market structure?
   A) There are few dominant sellers.
   B) Each firm need not react to the actions of rivals.
   C) Each firm sells a unique product.
   D) It is easy for new firms to enter the industry.
   Answer: A
   Diff: 1   Type: MC   Page Ref: 378/378
   Topic: Perfectly Competitive Markets
   Skill: Definition
   Objective: LO 1: Define a perfectly competitive market, and explain why a perfect competitor faces a horizontal demand curve.
   AACSB Coding: Reflective Thinking
   Special Feature: None

6. Which of the following is not a characteristic of a monopoly?
    A) There is only one seller in the market.
    B) It is easy for new firms to enter the market.
    C) The firm has no control over price.
    D) The product is not unique.
Answer: A
Diff: 1   Type: MC   Page Ref: 378/378
Topic: Perfectly Competitive Markets
Skill: Definition
Objective: LO 1: Define a perfectly competitive market, and explain why a perfect competitor
*   faces a horizontal demand curve.*
AACSB Coding: Reflective Thinking
Special Feature: None

7. Perfect competition is characterized by all of the following except
    A) horizontal demand for individual sellers.
    B) homogeneous products
    C) heavy advertising by individual sellers
    D) sellers are price takers
Answer: C
Diff: 1   Type: MC   Page Ref: 378/378
Topic: Perfectly Competitive Markets
Skill: Conceptual
Objective: LO 1: Define a perfectly competitive market, and explain why a perfect competitor
*   faces a horizontal demand curve.*
AACSB Coding: Reflective Thinking
Special Feature: None

8. A very large number of small sellers who sell identical products imply
    A) the inability of one seller to influence price.
    B) a downward sloping demand for each seller's product.
    C) a multitude of vastly different selling prices.
    D) chaos in the market.
Answer: A
Diff: 2   Type: MC   Page Ref: 378/378
Topic: Perfectly Competitive Markets
Skill: Conceptual
Objective: LO 1: Define a perfectly competitive market, and explain why a perfect competitor
*   faces a horizontal demand curve.*
AACSB Coding: Reflective Thinking
Special Feature: None

9. Which of the following is the best example of a perfectly competitive industry?
    A) steel production.
    B) airplane production.
    C) electricity production.
    D) wheat production.
Answer: D
Diff: 2   Type: MC   Page Ref: 378/378
Topic: Perfectly Competitive Markets
Skill: Conceptual
Objective: LO 1: Define a perfectly competitive market, and explain why a perfect competitor
*   faces a horizontal demand curve.*
AACSB Coding: Reflective Thinking
Special Feature: None

10. The price of a seller's product in perfect competition is determined by
    A) the individual seller.
    B) a few of the sellers.
    C) the individual demander.
    D) market demand and market supply.
Answer: D
Diff: 1   Type: MC   Page Ref: 379/379
Topic: Perfectly Competitive Markets
Skill: Conceptual
Objective: LO 1: Define a perfectly competitive market, and explain why a perfect competitor
*   faces a horizontal demand curve.*
AACSB Coding: Reflective Thinking
Special Feature: None

11. Both individual buyers and sellers in perfect competition
    A) can influence the market price by their own individual actions.
    B) have the market price dictated to them by government.
    C) can influence the market price by joining with a few of their competitors.
    D) have to take the market price as a given.
Answer: D
Diff: 1   Type: MC   Page Ref: 379/379
Topic: Perfectly Competitive Markets
Skill: Conceptual
Objective: LO 1: Define a perfectly competitive market, and explain why a perfect competitor
*   faces a horizontal demand curve.*
AACSB Coding: Reflective Thinking
Special Feature: None

12. Both buyers and sellers are price takers in a perfectly competitive market because
    A) the price is determined by government intervention and dictated to buyers and sellers.
    B) each buyer and seller is too small relative to others to independently affect the market price.
    C) each buyer and seller knows it is illegal to conspire to affect price.
    D) both buyers and sellers in a perfectly competitive market are concerned for the welfare of others.

Answer: B
Diff: 2   Type: MC   Page Ref: 379/379
Topic: Perfectly Competitive Markets
Skill: Conceptual
Objective: LO 1: Define a perfectly competitive market, and explain why a perfect competitor faces a horizontal demand curve.
AACSB Coding: Reflective Thinking
Special Feature: None

13. The demand for each seller's product in perfect competition is horizontal at the market price because
    A) each seller is too small to affect market price.
    B) all the demanders get together and set the price.
    C) all the sellers get together and set the price.
    D) the price is set by the government.

Answer: A
Diff: 1   Type: MC   Page Ref: 380/380
Topic: Perfectly Competitive Markets
Skill: Conceptual
Objective: LO 1: Define a perfectly competitive market, and explain why a perfect competitor faces a horizontal demand curve.
AACSB Coding: Reflective Thinking
Special Feature: None

14. An individual seller in perfect competition will not sell at a price lower than the market price because
    A) the seller can sell any quantity she wants at the prevailing market price.
    B) demand for the product will exceed supply.
    C) the seller would start a price war.
    D) demand is perfectly inelastic.

Answer: A
Diff: 2   Type: MC   Page Ref: 379/379
Topic: Perfectly Competitive Markets
Skill: Conceptual
Objective: LO 1: Define a perfectly competitive market, and explain why a perfect competitor faces a horizontal demand curve.
AACSB Coding: Reflective Thinking
Special Feature: None

15. Jason, a high-school student mows lawns for families in his neighborhood. The going rate is $12 for each lawn-mowing service. Jason would like to charge $20 because he believes he has more experience mowing lawns than the many other teenagers who also offer the same service. If the market for lawn mowing services is perfectly competitive, what would happen if Jason raised his price?
    A) If Jason raises his price he would lose all his customers.
    B) If Jason raises his price, then all others supplying the same service will also raise their prices.
    C) He would lose some but not all his customers.
    D) Initially, his customers might complain but over time they will come to accept the new rate.
Answer: A
Diff: 2   Type: MC   Page Ref: 377/377
Topic: Perfectly Competitive Markets
Skill: Conceptual
Objective: LO 1: Define a perfectly competitive market, and explain why a perfect competitor faces a horizontal demand curve.
AACSB Coding: Reflective Thinking
Special Feature: Economics in YOUR Life!: Are You an Entrepreneur?

16. The demand for an individual seller's product in perfect competition is
    A) downward sloping.
    B) vertical.
    C) the same as market demand.
    D) horizontal.
Answer: D
Diff: 2   Type: MC   Page Ref: 380/380
Topic: Perfectly Competitive Markets
Skill: Conceptual
Objective: LO 1: Define a perfectly competitive market, and explain why a perfect competitor faces a horizontal demand curve.
AACSB Coding: Reflective Thinking
Special Feature: None

17. In perfect competition
     A) the market demand curve is downward sloping while demand for an
        individual seller's product is perfectly elastic.
     B) the market demand curve is perfectly elastic while demand for an individual
        seller's product is perfectly inelastic.
     C) the market demand curve and the individual's demand are identical.
     D) the market demand curve is perfectly inelastic while demand for an individual
        seller's product is perfectly elastic.
    Answer: A
    Diff: 2   Type: MC   Page Ref: 380/380
    Topic: Perfectly Competitive Markets
    Skill: Conceptual
    Objective: LO 1: Define a perfectly competitive market, and explain why a perfect competitor
            faces a horizontal demand curve.
    AACSB Coding: Reflective Thinking
    Special Feature: Don't Let This Happen to YOU!: Don't Confuse the Demand Curve for Farmer
            Parker's Wheat with the Market Demand Curve for Wheat

18. Perfectly competitive industries tend to produce low–priced, low-technology
    products.
    Answer: True   ◉ False
    Diff: 2   Type: TF   Page Ref: 378/378
    Topic: Perfectly Competitive Markets
    Skill: Conceptual
    Objective: LO 1: Define a perfectly competitive market, and explain why a perfect competitor
            faces a horizontal demand curve.
    AACSB Coding: Reflective Thinking
    Special Feature: None

19. A perfectly competitive firm's horizontal demand curve implies that the firm does
    not have to lower its price to sell more output.
    Answer: ◉ True   False
    Diff: 2   Type: TF   Page Ref: 379/379
    Topic: Perfectly Competitive Markets
    Skill: Conceptual
    Objective: LO 1: Define a perfectly competitive market, and explain why a perfect competitor
            faces a horizontal demand curve.
    AACSB Coding: Reflective Thinking
    Special Feature: None

20. The market demand curve for a perfectly competitive industry is the horizontal
    summation of each individual firm's demand curve.
    Answer: True   ◉ False
    Diff: 2   Type: TF   Page Ref: 381/381
    Topic: Perfectly Competitive Markets
    Skill: Conceptual
    Objective: LO 1: Define a perfectly competitive market, and explain why a perfect competitor
            faces a horizontal demand curve.
    AACSB Coding: Reflective Thinking
    Special Feature: None

21. Why are individual buyers and sellers in perfect competition called price takers?
    Answer: They are called price takers because each firm is too small to influence the
    market price and have to take the market price as given.
    Diff: 2   Type: SA   Page Ref: 379/379
    Topic: Perfectly Competitive Markets
    Skill: Conceptual
    *Objective: LO 1: Define a perfectly competitive market, and explain why a perfect competitor
    faces a horizontal demand curve.*
    AACSB Coding: Reflective Thinking
    Special Feature: None

22. Consider the market for wheat which is a perfectly competitive market. Is the
    market demand curve the same as the demand curve facing an individual producer?
    If not, explain how and why they are different? Illustrate your answer graphically.
    Answer: The market demand is downward sloping while the demand for an
    individual firm's output is horizontal at the equilibrium market price. This is
    because an individual producer is too small to influence the market price and
    must take the market price as given. At the market price, the individual seller
    can sell all the output she desires. The figure below shows the market
    demand curve and the demand curve for a single firm.

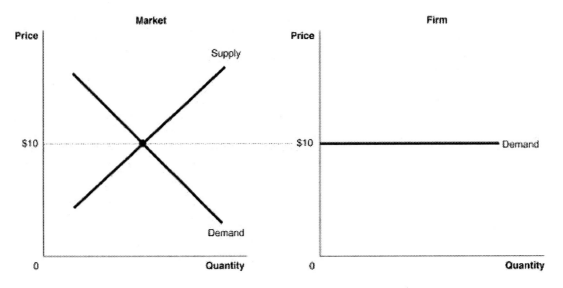

Diff: 2   Type: SA   Page Ref: 380-1/380-1
Topic: Perfectly Competitive Markets
Skill: Conceptual
*Objective: LO 1: Define a perfectly competitive market, and explain why a perfect competitor
faces a horizontal demand curve.*
AACSB Coding: Reflective Thinking
*Special Feature: Don't Let This Happen to YOU!: Don't Confuse the Demand Curve for Farmer
Parker's Wheat with the Market Demand Curve for Wheat*

11.2 How a Firm Maximizes Profit in a Perfectly Competitive Market

1. If the market price is $25, the average revenue of selling five units is
   A) $12.50.
   B) $5.
   C) $125.
   D) $25.
   Answer: D
   Diff: 2   Type: MC   Page Ref: 382/382
   Topic: How a Firm Maximizes Profit in a Perfectly Competitive Market
   Skill: Analytical
   Objective: LO 2: Explain how a firm maximizes profits in a perfectly competitive market.
   AACSB Coding: Reflective Thinking
   Special Feature: None

2. If the market price is $25 in a perfectly competitive market, the marginal revenue from selling the fifth unit is
   A) $25.
   B) $5.
   C) $125.
   D) $12.50.
   Answer: A
   Diff: 2   Type: MC   Page Ref: 382/382
   Topic: How a Firm Maximizes Profit in a Perfectly Competitive Market
   Skill: Analytical
   Objective: LO 2: Explain how a firm maximizes profits in a perfectly competitive market.
   AACSB Coding: Reflective Thinking
   Special Feature: None

3. Which of the following is not true for a firm in perfect competition?
   A) Average revenue is greater than marginal revenue.
   B) Profit equals total revenue minus total cost.
   C) Marginal revenue equals the change in total revenue from selling one more unit.
   D) Price equals average revenue.
   Answer: A
   Diff: 2   Type: MC   Page Ref: 382/382
   Topic: How a Firm Maximizes Profit in a Perfectly Competitive Market
   Skill: Conceptual
   Objective: LO 2: Explain how a firm maximizes profits in a perfectly competitive market.
   AACSB Coding: Reflective Thinking
   Special Feature: None

Table 11–1

Quantity	Total Cost (Dollars)	Variable Cost (Dollars)
0	$1,000	$0
100	1,360	360
200	1,560	560
300	1,960	960
400	2,760	1,760
500	4,000	3,000
600	5,800	4,800

Table 11–1 shows the short–run cost data of a perfectly competitive firm that produces plastic camera cases. Assume that output can only be increased in batches of 100 units.

4. *Refer to Table 11–1.* What is the fixed cost of production?
   A) $500
   B) $1,000
   C) $0
   D) It cannot be determined.
   Answer: B
   Diff: 3   Type: MC   Page Ref: 382–3/382–3
   Topic: How a Firm Maximizes Profit in a Perfectly Competitive Market
   Skill: Analytical
   Objective: LO 2: Explain how a firm maximizes profits in a perfectly competitive market.
   AACSB Coding: Analytic Skills
   Special Feature: None

5. *Refer to Table 11–1.* If the market price of each camera case is $8, what is the profit–maximizing quantity?
   A) 300 units
   B) 400 units
   C) 500 units
   D) 600 units
   Answer: B
   Diff: 2   Type: MC   Page Ref: 382–3/382–3
   Topic: How a Firm Maximizes Profit in a Perfectly Competitive Market
   Skill: Analytical
   Objective: LO 2: Explain how a firm maximizes profits in a perfectly competitive market.
   AACSB Coding: Analytic Skills
   Special Feature: None

6. *Refer to Table 11–1.* If the market price of each camera case is $8, what is the firm's total revenue?

    A) $2,400

    B) $3,200

    C) $4000

    D) $4,800

Answer: B

Diff: 2   Type: MC   Page Ref: 382–3/382–3

Topic: How a Firm Maximizes Profit in a Perfectly Competitive Market

Skill: Analytical

Objective: LO 2: Explain how a firm maximizes profits in a perfectly competitive market.

AACSB Coding: Analytic Skills

Special Feature: None

7. *Refer to Table 11–1.* If the market price of each camera case is $8 and the firm maximizes profit, what is the amount of the firm's profit or loss?

    A) $0 (it breaks even)

    B) loss of $1,000

    C) profit of $440

    D) loss of $440

Answer: C

Diff: 2   Type: MC   Page Ref: 382–3/382–3

Topic: How a Firm Maximizes Profit in a Perfectly Competitive Market

Skill: Analytical

Objective: LO 2: Explain how a firm maximizes profits in a perfectly competitive market.

AACSB Coding: Analytic Skills

Special Feature: None

8. *Refer to Table 11–1.* Suppose the fixed cost of production rises by $500 and if the price per unit is still $8. What happens to the firm's profit maximizing output level?

    A) It will remain the same.

    B) The firm will shut down.

    C) It must rise to offset the increased cost.

    D) It must fall.

Answer: A

Diff: 3   Type: MC   Page Ref: 382–3/382–3

Topic: How a Firm Maximizes Profit in a Perfectly Competitive Market

Skill: Analytical

Objective: LO 2: Explain how a firm maximizes profits in a perfectly competitive market.

AACSB Coding: Analytic Skills

Special Feature: None

9.

Refer to *Table 11–1.* The firm will not produce in the short run if the output price falls below
  A) $8.
  B) $4.
  C) $3.20.
  D) $2.80.
Answer: D
Diff: 2   *Type: MC*   *Page Ref: 382–3/382–3*
Topic: How a Firm Maximizes Profit in a Perfectly Competitive Market
Skill: Analytical
Objective: LO 2: Explain how a firm maximizes profits in a perfectly competitive market.
AACSB Coding: Analytic Skills
Special Feature: None

Figure 11–1

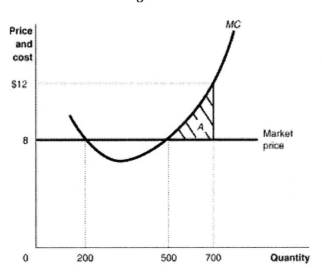

10. *Refer to Figure 11–1.* If the firm is producing 700 units,
      A) it should cut back its output to maximize profit.
      B) it should increase its output to maximize profit.
      C) it is making a profit.
      D) it is making a loss.
   Answer: A
   Diff: 1   *Type: MC*   *Page Ref: 384/384*
   Topic: How a Firm Maximizes Profit in a Perfectly Competitive Market
   Skill: Analytical
   Objective: LO 2: Explain how a firm maximizes profits in a perfectly competitive market.
   AACSB Coding: Analytic Skills
   Special Feature: None

11.

Refer to **11-1.** If the firm is producing 700 units, what is the amount of its profit or loss?
Figure
        A) loss equivalent to the area *A*.

        B) profit equivalent to the area *A*.

        C) loss of $280

        D) There is insufficient information to answer the question.

Answer: D
Diff: 1   Type: MC   Page Ref: 384/384
Topic: How a Firm Maximizes Profit in a Perfectly Competitive Market
Skill: Analytical
Objective: LO 2: Explain how a firm maximizes profits in a perfectly competitive market.
AACSB Coding: Analytic Skills
Special Feature: None

12. *Refer to Figure 11-1.* If the firm is producing 200 units,
        A) it breaks even.

        B) it should increase its output to maximize profit.

        C) it should cut back its output to maximize profit.

        D) it is making a loss.

Answer: B
Diff: 1   Type: MC   Page Ref: 384/384
Topic: How a Firm Maximizes Profit in a Perfectly Competitive Market
Skill: Analytical
Objective: LO 2: Explain how a firm maximizes profits in a perfectly competitive market.
AACSB Coding: Analytic Skills
Special Feature: None

13. A perfectly competitive firm produces 1,000 units of a good at a total cost of $36,000. The price of each good is $50. Calculate the firm's short run profit or loss.
        A) profit of $14,000

        B) profit of $50,000

        C) loss of $14,000

        D) There is insufficient information to answer the question.

Answer: A
Diff: 1   Type: MC   Page Ref: 383/383
Topic: How a Firm Maximizes Profit in a Perfectly Competitive Market
Skill: Analytical
Objective: LO 2: Explain how a firm maximizes profits in a perfectly competitive market.
AACSB Coding: Analytic Skills
Special Feature: None

14. A perfectly competitive firm produces 3,000 units of a good at a total cost of $36,000. The price of each good is $10. Calculate the firm's short run profit or loss.
    A) profit of $30,000
    B) profit of $6,000
    C) loss of $6,000
    D) There is insufficient information to answer the question.
    Answer: C
    Diff: 1   Type: MC   Page Ref: 383/383
    Topic: How a Firm Maximizes Profit in a Perfectly Competitive Market
    Skill: Analytical
    Objective: LO 2: Explain how a firm maximizes profits in a perfectly competitive market.
    AACSB Coding: Reflective Thinking
    Special Feature: None

15. If, for the last unit of a good produced by a perfectly competitive firm, MR > MC, then in producing it, the firm
    A) added more to total revenue than it added to total costs.
    B) is maximizing marginal profit.
    C) has minimized its losses.
    D) added more to total costs than it added to total revenue.
    Answer: A
    Diff: 2   Type: MC   Page Ref: 384/384
    Topic: How a Firm Maximizes Profit in a Perfectly Competitive Market
    Skill: Conceptual
    Objective: LO 2: Explain how a firm maximizes profits in a perfectly competitive market.
    AACSB Coding: Reflective Thinking
    Special Feature: None

16. If, for a perfectly competitive firm, if price exceeds the marginal cost of production, the firm should
    A) increase its output.
    B) lower the price.
    C) keep output constant and enjoy the above normal profit.
    D) reduce its output.
    Answer: A
    Diff: 1   Type: MC   Page Ref: 384/384
    Topic: How a Firm Maximizes Profit in a Perfectly Competitive Market
    Skill: Conceptual
    Objective: LO 2: Explain how a firm maximizes profits in a perfectly competitive market.
    AACSB Coding: Reflective Thinking
    Special Feature: None

Figure 11–2

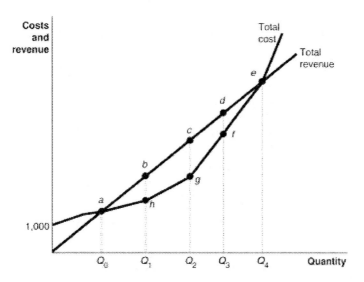

17. *Refer to Figure 11–2.* What is the amount of profit if the firm produces Q_2 units?

    A) It is equal to the vertical distance *c* to *g*.

    B) It is equal to the vertical distance *c* to Q_2.

    C) It is equal to the vertical distance *c* to *g* multiplied by Q_2 units.

    D) It is equal to the vertical distance *g* to Q_2.

    Answer: A

    Diff: 1   Type: MC   Page Ref: 384/384
    Topic: How a Firm Maximizes Profit in a Perfectly Competitive Market
    Skill: Analytical
    Objective: LO 2: Explain how a firm maximizes profits in a perfectly competitive market.
    AACSB Coding: Analytic Skills
    Special Feature: None

18. *Refer to Figure 11–2.* Suppose the firm is currently producing Q_2 units. What happens if it expands output to Q_3 units?

    A) It will be moving toward its profit maximizing output.

    B) It makes less profit.

    C) It incurs a loss.

    D) Its profit increases by the size of the vertical distance *df*.

    Answer: B

    Diff: 1   Type: MC   Page Ref: 384/384
    Topic: How a Firm Maximizes Profit in a Perfectly Competitive Market
    Skill: Analytical
    Objective: LO 2: Explain how a firm maximizes profits in a perfectly competitive market.
    AACSB Coding: Analytic Skills
    Special Feature: None

19. ***Refer to Figure 11–2.*** The firm breaks even at an output level of
    A) Q_3 units.
    B) Q_2 units.
    C) Q_1 units.
    D) Q_4 units.

Answer: D
Diff: 1   Type: MC   Page Ref: 384/384
Topic: How a Firm Maximizes Profit in a Perfectly Competitive Market
Skill: Analytical
Objective: LO 2: Explain how a firm maximizes profits in a perfectly competitive market.
AACSB Coding: Analytic Skills
Special Feature: None

20. ***Refer to Figure 11–2.*** What happens if the firm produces more than Q_4 units?
    A) It could make a profit or a loss depending on what happens to demand.
    B) Its total revenue is increasing faster than its total cost.
    C) Its profit increases.
    D) It makes a loss.

Answer: D
Diff: 1   Type: MC   Page Ref: 384/384
Topic: How a Firm Maximizes Profit in a Perfectly Competitive Market
Skill: Analytical
Objective: LO 2: Explain how a firm maximizes profits in a perfectly competitive market.
AACSB Coding: Analytic Skills
Special Feature: None

21. ***Refer to Figure 11–2.*** Why is the total revenue curve a ray from the origin?
    A) because the firm can sell its product at a constant price
    B) because revenue increases at an increasing rate
    C) because the firm must lower its price to sell more
    D) because revenue increases at an increasing rate

Answer: A
Diff: 2   Type: MC   Page Ref: 384/384
Topic: How a Firm Maximizes Profit in a Perfectly Competitive Market
Skill: Conceptual
Objective: LO 2: Explain how a firm maximizes profits in a perfectly competitive market.
AACSB Coding: Analytic Skills
Special Feature: None

22. In a graph with output on the horizontal axis and total revenue on the vertical axis, what is the shape of the total revenue curve for a perfectly competitive seller?
    A) inverted U-shaped.
    B) a horizontal line.
    C) U-shaped.
    D) a ray from the origin.
    Answer: D
    Diff: 2   Type: MC   Page Ref: 384/384
    Topic: Illustrating Profit or Loss on the Cost Curve Graph
    Skill: Conceptual
    Objective: LO 2: Explain how a firm maximizes profits in a perfectly competitive market.
    AACSB Coding: Reflective Thinking
    Special Feature: None

23. For a perfectly competitive firm, at profit maximization
    A) market price exceeds marginal cost.
    B) production must occur where average cost is minimized.
    C) marginal revenue equals marginal cost.
    D) total revenue is maximized.
    Answer: C
    Diff: 2   Type: MC   Page Ref: 384/384
    Topic: Illustrating Profit or Loss on the Cost Curve Graph
    Skill: Conceptual
    Objective: LO 2: Explain how a firm maximizes profits in a perfectly competitive market.
    AACSB Coding: Reflective Thinking
    Special Feature: None

24. For a perfectly competitive firm, which of the following is not true at profit maximization?
    A) Market price is greater than marginal cost.
    B) Price equals marginal cost.
    C) Total revenue minus total cost is maximized.
    D) Marginal revenue equals marginal cost.
    Answer: A
    Diff: 2   Type: MC   Page Ref: 384/384
    Topic: Illustrating Profit or Loss on the Cost Curve Graph
    Skill: Conceptual
    Objective: LO 2: Explain how a firm maximizes profits in a perfectly competitive market.
    AACSB Coding: Reflective Thinking
    Special Feature: None

25. Assume that price is greater than average variable cost. If a perfectly competitive seller is producing at an output where price is $11 and the marginal cost is $14.54, then to maximize profits the firm should
    A) produce a larger level of output.
    B) not enough information given to answer the question.
    C) continue producing at the current output.
    D) produce a smaller level of output.
    Answer: D
    Diff: 2   Type: MC   Page Ref: 384/384
    Topic: Illustrating Profit or Loss on the Cost Curve Graph
    Skill: Analytical
    Objective: LO 2: Explain how a firm maximizes profits in a perfectly competitive market.
    AACSB Coding: Reflective Thinking
    Special Feature: None

26. An increase in a firm's fixed cost will not change the firm's profit–maximizing output in the short run.
    Answer: ◉ True   False
    Diff: 1   Type: TF   Page Ref: 383/383
    Topic: How a Firm Maximizes Profit in a Perfectly Competitive Market
    Skill: Conceptual
    Objective: LO 2: Explain how a firm maximizes profits in a perfectly competitive market.
    AACSB Coding: Reflective Thinking
    Special Feature: None

27. Being a price–taker, a perfectly competitive firm cannot receive a producer surplus in the short run.
    Answer: True   ◉ False
    Diff: 2   Type: TF   Page Ref: 383/383
    Topic: How a Firm Maximizes Profit in a Perfectly Competitive Market
    Skill: Analytical
    Objective: LO 2: Explain how a firm maximizes profits in a perfectly competitive market.
    AACSB Coding: Analytic Skills
    Special Feature: None

28. For a perfectly competitive firm, at the profit maximizing output average revenue equals marginal cost
    Answer: ◉ True   False
    Diff: 2   Type: TF   Page Ref: 382/382
    Topic: How a Firm Maximizes Profit in a Perfectly Competitive Market
    Skill: Conceptual
    Objective: LO 2: Explain how a firm maximizes profits in a perfectly competitive market.
    AACSB Coding: Reflective Thinking
    Special Feature: None

29. A perfectly competitive firm's marginal revenue curve is downward sloping.
    Answer: True   ⊙ False
    Diff: 2   Type: TF   Page Ref: 383/383
    Topic: How a Firm Maximizes Profit in a Perfectly Competitive Market
    Skill: Conceptual
    Objective: LO 2: Explain how a firm maximizes profits in a perfectly competitive market.
    AACSB Coding: Reflective Thinking
    Special Feature: None

30. Assume that price is greater than average variable cost. If a perfectly competitive
    firm is producing at an output where price is $114 and the marginal cost is $102,
    then the firm is probably producing more than its profit-maximizing quantity.
    Answer: True   ⊙ False
    Diff: 2   Type: TF   Page Ref: 382-3/382-3
    Topic: How a Firm Maximizes Profit in a Perfectly Competitive Market
    Skill: Conceptual
    Objective: LO 2: Explain how a firm maximizes profits in a perfectly competitive market.
    AACSB Coding: Reflective Thinking
    Special Feature: None

31. How are market price, average revenue, and marginal revenue related for a
    perfectly competitive firm and why?
    Answer: They are all equal to each other. The market price for any firm equals average
            revenue. This can be verified by noting that average revenue = total revenue ÷
            quantity = (price x quantity) ÷ quantity. Further, a perfectly competitive firm
            faces a horizontal demand curve at the market price which means that it does
            not need to reduce the price to sell more. Therefore, its marginal revenue
            equals price.
    Diff: 2   Type: SA   Page Ref: 382/382
    Topic: How a Firm Maximizes Profit in a Perfectly Competitive Market
    Skill: Conceptual
    Objective: LO 2: Explain how a firm maximizes profits in a perfectly competitive market.
    AACSB Coding: Reflective Thinking
    Special Feature: None

11.3 Illustrating Profit or Loss on the Cost Curve Graph

1. A firm's total profit can be calculated as all of the following except
    A) (price minus average total cost) times quantity sold.
    B) average profit per unit times quantity sold.
    C) marginal profit times quantity sold.
    D) total revenue minus total cost.
    Answer: C
    Diff: 2   Type: MC   Page Ref: 385/385
    Topic: Illustrating Profit or Loss on the Cost Curve Graph
    Skill: Conceptual
    Objective: LO 3: Use graphs to show a firm's profit or loss.
    AACSB Coding: Reflective Thinking
    Special Feature: None

2. If a perfectly competitive firm's price is above its average total cost, the firm
    A) is incurring a loss.
    B) should shut down.
    C) is earning a profit.
    D) is breaking even.
Answer: C
Diff: 2   Type: MC   Page Ref: 385/385
Topic: Illustrating Profit or Loss on the Cost Curve Graph
Skill: Conceptual
Objective: LO 3: Use graphs to show a firm's profit or loss.
AACSB Coding: Reflective Thinking
Special Feature: None

Figure 11-3

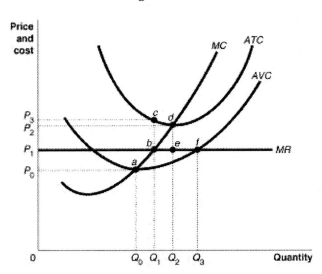

3. *Refer to Figure 11-3.* Suppose the prevailing price is P_1 and the firm is currently
    producing its loss-minimizing quantity. Identify the area that represents the loss.
    A) $0P_1 bQ_1$
    B) $P_2 deP_1$
    C) P_3caP_0
    D) P_3cbP_1
Answer: D
Diff: 2   Type: MC   Page Ref: 385/385
Topic: Illustrating Profit or Loss on the Cost Curve Graph
Skill: Analytical
Objective: LO 3: Use graphs to show a firm's profit or loss.
AACSB Coding: Analytic Skills
Special Feature: None

4. If a perfectly competitive firm's price is less than its average total cost but greater than its average variable cost, the firm
   A) is earning a profit.
   B) should shut down.
   C) is breaking even.
   D) is incurring a loss.
Answer: D
Diff: 2   Type: MC   Page Ref: 385/385
Topic: Illustrating Profit or Loss on the Cost Curve Graph
Skill: Conceptual
Objective: LO 3: Use graphs to show a firm's profit or loss.
AACSB Coding: Reflective Thinking
Special Feature: None

Figure 11–4

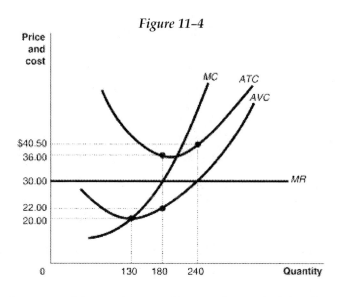

Figure 11–4 shows the cost and demand curves for a profit–maximizing firm in a perfectly competitive market.

5. ***Refer to Figure 11–4.*** If the market price is $30, the firm's profit maximizing output level is
   A) 0.
   B) 130.
   C) 180.
   D) 240.
Answer: C
Diff: 1   Type: MC   Page Ref: 385/385
Topic: Illustrating Profit or Loss on the Cost Curve Graph
Skill: Analytical
Objective: LO 3: Use graphs to show a firm's profit or loss.
AACSB Coding: Analytic Skills
Special Feature: Making the Connection: Losing Money in the Medical Screening Industry

6. ***Refer to Figure 11–4.*** If the market price is $30 and if the firm is producing output, what is the amount of its total variable cost?
    A) $7,200
    B) $6,480
    C) $5,400
    D) $3,960
Answer: D
Diff: 2   Type: MC   Page Ref: 385/385
Topic: Illustrating Profit or Loss on the Cost Curve Graph
Skill: Analytical
Objective: LO 3: Use graphs to show a firm's profit or loss.
AACSB Coding: Analytic Skills
Special Feature: None

7. ***Refer to Figure 11–4.*** What is the amount of its total fixed cost?
    A) $1,080
    B) $1,440
    C) $2,520
    D) It cannot be determined.
Answer: C
Diff: 2   Type: MC   Page Ref: 385/385
Topic: Illustrating Profit or Loss on the Cost Curve Graph
Skill: Analytical
Objective: LO 3: Use graphs to show a firm's profit or loss.
AACSB Coding: Analytic Skills
Special Feature: None

8. ***Refer to Figure 11–4.*** If the market price is $30 and the firm is producing output, what is the amount of the firm's profit or loss?
    A) loss of $1,080
    B) loss of $2,520
    C) profit of $1,440
    D) profit of $1,300
Answer: A
Diff: 2   Type: MC   Page Ref: 385/385
Topic: Illustrating Profit or Loss on the Cost Curve Graph
Skill: Analytical
Objective: LO 3: Use graphs to show a firm's profit or loss.
AACSB Coding: Analytic Skills
Special Feature: None

9. *Refer to Figure 11–4.* If the market price is $30, should the firm represented in the diagram continue to stay in business?
    A) No, it should shut down because it cannot cover its variable cost.
    B) Yes, because it is covering part of its fixed cost.
    C) Yes, because it is making a profit.
    D) No, it should shut down because it is making a loss.
Answer: B
Diff: 2   Type: MC   Page Ref: 385/385
Topic: Illustrating Profit or Loss on the Cost Curve Graph
Skill: Analytical
Objective: LO 3: Use graphs to show a firm's profit or loss.
AACSB Coding: Analytic Skills
Special Feature: None

10. A perfectly competitive firm earns a profit when price is
    A) above minimum average total cost.
    B) equal to minimum average total cost.
    C) equal to minimum average variable cost.
    D) equal to minimum average fixed costs.
Answer: A
Diff: 2   Type: MC   Page Ref: 385/385
Topic: Illustrating Profit or Loss on the Cost Curve Graph
Skill: Conceptual
Objective: LO 3: Use graphs to show a firm's profit or loss.
AACSB Coding: Reflective Thinking
Special Feature: None

11. All of the following can be used to compute average profit except
    A) total profit divided by quantity.
    B) marginal profit minus marginal cost.
    C) price minus average total cost.
    D) average revenue minus average total cost
Answer: B
Diff: 2   Type: MC   Page Ref: 388/388
Topic: Illustrating Profit or Loss on the Cost Curve Graph
Skill: Conceptual
Objective: LO 3: Use graphs to show a firm's profit or loss.
AACSB Coding: Reflective Thinking
Special Feature: Don't Let This Happen to YOU!: Remember That Firms Maximize Total Profit,
                Not Profit per Unit

Figure 11-5

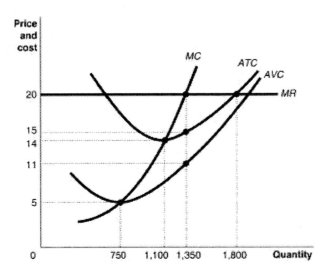

Figure 11-5 shows cost and demand curves facing a typical firm in a constant-cost perfectly competitive industry.

12. **Refer to Figure 11-5.** If the market price is $20, what is the firm's profit maximizing output?
    A) 750 units
    B) 1,100 units
    C) 1,350 units
    D) 1,800

Answer: C
Diff: 1   Type: MC   Page Ref: 386-7/386-7
Topic: Illustrating Profit or Loss on the Cost Curve Graph
Skill: Analytical
Objective: LO 3: Use graphs to show a firm's profit or loss.
AACSB Coding: Analytic Skills
Special Feature: Solved Problem: Determining Profit-Maximizing Price and Quantity

13. **Refer to Figure 11-5.** If the market price is $20, what is the amount of the firm's profit?
    A) $5,400
    B) $6,750
    C) $8,100
    D) $16,200

Answer: B
Diff: 2   Type: MC   Page Ref: 386-7/386-7
Topic: Illustrating Profit or Loss on the Cost Curve Graph
Skill: Analytical
Objective: LO 3: Use graphs to show a firm's profit or loss.
AACSB Coding: Analytic Skills
Special Feature: Solved Problem: Determining Profit-Maximizing Price and Quantity

14. *Refer to Figure 11–5.* If the market price is $20, what is the average profit at the profit maximizing quantity?
    A) $5
    B) $6
    C) $9
    D) $20
Answer: A
Diff: 2   Type: MC   Page Ref: 388/388
Topic: Illustrating Profit or Loss on the Cost Curve Graph
Skill: Analytical
Objective: LO 3: Use graphs to show a firm's profit or loss.
AACSB Coding: Analytic Skills
Special Feature: Don't Let This Happen to YOU!: Remember That Firms Maximize Total Profit,
            Not Profit per Unit

15. *Refer to Figure 11–5.* The firm's manager suggests that the firm's goal should be to maximize average profit. In that case, what is the output level and what is the average profit that will achieve the manger's goal?
    A) Q = 1,800 units, average profit =$20
    B) Q = 1,350 units, average profit =$9
    C) Q = 1,350 units, average profit =$5
    D) Q = 1,100 units, average profit =$6
Answer: D
Diff: 2   Type: MC   Page Ref: 388/388
Topic: Illustrating Profit or Loss on the Cost Curve Graph
Skill: Analytical
Objective: LO 3: Use graphs to show a firm's profit or loss.
AACSB Coding: Analytic Skills
Special Feature: Don't Let This Happen to YOU!: Remember That Firms Maximize Total Profit,
            Not Profit per Unit

16. *Refer to Figure 11–5.* The firm's manager suggests that the firm's goal should be to maximize average profit. If the firm does this, what is the amount of profit that it will earn?
    A) $6,600
    B) $36,000
    C) $6,750
    D) $12,150
Answer: A
Diff: 2   Type: MC   Page Ref: 388/388
Topic: Illustrating Profit or Loss on the Cost Curve Graph
Skill: Analytical
Objective: LO 3: Use graphs to show a firm's profit or loss.
AACSB Coding: Analytic Skills
Special Feature: Don't Let This Happen to YOU!: Remember That Firms Maximize Total Profit,
            Not Profit per Unit

17. ***Refer to Figure 11–5.*** What is the amount of the firm's fixed cost of production?
    A) $5,400
    B) $6,750
    C) $8,100
    D) It cannot be determined.
    Answer: A
    Diff: 2   Type: MC   Page Ref: 386–7/386–7
    Topic: Illustrating Profit or Loss on the Cost Curve Graph
    Skill: Analytical
    Objective: LO 3: Use graphs to show a firm's profit or loss.
    AACSB Coding: Analytic Skills
    Special Feature: None

18. ***Refer to Figure 11–5.*** If the firm's fixed cost increases by $1,000 due to a new environmental regulation, what happens in the diagram above?
    A) All the cost curves shift upward.
    B) Only the average total cost curve shifts upward; the marginal cost and average variable cost curves are not affected.
    C) Only the average variable cost and average total cost curves shift upward; marginal cost is not affected.
    D) None of the curves shifts; only the fixed cost curve, which is not shown here, is affected.
    Answer: B
    Diff: 2   Type: MC   Page Ref: 386–7/386–7
    Topic: Illustrating Profit or Loss on the Cost Curve Graph
    Skill: Conceptual
    Objective: LO 3: Use graphs to show a firm's profit or loss.
    AACSB Coding: Reflective Thinking
    Special Feature: None

19. ***Refer to Figure 11–5.*** The figure shows the cost structure of a firm in a perfectly competitive market. If the firm's fixed cost increases by $1,000 due to a new environmental regulation, what happens to its profit maximizing output level?
    A) It decreases.
    B) It increases.
    C) It remains the same.
    D) It could increase, decrease or remain constant, depending on whether the firm is able to cut cost somewhere else.
    Answer: C
    Diff: 2   Type: MC   Page Ref: 386–7/386–7
    Topic: Illustrating Profit or Loss on the Cost Curve Graph
    Skill: Conceptual
    Objective: LO 3: Use graphs to show a firm's profit or loss.
    AACSB Coding: Reflective Thinking
    Special Feature: None

20. ***Refer to Figure 11–5.*** What is the minimum price the firm requires to produce output?
    A) $14
    B) $5
    C) $20
    D) It cannot be determined
    Answer: B
    Diff: 2   Type: MC   Page Ref: 386-7/386-7
    Topic: Illustrating Profit or Loss on the Cost Curve Graph
    Skill: Analytical
    Objective: LO 3: Use graphs to show a firm's profit or loss.
    AACSB Coding: Analytic Skills
    Special Feature: None

21. A perfectly competitive firm breaks even at a price equals to its minimum average total cost.
    Answer: ◉ True   False
    Diff: 1   Type: TF   Page Ref: 388/388
    Topic: Illustrating Profit or Loss on the Cost Curve Graph
    Skill: Conceptual
    Objective: LO 3: Use graphs to show a firm's profit or loss.
    AACSB Coding: Reflective Thinking
    Special Feature: None

23. Maximizing average profit is equivalent to maximizing total profit.
    Answer: True   ◉ False
    Diff: 1   Type: TF   Page Ref: 388/388
    Topic: Illustrating Profit or Loss on the Cost Curve Graph
    Skill: Conceptual
    Objective: LO 3: Use graphs to show a firm's profit or loss.
    AACSB Coding: Reflective Thinking
    Special Feature: Don't Let This Happen to YOU!: Remember That Firms Maximize Total Profit,
    *   Not Profit per Unit*

24. In the short run, if price falls below a firm's minimum average total cost, the firm should shut down.
    Answer: True   ◉ False
    Diff: 1   Type: TF   Page Ref: 387/387
    Topic: Illustrating Profit or Loss on the Cost Curve Graph
    Skill: Conceptual
    Objective: LO 3: Use graphs to show a firm's profit or loss.
    AACSB Coding: Reflective Thinking
    Special Feature: Don't Let This Happen to YOU!: Remember That Firms Maximize Total Profit,
    *   Not Profit per Unit*

11.4 Deciding Whether to Produce or to Shut Down in the Short Run

1. If, for a given output level, a perfectly competitive firm's price is less than its average variable cost, the firm
    A) is earning a profit.
    B) should increase price.
    C) should increase output.
    D) should shut down.
   Answer: D
   Diff: 2   Type: MC   Page Ref: 390/390
   Topic: Deciding Whether to Produce or to Shut Down in the Short Run
   Skill: Conceptual
   Objective: LO 4: Explain why firms may shut down temporarily.
   AACSB Coding: Reflective Thinking
   Special Feature: None

2. How are sunk costs and fixed costs related?
    A) In the long run they are equal to each other.
    B) They are not related in any way.
    C) Sunk costs cannot be recovered and fixed costs can be avoided by shutting down.
    D) In the short run they are equal to each other.
   Answer: D
   Diff: 2   Type: MC   Page Ref: 390/390
   Topic: Deciding Whether to Produce or to Shut Down in the Short Run
   Skill: Conceptual
   Objective: LO 4: Explain why firms may shut down temporarily.
   AACSB Coding: Reflective Thinking
   Special Feature: None

3. A perfectly competitive firm's supply curve is its
    A) marginal cost curve.
    B) marginal cost curve above the minimum of its average fixed cost.
    C) marginal cost curve above its minimum average total cost.
    D) marginal cost curve above its minimum average variable cost.
   Answer: D
   Diff: 2   Type: MC   Page Ref: 391/391
   Topic: Deciding Whether to Produce or to Shut Down in the Short Run
   Skill: Conceptual
   Objective: LO 4: Explain why firms may shut down temporarily.
   AACSB Coding: Reflective Thinking
   Special Feature: None

4. When a perfectly competitive firm finds that its market price is below its minimum average variable cost, it will sell
    A) nothing at all; the firm shuts down.
    B) the output where average total costs equal price.
    C) any positive output the entrepreneur decides upon because all of it can be sold.
    D) the output level where marginal revenue equals marginal cost.
Answer: A
Diff: 2   Type: MC   Page Ref: 391/391
Topic: Deciding Whether to Produce or to Shut Down in the Short Run
Skill: Conceptual
Objective: LO 4: Explain why firms may shut down temporarily.
AACSB Coding: Reflective Thinking
Special Feature: None

5. Val Alvarado, an accountant quit his $80,000-a-year job and bought an existing laundry from its previous owner Ricky White. The lease has five years remaining and requires a monthly payment of $4,000. The lease
    A) is part of the marginal cost of operating the laundry.
    B) is a fixed cost of operating the laundry.
    C) is an implicit cost of operating the laundry.
    D) is a variable cost of operating the laundry.
Answer: B
Diff: 2   Type: MC   Page Ref: 390/390
Topic: Deciding Whether to Produce or to Shut Down in the Short Run
Skill: Conceptual
Objective: LO 4: Explain why firms may shut down temporarily.
AACSB Coding: Reflective Thinking
Special Feature: Making the Connection: When to Close a Laundry

6. Val Alvarado, an accountant quit his $80,000-a-year job and bought an existing laundry from its previous owner Ricky White. The lease has five years remaining and requires a monthly payment of $4,000. Val's explicit costs amounts to $3,000 per month more than his revenue. Should Val continue operating his business?
    A) Val's explicit cost exceeds his total revenue. He should shut down his laundry.
    B) If Val's marginal revenue is greater than or equal to his marginal cost, then he should stay in business.
    C) Val should continue to run the laundry until his lease runs out.
    D) Cannot be determined without information on his revenue.
Answer: C
Diff: 2   Type: MC   Page Ref: 390/390
Topic: Deciding Whether to Produce or to Shut Down in the Short Run
Skill: Conceptual
Objective: LO 4: Explain why firms may shut down temporarily.
AACSB Coding: Reflective Thinking
Special Feature: Making the Connection: When to Close a Laundry

Figure 11-6

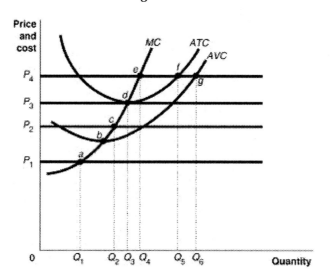

Figure 11-6 shows cost and demand curves facing a profit-maximizing perfectly competitive firm.

7. *Refer to Figure 11-6.* At price P_1, the firm would produce

    A) Q_3 units.

    B) zero units.

    C) Q_5 units.

    D) Q_1 units

Answer: B

Diff: 2   Type: MC   Page Ref: 390–1/390–1
Topic: Deciding Whether to Produce or to Shut Down in the Short Run
Skill: Conceptual
Objective: LO 4: Explain why firms may shut down temporarily.
AACSB Coding: Analytic Skills
Special Feature: None

8. *Refer to Figure 11-6.* At price P_1, the firm would

    A) Lose an amount less than fixed costs.

    B) break even.

    C) lose an amount equal to its fixed costs.

    D) lose an amount more than fixed costs.

Answer: C

Diff: 2   Type: MC   Page Ref: 390–1/390–1
Topic: Deciding Whether to Produce or to Shut Down in the Short Run
Skill: Conceptual
Objective: LO 4: Explain why firms may shut down temporarily.
AACSB Coding: Analytic Skills
Special Feature: None

9. *Refer to Figure 11-6.* At price P_2, the firm would produce

    A) Q_3 units.

    B) Q_2 units

    C) zero units.

    D) Q_4 units.

Answer: B

Diff: 2   Type: MC   Page Ref: 390-1/390-1
Topic: Deciding Whether to Produce or to Shut Down in the Short Run
Skill: Conceptual
Objective: LO 4: Explain why firms may shut down temporarily.
AACSB Coding: Analytic Skills
Special Feature: None

10. *Refer to Figure 11-6.* At price P_2, the firm would

    A) lose an amount more than fixed costs.

    B) lose an amount equal to its fixed costs.

    C) lose an amount less than fixed costs.

    D) break even.

Answer: C

Diff: 2   Type: MC   Page Ref: 390-1/390-1
Topic: Deciding Whether to Produce or to Shut Down in the Short Run
Skill: Conceptual
Objective: LO 4: Explain why firms may shut down temporarily.
AACSB Coding: Analytic Skills
Special Feature: None

11. *Refer to Figure 11-6.* At price P_3, the firm would produce

    A) Q_5 units.

    B) Q_2 units

    C) Q_4 units.

    D) Q_3 units.

Answer: D

Diff: 2   Type: MC   Page Ref: 390-1/390-1
Topic: Deciding Whether to Produce or to Shut Down in the Short Run
Skill: Conceptual
Objective: LO 4: Explain why firms may shut down temporarily.
AACSB Coding: Analytic Skills
Special Feature: None

12. *Refer to Figure 11–6.* At price P_3, the firm would
    A) lose an amount less than fixed costs.
    B) lose an amount more than fixed costs.
    C) break even.
    D) lose an amount equal to its fixed costs.
    Answer: C
    Diff: 2   Type: MC   Page Ref: 390–1/390–1
    Topic: Deciding Whether to Produce or to Shut Down in the Short Run
    Skill: Conceptual
    Objective: LO 4: Explain why firms may shut down temporarily.
    AACSB Coding: Analytic Skills
    Special Feature: None

13. *Refer to Figure 11–6.* At price P_4, the firm would produce
    A) Q_5 units.
    B) Q_6 units.
    C) Q_4 units.
    D) Q_3 units
    Answer: A
    Diff: 2   Type: MC   Page Ref: 390–1/390–1
    Topic: Deciding Whether to Produce or to Shut Down in the Short Run
    Skill: Conceptual
    Objective: LO 4: Explain why firms may shut down temporarily.
    AACSB Coding: Analytic Skills
    Special Feature: None

14. *Refer to Figure 11–6.* At price P_4, the firm would
    A) lose an amount less than fixed costs.
    B) make a normal profit
    C) lose an amount equal to its fixed costs.
    D) make a profit
    Answer: D
    Diff: 2   Type: MC   Page Ref: 390–1/390–1
    Topic: Deciding Whether to Produce or to Shut Down in the Short Run
    Skill: Conceptual
    Objective: LO 4: Explain why firms may shut down temporarily.
    AACSB Coding: Analytic Skills
    Special Feature: None

15. *Refer to Figure 11-6.* Identify the short run shut down point for the firm.
    A) *a*
    B) *b*.
    C) *c*
    D) *d*
    Answer: B
    Diff: 2   Type: MC   Page Ref: 390-1/390-1
    Topic: Deciding Whether to Produce or to Shut Down in the Short Run
    Skill: Conceptual
    Objective: LO 4: Explain why firms may shut down temporarily.
    AACSB Coding: Analytic Skills
    Special Feature: None

16. *Refer to Figure 11-6.* Identify the firm's short run supply curve.
    A) the marginal cost curve.
    B) the marginal cost curve from *a* and above.
    C) the marginal cost curve from *b* and above.
    D) the marginal cost curve from *d* and above.
    Answer: C
    Diff: 2   Type: MC   Page Ref: 390-1/390-1
    Topic: Deciding Whether to Produce or to Shut Down in the Short Run
    Skill: Conceptual
    Objective: LO 4: Explain why firms may shut down temporarily.
    AACSB Coding: Analytic Skills
    Special Feature: None

17. Market supply is found by
    A) horizontally summing each individual producer's average total cost curve.
    B) vertically summing each individual producer's average total cost curve.
    C) vertically summing the relevant part of each individual producer's marginal cost curve.
    D) horizontally summing the relevant part of each individual producer's marginal cost curve.
    Answer: D
    Diff: 2   Type: MC   Page Ref: 392/392
    Topic: Deciding Whether to Produce or to Shut Down in the Short Run
    Skill: Conceptual
    Objective: LO 4: Explain why firms may shut down temporarily.
    AACSB Coding: Reflective Thinking
    Special Feature: None

18. If total variable cost exceeds total revenue at all output levels, a perfectly competitive firm
    A) should produce in the short run.
    B) should shut down in the short run.
    C) is making short-run profits.
    D) has covered its fixed costs.
    Answer: A
    Diff: 2   Type: MC   Page Ref: 391/391
    Topic: Deciding Whether to Produce or to Shut Down in the Short Run
    Skill: Conceptual
    Objective: LO 4: Explain why firms may shut down temporarily.
    AACSB Coding: Reflective Thinking
    Special Feature: None

19. If total revenue exceeds fixed cost, a firm
    A) may or may not produce in the short run, depending on whether total revenue covers variable cost.
    B) should produce in the short run.
    C) is making short-run profits.
    D) has covered its variable costs.
    Answer: A
    Diff: 2   Type: MC   Page Ref: 391/391
    Topic: Deciding Whether to Produce or to Shut Down in the Short Run
    Skill: Conceptual
    Objective: LO 4: Explain why firms may shut down temporarily.
    AACSB Coding: Reflective Thinking
    Special Feature: None

20. If a firm shuts down in the short run,
    A) is makes zero economic profit.
    B) its loss equals zero.
    C) its total revenue is not large enough to cover its fixed costs.
    D) its loss equals its fixed cost.
    Answer: D
    Diff: 2   Type: MC   Page Ref: 391/391
    Topic: Deciding Whether to Produce or to Shut Down in the Short Run
    Skill: Conceptual
    Objective: LO 4: Explain why firms may shut down temporarily.
    AACSB Coding: Reflective Thinking
    Special Feature: None

21. A perfectly competitive firm produces 3,000 units of a good at a total cost of $36,000. The fixed cost of production is $20,000. The price of each good is $10. Should the firm continue to produce in the short run?
    A) Yes, it should continue to produce because its price exceeds its average fixed cost.
    B) Yes, it should continue to produce because it is minimizing its loss.
    C) No, it should shut down because it is making a loss.
    D) There is insufficient information to answer the question.
    Answer: B
    Diff: 2   Type: MC   Page Ref: 391/391
    Topic: Deciding Whether to Produce or to Shut Down in the Short Run
    Skill: Conceptual
    Objective: LO 4: Explain why firms may shut down temporarily.
    AACSB Coding: Analytic Skills
    Special Feature: None

22. In the short-run, a firm that incurs losses might choose to produce rather than shut down if the amount of its revenue is less than its fixed cost.
    Answer: True   ○ False
    Diff: 1   Type: TF   Page Ref: 391/391
    Topic: Deciding Whether to Produce or to Shut Down in the Short Run
    Skill: Conceptual
    Objective: LO 4: Explain why firms may shut down temporarily.
    AACSB Coding: Reflective Thinking
    Special Feature: None

23. In the short-run, if a firm shuts down it avoids its variable cost but not its fixed cost.
    Answer: ○ True   False
    Diff: 2   Type: TF   Page Ref: 391/391
    Topic: Deciding Whether to Produce or to Shut Down in the Short Run
    Skill: Conceptual
    Objective: LO 4: Explain why firms may shut down temporarily.
    AACSB Coding: Reflective Thinking
    Special Feature: None

24. In the short-run, if a firm shuts down its maximum loss equals the amount of its fixed cost.
    Answer: ○ True   False
    Diff: 1   Type: TF   Page Ref: 391/391
    Topic: Deciding Whether to Produce or to Shut Down in the Short Run
    Skill: Conceptual
    Objective: LO 4: Explain why firms may shut down temporarily.
    AACSB Coding: Reflective Thinking
    Special Feature: None

25. The minimum point on the average variable cost curve is called the loss-minimizing point.
Answer: True   ◉ False
Diff: 1   Type: TF   Page Ref: 391/391
Topic: Deciding Whether to Produce or to Shut Down in the Short Run
Skill: Conceptual
Objective: LO 4: Explain why firms may shut down temporarily.
AACSB Coding: Reflective Thinking
Special Feature: None

26. If a firm's fixed cost exceeds its total revenue, the firm should stop production by shutting down temporarily.
Answer: True   ◉ False
Diff: 2   Type: TF   Page Ref: 391/391
Topic: Deciding Whether to Produce or to Shut Down in the Short Run
Skill: Conceptual
Objective: LO 4: Explain why firms may shut down temporarily.
AACSB Coding: Reflective Thinking
Special Feature: None

27. In the short run, a firm might choose to produce rather than shut down even if its market price is less than its average total cost of production.
Answer: ◉ True   False
Diff: 1   Type: TF   Page Ref: 391/391
Topic: Deciding Whether to Produce or to Shut Down in the Short Run
Skill: Conceptual
Objective: LO 4: Explain why firms may shut down temporarily.
AACSB Coding: Reflective Thinking
Special Feature: None

28. If a firm's total variable cost exceeds its total revenue, the firm should stop production by shutting down temporarily.
Answer: ◉ True   False
Diff: 2   Type: TF   Page Ref: 391/391
Topic: Deciding Whether to Produce or to Shut Down in the Short Run
Skill: Conceptual
Objective: LO 4: Explain why firms may shut down temporarily.
AACSB Coding: Reflective Thinking
Special Feature: None

29. Under what conditions should a competitive firm shut down in the short run?
Answer: When market price is below average variable cost at the output where marginal revenue equals marginal cost, the firm should shut down in the short run.
Diff: 2   Type: SA   Page Ref: 391/391
Topic: Deciding Whether to Produce or to Shut Down in the Short Run
Skill: Conceptual
Objective: LO 4: Explain why firms may shut down temporarily.
AACSB Coding: Reflective Thinking, Ethical Reasoning
Special Feature: None

11.5 "If Everyone Can Do It, You Can't Make Money at It"- The Entry and Exit of Firms in the Long Run

1. Which of the following statements is correct?
   A) Economic profit takes into account all costs involved in producing a product.
   B) Accounting profit is not relevant in preparing the firm's financial statement.
   C) Accounting profit is the same as economic profit.
   D) Economic profit always exceeds accounting profit.
   Answer: A
   Diff: 2   Type: MC   Page Ref: 393/393
   Topic: "If Everyone Can Do It, You Can't Make Money at It" – The Entry and Exit of Firms in the Long Run
   Skill: Conceptual
   Objective: LO 5: Explain how entry and exit ensure that perfectly competitive firms earn zero economic profit in the long run.
   AACSB Coding: Reflective Thinking
   Special Feature: None

Figure 11-7

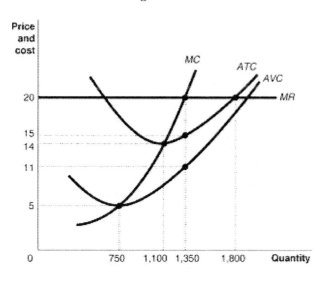

2. *Refer to Figure 11–7*. Suppose the prevailing price is $20 and the firm is currently producing 1,350 units. In the long run equilibrium, the firm represented in the diagram

    A) will reduce its output to 1,100 units.

    B) will cease to exist.

    C) will continue to produce the same quantity.

    D) will reduce its output to 750 units.

Answer: A

Diff: 2   Type: MC   Page Ref: 394/394

Topic: "If Everyone Can Do It, You Can't Make Money at It" – The Entry and Exit of Firms in the Long Run

Skill: Analytical

Objective: LO 5: Explain how entry and exit ensure that perfectly competitive firms earn zero economic profit in the long run.

AACSB Coding: Analytic Skills

Special Feature: None

3. *Refer to Figure 11–7*. Suppose the prevailing price is $20 and the firm is currently producing 1,350 units. In the long run equilibrium,

    A) there will be fewer firms in the industry and total industry output decreases.

    B) there will be more firms in the industry and total industry output remains constant.

    C) there will be fewer firms in the industry but total industry output increases.

    D) there will be more firms in the industry and total industry output increases.

Answer: D

Diff: 2   Type: MC   Page Ref: 394/394

Topic: "If Everyone Can Do It, You Can't Make Money at It" – The Entry and Exit of Firms in the Long Run

Skill: Analytical

Objective: LO 5: Explain how entry and exit ensure that perfectly competitive firms earn zero economic profit in the long run.

AACSB Coding: Analytic Skills

Special Feature: None

4. *Refer to Figure 11–7*. If this is a constant cost industry, what is the market price in the long run equilibrium?

    A) $5

    B) $20

    C) $15

    D) $14

Answer: D

Diff: 2   Type: MC   Page Ref: 394/394

Topic: "If Everyone Can Do It, You Can't Make Money at It" – The Entry and Exit of Firms in the Long Run

Skill: Analytical

Objective: LO 5: Explain how entry and exit ensure that perfectly competitive firms earn zero economic profit in the long run.

AACSB Coding: Analytic Skills

Special Feature: None

5. If a typical firm in a perfectly competitive industry is earning profits, then
- A) new firms will enter in the long run causing market supply to increase, market price to fall and profits to decrease.
- B) all firms will continue to earn profits.
- C) new firms will enter in the long run causing market supply to decrease, market price to rise and profits to increase.
- D) the number of firms in the industry will remain constant in the long run.

Answer: A
Diff: 2   Type: MC   Page Ref: 394/394
Topic: "If Everyone Can Do It, You Can't Make Money at It" – The Entry and Exit of Firms in the Long Run
Skill: Conceptual
Objective: LO 5: Explain how entry and exit ensure that perfectly competitive firms earn zero economic profit in the long run.
AACSB Coding: Reflective Thinking
Special Feature: None

Figure 11-8

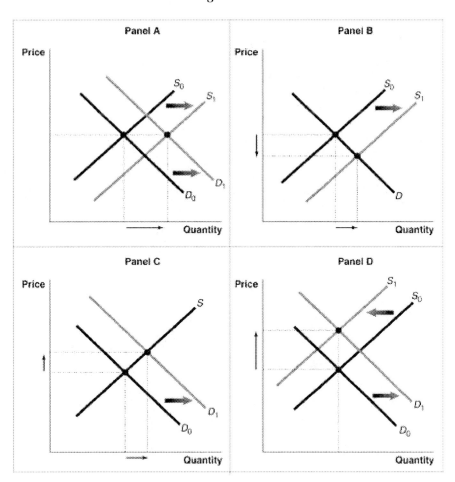

6. ***Refer to Figure 11–8.*** Consider a typical firm in a perfectly competitive industry that makes short run profits. Which of the diagrams in the Figure shows the effect on the industry as it transitions to a long run equilibrium?
    A) *Panel A*
    B) *Panel B*
    C) *Panel C*
    D) *Panel D*
Answer: B
Diff: 3   Type: MC   Page Ref: 394/394
Topic: "If Everyone Can Do It, You Can't Make Money at It" – The Entry and Exit of Firms in the Long Run
Skill: Analytical
Objective: LO 5: Explain how entry and exit ensure that perfectly competitive firms earn zero economic profit in the long run.
AACSB Coding: Analytic Skills
Special Feature: None

7. If, in a perfectly competitive industry, the market price facing a firm is above its average total cost at the output where marginal revenue equals marginal cost, then
    A) new firms are attracted to the industry.
    B) firms are breaking even.
    C) existing firms will exit the industry.
    D) market supply will remain constant.
Answer: A
Diff: 2   Type: MC   Page Ref: 394/394
Topic: "If Everyone Can Do It, You Can't Make Money at It" – The Entry and Exit of Firms in the Long Run
Skill: Conceptual
Objective: LO 5: Explain how entry and exit ensure that perfectly competitive firms earn zero economic profit in the long run.
AACSB Coding: Reflective Thinking
Special Feature: None

Figure 11-9

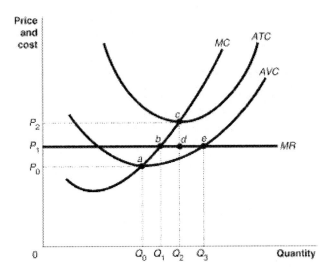

8. *Refer to Figure 11-9.* Suppose the prevailing price is P_1 and the firm is currently producing its loss-minimizing quantity. In the long run equilibrium,
    A) there will be fewer firms in the industry but total industry output increases.
    B) there will be more firms in the industry and total industry output increases.
    C) there will be more firms in the industry and total industry output remains constant.
    D) there will be fewer firms in the industry and total industry output decreases.
Answer: D
Diff: 2   *Type: MC*   *Page Ref: 395-6/395-6*
Topic: "If Everyone Can Do It, You Can't Make Money at It" – The Entry and Exit of Firms in the Long Run
Skill: Analytical
Objective: LO 5: Explain how entry and exit ensure that perfectly competitive firms earn zero economic profit in the long run.
AACSB Coding: Analytic Skills
Special Feature: None

9. ***Refer to Figure 11–9.*** Suppose the prevailing price is P_1 and the firm is currently producing its loss–minimizing quantity. If the firm represented in the diagram continues to stay in business, in the long run equilibrium,

    A) it will expand its output to Q_2 and face a price of P_2.

    B) it will continue to produce Q_1 but faces a higher price P_2.

    C) it will reduce its output to Q_0 and face a price of P_0.

    D) it will expand its output to Q_3 and face a price of P_1.

Answer: A
Diff: 2   Type: MC   Page Ref: 395–6/395–6
*Topic: "If Everyone Can Do It, You Can't Make Money at It" – The Entry and Exit of Firms in
      the Long Run*
Skill: Analytical
*Objective: LO 5: Explain how entry and exit ensure that perfectly competitive firms earn zero
      economic profit in the long run.*
AACSB Coding: Analytic Skills
Special Feature: None

10. If a typical firm in a perfectly competitive industry is incurring losses, then

    A) some firms will exit in the long run causing market supply to decrease and market price to fall increasing losses for the remaining firms.

    B) some firms will exit in the long run causing market supply to decrease and market price to rise increasing profits for the remaining firms.

    C) some firms will enter in the long run causing market supply to increase and market price to rise increasing profit for all firms.

    D) all firms will continue to lose money.

Answer: B
Diff: 2   Type: MC   Page Ref: 395–6/395–6
*Topic: "If Everyone Can Do It, You Can't Make Money at It" – The Entry and Exit of Firms in
      the Long Run*
Skill: Conceptual
*Objective: LO 5: Explain how entry and exit ensure that perfectly competitive firms earn zero
      economic profit in the long run.*
AACSB Coding: Reflective Thinking
Special Feature: None

11. A perfectly competitive market is in long run equilibrium. At present there are 100 identical firms each producing 5,000 units of output. The prevailing market price is $20. Assume that each firm faces increasing marginal cost. Now suppose there is a sudden increase in demand for the industry's product which causes the price of the good to rise to $24. Which of the following describes the effect of this increase in demand on a typical firm in the industry?

    A) In the short run, the typical firm increases its output but its total cost also rises, resulting in no change in profit.

    B) In the short run, the typical firm increases its output and makes an above normal profit.

    C) In the short run, the typical firm's output remains the same but because of the higher price, its profit increases.

    D) In the short run, the typical firm increases its output but its total cost also rises. Hence, the effect on the firm's profit cannot be determined without more information.

Answer: B

Diff: 3   Type: MC   Page Ref: 395–6/395–6

Topic: "If Everyone Can Do It, You Can't Make Money at It" – The Entry and Exit of Firms in the Long Run

Skill: Analytical

Objective: LO 5: Explain how entry and exit ensure that perfectly competitive firms earn zero economic profit in the long run.

AACSB Coding: Analytic Skills

Special Feature: None

12. In long–run perfectly competitive equilibrium, which of the following is false?

    A) Economies of scale are exhausted.

    B) Economic surplus is maximized.

    C) Firms earn economic profit.

    D) There is efficient, low–cost production at the minimum efficient scale.

Answer: C

Diff: 2   Type: MC   Page Ref: 395–6/395–6

Topic: "If Everyone Can Do It, You Can't Make Money at It" – The Entry and Exit of Firms in the Long Run

Skill: Conceptual

Objective: LO 5: Explain how entry and exit ensure that perfectly competitive firms earn zero economic profit in the long run.

AACSB Coding: Reflective Thinking

Special Feature: None

Figure 11-10

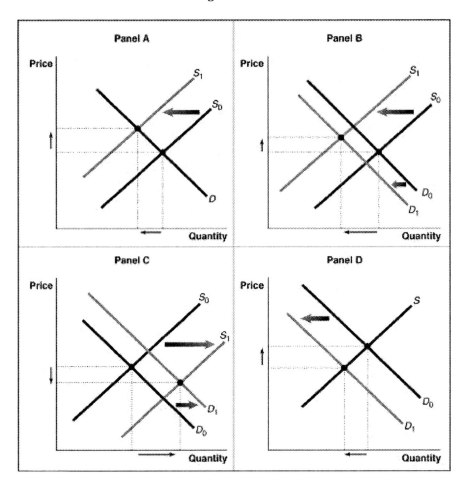

13. ***Refer to Figure 11-10.*** Consider a typical firm in a perfectly competitive industry is incurring short run losses. Which of the diagrams in the Figure shows the effect on the industry as it transitions to a long run equilibrium?

   A) *Panel A*
   B) *Panel B*
   C) *Panel C*
   D) *Panel D*

Answer: A
Diff: 3   Type: MC   Page Ref: 396/396
Topic: "If Everyone Can Do It, You Can't Make Money at It" – The Entry and Exit of Firms in
       the Long Run
Skill: Analytical
Objective: LO 5: Explain how entry and exit ensure that perfectly competitive firms earn zero
       economic profit in the long run.
AACSB Coding: Analytic Skills
Special Feature: None

14. If in a perfectly competitive industry, the market price facing a firm is below its average total cost but above average variable cost at the output where marginal cost equals marginal revenue
    A) the industry supply will not change.
    B) firms are breaking even.
    C) some existing firms will exit the industry.
    D) new firms are attracted to the industry.
Answer: C
Diff: 2   Type: MC   Page Ref: 395/395
Topic: "If Everyone Can Do It, You Can't Make Money at It" – The Entry and Exit of Firms in the Long Run
Skill: Conceptual
Objective: LO 5: Explain how entry and exit ensure that perfectly competitive firms earn zero economic profit in the long run.
AACSB Coding: Reflective Thinking
Special Feature: None

Figure 11–11

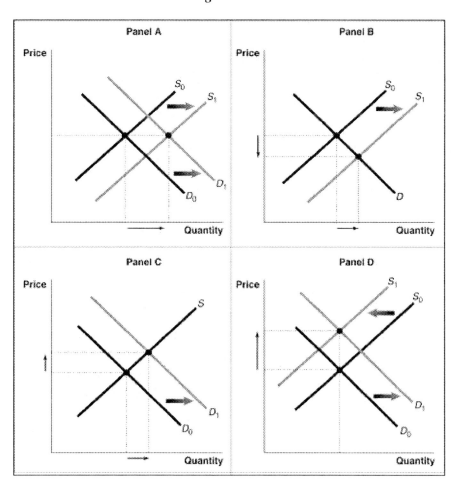

15. ***Refer to Figure 11–11.*** Assume that the medical screening industry is perfectly competitive and that some firms are making short run losses. Suppose the medical screening industry runs an effective advertising campaign which convinces a large number of people that yearly CT scans are critical for good health. Which of the diagrams in the Figure best describes what happens in the industry?

    A) Panel A

    B) Panel B

    C) Panel C

    D) Panel D

Answer: D

Diff: 3   Type: MC   Page Ref: 395/395

Topic: "If Everyone Can Do It, You Can't Make Money at It" – The Entry and Exit of Firms in the Long Run

Skill: Analytical

Objective: LO 5: Explain how entry and exit ensure that perfectly competitive firms earn zero economic profit in the long run.

AACSB Coding: Analytic Skills

Special Feature: Making the Connection: Losing Money in the Medical Screening Industry

16. ***Refer to Figure 11–11.*** Suppose typical firm in a perfectly competitive market is earning economic profits in the short run. Which of the diagrams in the Figure depicts what happens to in the industry as it transitions to along run equilibrium?

    A) Panel A

    B) Panel B

    C) Panel C

    D) Panel D

Answer: B

Diff: 3   Type: MC   Page Ref: 394/394

Topic: "If Everyone Can Do It, You Can't Make Money at It" – The Entry and Exit of Firms in the Long Run

Skill: Analytical

Objective: LO 5: Explain how entry and exit ensure that perfectly competitive firms earn zero economic profit in the long run.

AACSB Coding: Analytic Skills

Special Feature: None

17. Assume that the medical screening industry is perfectly competitive. Consider a typical firm in that is making short run losses. Suppose the medical screening industry runs an effective advertising campaign which convinces a large number of people that yearly CT scans are critical for good health. How will this affect a typical firm that remains in the industry?

    A) The marginal revenue curve shifts upwards, the firm's output increases along its marginal cost curve, it expands production until it breaks even.

    B) The marginal revenue curve shifts upwards, the firm's output increases along its marginal cost curve, it expands production and eventually starts making profits.

    C) The firm's marginal revenue curve and average cost curve shift upwards in response to the increase in market price and advertising expenditure. The firm increases output until it starts breaking even.

    D) The firm's supply curve shifts right and its marginal revenue curve shifts upwards t as the market price rises and ultimately the firm starts making profits.

Answer: A

Diff: 3   *Type: MC*   *Page Ref: 389/389*

Topic: "If Everyone Can Do It, You Can't Make Money at It" – The Entry and Exit of Firms in the Long Run

Skill: Analytical

Objective: LO 5: Explain how entry and exit ensure that perfectly competitive firms earn zero economic profit in the long run.

AACSB Coding: Analytic Skills

Special Feature: Making the Connection: Losing Money in the Medical Screening Industry

18. In a perfectly competitive industry, in the long-run equilibrium

    A) is maximizing its revenue.

    B) the typical firm is producing at the output where its long-run average total cost is not minimized.

    C) the typical firm earns zero profit.

    D) the typical firm is earning an accounting profit greater than its implicit costs.

Answer: C

Diff: 2   *Type: MC*   *Page Ref: 395/395*

Topic: "If Everyone Can Do It, You Can't Make Money at It" – The Entry and Exit of Firms in the Long Run

Skill: Conceptual

Objective: LO 5: Explain how entry and exit ensure that perfectly competitive firms earn zero economic profit in the long run.

AACSB Coding: Reflective Thinking

Special Feature: None

19. A constant cost perfectly competitive market is in long run equilibrium. At present, there are 1,000 firms each producing 400 units of output. The price of the good is $60. Now suppose there is a sudden increase in demand for the industry's product which causes the price of the good to rise to $64. In the new long run equilibrium, how will the average total cost of producing the good compare to what it was before the price of the good rose?
    A) The average total cost will be higher than it was before the price increase because of diseconomies of scale arising from the increased demand.
    B) The average total cost will be higher than it was before the price increase since the increase in demand will drive up input prices.
    C) The average total cost will be lower than it was before the price increase because of economies of scale.
    D) The average total cost will be the same as it was before the price increase.

Answer: D

Diff: 3   Type: MC   Page Ref: 397/397
Topic: "If Everyone Can Do It, You Can't Make Money at It" – The Entry and Exit of Firms in the Long Run
Skill: Analytical
Objective: LO 5: Explain how entry and exit ensure that perfectly competitive firms earn zero economic profit in the long run.
AACSB Coding: Analytic Skills
Special Feature: None

20. An industry's long-run supply curve shows
    A) how average productivity is changing.
    B) greater than normal profit.
    C) the relationship in the long run between market price and quantity supplied.
    D) how the government determines the price of the product.

Answer: C

Diff: 2   Type: MC   Page Ref: 397/397
Topic: "If Everyone Can Do It, You Can't Make Money at It" – The Entry and Exit of Firms in the Long Run
Skill: Conceptual
Objective: LO 5: Explain how entry and exit ensure that perfectly competitive firms earn zero economic profit in the long run.
AACSB Coding: Reflective Thinking
Special Feature: None

21. In the long run, a perfectly competitive market will
    A) produce only the quantity of output that yields a long run profit for the typical firm.
    B) supply whatever amount consumers demand at a price determined by the minimum point on the typical firm's average total cost curve.
    C) generate a long run equilibrium where the typical firm operates at a loss.
    D) supply whatever amount consumers will buy at an economic profit price.
    Answer: B
    Diff: 2   Type: MC   Page Ref: 397/397
    Topic: "If Everyone Can Do It, You Can't Make Money at It" – The Entry and Exit of Firms in the Long Run
    Skill: Conceptual
    Objective: LO 5: Explain how entry and exit ensure that perfectly competitive firms earn zero economic profit in the long run.
    AACSB Coding: Reflective Thinking
    Special Feature: None

22. A perfectly competitive firm in a constant-cost industry produces 3,000 units of a good at a total cost of $36,000. The prevailing market price is $15. What will happen to the market price of this good in the long run?
    A) The price rises above $15.
    B) The price falls to $12.
    C) The price remains constant at $15.
    D) There is insufficient information to answer the question.
    Answer: B
    Diff: 2   Type: MC   Page Ref: 394–5/394–5
    Topic: "If Everyone Can Do It, You Can't Make Money at It" – The Entry and Exit of Firms in the Long Run
    Skill: Analytical
    Objective: LO 5: Explain how entry and exit ensure that perfectly competitive firms earn zero economic profit in the long run.
    AACSB Coding: Analytic Skills
    Special Feature: None

23. A perfectly competitive firm in a constant-cost industry produces 1,000 units of a good at a total cost of $50,000. The prevailing market price is $48. What will happen to the market price of this good in the long run?
    A) The price falls below $48
    B) The price rises above $48.
    C) The price remains constant at $48.
    D) There is insufficient information to answer the question
    Answer: B
    Diff: 2   Type: MC   Page Ref: 394–394
    Topic: "If Everyone Can Do It, You Can't Make Money at It" – The Entry and Exit of Firms in the Long Run
    Skill: Analytical
    Objective: LO 5: Explain how entry and exit ensure that perfectly competitive firms earn zero economic profit in the long run.
    AACSB Coding: Analytic Skills
    Special Feature: None

24. A perfectly competitive firm in a constant-cost industry produces 1,000 units of a good at a total cost of $50,000. The prevailing market price is $48. Assuming that this firm continues to produce in the long run, what happens to output level in the long run?
    A) The firm's output increases.
    B) The firm produces the same output level.
    C) The firm's output falls.
    D) There is insufficient information to answer the question

    Answer: A
    Diff: 2   Type: MC   Page Ref: 394–394
    Topic: "If Everyone Can Do It, You Can't Make Money at It" – The Entry and Exit of Firms in the Long Run
    Skill: Analytical
    Objective: LO 5: Explain how entry and exit ensure that perfectly competitive firms earn zero economic profit in the long run.
    AACSB Coding: Analytic Skills
    Special Feature: None

25. A perfectly competitive firm in a constant-cost industry produces 3,000 units of a good at a total cost of $36,000. The prevailing market price is $15. What will happen to the number of firms in the industry and to the industry's output in the long run?
    A) The number of firms remains constant and the industry's output increases.
    B) The number of firms and the industry's output increase.
    C) The number of firms remains constant and the industry's output decreases.
    D) The number of firms and the industry's output decrease.

    Answer: B
    Diff: 2   Type: MC   Page Ref: 394–394
    Topic: "If Everyone Can Do It, You Can't Make Money at It" – The Entry and Exit of Firms in the Long Run
    Skill: Analytical
    Objective: LO 5: Explain how entry and exit ensure that perfectly competitive firms earn zero economic profit in the long run.
    AACSB Coding: Analytic Skills
    Special Feature: None

26. If, as a perfectly competitive industry expands, it can supply larger quantities at the same long-run market price, it is
    A) a constant-cost industry.
    B) a fixed-cost industry.
    C) a decreasing-cost industry.
    D) an increasing-cost industry.

    Answer: A
    Diff: 2   Type: MC   Page Ref: 394–394
    Topic: "If Everyone Can Do It, You Can't Make Money at It" – The Entry and Exit of Firms in the Long Run
    Skill: Definition
    Objective: LO 5: Explain how entry and exit ensure that perfectly competitive firms earn zero economic profit in the long run.
    AACSB Coding: Reflective Thinking
    Special Feature: None

27. If, as a perfectly competitive industry expands, it can supply larger quantities only at a higher long-run equilibrium price, it is
    A) a decreasing-cost industry.
    B) an increasing-cost industry.
    C) a fixed-cost industry.
    D) a constant-cost industry.
    Answer: B
    Diff: 2   Type: MC   Page Ref: 394–394
    Topic: "If Everyone Can Do It, You Can't Make Money at It" – The Entry and Exit of Firms in the Long Run
    Skill: Definition
    Objective: LO 5: Explain how entry and exit ensure that perfectly competitive firms earn zero economic profit in the long run.
    AACSB Coding: Reflective Thinking
    Special Feature: None

28. Assume that the tuna fishing industry is perfectly competitive. Which of the following best characterizes the industry if, as demand for tuna increases, fishing boats have to go farther into the ocean to harvest tuna?
    A) a fixed-cost industry
    B) an increasing-cost industry
    C) a constant-cost industry
    D) a decreasing-cost industry
    Answer: B
    Diff: 3   Type: MC   Page Ref: 394–394
    Topic: "If Everyone Can Do It, You Can't Make Money at It" – The Entry and Exit of Firms in the Long Run
    Skill: Conceptual
    Objective: LO 5: Explain how entry and exit ensure that perfectly competitive firms earn zero economic profit in the long run.
    AACSB Coding: Reflective Thinking
    Special Feature: None

29. If in the long run a firm makes zero profit, it should exit the industry.
    Answer: True   False
    Diff: 2   Type: TF   Page Ref: 395/395
    Topic: "If Everyone Can Do It, You Can't Make Money at It" – The Entry and Exit of Firms in the Long Run
    Skill: Conceptual
    Objective: LO 5: Explain how entry and exit ensure that perfectly competitive firms earn zero economic profit in the long run.
    AACSB Coding: Reflective Thinking
    Special Feature: None

30. A perfectly competitive firm in a constant–cost industry produces 1,000 units of a good at a total cost of $50,000. If the prevailing market price is $48, the number of firms and the industry's output will decrease in the long run.
    Answer: ⊚ True   False
    Diff: 2   *Type: TF*   *Page Ref: 394/394*
    Topic: "If Everyone Can Do It, You Can't Make Money at It" – The Entry and Exit of Firms in the Long Run
    Skill: Analytical
    Objective: LO 5: Explain how entry and exit ensure that perfectly competitive firms earn zero economic profit in the long run.
    AACSB Coding: Analytic Skills
    Special Feature: None

31. The assumption that there are no barriers to new firms entering the market or exiting a market guarantees that any excess profits will be eliminated.
    Answer: ⊚ True   False
    Diff: 2   *Type: TF*   *Page Ref: 395/395*
    Topic: "If Everyone Can Do It, You Can't Make Money at It" – The Entry and Exit of Firms in the Long Run
    Skill: Conceptual
    Objective: LO 5: Explain how entry and exit ensure that perfectly competitive firms earn zero economic profit in the long run.
    AACSB Coding: Reflective Thinking
    Special Feature: None

32. If a perfectly competitive industry has a downward sloping long–run supply curve, it suggests that the demand for the industry's product is decreasing over time.
    Answer: True   ⊚ False
    Diff: 1   *Type: TF*   *Page Ref: 398/398*
    Topic: "If Everyone Can Do It, You Can't Make Money at It" – The Entry and Exit of Firms in the Long Run
    Skill: Conceptual
    Objective: LO 5: Explain how entry and exit ensure that perfectly competitive firms earn zero economic profit in the long run.
    AACSB Coding: Reflective Thinking
    Special Feature: None

33. Suppose there are economies of scale in the production a specialized memory chip that is used in manufacturing microwaves. This suggests that the microwave industry is a decreasing–cost industry.
    Answer: ⊚ True   False
    Diff: 2   *Type: TF*   *Page Ref: 398/398*
    Topic: "If Everyone Can Do It, You Can't Make Money at It" – The Entry and Exit of Firms in the Long Run
    Skill: Conceptual
    Objective: LO 5: Explain how entry and exit ensure that perfectly competitive firms earn zero economic profit in the long run.
    AACSB Coding: Reflective Thinking
    Special Feature: None

34. A perfectly competitive firm in an increasing-cost industry faces an upward sloping long-run demand curve.

    Answer: True   ⊙ False
    Diff: 1   Type: TF   Page Ref: 398/398
    Topic: "If Everyone Can Do It, You Can't Make Money at It" – The Entry and Exit of Firms in the Long Run
    Skill: Conceptual
    Objective: LO 5: Explain how entry and exit ensure that perfectly competitive firms earn zero economic profit in the long run.
    AACSB Coding: Reflective Thinking
    Special Feature: None

35. In an increasing cost industry the long-run supply curve is upward sloping.

    Answer: ⊙ True   False
    Diff: 1   Type: TF   Page Ref: 398/398
    Topic: "If Everyone Can Do It, You Can't Make Money at It" – The Entry and Exit of Firms in the Long Run
    Skill: Conceptual
    Objective: LO 5: Explain how entry and exit ensure that perfectly competitive firms earn zero economic profit in the long run.
    AACSB Coding: Reflective Thinking
    Special Feature: None

36. If a perfectly competitive industry has a perfectly elastic long-run supply curve, then input prices remain constant as the industry expands.

    Answer: ⊙ True   False
    Diff: 2   Type: TF   Page Ref: 398/398
    Topic: "If Everyone Can Do It, You Can't Make Money at It" – The Entry and Exit of Firms in the Long Run
    Skill: Conceptual
    Objective: LO 5: Explain how entry and exit ensure that perfectly competitive firms earn zero economic profit in the long run.
    AACSB Coding: Reflective Thinking
    Special Feature: None

37. Assume that the personal computer industry is perfectly competitive. The fact that the price of personal computers over the last decade has fallen, despite increases in demand signifies that the industry is a decreasing-cost industry.

    Answer: ⊙ True   False
    Diff: 2   Type: TF   Page Ref: 398/398
    Topic: "If Everyone Can Do It, You Can't Make Money at It" – The Entry and Exit of Firms in the Long Run
    Skill: Conceptual
    Objective: LO 5: Explain how entry and exit ensure that perfectly competitive firms earn zero economic profit in the long run.
    AACSB Coding: Reflective Thinking
    Special Feature: None

11.6 Perfect Competition and Efficiency

1. How will an increase in the price of land for housing development affect apple growers who must use land to produce apples?
    A) Apple growers will earn higher profit because their land is now more valuable.
    B) It raises the opportunity cost of apple production.
    C) Apple growers will experience persistent losses if they do not sell their land to housing developers.
    D) It will raise the price of apples.
    Answer: B
    Diff: 2   Type: MC   Page Ref: 398-9/398-9
    Topic: Perfect Competition and Efficiency
    Skill: Analytical
    Objective: LO 6: Explain how perfect competition leads to economic efficiency.
    AACSB Coding: Reflective Thinking
    Special Feature: Making the Connection: The Decline of Apple Production in New York State

2. Which of the following describes a situation in which a good or service is produced at the lowest possible cost?
    A) productive efficiency
    B) allocative efficiency
    C) profit maximization
    D) marginal efficiency
    Answer: A
    Diff: 1   Type: MC   Page Ref: 399/399
    Topic: Perfect Competition and Efficiency
    Skill: Definition
    Objective: LO 6: Explain how perfect competition leads to economic efficiency.
    AACSB Coding: Reflective Thinking
    Special Feature: None

3. What is productive efficiency?
    A) a situation in which resources are allocated such the last unit of output produced provides a marginal benefit to consumers equal to the marginal cost of producing it
    B) a situation in which resources are allocated such that goods can be produced at their lowest possible average cost
    C) a situation in which resources are allocated to their highest profit use
    D) a situation in which firms produce as much as possible
    Answer: B
    Diff: 1   Type: MC   Page Ref: 399/399
    Topic: Perfect Competition and Efficiency
    Skill: Definition
    Objective: LO 6: Explain how perfect competition leads to economic efficiency.
    AACSB Coding: Reflective Thinking
    Special Feature: None

4. The perfectly competitive market structure benefits consumers because
    A) firms produce high quality goods at low prices.
    B) firms add a much smaller markup over average cost than firms in any other type of market structure.
    C) firms do not produce goods at the lowest possible price in the long run.
    D) firms are forced by competitive pressure to be as efficient as possible.
Answer: D
Diff: 2   Type: MC   Page Ref: 399/399
Topic: Perfect Competition and Efficiency
Skill: Conceptual
Objective: LO 6: Explain how perfect competition leads to economic efficiency.
AACSB Coding: Reflective Thinking
Special Feature: None

5. I the long-run average cost curve is U-shaped, the optimal scale of production from society's viewpoint is
    A) where firm profit is large enough to finance research and development.
    B) one which guarantees economic profit.
    C) where maximum economic profit is earned by producers.
    D) the minimum efficient scale.
Answer: D
Diff: 2   Type: MC   Page Ref: 399/399
Topic: Perfect Competition and Efficiency
Skill: Conceptual
Objective: LO 6: Explain how perfect competition leads to economic efficiency.
AACSB Coding: Reflective Thinking
Special Feature: None

6. Which of the following describes a situation in which every good or service is produced up to the point where the last unit provides a marginal benefit to consumers equal to the marginal cost of producing it?
    A) productive efficiency
    B) profit maximization
    C) marginal efficiency
    D) allocative efficiency
Answer: D
Diff: 1   Type: MC   Page Ref: 401/401
Topic: Perfect Competition and Efficiency
Skill: Definition
Objective: LO 6: Explain how perfect competition leads to economic efficiency.
AACSB Coding: Reflective Thinking
Special Feature: None

7. What is allocative efficiency?
   A) It refers to a situation in which resources are allocated such that goods can be produced at their lowest possible average cost.
   B) It refers to a situation in which resources are allocated to their highest profit use.
   C) It refers to a situation in which resources are allocated such the last unit of output produced provides a marginal benefit to consumers equal to the marginal cost of producing it.
   D) It refers to a situation in which resources are allocated fairly to all consumers in a society.
   Answer: C
   Diff: 1   Type: MC   Page Ref: 401/401
   Topic: Perfect Competition and Efficiency
   Skill: Definition
   Objective: LO 6: Explain how perfect competition leads to economic efficiency.
   AACSB Coding: Reflective Thinking
   Special Feature: None

8. A perfectly competitive industry achieves allocative efficiency because
   A) it produces where market price equals marginal production cost.
   B) firms carry production surpluses.
   C) goods and services are produced up to the point where the last unit provides a marginal benefit to consumers equal to the marginal cost of producing it.
   D) goods and services are produced at the lowest possible cost.
   Answer: C
   Diff: 2   Type: MC   Page Ref: 401/401
   Topic: Perfect Competition and Efficiency
   Skill: Conceptual
   Objective: LO 6: Explain how perfect competition leads to economic efficiency.
   AACSB Coding: Reflective Thinking
   Special Feature: None

Figure 11-12

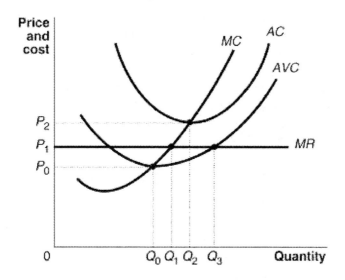

9. *Refer to Figure 11–12.* If the market price is P_1, what is the allocatively efficient output level?

   A) Q_1

   B) Q_0

   C) Q_2

   D) There is no allocatively efficient output level because the firm is making a loss.

Answer: A

Diff: 2   Type: MC   Page Ref: 401/401
Topic: Perfect Competition and Efficiency
Skill: Analytical
Objective: LO 6: Explain how perfect competition leads to economic efficiency.
AACSB Coding: Analytic Skills
Special Feature: None

10. Assume that the LCD and plasma television sets industry is perfectly competitive. Suppose a producer develops a successful innovation that enables it to lower its cost of production. What happens in the short run and in the long run?
    A) The firm will be able to increase its profits temporarily but in the long run, profits will be eliminated as other firms copy the innovation.
    B) The firm will probably incur losses temporarily because of the high cost of the innovation but in the long run it will start earning positive profits.
    C) Initially, the firm will be able to increase its profit significantly but in the long run its profits will still be greater than zero but lower than its short run profits because other firms would also innovate.
    D) This firm will be able to earn above normal profits indefinitely if it obtains a patent for its innovation.
    Answer: A
    Diff: 3   Type: MC   Page Ref: 399/399
    Topic: Perfect Competition and Efficiency
    Skill: Analytical
    Objective: LO 6: Explain how perfect competition leads to economic efficiency.
    AACSB Coding: Reflective Thinking
    Special Feature: Solved Problem: How Productive Efficiency Benefits Consumers

11. In early 2007, Pioneer and JVC, two Japanese electronics firms, each announced that their profits were going to be lower than expected because they had both had to cut prices for LCD and plasma television sets. Which of the following could explain why these firms did not simply raise their prices and increase their profits?
    A) In perfect competition, prices are determined by the market and firms will keep lowering prices until there are no profits to be earned.
    B) Most likely, intense competition between these two major producers probably pushed prices down. Thereafter, each feared that it would lose its customers to the other if it raised its prices.
    C) The firms are still making profits, just not as high as expected so there is room to lower prices until one can force the other out of business.
    D) The move to cut prices is probably just a temporary one to gain market share. In the long run the firms will raise prices and be able to increase their profits.
    Answer: B
    Diff: 3   Type: MC   Page Ref: 399/399
    Topic: Perfect Competition and Efficiency
    Skill: Analytical
    Objective: LO 6: Explain how perfect competition leads to economic efficiency.
    AACSB Coding: Reflective Thinking
    Special Feature: Solved Problem: How Productive Efficiency Benefits Consumers

12. Writing in the *New York Times* on the technology boom of the late 1990s, Michael Lewis argues, "The sad truth, for investors, seems to be that most of the benefits of new technologies are passed right through to consumers free of charge." What does Lewis means by the benefits of new technology being "passed right through to consumers free of charge"?

   A) Firms in perfect competition are price takers. Since they cannot influence price, they cannot dictate who benefits from new technologies, even if the benefits of new technology being "passed right through to consumers free of charge."

   B) In perfect competition, consumers place a value on the food equal to its marginal cost of production and since they are willing to pay the marginal valuation of the good, they are essentially receiving the new technology "free of charge."

   C) In the long run, price equals the lowest possible average cost of production. In this sense, consumers receive the new technology "free of charge."

   D) In perfect competition, price equals marginal cost of production. In this sense, consumers receive the new technology "free of charge."

Answer: C
Diff: 3   Type: MC   Page Ref: 399/399
Topic: Perfect Competition and Efficiency
Skill: Analytical
Objective: LO 6: Explain how perfect competition leads to economic efficiency.
AACSB Coding: Reflective Thinking
Special Feature: Solved Problem: How Productive Efficiency Benefits Consumers

13. According to Craig Johnson, president of retail consulting group Customer Growth Partners,
   "Wal–Mart's foray into organics should help to bring down prices for consumers."
   Which of the following statements supports Mr. Johnson's argument?
   Source: Parija Bhatnagar,"Wal–Mart's Next Conquest: Organics" CNNMoney.com, May 1, 2006

   A) Wal-Mart has a reputation for deliberately lowering prices to force its competitors out of the market.

   B) By expanding the organic market, Wal–Mart would bring in economies of scale that would, when added to a competitive market, drive down prices.

   C) Wal–Mart is large enough that it can successfully pressure the U.S. Department of Agriculture to force organic food farmers to lower their prices.

   D) Wal-Mart's core customer base is the low–income consumer. Therefore, to compete for this customer group, organic food farmers will be compelled to lower prices.

Answer: B
Diff: 2   Type: MC   Page Ref: 402-3/402-3
Topic: Perfect Competition and Efficiency
Skill: Analytical
Objective: LO 6: Explain how perfect competition leads to economic efficiency.
AACSB Coding: Analytic Skills
Special Feature: An Inside Look: Why are Organic Farmers Worried about Wal-mart?

14. While many small–scale organic farmers are concerned about Wal–Mart's entry into the organic food market, large corporations like Whole Foods and Wild Oats are not too worried. According to Sonja Tuitele, spokeswoman for Wild Oats, There's very little overlap between our shoppers and Wal-Mart's. We're a specialty retailer and our customers don't focus on price first." What does this imply about the price elasticity of demand for organic produce for the two groups of customers?

    Source: Parija Bhatnagar,"Wal–Mart's Next Conquest: Organics" CNNMoney.com, May 1, 2006

    A) No conclusions can be made about the relative price elasticities between Wal-Mart's customers and customers at Whole Foods and Wild Oats.

    B) For organic products, Wal-Mart's customers are likely to have the same price elasticity of demand as customers who shop at Whole Foods and Wild Oats, although the two groups may have different income elasticities.

    C) Wal-Mart's customers are likely to have a higher price elasticity of demand compared to customers who shop at Whole Foods and Wild Oats.

    D) Wal-Mart's customers are likely to have a lower price elasticity of demand compared to customers who shop at Whole Foods and Wild Oats.

    Answer: C

    Diff: 2   Type: MC   Page Ref: 402–3/402–3
    Topic: Perfect Competition and Efficiency
    Skill: Analytical
    Objective: LO 6: Explain how perfect competition leads to economic efficiency.
    AACSB Coding: Analytic Skills
    Special Feature: An Inside Look: Why are Organic Farmers Worried about Wal-mart?

15. Farmers in California are taking resources out of non-organic produce farming and putting them into organic produce farming. This suggests that at present, organic produce farmers earn economic profits.

    Answer: ◉ True   False

    Diff: 2   Type: TF   Page Ref: 402–3/402–3
    Topic: Perfect Competition and Efficiency
    Skill: Analytical
    Objective: LO 6: Explain how perfect competition leads to economic efficiency.
    AACSB Coding: Analytic Skills
    Special Feature: An Inside Look: Why are Organic Farmers Worried about Wal-mart?

16. In a market system, entrepreneurs will not continue to employ resources to produce a product unless consumers are willing to pay a price at least high enough for them to break even.

    Answer: ◉ True   False

    Diff: 2   Type: TF   Page Ref: 399/399
    Topic: Perfect Competition and Efficiency
    Skill: Conceptual
    Objective: LO 6: Explain how perfect competition leads to economic efficiency.
    AACSB Coding: Reflective Thinking
    Special Feature: Making the Connection: The Decline of Apple Production in New York State

17. If a firm in a perfectly competitive industry introduces a lower-cost way of producing an existing product, the firm will be able to earn economic profits in the long run.
    Answer: True   ⊚ False
    Diff: 2   Type: TF   Page Ref: 399/399
    Topic: Perfect Competition and Efficiency
    Skill: Conceptual
    Objective: LO 6: Explain how perfect competition leads to economic efficiency.
    AACSB Coding: Reflective Thinking
    Special Feature: None

18. If productive efficiency characterizes an industry, firms in that industry are using the best technology available to produce the goods.
    Answer: True   ⊚ False
    Diff: 1   Type: TF   Page Ref: 399/399
    Topic: Perfect Competition and Efficiency
    Skill: Definition
    Objective: LO 6: Explain how perfect competition leads to economic efficiency.
    AACSB Coding: Reflective Thinking
    Special Feature: None

19. A perfectly competitive firm in long-run equilibrium produces output at the lowest possible average total cost.
    Answer: ⊚ True   False
    Diff: 1   Type: TF   Page Ref: 399/399
    Topic: Perfect Competition and Efficiency
    Skill: Conceptual
    Objective: LO 6: Explain how perfect competition leads to economic efficiency.
    AACSB Coding: Reflective Thinking
    Special Feature: None

20. Firms in perfect competition produce the productively efficient output level in the short run and in the long run.
    Answer: True   ⊚ False
    Diff: 2   Type: TF   Page Ref: 399/399
    Topic: Perfect Competition and Efficiency
    Skill: Analytical
    Objective: LO 6: Explain how perfect competition leads to economic efficiency.
    AACSB Coding: Analytic Skills
    Special Feature: None

21. Firms in perfect competition produce the allocatively efficient output in the short run and in the long run.
    Answer: ⊚ True   False
    Diff: 2   Type: TF   Page Ref: 401/401
    Topic: Perfect Competition and Efficiency
    Skill: Analytical
    Objective: LO 6: Explain how perfect competition leads to economic efficiency.
    AACSB Coding: Analytic Skills
    Special Feature: None

Chapter 12   Monopolistic Competition: The Competitive Model in a More Realistic Setting

12.1   Demand and Marginal Revenue for a Firm in a Monopolistically Competitive Market

1. One reason why the coffeehouse market is competitive is that
   A) demand for specialty coffee is very high.
   B) barriers to entry are low.
   C) consumption takes place in public.
   D) it is trendy and therefore is likely to have a customer following.
   Answer: B
   Diff: 1   Type: MC   Page Ref: 410/410
   Topic: Demand and Marginal Revenue for a Firm in a Monopolistically Competitive Market
   Skill: Conceptual
   Objective: LO 1: Explain why a monopolistically competitive firm has downward–sloping
   *   demand and marginal revenue curve.*
   AACSB Coding: Reflective Thinking
   Special Feature: Chapter Opener: Starbucks: Growth through Product Differentiation

2. Firms such as Caribou Coffee and Diedrich Coffee operate hundreds of coffeehouses nationwide while firms such as Dunn Brothers Coffee operate only in four states. How would you characterize these stores?
   A) Caribou Coffee and Diedrich Coffee are oligopolists while Dunn Brothers is a monopolistic competitor.
   B) Caribou Coffee and Diedrich Coffee are duopolists while Dunn Brothers is an oligopolist
   C) Caribou Coffee and Diedrich Coffee are duopolists while Dunn Brothers is a monopolistic competitor.
   D) They are all monopolistic competitor.
   Answer: D
   Diff: 1   Type: MC   Page Ref: 410/410
   Topic: Demand and Marginal Revenue for a Firm in a Monopolistically Competitive Market
   Skill: Conceptual
   Objective: LO 1: Explain why a monopolistically competitive firm has downward–sloping
   *   demand and marginal revenue curve.*
   AACSB Coding: Reflective Thinking
   Special Feature: Chapter Opener: Starbucks: Growth through Product Differentiation

3. The key characteristics of a monopolistically competitive market structure include
    A) many small (relative to the total market) sellers acting independently.
    B) sellers have no incentive to advertise their products.
    C) barriers to entry are strong.
    D) all sellers sell a homogeneous product.
Answer: A
Diff: 1   Type: MC   Page Ref: 412/412
Topic: Demand and Marginal Revenue for a Firm in a Monopolistically Competitive Market
Skill: Conceptual
Objective: LO 1: Explain why a monopolistically competitive firm has downward-sloping
            demand and marginal revenue curve.
AACSB Coding: Reflective Thinking
Special Feature: None

4. Which of the following characteristics is not common to monopolistic competition
    and perfect competition?
    A) Firms take market prices as given.
    B) Entry barriers into the industry are low.
    C) Firms act to maximize profit.
    D) The market demand curve is downward –sloping.
Answer: A
Diff: 2   Type: MC   Page Ref: 412/412
Topic: Demand and Marginal Revenue for a Firm in a Monopolistically Competitive Market
Skill: Conceptual
Objective: LO 1: Explain why a monopolistically competitive firm has downward-sloping
            demand and marginal revenue curve.
AACSB Coding: Reflective Thinking
Special Feature: None

5. Which of the following characteristics is common to monopolistic competition and
    perfect competition?
    A) Entry barriers into the industry are low.
    B) Firms produce identical products.
    C) Firms take market prices as given.
    D) Each firm faces a downward –sloping demand curve.
Answer: A
Diff: 2   Type: MC   Page Ref: 412/412
Topic: Demand and Marginal Revenue for a Firm in a Monopolistically Competitive Market
Skill: Conceptual
Objective: LO 1: Explain why a monopolistically competitive firm has downward-sloping
            demand and marginal revenue curve.
AACSB Coding: Reflective Thinking
Special Feature: None

6. A major difference between monopolistic competition and perfect competition is
   A) that products are not standardized in monopolistic competition unlike in perfect competition
   B) the degree by which the market demand curves slope downwards
   C) the barriers to entry in the two markets
   D) the number of sellers in the markets
   Answer: A
   Diff: 2   Type: MC   Page Ref: 412/412
   Topic: Demand and Marginal Revenue for a Firm in a Monopolistically Competitive Market
   Skill: Conceptual
   Objective: LO 1: Explain why a monopolistically competitive firm has downward-sloping demand and marginal revenue curve.
   AACSB Coding: Reflective Thinking
   Special Feature: None

7. The key characteristics of a monopolistically competitive market structure include
   A) high barriers to entry.
   B) few sellers.
   C) sellers acting to maximize revenue.
   D) sellers selling similar but differentiated products.
   Answer: D
   Diff: 1   Type: MC   Page Ref: 412/412
   Topic: Demand and Marginal Revenue for a Firm in a Monopolistically Competitive Market
   Skill: Conceptual
   Objective: LO 1: Explain why a monopolistically competitive firm has downward-sloping demand and marginal revenue curve.
   AACSB Coding: Reflective Thinking
   Special Feature: None

8. In what sense is a firm in monopolistically competition a monopoly in its market?
   A) It acts independently of other sellers.
   B) It sells a unique product.
   C) It acts to maximize market share.
   D) It is able to erect entry barriers by deliberately lowering its price.
   Answer: B
   Diff: 1   Type: MC   Page Ref: 412/412
   Topic: Demand and Marginal Revenue for a Firm in a Monopolistically Competitive Market
   Skill: Conceptual
   Objective: LO 1: Explain why a monopolistically competitive firm has downward-sloping demand and marginal revenue curve.
   AACSB Coding: Reflective Thinking
   Special Feature: None

9. Which of the following firms is not an example of a monopolistically competitive market?
    A) Makers of women's clothing
    B) Video stores
    C) Automobile producers
    D) Supermarkets
Answer: C
Diff: 2   Type: MC   Page Ref: 412/412
Topic: Demand and Marginal Revenue for a Firm in a Monopolistically Competitive Market
Skill: Conceptual
Objective: LO 1: Explain why a monopolistically competitive firm has downward–sloping demand and marginal revenue curve.
AACSB Coding: Reflective Thinking
Special Feature: None

10. In the United States, the average person mostly patronizes firms that operate in
    A) perfectly competitive markets.
    B) monopolistically competitive markets.
    C) monopoly markets.
    D) oligopoly markets.
Answer: B
Diff: 1   Type: MC   Page Ref: 412/412
Topic: Demand and Marginal Revenue for a Firm in a Monopolistically Competitive Market
Skill: Factual
Objective: LO 1: Explain why a monopolistically competitive firm has downward–sloping demand and marginal revenue curve.
AACSB Coding: Reflective Thinking
Special Feature: None

11. In monopolistic competition there is/are
    A) only one seller who faces a downward–sloping demand curve.
    B) a few sellers who each face a downward–sloping demand curve.
    C) many sellers who each face a perfectly elastic demand curve.
    D) many sellers who each face a downward–sloping demand curve.
Answer: D
Diff: 1   Type: MC   Page Ref: 412/412
Topic: Demand and Marginal Revenue for a Firm in a Monopolistically Competitive Market
Skill: Conceptual
Objective: LO 1: Explain why a monopolistically competitive firm has downward–sloping demand and marginal revenue curve.
AACSB Coding: Reflective Thinking
Special Feature: None

12. Which of the following is true for a firm with a downward–sloping demand curve for its product?
    A) Price, average revenue, and marginal revenue are all equal.
    B) Price equals average revenue but is greater than marginal revenue.
    C) Price, average revenue, and marginal revenue are all different.
    D) Price equals average revenue but is less than marginal revenue.
    Answer: B
    Diff: 2   Type: MC   Page Ref: 413/413
    Topic: Demand and Marginal Revenue for a Firm in a Monopolistically Competitive Market
    Skill: Conceptual
    Objective: LO 1: Explain why a monopolistically competitive firm has downward–sloping demand and marginal revenue curve.
    AACSB Coding: Reflective Thinking
    Special Feature: None

13. If a firm faces a downward–sloping demand curve,
    A) the demand for its product must be inelastic.
    B) it must reduce its price to sell more units.
    C) it can control both price and quantity sold.
    D) it will always make a profit.
    Answer: B
    Diff: 2   Type: MC   Page Ref: 413/413
    Topic: Demand and Marginal Revenue for a Firm in a Monopolistically Competitive Market
    Skill: Conceptual
    Objective: LO 1: Explain why a monopolistically competitive firm has downward–sloping demand and marginal revenue curve.
    AACSB Coding: Reflective Thinking
    Special Feature: None

14. A monopolistically competitive firm faces a downward–sloping demand curve because
    A) it is able to control price and quantity demanded.
    B) of product differentiation.
    C) its market decisions are affected by the decisions of its rivals.
    D) there are few substitutes for its product.
    Answer: B
    Diff: 1   Type: MC   Page Ref: 412/412
    Topic: Demand and Marginal Revenue for a Firm in a Monopolistically Competitive Market
    Skill: Conceptual
    Objective: LO 1: Explain why a monopolistically competitive firm has downward–sloping demand and marginal revenue curve.
    AACSB Coding: Analytic Skills
    Special Feature: None

15. What type of demand curve does a monopolistically competitive firm face?
    A) Vertical
    B) Downward sloping
    C) Horizontal
    D) Upward sloping
    Answer: B
    Diff: 2   Type: MC   Page Ref: 412/412
    Topic: Demand and Marginal Revenue for a Firm in a Monopolistically Competitive Market
    Skill: Conceptual
    Objective: LO 1: Explain why a monopolistically competitive firm has downward–sloping
              demand and marginal revenue curve.
    AACSB Coding: Reflective Thinking
    Special Feature: None

16. A monopolistically competitive firm will
    A) always produce at the minimum efficient scale of production.
    B) have some control over its price because its product is differentiated.
    C) produce an output level that is productively and allocatively efficient.
    D) charge the same price as its competitors do.
    Answer: B
    Diff: 2   Type: MC   Page Ref: 412/412
    Topic: Demand and Marginal Revenue for a Firm in a Monopolistically Competitive Market
    Skill: Conceptual
    Objective: LO 1: Explain why a monopolistically competitive firm has downward–sloping
              demand and marginal revenue curve.
    AACSB Coding: Reflective Thinking
    Special Feature: None

17. Which of the following is true of a typical firm in a monopolistically competitive industry?
    A) Each firm acts independently.
    B) The more successful firms have an incentive to merge in order to exert greater market power.
    C) Product differentiation allows a successful firm to emerge as a market leader in the industry.
    D) All firms have identical cost structures.
    Answer: A
    Diff: 1   Type: MC   Page Ref: 412/412
    Topic: Demand and Marginal Revenue for a Firm in a Monopolistically Competitive Market
    Skill: Conceptual
    Objective: LO 1: Explain why a monopolistically competitive firm has downward–sloping
              demand and marginal revenue curve.
    AACSB Coding: Reflective Thinking
    Special Feature: None

18. For a monopolistically competitive firm, marginal revenue
    A) is greater than the price.
    B) is less than the price.
    C) and price are unrelated.
    D) equals the price.
    Answer: B
    Diff: 2   Type: MC   Page Ref: 414/414
    Topic: Demand and Marginal Revenue for a Firm in a Monopolistically Competitive Market
    Skill: Conceptual
    Objective: LO 1: Explain why a monopolistically competitive firm has downward-sloping
                demand and marginal revenue curve.
    AACSB Coding: Reflective Thinking
    Special Feature: None

19. If the demand curve for a firm is downward-sloping, its marginal revenue curve
    A) will lie below the demand curve.
    B) is coincident with the demand curve.
    C) is horizontal.
    D) will lie above the demand curve,
    Answer: A
    Diff: 2   Type: MC   Page Ref: 414/414
    Topic: Demand and Marginal Revenue for a Firm in a Monopolistically Competitive Market
    Skill: Conceptual
    Objective: LO 1: Explain why a monopolistically competitive firm has downward-sloping
                demand and marginal revenue curve.
    AACSB Coding: Reflective Thinking
    Special Feature: None

20. When a monopolistically competitive firm cuts its price to increase its sales, it
    experiences a gain in revenue due to the
    A) income effect.
    B) substitution effect.
    C) price effect.
    D) output effect.
    Answer: D
    Diff: 2   Type: MC   Page Ref: 413/413
    Topic: Demand and Marginal Revenue for a Firm in a Monopolistically Competitive Market
    Skill: Conceptual
    Objective: LO 1: Explain why a monopolistically competitive firm has downward-sloping
                demand and marginal revenue curve.
    AACSB Coding: Reflective Thinking
    Special Feature: None

21. When a monopolistically competitive firm cuts its price to increase its sales, it experiences a loss in revenue due to the
    A) substitution effect.
    B) price effect.
    C) output effect.
    D) income effect.
Answer: B
Diff: 2   Type: MC   Page Ref: 413/413
Topic: Demand and Marginal Revenue for a Firm in a Monopolistically Competitive Market
Skill: Conceptual
Objective: LO 1: Explain why a monopolistically competitive firm has downward–sloping demand and marginal revenue curve.
AACSB Coding: Reflective Thinking
Special Feature: None

22. Suppose a monopolistically competitive firm sells 25 units at a price of $10. Calculate its marginal revenue per unit of output if it sells 5 more units of output when it reduced its price to $9.
    A) $20.
    B) $2.50
    C) $4.
    D) $270.
Answer: C
Diff: 3   Type: MC   Page Ref: 413/413
Topic: Demand and Marginal Revenue for a Firm in a Monopolistically Competitive Market
Skill: Analytical
Objective: LO 1: Explain why a monopolistically competitive firm has downward–sloping demand and marginal revenue curve.
AACSB Coding: Analytic Skills
Special Feature: None

Table 12–1

Quantity	Price (Dollars)	Total Revenue (Dollars)
1	$7.50	$7.50
2	7.00	14.00
3	6.50	19.50
4	6.00	24.00
5	5.50	27.50
6	5.00	30.00

23. *Refer to Table 12–1.* What is the marginal revenue of the 3rd unit?
    A) $0.50
    B) $5.50
    C) $1.83
    D) $6.50
    Answer: B
    Diff: 1   Type: MC   Page Ref: 413/413
    Topic: Demand and Marginal Revenue for a Firm in a Monopolistically Competitive Market
    Skill: Analytical
    *Objective: LO 1: Explain why a monopolistically competitive firm has downward–sloping
                demand and marginal revenue curve.*
    AACSB Coding: Analytic Skills
    Special Feature: None

24. *Refer to Table 12–1.* The Table shows
    A) a demand curve with an elastic segment of the demand curve from $7.50 to
        $6.50 followed by an inelastic segment.
    B) an inelastic segment of the demand curve.
    C) a demand curve with an inelastic segment of the demand curve from $7.50 to
        $6.50 followed by an elastic segment.
    D) an elastic segment of the demand curve.
    Answer: D
    Diff: 1   Type: MC   Page Ref: 413/413
    Topic: Demand and Marginal Revenue for a Firm in a Monopolistically Competitive Market
    Skill: Analytical
    *Objective: LO 1: Explain why a monopolistically competitive firm has downward–sloping
                demand and marginal revenue curve.*
    AACSB Coding: Analytic Skills
    Special Feature: None

25. ***Refer to Table 12–1.*** What portion of the marginal revenue of the 4th unit is due to the output effect and what portion is due to the price effect?
    A) Output effect = $6.50; Price effect = $2.00
    B) Output effect = -$0.50; Price effect = $5.00
    C) Output effect = $24.00; Price effect = $19.50
    D) Output effect = $6.00; Price effect = -$1.50
    Answer: D
    Diff: 2   Type: MC   Page Ref: 413/413
    Topic: Demand and Marginal Revenue for a Firm in a Monopolistically Competitive Market
    Skill: Analytical
    Objective: LO 1: Explain why a monopolistically competitive firm has downward–sloping
        demand and marginal revenue curve.
    AACSB Coding: Analytic Skills
    Special Feature: None

26. ***Refer to Table 12–1.*** What portion of the marginal revenue of the 5th unit is due to the output effect and what portion is due to the price effect?
    A) Output effect = $4.00; Price effect = -$0.50
    B) Output effect = $5.50; Price effect = -$2.00
    C) Output effect = $3.00; Price effect = $0.50
    D) Output effect = $1.50; Price effect = $2.00
    Answer: B
    Diff: 2   Type: MC   Page Ref: 413/413
    Topic: Demand and Marginal Revenue for a Firm in a Monopolistically Competitive Market
    Skill: Analytical
    Objective: LO 1: Explain why a monopolistically competitive firm has downward–sloping
        demand and marginal revenue curve.
    AACSB Coding: Analytic Skills
    Special Feature: None

Figure 12–1

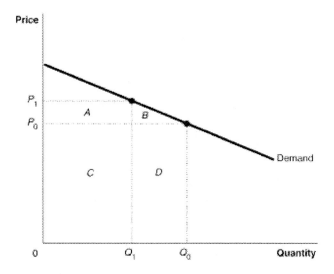

27. **Refer to Figure 12–1.** The marginal revenue from the increase in price from P_0 to P_1 equals

    A) the area $(A-D)$.

    B) the area $(C-B)$.

    C) the area $(B+D-A)$

    D) the area A.

Answer: A

Diff: 2   Type: MC   Page Ref: 414/414

Topic: Demand and Marginal Revenue for a Firm in a Monopolistically Competitive Market

Skill: Analytical

Objective: LO 1: Explain why a monopolistically competitive firm has downward-sloping demand and marginal revenue curve.

AACSB Coding: Analytic Skills

Special Feature: None

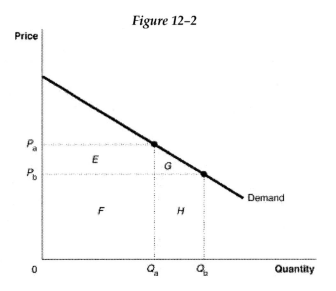

Figure 12–2

28. ***Refer to Figure 12–2.*** The marginal revenue from selling the additional unit Q_b instead of Q_a equals
    A) the area G.
    B) the area $(G+H)$.
    C) the area $(H-E)$.
    D) the area $(E+F) - (G+H)$.
    Answer: C
    Diff: 2   Type: MC   Page Ref: 414/414
    Topic: Demand and Marginal Revenue for a Firm in a Monopolistically Competitive Market
    Skill: Analytical
    Objective: LO 1: Explain why a monopolistically competitive firm has downward–sloping demand and marginal revenue curve.
    AACSB Coding: Analytic Skills
    Special Feature: None

29. Which of the following statements is true about marginal revenue?
    A) If marginal revenue is zero, it means that quantity demanded falls to zero when a firm changes its price.
    B) If marginal revenue is positive, the additional revenue received from selling 1 more unit of the good is smaller than the revenue lost from receiving a lower price on all the units that could have been sold at the original price.
    C) If marginal revenue is negative, the additional revenue received from selling 1 more unit of the good is smaller than the revenue lost from receiving a lower price on all the units that could have been sold at the original price.
    D) Marginal revenue increases as price falls and quantity sold increases.
    Answer: C
    Diff: 2   Type: MC   Page Ref: 413–4/413–4
    Topic: Demand and Marginal Revenue for a Firm in a Monopolistically Competitive Market
    Skill: Conceptual
    Objective: LO 1: Explain why a monopolistically competitive firm has downward–sloping demand and marginal revenue curve.
    AACSB Coding: Reflective Thinking
    Special Feature: None

30. Firms in monopolistic competition compete by selling similar, but not identical products.
    Answer: ◦ True   False
    Diff: 1   Type: TF   Page Ref: 412/412
    Topic: Demand and Marginal Revenue for a Firm in a Monopolistically Competitive Market
    Skill: Conceptual
    Objective: LO 1: Explain why a monopolistically competitive firm has downward-sloping
    *   demand and marginal revenue curve.*
    AACSB Coding: Reflective Thinking
    Special Feature: None

31. In monopolistic competition, if a firm produces a highly desirable product relative to its competitors, the firm will be able to raise its price without losing any customers.
    Answer: True   ◦ False
    Diff: 1   Type: TF   Page Ref: 413/413
    Topic: Demand and Marginal Revenue for a Firm in a Monopolistically Competitive Market
    Skill: Conceptual
    Objective: LO 1: Explain why a monopolistically competitive firm has downward-sloping
    *   demand and marginal revenue curve.*
    AACSB Coding: Reflective Thinking
    Special Feature: None

32. For a downward-sloping demand curve, marginal revenue decreases as quantity sold increases.
    Answer: ◦ True   False
    Diff: 1   Type: TF   Page Ref: 413/413
    Topic: Demand and Marginal Revenue for a Firm in a Monopolistically Competitive Market
    Skill: Conceptual
    Objective: LO 1: Explain why a monopolistically competitive firm has downward-sloping
    *   demand and marginal revenue curve.*
    AACSB Coding: Reflective Thinking
    Special Feature: None

33. When a monopolistically competitive firm cuts its price to increase its sales, it experiences a
    loss in revenue due to the income effect and a gain in revenue due to the substitution effect
    Answer: True   ◦ False
    Diff: 1   Type: TF   Page Ref: 413/413
    Topic: Demand and Marginal Revenue for a Firm in a Monopolistically Competitive Market
    Skill: Conceptual
    Objective: LO 1: Explain why a monopolistically competitive firm has downward-sloping
    *   demand and marginal revenue curve.*
    AACSB Coding: Reflective Thinking
    Special Feature: None

34. If marginal revenue is negative then the revenue lost from receiving a lower price on all the units that could have been sold at the original price is smaller than the additional revenue from selling one more unit of the good.
    Answer: True   ⊚ False
    Diff: 2   *Type: TF*   *Page Ref: 415/415*
    Topic: Demand and Marginal Revenue for a Firm in a Monopolistically Competitive Market
    Skill: Conceptual
    Objective: LO 1: Explain why a monopolistically competitive firm has downward-sloping demand and marginal revenue curve.
    AACSB Coding: Reflective Thinking
    Special Feature: None

12.2   How a Monopolistically Competitive Firm Maximizes Profits in the Short Run

1. What is the profit-maximizing rule for a monopolistically competitive firm?
    A) to produce a quantity that maximizes market share
    B) to produce a quantity such that marginal revenue equals marginal cost
    C) to produce a quantity such that price equals marginal cost
    D) to produce a quantity that maximizes total revenue
    Answer: B
    Diff: 1   *Type: MC*   *Page Ref: 415/415*
    Topic: How a Monopolistically Competitive Firm Maximizes Profits in the Short Run
    Skill: Conceptual
    Objective: LO 2: Explain how a monopolistically competitive firm maximizes profits in the short run.
    AACSB Coding: Reflective Thinking
    Special Feature: None

2. A monopolistically competitive firm maximizes profit where
    A) total revenue > marginal cost.
    B) price > marginal cost.
    C) marginal revenue > average revenue.
    D) price = marginal revenue.
    Answer: B
    Diff: 2   *Type: MC*   *Page Ref: 415/415*
    Topic: How a Monopolistically Competitive Firm Maximizes Profits in the Short Run
    Skill: Conceptual
    Objective: LO 2: Explain how a monopolistically competitive firm maximizes profits in the short run.
    AACSB Coding: Reflective Thinking
    Special Feature: None

3. Unlike a perfectly competitive firm, for a monopolistically competitive firm
    A) marginal revenue = marginal cost at the profit maximizing output.
    B) price ≠ marginal revenue for all output levels.
    C) price ≠ average revenue for all output levels.
    D) price ≠ marginal cost for all output levels.
Answer: B
Diff: 3   Type: MC   Page Ref: 415/415
Topic: How a Monopolistically Competitive Firm Maximizes Profits in the Short Run
Skill: Conceptual
Objective: LO 2: Explain how a monopolistically competitive firm maximizes profits in the
        short run.
AACSB Coding: Reflective Thinking
Special Feature: None

Table 12–2

Quantity (Cases)	Price (Dollars)	Total Revenue (Dollars)	Total Cost (Dollars)
1	$75	$75	$60
2	70	140	85
3	65	195	105
4	60	240	115
5	55	275	130
6	50	300	155
7	45	315	190
8	40	320	230
9	35	315	280

Eco Energy is a monopolistically competitive producer of a sports beverage called Power On.
Table 12–2 shows the firm's demand and cost schedules.

4. *Refer to Table 12–2.* What is the maximum output (Q) that maximizes profit and
    what is the price (P) charged?
    A) P=$55; Q=5 cases
    B) P=$50; Q=6 cases
    C) P=$45; Q=7 cases
    D) P=$40; Q=8 cases
Answer: B
Diff: 2   Type: MC   Page Ref: 416/416
Topic: How a Monopolistically Competitive Firm Maximizes Profits in the Short Run
Skill: Analytical
Objective: LO 2: Explain how a monopolistically competitive firm maximizes profits in the
        short run.
AACSB Coding: Analytic Skills
Special Feature: None

5. ***Refer to Table 12–2.*** What is Eco Energy's profit?
   A) $125
   B) $140
   C) $145
   D) $150
   Answer: C
   Diff: 2   Type: MC   Page Ref: 416/416
   Topic: How a Monopolistically Competitive Firm Maximizes Profits in the Short Run
   Skill: Analytical
   Objective: LO 2: Explain how a monopolistically competitive firm maximizes profits in the
   *   short run.*
   AACSB Coding: Analytic Skills
   Special Feature: None

6. ***Refer to Table 12–2.*** What is the marginal profit from producing and selling the 5th case?
   A) $275
   B) $145
   C) $35
   D) $20
   Answer: D
   Diff: 2   Type: MC   Page Ref: 416/416
   Topic: How a Monopolistically Competitive Firm Maximizes Profits in the Short Run
   Skill: Analytical
   Objective: LO 2: Explain how a monopolistically competitive firm maximizes profits in the
   *   short run.*
   AACSB Coding: Analytic Skills
   Special Feature: None

7. ***Refer to Table 12–2.*** What is likely to happen to the product's price in the long run?
   A) Cannot be determined without information on its long run demand curve.
   B) It will increase.
   C) It will fall.
   D) It will remain constant.
   Answer: C
   Diff: 2   Type: MC   Page Ref: 416/416
   Topic: How a Monopolistically Competitive Firm Maximizes Profits in the Short Run
   Skill: Analytical
   Objective: LO 2: Explain how a monopolistically competitive firm maximizes profits in the
   *   short run.*
   AACSB Coding: Analytic Skills
   Special Feature: None

Figure 12–3

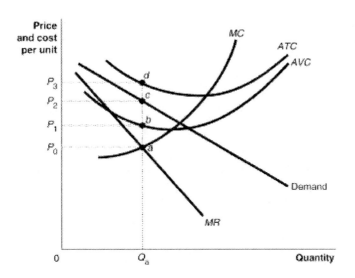

Figure 12–3 shows short run cost and demand curves for a monopolistically competitive firm in the market for designer watches.

8. ***Refer to Figure 12–3.*** If the firm represented in the diagram is currently producing and selling Q_a units, what is the price charged?

   A) $\$P_0$
   B) $\$P_1$
   C) $\$P_2$
   D) $\$P_3$

Answer: C
Diff: 1   Type: MC   Page Ref: 416/416
Topic: How a Monopolistically Competitive Firm Maximizes Profits in the Short Run
Skill: Analytical
Objective: LO 2: Explain how a monopolistically competitive firm maximizes profits in the
*   short run.*
AACSB Coding: Analytic Skills
Special Feature: None

9. **Refer to Figure 12–3.** What is the area that represents the total revenue made by the firm?
    A) $0P_3dQ_a$
    B) $0P_2cQ_a$
    C) $0P_0aQ_a$
    D) $0P_1bQ_a$

Answer: B
Diff: 2   Type: MC   Page Ref: 416/416
Topic: How a Monopolistically Competitive Firm Maximizes Profits in the Short Run
Skill: Analytical
Objective: LO 2: Explain how a monopolistically competitive firm maximizes profits in the short run.
AACSB Coding: Analytic Skills
Special Feature: None

10. **Refer to Figure 12–3.** What is the area that represents the total variable cost of production?
    A) P_0abP_1
    B) $0P_1bQ_a$
    C) $0P_0aQ_a$
    D) P_1bdP_3

Answer: B
Diff: 2   Type: MC   Page Ref: 416/416
Topic: How a Monopolistically Competitive Firm Maximizes Profits in the Short Run
Skill: Analytical
Objective: LO 2: Explain how a monopolistically competitive firm maximizes profits in the short run.
AACSB Coding: Analytic Skills
Special Feature: None

11. **Refer to Figure 12–3.** What is the area that represents the total fixed cost of production?
    A) P_0adP_3
    B) $0P_1aQ_a$
    C) P_1bdP_3
    D) That information cannot be determined from the graph.

Answer: C
Diff: 2   Type: MC   Page Ref: 416/416
Topic: How a Monopolistically Competitive Firm Maximizes Profits in the Short Run
Skill: Analytical
Objective: LO 2: Explain how a monopolistically competitive firm maximizes profits in the short run.
AACSB Coding: Analytic Skills
Special Feature: None

12. **Refer to Figure 12-3.** What is the area that represents the loss made by the firm?

    A) the area P_1bcP_2

    B) the area P_0adP_3

    C) the area P_0acP_2

    D) the area P_2cdP_3

Answer: D

Diff: 2   Type: MC   Page Ref: 416/416
Topic: How a Monopolistically Competitive Firm Maximizes Profits in the Short Run
Skill: Analytical
Objective: LO 2: Explain how a monopolistically competitive firm maximizes profits in the
        short run.
AACSB Coding: Analytic Skills
Special Feature: None

13. **Refer to Figure 12-3.** Should the firm represented in the diagram continue to stay in business despite its losses?

    A) Yes, its total revenue covers its variable cost.

    B) No, it is not able to cover its fixed cost.

    C) No, it should shut down.

    D) Yes, it should increase its revenue by raising its price.

Answer: A

Diff: 2   Type: MC   Page Ref: 416/416
Topic: How a Monopolistically Competitive Firm Maximizes Profits in the Short Run
Skill: Conceptual
Objective: LO 2: Explain how a monopolistically competitive firm maximizes profits in the
        short run.
AACSB Coding: Analytic Skills
Special Feature: None

14. In the short run, a profit maximizing firm's decision to produce should be guided by whether

    A) its total revenue exceeds its fixed cost.

    B) its marginal profit is maximized.

    C) its total revenue covers its variable cost.

    D) it makes a profit.

Answer: C

Diff: 2   Type: MC   Page Ref: 415/415
Topic: How a Monopolistically Competitive Firm Maximizes Profits in the Short Run
Skill: Conceptual
Objective: LO 2: Explain how a monopolistically competitive firm maximizes profits in the
        short run.
AACSB Coding: Reflective Thinking
Special Feature: None

15. Suppose a publishing firm is considering expanding its production of an already published book. The firm's manager wants to estimate the marginal cost of production. How can she best do this?
    A) by adding up every expense associated with the book, including the overhead like rent and editors' salaries, and then dividing by the planned number of copies to be published
    B) by using the book's selling price as an indicator of the marginal cost since price equals marginal cost is a profit maximizing rule
    C) by adding a desirable profit margin to the book's selling price to cover overheads such as rent and editor's salaries and dividing that amount by the planned number of copies to be published
    D) by adding up only the variable costs associated with a book, such as printing cost, and excluding overheads like rent and editors' salaries, and then dividing the total variable costs by the planned number of copies number of copies to be published

    Answer: D
    Diff: 2   Type: MC   Page Ref: 416/416
    Topic: How a Monopolistically Competitive Firm Maximizes Profits in the Short Run
    Skill: Conceptual
    Objective: LO 2: Explain how a monopolistically competitive firm maximizes profits in the short run.
    AACSB Coding: Reflective Thinking
    Special Feature: Solved Problem: How Not to Maximize Profits at a Publishing Company

16. If price exceeds average variable cost but is less than average total cost, a firm
    A) should shut down.
    B) should stay in business for a while longer until its fixed costs expire.
    C) is making some profit but less than maximum profit.
    D) should further differentiate its product.

    Answer: B
    Diff: 2   Type: MC   Page Ref: 415/415
    Topic: How a Monopolistically Competitive Firm Maximizes Profits in the Short Run
    Skill: Conceptual
    Objective: LO 2: Explain how a monopolistically competitive firm maximizes profits in the short run.
    AACSB Coding: Reflective Thinking
    Special Feature: None

Table 12–3

Quantity	Price (Dollars)	Total Revenue (Dollars)	Total Variable Cost (Dollars)	Total Cost (Dollars)
0	$22	$0	$0	$50
1	20	20	16	66
2	19	38	31	81
3	18	54	45	95
4	17	68	59	109
5	16	80	75	125
6	15	90	93	143
7	14	98	112	162
8	13	104	140	190
9	12	108	180	230
10	11	110	230	280

Table 12–3 shows the firm's demand and cost schedules for a firm in monopolistic competition.

17. *Refer to Table 12–3.* What is the maximum profit-maximizing/loss-minimizing output level and what is the output price (P)?
    A) Q=0 (firm should not produce)
    B) Q=3; P=$18
    C) Q=4; P=$17
    D) Q=5; P=$16
    Answer: C
    Diff: 2   Type: MC   Page Ref: 416/416
    Topic: How a Monopolistically Competitive Firm Maximizes Profits in the Short Run
    Skill: Analytical
    Objective: LO 2: Explain how a monopolistically competitive firm maximizes profits in the short run.
    AACSB Coding: Analytic Skills
    Special Feature: None

18. *Refer to Table 12–3.* What is the amount of the firm's loss at its optimal output level?
    A) $0
    B) $31
    C) $45
    D) $50
    Answer: B
    Diff: 2   Type: MC   Page Ref: 416/416
    Topic: How a Monopolistically Competitive Firm Maximizes Profits in the Short Run
    Skill: Analytical
    Objective: LO 2: Explain how a monopolistically competitive firm maximizes profits in the short run.
    AACSB Coding: Analytic Skills
    Special Feature: None

19.   *Refer to Table 12-3.* What is its average variable cost of production at its optimal output level?
      A) $0 (because its optimal output =0)
      B) $15
      C) $14.75
      D) $29
      Answer: C
      Diff: 2   Type: MC   Page Ref: 416/416
      Topic: How a Monopolistically Competitive Firm Maximizes Profits in the Short Run
      Skill: Analytical
      Objective: LO 2: Explain how a monopolistically competitive firm maximizes profits in the
                  short run.
      AACSB Coding: Analytic Skills
      Special Feature: None

20.   *Refer to Table 12-3.* What is the best course of action for the firm in the short run?
      A) It should shut down.
      B) It should not cut its price but it should increase its sales by advertising.
      C) It should increase its sales by lowering its price.
      D) It should stay in business because it covers some of its fixed cost.
      Answer: D
      Diff: 2   Type: MC   Page Ref: 416/416
      Topic: How a Monopolistically Competitive Firm Maximizes Profits in the Short Run
      Skill: Analytical
      Objective: LO 2: Explain how a monopolistically competitive firm maximizes profits in the
                  short run.
      AACSB Coding: Analytic Skills
      Special Feature: None

21.   *Refer to Table 12-3.* If this firm continue to produce, what is likely to happen to the product's price in the long run?
      A) It will remain constant.
      B) It will increase
      C) It will fall.
      D) It cannot be determined without information on its long run demand curve.
      Answer: B
      Diff: 2   Type: MC   Page Ref: 416/416
      Topic: How a Monopolistically Competitive Firm Maximizes Profits in the Short Run
      Skill: Analytical
      Objective: LO 2: Explain how a monopolistically competitive firm maximizes profits in the
                  short run.
      AACSB Coding: Analytic Skills
      Special Feature: None

22. Assume price exceeds average variable cost over the relevant range of demand. If a monopolistically competitive firm is producing at an output where marginal revenue is $23 and marginal cost is $19, then to maximize profits the firm should
    A) decrease output.
    B) continue to produce the same quantity.
    C) increase output.
    D) shutdown.
    Answer: C
    Diff: 2   Type: MC   Page Ref: 415/415
    Topic: How a Monopolistically Competitive Firm Maximizes Profits in the Short Run
    Skill: Analytical
    Objective: LO 2: Explain how a monopolistically competitive firm maximizes profits in the
             short run.
    AACSB Coding: Reflective Thinking
    Special Feature: None

23. Suppose a monopolistically competitive firm's output where marginal revenue equals marginal is 66 units and the output price corresponding tot this quantity is $18. If the average total cost at this output is $16.55, then its total profit is
    A) $1.45.
    B) $1,188.
    C) $95.70.
    D) $1,092.30.
    Answer: C
    Diff: 2   Type: MC   Page Ref: 415/415
    Topic: How a Monopolistically Competitive Firm Maximizes Profits in the Short Run
    Skill: Analytical
    Objective: LO 2: Explain how a monopolistically competitive firm maximizes profits in the
             short run.
    AACSB Coding: Analytic Skills
    Special Feature: None

24. If a monopolistically competitive firm is producing 50 units of output where marginal cost equals marginal revenue, total cost is $1,674 and total revenue is $2,000, its average profit is
    A) $40.
    B) $6.52.
    C) $326.
    D) impossible to determine without additional information.
    Answer: B
    Diff: 2   Type: MC   Page Ref: 415/415
    Topic: How a Monopolistically Competitive Firm Maximizes Profits in the Short Run
    Skill: Analytical
    Objective: LO 2: Explain how a monopolistically competitive firm maximizes profits in the
             short run.
    AACSB Coding: Analytic Skills
    Special Feature: None

Figure 12–4

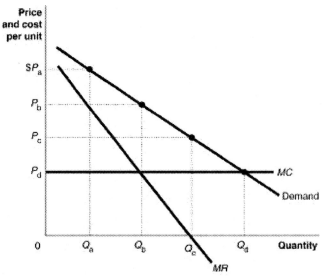

25. *Refer to Figure 12–4.* The firm represented in the diagram is currently selling Q_a units at a price of $\$P_a$. Is this firm maximizing its profit and if it is not, what would you recommend to the firm?

   A) No, it is not; it should lower its price to $\$P_b$ and sell Q_b units.

   B) No, it is not; it should lower its price to $\$P_c$ and sell Q_c units.

   C) Yes, it is maximizing its profit by charging the highest price possible.

   D) No, it is not; since its marginal cost is constant, it should produce and sell as much as it can. It should sell Q_d units at a price of $\$P_d$.

Answer: A
Diff: 2   Type: MC   Page Ref: 415/415
Topic: How a Monopolistically Competitive Firm Maximizes Profits in the Short Run
Skill: Analytical
Objective: LO 2: Explain how a monopolistically competitive firm maximizes profits in the short run.
AACSB Coding: Analytic Skills
Special Feature: None

26. For a monopolistically competitive firm, price equals average revenue.
   Answer: ⊙ True   False
Diff: 1   Type: TF   Page Ref: 415/415
Topic: How a Monopolistically Competitive Firm Maximizes Profits in the Short Run
Skill: Conceptual
Objective: LO 2: Explain how a monopolistically competitive firm maximizes profits in the short run.
AACSB Coding: Reflective Thinking
Special Feature: None

27. A profit maximizing monopolistically competitive firm produces and sells an allocatively efficient quantity of output.
    Answer: True   ⊙ False
    Diff: 1   *Type: TF*   *Page Ref: 415/415*
    Topic: How a Monopolistically Competitive Firm Maximizes Profits in the Short Run
    Skill: Conceptual
    Objective: LO 2: Explain how a monopolistically competitive firm maximizes profits in the short run.
    AACSB Coding: Reflective Thinking
    Special Feature: None

28. For a profit maximizing monopolistically competitive firm, for the last unit sold, the marginal cost of production is less than the marginal benefit received by a customer from the purchase of that unit.
    Answer: ⊙ True   False
    Diff: 1   *Type: TF*   *Page Ref: 416/416*
    Topic: How a Monopolistically Competitive Firm Maximizes Profits in the Short Run
    Skill: Conceptual
    Objective: LO 2: Explain how a monopolistically competitive firm maximizes profits in the short run.
    AACSB Coding: Reflective Thinking
    Special Feature: None

29. Unlike a perfectly competitive firm, a monopolistic competitor does not have a short run shut down point.
    Answer: True   ⊙ False
    Diff: 1   *Type: TF*   *Page Ref: 416/416*
    Topic: How a Monopolistically Competitive Firm Maximizes Profits in the Short Run
    Skill: Conceptual
    Objective: LO 2: Explain how a monopolistically competitive firm maximizes profits in the short run.
    AACSB Coding: Reflective Thinking
    Special Feature: None

30. Consumers in a monopolistically competitive market do not receive any consumer surplus because the price paid for the product exceeds the marginal cost of production.
    Answer: True   ⊙ False
    Diff: 2   *Type: TF*   *Page Ref: 416/416*
    Topic: How a Monopolistically Competitive Firm Maximizes Profits in the Short Run
    Skill: Conceptual
    Objective: LO 2: Explain how a monopolistically competitive firm maximizes profits in the short run.
    AACSB Coding: Reflective Thinking
    Special Feature: None

31. Assume that price exceeds average variable cost over the relevant range of demand. If a monopolistically competitive firm is producing at an output where marginal revenue is $111.11 and marginal cost is $118, then to maximize profits the firm should increase its output.

Answer: True   ○ False

Diff: 2   Type: TF   Page Ref: 416/416
Topic: How a Monopolistically Competitive Firm Maximizes Profits in the Short Run
Skill: Conceptual
Objective: LO 2: Explain how a monopolistically competitive firm maximizes profits in the short run.
AACSB Coding: Reflective Thinking
Special Feature: None

12.3   What Happens to Profits in the Long Run

1. A monopolistically competitive industry that earns economic profits in the short run will

A) experience the entry of new rival firms into the industry in the long run.
B) experience the exit of old firms out of the industry in the long run.
C) experience a rise in demand in the long run.
D) continue to earn economic profits in the long run.

Answer: A

Diff: 2   Type: MC   Page Ref: 417/417
Topic: What Happens to Profits in the Long Run?
Skill: Conceptual
Objective: LO 3: Analyze the situation of a monopolistically competitive firm in the long run.
AACSB Coding: Reflective Thinking
Special Feature: None

2. In the long run, if price is less than average cost.

A) there is no incentive for the number of firms in the market to change.
B) there is profit incentive for firms to enter the market.
C) the market must be in long–run equilibrium.
D) there is an incentive for firms to exit the market.

Answer: D

Diff: 2   Type: MC   Page Ref: 417/417
Topic: What Happens to Profits in the Long Run?
Skill: Conceptual
Objective: LO 3: Analyze the situation of a monopolistically competitive firm in the long run.
AACSB Coding: Reflective Thinking
Special Feature: None

3. A monopolistically competitive firm that is earning profits will, in the long run, experience all of the following except
    A) a decrease in the number of rival products.
    B) a decrease in demand for its product.
    C) new rivals entering the market.
    D) demand for the firm's product becomes more elastic.
Answer: A
Diff: 2   Type: MC   Page Ref: 417/417
Topic: What Happens to Profits in the Long Run?
Skill: Conceptual
Objective: LO 3: Analyze the situation of a monopolistically competitive firm in the long run.
AACSB Coding: Reflective Thinking
Special Feature: None

4. Assuming that the total market size remains constant, a monopolistically competitive firm earning profits in the short run will find the demand for its product decreasing in the long run because
    A) some of its customers have switched to purchasing the products of new entrants in the market.
    B) new entrants into the market are more likely to have cutting edge products.
    C) as the firm raises its price in the long run, it will lose some customers to new entrants in the market.
    D) its costs of production rises.
Answer: A
Diff: 2   Type: MC   Page Ref: 417/417
Topic: What Happens to Profits in the Long Run?
Skill: Conceptual
Objective: LO 3: Analyze the situation of a monopolistically competitive firm in the long run.
AACSB Coding: Reflective Thinking
Special Feature: None

5. You are planning to open a new Italian restaurant in your hometown where there are three other Italian restaurants. You plan to distinguish your restaurant from your competitors by offering northern Italian cuisine and using locally grown organic produce. What is likely to happen in the restaurant market in your hometown after you open?
    A) Your competitors are likely to change their menus to make their products more similar to yours.
    B) The demand curve facing each restaurant owner becomes more elastic.
    C) The demand curve facing each restaurant owner shifts to the right.
    D) While the demand curves facing your competitors becomes more elastic, your demand curve will be inelastic.
Answer: B
Diff: 2   Type: MC   Page Ref: 411/411
Topic: What Happens to Profits in the Long Run?
Skill: Conceptual
Objective: LO 3: Analyze the situation of a monopolistically competitive firm in the long run.
AACSB Coding: Reflective Thinking
Special Feature: Economics in YOUR Life!: Opening Your Own Restaurant

6. You have just opened a new Italian restaurant in your hometown where there are three other Italian restaurants. Your restaurant is doing a brisk business and you attribute your success to your distinctive northern Italian cuisine using locally grown organic produce. What is likely to happen to your business in the long run?
   A) If you continue to maintain consistent quality, you will be able to earn profits indefinitely.
   B) Your success will invite others to open competing restaurants and ultimately your profits will be driven to zero.
   C) Your competitors are likely to change their menus to make their products more similar to yours.
   D) If your success continues, you will be likely to establish a franchise and expand your market size.

Answer: B
Diff: 2   Type: MC   Page Ref: 411/411
Topic: What Happens to Profits in the Long Run?
Skill: Conceptual
Objective: LO 3: Analyze the situation of a monopolistically competitive firm in the long run.
AACSB Coding: Reflective Thinking
Special Feature: Economics in YOUR Life!: Opening Your Own Restaurant

Figure 12–5

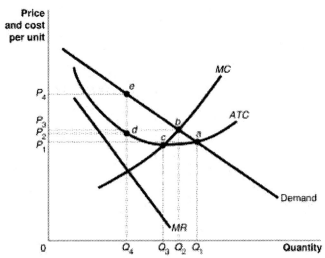

7. *Refer to Figure 12–5.* What is the profit maximizing output level?
   A) Q_1 units
   B) Q_2 units
   C) Q_3 units
   D) Q_4 units

Answer: D
Diff: 1   Type: MC   Page Ref: 418/418
Topic: What Happens to Profits in the Long Run?
Skill: Analytical
Objective: LO 3: Analyze the situation of a monopolistically competitive firm in the long run.
AACSB Coding: Analytic Skills
Special Feature: None

8. *Refer to Figure 12–5.* What is the output price?
    A) P_4
    B) P_3
    C) P_2
    D) P_1
    Answer: A
    Diff: 1   Type: MC   Page Ref: 418/418
    Topic: What Happens to Profits in the Long Run?
    Skill: Analytical
    Objective: LO 3: Analyze the situation of a monopolistically competitive firm in the long run.
    AACSB Coding: Analytic Skills
    Special Feature: None

9. *Refer to Figure 12–5.* What is the area that represents the firm's profit?
    A) P_4edP_2
    B) P_4eaP_1
    C) $Profit = 0$
    D) P_3baP_2
    Answer: A
    Diff: 2   Type: MC   Page Ref: 418/418
    Topic: What Happens to Profits in the Long Run?
    Skill: Analytical
    Objective: LO 3: Analyze the situation of a monopolistically competitive firm in the long run.
    AACSB Coding: Analytic Skills
    Special Feature: None

10. *Refer to Figure 12–5.* Economies of scale are exhausted at which output level?
    A) Q_1 units
    B) Q_2 units
    C) Q_3 units
    D) more than Q_1 units
    Answer: C
    Diff: 2   Type: MC   Page Ref: 418/418
    Topic: What Happens to Profits in the Long Run?
    Skill: Analytical
    Objective: LO 3: Analyze the situation of a monopolistically competitive firm in the long run.
    AACSB Coding: Analytic Skills
    Special Feature: None

11. ***Refer to Figure 12-5.*** If the diagram represents a typical firm in the market, what is likely to happen in the long run?
    A) New firms will enter the market causing the demand to decrease for existing firms.
    B) Competition will be intensified as firms strive to make long run profits.
    C) Inefficient firms will exit the market and new cost efficient firms will enter the market.
    D) Some firms will exit the market causing the demand to increase for firms remaining in the market.
    Answer: A
    Diff: 2   Type: MC   Page Ref: 418/418
    Topic: What Happens to Profits in the Long Run?
    Skill: Analytical
    Objective: LO 3: Analyze the situation of a monopolistically competitive firm in the long run.
    AACSB Coding: Analytic Skills
    Special Feature: None

12. ***Refer to Figure 12-5.*** If the diagram represents a typical firm in the market, what is likely to happen to its average cost of production in the long run?
    A) It will probably rise since the firm will be producing less than its current amount.
    B) It will probably fall since the firm must be cost efficient to remain competitive.
    C) It will probably fall since the firm will be selling less than its current amount.
    D) It will probably rise since its long run demand is likely to be higher.
    Answer: A
    Diff: 2   Type: MC   Page Ref: 418/418
    Topic: What Happens to Profits in the Long Run?
    Skill: Analytical
    Objective: LO 3: Analyze the situation of a monopolistically competitive firm in the long run.
    AACSB Coding: Analytic Skills
    Special Feature: None

13. A monopolistically competitive firm earning profits in the short run will find the demand for its product decreasing and becoming more elastic in the long run as new firms move into the industry until
    A) the firm exits the market.
    B) the firm's demand curve is tangent to its average total cost curve.
    C) the original firm is driven into bankruptcy.
    D) the firm's demand curve is perfectly elastic.
    Answer: B
    Diff: 2   Type: MC   Page Ref: 418/418
    Topic: What Happens to Profits in the Long Run?
    Skill: Conceptual
    Objective: LO 3: Analyze the situation of a monopolistically competitive firm in the long run.
    AACSB Coding: Reflective Thinking
    Special Feature: None

14. In the long run, what happens to the demand curve facing a monopolistically competitive firm that is earning short run profits?
    A) The demand curve will shift to the left and became more elastic throughout the relevant
        range of prices.
    B) The demand curve will shift to the right and became less elastic throughout the relevant
        range of prices.
    C) The demand curve will shift to the right and became more elastic throughout the relevant
        range of prices.
    D) The demand curve will shift to the left and became less elastic throughout the relevant
        range of prices.
    Answer: A
    Diff: 2   Type: MC   Page Ref: 418/418
    Topic: What Happens to Profits in the Long Run?
    Skill: Conceptual
    Objective: LO 3: Analyze the situation of a monopolistically competitive firm in the long run.
    AACSB Coding: Reflective Thinking
    Special Feature: None

15. If a typical monopolistically competitive firm is making short run losses, then
    A) as some firms leave, the demand for the products of the remaining firms will become more elastic.
    B) the industry will eventually cease to exist.
    C) as some firms leave, the remaining firms will experience an increase in the demand for their products.
    D) other more competitive firms will enter the market.
    Answer: C
    Diff: 2   Type: MC   Page Ref: 419/419
    Topic: What Happens to Profits in the Long Run?
    Skill: Conceptual
    Objective: LO 3: Analyze the situation of a monopolistically competitive firm in the long run.
    AACSB Coding: Reflective Thinking
    Special Feature: None

Figure 12–6

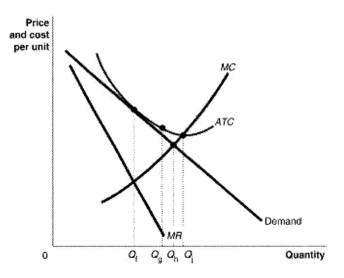

16. *Refer to Figure 12–6.* What is the monopolistic competitor's profit maximizing output?

    A) Q_1 units

    B) Q_2 units

    C) Q_3 units

    D) Q_4 units

    Answer: B
    Diff: 1   Type: MC   Page Ref: 418–9/418–9
    Topic: What Happens to Profits in the Long Run?
    Skill: Analytical
    Objective: LO 3: Analyze the situation of a monopolistically competitive firm in the long run.
    AACSB Coding: Analytic Skills
    Special Feature: None

17. *Refer to Figure 12–6.* What is the monopolistic competitor's profit maximizing price?

    A) $\$P_1$

    B) $\$P_2$

    C) $\$P_3$

    D) $\$P_4$

    Answer: D
    Diff: 1   Type: MC   Page Ref: 418–9/418–9
    Topic: What Happens to Profits in the Long Run?
    Skill: Analytical
    Objective: LO 3: Analyze the situation of a monopolistically competitive firm in the long run.
    AACSB Coding: Analytic Skills
    Special Feature: None

18. *Refer to Figure 12–6.* The firm represented in the diagram makes
    A) should exit the industry.
    B) should expand its output to take advantage of economies of scale.
    C) makes zero economic profit.
    D) makes zero accounting profit.
    Answer: C
    Diff: 1   Type: MC   Page Ref: 418–9/418–9
    Topic: What Happens to Profits in the Long Run?
    Skill: Analytical
    Objective: LO 3: Analyze the situation of a monopolistically competitive firm in the long run.
    AACSB Coding: Analytic Skills
    Special Feature: None

19. *Refer to Figure 12–6.* What is the productively efficient output for the firm
    represented in the diagram?
    A) Q_1 units
    B) Q_2 units
    C) Q_3 units
    D) Q_4 units
    Answer: D
    Diff: 2   Type: MC   Page Ref: 418–9/418–9
    Topic: What Happens to Profits in the Long Run?
    Skill: Analytical
    Objective: LO 3: Analyze the situation of a monopolistically competitive firm in the long run.
    AACSB Coding: Analytic Skills
    Special Feature: None

20. *Refer to Figure 12–6.* What is the allocatively efficient output for the firm
    represented in the diagram?
    A) Q_1 units
    B) Q_2 units
    C) Q_3 units
    D) Q_4 units
    Answer: C
    Diff: 2   Type: MC   Page Ref: 418–9/418–9
    Topic: What Happens to Profits in the Long Run?
    Skill: Analytical
    Objective: LO 3: Analyze the situation of a monopolistically competitive firm in the long run.
    AACSB Coding: Analytic Skills
    Special Feature: None

21. **Refer to Figure 12–6.** The diagram depicts a firm
    A) in an increasing cost industry.
    B) in a constant cost industry.
    C) that is making short run losses.
    D) in long run equilibrium.
    Answer: D
    Diff: 2   Type: MC   Page Ref: 418–9/418–9
    Topic: What Happens to Profits in the Long Run?
    Skill: Analytical
    Objective: LO 3: Analyze the situation of a monopolistically competitive firm in the long run.
    AACSB Coding: Analytic Skills
    Special Feature: None

22. **Refer to Figure 12–6.** What is the amount of excess capacity?
    A) $Q_4 - Q_3$ units
    B) $Q_3 - Q_1$ units
    C) $Q_4 - Q_2$ units
    D) $Q_3 - Q_2$ units
    Answer: C
    Diff: 2   Type: MC   Page Ref: 418–9/418–9
    Topic: What Happens to Profits in the Long Run?
    Skill: Analytical
    Objective: LO 3: Analyze the situation of a monopolistically competitive firm in the long run.
    AACSB Coding: Analytic Skills
    Special Feature: None

23. Why do most firms in monopolistic competition typically make zero profit in the
    long run?
    A) because firms do not produce at their minimum efficient scale
    B) because the total market is not large enough to accommodate so many firms
    C) because the lack of entry barriers would compete away profits
    D) because firms produce differentiated products
    Answer: C
    Diff: 2   Type: MC   Page Ref: 418–9/418–9
    Topic: What Happens to Profits in the Long Run?
    Skill: Conceptual
    Objective: LO 3: Analyze the situation of a monopolistically competitive firm in the long run.
    AACSB Coding: Reflective Thinking
    Special Feature: None

24. If a monopolistically competitive firm breaks even, the firm
    A) is earning zero accounting and zero economic profit.
    B) should advertise its product to stimulate demand.
    C) expand production.
    D) is earning an accounting profit and will have to pay taxes on that profit.
    Answer: D
    Diff: 2   Type: MC   Page Ref: 418/418
    Topic: What Happens to Profits in the Long Run?
    Skill: Conceptual
    Objective: LO 3: Analyze the situation of a monopolistically competitive firm in the long run.
    AACSB Coding: Reflective Thinking
    Special Feature: Don't Let This Happen to You! : Don't Confuse Zero economic Profit with Zero
    *   Accounting Profit*

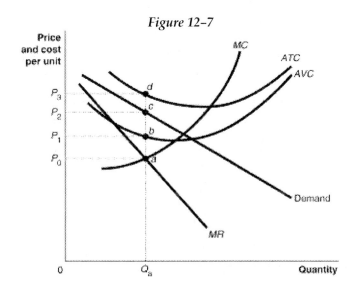

Figure 12–7

Figure 12–7 shows short run cost and demand curves for a monopolistically competitive firm in the market for designer watches.

25. ***Refer to Figure 12–7.*** If the diagram represents a typical firm in the designer watch market, what is likely to happen in the long run?
    A) Inefficient firms will exit the market and new cost efficient firms will enter the market.
    B) Firms will have to raise their prices to cover costs of production.
    C) The firms that are making losses will be purchased by their more successful rivals.
    D) Some firms will exit the market causing the demand to increase for firms remaining in the market.
    Answer: D
    Diff: 2   Type: MC   Page Ref: 419/419
    Topic: What Happens to Profits in the Long Run?
    Skill: Conceptual
    Objective: LO 3: Analyze the situation of a monopolistically competitive firm in the long run.
    AACSB Coding: Reflective Thinking
    Special Feature: None

26. In 1984 when Apple Computer introduced the Macintosh, it was able to sell the product at a hefty premium while comparable personal computers were priced at less than half the price of a Macintosh. Despite its much higher price, Apple was able to achieve a 15 percent market share. Which of the following contributed to Apple's initial success?
    A) Apple spent heavily on advertising to inform consumers about its product.
    B) Apple had successfully introduced a personal computer that was strongly differentiated from its competitors.
    C) Apple used superior materials to produce its product which justified the higher price.
    D) Apple was catering to a small segment of the market in which demand is relatively inelastic.
    Answer: B
    Diff: 2   Type: MC   Page Ref: 419–20/419–20
    Topic: What Happens to Profits in the Long Run?
    Skill: Conceptual
    Objective: LO 3: Analyze the situation of a monopolistically competitive firm in the long run.
    AACSB Coding: Reflective Thinking
    Special Feature: Making the Connection: The Rise and Fall of Apple's Macintosh Computer

27. At the peak of its success in the mid–1980s to the early 1990s, Apple Computer commanded a
    15 percent share of the personal computers market. Today, in 2007, its share of the growing personal computer market is estimated at 6 percent. During this period what happened to Apple's demand curve?
    A) The demanded curve shifted to the right and became less elastic throughout the relevant range of prices.
    B) The demanded curve stagnated which is why Apple lost market share.
    C) The demanded curve shifted to the left and became less elastic throughout the relevant range of prices.
    D) The demanded curve shifted to the left and became more elastic throughout the relevant range of prices.
    Answer: D
    Diff: 2   Type: MC   Page Ref: 420/420
    Topic: What Happens to Profits in the Long Run?
    Skill: Conceptual
    Objective: LO 3: Analyze the situation of a monopolistically competitive firm in the long run.
    AACSB Coding: Reflective Thinking
    Special Feature: Solved Problem: The Short Run and the Long Run for the Macintosh

28. At the peak of its success in the mid–1980s to the early 1990s, Apple Computer commanded a 15 percent share of the personal computers market. Today, in 2007, its share of the growing personal computer market is estimated at 6 percent. Which of the following best accounts for its dwindling market share?
    A) The entry of rivals eliminated Apple's product differentiation.
    B) Rivals engaged in predatory pricing but Apple was not willing to engage in a price war.
    C) Apple was not able to keep up with technological advancements in the personal computers market.
    D) The entry of rivals revealed that Apples was producing sub-standard computers.
    Answer: A
    Diff: 2   Type: MC   Page Ref: 420–1/420–1
    Topic: What Happens to Profits in the Long Run?
    Skill: Analytical
    Objective: LO 6: Identify key factors that determine a firm's success.
    AACSB Coding: Analytic Skills
    Special Feature: Solved Problem: The Short Run and the Long Run for the Macintosh

29. The economic analysis of monopolistic competition shows that market forces tend to eliminate profits in the long run. However, in reality it is possible for some firms to continue to reap profits in the long run. The text cites the example of L'Oreal, the world's largest cosmetics and beauty products firm as one that has experienced substantial profits even in the long run. Which of the following strategies contributed to L'Oreal's success?
    A) making its products similar to those of its competitors
    B) developing new products or improving existing products to cater to changing consumer tastes
    C) advertising heavily using celebrities
    D) focusing only on wealthy markets like the United States and Europe
    Answer: B
    Diff: 2   Type: MC   Page Ref: 423/423
    Topic: What Happens to Profits in the Long Run?
    Skill: Analytical
    Objective: LO 3: Analyze the situation of a monopolistically competitive firm in the long run.
    AACSB Coding: Analytic Skills
    Special Feature: Making the Connection: Staying One Step Ahead of the Competition: Eugene Schuller and L'Oreal

30. In theory, in the long run, monopolistically competitive firm earns zero profits.
    However, in reality there are some ways by which a firm can avoid losing profits.
    Which of the following is one such way?
    - A) gradually increase the mark up on the goods produced
    - B) find a market niche and keep it as narrow as possible so as to prevent other
      producers from entering this market segment
    - C) lower the price of its products to expand its market share
    - D) identify new markets and develop products precisely for those markets

    Answer: D
    Diff: 2   Type: MC   Page Ref: 421/421
    Topic: What Happens to Profits in the Long Run?
    Skill: Conceptual
    Objective: LO 3: Analyze the situation of a monopolistically competitive firm in the long run.
    AACSB Coding: Reflective Thinking
    Special Feature: None

31. A monopolistically competitive firm can increase its profits beyond the long–run
    equilibrium
    breakeven level by deliberately lowering its price to force some of its competitors
    out of the market.

    Answer: True   ○ False
    Diff: 2   Type: TF   Page Ref: 421/421
    Topic: What Happens to Profits in the Long Run?
    Skill: Conceptual
    Objective: LO 3: Analyze the situation of a monopolistically competitive firm in the long run.
    AACSB Coding: Reflective Thinking
    Special Feature: None

32. If a monopolistically competitive firm breaks even, the firm is earning as much in
    this industry as it could in any other comparable industry.

    Answer: ○ True   False
    Diff: 1   Type: TF   Page Ref: 418/418
    Topic: What Happens to Profits in the Long Run?
    Skill: Conceptual
    Objective: LO 3: Analyze the situation of a monopolistically competitive firm in the long run.
    AACSB Coding: Reflective Thinking
    Special Feature: None

33. A monopolistically competitive industry that earns economic profits in the short run
    will be able to expand its market share even if the market size remains constant.

    Answer: True   ○ False
    Diff: 1   Type: TF   Page Ref: 418/418
    Topic: What Happens to Profits in the Long Run?
    Skill: Conceptual
    Objective: LO 3: Analyze the situation of a monopolistically competitive firm in the long run.
    AACSB Coding: Reflective Thinking
    Special Feature: None

34. A monopolistically competitive industry that earns economic profits in the short run will face a more elastic demand curve in the long run.
    Answer: ☉ True   False
    Diff: 1   Type: TF   Page Ref: 418/418
    Topic: What Happens to Profits in the Long Run?
    Skill: Conceptual
    Objective: LO 3: Analyze the situation of a monopolistically competitive firm in the long run.
    AACSB Coding: Reflective Thinking
    Special Feature: None

12.4 Comparing Perfect Competition and Monopolistic Competition

1. How does the long run equilibrium of a monopolistically competitive industry differ from that of a perfectly competitive industry?
    A) A firm in monopolistic competition will charge a price higher than the average cost of production but a firm in perfect competition charges a price equal to the average cost of production.
    B) A firm in monopolistic competition produces an allocatively efficient output level while a firm in perfect competition produces a productively efficient output level.
    C) A firm in monopolistic competition does not take full advantage of its economies of scale but a firm in perfect competition produces at the lowest average cost possible.
    D) A firm in monopolistic competition will earn economic profits but a firm in perfect competition earns zero profit.
    Answer: C
    Diff: 2   Type: MC   Page Ref: 423–4/423–4
    Topic: Comparing Perfect Competition and Monopolistic Competition
    Skill: Conceptual
    Objective: LO 4: Compare the efficiency of monopolistic competition and perfect competition.
    AACSB Coding: Reflective Thinking
    Special Feature: None

2. Long run equilibrium under monopolistic competition is similar to that under perfect competition in that
    A) firms earn normal profits.
    B) price equals marginal cost.
    C) price equals marginal revenue.
    D) firms produce at the minimum point of their average cost curves.
    Answer: A
    Diff: 2   Type: MC   Page Ref: 423–4/423–4
    Topic: Comparing Perfect Competition and Monopolistic Competition
    Skill: Conceptual
    Objective: LO 4: Compare the efficiency of monopolistic competition and perfect competition.
    AACSB Coding: Reflective Thinking
    Special Feature: None

3. Which of the following is not a characteristic of long-run equilibrium in a monopolistically competitive market?
    A) Marginal revenue equals marginal cost.
    B) Selling price is greater than marginal cost.
    C) Production is at minimum average total cost.
    D) Selling price equals average total cost.
Answer: C
Diff: 2   Type: MC   Page Ref: 423–4/423–4
Topic: Comparing Perfect Competition and Monopolistic Competition
Skill: Conceptual
Objective: LO 4: Compare the efficiency of monopolistic competition and perfect competition.
AACSB Coding: Reflective Thinking
Special Feature: None

4. For productive efficiency to hold,
    A) price must equal marginal revenue of the last unit sold.
    B) average variable cost is minimized in production.
    C) price must equal the marginal cost of the last unit produced.
    D) average total cost is minimized in production.
Answer: D
Diff: 2   Type: MC   Page Ref: 424/424
Topic: Comparing Perfect Competition and Monopolistic Competition
Skill: Conceptual
Objective: LO 4: Compare the efficiency of monopolistic competition and perfect competition.
AACSB Coding: Reflective Thinking
Special Feature: None

5. For allocative efficiency to hold,
    A) average variable cost is minimized in production.
    B) price must equal the marginal cost of the last unit produced.
    C) price must equal marginal revenue of the last unit sold.
    D) average total cost is minimized in production.
Answer: B
Diff: 2   Type: MC   Page Ref: 424/424
Topic: Comparing Perfect Competition and Monopolistic Competition
Skill: Conceptual
Objective: LO 4: Compare the efficiency of monopolistic competition and perfect competition.
AACSB Coding: Reflective Thinking
Special Feature: None

6. Is a monopolistically competitive firm productively efficient?
    A) No, because it does not produce at minimum average total cost.
    B) Yes, because it produces where marginal cost equals marginal revenue.
    C) Yes, because price equals average total costs.
    D) No, because price is greater than marginal cost.
Answer: A
Diff: 2   Type: MC   Page Ref: 424/424
Topic: Comparing Perfect Competition and Monopolistic Competition
Skill: Conceptual
Objective: LO 4: Compare the efficiency of monopolistic competition and perfect competition.
AACSB Coding: Reflective Thinking
Special Feature: None

7. Is a monopolistically competitive firm allocatively efficient?
    A) No, because it does not produce at minimum average total cost.
    B) No, because price is greater than marginal cost.
    C) Yes, because it produces where marginal cost equals marginal revenue.
    D) Yes, because price equals average total costs.
Answer: B
Diff: 2   Type: MC   Page Ref: 424/424
Topic: Comparing Perfect Competition and Monopolistic Competition
Skill: Conceptual
Objective: LO 4: Compare the efficiency of monopolistic competition and perfect competition.
AACSB Coding: Reflective Thinking
Special Feature: None

8. If   a   firm   has   excess   capacity,   it   means
    A) that the firm's quantity supplied exceeds its quantity demanded.
    B) that the firm expends too much of their resources on advertising its product
       without seeing an appreciable increase in sales.
    C) that the firm's long run average cost of producing a given quantity exceeds its
       short run cost of producing that same quantity.
    D) that the firm is not producing its minimum efficient scale of output.
Answer: D
Diff: 2   Type: MC   Page Ref: 424/424
Topic: Comparing Perfect Competition and Monopolistic Competition
Skill: Definition
Objective: LO 4: Compare the efficiency of monopolistic competition and perfect competition.
AACSB Coding: Reflective Thinking
Special Feature: None

9. Economists agree that a monopolistically competitive market structure
    A) benefits consumers because firms to produce products that appeal to a wide range of consumers tastes.
    B) lowers consumer' utility because consumers pay a price higher than the marginal cost of production.
    C) can eliminate any excess capacity if all firms in the industry devote more funds to differentiating their products.
    D) is detrimental to society because it leads to a waste of scarce resources.
    Answer: A
    Diff: 2   Type: MC   Page Ref: 424/424
    Topic: Comparing Perfect Competition and Monopolistic Competition
    Skill: Conceptual
    Objective: LO 4: Compare the efficiency of monopolistic competition and perfect competition.
    AACSB Coding: Reflective Thinking
    Special Feature: None

10. Consumers benefit from monopolistic competition by
    A) paying the lowest possible price for the product.
    B) being able to purchase high quality products at low prices.
    C) paying the same price as everyone else.
    D) being able to choose from products more closely suited to their tastes.
    Answer: D
    Diff: 2   Type: MC   Page Ref: 424/424
    Topic: Comparing Perfect Competition and Monopolistic Competition
    Skill: Conceptual
    Objective: LO 4: Compare the efficiency of monopolistic competition and perfect competition.
    AACSB Coding: Reflective Thinking
    Special Feature: None

Figure 12-8

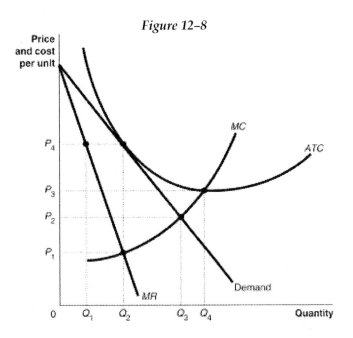

11. *Refer to Figure 12-8.* What is the productively efficient output for the firm represented in the diagram?

    A) Q_f units

    B) Q_g units

    C) Q_h units

    D) Q_j units

Answer: D

Diff: 2   Type: MC   Page Ref: 424/424
Topic: Comparing Perfect Competition and Monopolistic Competition
Skill: Analytical
Objective: LO 4: Compare the efficiency of monopolistic competition and perfect competition.
AACSB Coding: Analytic Skills
Special Feature: None

12. *Refer to Figure 12-8.* What is the allocatively efficient output for the firm represented in the diagram?

    A) Q_f units

    B) Q_g units

    C) Q_h units

    D) Q_j units

Answer: C

Diff: 2   Type: MC   Page Ref: 424/424
Topic: Comparing Perfect Competition and Monopolistic Competition
Skill: Analytical
Objective: LO 4: Compare the efficiency of monopolistic competition and perfect competition.
AACSB Coding: Analytic Skills
Special Feature: None

13. *Refer to Figure 12–8.* What is the amount of excess capacity?
    A) $Q_h - Q_g$ units
    B) $Q_h - Q_f$ units
    C) $Q_j - Q_f$ units
    D) $Q_j - Q_h$ units
    Answer: C
    Diff: 2   Type: MC   Page Ref: 424/424
    Topic: Comparing Perfect Competition and Monopolistic Competition
    Skill: Analytical
    Objective: LO 4: Compare the efficiency of monopolistic competition and perfect competition.
    AACSB Coding: Analytic Skills
    Special Feature: None

14. *Refer to Figure 12–8.* Suppose the firm is currently producing Q_f units. What happens if it increases its output to Q_g units?
    A) It will be taking advantage of economies of scale and will be able to lower the price of its product.
    B) It will move from a zero profit situation to a loss situation
    C) Its average cost of production will fall and its profit will rise.
    D) It will move from a zero profit situation to a profit situation
    Answer: B
    Diff: 2   Type: MC   Page Ref: 424/424
    Topic: Comparing Perfect Competition and Monopolistic Competition
    Skill: Analytical
    Objective: LO 4: Compare the efficiency of monopolistic competition and perfect competition.
    AACSB Coding: Analytic Skills
    Special Feature: None

15. *Refer to Figure 12–8.* In the long run, why will the firm produce Q_f units and not Q_g units, which has a lower its average cost of production?
    A) At Q_g, average cost exceeds marginal cost so the firm will actually make a loss.
    B) Although its average cost of production is lower when the firm produces Q_g units, to be able to sell its output the firm will have to charge a price below average cost, resulting in a loss.
    C) At Q_g, marginal revenue t is less than average revenue cost which will result in a loss for the firm.
    D) The firm's goal is to charge a high price and make a small profit rather than a low price and no profit.
    Answer: B
    Diff: 3   Type: MC   Page Ref: 424/424
    Topic: Comparing Perfect Competition and Monopolistic Competition
    Skill: Analytical
    Objective: LO 4: Compare the efficiency of monopolistic competition and perfect competition.
    AACSB Coding: Analytic Skills
    Special Feature: None

Figure 12–9

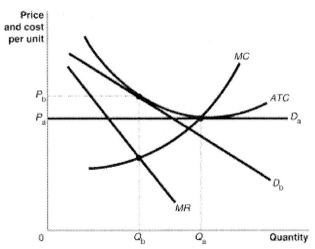

16. *Refer to Figure 12–9.* Which of the following statements is true?

   A) D_a represents the long run supply curve in a perfectly competitive constant cost industry while D_b depicts the long run demand curve facing a monopolizing competitor in a decreasing cost industry.

   B) D_a represents the long run demand curve facing a perfect competitor while D_b depicts the long run demand curve facing a monopolizing competitor.

   C) D_a represents the long run demand curve facing a monopolistic competitor in a constant cost industry while D_b depicts the long run demand curve in an increasing cost industry.

   D) D_a represents the long run demand curve facing a monopolistic competitor in a constant cost industry while D_b depicts the demand curve in the short run.

Answer: B
Diff: 3   Type: MC   Page Ref: 424/424
Topic: Comparing Perfect Competition and Monopolistic Competition
Skill: Analytical
Objective: LO 4: Compare the efficiency of monopolistic competition and perfect competition.
AACSB Coding: Analytic Skills
Special Feature: None

17. ***Refer to Figure 12–9.*** The diagram demonstrates that
    A) in the long run the monopolistic competitor produces the minimum cost output level, Q_a, but in the short run its output of Q_b is not cost minimizing.
    B) in the short run the monopolistic competitor produces an output Q_b but in the long run after it adjusts its capacity, it will produce run the allocatively efficient output, Q_a.
    C) it is not possible for a monopolistic competitor to produce the productively efficient output level, Q_a, because of product differentiation.
    D) it is possible for a monopolistic competitor to produce the productively efficient output level, Q_a, if it is willing to lower its price from P_b to P_a.
    Answer: C
    Diff: 3   Type: MC   Page Ref: 424/424
    Topic: Comparing Perfect Competition and Monopolistic Competition
    Skill: Analytical
    Objective: LO 4: Compare the efficiency of monopolistic competition and perfect competition.
    AACSB Coding: Analytic Skills
    Special Feature: None

18. Consumers in monopolistically competitive markets face a tradeoff between paying prices greater than marginal costs and purchasing products that are more closely suited to their tastes.
    Answer: ◉ True   False
    Diff: 2   Type: TF   Page Ref: 425/425
    Topic: Comparing Perfect Competition and Monopolistic Competition
    Skill: Conceptual
    Objective: LO 4: Compare the efficiency of monopolistic competition and perfect competition.
    AACSB Coding: Reflective Thinking
    Special Feature: None

19. One way by which firms differentiate their product is to find a market niche.
    Answer: ◉ True   False
    Diff: 1   Type: TF   Page Ref: 425/425
    Topic: Comparing Perfect Competition and Monopolistic Competition
    Skill: Conceptual
    Objective: LO 4: Compare the efficiency of monopolistic competition and perfect competition.
    AACSB Coding: Reflective Thinking
    Special Feature: Making the Connection: Abercrombie& Fitch: Can the Product Be Too Differentiated?

20. A monopolistic competitor does not earn profits in the long run unless it can successfully differentiate its product in the minds of its consumers.
    Answer: ◉ True   False
    Diff: 1   Type: TF   Page Ref: 424/424
    Topic: Comparing Perfect Competition and Monopolistic Competition
    Skill: Conceptual
    Objective: LO 4: Compare the efficiency of monopolistic competition and perfect competition.
    AACSB Coding: Reflective Thinking
    Special Feature: None

21. In the long run equilibrium a monopolistic ally competitive firm earning normal profit produces the allocatively efficient output level.
    Answer: True   ⊚ False
    Diff: 1   Type: TF   Page Ref: 424/424
    Topic: Comparing Perfect Competition and Monopolistic Competition
    Skill: Conceptual
    Objective: LO 4: Compare the efficiency of monopolistic competition and perfect competition.
    AACSB Coding: Reflective Thinking
    Special Feature: None

22. Productive efficiency does not hold for a profit-maximizing, monopolistically competitive firm in the long run equilibrium because the firm operates along the diseconomies of scale region of its average total cost curve
    Answer: True   ⊚ False
    Diff: 2   Type: TF   Page Ref: 424/424
    Topic: Comparing Perfect Competition and Monopolistic Competition
    Skill: Conceptual
    Objective: LO 4: Compare the efficiency of monopolistic competition and perfect competition.
    AACSB Coding: Reflective Thinking
    Special Feature: None

23. In the long run equilibrium, both the perfectly competitive firm and the monopolistically competitive firm produce the output at which MR=MC and charge a price equal to the average total cost of production.
    Answer: ⊚ True   False
    Diff: 2   Type: TF   Page Ref: 424/424
    Topic: Comparing Perfect Competition and Monopolistic Competition
    Skill: Conceptual
    Objective: LO 4: Compare the efficiency of monopolistic competition and perfect competition.
    AACSB Coding: Reflective Thinking
    Special Feature: None

12.5   How Marketing Differentiates Products

1. A franchise is
    A) a branch of a national company.
    B) a firm with no competitors.
    C) a firm that buys and operates a brand name business in a new market.
    D) a firm with the legal right to sell a good or service in a particular area.
    Answer: D
    Diff: 2   Type: MC   Page Ref: 426/426
    Topic: How Marketing Differentiates Products
    Skill: Definition
    Objective: LO 5: Define marketing and explain how firms use it to differentiate their products.
    AACSB Coding: Reflective Thinking
    Special Feature: None

2. A trademark is
    A) a patent on a firm's product.
    B) a legal instrument which grants a firm the right to differentiate its product.
    C) a legal right to position a firm's product in high traffic public areas such as airports and post offices.
    D) a distinguishing attribute such as a sign or logo that allows a firm to uniquely identify its product.
Answer: D
Diff: 2   Type: MC   Page Ref: 426/426
Topic: How Marketing Differentiates Products
Skill: Definition
Objective: LO 5: Define marketing and explain how firms use it to differentiate their products.
AACSB Coding: Reflective Thinking
Special Feature: None

3. Which of the following is true of trademarks?
    A) A successful trademark is one that allows consumers to immediately identify the source or producer of the products.
    B) If a firm is granted a trademark, then no other firms can legally sell in the same geographic area for a given period of time.
    C) A successful trademark is one that becomes a generic name for a product, for example, "Xerox" has become a generic term for making photocopies.
    D) If a firm is granted a trademark, then no other firms can legally produce similar products for a given period of time.
Answer: A
Diff: 2   Type: MC   Page Ref: 426/426
Topic: How Marketing Differentiates Products
Skill: Conceptual
Objective: LO 5: Define marketing and explain how firms use it to differentiate their products.
AACSB Coding: Reflective Thinking
Special Feature: None

4. Which of the following is a disadvantage of trademarking a firm's product?
    A) A trademark may become so widely used to denote a particular type of product that the trademark may no longer be a legally protected brand name.
    B) A trademark conveys information about the product to the public.
    C) A trademark does not affect demand for the firm's product.
    D) A trademark differentiates a firm's product.
Answer: A
Diff: 2   Type: MC   Page Ref: 426/426
Topic: How Marketing Differentiates Products
Skill: Conceptual
Objective: LO 5: Define marketing and explain how firms use it to differentiate their products.
AACSB Coding: Reflective Thinking
Special Feature: None

5. Nike has used Michael Jordan to create the impression that Air Jordan basketball shoes are superior to any other basketball shoe. Nike is attempting to
    A) convince consumers that Air Jordan basketball shoes are no different from other basketball shoes favored by celebrities.
    B) increase its profit by raising the price of Air Jordan basketball shoes.
    C) lower the marginal cost of producing Air Jordan basketball shoes.
    D) differentiate Air Jordan basketball shoes from other types of basketball shoes.
Answer: D
Diff: 2   Type: MC   Page Ref: 426/426
Topic: How Marketing Differentiates Products
Skill: Analytical
Objective: LO 5: Define marketing and explain how firms use it to differentiate their products.
AACSB Coding: Analytic Skills, Communication
Special Feature: None

6. When a credit card company offers different services with its card, like travel insurance for air travel tickets purchased with the credit card or product insurance for items purchased with the card, the credit card company is trying to
    A) create a barrier to entry for competing firms.
    B) convince customers that its card has greater value than those offered by rival firms.
    C) create a perfectly competitive market in which to sell its credit card.
    D) shift the demand curve for competing firms to the right.
Answer: B
Diff: 2   Type: MC   Page Ref: 426/426
Topic: How Marketing Differentiates Products
Skill: Analytical
Objective: LO 5: Define marketing and explain how firms use it to differentiate their products.
AACSB Coding: Analytic Skills
Special Feature: None

7. Juicy Couture has been successful in selling women's clothing using an unusual strategy. According to an article in the Wall Street Journal the key to the firm's strategy is to "limit distribution to maintain the brand's exclusive cachet, even if that means sacrificing sales, a brand–management technique once used only for high–end luxury brands." In 2006, Juicy clothes were sold in only four department stores: Neiman Marcus, Saks, Bloomingdale's, and Nordstrom. In 2006, its sales have more than quadrupled since 2202.
   Source: Rachel Dodes, "From Track Suits to Fast Track," Wall Street Journal, September 13, 2006.

   How does limiting the number of stores Juicy's products are sold contribute to its success?
      A) Because it helps establish Juicy's products as luxury items favored by the very wealthy
      B) Because it enables Juicy to price its products at a premium and differentiated them from lower priced products.
      C) By sacrificing sales, the company was able to focus on producing high quality products
      D) Because maintaining the exclusivity of a product increases the demand for the product
   Answer: B
   Diff: 3   Type: MC   Page Ref: 426/426
   Topic: How Marketing Differentiates Products
   Skill: Analytical
   Objective: LO 5: Define marketing and explain how firms use it to differentiate their products.
   AACSB Coding: Analytic Skills
   Special Feature: None

8. Brand management refers to
      A) efforts to reduce the cost of production.
      B) picking a brand name for a new product that will attract attention.
      C) the efforts to maintain the differentiation of a product over time.
      D) selling the right to use a brand name in a particular market.
   Answer: C
   Diff: 1   Type: MC   Page Ref: 426/426
   Topic: How Marketing Differentiates Products
   Skill: Definition
   Objective: LO 5: Define marketing and explain how firms use it to differentiate their products.
   AACSB Coding: Reflective Thinking
   Special Feature: None

9. Which of the following statements is true about advertising by a monopolistically competitive firm?
    A) Monopolistically competitive firms tend to shun advertising because advertising draws attention to the variety of differentiated products available in the industry.
    B) Since the monopolistic competitor, like the perfect competitor, makes zero profit in the long run, it is a waste of resources to advertise its products.
    C) Advertising could make the monopolistic competitor's demand more inelastic but advertising has no effect on a perfect competitor's demand.
    D) Advertising will be more beneficial if a monopolistic competitor colludes with other firms to advertise the products of the industry as a whole rather than an individual firm's product.

Answer: C
Diff: 2   Type: MC   Page Ref: 426/426
Topic: How Marketing Differentiates Products
Skill: Conceptual
Objective: LO 5: Define marketing and explain how firms use it to differentiate their products.
AACSB Coding: Reflective Thinking
Special Feature: None

10. Although advertising raises the price of a monopolistic competitor's product, it does confer a benefit to consumers. Which of the following is a benefit to consumers?
    A) Advertising could provide consumers with useful information about new products and enable them to comparison shop.
    B) Advertised products tend to be of higher quality so consumers feel special when they consume advertised products.
    C) Advertising act as a barrier to entry.
    D) Advertising engenders brand loyalty.

Answer: A
Diff: 2   Type: MC   Page Ref: 426/426
Topic: How Marketing Differentiates Products
Skill: Conceptual
Objective: LO 5: Define marketing and explain how firms use it to differentiate their products.
AACSB Coding: Reflective Thinking
Special Feature: None

11. One of your classmates asserts that advertising, marketing research, and brand management are redundant expenditures because a firm can obtain the same information by simply looking at what customers are already buying. Which of the following is not a response you might offer her?
    A) Advertising and brand management allow a firm to create an entry barrier which will insulate the firm from competition and from undertaking further product innovations.
    B) Conducting market research is a good way for firms to keep abreast of changing consumer tastes and preferences.
    C) If a firm successfully manages its brand, customers become less price sensitive as they perceive fewer substitutes for the firm's brand.
    D) Marketing research could allow a firm to identify new market opportunities and at least, in the short run, a firm can make a profit supplying products to this market segment.
    Answer: A
    Diff: 2   *Type: MC*   *Page Ref: 426/426*
    Topic: How Marketing Differentiates Products
    Skill: Analytical
    Objective: LO 5: Define marketing and explain how firms use it to differentiate their products.
    AACSB Coding: Analytic Skills, Ethical Reasoning
    Special Feature: None

12. What is a "niche" market?
    A) a narrowly defined portion of a common market
    B) a market comprising wealthy college educated adults under the age of thirty
    C) a group of customers who are highly sensitive to marketing
    D) a group of customers who are drawn to counter culture
    Answer: A
    Diff: 2   *Type: MC*   *Page Ref: 425/425*
    Topic: How Marketing Differentiates Products
    Skill: Definition
    Objective: LO 5: Define marketing and explain how firms use it to differentiate their products.
    AACSB Coding: Reflective Thinking
    Special Feature: Making the Connection: Abercrombie& Fitch: Can the Product Be Too
                     Differentiated?

13. Which of the following is not an example of a "niche" market?
    A) commuter airlines
    B) economy class on commercial airlines
    C) sale of pasteurized goat milk for those allergic to cow milk
    D) dairy operation supplying kosher milk to a large Jewish population in New York City
    Answer: B
    Diff: 2   *Type: MC*   *Page Ref: 425/425*
    Topic: How Marketing Differentiates Products
    Skill: Conceptual
    Objective: LO 5: Define marketing and explain how firms use it to differentiate their products.
    AACSB Coding: Reflective Thinking
    Special Feature: Making the Connection: Abercrombie& Fitch: Can the Product Be Too
                     Differentiated?

14. A successful trademark is one that becomes a generic name for a product, for example,
    "Kleenex" has become a generic term for tissues.
    Answer: True   ◎ False
    Diff: 2   *Type: TF*   *Page Ref: 426/426*
    Topic: How Marketing Differentiates Products
    Skill: Conceptual
    Objective: LO 5: Define marketing and explain how firms use it to differentiate their products.
    AACSB Coding: Reflective Thinking
    Special Feature: None

15. In the highly competitive fast-food restaurant market, brand name restaurants have a strong profit incentive to maintain high sanitary conditions and avoid any negative consequences.
    Answer: ◎ True   False
    Diff: 2   *Type: TF*   *Page Ref: 427/427*
    Topic: How Marketing Differentiates Products
    Skill: Analytical
    Objective: LO 5: Define marketing and explain how firms use it to differentiate their products.
    AACSB Coding: Reflective Thinking
    Special Feature: None

12.6 What Makes a Firm Successful?

1. If buyers of a monopolistically competitive product feel the products of different sellers are strongly differentiated, then
    A) the demand for each seller's product is relatively elastic.
    B) the demand for each seller's product is perfectly inelastic.
    C) the demand for each seller's product is relatively inelastic.
    D) the demand for each seller's product is perfectly elastic.
    Answer: C
    Diff: 2   *Type: MC*   *Page Ref: 427/427*
    Topic: What Makes a Firm Successful?
    Skill: Analytical
    Objective: LO 6: Identify key factors that determine a firm's success.
    AACSB Coding: Analytic Skills
    Special Feature: None

2. Which of the following is an example of a factor that a firm's owners and managers can control in making the firm successful?
    A) a rise in the price of a key input for example, a rise in the price of oil leads to higher energy costs
    B) the choice of technology used to produce the product
    C) the ability to produce the product at a lower cost
    D) changing consumer tastes
Answer: C
Diff: 2   Type: MC   Page Ref: 427/427
Topic: What Makes a Firm Successful?
Skill: Analytical
Objective: LO 6: Identify key factors that determine a firm's success.
AACSB Coding: Analytic Skills
Special Feature: None

3. A firm that is first to the market with a new product frequently discovers that there are design flaws or problems with the product that were not anticipated. How do these problems affect the innovating firm?
    A) The firm is protected by a first–mover advantage: initial design flaws tend not to harm a firm significantly because consumers resist changing products for fear of incurring high switching costs.
    B) They reduce profits for the new innovations and open the door to competitors who can enter the new market with a better product.
    C) The firm's cost increases as it improves the product but it will not be able to raise its price for fear of alienating customers. Consequently, its profits will erode although its market share remains secure.
    D) Because these design flaws were not anticipated, consumers tend to be more forgiving and are likely to remain loyal to the company and its products.
Answer: B
Diff: 2   Type: MC   Page Ref: 428/428
Topic: What Makes a Firm Successful?
Skill: Analytical
Objective: LO 6: Identify key factors that determine a firm's success.
AACSB Coding: Analytic Skills
Special Feature: Making the Connection: Is Being the First Firm in the Market a Key to Success?

Figure 12–10

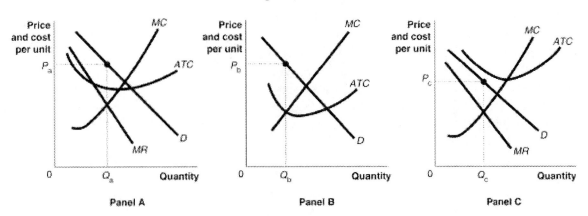

Panel A   Panel B   Panel C

4. *Refer to Figure 12–10.* Currently, upscale coffeehouses like Starbucks are earning an economic profit. Which of the graphs in the Figure above reflects this?
   A) Panel A
   B) Panel B
   C) Panel C
   D) Either Panel A or Panel B.

Answer: A
Diff: 1   Type: MC   Page Ref: 430–1/430–1
Topic: MComp in the Short Run
Skill: Analytical
Objective: LO 6: Identify key factors that determine a firm's success.
AACSB Coding: Analytic Skills
Special Feature: An Inside Look: Brewing Battle: Dunkin' Donuts Tries to Go Upscale, but Not too Far

5. Assume that the coffeehouse market is monopolistically competitive and that there are three major customer groups: the Starbucks tribe, the Dunkin' Donuts tribe and the Lost tribe (no allegiance to any particular coffeehouse). Suppose that the number of people in the Dunkin' Donuts tribe increases as people begin to prefer donuts with their coffee. How would Starbucks likely respond to this change in tastes?
   A) Starbucks is likely to pursue aggressive advertising to inform customers about its "socially responsible" business philosophy and its commitment to serving healthy products in an attempt to sway customers to choose Starbucks over Dunkin' Donuts.
   B) Starbucks is likely to lower the prices of its products to entice customers away from Dunkin' Donuts.
   C) Starbucks is likely to move closer to the Dunkin' Donuts product. For instance, they could introduce more donuts and similar baked goods into their coffee shops.
   D) Starbucks is likely to further differentiate its product to create value for its customers.

Answer: C
Diff: 2   Type: MC   Page Ref: 430-1/430-1
Topic: What Makes a Firm Successful?
Skill: Analytical
Objective: LO 6: Identify key factors that determine a firm's success.
AACSB Coding: Analytic Skills
Special Feature: An Inside Look: Brewing Battle: Dunkin' Donuts Tries to Go Upscale, but Not too Far

6. If buyers of a monopolistically competitive product feel the products of different sellers have little differences between them, then the demand for each seller's product is relatively elastic over the relevant range of prices.
Answer: ● True   False
Diff: 2   Type: TF   Page Ref: 427/427
Topic: What Makes a Firm Successful?
Skill: Conceptual
Objective: LO 6: Identify key factors that determine a firm's success.
AACSB Coding: Reflective Thinking
Special Feature: None

7. A monopolistically competitive firm can convince buyers that its product has value by differentiating its product to suit consumers' preferences.
Answer: ● True   False
Diff: 2   Type: TF   Page Ref: 426/426
Topic: What Makes a Firm Successful?
Skill: Conceptual
Objective: LO 6: Identify key factors that determine a firm's success.
AACSB Coding: Reflective Thinking
Special Feature: None

Chapter 13   Oligopoly: Firms in Less Competitive Markets

13.1   Oligopoly and Barrier to Entry

1. What do Wal-Mart, the Microsoft Corporation, and the Dell computer company have in common?
   - A) Each achieved a dominant position in its industry because it owned a key input in the production of its product.
   - B) The industry in which each firm competes is an oligopoly because of government-imposed barriers to entry.
   - C) Each company was founded in the same state.
   - D) The profitability of each firm depends on its interactions with other firms.

   Answer: D
   Diff: 1   Type: MC   Page Ref: 440-1/440-1
   Topic: Characteristics of oligopoly
   Skill: Fact
   Objective: LO 1: Show how barriers to entry explain the existence of oligopolies
   AACSB Coding: Reflective Thinking
   Special Feature: Chapter Opener: Competing with Wal-Mart

2. Beginning in the 1970s, Wal-Mart began to develop a computerized system for tracking the goods sold in its stores. Which of the following actions did Wal-Mart take to aid in the development of this system?
   - A) In the early 1980s Wal-Mart insisted that its suppliers use UPC barcodes on its products.
   - B) In the early 1980s Wal-Mart insisted that its suppliers purchase Dell computers for its stores' checkout lines.
   - C) It obtained a patent on the tracking system it developed in order to create a barrier to entry.
   - D) Engineers from Wal-Mart met with engineers from the Dell computer company and the Microsoft Corporation to develop a system that other retailers would not be able to copy.

   Answer: A
   Diff: 2   Type: MC   Page Ref: 440-1/440-1
   Topic: Characteristics of oligopoly
   Skill: Fact
   Objective: LO 1: Show how barriers to entry explain the existence of oligopolies
   AACSB Coding: Reflective Thinking
   Special Feature: Chapter Opener: Competing with Wal-Mart

3. Oligopoly differs from perfect competition and monopolistic competition in that
   A) barriers to entry are lower in oligopoly industries than they are in perfectly competitive and monopolistically competitive industries.
   B) demand and marginal revenue curves are more useful for analyzing oligopoly than they are for analyzing perfect competition and monopolistic competition.
   C) because oligopoly firms often react when other firms in their industry when change their prices, it is difficult to know what the oligopolist's demand curve looks like.
   D) the concentration ratios of oligopoly industries are lower than they are for perfectly competitive and monopolistically competitive firms.

Answer: C
Diff: 1   Type: MC   Page Ref: 442/442
Topic: Characteristics of oligopoly
Skill: Conceptual
Objective: LO 1: Show how barriers to entry explain the existence of oligopolies
AACSB Coding: Reflective Thinking
Special Feature: None

4. We can draw demand curves for firms in perfectly competitive and monopolistically competitive industries, but not for oligopoly firms. The reason for this is
   A) there are no barriers to entry in perfectly competitive and monopolistically competitive industries. There are high barriers to entry in oligopoly industries.
   B) we can assume that the prices charged by perfectly competitive and monopolistically competitive firms have no impact on rival firms. For oligopoly this assumption is unrealistic.
   C) that perfectly competitive and monopolistically competitive firms are price takers. Oligopoly firms are price makers.
   D) perfectly competitive and monopolistically competitive firms sell standardized products. Oligopoly firms sell differentiated products.

Answer: B
Diff: 3   Type: MC   Page Ref: 442/442
Topic: Characteristics of oligopoly
Skill: Conceptual
Objective: LO 1: Show how barriers to entry explain the existence of oligopolies
AACSB Coding: Reflective Thinking
Special Feature: None

5. When large firms in oligopoly markets cut their prices
    A) rival firms will also cut their prices to avoid losing sales.
    B) rival firms will not change their prices because most of their customers have signed contracts that commit them to doing business with the same firms for the life of their contracts.
    C) we don't know for sure how rival firms will respond.
    D) rival firms will not cut their prices because they fear that the federal government will accuse them of collusion.
Answer: C
Diff: 2   Type: MC   Page Ref: 442/442
Topic: Characteristics of oligopoly
Skill: Conceptual
Objective: LO 1: Show how barriers to entry explain the existence of oligopolies
AACSB Coding: Reflective Thinking
Special Feature: None

6. The fraction of an industry's sales that are accounted for by the largest firms is called
    A) the four-firm competition ratio.
    B) the four-firm concentration ratio.
    C) the four-firm industry ratio.
    D) the four-firm oligopoly ratio.
Answer: B
Diff: 1   Type: MC   Page Ref: 442-3/442-3
Topic: Concentration ratio
Skill: Definition
Objective: LO 1: Show how barriers to entry explain the existence of oligopolies
AACSB Coding: Reflective Thinking
Special Feature: None

7. A four-firm concentration ratio measures
    A) the extent to which industry sales are concentrated among a few large firms.
    B) the price elasticity of demand among the four largest firms in an industry.
    C) the number of firms in an industry.
    D) the price elasticity of demand in an industry.
Answer: A
Diff: 1   Type: MC   Page Ref: 442-3/442-3
Topic: Concentration ratio
Skill: Conceptual
Objective: LO 1: Show how barriers to entry explain the existence of oligopolies
AACSB Coding: Reflective Thinking
Special Feature: None

8. As a measure of competition in an industry concentration ratios have several flaws. One of these flaws is that concentration ratios
   A) assume that all industries have low barriers to entry.
   B) assume that a ratio less than .40 (40 percent) means an industry is perfectly competitive.
   C) assume there are only four firms in an industry.
   D) are calculated for the national market, even though competition in some industries is mainly local.

Answer: D
Diff: 2   Type: MC   Page Ref: 442-3/442-3
Topic: Concentration ratio
Skill: Conceptual
Objective: LO 1: Show how barriers to entry explain the existence of oligopolies
AACSB Coding: Reflective Thinking
Special Feature: None

9. Which of the following is *not* a characteristic of oligopoly?
   A) The ability to influence price.
   B) A small number of firms.
   C) Low barriers to entry.
   D) Interdependent firms.

Answer: C
Diff: 1   Type: MC   Page Ref: 442/442
Topic: Characteristics of oligopoly
Skill: Conceptual
Objective: LO 1: Show how barriers to entry explain the existence of oligopolies
AACSB Coding: Reflective Thinking
Special Feature: None

10. Which of the following is not a barrier to entry?
   A) An inelastic demand curve.
   B) Economies of scale.
   C) Ownership of a key input.
   D) A patent.

Answer: A
Diff: 1   Type: MC   Page Ref: 443/443
Topic: Barriers to entry
Skill: Fact
Objective: LO 1: Show how barriers to entry explain the existence of oligopolies
AACSB Coding: Reflective Thinking
Special Feature: None

11. Economies of scale will create a barrier to entry in an oligopoly industry when
    A) a firm's minimum efficient scale occurs where long-run average total costs are constant.
    B) the typical firm's long-run average total cost curve reaches a minimum at a level of output that is a large fraction of total industry sales.
    C) the typical firm's long-run average total cost curve reaches a minimum at a level of output that is a small fraction of total industry sales.
    D) the industry's four-firm concentration ratio is less than 40 percent.
    Answer: B
    Diff: 2   Type: MC   Page Ref: 443/443
    Topic: Economies of scale
    Skill: Conceptual
    Objective: LO 1: Show how barriers to entry explain the existence of oligopolies
    AACSB Coding: Reflective Thinking
    Special Feature: None

12. If economies of scale are relatively important in an industry the typical firm's
    A) marginal cost curve will decline continuously until it reaches minimum efficient scale.
    B) long-run average cost curve will begin rising before it reaches minimum efficient scale.
    C) long-run average cost curve will reach a minimum at a level of output that leaves room for a large number of firms to enter the industry.
    D) long-run average cost curve will reach a minimum at a level of output that is a relatively large fraction of total industry sales.
    Answer: D
    Diff: 2   Type: MC   Page Ref: 443/443
    Topic: Economies of scale
    Skill: Conceptual
    Objective: LO 1: Show how barriers to entry explain the existence of oligopolies
    AACSB Coding: Reflective Thinking
    Special Feature: None

13. A patent is an example of
    A) how ownership of a key input creates a barrier to entry.
    B) a government-imposed barrier to entry.
    C) occupational licensing.
    D) how market failure can lead to oligopoly.
    Answer: B
    Diff: 1   Type: MC   Page Ref: 444/444
    Topic: Barriers to entry
    Skill: Conceptual
    Objective: LO 1: Show how barriers to entry explain the existence of oligopolies
    AACSB Coding: Reflective Thinking
    Special Feature: None

14. For many years the Aluminum Company of America (Alcoa) controlled most of the world's supply of high quality bauxite, the ore needed to produce aluminum. What type of entry barrier was responsible for Alcoa's position in the aluminum industry?
    A) Ownership of a key input.
    B) A government–imposed barrier.
    C) A patent on the manufacture of aluminum.
    D) Economies of scale.
    Answer: A
    Diff: 1   Type: MC   Page Ref: 444/444
    Topic: Barriers to entry
    Skill: Conceptual
    Objective: LO 1: Show how barriers to entry explain the existence of oligopolies
    AACSB Coding: Reflective Thinking
    Special Feature: None

15. Which of the following is *not* an example of a government–imposed entry barrier?
    A) Patents.
    B) Occupational licensing.
    C) Barriers to international trade.
    D) Antitrust legislation.
    Answer: D
    Diff: 1   Type: MC   Page Ref: 444–5/444–5
    Topic: Barriers to entry
    Skill: Fact
    Objective: LO 1: Show how barriers to entry explain the existence of oligopolies
    AACSB Coding: Reflective Thinking
    Special Feature: None

16. Consider a U–shaped long–run average cost curve that has a minimum efficient scale at 6,000 units of output. In this case, this industry would be
    A) perfectly competitive if the market quantity demanded is 20,000 units.
    B) monopolistically competitive if the market quantity demanded is 12,000 units.
    C) an oligopoly if the market quantity demanded is 18,000 units.
    D) an oligopoly if the four–firm concentration ratio is more than 10 percent.
    Answer: C
    Diff: 1   Type: MC   Page Ref: 443–4/443–4
    Topic: Economies of scale
    Skill: Conceptual
    Objective: LO 1: Show how barriers to entry explain the existence of oligopolies
    AACSB Coding: Reflective Thinking
    Special Feature: None

17. Hewlett–Packard will not raise the prices of its personal computers without first considering how Dell might respond. This is evidence of
    A) interdependence.
    B) collusion.
    C) cutthroat competition.
    D) price fixing.
    Answer: A
    Diff: 1   Type: MC   Page Ref: 444/444
    Topic: Interdependence
    Skill: Fact
    Objective: LO 1: Show how barriers to entry explain the existence of oligopolies
    AACSB Coding: Reflective Thinking
    Special Feature: None

18. If economies of scale are relatively unimportant in an industry, the typical firm's long–run average total cost curve will reach a minimum at a level of output that is a _____ fraction of total industry sales. The industry will be _____.
    A) large; competitive.
    B) large; an oligopoly.
    C) small; competitive.
    D) small; an oligopoly.
    Answer: C
    Diff: 2   Type: MC   Page Ref: 443–4/443–4
    Topic: Economies of scale
    Skill: Analytical
    Objective: LO 1: Show how barriers to entry explain the existence of oligopolies
    AACSB Coding: Reflective Thinking
    Special Feature: None

19. A patent is a government–imposed entry barrier because
    A) it allows a firm to achieve economies of scale.
    B) it is a key input owned by the firm that is granted the patent.
    C) it limits the quantity of a good that can be imported into a country.
    D) it gives a firm the exclusive right to a new product for a period of 20 years from the date the product is invented.
    Answer: D
    Diff: 1   Type: MC   Page Ref: 444/444
    Topic: Barriers to entry
    Skill: Conceptual
    Objective: LO 1: Show how barriers to entry explain the existence of oligopolies
    AACSB Coding: Reflective Thinking
    Special Feature: None

20. An example of a government-imposed barrier to entry gives a firm the exclusive right to a new product for a period of 20 years from the date the product is invented. This entry barrier is known as
    A) a copyright.
    B) a patent.
    C) an exclusive marketing agreement.
    D) a tariff.
    Answer: B
    Diff: 1   Type: MC   Page Ref: 444/444
    Topic: Government-imposed barriers
    Skill: Definition
    Objective: LO 1: Show how barriers to entry explain the existence of oligopolies
    AACSB Coding: Reflective Thinking
    Special Feature: None

21. The De Beers Company blocked competition
    A) in the diamond market by controlling the output of most of the world's diamond mines.
    B) by controlling the supply of most of the world's high-quality bauxite, the mineral used to produce aluminum.
    C) in the market for fresh and frozen cranberries because it controls about 80 percent of the cranberry crop.
    D) because it has lower costs of producing than other department stores due to economies of scale.
    Answer: A
    Diff: 1   Type: MC   Page Ref: 444/444
    Topic: Barriers to entry
    Skill: Fact
    Objective: LO 1: Show how barriers to entry explain the existence of oligopolies
    AACSB Coding: Reflective Thinking
    Special Feature: None

22. Of all barriers to entry the most important are those that are due to
    A) ownership of a key input.
    B) economies of scale.
    C) government-imposed barriers.
    D) the Herfindahl-Hirschman Index.
    Answer: B
    Diff: 1   Type: MC   Page Ref: 443/443
    Topic: Barriers to entry
    Skill: Conceptual
    Objective: LO 1: Show how barriers to entry explain the existence of oligopolies
    AACSB Coding: Reflective Thinking
    Special Feature: None

23. Which industry has the highest four-firm concentration ratio?
    A) Discount department stores.
    B) College bookstores.
    C) Retail gasoline stations.
    D) Cigarettes.
    Answer: D
    Diff: 1   Type: MC   Page Ref: 443/443
    Topic: Concentration ratio
    Skill: Fact
    Objective: LO 1: Show how barriers to entry explain the existence of oligopolies
    AACSB Coding: Reflective Thinking
    Special Feature: None

24. Which government agency publishes four-firm concentration ratios?
    A) The Economic Council.
    B) The Federal Reserve System.
    C) The U.S. Bureau of the Census.
    D) The Treasury Department.
    Answer: C
    Diff: 1   Type: MC   Page Ref: 443/443
    Topic: Concentration ratio
    Skill: Fact
    Objective: LO 1: Show how barriers to entry explain the existence of oligopolies
    AACSB Coding: Reflective Thinking
    Special Feature: None

25. The profit-maximizing level of output and the profit-maximizing price for an oligopolist cannot be calculated when we don't know
    A) what the concentration ratio for the oligopolist's industry is.
    B) what the minimum efficient scale in the oligopolist's industry is.
    C) the demand curve and the marginal revenue curve of the oligopolist.
    D) the type of barrier to entry that exists in the oligopolist's industry.
    Answer: C
    Diff: 2   Type: MC   Page Ref: 442/442
    Topic: Characteristics of oligopoly
    Skill: Conceptual
    Objective: LO 1: Show how barriers to entry explain the existence of oligopolies
    AACSB Coding: Reflective Thinking
    Special Feature: None

26. Because of the shortcomings of concentration ratios some economists prefer another measure of competition called
    A) the Competition Index.
    B) the Marginal Revenue–Marginal Cost Index.
    C) the Economic Profit Index.
    D) the Herfindahl–Hirschman Index.

Answer: A
Diff: 1   Type: MC   Page Ref: 443/443
Topic: Concentration ratio
Skill: Fact
Objective: LO 1: Show how barriers to entry explain the existence of oligopolies
AACSB Coding: Reflective Thinking
Special Feature: None

27. Ocean Spray is considered to be an oligopoly firm because, until the 1990s, it faced little competition in the market for fresh and frozen cranberries. Why?
    A) Ocean Spray had a patent on the production of cranberries that gave the company the exclusive right to market its product for 20 years. The 20-year period ended in the 1990s.
    B) Until the 1990s, Ocean Spray controlled almost the entire supply of cranberries.
    C) Ocean Spray was able to achieve significant economies of scale in the production of cranberries. Beginning in the 1990s, other firms finally achieved economies of scale as well, but Ocean Spray still controls about 80 percent of the cranberry market.
    D) The federal government imposed a high tariff on cranberry imports. During the 1990s the tariff was eliminated, but Ocean Spray still controls about 80 percent of the cranberry market.

Answer: B
Diff: 3   Type: MC   Page Ref: 444/444
Topic: Barriers to entry
Skill: Fact
Objective: LO 1: Show how barriers to entry explain the existence of oligopolies
AACSB Coding: Reflective Thinking
Special Feature: None

28. The people firms hire to attempt to convince state legislators and members of Congress to pass laws that are favorable to the economic interests of the firms are called
    A) economic advisors.
    B) legislative assistants.
    C) government bureaucrats.
    D) lobbyists.

Answer: D
Diff: 1   Type: MC   Page Ref: 444/444
Topic: Government–imposed barriers
Skill: Fact
Objective: LO 1: Show how barriers to entry explain the existence of oligopolies
AACSB Coding: Reflective Thinking
Special Feature: None

29. Doctors and lawyers in every state need a license to practice. This is an example of
    A) consumer protection laws.
    B) consumer advocacy.
    C) occupational licensing.
    D) ownership of a key input.
    Answer: C
    Diff: 1   Type: MC   Page Ref: 444/444
    Topic: Government–imposed barriers
    Skill: Fact
    Objective: LO 1: Show how barriers to entry explain the existence of oligopolies
    AACSB Coding: Reflective Thinking
    Special Feature: None

30. The justification for occupational licensing laws is that they protect the public from incompetent practitioners (for example, lawyers and medical doctors), but the laws also result in
    A) higher prices and restrictions on the number of people who can enter the professions affected by the laws.
    B) economies of scale.
    C) ownership of a key input.
    D) an increase in the amount of output required to achieve minimum efficient scale.
    Answer: A
    Diff: 1   Type: MC   Page Ref: 445/445
    Topic: Government–imposed barriers
    Skill: Conceptual
    Objective: LO 1: Show how barriers to entry explain the existence of oligopolies
    AACSB Coding: Reflective Thinking
    Special Feature: None

31. A consequence of the quota that has been imposed on the importation of sugar into the United States is
    A) consumers are protected from eating unsafe products made from cheap imported sugar.
    B) competition in the U.S. sugar market is reduced.
    C) the cost of producing cereal, chocolate and candy products in the United States is reduced.
    D) the market for sugar in the U.S. has become monopolistically competitive rather than oligopolistic.
    Answer: B
    Diff: 1   Type: MC   Page Ref: 445/445
    Topic: Government–imposed barriers
    Skill: Conceptual
    Objective: LO 1: Show how barriers to entry explain the existence of oligopolies
    AACSB Coding: Reflective Thinking
    Special Feature: None

32. If firms are protected by substantial barriers to entry, short-run profits can turn into long-run profits.
    Answer: ⊙ True   False
    Diff: 1   Type: TF   Page Ref: 442–3/442–3
    Topic: Barriers to entry
    Skill: Conceptual
    Objective: LO 1: Show how barriers to entry explain the existence of oligopolies
    AACSB Coding: Reflective Thinking
    Special Feature: None

33. The four-firm concentration ratio of the aircraft industry is over 80 percent. Most economists would consider this industry an oligopoly.
    Answer: ⊙ True   False
    Diff: 1   Type: TF   Page Ref: 442–3/442–3
    Topic: Concentration ratio
    Skill: Fact
    Objective: LO 1: Show how barriers to entry explain the existence of oligopolies
    AACSB Coding: Reflective Thinking
    Special Feature: None

34. The most important barrier to entry is economies of scale.
    Answer: ⊙ True   False
    Diff: 1   Type: TF   Page Ref: 443/443
    Topic: Concentration ratio
    Skill: Fact
    Objective: LO 1: Show how barriers to entry explain the existence of oligopolies
    AACSB Coding: Reflective Thinking
    Special Feature: None

35. Because of the flaws of the concentration ratio as a measure of the extent of competition in an industry, some economists prefer another measure of competition, the Herfindahl-Hirschman Index.
    Answer: ⊙ True   False
    Diff: 2   Type: TF   Page Ref: 443/443
    Topic: Oligopoly
    Skill: Conceptual
    Objective: LO 1: Show how barriers to entry explain the existence of oligopolies
    AACSB Coding: Reflective Thinking
    Special Feature: None

36. In an oligopoly minimum efficient scale is likely to occur at a level of output that is a large fraction of industry sales.
    Answer: ⊙ True   False
    Diff: 2   Type: TF   Page Ref: 443/443
    Topic: Characteristics of oligopoly
    Skill: Conceptual
    Objective: LO 1: Show how barriers to entry explain the existence of oligopolies
    AACSB Coding: Reflective Thinking
    Special Feature: None

37. The breakfast cereal industry has a four-firm concentration ratio greater than 80 percent. Is this enough information to classify the industry as an oligopoly? Is a high concentration ratio evidence that an industry is not competitive?

Answer: Most economists classify an industry with a four-firm concentration ratio greater than 40 percent as an oligopoly; therefore, the breakfast cereal industry would be considered an oligopoly. But the concentration ratio is a flawed measure of the extent of competition in the breakfast cereal industry. For example, concentration ratios do not include sales in the United States by foreign firms so to the extent that foreign firms sell breakfast cereal in the U.S. the concentration ratio understates the degree of competition in this industry. Also, since concentration ratios are calculated for the national market, regional or local competition is ignored. Concentration ratios are useful for providing a general idea of the extent of competition in an industry.

Diff: 2   Type: ES   Page Ref: 442–5/442–5
Topic: Concentration ratio
Skill: Analytical
Objective: LO 1: Show how barriers to entry explain the existence of oligopolies
AACSB Coding: Analytic Skills
Special Feature: None

38. Firms in an oligopoly are said to be interdependent. What does this mean?

Answer: Interdependence among firms means that the decisions and business strategies of each firm have a significant impact on the decisions, strategies, and profits of the other firms in the oligopoly industry.

Diff: 1   Type: ES   Page Ref: 442/442
Topic: Characteristics of oligopoly
Skill: Definition
Objective: LO 1: Show how barriers to entry explain the existence of oligopolies
AACSB Coding: Reflective Thinking
Special Feature: None

39. Most economists are concerned about entry barriers. Why is this so important to them?

Answer: Entry barriers enable a firm to earn long–run profits. Furthermore, when there are entry barriers in a market, the industry output does not achieve allocative or productive efficiency, resulting in deadweight losses.

Diff: 3   Type: ES   Page Ref: 442–5/442–5
Topic: Barriers to entry
Skill: Conceptual
Objective: LO 1: Show how barriers to entry explain the existence of oligopolies
AACSB Coding: Reflective Thinking
Special Feature: None

13.2 Using Game theory to Analyze Oligopoly

1. Game theory was developed in the 1940s by John von Neuman, a mathematician, and an economist named
   A) John Nash.
   B) John Maynard Keynes.
   C) Oskar Morgenstern.
   D) Milton Friedman.
   Answer: C
   Diff: 1   Type: MC   Page Ref: 445/445
   Topic: Game theory
   Skill: Fact
   Objective: LO 2: Use game theory to analyze the actions of oligopolistic firms
   AACSB Coding: Reflective Thinking
   Special Feature: None

2. An oligopoly between two firms is called
   A) a biopoly.
   B) an oligopoly; there are no special terms used for oligopolies with different numbers of firms.
   C) a dual–firm oligopoly.
   D) a duopoly.
   Answer: D
   Diff: 1   Type: MC   Page Ref: 445/445
   Topic: Characteristics of oligopoly
   Skill: Definition
   Objective: LO 2: Use game theory to analyze the actions of oligopolistic firms
   AACSB Coding: Reflective Thinking
   Special Feature: None

3. The study of how people make decisions in situations in which attaining their goals depends on their interactions with others is called
   A) game theory.
   B) oligopoly.
   C) competitive analysis.
   D) strategic analysis.
   Answer: A
   Diff: 1   Type: MC   Page Ref: 445/445
   Topic: Game theory
   Skill: Definition
   Objective: LO 2: Use game theory to analyze the actions of oligopolistic firms
   AACSB Coding: Reflective Thinking
   Special Feature: None

4. In economics, the study of the decisions of firms in industries where the profits of each firm depend on its interactions with other firms is called
   A) decision theory.
   B) game theory.
   C) market structure analysis.
   D) profit analysis.
   Answer: B
   Diff: 1   Type: MC   Page Ref: 445/445
   Topic: Game theory
   Skill: Definition
   Objective: LO 2: Use game theory to analyze the actions of oligopolistic firms
   AACSB Coding: Reflective Thinking
   Special Feature: None

5. The approach economists use to analyze competition among oligopolists is called
   A) marginal analysis.
   B) game theory.
   C) oligopoly theory.
   D) competition among the few.
   Answer: B
   Diff: 2   Type: MC   Page Ref: 445/445
   Topic: Game theory
   Skill: Fact
   Objective: LO 2: Use game theory to analyze the actions of oligopolistic firms
   AACSB Coding: Reflective Thinking
   Special Feature: None

6. Economists use game theory to analyze oligopolies because
   A) real markets are too complicated to analyze without using games.
   B) it is more enjoyable for economists and students to learn by playing games.
   C) game theory helps us to understand why interactions among firms are crucial in determining profitable business strategies.
   D) game theory is useful in understanding the actions of firms that are price takers.
   Answer: C
   Diff: 1   Type: MC   Page Ref: 445-6/445-6
   Topic: Game theory
   Skill: Conceptual
   Objective: LO 2: Use game theory to analyze the actions of oligopolistic firms
   AACSB Coding: Reflective Thinking
   Special Feature: None

7. In game theory, the three key characteristics of a game are
    A) rules, strategies, and payoffs.
    B) rules, regulations, and payoffs.
    C) winners, losers, and rules.
    D) risks, rewards, and penalties.
   Answer: A
   Diff: 1   Type: MC   Page Ref: 445/445
   Topic: Game theory
   Skill: Fact
   Objective: LO 2: Use game theory to analyze the actions of oligopolistic firms
   AACSB Coding: Reflective Thinking
   Special Feature: None

8. All games share three characteristics. Two of these characteristics are rule and strategies. What is the third characteristic called?
    A) Competition.
    B) Collusion.
    C) Results.
    D) Payoffs.
   Answer: D
   Diff: 2   Type: MC   Page Ref: 445/445
   Topic: Game theory
   Skill: Fact
   Objective: LO 2: Use game theory to analyze the actions of oligopolistic firms
   AACSB Coding: Reflective Thinking
   Special Feature: None

9. A set of actions that a firm takes to achieve a goal is the definition of a
    A) business plan.
    B) business strategy.
    C) business prospectus.
    D) business goal.
   Answer: B
   Diff: 1   Type: MC   Page Ref: 445/445
   Topic: Business strategy
   Skill: Definition
   Objective: LO 2: Use game theory to analyze the actions of oligopolistic firms
   AACSB Coding: Reflective Thinking
   Special Feature: None

10. A situation in which each firm chooses the best strategy given the strategies chosen by other firms is called a
    A) Nash equilibrium.
    B) dominant strategy.
    C) collusion.
    D) pay-off matrix.
    Answer: A
    Diff: 2   Type: MC   Page Ref: 446/446
    Topic: Nash equilibrium
    Skill: Definition
    Objective: LO 2: Use game theory to analyze the actions of oligopolistic firms
    AACSB Coding: Reflective Thinking
    Special Feature: None

11. Collusion occurs when
    A) a firm chooses a level of output to maximize its own profit.
    B) two firms' price and output decisions come into conflict.
    C) there is an agreement among firms to charge the same price or otherwise not to compete.
    D) firms refuse to follow their price leaders.
    Answer: C
    Diff: 1   Type: MC   Page Ref: 446/446
    Topic: Collusion
    Skill: Definition
    Objective: LO 2: Use game theory to analyze the actions of oligopolistic firms
    AACSB Coding: Reflective Thinking
    Special Feature: None

12. An agreement among firms to charge the same price or to otherwise not compete is called
    A) a pay-off matrix.
    B) a subgame-perfect equilibrium.
    C) a Nash equilibrium.
    D) collusion.
    Answer: D
    Diff: 1   Type: MC   Page Ref: 446/446
    Topic: Collusion
    Skill: Definition
    Objective: LO 2: Use game theory to analyze the actions of oligopolistic firms
    AACSB Coding: Reflective Thinking
    Special Feature: None

13. A table that shows the possible payoffs each firm earns from every combination of strategies by all firms is called
    A) an earnings table.
    B) a payoff table.
    C) a payoff matrix.
    D) a strategic matrix.
Answer: C
Diff: 1   Type: MC   Page Ref: 446/446
Topic: Payoff matrix
Skill: Definition
Objective: LO 2: Use game theory to analyze the actions of oligopolistic firms
AACSB Coding: Reflective Thinking
Special Feature: None

14. A dominant strategy is
    A) an equilibrium where each firm chooses the best strategy, given the strategies of other firms.
    B) a strategy chosen by two firms that decide to charge the same price or otherwise not to compete.
    C) a strategy that is obviously the best for each firm that is a party to a business decision.
    D) a strategy that is the best for a firm no matter what strategies other firms use.
Answer: D
Diff: 2   Type: MC   Page Ref: 446/446
Topic: Business strategy
Skill: Definition
Objective: LO 2: Use game theory to analyze the actions of oligopolistic firms
AACSB Coding: Reflective Thinking
Special Feature: None

15. Who won a Nobel Prize in economics for his work in the development of game theory?
    A) John von Neuman.
    B) Oskar Morgenstern.
    C) John Nash.
    D) Howard Schultz.
Answer: A
Diff: 1   Type: MC   Page Ref: 445/445
Topic: Game theory
Skill: Fact
Objective: LO 2: Use game theory to analyze the actions of oligopolistic firms
AACSB Coding: Reflective Thinking
Special Feature: None

16. Two firms would sometimes be better off if they got together and agreed to charge a high price, rather than to compete and risk having to charge a lower, competitive price. What is the greatest deterrent to this strategy?
    A) The firms may find that the price they charge is greater than the price that would maximize their profits.
    B) An agreement by firms to charge high prices is illegal. The government can fine the firms and send their managers to jail.
    C) Consumers may resent having to pay high prices and not buy from either of the firms.
    D) One of the firms may decide to lower its price and take business away from the firm that charged the high price.
    Answer: B
    Diff: 3   Type: MC   Page Ref: 446/446
    Topic: Collusion
    Skill: Conceptual
    Objective: LO 2: Use game theory to analyze the actions of oligopolistic firms
    AACSB Coding: Reflective Thinking
    Special Feature: None

17. John Nash is famous because of his contributions to game theory as well as a book and movie based on his life. What is the title of the book and the movie?
    A) The Games People Play.
    B) A Beautiful Mind.
    C) Fear Strikes Out.
    D) Beloved Infidel.
    Answer: B
    Diff: 1   Type: MC   Page Ref: 447/447
    Topic: Game theory
    Skill: Fact
    Objective: LO 2: Use game theory to analyze the actions of oligopolistic firms
    AACSB Coding: Reflective Thinking
    Special Feature: Making the Connection: A Beautiful Mind: Game Theory Goes to the Movies

18. At one point in the movie *A Beautiful Mind* John Nash (played by Russell Crowe) describes what has become known as the Nash equilibrium: "The best result comes from everyone in the group doing what's best for himself and the group." This statement is
    A) correct, but it should have been attributed to John von Neumann and Oskar Morgenstern, not John Nash.
    B) incorrect. An accurate statement of the Nash equilibrium is: "The best result comes from everyone in the group doing what's best for himself."
    C) incorrect. An accurate statement of the Nash equilibrium is: "The best result comes from everyone using a strategy that will make himself as well off as possible, given the strategies of the other individuals."
    D) incorrect. An accurate statement of the Nash equilibrium is: "The best result comes from everyone doing what is best from himself, no matter what the strategies of the other individuals are."

    Answer: A
    Diff: 2   Type: MC   Page Ref: 447/447
    Topic: Game theory
    Skill: Conceptual
    Objective: LO 3: use sequential games to analyze business strategies
    AACSB Coding: Reflective Thinking
    Special Feature: Making the Connection: A Beautiful Mind: Game Theory Goes to the Movies

19. An equilibrium in a game in which players pursue their own self-interest is called
    A) a Nash equilibrium.
    B) a cooperative equilibrium.
    C) a noncooperative equilibrium.
    D) a Prisoners' dilemma.

    Answer: C
    Diff: 1   Type: MC   Page Ref: 448/448
    Topic: Game theory
    Skill: Definition
    Objective: LO 2: Use game theory to analyze the actions of oligopolistic firms
    AACSB Coding: Reflective Thinking
    Special Feature: None

20. When an oligopoly market is in Nash equilibrium,
    A) firms have colluded to set their prices.
    B) firms will not behave as profit maximizers.
    C) a firm will not take into account the strategies of its rivals.
    D) a firm will choose its best pricing strategy, given the strategies that it observes other firms have taken.

    Answer: D
    Diff: 1   Type: MC   Page Ref: 446/446
    Topic: Nash equilibrium
    Skill: Definition
    Objective: LO 2: Use game theory to analyze the actions of oligopolistic firms
    AACSB Coding: Reflective Thinking
    Special Feature: None

21. The Brooks Appliance Store and the Lefingwell Appliance Store (both are located in the same city) each sell an identical washer–dryer. The owner of each store considered offering the washer–dryer for $700, but decided on a price of $500. If this is a Nash equilibrium we can conclude that
    A) each store owner feared charging the higher price would result in being undercut by the other store charging the lower price.
    B) the owners of the stores feared that charging $700 could be used as evidence of collusion.
    C) charging $500 was the most profitable strategy for each store, regardless of what price was charged by the other store.
    D) the stores were less concerned about making a profit from the washer–dryers than they were with attracting customers who would also buy other appliances.
    Answer: C
    Diff: 2   Type: MC   Page Ref: 445/445
    Topic: Nash equilibrium
    Skill: Conceptual
    Objective: LO 2: Use game theory to analyze the actions of oligopolistic firms
    AACSB Coding: Analytic Skills
    Special Feature: Don't Let This Happen to YOU!: Don't Misunderstand Why Each Manager Ends up Charging a Price of $400

22. eBay is an online auction site where more than 200 million items are auctioned annually. What type of auctions are run on eBay?
    A) Noncooperative auctions.
    B) Second–price auctions.
    C) Cooperative auctions.
    D) Double–blind auctions.
    Answer: B
    Diff: 1   Type: MC   Page Ref: 449–50/449–50
    Topic: Game theory
    Skill: Fact
    Objective: LO 2: Use game theory to analyze the actions of oligopolistic firms
    AACSB Coding: Reflective Thinking
    Special Feature: Making the Connection: Is There a Dominant Strategy for Bidding on eBay?

23. A baseball hat worn by the Boston Red Sox Hall of Fame outfielder Ted Williams was auctioned on eBay. The three highest bidders and their bids were:

Roger Bulava $5,000
Tony Millasiti $4,900
Joe Albano $4,200

What price did Roger have to pay for the Ted Williams hat?
   A) $4,200.
   B) $5,000.
   C) $4,700 (the average of the three highest bids).
   D) $4,900.
Answer: D
Diff: 2   Type: MC   Page Ref: 449–50/449–50
Topic: Game theory
Skill: Analytical
Objective: LO 2: Use game theory to analyze the actions of oligopolistic firms
AACSB Coding: Analytic Skills
Special Feature: Making the Connection: Is There a Dominant Strategy for Bidding on eBay?

24. A game in which pursuing dominant strategies results in noncooperation that leaves all parties worse off is a
   A) a prisoners' dilemma.
   B) cooperative equilibrium.
   C) a first-price auction.
   D) a zero-sum game.
Answer: A
Diff: 1   Type: MC   Page Ref: 448/448
Topic: Prisoners' dilemma
Skill: Definition
Objective: LO 2: Use game theory to analyze the actions of oligopolistic firms
AACSB Coding: Reflective Thinking
Special Feature: None

25. Prisoners' dilemma games imply that cooperative behavior between two people or two firms always breaks down. But reality teaches us that people and firms often cooperate successfully to achieve their goals. Why do the results from prisoners' dilemma games fail to predict real world results?

    A) Prisoners' dilemma games do not permit people or firms from reneging on agreements, which often occurs in real word situations.

    B) The prisoners' dilemma does not apply to most business situations that are repeated over and over.

    C) Prisoners' dilemma games predict the behavior of people and firms that engage in illegal activity; most people and firms do not resort to illegal activity.

    D) Most real world situations involve more than two people or firms; the prisoners' dilemma is only applicable to situations that involve two parties.

Answer: B

Diff: 2   Type: MC   Page Ref: 448–9/448–9
Topic: Prisoners' dilemma
Skill: Conceptual
Objective: LO 2: Use game theory to analyze the actions of oligopolistic firms
AACSB Coding: Reflective Thinking
Special Feature: Solved Problem: Is Advertising a Prisoners' Dilemma for Coca–Cola and Pepsi?

Figure 13–1

		Ming	
		offers free pickup and delivery	*does not offer free pickup and delivery*
Henri	*offers free pickup and delivery*	Ming:$20,000 Henri:$50,000	Ming:$10,000 Henri:$25,000
	does not offer free pickup and delivery	Ming:$30,000 Henri:$40,000	Ming:$15,000 Henri:$45,000

Ming and Henri each run one of the two dry cleaning facilities in the town of Scaraby. Both consider offering free pickup and delivery services. Figure 13–1 shows the payoff matrix containing the expected quarterly profits for each firm.

26. **Refer to Figure 13–1.** Does Ming have a dominant strategy? If yes, what is it?

    A) Yes, Ming's dominant strategy is to offer free pickup and delivery.

    B) No, Ming does not a dominant strategy – his best outcome depends on what Henri does.

    C) Yes, Ming's dominant strategy is to not to offer free pickup and delivery.

    D) Yes, Ming's dominant strategy is to wait to see what Henri does first.

Answer: A

Diff: 3   Type: MC   Page Ref: 445–51/445–51
Topic: Game theory
Skill: Analytical
Objective: LO 2: Use game theory to analyze the actions of oligopolistic firms
AACSB Coding: Analytic Skills
Special Feature: None

27. *Refer to Figure 13–1.* Does Henri have a dominant strategy? If yes, what is it?
    A) Yes, Henri's dominant strategy is to not offer free pickup and delivery.
    B) Yes, Henri's dominant strategy is to offer free pickup and delivery.
    C) No, Henri does not a dominant strategy – his best outcome depends on what Ming does.
    D) Yes, Henri's dominant strategy is to wait and see what Ming does first.
    Answer: C
    Diff: 3   Type: MC   Page Ref: 445–51/445–51
    Topic: Game Theory
    Skill: Analytical
    Objective: LO 2: Use game theory to analyze the actions of oligopolistic firms
    AACSB Coding: Analytic Skills
    Special Feature: None

28. *Refer to Figure 13–1.* What is the Nash equilibrium in this game?
    A) There is no Nash equilibrium.
    B) Ming offers free pickup and delivery, but Henri does not.
    C) Henri offers free pickup and delivery, but Ming does not.
    D) Both Ming and Henri offer free pickup and delivery.
    Answer: D
    Diff: 3   Type: MC   Page Ref: 445–51/445–51
    Topic: Game Theory
    Skill: Analytical
    Objective: LO 2: Use game theory to analyze the actions of oligopolistic firms
    AACSB Coding: Analytic Skills
    Special Feature: None

29. An equilibrium in a game in which players pursue their own self–interest and do not cooperate is called a
    A) cartel equilibrium.
    B) noncooperative equilibrium.
    C) prisoners' dilemma equilibrium.
    D) dominant strategy equilibrium.
    Answer: B
    Diff: 1   Type: MC   Page Ref: 448/448
    Topic: Game theory
    Skill: Definition
    Objective: LO 2: Use game theory to analyze the actions of oligopolistic firms
    AACSB Coding: Reflective Thinking
    Special Feature: None

Figure 13-2

		Sturdy Homes (S) Strategies		
		$8,000	$10,000	$12,000
My Haven's (M) Strategies	$8,000	S: $4 million M: $4 million	S: $2 million M: $6 million	S: $1 million M: $7 million
	$10,000	S: $6 million M: $2 million	S: $5 million M: $5 million	S: $2 million M: $6 million
	$12,000	S: $7 million M: $1 million	S: $6 million M: $2 million	S: $3 million M: $3 million

There are two mobile home manufacturers in Nevada, Sturdy Homes (S) and My Haven (M). Sturdy Homes has been in the market for a long time and must now compete with newcomer, My Haven. Suppose that Sturdy Homes believes that My Haven will match any price it sets. Use Figure 13-2 to answer the following question(s) and assume throughout that Sturdy Homes believes that My Haven will match any price it sets.

30. *Refer to Figure 13-2.* What price will Sturdy Homes charge and what profit does Sturdy Homes expect to make?
    A) Price = $8, 000; expected profit = $7 million
    B) Price = $8,000; expected profit = $4 million
    C) Price = $10,000; expected profit = $5 million
    D) Price = $12,000; expected profit = $3 million
    Answer: C
    Diff: 3   Type: MC   Page Ref: 445–51/451–51
    Topic: Game theory
    Skill: Analytical
    Objective: LO 2: Use game theory to analyze the actions of oligopolistic firms
    AACSB Coding: Analytic Skills
    Special Feature: None

31.   *Table 13-1*

		Pepsi	Pepsi
		Don't Advertise	**Advertise**
Coca-Cola	Don't advertise	Coca-Cola earns $1,500 million profit/Pepsi earns $1,500 million profit	Coca-Cola earns $800 million profit/Pepsi earns $1,800 million profit
Coca-Cola	Advertise	Coca-Cola earns $1,800 profit/Pepsi earns $800 million profit	Coca-Cola earns $1,000 million profit/Pepsi earns $1,000 million profit

Refer to Table13-1. The payoff matrix shown above assumes that Pepsi and Cocoa-Cola must decide whether to advertise their products. The matrix shows how much profit each firm will earn if it does or does not advertise. The amount of profit for one firm depends on whether the other firm advertises. Which of the following statements is true?
   A) Neither Pepsi nor Coca-cola have a dominant strategy.
   B) Pepsi's dominant strategy is to advertise; Coca-Cola's dominant strategy is to not advertise.
   C) Coca-Cola's dominant strategy is to advertise; Pepsi's dominant strategy is to not advertise.
   D) The dominant strategy for both firms is to advertise.
Answer: D
Diff: 3   Type: MC   Page Ref: 448-9/448-9
Topic: Game theory
Skill: Analytical
Objective: LO 2: Use game theory to analyze the actions of oligopolistic firms
AACSB Coding: Analytic Skills
Special Feature: Solved Problem: Is Advertising a Prisoners' Dilemma for Coca-Cola and Pepsi?

32. *Refer to Table 13-1.* The payoff matrix shown above assumes that Pepsi and Cocoa-Cola must decide whether to advertise their products. The matrix shows how much profit each firm will earn if it does or does not advertise. The amount of profit for one firm depends on whether the other firm advertises. Which of the following statements is true?
   A) Given that Coca-cola advertises, Pepsi's best strategy is to not advertise.
   B) Given that Pepsi advertises, Coca-Cola's best strategy is to advertise.
   C) Pepsi and Coca-Cola will agree to collude in order to maximize their profits.
   D) Neither Pepsi nor Coca-cola will advertise; this decision will decrease their costs and allow each firm to earn more than $1,800 million in profits.
Answer: B
Diff: 3   Type: MC   Page Ref: 448-9/448-9
Topic: Game theory
Skill: Analytical
Objective: LO 2: Use game theory to analyze the actions of oligopolistic firms
AACSB Coding: Analytic Skills
Special Feature: Solved Problem: Is Advertising a Prisoners' Dilemma for Coca-Cola and Pepsi?

33. Which of the following explains why two firms (Firm A and Firm B) would engage in implicit collusion, rather than explicit collusion?
    A) Implicit collusion allows Firm A to increase its profits at the expense of Firm B without Firm B knowing that collusion has occurred; if Firm A engages in explicit collusion, Firm B will realize collusion has taken place and retaliate against Firm A.
    B) Implicit collusion is less costly to both firms than explicit collusion; therefore, profits will be greater for both firms if they engage in implicit collusion.
    C) explicit collusion is illegal; if the managers of Firm A and Firm B engage in implicit collusion they may be within the law.
    D) Implicit collusion always has an enforcement mechanism that forces both firms to collude; explicit collusion does not have an enforcement mechanism.
    Answer: C
    Diff: 2   Type: MC   Page Ref: 450/450
    Topic: Collusion
    Skill: Conceptual
    Objective: LO 2: Use game theory to analyze the actions of oligopolistic firms
    AACSB Coding: Reflective Thinking
    Special Feature: None

34. Which of the following is an example of implicit collusion?
    A) Product differentiation.
    B) A retaliation strategy.
    C) A second-price auction.
    D) Price leadership.
    Answer: D
    Diff: 2   Type: MC   Page Ref: 450-1/450-1
    Topic: Collusion
    Skill: Conceptual
    Objective: LO 2: Use game theory to analyze the actions of oligopolistic firms
    AACSB Coding: Reflective Thinking
    Special Feature: None

35. A form of implicit collusion where one firm in an oligopoly announces a price change which is matched by other firms in the same industry is
    A) "follow the leader" pricing.
    B) price leadership.
    C) retaliation pricing.
    D) "tit-for-tat" pricing.
    Answer: B
    Diff: 1   Type: MC   Page Ref: 450-1/450-1
    Topic: Collusion
    Skill: Definition
    Objective: LO 2: Use game theory to analyze the actions of oligopolistic firms
    AACSB Coding: Reflective Thinking
    Special Feature: None

36. Which of the following best explains why airlines often cut their ticket prices at the last-minute in order to fill the remaining empty seats on their flights?
    A) Fixed costs in the airline industry are very large, but the marginal cost of flying one more passenger is very low.
    B) Airlines receive a subsidy from the government for each flight that is fully booked and departs on time.
    C) The Federal Aviation Administration ranks each airline based on the percentage of flights that are fully booked. These rankings affect the decisions of firms to use a particular airline to fly their employees to business meetings.
    D) Cutting prices makes the airlines more popular with their customers, who may fly with the same airline in the future as the result of buying low-price tickets.

Answer: A
Diff: 2   Type: MC   Page Ref: 451-2/451-2
Topic: Game theory
Skill: Fact
Objective: LO 2: Use game theory to analyze the actions of oligopolistic firms
AACSB Coding: Reflective Thinking
Special Feature: Making the Connection: American Airlines and Northwest Airlines Fail to Cooperate on a Price Increase

37. In 2002 American Airlines indirectly raised some of their ticket prices by increasing the number of days business travelers would have to make their reservations prior to their flights from 3 days to 7 days. Since many business travelers cannot make their reservations 7 days in advance they were forced to buy full-fare tickets. How did other airlines respond to American Airlines' pricing change?
    A) All major airlines except Continental Airlines matched the change; Continental hoped to gain customers at the expense of American Airlines.
    B) Continental Airlines matched the change, but other airlines refused to go along, hoping to gain customers at the expense of American Airlines.
    C) All other major airlines matched American Airlines change; this led the federal government to accuse the airlines of collusion. Eventually, the airlines were found guilty of collusion but only American Airlines was fined for its actions.
    D) None of the other airlines followed the change. American Airlines quickly returned to its previous pricing policy. No further pricing policy changes followed.

Answer: B
Diff: 3   Type: MC   Page Ref: 451-2/451-2
Topic: Game theory
Skill: Fact
Objective: LO 2: Use game theory to analyze the actions of oligopolistic firms
AACSB Coding: Reflective Thinking
Special Feature: Making the Connection: American Airlines and Northwest Airlines Fail to Cooperate on a Price Increase

38. The Organization of Petroleum Exporting Countries (OPEC) controls about 75 percent of the world's proven oil reserves. Economists refer to OPEC as a cartel because
    A) OPEC is a monopoly, but it is located outside of the boundaries of any one country. This is the definition of a cartel.
    B) this is the term used for an oligopoly that is controlled by national governments rather than private firms.
    C) it is a group of firms that collude to restrict output to increase prices and profits.
    D) this is the term economists use to describe an oligopoly that sells a standardized product, such as oil, rather than a differentiated product, such as automobiles.
    Answer: C
    Diff: 1   *Type: MC*   *Page Ref: 452/452*
    Topic: Cartels
    Skill: Definition
    Objective: LO 2: Use game theory to analyze the actions of oligopolistic firms
    AACSB Coding: Reflective Thinking
    Special Feature: None

39. From 1972 the world price of oil has been largely determined by OPEC, which controls about 75 percent of the world's proven oil reserves. Since 1972 the price of oil has
    A) fluctuated. OPEC's situation is an example of a prisoners' dilemma.
    B) risen slowly, but steadily. Members of OPEC fear that if they raise the price of oil too quickly this will lead oil–buying nations to accuse OPEC of price gouging, which is illegal under international law.
    C) steadily fallen through the 1970s, then risen continually in the years since then. OPEC's actions are an example of implicit collusion.
    D) been tied by OPEC to the rate of inflation in the United States. If, for example, the rate of inflation is 5 percent in one year OPEC will raise the price of oil by 5 percent the next year.
    Answer: A
    Diff: 2   *Type: MC*   *Page Ref: 452–4/452–4*
    Topic: Cartels
    Skill: Conceptual
    Objective: LO 2: Use game theory to analyze the actions of oligopolistic firms
    AACSB Coding: Reflective Thinking
    Special Feature: None

40. Collusion makes firms better off because if they act as a single entity (a cartel) they can reduce output and increase their prices and profits. But some cartels have failed and others are unstable. Which of the following is a reason why cartels often break down?
    A) Most cartels do not have a dominant strategy.
    B) When a cartel is profitable the amount of competition it faces increases.
    C) Members of a cartel may resent having to share their profits equally.
    D) Each member of a cartel has an incentive to "cheat" on the collusive agreement by producing more than its share when everyone else sticks with the collusive agreement.
Answer: D
Diff: 2   Type: MC   Page Ref: 452–4/452–4
Topic: Cartel
Skill: Conceptual
Objective: LO 2: Use game theory to analyze the actions of oligopolistic firms
AACSB Coding: Reflective Thinking
Special Feature: None

Figure 13–4

		Power Fuel's (P) Strategy	
		High Price	Low Price
Brawny Juice's (B) Strategy	High Price	P: $12m B: $12m	P: $16m B: $4m
	Low Price	P: $4m B: $16m	P: $8m B: $8m

Two rival oligopolists in the athletic supplements industry, the Power Fuel Company and the Brawny Juice Company, have to decide on their pricing strategy. Each can choose either a high price or a low price. Figure 13–4 shows the payoff matrix with the profits that each firm can expect to earn depending on the pricing strategy it adopts.

41. *Refer to Figure 13–4.* If the firms act out of individual self–interest, which prices will they select?
    A) Both firms will select a high price.
    B) Brawny Juice will select a high price, Power Fuel will select a low price.
    C) Brawny Juice will select a low price, Power Fuel will select a high price.
    D) Both firms will select a low price.
Answer: D
Diff: 2   Type: MC   Page Ref: 452–4/452–4
Topic: Game theory
Skill: Analytical
Objective: LO 2: Use game theory to analyze the actions of oligopolistic firms
AACSB Coding: Reflective Thinking
Special Feature: None

42. ***Refer to Figure 13–4.*** Which of the following is true?
    A) Power Fuel's dominant strategy is to select a low price.
    B) Brawny Juice's dominant strategy is to select a high price.
    C) Power Fuel does not have a dominant strategy.
    D) Brawny Juice does not have a dominant strategy.
    Answer: A
    Diff: 2   Type: MC   Page Ref: 452–4/452–4
    Topic: Game theory
    Skill: Analytical
    Objective: LO 2: Use game theory to analyze the actions of oligopolistic firms
    AACSB Coding: Analytic Skills
    Special Feature: None

43. ***Refer to Figure 13–4.*** If Brawny Juice selects a high price, what is Power Fuel's best strategy and what will Power Fuel earn as a result of this strategy?
    A) Power Fuel will select a low price and earn $8 million.
    B) Power Fuel will select a low price and earn $16 million.
    C) Power Fuel will select a high price and earn $12 million.
    D) Power Fuel will select a high price and earn $16 million.
    Answer: B
    Diff: 2   Type: MC   Page Ref: 452–4/452–4
    Topic: Game theory
    Skill: Analytical
    Objective: LO 2: Use game theory to analyze the actions of oligopolistic firms
    AACSB Coding: Analytic Skills
    Special Feature: None

44. ***Refer to Figure 13–4.*** If the firms cooperate, what prices will they select?
    A) Both firms will select a low price.
    B) Brawny Juice will select a high price, Power Fuel a low price.
    C) Both firms will select a high price.
    D) Brawny Juice will select a low price, Power Fuel a high price.
    Answer: C
    Diff: 2   Type: MC   Page Ref: 452–4/452–4
    Topic: Game theory
    Skill: Analytical
    Objective: LO 2: Use game theory to analyze the actions of oligopolistic firms
    AACSB Coding: Analytic Skills
    Special Feature: None

45. *Refer to Figure 13-4.* If the two firms collude, is there an incentive for either to cheat on the collusion agreement?
    A) No, neither firm can gain by cheating.
    B) Yes, but only Brawny Juice is in a position to gain by cheating.
    C) Yes, but only Power Fuel is in a position to gain by cheating.
    D) Yes, either firm can gain if it alone cheats.
    Answer: D
    Diff: 2   Type: MC   Page Ref: 452-4/452-4
    Topic: Game theory
    Skill: Analytical
    Objective: LO 2: Use game theory to analyze the actions of oligopolistic firms
    AACSB Coding: Analytic Skills
    Special Feature: None

46. Natural resource cartels such as OPEC are inherently unstable because their members operate with excess capacity and have an incentive to cheat on their output quotas.
    Answer: ◌ True   False
    Diff: 2   Type: TF   Page Ref: 452-4/452-4
    Topic: Cartels
    Skill: Fact
    Objective: LO 2: Use game theory to analyze the actions of oligopolistic firms
    AACSB Coding: Reflective Thinking
    Special Feature: None

47. Because many business situations are repeated games, firms may be able to avoid the prisoners' dilemma and implicitly collude to keep prices high.
    Answer: ◌ True   False
    Diff: 2   Type: TF   Page Ref: 445-51/445-51
    Topic: Prisoners' dilemma
    Skill: Conceptual
    Objective: LO 2: Use game theory to analyze the actions of oligopolistic firms
    AACSB Coding: Reflective Thinking
    Special Feature: None

48. Firms are more likely to find themselves in a prisoners' dilemma in sequential games as opposed to simultaneous games.
    Answer: True   ◌ False
    Diff: 2   Type: TF   Page Ref: 450-1/450-1
    Topic: Prisoners' dilemma
    Skill: Conceptual
    Objective: LO 2: Use game theory to analyze the actions of oligopolistic firms
    AACSB Coding: Reflective Thinking
    Special Feature: None

49. Consider two single-malt whiskey distillers, Laphroaig and Knockando. If they advertise, they can both sell more whiskey and increase their revenue. However, the cost of advertising more than offsets the increased revenue so that each distiller ends up with a lower profit than if they do not advertise. On the other hand, if only one advertises, that distiller increases its market share and also its profit.

    a. Construct a payoff matrix using the following hypothetical information:

        If neither distiller advertises, each earns a profit of $35 million per year.

        If both advertise, each earns a profit of $20 million per year.

        If one advertises and the other does not, the distiller who advertises earns a profit of $50 million and the distiller who does not advertise earns a profit of $9 million.

    b. If Laphroaig wants to maximize profit, will it advertise? Briefly explain.

    c. If Knockando wants to maximize profit, will it advertise? Briefly explain.

    d. Is there a dominant strategy for each distiller? Briefly explain.

Answer: a. The payoff matrix:

		Laphroaig's (L) Strategies	
		Advertise	*Don't Advertise*
Knockando's (K) Strategies	*Advertise*	L: $20m K: $20m	L: $9m K: $50m
	Don't Advertise	L: $50m K: $9m	L: $35m K: $35m

    b. If Laphroaig wants to maximize profit, it will advertise. If Knockando advertises, then Laphroaig will make $9 million if it does not advertise, and $20 million if it does. Therefore, it will choose to advertise. If Knockando does not advertise, then Laphroaig will make $50 million if it advertises and $35 million if it does not. Therefore, it will choose to advertise.

    c. If Knockando wants to maximize profit, it will advertise. Same reasoning as used in (b).

    d. Yes, the dominant strategy is to advertise. Same reasoning as in part b.

Diff: 3   Type: ES   Page Ref: 445–51/445–51
Topic: Game theory
Skill: Analytical
Objective: LO 2: Use game theory to analyze the actions of oligopolistic firms
AACSB Coding: Analytic Skills
Special Feature: None

50. Consider two single-malt whiskey distillers, Laphroaig and Knockando. If they advertise, they can both sell more whiskey and increase their revenue. However, the cost of advertising more than offsets the increased revenue so that each distiller ends up with a lower profit than if they do not advertise. On the other hand, if only one advertises, that distiller increases its market share and also its profit.

   a.   Construct a payoff matrix using the following hypothetical information:
          If neither distiller advertises: each earns a profit of $35 million per year.
          If both advertise: each earns a profit of $20 million per year.
          If one advertises and the other does not: the distiller who advertises earns a profit of $50 million and the distiller who does not advertise earns a profit of $9 million.

   b.   If the two distillers agree to coordinate their strategies, what is the outcome?

   Answer: a.   The payoff matrix:

		Laphroaig's (L) Strategies	
		Advertise	*Don't Advertise*
Knockando's (K) Strategies	*Advertise*	L: $20m K: $20m	L: $9m K: $50m
	Don't Advertise	L: $50m K: $9m	L: $35m K: $35m

   b. If the two distillers agree to coordinate their strategies, then they would choose not to advertise.

Diff: 2   Type: ES   Page Ref: 445–51/445–51
Topic: Game theory
Skill: Analytical
Objective: LO 2: Use game theory to analyze the actions of oligopolistic firms
AACSB Coding: Analytic Skills
Special Feature: None

51.

Figure 13–5

		Yemen (Y)	
		Low Output	**High Output**
Saudi Arabia (S)	**Low Output**	S: $200 million Y: $30 million	S: $100 million Y: $50 million
	High Output	S: $120 million Y: $10 million	S: $70 million Y: $20 million

Refer to Figure 13–5. Saudi Arabia and Yemen must decide how much oil to produce. Since the demand for oil is inelastic, relatively low production rates drive up prices and profits. Saudi Arabia, the world's largest and lowest cost producer, is able to influence market price; it has an incentive to keep output low. Yemen, on the other hand, is a relatively high cost producer with much smaller reserves. Use the payoff matrix in Figure 13–5 to answer the following questions.

a. What is the dominant strategy for Saudi Arabia?
b. What is the dominant strategy for Yemen?
c. What is the Nash equilibrium?

Answer: a. Saudia Arabia's dominant strategy is to produce a low output

b. Yemen's dominant strategy is to produce a high output.
c. The Nash equilibrium has Saudi Arabia producing a low output and Yemen a high output.

Diff: 3   Type: ES   Page Ref: 445–51/445–51
Topic: Game theory
Skill: Analytical
Objective: LO 2: Use game theory to analyze the actions of oligopolistic firms
AACSB Coding: Analytic Skills
Special Feature: None

52. *Refer to Figure 13–5.*
   a.   Create a new payoff matrix that reflects Saudi Arabia's willingness to pay Yemen $25 million to   produce a low output.
   b.   What is the dominant strategy for each country in this new game?
   c.   What is the new Nash equilibrium?

Answer: a. See payoff matrix below.

b. The dominant strategy for both countries is to produce a low output.

c.   The Nash equilibrium has both countries producing low output.

		Yemen (Y)	
		Low Output	**High Output**
Saudi Arabia (S)	**Low Output**	S: $175 million Y: $55 million	S: $100 million Y: $50 million
	High Output	S: $95 million Y: $35 million	S: $70 million Y: $20 million

Diff: 3   Type: ES   Page Ref: 452–4/452–4
Topic: Game theory
Skill: Analytical
Objective: LO 2: Use game theory to analyze the actions of oligopolistic firms
AACSB Coding: Analytic Skills
Special Feature: None

53. There are two firms in the residential paint industry, Cool Shades (C) and Warm Hues (W). They collude to share the market equally. They jointly set a monopoly price and split the quantity demanded at that price. Here are their options:

   i.   They continue to collude (no cheating) and make $12 million each in profits.
   ii. One firm cheats and the other does not. The firm that cheats makes a profit of $14 million whereas the firm that doesn't makes a profit of $9 million.
   iii. They both cheat and each firm makes a profit of $7 million.

   a.   Construct a payoff matrix for these two firms.
   b.   How does this situation relate to the prisoners' dilemma?
   c.   If each firm acted noncooperatively, how much profit would each make?
   d.   Are the firms better off colluding (with no cheating) or competing? Explain.

   Answer: a.   The payoff matrix:

		Cool Shades' (C) Strategies	
		Cheat	**Don't Cheat**
Warm Hues' (W) Strategies	**Cheat**	C: $7m R: $7m	C: $9m R: $14m
	Don't Cheat	C: $14m R: $9m	C: $12m R: $12m

b. With a prisoner's dilemma cooperative behavior – each prisoner standing firm without admitting to anything – leads to the best outcome for each player. But each player stands to gain by cheating. Similarly, in this case, each firm has the potential to make a profit of $14 m ($2 m above the outcome with collusion) if it unilaterally increases output. But if both acted on this incentive, then each ends up with only $7 m in profit. This outcome is inferior to cooperation.

c. Each firm has the potential to make a profit of $14 m if one cheats and the other does not. But if both cheat, then profits fall to $7 m each.

d. If they colluded (no cheating), each firm stands to make $12 m, an outcome which is superior to the cheating outcome.

Diff: 3   Type: ES   Page Ref: 445–51/445–51
Topic: Game theory
Skill: Analytical
Objective: LO 2: Use game theory to analyze the actions of oligopolistic firms
AACSB Coding: Analytic Skills
Special Feature: None

13.3   Sequential Games and Business Strategy

1. In many business situations one firm will act first, and then other firms will respond. To help analyze these types of situations economists use
    A) retaliation games.
    B) follow–the–leader–games.
    C) sequential games.
    D) bargaining games.
Answer: C
Diff: 1   Type: MC   Page Ref: 454/454
Topic: Sequential games and business strategy
Skill: Definition
Objective: LO 3: use sequential games to analyze business strategies
AACSB Coding: Reflective Thinking
Special Feature: None

2. Sequential games are used to analyze
    A) firms that are subject to the prisoners' dilemma.
    B) cartels.
    C) second–price auctions.
    D) situations in which one firm acts and other firms respond.
Answer: D
Diff: 1   Type: MC   Page Ref: 454/454
Topic: Sequential games and business strategy
Skill: Definition
Objective: LO 3: use sequential games to analyze business strategies
AACSB Coding: Reflective Thinking
Special Feature: None

3. A sequential game can be used to analyze whether a retail firm should build a large store or a small store in a city, when the correct choice depends on whether a competing firm will build a new store in the same city. Which of the following is used to analyze this type of decision?
    A) A decision tree.
    B) A decision matrix.
    C) A sequential matrix.
    D) An either-or graph.
    Answer: A
    Diff: 1   Type: MC   Page Ref: 454/454
    Topic: Sequential games and business strategy
    Skill: Conceptual
    Objective: LO 3: use sequential games to analyze business strategies
    AACSB Coding: Reflective Thinking
    Special Feature: None

4. Decision trees are commonly used to illustrate how firms make business decisions that depend on the actions of rival firms. A decision tree has boxes that contain points that represent when firms must make the decisions contained in the boxes. What are these points called?
    A) Option points.
    B) Decision nodes.
    C) Either-or terminals.
    D) Decision options.
    Answer: B
    Diff: 1   Type: MC   Page Ref: 454/454
    Topic: Sequential games and business strategy
    Skill: Definition
    Objective: LO 3: use sequential games to analyze business strategies
    AACSB Coding: Reflective Thinking
    Special Feature: None

5. When Wal-Mart decides to build a new retail store in a town it will decide to build a large store rather than a small store if the large store is expected to earn a greater economic profit. What other motive would Wal-Mart have for choosing to build a large store?
    A) A larger store will help Wal-Mart maintain its position as the leading retail company in the world more than a smaller store would.
    B) A larger store will give Wal-Mart greater political influence in the community.
    C) A larger store may deter entry into the town by a rival firm.
    D) Because of economies of scale, the average total cost of production is less for a larger store than a smaller store.
    Answer: C
    Diff: 2   Type: MC   Page Ref: 455-6/455-6
    Topic: Sequential games and business strategy
    Skill: Analytical
    Objective: LO 3: use sequential games to analyze business strategies
    AACSB Coding: Analytic Skills
    Special Feature: Solved Problem: Is Deterring Entry Always a Good Idea?

6. Sequential games are often used to analyze which two types of business strategies?
   A) Whether to invest in research and development and whether to offer employees an early retirement package.
   B) Deciding to merge with another firm and deciding how much to spend on an advertising campaign.
   C) Deciding to end production of an unprofitable product and deciding to shut down temporarily.
   D) Deterring entry by another firm and bargaining between firms.

Answer: D

Diff: 2   Type: MC   Page Ref: 454–7/454–7
Topic: Sequential games and business strategy
Skill: Conceptual
Objective: LO 3: use sequential games to analyze business strategies
AACSB Coding: Reflective Thinking
Special Feature: None

Figure 13–6

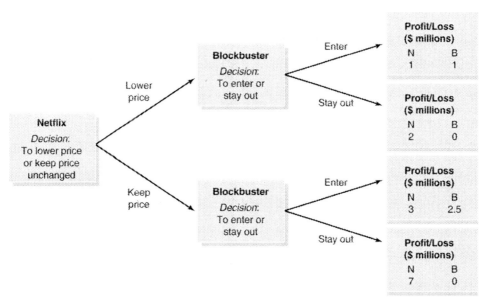

A few years ago Netflix (N) pioneered an online DVD rental service. Blockbuster (B), a brick and mortar DVD/video rental company, waited until Netflix had been in business for over a year before deciding whether to establish its own online rental service. At this point, Netflix had to decide whether or not to lower its subscription price in order to deter Blockbuster's entry into the market. Figure 13–6 shows the decision tree for the Netflix–Blockbuster entry game.

7. *Refer to Figure 13–6.* If Netflix lowers its price will this deter Blockbuster from setting up an online DVD rental service?
   A) Yes, because Blockbuster stands to lose $1 million if it competes with Netflix.
   B) Yes, because Blockbuster will make a smaller profit than Netflix if it chooses to compete.
   C) No, because Blockbuster will make a profit if it competes with Netflix.
   D) No, because Blockbuster will make a larger profit than Netflix if it chooses to compete.

Answer: A
Diff: 2   Type: MC   Page Ref: 454-7/454-7
Topic: Payoff matrix
Skill: Analytical
Objective: LO 3: use sequential games to analyze business strategies
AACSB Coding: Analytic Skills
Special Feature: None

8. *Refer to Figure 13-6.* Does it make sense for Netflix to lower its price in order to deter Blockbuster's entry into the online DVD rental market?
   A) Yes, because Netflix stands to make a profit of $7 million by lowering its price and keeping Blockbuster out of the market.
   B) No, because Netflix will make a higher profit by keeping its subscription price unchanged, whether Blockbuster enters the market or not.
   C) Yes, because it is always profitable to remain a monopoly.
   D) No, because Blockbuster will enter the market regardless of Netflix's decision about its subscription price.

   Answer: B
   Diff: 3   Type: MC   Page Ref: 454-7/454-7
   Topic: Game theory
   Skill: Analytical
   Objective: LO 3: use sequential games to analyze business strategies
   AACSB Coding: Analytic Skills
   Special Feature: None

9. Why are decision trees useful to managers who plan business strategies?
   A) Decision trees explain the level of concentration in an industry.
   B) Decision trees can be used to increase the amount of product differentiation; this enables managers to charge higher prices for their products.
   C) Decision trees provide a systematic way of thinking through the implications of a strategy.
   D) Using a decision tree always leads to a dominant strategy.

   Answer: C
   Diff: 2   Type: MC   Page Ref: 454-7/454-7
   Topic: Sequential games and business strategy
   Skill: Conceptual
   Objective: LO 3: use sequential games to analyze business strategies
   AACSB Coding: Reflective Thinking
   Special Feature: None

10. A subgame-perfect equilibrium is a Nash equilibrium in which no player can make himself better off by changing his decision at any decision mode.
    Answer: ⊙ True   False
    Diff: 2   Type: TF   Page Ref: 457/457
    Topic: Nash equilibrium
    Skill: Definition
    Objective: LO 3: use sequential games to analyze business strategies
    AACSB Coding: Reflective Thinking
    Special Feature: None

11. The prisoners' dilemma is used to analyze business situations in which one firm acts first and then other firms respond.

Answer: True   ⊘ False
Diff: 2   Type: TF   Page Ref: 454/454
Topic: Sequential games and business strategy
Skill: Conceptual
Objective: LO 3: use sequential games to analyze business strategies
AACSB Coding: Reflective Thinking
Special Feature: None

12. Explain why selling output at a price below that at which marginal revenue equals marginal cost (MR = MC) might serve to deter entry of a potential competitor.

Answer: If a potential entrant is unsure about the existing firm's marginal cost it might believe that the firm is maximizing profits at its chosen price and quantity combination and will conclude that profits are low in this industry. As a result, the potential entrant might believe it cannot compete with the existing firm. Alternatively, the potential entrant might view the low profits as inadequate incentive to enter the industry.

Diff: 3   Type: ES   Page Ref: 454–7/454–7
Topic: Sequential games and business strategy
Skill: Analytical
Objective: LO 3: use sequential games to analyze business strategies
AACSB Coding: Analytic Skills
Special Feature: None

13.5   The Five Competitive Forces Model

1. A large majority of the personal computers (PCs) in the USA use an operating system purchased from Microsoft. Microsoft's relationship with PC manufacturers is an example of which of Porter's competitive forces?

    A) The threat from new entrants.
    B) The bargaining power of suppliers.
    C) The bargaining power of buyers.
    D) Competition from substitute goods or services.

Answer: B
Diff: 1   Type: MC   Page Ref: 459/459
Topic: Five competitive forces model
Skill: Conceptual
Objective: LO 4: Use the five competitive forces model to analyze competition in an industry
AACSB Coding: Reflective Thinking
Special Feature: None

2. The five competitive forces model was developed by
   A) Michael Porter.
   B) John Nash.
   C) Michael Spence.
   D) Porter Smith.
   Answer: A
   Diff: 1   Type: MC   Page Ref: 457/457
   Topic: Five competitive forces model
   Skill: Fact
   Objective: LO 4: Use the five competitive forces model to analyze competition in an industry
   AACSB Coding: Reflective Thinking
   Special Feature: None

3. Which of the following is *not* one of the five competitive forces?
   A) The threat from potential entrants.
   B) The bargaining power of buyers.
   C) The firm's ability to differentiate its product.
   D) The bargaining power of suppliers.
   Answer: C
   Diff: 1   Type: MC   Page Ref: 457–9/457–9
   Topic: Five competitive forces model
   Skill: Fact
   Objective: LO 4: Use the five competitive forces model to analyze competition in an industry
   AACSB Coding: Reflective Thinking
   Special Feature: None

4. Assume that the four-firm concentration ratio in an industry is 0.85. Which of the following statements uses one of the five competitive forces to argue that this industry may be more competitive than its concentration ratio suggests?
   A) The high concentration may be due to patents owned by the largest firms but competition will increase when patent rights expire.
   B) If high concentration is the result of large firms owning much of the available supply of a key input, the industry will become more competitive when new sources of the input are discovered by other firms.
   C) Even though concentration is high, large firms in the industry may act competitively by spending large sums on advertising.
   D) The threat of entry into this industry can cause firms in the industry to lower their prices and profits in order to deter entry.
   Answer: D
   Diff: 2   Type: MC   Page Ref: 458–9/458–9
   Topic: Five competitive forces model
   Skill: Conceptual
   Objective: LO 4: Use the five competitive forces model to analyze competition in an industry
   AACSB Coding: Reflective Thinking
   Special Feature: None

5. Which of the following statements is generally true?
    A) Rivalry is less the larger the number of firms in an industry.
    B) The smaller the number of firms in an industry, the greater the rivalry.
    C) The larger the number of firms in an industry, the greater the rivalry.
    D) The degree of rivalry in an industry is largely independent of the number of firms.
   Answer: C
   Diff: 2   Type: MC   Page Ref: 457–8/457–8
   Topic: Five competitive forces model
   Skill: Conceptual
   Objective: LO 4: Use the five competitive forces model to analyze competition in an industry
   AACSB Coding: Reflective Thinking
   Special Feature: None

6. A supplier of an input is unlikely to have bargaining power if
    A) the input supplied is specialized.
    B) many firms can supply the input.
    C) it is the sole supplier of the input.
    D) it has a patent on the input.
   Answer: B
   Diff: 1   Type: MC   Page Ref: 458–9/458–9
   Topic: Five competitive forces model
   Skill: Conceptual
   Objective: LO 4: Use the five competitive forces model to analyze competition in an industry
   AACSB Coding: Reflective Thinking
   Special Feature: None

7. In 2007 the Educational Testing Service (ETS) charged $43 to take the Scholastic Aptitude Test (SAT) but $140 to take the Graduate Record Exam (GRE). One reason for this difference in price is
    A) more people took the SAT than the GRE in 2007.
    B) the GRE is a longer test with more questions.
    C) an average, those who take the GRE have higher incomes than those who take the SAT.
    D) the ETS faces competition in the market for the SAT but no competition for the GRE.
   Answer: D
   Diff: 2   Type: MC   Page Ref: 458/458
   Topic: Five competitive forces model
   Skill: Conceptual
   Objective: LO 4: Use the five competitive forces model to analyze competition in an industry
   AACSB Coding: Reflective Thinking
   Special Feature: None

8. By the 21st century few people purchased printed encyclopedias. Which of the following competitive forces best explains this?
   A) Competition from substitutes.
   B) The bargaining power of buyers.
   C) The bargaining power of suppliers.
   D) The threat from potential entrants.
   Answer: A
   Diff: 2   Type: MC   Page Ref: 459/459
   Topic: Five competitive forces model
   Skill: Conceptual
   Objective: LO 4: Use the five competitive forces model to analyze competition in an industry
   AACSB Coding: Reflective Thinking
   Special Feature: None

9. For years economists believed that market structure explained the ability of some firms to earn economic profits. For example, firms in industries with little competition and high barriers to entry would earn higher profits than firms in competitive industries with low entry barriers. Which of the following has caused economists to question this explanation and seek other explanations for why firms are profitable?
   A) Studies have shown that, on average, firms in competitive industries earn higher profit rates than firms in industries with little competition.
   B) In recent years new technologies have increased the potential entry of new firms in industries with high entry barriers.
   C) Studies have shown that firms in industries that have little competition and high entry barriers are not very profitable. Economists conclude from this that some competition is necessary in order to force firms to lower their costs and develop products that satisfy new consumer demands.
   D) The market structure explanation fails to explain how firms in the same industry can have very different levels of profit.
   Answer: D
   Diff: 3   Type: MC   Page Ref: 458–9/458–9
   Topic: Business strategy
   Skill: Conceptual
   Objective: LO 4: Use the five competitive forces model to analyze competition in an industry
   AACSB Coding: Reflective Thinking
   Special Feature: Making the Connection: Is Southwest's Business Strategy More Important Than the Structure of the Airline Industry?

10. Southwest Airlines earns economic profits despite a decline in the demand for air travel due to fears of terrorism and higher fuel costs. In contrast, in recent years other airlines have suffered losses and declared bankruptcy. Which of the following is not part of the strategy Southwest has used to be successful?
    A) The firm charges higher prices to customers willing to pay for more luxurious first-class accommodations on all of its flights.
    B) Southwest lowers its costs by flying only Boeing 737s in order to minimize maintenance costs.
    C) Southwest caters to customers who fly relatively short distances between midsize cities.
    D) Southwest keeps its costs low by offering customers only coach seats.

Answer: A

Diff: 1   Type: MC   Page Ref: 459–60/459–60
Topic: Business strategy
Skill: Fact
Objective: LO 4: Use the five competitive forces model to analyze competition in an industry
AACSB Coding: Reflective Thinking
Special Feature: Making the Connection: Is Southwest's Business Strategy More Important Than the Structure of the Airline Industry?

11. The success of Southwest Airlines provides evidence for which of the following?
    A) Firms in industries with high entry barriers and little competition are more profitable than firms in competitive industries with lower entry barriers.
    B) Because of economies of scale, large firms in an oligopoly industry earn higher profits than small firms in the same industry.
    C) Government regulation can enable small firms in competitive industries to be as profitable as large firms in the same industry.
    D) Characteristics of individual firms, rather than characteristics of the industry in which the firms operate, explain why firms are profitable.

Answer: D

Diff: 2   Type: MC   Page Ref: 459–60/459–60
Topic: Five competitive forces model
Skill: Conceptual
Objective: LO 4: Use the five competitive forces model to analyze competition in an industry
AACSB Coding: Reflective Thinking
Special Feature: Making the Connection: Is Southwest's Business Strategy More Important Than the Structure of the Airline Industry?

12. In recent years online bookseller Amazon.com has lowered its profits by offering some of its customers free shipping and building more warehouses to hold its inventories. Which of the following explains Amazon.com's actions?
    A) Amazon.com feared government regulation if its profits were too high.
    B) Amazon.com took these actions to deter entry into its market by new online booksellers.
    C) Amazon.com took these actions to compete more effectively with existing online booksellers.
    D) Amazon.com was forced to take these actions because of the bargaining power of its suppliers.
    Answer: C
    Diff: 1   Type: MC   Page Ref: 458/458
    Topic: Five competitive forces model
    Skill: Conceptual
    Objective: LO 4: Use the five competitive forces model to analyze competition in an industry
    AACSB Coding: Reflective Thinking
    Special Feature: None

13. An example of a supplier that used its bargaining power to charge high prices to its customers is
    A) Wal-Mart, which required many of its suppliers to alter their distribution systems to accommodate Wal-Mart's need to control the flow of goods to its stores.
    B) the firms that supply paper napkins to McDonald's restaurants.
    C) the Technicolor Company, the sole producer of cameras and film that movie studios needed to produce color movies in the 1930s and 1940s.
    D) the publishers of the Encyclopedia Britannica.
    Answer: A
    Diff: 2   Type: MC   Page Ref: 459/459
    Topic: Five competitive forces model
    Skill: Fact
    Objective: LO 4: Use the five competitive forces model to analyze competition in an industry
    AACSB Coding: Reflective Thinking
    Special Feature: None

14. Prices of PlayStation 3 game systems are similar at almost every large retailer and little price competition occurs among these retailers. An explanation for this is
    A) retailers are all price takers.
    B) retailers have lobbied state governments to allow them to collude legally to set the prices of certain products.
    C) pricing PlayStation 3 game systems is a repeated game. Over a long period of time a cooperative equilibrium has been reached where retailers charge high prices for these systems.
    D) retailers are in a prisoner's dilemma which causes them to all charge the same price for PlayStation 3 game systems.
    Answer: C
    Diff: 2   Type: MC   Page Ref: 461/461
    Topic: Business strategy
    Skill: Conceptual
    Objective: LO 4: Use the five competitive forces model to analyze competition in an industry
    AACSB Coding: Reflective Thinking
    Special Feature: Economics in YOUR Life!: Why Can't You Find a Cheap PlayStation 3?

15. In 2006 Wal-Mart began offering low prices on about 150 generic drugs in the Tampa Bay area. Wal-Mart later expanded this offer nationwide. Wal-Mart
    A) is using this program as a "loss leader." That is, it expects to lose money from the sale of the generic drugs but hopes that customers will buy other products when they buy drugs.
    B) doesn't expect to lose money on the sale of generic drugs because they buy the drugs at low prices in wholesale markets.
    C) took this action to respond to its rival Target, which was the first store chain to sell generic drugs at the same $4 price.
    D) sold the drugs at such low prices that no rival store chain matched Wal-Mart's price.
    Answer: B
    Diff: 2   Type: MC   Page Ref: 462-3/462-3
    Topic: Game theory
    Skill: Conceptual
    Objective: LO 4: Use the five competitive forces model to analyze competition in an industry
    AACSB Coding: Reflective Thinking
    Special Feature: An Inside Look: can Target Compete with Wal-Mart in the Market for Generic Drugs?

16. The four-firm concentration ratio in the breakfast cereal industry is just over 80 percent. How does the five competitive forces model provide better insight into the degree of competition in the breakfast cereal industry than just observing the concentration ratio?

    Answer: The concentration ratio only measures the market share of the largest firms in an industry; it does not describe the degree of competition among the existing firms (one of the five forces), which may come in the form of advertising, service, price, etc. The concentration ratio does not assess the threat firms in the breakfast cereal industry face from potential entrants (another of the five forces) into their market. Existing firms may keep their prices low in order to discourage new firms from entering. The concentration ratio cannot be used to evaluate any of the other three competitive forces – competition from substitute goods (for example, frozen breakfast foods), and the bargaining powers of buyers and suppliers.

    Diff: 2   *Type: ES*   *Page Ref: 454–459/454–459*
    Topic: Five competitive forces model
    Skill: Analytical
    Objective: LO 4: Use the five competitive forces model to analyze competition in an industry
    AACSB Coding: Reflective Thinking
    Special Feature: None

Chapter 14 Monopoly and Antitrust Policy

14.1 Is Any Firm Ever Really a Monopoly?

1. By 1970, few households in the United States had cable television but two developments
would lead to a substantial increase in the growth of the cable television industry. One of
these developments was satellite relay technology that made it feasible for local systems to
receive signals from distant broadcast stations. What was the second development?
   A) The introduction of Home Box Office (HBO) and other premium cable channels.
   B) The U.S. Congress relaxed restrictions on rebroadcasting distant stations and premium
   channels.
   C) Ted Turner purchased the WTBS, which became the first cable "superstation."
   D) The U.S. Congress granted an antitrust exemption that enabled cable stations to merge.
   As a result, several "superstations" were able to take advantage of economies of scale to
   lower their average costs and prices.
   Answer: B
   Diff: 1   Type: MC   Page Ref: 472–3/472–3
   Topic: Chapter Opener
   Skill: Fact
   Objective: LO 1: Define monopoly.
   AACSB Coding: Reflective Thinking
   Special Features: Chapter Opener: Time Warner Rules Manhattan

2. Few firms in the United States are monopolies because
   A) few firms experience economies of scale.
   B) of antitrust laws.
   C) when a firm earns profits, other firms will enter its market.
   D) most products that firms produce have substitutes.
   Answer: C
   Diff: 1   Type: MC   Page Ref: 472–3/472–3
   Topic: Characteristics of monopoly
   Skill: Fact
   Objective: LO 1: Define monopoly.
   AACSB Coding: Reflective Thinking
   Special Features: Chapter Opener: Time Warner Rules Manhattan

3. Time Warner Cable is the only provider of cable TV in Manhattan. Other cable stations
   A) could ask the New York City government for a license to compete with Time Warner Cable but have chosen not to do so.
   B) have chosen not to offer cable service in Manhattan because there are not enough potential customers for them to make a profit.
   C) have expressed interest in offering cable service in Manhattan but Time Warner has a license from the city government that prohibits other firms from entering the market.
   D) have requested licenses from the New York City government to compete with Time Warner Cable. These firms will begin offering cable television service after 2010.

Answer: A
Diff: 1   Type: MC   Page Ref: 472-3/472-3
Topic: Monopoly
Skill: Fact
Objective: LO 1: Define monopoly.
AACSB Coding: Reflective Thinking
Special Features: Chapter Opener: Time Warner Rules Manhattan

4. A monopoly is a firm that is the only seller of a good or service that does not have
   A) a patent.
   B) a close complement.
   C) a barrier to entry.
   D) a close substitute.

Answer: D
Diff: 1   Type: MC   Page Ref: 474/474
Topic: Monopoly
Skill: Definition
Objective: LO 1: Define monopoly.
AACSB Coding: Reflective Thinking
Special Features: None

5. A narrow definition of monopoly is that a firm is a monopoly if it can ignore
   A) government antitrust laws.
   B) the pricing decisions of its suppliers.
   C) the pricing decisions of firms that produce complementary products.
   D) the actions of all other firms.

Answer: D
Diff: 1   Type: MC   Page Ref: 474/474
Topic: Monopoly
Skill: Definition
Objective: LO 1: Define monopoly.
AACSB Coding: Reflective Thinking
Special Features: None

6. Using a broad definition, a firm would have a monopoly if
   A) it produced a product that has no close substitutes.
   B) it does not have to collude with any other producer to earn an economic profit.
   C) there is no other firm selling a substitute for its product close enough that its economic profits are competed away in the long run.
   D) it can make decisions regarding price and output without violating antitrust laws.
   Answer: C
   Diff: 2   Type: MC   Page Ref: 474/474
   Topic: Monopoly
   Skill: Definition
   Objective: LO 1: Define monopoly.
   AACSB Coding: Reflective Thinking
   Special Features: None

7. In the early 2000s Microsoft suffered losses from its sales of its Xbox while another video game console, Sony's PlayStation 2, was profitable. Which of the following is one reason for Microsoft's losses from the Xbox?
   A) The Xbox used technology that was inferior to that of the PlayStation2.
   B) Microsoft was forced to charge the same price for the Xbox that the PlayStation2 sold for but the Xbox was more costly to produce.
   C) Sony charged a much lower price for the PlayStation2 than Microsoft charged for the Xbox.
   D) Sony spent more on advertising the PlayStation2 than Microsoft spent on the Xbox. As a result, sales of the Xbox were much lower than PlayStation2 sales.
   Answer: B
   Diff: 1   Type: MC   Page Ref: 474–5/474–5
   Topic: Close substitutes
   Skill: Fact
   Objective: LO 1: Define monopoly.
   AACSB Coding: Reflective Thinking
   Special Features: Making the Connection: Is Xbox 360 a Close Substitute for PlayStation 3?

8. In the early 2000s Microsoft suffered losses from selling its Xbox video game consoles while Sony made a profit from sales of its video game console, the PlayStation2. When Sony and Microsoft developed the next generation of video game consoles, early sales indicated that the Xbox was more profitable than the PlayStation3. What was the reason for the change in profitability of the two generations of video game consoles?
    A) The Xbox sold for a lower price than the PlayStation3 and consumers considered both products to be close substitutes.
    B) Sony decided to charge a much lower price for the PlayStation3 than Microsoft sold for the newer Xbox. Though its sales were greater, Sony was not able to earn enough profit to make up for the lower prices.
    C) Microsoft used the latest technology for the later version of the Xbox; it is capable of playing high definition (HD) DVDs as well as older DVDs. More consumers preferred the Xbox to the PlayStation3, which sold at a lower price but only played older-format DVDs.
    D) Microsoft spent much more on advertising for Xbox via Web sites. This proved to be more successful than advertising on television, where Sony advertised the PlayStation3.

Answer: A
Diff: 2   Type: MC   Page Ref: 474–5/474–5
Topic: Close substitutes
Skill: Fact
Objective: LO 1: Define monopoly.
AACSB Coding: Reflective Thinking
Special Features: Making the Connection: Is Xbox 360 a Close Substitute for PlayStation 3?

9. A monopoly firm is the only seller of a good or service that
    A) has a perfectly elastic demand.
    B) has no close complements.
    C) does not need to be advertised.
    D) does not have a close substitute.

Answer: D
Diff: 1   Type: MC   Page Ref: 474/474
Topic: Monopoly
Skill: Definition
Objective: LO 1: Define monopoly.
AACSB Coding: Reflective Thinking
Special Features: None

10. A firm that is the only seller of a good or service that does not have a close substitute is called
    A) a monopoly.
    B) an oligopolist.
    C) a market maker.
    D) a price maker.
    Answer: A
    Diff: 1   Type: MC   Page Ref: 474/474
    Topic: Monopoly
    Skill: Definition
    Objective: LO 1: Define monopoly.
    AACSB Coding: Reflective Thinking
    Special Features: None

14.2   Where Do Monopolies Come From?

1. To have a monopoly in an industry there must be
    A) barriers to entry so high that no other firms can enter the industry.
    B) a patent or copyright giving the firm exclusive rights to sell a product for 20 years.
    C) an inelastic demand for the industry's product.
    D) a public franchise, making the monopoly the exclusive legal provider of a good or service.
    Answer: A
    Diff: 1   Type: MC   Page Ref: 475/475
    Topic: Barriers to entry
    Skill: Fact
    Objective: LO 2: Explain the four main reasons monopolies arise.
    AACSB Coding: Reflective Thinking
    Special Features: None

2. Which one of the following is *not* a possible barrier to entry high enough to keep competing firms out of a monopoly industry?
    A) The monopoly firm has control of a key resource necessary to produce a good.
    B) There are important network externalities in supplying a good or service.
    C) Large economies of scale that result in a natural monopoly.
    D) A high concentration ratio.
    Answer: D
    Diff: 1   Type: MC   Page Ref: 475/475
    Topic: Barriers to entry
    Skill: Conceptual
    Objective: LO 2: Explain the four main reasons monopolies arise.
    AACSB Coding: Reflective Thinking
    Special Features: None

3. When the government wants to give an exclusive right to one firm to produce a product it
   A) imposes a tariff on imports of the product.
   B) imposes a quota on imports of the product.
   C) grants a patent or copyright to an individual or firm.
   D) uses antitrust laws to keep other firms from entering the market.
   Answer: C
   Diff: 1   Type: MC   Page Ref: 475–6/475–6
   Topic: Barriers to entry
   Skill: Fact
   Objective: LO 2: Explain the four main reasons monopolies arise.
   AACSB Coding: Reflective Thinking
   Special Features: None

4. There are several types of barriers to entry that can create a monopoly. Which of the
   following barriers is the result of government action?
   A) Network externalities.
   B) Public franchise.
   C) Economies of scale.
   D) Control of a key resource.
   Answer: B
   Diff: 1   Type: MC   Page Ref: 475–6/475–6
   Topic: Barriers to entry
   Skill: Conceptual
   Objective: LO 2: Explain the four main reasons monopolies arise.
   AACSB Coding: Reflective Thinking
   Special Features: None

5. When the government makes a firm the exclusive legal provider of a good or service it
   grants the firm
   A) a copyright.
   B) a network externality.
   C) a quota.
   D) a public franchise.
   Answer: D
   Diff: 1   Type: MC   Page Ref: 477/477
   Topic: Barriers to entry
   Skill: Fact
   Objective: LO 2: Explain the four main reasons monopolies arise.
   AACSB Coding: Reflective Thinking
   Special Features: None

6. A patent
   A) grants the creator of a book, film, or piece of music the exclusive right to use the creation for 20 years.
   B) grants the creator of a book, film, or piece of music the exclusive right to use the creation during the creator's lifetime.
   C) gives a firm the exclusive right to a new product for 20 years from the date the product is invented.
   D) gives the firm the exclusive right to a new product during the product inventor's lifetime.

Answer: C
Diff: 1   Type: MC   Page Ref: 476/476
Topic: Patents and copyrights
Skill: Definition
Objective: LO 2: Explain the four main reasons monopolies arise.
AACSB Coding: Reflective Thinking
Special Features: None

7. Ordinarily, governments attempt to promote competition in markets. Why do governments use patents to block entry into some markets when this prohibits competition?
   A) Patents encourage firms to spend money on research necessary to create new products.
   B) Politicians sometimes succumb to pressure from lobbyists to grant favors to businesses for political reasons.
   C) Patents are an important source of government revenue.
   D) Patents are justified because they are an important means for creating network externalities.

Answer: A
Diff: 2   Type: MC   Page Ref: 476/476
Topic: Patents and copyrights
Skill: Conceptual
Objective: LO 2: Explain the four main reasons monopolies arise.
AACSB Coding: Reflective Thinking
Special Features: None

8. One reason patent protection is vitally important to pharmaceutical firms is
   A) successful new drugs are not profitable. If firms are not granted patents many would go out of business and health care would be severely diminished.
   B) the approval process for new drugs through the Food and Drug Administration can take more than 10 years and is very costly. Patents enable firms to recover costs incurred during this process.
   C) that taxes on profits from drugs are very high; profits from patent protection enable firms to pay these taxes.
   D) the high salaries pharmaceutical firms pay to scientists and doctors make their labor costs higher than for any other business. Profits from patents are needed to pay these labor costs.

Answer: B
Diff: 2   Type: MC   Page Ref: 476/476
Topic: Patents and copyrights
Skill: Conceptual
Objective: LO 2: Explain the four main reasons monopolies arise.
AACSB Coding: Reflective Thinking
Special Features: None

9. Experience with patents in the pharmaceutical industry shows that when patents on drugs expire
   A) most patients will continue to buy the drugs from the same firms because their doctors recommend they buy brand-name drugs.
   B) prices remain high without patent protection because of a lack of competition. Firms that are not granted patents cannot compete with firms that are granted patents.
   C) other firms are free to produce chemically identical drugs. Competition reduces the profits that had been earned by the firms that received patents.
   D) firms will find ways to obtain additional patent protection - often by making cosmetic changes in drugs that were patented - so that they can continue charging high prices.

Answer: C
Diff: 1   Type: MC   Page Ref: 476/476
Topic: Patents and copyrights
Skill: Conceptual
Objective: LO 2: Explain the four main reasons monopolies arise.
AACSB Coding: Reflective Thinking
Special Features: None

10. Research has shown that most economic profits from selling a prescription drug are eliminated 20 years after the drug is first offered for sale. The main reason for the elimination of profits is
    A) after 20 years most people who have taken the drug have passed away or are cured of the illness the drug was intended to treat.
    B) firms sell their patent rights to other firms so that they can concentrate on finding drugs to treat new illnesses.
    C) the quantity demanded of the drug has increased enough that the demand becomes inelastic and revenue falls.
    D) after 20 years patent protection is ended and other firms can produce less expensive generic versions of the drug.

Answer: D
Diff: 1   Type: MC   Page Ref: 476/476
Topic: Patents and copyrights
Skill: Conceptual
Objective: LO 2: Explain the four main reasons monopolies arise.
AACSB Coding: Reflective Thinking
Special Features: None

11. For years the Paul Ecke Ranch had a monopoly on poinsettias. What was the reason for the monopoly the Ranch had on poinsettia sales?
    A) The Paul Ecke Ranch was granted a public franchise which made it the sole legal provider of poinsettias.
    B) Paul Ecke discovered a technique for growing poinsettias that had more leaves and were more colorful than other poinsettias.
    C) The Paul Ecke Ranch was granted a patent that gave it the exclusive right to produce and sell poinsettias.
    D) The Paul Ecke Ranch was able to take advantage of network externalities in supplying poinsettias.

Answer: B
Diff: 1   Type: MC   Page Ref: 476-7/476-7
Topic: Barriers to entry
Skill: Fact
Objective: LO 2: Explain the four main reasons monopolies arise.
AACSB Coding: Reflective Thinking
Special Features: Making the Connection: The End of the Christmas Plant Monopoly.

12. For years the Paul Ecke Ranch had a monopoly on poinsettias. What event was responsible for the end of this monopoly?
    A) A university researcher discovered the special technique the Ecke Ranch used for growing poinsettias. After the researcher published the technique other firms were able to compete with the Ecke Ranch.
    B) Other poinsettia sellers were finally able to take advantage of the network externalities that had given the Ecke Ranch its monopoly.
    C) After 20 years, the patent the Ecke Ranch had been granted for its poinsettias expired.
    D) The government took away the public franchise it had earlier given to the Ecke Ranch to be the sole legal provider of poinsettias.

    Answer: A
    Diff: 1   Type: MC   Page Ref: 476–7/476–7
    Topic: Barriers to entry
    Skill: Fact
    Objective: LO 2: Explain the four main reasons monopolies arise.
    AACSB Coding: Reflective Thinking
    Special Features: Making the Connection: The End of the Christmas Plant Monopoly.

13. Network externalities
    A) can only exist when there are economies of scale.
    B) prevent the dominance of a market by one firm.
    C) exist when the usefulness of a product increases with the number of consumers who use it.
    D) are created when celebrity endorsements of products lead to a surge in the demand for those products.

    Answer: C
    Diff: 1   Type: MC   Page Ref: 478–9/478–9
    Topic: Network externalities
    Skill: Definition
    Objective: LO 2: Explain the four main reasons monopolies arise.
    AACSB Coding: Reflective Thinking
    Special Features: None

14. What type of protection does U.S. law grant the creator of a book, film or piece of music?
    A) A public franchise, which grants the exclusive right to use the creation during the author's lifetime and to his or her heirs for 70 years after the author's death.
    B) A copyright, which grants exclusive rights to the creation's author for 20 years after the work is created.
    C) A patent, which grants the exclusive right to use the creation during the author's lifetime and to his or her heirs for 70 years after the author's death.
    D) A copyright, which grants the exclusive right to use the creation during the author's lifetime and to his or her heirs for 70 years after the author's death.

    Answer: D
    Diff: 1   Type: MC   Page Ref: 476/476
    Topic: Patents and copyrights
    Skill: Definition
    Objective: LO 2: Explain the four main reasons monopolies arise.
    AACSB Coding: Reflective Thinking
    Special Features: None

15. A designation by the government that a firm is the only legal provider of a good or service is called a
    A) patent.
    B) public franchise.
    C) public enterprise.
    D) copyright.
    Answer: B
    Diff: 1   Type: MC   Page Ref: 477/477
    Topic: Public franchise
    Skill: Definition
    Objective: LO 2: Explain the four main reasons monopolies arise.
    AACSB Coding: Reflective Thinking
    Special Features: None

16. What is the difference between a public franchise and a public enterprise?
    A) A public franchise grants a firm the right to be the sole legal provider of a good or service. A public enterprise refers to a service that is provided directly to consumers through the government.
    B) A public enterprise grants a firm the right to be the sole legal provider of a good or service. A public franchise refers to a service that is provided directly to consumers through the government.
    C) A public enterprise is owned by the public through its holdings of shares of stock in the enterprise. A public franchise is a firm owned by the government.
    D) Both refer to a service provided directly to consumers through the government, but "public franchise" is a term more commonly used in the U.S. while "public enterprise" is more commonly used in European countries.
    Answer: A
    Diff: 1   Type: MC   Page Ref: 477/477
    Topic: Public franchise
    Skill: Definition
    Objective: LO 2: Explain the four main reasons monopolies arise.
    AACSB Coding: Reflective Thinking
    Special Features: None

17. The International Nickel Company of Canada is often cited as an example of monopoly. What was the source of the barrier to entry that gave this firm monopoly power?
    A) It was a public enterprise; therefore, the Canadian government blocked entry into the market for nickel.
    B) There were important network externalities in the production of nickel.
    C) Economies of scale resulted in the company becoming a natural monopoly.
    D) Control of a key resource.
    Answer: D
    Diff: 1   Type: MC   Page Ref: 477/477
    Topic: Barriers to entry
    Skill: Fact
    Objective: LO 2: Explain the four main reasons monopolies arise.
    AACSB Coding: Reflective Thinking
    Special Features: None

18. The International Nickel Company of Canada is often cited as an example of monopoly. But International Nickel eventually lost its monopoly. What event was responsible for this?
    A) New technology allowed other firms to achieve network externalities after World War II.
    B) The Canadian government, which had owned International Nickel, sold the company after World War II. The government no longer blocked entry into the market for nickel.
    C) Competition in the market for nickel increased after nickel fields were developed in Russia after World War II.
    D) Competition in the market for nickel increased after Canada signed the North American Free Trade Agreement with the United States and Mexico in 1994.
    Answer: C
    Diff: 1   Type: MC   Page Ref: 477/477
    Topic: Barriers to entry
    Skill: Fact
    Objective: LO 2: Explain the four main reasons monopolies arise.
    AACSB Coding: Reflective Thinking
    Special Features: None

19. In the United States barriers to entry in professional team sports (for example, football and baseball) result from
    A) the draft of college players, which grants teams exclusive signing rights to individual players.
    B) long–term leases teams sign for stadiums and ballparks in major cities.
    C) television contracts, which give networks the exclusive rights to broadcast games.
    D) the reserve clause, which is a provision in contracts of professional athletes that require them to play for specific teams over the length of their contracts.
    Answer: B
    Diff: 1   Type: MC   Page Ref: 477/477
    Topic: Barriers to entry
    Skill: Conceptual
    Objective: LO 2: Explain the four main reasons monopolies arise.
    AACSB Coding: Reflective Thinking
    Special Features: None

20. The De Beers diamond mining and marketing company of South Africa became one of the most profitable and longest-lived monopolies in history. Which of the following has always threatened DeBeers' control of the diamond market?

    A) Since few diamonds are ever destroyed, DeBeers has constantly faced possible competition from other firms reselling diamonds.

    B) Competition from imitation diamonds. Technology has made it possible to make fake diamonds look exactly like real diamonds.

    C) Competition from other gemstones, including rubies and emeralds, that have become more popular over time.

    D) At different times in the past some countries have banned the importation of diamonds from South Africa for political reasons.

Answer: A

Diff: 1   Type: MC   Page Ref: 477-8/477-8
Topic: Barriers to entry
Skill: Fact
Objective: LO 2: Explain the four main reasons monopolies arise.
AACSB Coding: Reflective Thinking
Special Features: Making the Connection; Are Diamond Profits Forever? The De Beers Diamond Monopoly

21. BHP Billiton is a Canadian company that owns mines in Canada that

    A) produce nickel. After World War BHP Billiton began to compete with another Canadian firm, the International Nickel Company. This competition eventually ended International Nickel's monopoly in this market.

    B) produces bauxite, the mineral needed to produce aluminum. BHP Billiton began to mine bauxite after World War II. This competition eventually ended the Aluminum Company of America (ALCOA)'s monopoly in this market.

    C) coal. Until World War II BHP Billiton had a monopoly on coal in Canada.

    D) produce diamonds.

Answer: D

Diff: 3   Type: MC   Page Ref: 477-8/477-8
Topic: Barriers to entry
Skill: Fact
Objective: LO 2: Explain the four main reasons monopolies arise.
AACSB Coding: Reflective Thinking
Special Features: Making the Connection; Are Diamond Profits Forever? The De Beers Diamond Monopoly

22. After having a monopoly in the diamond market for many years, by 2000 the DeBeers company faced competition from other companies. To maintain its market share DeBeers
    A) began buying so-called "blood diamonds" in order to keep these diamonds out of the control of other diamond companies.
    B) adopted a strategy of differentiating its diamonds. Each of its diamonds is now marked with a microscopic brand.
    C) bought diamond mines in Canada and Russia that had been its competitors.
    D) lowered the prices of its diamonds to make the market appear less profitable to potential competitors.
    Answer: B
    Diff: 1   Type: MC   Page Ref: 477–8/477–8
    Topic: Barriers to entry
    Skill: Fact
    Objective: LO 2: Explain the four main reasons monopolies arise.
    AACSB Coding: Reflective Thinking
    Special Features: Making the Connection; Are Diamond Profits Forever? The De Beers Diamond Monopoly

23. Some economists argue that Microsoft become a monopoly in the market for computer software by developing MS-DOS, an operating system used for the first IBM personal computers. The more people who used MS-DOS-based programs, the greater the usefulness of a using a computer with an MS-DOS operating system. The explanation for Microsoft's monopoly is
    A) the development of new technology that other firms could not copy.
    B) control of a key resource which, in this case, is the MS-DOS operating system.
    C) network externalities.
    D) patents Microsoft obtained when it developed the MS-DOS operating system.
    Answer: C
    Diff: 2   Type: MC   Page Ref: 478–9/478–9
    Topic: Network externalities
    Skill: Conceptual
    Objective: LO 2: Explain the four main reasons monopolies arise.
    AACSB Coding: Reflective Thinking
    Special Features: None

24. Although some economists believe network externalities are important barriers to entry other economists disagree because

    A) they believe that the dominant positions of firms that are supposedly due to network externalities are to a greater extent the result of the efficiency of firms in offering products that satisfy consumer preferences.

    B) they believe that most examples of network externalities are really barriers to entry caused by the control of a key resource.

    C) network externalities are really negative externalities.

    D) they believe that the dominant positions of firms that are supposedly due to network externalities are to a greater extent the result of economies of scale.

Answer: A

Diff: 1   *Type: MC*   *Page Ref: 478–9/478–9*
Topic: Network externalities
Skill: Conceptual
Objective: LO 2: Explain the four main reasons monopolies arise.
AACSB Coding: Reflective Thinking
Special Features: None

25. In discussions of barriers to entry, what is meant by the term "virtuous cycle"?

    A) A virtuous cycle refers to successful research and development that leads to information that is used to develop other new products.

    B) A virtuous cycle refers to a firm using the profits from a monopoly in one market to establish a monopoly in another market.

    C) A virtuous cycle refers to the situation where the pursuit of self–interest in establishing an entry barrier leads to an increase in social welfare (the "invisible hand").

    D) A virtuous cycle refers to a situation where if a firm can attract enough customers initially, it can attract additional customers because its product's value has been increased by other customers using it, which attracts even more customers.

Answer: D

Diff: 1   *Type: MC*   *Page Ref: 478–9/478–9*
Topic: Network externalities
Skill: Definition
Objective: LO 2: Explain the four main reasons monopolies arise.
AACSB Coding: Reflective Thinking
Special Features: None

26. In a natural monopoly, throughout the range of market demand

    A) marginal cost is above average total cost and pulls average total cost upward.

    B) average total cost is above marginal cost and pulls marginal cost upward.

    C) marginal cost is below average total cost and pulls average total cost downward.

    D) there are diseconomies of scale.

Answer: C

Diff: 1   *Type: MC*   *Page Ref: 479–80/479–80*
Topic: Natural monopoly
Skill: Conceptual
Objective: LO 2: Explain the four main reasons monopolies arise.
AACSB Coding: Reflective Thinking
Special Features: None

27. To be a natural monopoly a firm must
    A) control a key resource input.
    B) have economies of scale that are so large that it can supply the entire market at a lower cost than two or more firms.
    C) have significant network externalities.
    D) be very large relative to the total market.
  Answer: B
  Diff: 1   Type: MC   Page Ref: 479–80/479–80
  Topic: Natural monopoly
  Skill: Definition
  Objective: LO 2: Explain the four main reasons monopolies arise.
  AACSB Coding: Reflective Thinking
  Special Features: None

Figure 14–1

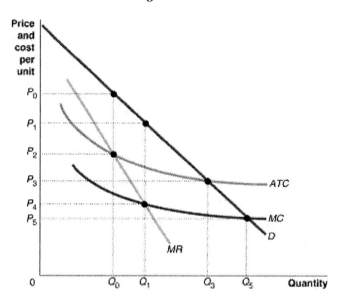

Figure 14–1 shows the market demand and cost curves facing a natural monopoly.

28. ***Refer to Figure 14–1.*** Which of the following statements about the firm depicted in the diagram is true?
    A) The fact that this firm is a natural monopoly is shown by the continually declining long–run average total cost as output rises.
    B) The fact that this firm is a natural monopoly is shown by the continually declining market demand curve as output rises.
    C) The fact that this firm is a natural monopoly is shown by the continually declining marginal revenue curve as output rises.
    D) The fact that this firm is a natural monopoly is shown by the fact that marginal cost lies below the long–run average total cost where the firm maximizes its profits.
  Answer: A

Diff: 1   Type: MC   Page Ref: 479–80/479–80
Topic: Natural monopoly
Skill: Analytical
Objective: LO 2: Explain the four main reasons monopolies arise.
AACSB Coding: Reflective Thinking
Special Features: None

29. A natural monopoly is most likely to occur in which of the following industries?
    A) The pharmaceutical industry because the development and approval of new drugs through the Food and Drug Administration can take more than 10 years.
    B) The diamond mining and marketing industry because one firm can control a key resource.
    C) The software industry because of the importance of network externalities.
    D) An industry where fixed costs are very large relative to variable costs.
    Answer: D
    Diff: 2   Type: MC   Page Ref: 479–80/479–80
    Topic: Natural monopoly
    Skill: Conceptual
    Objective: LO 2: Explain the four main reasons monopolies arise.
    AACSB Coding: Reflective Thinking
    Special Features: None

30. Automatic Data Processing, Inc. (ADP) is an example of a monopoly. What is the reason for ADP's monopoly?
    A) ADP developed a popular type of software. As more and more consumers bought the software a virtuous cycle allowed the firm to sell even more of its software. This made it difficult for other firms to enter ADP's market.
    B) ADP provides annual reports and other information to corporations' shareholders prior to their annual meetings. Economies of scale in this business are the reason for ADP's monopoly.
    C) ADP has been successful in acquiring patents for its data processing software. These patents give the company an exclusive right to produce and sell its software for 20 years.
    D) ADP is a public franchise which means it is the only legal provider of documents (for example, annual reports and proxy statements) to corporations prior to their annual meetings.
    Answer: B
    Diff: 1   Type: MC   Page Ref: 480–1/480–1
    Topic: Natural monopoly
    Skill: Fact
    Objective: LO 2: Explain the four main reasons monopolies arise.
    AACSB Coding: Reflective Thinking
    Special Features: None

31. An article in the *Wall Street Journal* quoted an analyst who claimed that Automatic Data Processing, Inc. (ADP) had a virtual monopoly in its industry because "The economies of scale and the efficiencies achieved by ADP...handling all of the...business–rather than multiple companies – resulted in savings..." What services does ADP offer its customers?
    A) ADP sells computer software to businesses.
    B) ADP provides data processing consulting services to computer software companies.
    C) ADP supplies reports and forms that allow shareholders to vote by mail on business conducted at corporations' annual meetings.
    D) ADP supplies the paper products (forms, reports, etc.,) used by Microsoft and other computer software companies.
    Answer: C
    Diff: 1   Type: MC   Page Ref: 480–1/480–1
    Topic: Natural monopoly
    Skill: Fact
    Objective: LO 2: Explain the four main reasons monopolies arise.
    AACSB Coding: Reflective Thinking
    Special Features: Solved Problem: Is the "Proxy Business" a Natural Monopoly?

32. Network externalities refer to the situation where the usefulness of a product increases with the number of consumers who use it.
    Answer: ⊚ True   False
    Diff: 1   Type: TF   Page Ref: 478–9/478–9
    Topic: Network externalities
    Skill: Definition
    Objective: LO 2: Explain the four main reasons monopolies arise.
    AACSB Coding: Reflective Thinking
    Special Features: None

33. A public franchise gives the exclusive right to produce a product for 20 years from the date the product is invented.
    Answer: True   ⊚ False
    Diff: 1   Type: TF   Page Ref: 477/477
    Topic: Barriers to entry
    Skill: Definition
    Objective: LO 2: Explain the four main reasons monopolies arise.
    AACSB Coding: Reflective Thinking
    Special Features: None

34. A virtuous cycle refers to the development of new products that follows when a monopoly earns economic profits.
    Answer: True   ⊚ False
    Diff: 2   Type: TF   Page Ref: 479/479
    Topic: Network externalities
    Skill: Definition
    Objective: LO 2: Explain the four main reasons monopolies arise.
    AACSB Coding: Reflective Thinking
    Special Features: None

35. Natural monopolies are most likely to occur in markets where fixed costs are very large relative to variable costs.

    Answer: ◌ True   False
    Diff: 1   Type: TF   Page Ref: 479-80/479-80
    Topic:
    Skill: Conceptual
    Objective: LO 2: Explain the four main reasons monopolies arise.
    AACSB Coding: Reflective Thinking
    Special Features: None

36. U.S. antitrust laws are designed to prohibit monopolization and encourage competition. Why, then, does the government erect barriers to entry and create monopoly power by granting firms patents?

    Answer: Patents are designed to encourage creative activity and promote the development of new technologies. Firms can spend years on research and development in the search for new and better production processes and consumer products. Research and development is costly – many potential new ideas are ultimately not technically feasible or never become commercially successful. If research and development results in a successful product, competing firms can easily copy the product and sell it without incurring the research costs of the firm that developed the product, if patent protection is not granted. Most people would object to this form of "free riding" on equity grounds; but patents also encourage firms to conduct research that leads to social benefits: new technologies result in a higher standard of living for all and a more efficient allocation of society's scarce resources.
    Diff: 2   Type: ES   Page Ref: 476/476
    Topic: Patents and copyrights
    Skill: Conceptual
    Objective: LO 2: Explain the four main reasons monopolies arise.
    AACSB Coding: Reflective Thinking
    Special Features: None

37. Identify four reasons for high entry barriers? Briefly explain each reason.

    Answer: 1. Economies of scale. This occurs when a firm faces declining average total cost over the entire range of output that consumers are willing to buy. When this happens, the larger the firm's output, the smaller its per unit costs, making it difficult for small firms to enter the market since the small firms face much higher average costs. Thus, only a single firm will survive.

    2. Government can block entry via legal barriers such as public franchise, government license, patent, or copyright. A public franchise is a firm the government designates will be the only legal provider of a good or service. A government license controls entry into particular occupations, professions, and industries. Patents and copyrights grant exclusive rights to a product that is invented or created.

    3. Control over a key resource. If one firm owns the entire (or a great percentage of the) resource needed to produce a final good, it creates a barrier to entry because it limits other producers' access to that resource.

    4. Network externalities in supplying the good or service. If a product becomes more valuable when more people use it, then firms with larger outputs (networks) may have advantages over smaller firms.

Diff: 2   Type: ES   Page Ref: 475–80/475–80
Topic: Barriers to entry
Skill: Conceptual
Objective: LO 1: Define monopoly.
AACSB Coding: Reflective Thinking
Special Features: None

14.3   How Does a Monopoly Choose Price and Output?

1. A monopoly firm's demand curve
   A) is the same as the demand curve for the product it sells.
   B) is perfectly inelastic.
   C) is more inelastic than the demand curve for the product.
   D) is inelastic at high prices and elastic at lower prices.
   Answer: A
   Diff: 1   Type: MC   Page Ref: 481/481
   Topic: Characteristics of monopoly
   Skill: Conceptual
   Objective: LO 3: Explain how a monopoly chooses price and output.
   AACSB Coding: Reflective Thinking
   Special Features: None

2. Which of the following is true for a monopolist?
   A) Being the only seller in the market, the monopolist faces a perfectly inelastic demand
      curve.
   B) Being the only seller in the market, the monopolist faces a perfectly elastic demand
      curve.
   C) Being the only seller in the market, the monopolist faces the market demand curve.
   D) Being the only seller in the market, the monopolist faces a downward sloping demand
      curve that lies below the marginal revenue curve.
   Answer: C
   Diff: 1   Type: MC   Page Ref: 481–3/481–3
   Topic: Characteristics of monopoly
   Skill: Conceptual
   Objective: LO 3: Explain how a monopoly chooses price and output.
   AACSB Coding: Reflective Thinking
   Special Features: None

3. A price maker is
  A) a person who actively seeks out the best price for a product that he or she wishes to buy.
  B) a firm that has some control over the price of the product it sells.
  C) a firm that is able to sell any quantity at the highest possible price.
  D) a consumer who participates in an auction where she announces her willingness to pay for a product.

Answer: B
Diff: 1   Type: MC   Page Ref: 481/481
Topic: Characteristics of monopoly
Skill: Definition
Objective: LO 3: Explain how a monopoly chooses price and output.
AACSB Coding: Reflective Thinking
Special Features: None

4. Firms that face downward–sloping demand curves for their output in the product market are called
  A) price takers.
  B) price dictators.
  C) monopolists.
  D) price makers.

Answer: D
Diff: 1   Type: MC   Page Ref: 481/481
Topic: Demand and marginal revenue
Skill: Conceptual
Objective: LO 3: Explain how a monopoly chooses price and output.
AACSB Coding: Reflective Thinking
Special Features: None

5. Wendell can sell five motor homes per week at a price of $22,000. If he lowers the price of motor homes to $20,000 per week he will sell six motor homes. What is the marginal revenue of the sixth motor home?
  A) $20,000
  B) $12,000
  C) $10,000
  D) $22,000

Answer: C
Diff: 2   Type: MC   Page Ref: 481–3/481–3
Topic: Demand and marginal revenue
Skill: Analytical
Objective: LO 3: Explain how a monopoly chooses price and output.
AACSB Coding: Analytic Skills
Special Features: None

6.   *Figure 14–2*

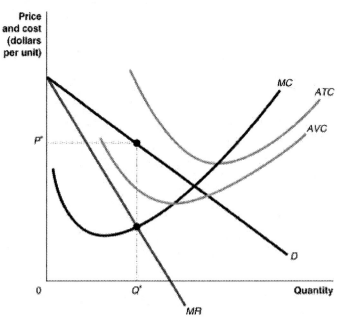

Refer to Figure 14–2. If the monopolist charges price P* for output Q*, in order to maximize profit or minimize loss in the short run, it should

    A) continue to produce because price is greater than average variable cost.

    B) shut down because price is greater than marginal cost.

    C) shut down because price is less than average total cost.

    D) continue to produce because a monopolist always earns a profit.

Answer: A

Diff: 2   *Type: MC*   *Page Ref: 481–3/481–3*
Topic: Profit maximization
Skill: Analytical
Objective: LO 3: Explain how a monopoly chooses price and output.
AACSB Coding: Analytic Skills
Special Features: None

Table 14–1

Quantity per day (cases)	Price per case ($)	Total Cost ($)
1	$16	$7.00
2	15	9.50
3	14	11.00
4	13	12.00
5	12	14.50
6	11	17.50
7	10	21.00
8	9	25.00
9	8	30.00
10	7	35.50

The government of a small developing country has granted exclusive rights to Linden Enterprises for the production of plastic syringes. Table 14–1 shows the cost and demand data for this government protected monopolist.

7. *Refer to Table 14–1.* What is the profit–maximizing quantity and price for the monopolist?
   A) Quantity = 8 cases, Price = $9
   B) Quantity = 7 cases, Price = $10
   C) Quantity = 9 cases, Price = $8
   D) Quantity = 10 cases, Price = $7
   Answer: B
   Diff: 2   Type: MC   Page Ref: 481–3/481–3
   Topic: Profit maximization
   Skill: Analytical
   Objective: LO 3: Explain how a monopoly chooses price and output.
   AACSB Coding: Analytic Skills
   Special Features: None

8. *Refer to Table 14–1.* What is the amount of profit that the firm earns?
   A) $47
   B) $42
   C) $34.50
   D) $49
   Answer: D
   Diff: 2   Type: MC   Page Ref: 481–3/481–3
   Topic: Profit maximization
   Skill: Conceptual
   Objective: LO 3: Explain how a monopoly chooses price and output.
   AACSB Coding: Analytic Skills
   Special Features: None

Figure 14–3

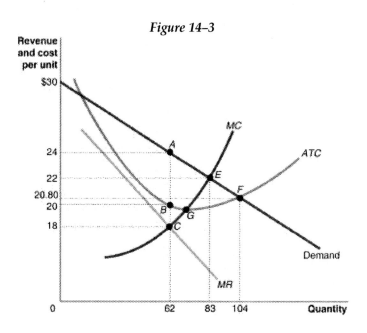

Figure 14–3 shows the cost and demand curves for a monopolist.

9. *Refer to Figure 14–3.* The profit-maximizing output and price for the monopolist are
 A) output = 62; price = $24
 B) output = 62; price = $18
 C) output = 83; price = $22
 D) output = 104; price = $20.80
Answer: A
Diff: 1 Type: MC Page Ref: 483/483
Topic: Profit maximization
Skill: Analytical
Objective: LO 3: Explain how a monopoly chooses price and output.
AACSB Coding: Analytic Skills
Special Features: None

10. *Refer to Figure 14–3.* The monopolist's total revenue is
 A) $1,116
 B) $1,488
 C) $1,826
 D) $1,726.40
Answer: B
Diff: 2 Type: MC Page Ref: 481-3/481-3
Topic: Profit Maximization
Skill: Analytical
Objective: LO 3: Explain how a monopoly chooses price and output.
AACSB Coding: Analytic Skills
Special Features: None

11. ***Refer to Figure 14-3.*** The monopolist's total cost is
     A) $1,116
     B) $1,660
     C) $1,726.40
     D) $1,240
Answer: D
Diff: 2   Type: MC   Page Ref: 481-3/481-3
Topic: Profit maximization
Skill: Analytical
Objective: LO 3: Explain how a monopoly chooses price and output.
AACSB Coding: Analytic Skills
Special Features: None

12. ***Refer to Figure 14-3.*** The monopolist earns a profit of
     A) $0
     B) $372
     C) $248
     D) $170
Answer: C
Diff: 2   Type: MC   Page Ref: 481-3/481-3
Topic: Profit maximization
Skill: Analytical
Objective: LO 3: Explain how a monopoly chooses price and output.
AACSB Coding: Analytic Skills
Special Features: None

13.   *Table 14-2*

Price	Quantity	Total Revenue	Marginal Revenue	Total Cost	Marginal Cost
$17	3	$51	-----	$56	-----
16	4	64	$13	63	$7
15	5	75	11	71	8
14	6	84	9	80	9
13	7	91	7	90	10
12	8	96	5	101	11

Refer to Figure 14-2. Assume that the table above gives the monthly demand and costs for subscriptions to basic cable for Comcast, a cable television monopoly in Philadelphia. If Comcast wants to maximize its profits, what price (P) should it charge and how many cable subscriptions per month (Q) should it sell?
     A) P = $12; Q = 8
     B) P = $14; Q = 6
     C) P = $16; Q = 4
     D) P = $15: Q = 5
Answer: B
Diff: 1   Type: MC   Page Ref: 484-5/484-5
Topic: Profit maximization
Skill: Analytical

Objective: LO 3: Explain how a monopoly chooses price and output.
AACSB Coding: Analytic Skills
Special Features: Solved Problem: Finding the Profit–Maximizing Price for the Output for a Monopolist

14. *Refer to Figure 14–2.* Assume that the table above gives the monthly demand and costs for subscriptions to basic cable for Comcast, a cable television monopoly in Philadelphia. If Comcast maximizes its profits how much profit will it earn?
    A) $84
    B) $40
    C) $4
    D) Comcast will break even.
    Answer: C
    Diff: 1   Type: MC   Page Ref: 484–5/484–5
    Topic: Profit maximization
    Skill: Analytical
    Objective: LO 3: Explain how a monopoly chooses price and output.
    AACSB Coding: Analytic Skills
    Special Features: Solved Problem: Finding the Profit–Maximizing Price for the Output for a Monopolist

15. To maximize profit a monopolist will produce where
    A) marginal revenue is equal to marginal cost.
    B) demand for its product is unit–elastic.
    C) revenue per unit is maximized.
    D) average total cost is equal to average revenue.
    Answer: A
    Diff: 1   Type: MC   Page Ref: 483/483
    Topic: Profit maximization
    Skill: Conceptual
    Objective: LO 3: Explain how a monopoly chooses price and output.
    AACSB Coding: Reflective Thinking
    Special Features: None

16. The most profitable price for a monopolist is
    A) the highest price a consumer is willing to pay for the monopolist's product.
    B) the price at which demand is unit–elastic.
    C) a price that maximizes the quantity sold.
    D) the price for which marginal revenue equals marginal cost.
    Answer: D
    Diff: 1   Type: MC   Page Ref: 485/485
    Topic: Profit maximization
    Skill: Conceptual
    Objective: LO 3: Explain how a monopoly chooses price and output.
    AACSB Coding: Reflective Thinking
    Special Features: Don't Let This Happen to YOU!: Don't Assume That Charging a Higher Price Is Always More Profitable for a Monopolist

17. Which of the following statements is true?
    A) Monopolists are price makers. All other firms are price takers.
    B) Unlike other industries, monopoly industries have high barriers to entry.
    C) Only monopoly firms are granted patents and copyrights.
    D) Unlike other firms, a monopolist's demand curve is the same as the demand curve for its product.

    Answer: D
    Diff: 1   Type: MC   Page Ref: 481/481
    Topic: Characteristics of monopoly
    Skill: Conceptual
    Objective: LO 3: Explain how a monopoly chooses price and output.
    AACSB Coding: Reflective Thinking
    Special Features: None

18. The demand curve for a monopoly firm
    A) is perfectly inelastic.
    B) lies below its marginal revenue curve.
    C) is the same as the demand curve for the product the firms sells.
    D) is horizontal.

    Answer: C
    Diff: 1   Type: MC   Page Ref: 481/481
    Topic: Demand and marginal revenue
    Skill: Analytical
    Objective: LO 3: Explain how a monopoly chooses price and output.
    AACSB Coding: Reflective Thinking
    Special Features: None

19. A monopolist will maximize profit where marginal revenue equals marginal cost.
    Answer: ⊙ True   False
    Diff: 1   Type: TF   Page Ref: 481–3/481–3
    Topic: Profit maximization
    Skill: Conceptual
    Objective: LO 3: Explain how a monopoly chooses price and output.
    AACSB Coding: Reflective Thinking
    Special Features: None

20. A monopolist's demand curve is the same at the marginal revenue curve for the product.
    Answer: True   ⊙ False
    Diff: 1   Type: TF   Page Ref: 481–3/481–3
    Topic: Characteristics of monopoly
    Skill: Conceptual
    Objective: LO 3: Explain how a monopoly chooses price and output.
    AACSB Coding: Reflective Thinking
    Special Features: None

21.   *Figure 14–4*

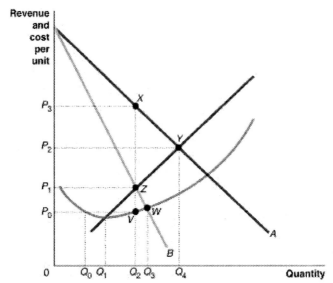

Figure 14–4 below reflects the cost and revenue structure for a monopoly that has been in business for a very long time.

Refer to Figure 14–4. Use the figure above to answer the following questions.
a.   Identify the curves labeled A, B, C, and D.
b.   What is the profit-maximizing quantity and what price will the monopolist charge?
c.   What area represents total revenue at the profit–maximizing output level?
d.   What area represents total cost at the profit–maximizing output level?
e.   What area represents profit?
f.   What is the profit per unit (average profit) at the profit–maximizing output level?
g.   If this industry was organized as a perfectly competitive industry, what would be the profit-maximizing price and quantity?
h.   What area represents the deadweight loss as a result of a monopoly?
Answer: a.   A = Demand curve; B = Marginal revenue curve; C = Marginal cost curve; D = Average total   cost curve.
        b.   Quantity = Q_2 units; Price = P_3
        c. $P_3 \times Q_2$
        d. $P_0 \times Q_2$
        e. $(P_3 - P_0) \times Q_2$
        f. $P_3 - P_0$
        g.   Quantity = Q_4 and Price = P_2
        h.   The triangle xyz
Diff: 3   Type: ES   Page Ref: 481–5/481–5
Topic: Profit maximization
Skill: Analytical
Objective: LO 3: Explain how a monopoly chooses price and output.
AACSB Coding: Analytic Skills
Special Features: None

22. "Being the only seller in the market, the monopolist can choose any price and quantity it desires." Evaluate this statement: is it true or false? Explain your answer.

Answer: The statement is false. The monopolist cannot choose both the price and quantity. The monopolist has some market power and therefore has some ability to affect market price but it does not control the demand curve. If the monopolist sets a price, the quantity sold will be indicated by the demand curve.

Diff: 2   Type: SA   Page Ref: 481–5/481–5
Topic: Monopoly
Skill: Conceptual
Objective: LO 3: Explain how a monopoly chooses price and output.
AACSB Coding: Reflective Thinking
Special Features: None

14.4   Does Monopoly Reduce Economic Efficiency?

1. Assume a hypothetical case where an industry begins as perfectly competitive and then becomes a monopoly. Which of the following statements regarding economic surplus in each market structure is true?
   A) Under perfectly competitive conditions, economic surplus in this industry equals consumer surplus plus producer surplus. Under monopoly conditions, some consumer surplus is transferred to producer surplus, but economic surplus is the same as it was under perfectly competitive conditions.
   B) Under perfectly competitive conditions, economic surplus in this industry is maximized. Under monopoly conditions economic surplus is minimized.
   C) Under perfectly competitive conditions, economic surplus is equal to consumer surplus; there is no producer surplus because firms are price-takers. Under monopoly conditions, economic surplus is equal to producer surplus.
   D) Under perfectly competitive conditions, economic surplus is maximized. Under monopoly conditions economic surplus is less than under perfect competition and there is a deadweight loss.

Answer: D
Diff: 2   Type: MC   Page Ref: 485–7/485–7
Topic: Comparing monopoly and perfect competition
Skill: Conceptual
Objective: LO 4: Use a graph to illustrate how a monopoly affects economic efficiency.
AACSB Coding: Reflective Thinking
Special Features: None

2. Assume a hypothetical case where an industry begins as perfectly competitive and then becomes a monopoly. Which of the following statements comparing the conditions in the industry under both market structures is true?
   A) A monopoly will produce more and charge a higher price than would a perfectly competitive industry producing the same good.
   B) A monopoly will produce more and advertise more than would a perfectly competitive industry producing the same good.
   C) A monopoly will produce less and charge a higher price than would a perfectly competitive industry producing the same good.
   D) A monopoly will produce less and charge a lower price than would a perfectly competitive industry producing the same good.

Answer: C
Diff: 1   Type: MC   Page Ref: 485–6/485–6
Topic: Comparing monopoly and perfect competition
Skill: Conceptual
Objective: LO 4: Use a graph to illustrate how a monopoly affects economic efficiency.
AACSB Coding: Reflective Thinking
Special Features: None

3. Assume a hypothetical case where an industry begins as perfectly competitive and then becomes a monopoly. As a result of this change
   A) Price will be higher, output will be lower and the deadweight loss will be eliminated.
   B) Consumer surplus will be smaller, producer surplus will be greater and there will be a reduction in economic efficiency.
   C) Price will be higher, consumer surplus will be greater and output will be greater.
   D) Consumer surplus will be smaller and producer surplus will be greater. There will be a net increase in economic surplus.

Answer: B
Diff: 2   Type: MC   Page Ref: 485–7/485–7
Topic: Monopoly and economic efficiency
Skill: Conceptual
Objective: LO 4: Use a graph to illustrate how a monopoly affects economic efficiency.
AACSB Coding: Reflective Thinking
Special Features: None

4. Which of the following statements is true?
   A) If a tax is imposed on a product sold by a monopolist, the monopolist will maximize its profits by producing where marginal revenue equals marginal cost.
   B) A monopolist will always charge the highest possible price.
   C) If a tax is imposed on a product sold by a monopolist, the monopolist can increase its price to pass along the entire tax to consumers.
   D) Because a monopolist faces no competition the demand for its product is perfectly inelastic.

Answer: A

Diff: 2   Type: MC   Page Ref: 485/485
Topic: Monopoly and economic efficiency
Skill: Conceptual
Objective: LO 4: Use a graph to illustrate how a monopoly affects economic efficiency.
AACSB Coding: Reflective Thinking
Special Features: None

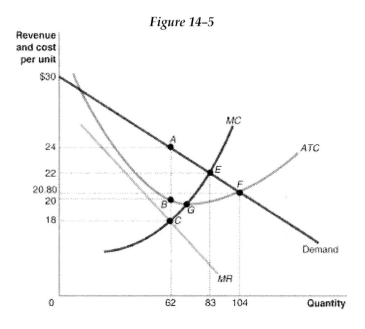

Figure 14–5

Figure 14–5 shows the cost and demand curves for a monopolist.

5. *Refer to Figure 14–5.* Assume the firm maximizes its profits. What is the amount of consumer surplus?
   A) $21
   B) $124
   C) $186
   D) $332

Answer: C

Diff: 2   Type: MC   Page Ref: 485–7/485–7
Topic: Monopoly and economic efficiency
Skill: Analytical
Objective: LO 4: Use a graph to illustrate how a monopoly affects economic efficiency.
AACSB Coding: Analytic Skills
Special Features: None

6. ***Refer to Figure 14–5.*** What is the amount of consumer surplus if, instead of monopoly, the industry was organized as a perfectly competitive industry?

    A) $21

    B) $124

    C) $186

    D) $332

Answer: D

Diff: 3   Type: MC   Page Ref: 485–7/485–7

Topic: Monopoly and economic efficiency

Skill: Analytical

Objective: LO 4: Use a graph to illustrate how a monopoly affects economic efficiency.

AACSB Coding: Analytic Skills

Special Features: None

7. ***Refer to Figure 14–5.*** If this industry was organized as a perfectly competitive industry, the market output and market price would be

    A) output = 62; price = $24

    B) output = 83; price = $22

    C) output = 62; price = $18

    D) output = 104; price = $20.80

Answer: B

Diff: 2   Type: MC   Page Ref: 485–7/485–7

Topic: Monopoly and economic efficiency

Skill: Analytical

Objective: LO 4: Use a graph to illustrate how a monopoly affects economic efficiency.

AACSB Coding: Analytic Skills

Special Features: None

8. ***Refer to Figure 14–5.*** If the monopoly firm maximizes its profits, total revenue would be

    A) $1,488

    B) $1,116

    C) $1,826

    D) $1,726.40

Answer: A

Diff: 1   Type: MC   Page Ref: 485–7/485–7

Topic: Monopoly and economic efficiency

Skill: Analytical

Objective: LO 4: Use a graph to illustrate how a monopoly affects economic efficiency.

AACSB Coding: Analytic Skills

Special Features: None

Figure 14–3

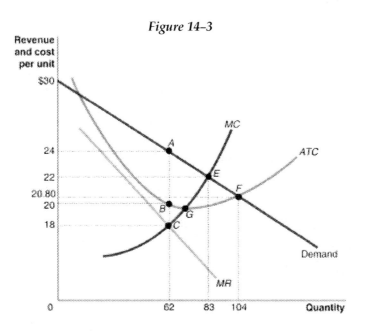

Figure 14–3 shows the cost and demand curves for a monopolist.

9. *Refer to Figure 14–5.* If the firm maximizes its profits total cost would be
     A) $1,116
     B) $1,240
     C) $1,660
     D) $1,726.40
   Answer: B
   Diff: 1   Type: MC   Page Ref: 485–7/485–7
   Topic: Monopoly and economic efficiency
   Skill: Analytical
   Objective: LO 4: Use a graph to illustrate how a monopoly affects economic efficiency.
   AACSB Coding: Analytic Skills
   Special Features: None

10. *Refer to Figure 14–5.* If the firm maximizes its profits its total profit would be
     A) $248
     B) $0
     C) $372
     D) $170
   Answer: A
   Diff: 1   Type: MC   Page Ref: 485–7/485–7
   Topic: Monopoly and economic efficiency
   Skill: Analytical
   Objective: LO 4: Use a graph to illustrate how a monopoly affects economic efficiency.
   AACSB Coding: Analytic Skills
   Special Features: None

11. ***Refer to Figure 14–5.*** If the firm maximizes its profits the deadweight loss to society due to this monopoly is equal to the area
    A) abf
    B) abeg
    C) aec
    D) efg
Answer: C
Diff: 3   Type: MC   Page Ref: 485–7/485–7
Topic: Monopoly and economic efficiency
Skill: Analytical
Objective: LO 4: Use a graph to illustrate how a monopoly affects economic efficiency.
AACSB Coding: Analytic Skills
Special Features: None

12. The ability of a firm to charge a price greater than marginal cost is called
    A) monopoly power.
    B) price–making power.
    C) cost–plus pricing.
    D) market power.
Answer: D
Diff: 1   Type: MC   Page Ref: 487/487
Topic: Market power
Skill: Definition
Objective: LO 4: Use a graph to illustrate how a monopoly affects economic efficiency.
AACSB Coding: Reflective Thinking
Special Features: None

13. Whenever a firm can charge a price greater than marginal cost
    A) the firm must be a monopolist.
    B) there is some loss of economic efficiency.
    C) consumers have the ability to choose a close substitute.
    D) the firm will earn economic profits.
Answer: B
Diff: 2   Type: MC   Page Ref: 487/487
Topic: Market power
Skill: Conceptual
Objective: LO 4: Use a graph to illustrate how a monopoly affects economic efficiency.
AACSB Coding: Reflective Thinking
Special Features: None

14. The only firms that do not have market power are
    A) firms in industries with low barriers to entry.
    B) firms that do not advertise their products.
    C) firms in perfectly competitive markets.
    D) firms that sell identical products.
    Answer: C
    Diff: 1   Type: MC   Page Ref: 487/487
    Topic: Market power
    Skill: Conceptual
    Objective: LO 4: Use a graph to illustrate how a monopoly affects economic efficiency.
    AACSB Coding: Reflective Thinking
    Special Features: None

15. Arnold Harberger was the first economist to estimate the loss of economic efficiency due to market power. Harberger found that
    A) the loss of economic efficiency in the U.S. economy due to market power was less than 1 percent of the value of production.
    B) because of the increase in the average size of firms since World War II, the loss of economic efficiency has been relatively large, about 10 percent of the value of total production in the United States.
    C) although the number of monopolies was small, the large number of other non–competitive firms in the United States resulted in a large loss of economic efficiency, about 20 percent of the value of total production.
    D) the loss of economic efficiency in the U.S. economy due to market power was small around 1973, about 1 percent of the value of production, but has since grown to about 10 percent.
    Answer: A
    Diff: 1   Type: MC   Page Ref: 487/487
    Topic: Market power
    Skill: Fact
    Objective: LO 4: Use a graph to illustrate how a monopoly affects economic efficiency.
    AACSB Coding: Reflective Thinking
    Special Features: None

16. Arnold Harberger was the first economist to estimate the loss of economic efficiency due to market power. Since Harberger's findings were published, other researchers have studied this same issue. How do the results of these researchers compare to Harberger's results?
    A) The other researchers reached conclusions similar to Harberger's; namely, the loss of economic efficiency due to market power is about 10 percent of the value of production in the United States.
    B) The other researchers reached conclusions different from Harberger's; namely, they found that the loss of economic efficiency due to market power is only about 1 percent of the value of production in the United States, much less than Harberger's estimate.
    C) The other researchers reached conclusions different from Harberger's; namely, the loss of economic efficiency due to market power is about 10 percent of the value of production in the United States, significantly greater than Harberger's estimate.
    D) The other researchers reached conclusions similar to Harberger's; namely, the loss of economic efficiency due to market power is about 1 percent of the value of production in the United States.
    Answer: D
    Diff: 2   Type: MC   Page Ref: 487/487
    Topic: Market Power
    Skill: Fact
    Objective: LO 4: Use a graph to illustrate how a monopoly affects economic efficiency.
    AACSB Coding: Reflective Thinking
    Special Features: None

17. In evaluating the degree of economic efficiency in a market we can state that the size of the deadweight loss in a market will be smaller
    A) the greater the difference between marginal cost and price.
    B) the smaller the difference between marginal cost and average total cost.
    C) the smaller the difference between marginal cost and price.
    D) the greater the difference between marginal cost and average revenue.
    Answer: C
    Diff: 2   Type: MC   Page Ref: 487/487
    Topic: Market power
    Skill: Conceptual
    Objective: LO 4: Use a graph to illustrate how a monopoly affects economic efficiency.
    AACSB Coding: Reflective Thinking
    Special Features: None

18. The possibility that the economy may benefit from having market power, rather than being very competitive, is closely identified with which famous economist?
    A) Arnold Harberger
    B) Joseph Schumpeter
    C) Sergey Brin
    D) Donald Turner
    Answer: B
    Diff: 1   Type: MC   Page Ref: 488/488
    Topic: Monopoly and economic efficiency
    Skill: Fact
    Objective: LO 4: Use a graph to illustrate how a monopoly affects economic efficiency.
    AACSB Coding: Reflective Thinking
    Special Features: None

19. Some economists believe that the economy benefits from firms having market power. Which of the following is an argument that has been made to support this position?
    A) Large firms are better able than small firms to spend funds on research and development required to develop new products.
    B) Competition is very rare in the U.S. economy and few new products are produced by smaller, competitive firms.
    C) Research has shown that the deadweight loss from monopolies is a small percentage of the value of production in the U.S.
    D) Large firms can afford to lobby the U.S. government in order to impose restrictions on imports and reduce the outsourcing of jobs to other countries.
    Answer: A
    Diff: 1   Type: MC   Page Ref: 488/488
    Topic: Monopoly and economic efficiency
    Skill: Conceptual
    Objective: LO 4: Use a graph to illustrate how a monopoly affects economic efficiency.
    AACSB Coding: Reflective Thinking
    Special Features: None

20. If the market for a product begins as perfectly competitive and then becomes a monopoly there will be a reduction in economic efficiency and a deadweight loss.
    Answer: ○ True   False
    Diff: 2   Type: TF   Page Ref: 485–6/485–6
    Topic: Monopoly and economic efficiency
    Skill: Conceptual
    Objective: LO 4: Use a graph to illustrate how a monopoly affects economic efficiency.
    AACSB Coding: Reflective Thinking
    Special Features: None

21. According to research conducted by economists, if every industry in the U.S. economy were perfectly competitive, the gain in economic efficiency would be less than 1 percent of the value of total production.
Answer: True   ⊙ False
Diff: 2   Type: TF   Page Ref: 487/487
Topic: Monopoly and economic efficiency
Skill: Fact
Objective: LO 4: Use a graph to illustrate how a monopoly affects economic efficiency.
AACSB Coding: Reflective Thinking
Special Features: None

22. Equilibrium in a perfectly competitive market results in the greatest amount of economic surplus, or total benefit to society, from the production of a good. Why, then, did Joseph Schumpeter argue that an economy may benefit more from firms that have market power than from firms that are perfectly competitive?
Answer: Schumpeter did not deny that perfectly competitive firms produced the greatest amount of consumer surplus, but this result does not address which type of market structure is best for developing new products. Schumpeter pointed to the large costs of product development; how can small, perfectly competitive firms afford the monetary cost and the risk of failure that product development requires? Only large firms in monopoly or oligopoly industries can afford investments in research and development, and the inevitable failures that accompany research. According to Schumpeter, the higher prices firms with market power charge are less important than the benefits from new products these firms introduce to the market.
Diff: 2   Type: ES   Page Ref: 488/488
Topic: Comparing monopoly and perfect competition
Skill: Conceptual
Objective: LO 4: Use a graph to illustrate how a monopoly affects economic efficiency.
AACSB Coding: Reflective Thinking
Special Features: None

14.5   Government Policy Toward Monopoly

1. Collusion is
    A) common among monopoly firms.
    B) an agreement among firms to charge the same price or otherwise not to compete.
    C) necessary for firms to raise money by borrowing from investors or from banks in order to fund research and development required to develop new products.
    D) legal under U.S. antitrust laws if the intent is to increase competition.
Answer: B
Diff: 1   Type: MC   Page Ref: 488/488
Topic: Antitrust law and enforcement
Skill: Definition
Objective: LO 5: Discuss government policies toward monopoly.
AACSB Coding: Reflective Thinking
Special Features: None

2. In the United States, government policies with respect to monopolies and collusion are embodied in
   A) the U.S. Constitution.
   B) common law, which the U.S. adopted from English law.
   C) the Supreme Court.
   D) antitrust laws.
   Answer: D
   Diff: 1   *Type: MC*   *Page Ref: 488/488*
   Topic: Antitrust law and enforcement
   Skill: Fact
   Objective: LO 5: Discuss government policies toward monopoly.
   AACSB Coding: Reflective Thinking
   Special Features: None

3. The first important law regulating monopolies in the United States was
   A) the Grant Act, which was passed in 1890.
   B) the Clayton Act, which was passed in 1890.
   C) the Sherman Act, which was passed in 1890.
   D) the Federal Trade Commission Act, which was passed in 1914.
   Answer: C
   Diff: 1   *Type: MC*   *Page Ref: 488/488*
   Topic: Antitrust law and enforcement
   Skill: Fact
   Objective: LO 5: Discuss government policies toward monopoly.
   AACSB Coding: Reflective Thinking
   Special Features: None

4. Which antitrust law prohibited firms from buying stock in competitors and from having directors serve on the boards of competing firms?
   A) The Clayton Act
   B) The Securities and Exchange Act
   C) The Sherman Act
   D) The Robinson–Patman Act
   Answer: A
   Diff: 1   *Type: MC*   *Page Ref: 489/489*
   Topic: Antitrust law and enforcement
   Skill: Fact
   Objective: LO 5: Discuss government policies toward monopoly.
   AACSB Coding: Reflective Thinking
   Special Features: None

5. The Clayton Act is an antitrust law that was passed to
    A) outlaw monopolization.
    B) address loopholes in the Sherman Act.
    C) prohibit charging buyers different prices if the result would reduce competition.
    D) toughen restrictions on mergers by prohibiting mergers that reduce competition.
Answer: B
Diff: 1   Type: MC   Page Ref: 489/489
Topic: Antitrust law and enforcement
Skill: Fact
Objective: LO 5: Discuss government policies toward monopoly.
AACSB Coding: Reflective Thinking
Special Features: None

6. Why are laws aimed at regulating monopolies called "antitrust" laws?
    A) The rise of large firms (e.g., Standard Oil) in the late 1800s in the United States caused consumers to lose trust in private business.
    B) "Trust" was a word in Old English that meant monopoly in the Middle Ages. Therefore, "antitrust" is a term that means "against monopoly."
    C) In the late 1800s firms in several industries formed trusts; the firms were independent but gave voting control to a board of trustees.   Antitrust laws were passed to regulate these trusts.
    D) In the late 1800s firms in several industries formed trusts; they were called "trusts" because when corporate officials were questioned about their business they would clam that business was good for the country and that they should trusted.
Answer: C
Diff: 1   Type: MC   Page Ref: 489/489
Topic: Antitrust law and enforcement
Skill: Fact
Objective: LO 5: Discuss government policies toward monopoly.
AACSB Coding: Reflective Thinking
Special Features: None

7. The U.S. Congress has given two government entities the authority to police mergers. These two entities are
    A) the antitrust division of the Department of State and the Securities and Exchange Commission.
    B) the Federal Trade Commission and the Internal Revenue Service.
    C) the Antitrust Division of the U.S. Department of Justice and the Council of Economic Advisors.
    D) the Federal Trade Commission and the Antitrust Division of the U.S. Department of Justice.
Answer: D
Diff: 1   Type: MC   Page Ref: 489/489
Topic: Antitrust law and enforcement
Skill: Fact
Objective: LO 5: Discuss government policies toward monopoly.
AACSB Coding: Reflective Thinking
Special Features: None

8. A merger between firms at different stages of production of a good
    A) is a vertical merger.
    B) was made illegal by the Sherman Act.
    C) was made legal by the Clayton Act.
    D) is a horizontal merger.
    Answer: A
    Diff: 1   Type: MC   Page Ref: 489/489
    Topic: Antitrust law and enforcement
    Skill: Fact
    Objective: LO 5: Discuss government policies toward monopoly.
    AACSB Coding: Reflective Thinking
    Special Features: None

9. A horizontal merger
    A) is a merger between firms in the same industry.
    B) results in a trust (for example, the Standard Oil Company).
    C) is a merger between firms at different stages of production of a good.
    D) was illegal in the United States until the Federal Trade Commission Act was passed by Congress in 1914.
    Answer: A
    Diff: 1   Type: MC   Page Ref: 489/489
    Topic: Antitrust law and enforcement
    Skill: Definition
    Objective: LO 5: Discuss government policies toward monopoly.
    AACSB Coding: Reflective Thinking
    Special Features: None

10. Baxter International, a manufacturer of hospital supplies, acquired American Hospital Supply, a distributor of hospital supplies. This is an example of
    A) a conglomerate merger.
    B) a horizontal merger.
    C) a vertical merger.
    D) a two-dimensional merger.
    Answer: C
    Diff: 1   Type: MC   Page Ref: 489–90/489–90
    Topic: Mergers
    Skill: Conceptual
    Objective: LO 5: Discuss government policies toward monopoly.
    AACSB Coding: Reflective Thinking
    Special Features: None

11. Congress has divided the authority to police mergers between the Antitrust Division of the U.S. Department of Justice (AD) and the Federal Trade Commission (FTC). How is this authority divided?
    A) The AD decides whether proposed horizontal mergers will be challenged; the FTC decides whether proposed vertical mergers will be challenged.
    B) Both the AD and the FTC are responsible for merger policy.
    C) The AD always renders its opinion on any proposed merger first. If the AD approves the merger the case then goes to the FTC for final approval. If the AD disallows the merger, the decision stands and the FTC does not become involved.
    D) The AD establishes the guidelines that are used to evaluate proposed mergers; the FTC uses these guidelines to decide whether a proposed merger will be allowed to take place.

Answer: B
Diff: 2   Type: MC   Page Ref: 489–92/489–92
Topic: Antitrust law and enforcement
Skill: Fact
Objective: LO 5: Discuss government policies toward monopoly.
AACSB Coding: Reflective Thinking
Special Features: None

12. Which two factors make regulating mergers complicated?
    A) First, firms may lobby government officials to influence their decision to approve the merger. Second, by the time the government officials reach a decision regarding the merger, the firms often decide not to merge.
    B) First, the time it takes to reach a decision to approve a merger is so long that the firms' often have new owners and mangers. Second, by law government officials are not allowed to consider the impact of foreign trade (exports and imports) on the degree of competition in the markets of the merged firms.
    C) First, the Federal Trade Commission and the Antitrust Division of the U.S. Department of Justice must both approve mergers. Second, the concentration ratios that are used to evaluate the degree of competition the merged firms face are flawed.
    D) First, it is not always clear what market firms are in. Second, the newly merged firm might be more efficient than the merging firms were individually.

Answer: D
Diff: 2   Type: MC   Page Ref: 490/490
Topic: Merger guidelines
Skill: Conceptual
Objective: LO 5: Discuss government policies toward monopoly.
AACSB Coding: Reflective Thinking
Special Features: None

13. Beginning in 1965 the head of the Antitrust Division of the U.S. Department of Justice began to change antitrust policy. How did antitrust policy change?
    A) For the first time horizontal mergers were allowed – with government approval – and vertical mergers were allowed without need for approval from the government.
    B) For the first time concentration ratios were used to evaluate the degree of competition in the industries of firms that proposed mergers.
    C) The Division began to systematically consider the economic consequences of proposed mergers.
    D) Proposed mergers no longer needed the approval of the Federal Trade Commission or the court system.
    Answer: C
    Diff: 2   Type: MC   Page Ref: 491/491
    Topic: Merger guidelines
    Skill: Fact
    Objective: LO 5: Discuss government policies toward monopoly.
    AACSB Coding: Reflective Thinking
    Special Features: None

14. Economists played a key role in the development of merger guidelines by the Department of Justice and the Federal Trade Commission in 1982. These guidelines have three main parts. What are these parts?
    A) Concentration ratios; the Herfindahl–Hirschman Index; market standards.
    B) Concentration standards; concentration ratios; competitive analysis.
    C) Economic analysis; political analysis; dynamic analysis.
    D) Market definition; measure of concentration; merger standards.
    Answer: D
    Diff: 1   Type: MC   Page Ref: 491/491
    Topic: Merger guidelines
    Skill: Fact
    Objective: LO 5: Discuss government policies toward monopoly.
    AACSB Coding: Reflective Thinking
    Special Features: None

15. Merger guidelines developed by the U.S. Department of Justice and the Federal Trade Commission use the Herfindahl–Hirschman Index as a measure of concentration.   This index measures concentration in an industry by
    A) adding up the market shares of all firms in the industry, squaring this number and then dividing by the number of firms in the industry.
    B) squaring the market shares of each firm in an industry and then adding up the values of the squares.
    C) squaring the four–firm concentration ratio of the industry and dividing this number by the total number of firms in the industry.
    D) determining the market shares of the four largest firms in the industry but unlike the concentration ratio, the Index includes sales in the United States by foreign firms.
    Answer: B
    Diff: 1   Type: MC   Page Ref: 492/492
    Topic: Merger guidelines
    Skill: Definition
    Objective: LO 5: Discuss government policies toward monopoly.
    AACSB Coding: Reflective Thinking
    Special Features: None

16. The Herfindahl–Hirschman Index is one factor used to determine whether a merger between two firms should be allowed. Which of the following statements regarding the value of the Index for a given industry is true?
    A) If a merger would result in an Index value less than 1,000 the merger would not be challenged.
    B) If a merger would result in an Index value of 1,000 or more, the industry would be considered a monopoly and the merger would be challenged.
    C) If a merger resulted in an Index of between 1,000 and 1,800, the industry would be considered competitive and the merger would not be challenged.
    D) If a merger would increase the Index by 100 the industry would be considered a monopoly and the merger would be challenged.
    Answer: A
    Diff: 2   Type: MC   Page Ref: 492/492
    Topic: Merger guidelines
    Skill: Fact
    Objective: LO 5: Discuss government policies toward monopoly.
    AACSB Coding: Reflective Thinking
    Special Features: None

17. According to the Department of Justice merger guidelines, a proposed merger between two firms may be challenged if the post-merger Herfindahl–Hirschman Index
    A) lies between 1,000 and 1,800 and the merger raises the Index by 50 points.
    B) lies between 1,000 and 1,800 and the merger raises the Index by more than 100 points.
    C) lies above 1,800 and the merger raises the Index by less than 50 points.
    D) lies below 1,000 and the merger raises the Index by 100 points.
    Answer: B
    Diff: 2   Type: MC   Page Ref: 492/492
    Topic: Merger guidelines
    Skill: Fact
    Objective: LO 5: Discuss government policies toward monopoly.
    AACSB Coding: Reflective Thinking
    Special Features: None

18. Consider an industry that is made up of six firms with the following market shares: Firm A – 50%, Firm B – 20%, Firms C and D – 10% each, and Firms E and F – 5% each. What is the value of the Herfindahl–Hirschman Index and how will the industry be categorized?
    A) 2,500; mildly concentrated
    B) 8,100; highly concentrated
    C) 3,150; highly concentrated
    D) 10,000; effectively competitive
    Answer: C
    Diff: 2   Type: MC   Page Ref: 492/492
    Topic: Herfindahl–Hirschman Index
    Skill: Analytical
    Objective: LO 5: Discuss government policies toward monopoly.
    AACSB Coding: Analytic Skills
    Special Features: None

19. If a firm is a natural monopoly, competition from other firms cannot be counted on to force price down to the level where the company earns zero economic profit. How are prices usually set in natural monopoly markets in the U.S.?
    A) Each natural monopoly is made a public franchise. The public franchise is then required to set its price equal to its marginal cost.
    B) Natural monopolies are privately owned, but prices proposed by the firms must be approved by the Antitrust Division of the Department of Justice.
    C) Natural monopolies are privately owned and allowed to set their own prices. Government regulation of the firms would result in greater deadweight losses.
    D) Local or state regulatory commissions usually set prices for natural monopolies.
    Answer: D
    Diff: 1   Type: MC   Page Ref: 494/494
    Topic: Natural monopoly
    Skill: Conceptual
    Objective: LO 5: Discuss government policies toward monopoly.
    AACSB Coding: Reflective Thinking
    Special Features: None

Figure 14-1

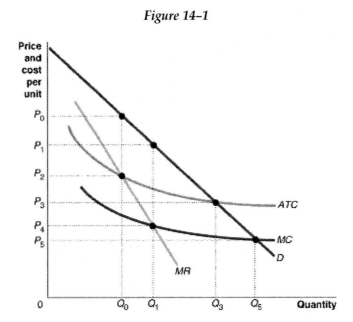

Figure 14-1 shows the market demand and cost curves facing a natural monopoly.

20. ***Refer to Figure 14-6.*** Suppose the government regulates this industry in order to remove the inefficiency implied by the behavior of the profit maximizing owners. If regulators require that the firm produces the economically efficient output level, what is this level and what price will be charged?

   A) Q_5 units; $\$P_5$

   B) Q_1 units; $\$P_4$

   C) Q_1 units; $\$P_1$

   D) Q_3 units; $\$P_3$

Answer: A
Diff: 2   Type: MC   Page Ref: 494/494
Topic: Natural monopoly
Skill: Analytical
Objective: LO 5: Discuss government policies toward monopoly.
AACSB Coding: Analytic Skills
Special Features: None

21. *Refer to Figure 14–6.* Which of the following would be true if government regulators require the natural monopoly to produce at the economically efficient output level?
    A) This results in a misallocation of resources.
    B) The marginal cost of producing the last unit sold exceeds the marginal benefit.
    C) The firm will sustain persistent losses and will not continue in business in the long run.
    D) The firm will break even.
    Answer: C
    Diff: 2   Type: MC   Page Ref: 494/494
    Topic: Natural monopoly
    Skill: Analytical
    Objective: LO 5: Discuss government policies toward monopoly.
    AACSB Coding: Analytic Skills
    Special Features: None

22. *Refer to Figure 14–6.* If the regulators of the natural monopoly allow the owners of the firm to break even on their investment the firm will produce an output of _____ and charge a price of _____.
    A) Q_1 units; P_4
    B) Q_1 units; P_1
    C) Q_5 units; P_5
    D) Q_3 units; P_3
    Answer: D
    Diff: 2   Type: MC   Page Ref: 494/494
    Topic: Natural monopoly
    Skill: Analytical
    Objective: LO 5: Discuss government policies toward monopoly.
    AACSB Coding: Analytic Skills
    Special Features: None

23. *Refer to figure 14–6.* In the absence of any government regulation, the profit–maximizing owners of this firm will produce _____ units and charge a price of _____.
    A) Q_0 units; P_0
    B) Q_1 units; P_1
    C) Q_1 units; P_4
    D) Q_3 units; P_3
    Answer: B
    Diff: 2   Type: MC   Page Ref: 494/494
    Topic: Natural monopoly
    Skill: Analytical
    Objective: LO 2: Explain the four main reasons monopolies arise.
    AACSB Coding: Analytic Skills
    Special Features: None

24. Until the 1990s federal regulations placed restrictions on commercial banks that did not allow
    A) any bank to have a branch in more than one state.
    B) banks to make mortgages loans. Only savings banks could do this.
    C) banks to offer customers free checking.
    D) banks to pay customers more than 6 percent interest on any of their accounts.
    Answer: A
    Diff: 1   Type: MC   Page Ref: 493–4/493–4
    Topic: Government policy toward monopoly
    Skill: Fact
    Objective: LO 5: Discuss government policies toward monopoly.
    AACSB Coding: Reflective Thinking
    Special Features: None

25. The elimination of government restrictions on banks in the 1990s has led to
    A) bank mergers that resulted in two banks that each have more than 10 percent of all bank deposits.
    B) a sharp increase in the number of banks nationwide.
    C) a large increase in the percentage of people who have savings and checking accounts.
    D) a sharp decline in the number of banks nationwide.
    Answer: D
    Diff: 1   Type: MC   Page Ref: 493–4/493–4
    Topic: Government policy toward monopoly
    Skill: Fact
    Objective: LO 5: Discuss government policies toward monopoly.
    AACSB Coding: Reflective Thinking
    Special Features: Making the Connection: Should the Government Prevent Banks from Becoming Too Big?

26. Despite the popularity of the National Football League many cable television systems do not offer their customers the NFL Network. In most cities, cable systems are monopolies so their customers cannot switch to another system that carries the NFL Network. One reason why cable systems don't offer the NFL Network is
    A) it would violate antitrust laws.
    B) cable systems can make greater profits by not offering the NFL network as part of its normal package but forcing consumers to upgrade their service in order to watch it.
    C) the marginal cost of adding the NFL Network to their programming packages would exceed the marginal revenue cable systems would receive.
    D) consumer surveys convinced cable systems that the NFL Network is not as popular as NFL games that are not carried on the NFL network.
    Answer: B
    Diff: 1   Type: MC   Page Ref: 495/495
    Topic: Monopoly
    Skill: Fact
    Objective: LO 5: Discuss government policies toward monopoly.
    AACSB Coding: Reflective Thinking
    Special Features: Economics in YOUR Life!: Why Can't I Watch the NFL Network?

27. In 2006 the California legislature passed a law that allowed greater competition in the cable television market. Several other states have passed similar laws. A likely outcome of these laws is
    A) an increase in the number of state laws that allow for greater competition in the satellite television market.
    B) an increase in campaign contributions from cable television company officials to state legislators.
    C) lower prices for cable television and an improvement in the services cable companies offer to their customers.
    D) higher cable prices but an increase in the number of stations offered by cable television companies to their customers.

    Answer: C
    Diff: 1   Type: MC   Page Ref: 496–7/496–7
    Topic: Monopoly and economic efficiency
    Skill: Conceptual
    Objective: LO 5: Discuss government policies toward monopoly.
    AACSB Coding: Reflective Thinking
    Special Features: An Inside Look: As Barriers Fall, Will Cable TV Competition Rise?

28. Merger guidelines developed by the Antitrust Division of the U.S. Department of Justice use four–firm concentration ratios as measures of concentration.

    Answer: True   ◎ False
    Diff: 1   Type: TF   Page Ref: 492/492
    Topic: Merger guidelines
    Skill: Fact
    Objective: LO 5: Discuss government policies toward monopoly.
    AACSB Coding: Reflective Thinking
    Special Features: None

29. Local or state offices of the Department of Justice usually set prices for natural monopolies in their jurisdictions.

    Answer: True   ◎ False
    Diff: 1   Type: TF   Page Ref: 494/494
    Topic: Regulating natural monopolies
    Skill: Fact
    Objective: LO 5: Discuss government policies toward monopoly.
    AACSB Coding: Reflective Thinking
    Special Features: None

30. Identify the type of merger in each of the following situations and indicate how the post-merger concentration ratio for the industry is affected.
    a. A steel company merges with a coal and iron ore mining company.
    b. Staples, a retailer of office supplies, acquires Office Depot, another retailer of office supplies.
    c. An oil company merges with pipeline, shipping, and railroad companies as well as refineries and gas stations.

    Answer: a. This would be a vertical merger; the concentration ratio of the steel industry is not likely to change.
    b. This is a horizontal merger; the concentration ratio would increase.
    c. This is a vertical merger; the concentration ratio for the oil industry is not likely to change.

Diff: 2   Type: ES   Page Ref: 489/489
Topic: Mergers
Skill: Conceptual
Objective: LO 5: Discuss government policies toward monopoly.
AACSB Coding: Reflective Thinking
Special Features: None

31. a. What is the defining characteristic of a natural monopoly?
    b. Should the government break up a natural monopoly into two or more firms to make the industry more competitive?
    c. Suppose the government wants to ensure that some of the benefits of declining average total cost are passed on to consumers. To achieve this goal, it requires that the natural monopoly
    set its price equal to marginal cost. Is this a feasible goal? Explain.
    d. What is an alternative to marginal cost pricing that ensures that consumers reap some of the benefits of declining average total cost?

    Answer: a. The defining characteristic is the presence of significant economies of scale such that the average total cost of production declines over the relevant range of market demand.
    b. No, given the importance of economies of scale, society is better of with one big firm producing the output rather than several small firms.
    c. Setting price equals to marginal cost is not feasible because the natural monopoly will incur persistent losses and will not continue to produce in the long run.
    d. An alternative solution is to require average total cost pricing; that is, price is set equal to the average cost of production (where the average cost includes the opportunity cost of funds invested in the firm by its owners). This will allow the monopolist to break even on its   investment and stay in business.

Diff: 3   Type: ES   Page Ref: 494/494
Topic: Natural monopoly
Skill: Conceptual
Objective: LO 5: Discuss government policies toward monopoly.
AACSB Coding: Reflective Thinking
Special Features: None

32. Consider two industries, industry W and industry X. In industry W there are five companies, each with a market share of 20% of total sales. In industry X, there are six companies. One company has a 50% market share and each of the other five firms has a market share of 10%.

   a. Calculate the four-firm concentration ratio for each industry.
   b. Calculate the Herfindahl–Hirschman Index (HHI) for each industry.
   c. What do the values of the two concentration measures imply about the degree of market power in the two industries?

   Answer: a.   The concentration ratio in industry W = 20% + 20% + 20% + 20% = 80%.
   The concentration ratio for industry X = 50% + 10% + 10% + 10% = 80%.

   b.   The HHI for industry W = 400 × 5 = 2,000 and the HHI for industry X = 2,500 + (100 x 5) = 3,000.

   c.   Both industries are highly concentrated. Although the concentration ratios are the same for each industry, market power is more significant in industry X. The ability to raise prices is greater in industry X.

   Diff: 3   Type: ES   Page Ref: 492/492
   Topic: Characteristics of monopoly
   Skill: Analytical
   Objective: LO 5: Discuss government policies toward monopoly.
   AACSB Coding: Analytic Skills
   Special Features: None

33. a.   What is the difference between a horizontal merger and a vertical merger?
   b.   Give an example of each type of merger.
   c.   Could a horizontal merger be welfare improving?

   Answer: a.   A horizontal merger is a merger between firms in the same industry. A vertical merger is a merger between firms at different stages of production of a good.

   b.   Students can offer many different examples.

   c.   Yes, if there are economies of scale so that the merged firm can produce output at a lower average total cost.

   Diff: 2   Type: ES   Page Ref: 489–491/489–491
   Topic: Mergers
   Skill: Conceptual
   Objective: LO 5: Discuss government policies toward monopoly.
   AACSB Coding: Reflective Thinking
   Special Features: None

34.   *Figure 14–7*

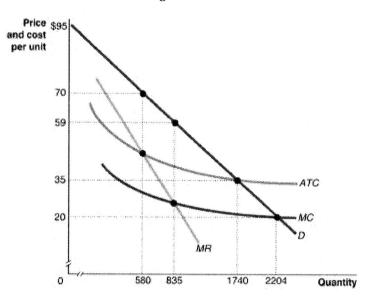

Refer to Figure 14–7 to answer the following questions.

a. What quantity will the monopoly represented in Figure 14–8 produce and what price will it charge?

b. Suppose the monopoly is regulated. If the regulatory agency wants to achieve economic efficiency, what price should it require the monopoly to charge?

c. To achieve economic efficiency, what quantity would the regulated monopoly produce?

d. Will the regulated monopoly make a profit if it charges the price that will achieve economic efficiency?

e. Suppose the government decides to regulate the monopoly by imposing a price ceiling of $35. What quantity would the monopoly produce and what price will the monopoly charge?

f. With the price ceiling of $35, what profit will the monopoly earn?

Answer: a. Quantity = 835 units and Price = $59.

b. To achieve economic efficiency, the price = $20.

c. The quantity produced = 2,204 units.

d. No, the regulated monopoly will make a loss.

e. If the ceiling price is set at $35, the monopoly would produce a quantity of 1,740 units and charge the ceiling price of $35.

f. The monopoly would break even.

Diff: 2   Type: ES   Page Ref: 494/494
Topic: Natural monopoly
Skill: Analytical
Objective: LO 5: Discuss government policies toward monopoly.
AACSB Coding: Analytic Skills
Special Features: None

Chapter 15   Pricing Strategy

15.1   Pricing Strategy, the Law of One Price, and Arbitration

1. The price of admission to Walt Disney World
    A) can vary by your age and address.
    B) is the same for everyone.
    C) is kept low to attract customers but Disney earns most of its profits by selling tickets to rides and attractions inside the park.
    D) is kept low to attract customers, but prices of rides and attractions inside the park vary by your age, address and other factors.
    Answer: A
    Diff: 1   Type: MC   Page Ref: 506–7/506–7
    Topic: Pricing strategy
    Skill: Fact
    Objective: LO 1: Define the low of one price and explain the role of arbitration
    AACSB Coding: Reflective Thinking
    Special Feature: Chapter Opener: Getting into Walt Disney World: One Price Does Not Fit All

2. In the 1950s Walt Disney began to plan the development of a theme park that would eventually become Disneyland. Disney hired an economist to help determine whether the park would be a financial success. This economist surveyed managers of existing amusement parks for advice. Many of these managers
    A) believed that a theme park would be very successful because the Disney name created a market among children and parents who had watched Disney cartoons and movies such as *Snow White.*
    B) recommended that the theme park be located in California because population in the state would increase greatly in the future. Disney followed this advice.
    C) recommended that Disney not build the park and leave the amusement park business to those who knew what they were doing.
    D) recommended that Disney first build an audience for his park by offering the ABC television network a weekly program that would feature Disney movies, cartoons and original programming. Walt Disney followed this advice. Both the television program and Disneyland were financial successes.
    Answer: C
    Diff: 1   Type: MC   Page Ref: 506–7/506–7
    Topic: Pricing strategy
    Skill: Fact
    Objective: LO 1: Define the low of one price and explain the role of arbitration
    AACSB Coding: Reflective Thinking
    Special Feature: Chapter Opener: Getting into Walt Disney World: One Price Does Not Fit All

3. Walt Disney began planning for Disneyland in the early 1950s. When he began to consider how the amusement park would be funded
    A) he decided to use the profits earned from his company's cartoons and motion pictures.
    B) he had trouble raising the required funds. Eventually, he convinced a television network to fund the amusement park in exchange for providing a weekly television program.
    C) he decided to borrow money from Hollywood banks. The banks quickly agreed to loan Disney the money because of Disney's reputation and previous success.
    D) he had trouble raising the required funds from banks, so he decided to issue "Disney bonds." He had no trouble paying the interest and principal on the bonds with profits from Disneyland.

Answer: B
Diff: 1   Type: MC   Page Ref: 506-7/506-7
Topic: Price discrimination
Skill: Fact
Objective: LO 1: Define the low of one price and explain the role of arbitration
AACSB Coding: Reflective Thinking
Special Feature: Chapter Opener: Getting into Walt Disney World: One Price Does Not Fit All

4. When Disneyland opened in 1955, what prices were charged for admission and rides?
    A) Admission was free; customers paid for rides.
    B) All customers paid the same price for admission; rides were free.
    C) Admission prices varied by your age, home address and occupation; rides were free.
    D) All customers paid the same low price for admission; customers were also charged prices for rides.

Answer: D
Diff: 1   Type: MC   Page Ref: 506-7/506-7
Topic: Pricing strategy
Skill: Fact
Objective: LO 1: Define the low of one price and explain the role of arbitration
AACSB Coding: Reflective Thinking
Special Feature: Chapter Opener: Getting into Walt Disney World: One Price Does Not Fit All

5. Today Walt Disney World charges different customers different prices for admission. This pricing strategy is called
    A) arbitrage.
    B) odd pricing.
    C) cost-price pricing.
    D) price discrimination.

Answer: D
Diff: 1   Type: MC   Page Ref: 508/508
Topic: Price discrimination
Skill: Conceptual
Objective: LO 1: Define the low of one price and explain the role of arbitration
AACSB Coding: Reflective Thinking
Special Feature: None

6. Many firms use technology to gather information on the preferences of consumers and their responses to changes in prices. This information is then used to adjust prices of the firms' goods and services. This practice is called
   A) price discovery.
   B) empirical research.
   C) yield management.
   D) econometrics.
   Answer: C
   Diff: 1   Type: MC   Page Ref: 508/508
   Topic: Price discrimination
   Skill: Definition
   Objective: LO 1: Define the low of one price and explain the role of arbitration
   AACSB Coding: Reflective Thinking
   Special Feature: None

7. Which of the following will prevent firms from engaging in price discrimination?
   A) Yield management
   B) Arbitrage
   C) Transactions costs
   D) Odd pricing
   Answer: B
   Diff: 1   Type: MC   Page Ref: 508/508
   Topic: Arbitrage
   Skill: Conceptual
   Objective: LO 1: Define the low of one price and explain the role of arbitration
   AACSB Coding: Reflective Thinking
   Special Feature: None

8. What is meant by the "law of one price"?
   A) Identical products should sell for the same price everywhere.
   B) A law was passed in 1913 that made it illegal to sell the same good or service to different people for different prices.
   C) This is a section of the Sherman Act that forced trusts (for example, the Standard Oil Company) to charge the same price for the same good or service in different states.
   D) Foreign companies should not be allowed to sell a product in the United States for prices different from prices these companies charge in other countries.
   Answer: A
   Diff: 1   Type: MC   Page Ref: 508/508
   Topic: Arbitrage
   Skill: Definition
   Objective: LO 1: Define the low of one price and explain the role of arbitration
   AACSB Coding: Reflective Thinking
   Special Feature: None

9. The costs in time and other resources that parties incur in the process of agreeing to and carrying out an exchange of goods or services are called
    A) exchange costs.
    B) implicit costs.
    C) transactions costs.
    D) selling costs.
Answer: C

Diff: 1   *Type: MC*   *Page Ref: 508/508*
Topic: Transactions costs
Skill: Definition
Objective: LO 1: Define the low of one price and explain the role of arbitration
AACSB Coding: Reflective Thinking
Special Feature: None

10. Harry attended a baseball card show in New York City where he bought a number of rookie cards of Pittsburgh Pirates baseball players from the 1950s and 1960s. Harry then sold the cards in Pittsburgh, Harry's hometown, where he knew the cards sold for higher prices. The profits Harry earned from these transactions are called
    A) arbitrage profits.
    B) normal profits.
    C) accounting profits.
    D) implicit profits.
Answer: A

Diff: 1   *Type: MC*   *Page Ref: 508/508*
Topic: Arbitrage
Skill: Conceptual
Objective: LO 1: Define the low of one price and explain the role of arbitration
AACSB Coding: Reflective Thinking
Special Feature: None

11. The law of one price
    A) states that consumers can only buy one good or service at a time.
    B) is a law passed by Congress that prohibits firms from selling a product at two different prices in the same market at the same time.
    C) states that consumers will pay any price for a product that has a perfectly inelastic demand curve.
    D) states that identical products should sell for the same price everywhere.
Answer: D

Diff: 1   *Type: MC*   *Page Ref: 508/508*
Topic: The law of one price
Skill: Definition
Objective: LO 1: Define the low of one price and explain the role of arbitration
AACSB Coding: Reflective Thinking
Special Feature: None

12. According to the law of one price, identical products should sell for the same price everywhere if
    A) consumers have knowledge of the prices charged for products in different markets.
    B) transactions costs are zero.
    C) firms can prevent consumers from engaging in arbitrage.
    D) there are no tariffs or other restrictions on imports or exports.
    Answer: B
    Diff: 1   Type: MC   Page Ref: 508/508
    Topic: The law of one price
    Skill: Conceptual
    Objective: LO 1: Define the low of one price and explain the role of arbitration
    AACSB Coding: Reflective Thinking
    Special Feature: None

13. Many people sell goods through eBay at prices that are higher than the prices they paid for these goods. Economists consider these transactions as
    A) examples of zero sum games, since the value of the goods sold is exactly equal to the prices paid for them.
    B) unproductive since the goods sold have been produced in the past.
    C) examples of exploitation of buyers of the goods by the sellers.
    D) examples of arbitrage.
    Answer: D
    Diff: 2   Type: MC   Page Ref: 509/509
    Topic: Arbitrage
    Skill: Conceptual
    Objective: LO 1: Define the low of one price and explain the role of arbitration
    AACSB Coding: Reflective Thinking
    Special Feature: Solved Problem: Is Arbitrage Just a Rip-off?

14. Harvey Morris bought dishes and pitchers made of blue glass during the Great Depression at a flea market. He later resold these items on eBay. The profits Harvey earned from these sales are
    A) subject to a retail profits tax.
    B) are not economic profits because Harvey did not add value to the items but took advantage of the buyers who were not aware of how much Harvey paid for the items.
    C) the result of arbitrage.
    D) accounting profits but not economic profits.
    Answer: C
    Diff: 1   Type: MC   Page Ref: 509/509
    Topic: Arbitrage
    Skill: Conceptual
    Objective: LO 1: Define the low of one price and explain the role of arbitration
    AACSB Coding: Reflective Thinking
    Special Feature: Solved Problem: Is Arbitrage Just a Rip-off?

15. According to the law of one price
    A) if transaction costs are zero, identical goods should sell for the same price everywhere.
    B) if transactions costs are zero, firms must sell a product at a price equal to its marginal cost.
    C) if transactions costs are zero, all firms must earn the same profit margin.
    D) there must be no differences in the cost of producing identical goods by different producers.

    Answer: A
    Diff: 1   Type: MC   Page Ref: 508/508
    Topic: The law of one price
    Skill: Definition
    Objective: LO 1: Define the low of one price and explain the role of arbitration
    AACSB Coding: Reflective Thinking
    Special Feature: None

16. Arbitrage refers to the act of
    A) resolving a dispute in front of an arbitrator instead of a court of law.
    B) buying a product in one market at a low price and reselling in another market at a higher price.
    C) trading in the foreign exchange market.
    D) suing a producer for illegal business practices.

    Answer: B
    Diff: 1   Type: MC   Page Ref: 508/508
    Topic: Arbitrage
    Skill: Definition
    Objective: LO 1: Define the low of one price and explain the role of arbitration
    AACSB Coding: Reflective Thinking
    Special Feature: None

17. The process of rapidly adjusting prices based on information gathered on consumers' preferences and their responsiveness to changes in price is called
    A) yield management.
    B) elasticity management.
    C) brand management.
    D) marketing.

    Answer: A
    Diff: 1   Type: MC   Page Ref: 508/508
    Topic: Yield management
    Skill: Definition
    Objective: LO 1: Define the low of one price and explain the role of arbitration
    AACSB Coding: Reflective Thinking
    Special Feature: None

18. Transactions costs refer to
    A) the implicit costs of production.
    B) the costs in time and other resources that parties incur in the process of agreeing to and carrying out an exchange of goods or services.
    C) the raw material cost of production.
    D) the cost of transporting goods from one destination to another.
    Answer: B
    Diff: 1   Type: MC   Page Ref: 508/508
    Topic: Transaction costs
    Skill: Definition
    Objective: LO 1: Define the low of one price and explain the role of arbitration
    AACSB Coding: Reflective Thinking
    Special Feature: None

19. The law of one price holds exactly only if there are transactions costs associated with buying a product in one location and selling it in another location.
    Answer: True   ○ False
    Diff: 2   Type: TF   Page Ref: 508/508
    Topic: The law of one price
    Skill: Definition
    Objective: LO 1: Define the low of one price and explain the role of arbitration
    AACSB Coding: Reflective Thinking
    Special Feature: None

20. Charging different prices to different consumers for the same product when the price differences are not due to differences in cost is called arbitrage.
    Answer: True   ○ False
    Diff: 1   Type: TF   Page Ref: 508/508
    Topic: Price discrimination
    Skill: Definition
    Objective: LO 1: Define the low of one price and explain the role of arbitration
    AACSB Coding: Reflective Thinking
    Special Feature: None

21. "Buy low and sell high is advice given to people who want to make a profit by buying and selling shares of stock. Arbitrage is defined as buying a product in one market at a low price and reselling it in another market at a high price. Therefore, when stock brokers buy and sell stocks to earn a profit they are engaging in arbitrage." Evaluate this statement; state whether it is true or false and explain your answer.

Answer: The statement is false. Buying and selling shares of stock is not arbitrage. Arbitrage profits are earned when someone buys a product where its price is low and selling where it is high at the same time; there is no risk involved in arbitrage trades. If transactions costs are zero, arbitrage trades will cause prices to adjust so that they are equal in all markets. When shares of stock are purchased, the buyers do not know whether the price will increase or decrease in the future. There is a risk in buying stocks that their prices will fall; traders will earn a profit if prices rise but will suffer losses if prices fall.

Diff: 2   Type: ES   Page Ref: 508–9/508–9
Topic: Arbitrage
Skill: Conceptual
Objective: LO 1: Define the low of one price and explain the role of arbitration
AACSB Coding: Reflective Thinking
Special Feature: None

22. What is meant by the "law of one price"? In discussing the law of demand, Hubbard and O'Brien claim there has been no evidence of an exception to the law (that is, no evidence of an upward–sloping demand curve). Are there exceptions to the law of one price?

Answer: The law of demand states that identical products should sell for the same price everywhere. But this law refers to a tendency for prices to be equal in different locations, not that such differences never occur. If identical products do sell for different prices in different locations arbitrage profits can be earned by people who buy where the price is low and sell where the price is high. Arbitrage will eventually cause prices to move toward equality, but the law of one price will hold exactly only if transactions costs associated with arbitrage trade are zero. If there are transactions costs, price differences will persist.

Diff: 2   Type: ES   Page Ref: 508–9/508–9
Topic: The law of one price
Skill: Conceptual
Objective: LO 1: Define the low of one price and explain the role of arbitration
AACSB Coding: Reflective Thinking
Special Feature: None

15.2   Price Discrimination: Charging Different Prices for the Same Product

1. If Mort's House of Flowers sells one dozen roses to different customers at different prices economists would consider this an example of
   A) price gouging.
   B) rational ignorance.
   C) arbitrage.
   D) price discrimination.
   Answer: D
   Diff: 1   Type: MC   Page Ref: 511/511
   Topic: Price discrimination
   Skill: Definition
   Objective: LO 2: Explain how a firm can increase its profits through price discrimination
   AACSB Coding: Reflective Thinking
   Special Feature: None

2. Price discrimination is the practice of
   A) charging different prices for the same good when the price differences are not due to differences in cost.
   B) charging different prices for the same good when the price differences arise because of differences in cost.
   C) charging different prices for different qualities of a product.
   D) charging higher prices for brand named goods and lower prices for generic versions of the goods.
   Answer: A
   Diff: 1   Type: MC   Page Ref: 510/510
   Topic: Price Discrimination
   Skill: Definition
   Objective: LO 2: Explain how a firm can increase its profits through price discrimination
   AACSB Coding: Reflective Thinking
   Special Feature: None

3. Which of the following is necessary in order for a firm to successfully practice price discrimination?
   A) The firm must practice product differentiation.
   B) The demand for the firm's product is inelastic.
   C) The firm must be able to segment the market for the product.
   D) The firm's transactions costs must be zero.
   Answer: C
   Diff: 2   Type: MC   Page Ref: 511/511
   Topic: Price discrimination
   Skill: Fact
   Objective: LO 2: Explain how a firm can increase its profits through price discrimination
   AACSB Coding: Reflective Thinking
   Special Feature: None

4. Arnold Marion, a first-year economics student at Fazer College, was given an assignment to find an example of price discrimination and present it to his class. When asked for his example Arnold said "I went to a Milwaukee Brewers baseball game with my cousin last week. We paid $25 each for our seats in left field. My aunt and uncle paid $50 each for their tickets; they sat five rows behind the first base dugout. This is an example of price discrimination since we paid different prices for the same product, and the differences were not due to differences in costs." How would Arnold's economics instructor assess Arnold's example?

   A) He would agree with Arnold that he had found an example of price discrimination, but would add that arbitrage would occur if ticket scalpers sold Brewers tickets for more than the prices Arnold and his uncle paid.

   B) He would disagree with Arnold's example because the $25 seats and the $50 seats were not the same products.

   C) He would agree with Arnold that he had found an example of price discrimination and would explain that the elasticity of demand for Brewers tickets is different for Arnold and his uncle.

   D) He would disagree with Arnold's example because there were differences in transactions costs for the $50 tickets and the $25 tickets.

   Answer: B
   Diff: 2   Type: MC   Page Ref: 510–1/510–1
   Topic: Price discrimination
   Skill: Conceptual
   Objective: LO 2: Explain how a firm can increase its profits through price discrimination
   AACSB Coding: Reflective Thinking
   Special Feature: None

5. Which of the following is not a requirement for a successful price discrimination strategy?

   A) A firm must have the ability to charge a price greater than marginal cost.

   B) Some consumers must have a greater willingness to pay for the product than other consumers, and the firm must be able to know what prices consumers are willing to pay.

   C) The firm must be able to prevent arbitrage.

   D) Transactions costs must be the same for all consumers.

   Answer: D
   Diff: 2   Type: MC   Page Ref: 511/511
   Topic: Price discrimination
   Skill: Conceptual
   Objective: LO 2: Explain how a firm can increase its profits through price discrimination
   AACSB Coding: Reflective Thinking
   Special Feature: None

6. Which of the following is *not* a requirement for a successful price discrimination strategy?
   A) A firm must have market power.
   B) The firm must be able to prevent consumers who buy a product at a low price from reselling it to other consumers at a high price.
   C) Managers must practice yield management.
   D) Some consumers must have greater willingness to pay for the product than other consumers, and the firm must be able to know what prices consumers are willing to pay.

Answer: C
Diff: 2   Type: MC   Page Ref: 511/511
Topic: Price discrimination
Skill: Conceptual
Objective: LO 2: Explain how a firm can increase its profits through price discrimination
AACSB Coding: Reflective Thinking
Special Feature: None

7. Which of the following is a reason why a firm would not engage in price discrimination?
   A) Price discrimination is illegal in some western states and the owners of firms in these states face civil or criminal prosecution if they engage in price discrimination.
   B) Some firms are not able to segment the market for the products they sell.
   C) Some firms do not want to violate the law of one price.
   D) The transactions costs associated with selling the product exceed the price of the product.

Answer: B
Diff: 2   Type: MC   Page Ref: 511/511
Topic: Price discrimination
Skill: Conceptual
Objective: LO 2: Explain how a firm can increase its profits through price discrimination
AACSB Coding: Reflective Thinking
Special Feature: None

8. Insurance companies typically charge women lower prices than men for automobile insurance. Is this an example of price discrimination?
   A) No, because, on average, women have better driving records than men and the costs of insuring men are greater than the costs of insuring women.
   B) Yes, because the costs of selling insurance to men and women are the same.
   C) Yes, because insurance companies can prevent arbitrage; that is, women cannot transfer their insurance coverage to men.
   D) No, because there are too many insurance companies for any one company to have market power. A firm must possess market power in order to practice price discrimination.

Answer: A
Diff: 2   Type: MC   Page Ref: 510/510
Topic: Price discrimination
Skill: Conceptual
Objective: LO 2: Explain how a firm can increase its profits through price discrimination
AACSB Coding: Reflective Thinking
Special Feature: Don't Let This Happen to YOU!: Don't Confuse Price Discrimination with Other Types of Discrimination

9. Price discrimination is a rational strategy for a profit–maximizing firm when
    A) it is possible to engage in arbitrage across market segments.
    B) it is not possible to segment consumers into identifiable markets.
    C) there is no opportunity for arbitrage across market segments.
    D) firms want to increase the amount of consumer surplus received by its customers.
    Answer: C
    Diff: 2   Type: MC   Page Ref: 510–1/510–1
    Topic: Price discrimination
    Skill: Conceptual
    Objective: LO 2: Explain how a firm can increase its profits through price discrimination
    AACSB Coding: Reflective Thinking
    Special Feature: None

10. One reason why airlines charge business travelers and leisure travelers different prices is
    A) business travelers fly according to schedules that are planned months in advance. Many leisure travelers buy their tickets at the last minute.
    B) business travelers usually travel alone. Leisure travelers often fly with friends and family members; therefore, they have a more inelastic demand for airline tickets than business travelers.
    C) business travelers fly more often than most leisure travelers. As a result, their employers are able to bargain with airlines for lower fares than leisure travelers pay.
    D) business travelers often have inflexible schedules and have to travel on a particular day. The opposite is true for leisure travelers.
    Answer: D
    Diff: 1   Type: MC   Page Ref: 513–4/513–4
    Topic: Price discrimination
    Skill: Conceptual
    Objective: LO 2: Explain how a firm can increase its profits through price discrimination
    AACSB Coding: Reflective Thinking
    Special Feature: None

11. Perfect price discrimination is also known as
    A) monopoly.
    B) first–degree price discrimination.
    C) third–degree price discrimination.
    D) yield management.
    Answer: B
    Diff: 1   Type: MC   Page Ref: 515/515
    Topic: Perfect price discrimination
    Skill: Fact
    Objective: LO 2: Explain how a firm can increase its profits through price discrimination
    AACSB Coding: Reflective Thinking
    Special Feature: None

12. The prices college students pay for Dell computers are higher than the prices Dell charges its
    health–care customers. Dell charges lower prices to health–care customers because
    A) health–care customers have a more elastic demand for computers than college
       students.
    B) Dell can deduct from its federal taxes some of the costs of the computers it sells to
       health–care customers.
    C) health–care customers have a more inelastic demand for computers than college
       students.
    D) health–care customers typically buy more supplies from Dell (print cartridges, paper,
       etc.,) than college students.
    Answer: A
    Diff: 2   *Type: MC*   *Page Ref: 512–3/512–3*
    Topic: Price discrimination
    Skill: Fact
    Objective: LO 2: Explain how a firm can increase its profits through price discrimination
    AACSB Coding: Reflective Thinking
    Special Feature: Solved Problem: How Dell Computer Uses Price Discrimination to Increase Profits

13. Health–care customers have a more elastic demand than college students for Dell's Optiplex
    business desktop computers.   From this we can conclude that
    A) Dell will charge health care customers higher prices than it charges college students.
    B) Dell will charge health care customers lower prices than it charges college students.
    C) college students will earn arbitrage profits by buying Optiplex business desktop
       computers from Dell and reselling them to health–care customers.
    D) Dell will earn economic profits from the computers it sells to college students but will
       break even on the computers it sells to health–care customers.
    Answer: B
    Diff: 2   *Type: MC*   *Page Ref: 512–3/512–3*
    Topic: Price discrimination
    Skill: Conceptual
    Objective: LO 2: Explain how a firm can increase its profits through price discrimination
    AACSB Coding: Reflective Thinking
    Special Feature: Solved Problem: How Dell Computer Uses Price Discrimination to Increase Profits

14. Many colleges and universities practice yield management to maximize the revenue they
    receive from tuition and
    A) to maximize the amount of aid they receive from the federal government.
    B) to maximize the amount of their student loans.
    C) to maximize the size of their endowments.
    D) to increase the academic quality of the students who enroll in their schools.
    Answer: D
    Diff: 1   *Type: MC*   *Page Ref: 515/515*
    Topic: Yield management
    Skill: Fact
    Objective: LO 2: Explain how a firm can increase its profits through price discrimination
    AACSB Coding: Reflective Thinking
    Special Feature: Making the Connection: How Colleges Use Yield Management

15. Many colleges and universities practice yield management. As a result, they offer different financial aid packages to different students. One result of yield management is that colleges often
    A) offer a less generous financial aid package to students who apply for an early admission decision.
    B) offer a more generous financial aid package to students who apply for an early admission decision.
    C) offer a less generous financial aid package to students with relatively high family incomes.
    D) offer a less generous financial aid package to students who don't participate in many extracurricular activities when they are in high school.
    Answer: A
    Diff: 2   Type: MC   Page Ref: 515/515
    Topic: Yield management
    Skill: Fact
    Objective: LO 2: Explain how a firm can increase its profits through price discrimination
    AACSB Coding: Reflective Thinking
    Special Feature: Making the Connection: How Colleges Use Yield Management

16. If a firm knew every consumer's willingness to pay and could prevent arbitrage it could charge every consumer a different price. This practice is known as
    A) first–degree exploitation, or perfect price discrimination.
    B) maximization of producer surplus, or perfect price discrimination.
    C) first–degree price discrimination, or perfect price discrimination.
    D) first–degree transfer of consumer surplus, or perfect price discrimination.
    Answer: C
    Diff: 2   Type: MC   Page Ref: 515/515
    Topic: Perfect price discrimination
    Skill: Definition
    Objective: LO 2: Explain how a firm can increase its profits through price discrimination
    AACSB Coding: Reflective Thinking
    Special Feature: None

17. A price-discriminating firm charges the highest price to
    A) the group with the largest demand.
    B) the group with the most elastic demand.
    C) the group with the least elastic demand.
    D) the group with demand that is unit–elastic.
    Answer: C
    Diff: 2   Type: MC   Page Ref: 515-6/515-6
    Topic: Price discrimination
    Skill: Conceptual
    Objective: LO 2: Explain how a firm can increase its profits through price discrimination
    AACSB Coding: Reflective Thinking
    Special Feature: None

18. In which market structure is it not possible to practice price discrimination?
    A) perfect competition
    B) monopolistic competition
    C) oligopoly
    D) monopoly
    Answer: A
    Diff: 1   Type: MC   Page Ref: 511/511
    Topic: Price discrimination
    Skill: Conceptual
    Objective: LO 2: Explain how a firm can increase its profits through price discrimination
    AACSB Coding: Reflective Thinking
    Special Feature: None

19. Which of the following is not an example of price discrimination?
    A) Adobe Systems offers software at discounted prices to students and faculty at K–12 and university levels.
    B) Unlike foreign tourists, citizens of Cambodia are exempted from paying an admission fee to the temples of Angkor.
    C) Senior citizens may purchase special fare tickets for public transportation that are not available to others.
    D) Buyers at an automotive parts store receive a discount for bulk buying because the store is able to pass on to its customers some of the lower average cost for producing large quantities.
    Answer: D
    Diff: 2   Type: MC   Page Ref: 511/511
    Topic: Price discrimination
    Skill: Conceptual
    Objective: LO 2: Explain how a firm can increase its profits through price discrimination
    AACSB Coding: Reflective Thinking
    Special Feature: None

20. Erin and Deidre, two residents in Ithaca, New York, are planning a trip to Boston. Erin, the sales manager for a large retailer, has to attend a business meeting. Deidre, a college student on vacation, is planning a leisurely trip to visit friends and relatives. Whose demand curve for air travel is likely to be more elastic?
    A) Erin
    B) Deidre
    C) There is no difference in their price elasticities of demand.
    D) The elasticity of the demand curves for Erin and Deidre cannot be determined without more information.
    Answer: B
    Diff: 2   Type: MC   Page Ref: 514–5/514–5
    Topic: Price discrimination
    Skill: Conceptual
    Objective: LO 2: Explain how a firm can increase its profits through price discrimination
    AACSB Coding: Reflective Thinking
    Special Feature: None

21. Erin and Deidre, two residents of Ithaca, New York, are planning a trip to Boston. Erin, the sales manager for a large retailer, has to attend a business meeting. Deidre, a college student on vacation, is planning a leisurely trip to visit friends and relatives. Which of the following statements is true?
    A) An airline that price discriminates will charge Erin a higher price.
    B) An airline that price discriminates will charge Deidre a higher price.
    C) Since there is no difference in the cost of producing air travel, airlines will not charge different prices to Erin and Deidre.
    D) An airline cannot price discriminate because buyers can resell their tickets through the Internet.

Answer: A

Diff: 1   Type: MC   Page Ref: 513–4/513–4
Topic: Price discrimination
Skill: Conceptual
Objective: LO 2: Explain how a firm can increase its profits through price discrimination
AACSB Coding: Reflective Thinking
Special Feature: None

22. Suppose Dublin Electronics charges regular customers $120 for a DVD player but allows senior citizens to purchase the same item for $80. Is this likely to be a successful price discriminating strategy?
    A) Yes, firms price discriminate to maximize profits.
    B) No, price discrimination will not be effective because the store cannot prevent senior citizens from buying large quantities of DVDs and reselling them for a profit.
    C) Yes, because senior citizens are likely to have a more elastic demand and therefore will be willing to pay a lower price compared to regular customers.
    D) No, because there are many different brands of DVDs and consumers will shop around.

Answer: B

Diff: 2   Type: MC   Page Ref: 510–1/510–1
Topic: Price discrimination
Skill: Conceptual
Objective: LO 2: Explain how a firm can increase its profits through price discrimination
AACSB Coding: Reflective Thinking
Special Feature: None

23. Which of the following products allows the seller to identify different groups of consumers (segment the market) and practice price discrimination?
    A) Clothing items sold through Macy's Department Store.
    B) A hamburger sold at Burger King.
    C) A cafe latte sold at Starbucks.
    D) Tickets to matinee shows at a movie theatre.

Answer: D

Diff: 2   Type: MC   Page Ref: 511/511
Topic: Price discrimination
Skill: Conceptual
Objective: LO 2: Explain how a firm can increase its profits through price discrimination
AACSB Coding: Reflective Thinking
Special Feature: None

24. Why might a producer practice price discrimination?
     A) To make its products more affordable to those with low incomes.
     B) To maximize economic efficiency.
     C) To maximize profits.
     D) To maximize quantity demanded.
   Answer: C
   Diff: 1   Type: MC   Page Ref: 510–1/510–1
   Topic: Price discrimination
   Skill: Conceptual
   Objective: LO 2: Explain how a firm can increase its profits through price discrimination
   AACSB Coding: Reflective Thinking
   Special Feature: None

25. Which of the following pricing strategies allows a firm to earn economic profit?
     A) Price discrimination.
     B) Charging a price equal to marginal cost.
     C) Charging a price equal to the average total cost of production.
     D) Charging a price equal to the average variable cost of production.
   Answer: A
   Diff: 2   Type: MC   Page Ref: 510–1/510–1
   Topic: Price Discrimination
   Skill: Conceptual
   Objective: LO 2: Explain how a firm can increase its profits through price discrimination
   AACSB Coding: Reflective Thinking
   Special Feature: None

Figure 15-1

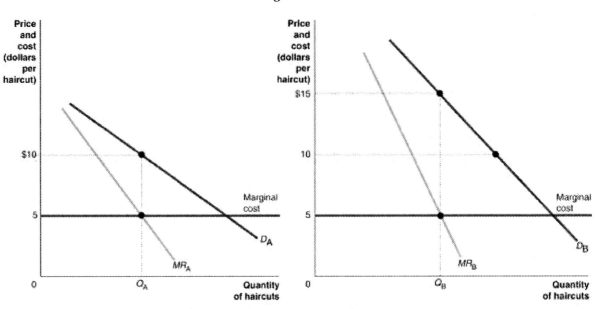

Market A: Customers from "The Chateau"   Market B: Customers from the neighborhood

Chantal owns a hairdressing salon which caters to two main groups of customers: residents of "The Chateau," a retirement community, and other residents in the neighborhood. Figure 15-1 shows the demand curves for the residents of the retirement community, labeled Market A, and other residents in the neighborhood, labeled Market B. The demand curves are not identical.

26. *Refer to Figure 15-1.* What prices are charged in the two markets?
    A) price in market A = price in market B = $15
    B) price in market A = $10; price in market B = $15
    C) price in market A = price in market B = $5
    D) price in market A = price in market B = $10
    Answer: B
    Diff: 2   Type: MC   Page Ref: 510-7/510-7
    Topic: Price discrimination
    Skill: Analytical
    Objective: LO 2: Explain how a firm can increase its profits through price discrimination
    AACSB Coding: Analytic Skills
    Special Feature: None

27. *Refer to Figure 15–1.* Which group of customers is likely to have a more elastic demand curve (more sensitive to price)?
    A) The other residents of the neighborhood – market B.
    B) There is no difference in the elasticity of demand between the two groups.
    C) The customers from "The Chateau" – market A.
    D) There is insufficient information to answer this question.
    Answer: C
    Diff: 2   Type: MC   Page Ref: 510–7/510–7
    Topic: Price discrimination
    Skill: Conceptual
    Objective: LO 2: Explain how a firm can increase its profits through price discrimination
    AACSB Coding: Analytic Skills
    Special Feature: None

28. *Refer to Figure 15–1.* Suppose Chantal practices price discrimination. Which of the following statements is true?
    A) Chantal's profits will be higher if she has uniform pricing instead of different prices for different groups of customers.
    B) By charging a higher price in market B, Chantal has transferred some of the consumer surplus from customers in market B to customers in market A.
    C) By charging different prices in markets A and B Chantal can transfer some producer surplus into economic profit.
    D) By charging a higher price in market B, Chantal can convert some consumer surplus into economic profit.
    Answer: D
    Diff: 2   Type: MC   Page Ref: 510–7/510–7
    Topic: Price discrimination
    Skill: Analytical
    Objective: LO 2: Explain how a firm can increase its profits through price discrimination
    AACSB Coding: Analytic Skills
    Special Feature: None

29. *Refer to Figure 15–1.* Suppose Chantal charges all her customers a uniform price of $10 for a haircut. Which of the following statements is true?
    A) Chantal is selling more than the profit–maximizing quantity of haircuts in market B.
    B) Chantal is selling less than the profit–maximizing quantity of haircuts in market B.
    C) Chantal is maximizing revenue in market B.
    D) Chantal will earn a greater profit through uniform pricing than if she practices price discriminates.
    Answer: A
    Diff: 2   Type: MC   Page Ref: 510–7/510–7
    Topic: Price discrimination
    Skill: Analytical
    Objective: LO 2: Explain how a firm can increase its profits through price discrimination
    AACSB Coding: Analytic Skills
    Special Feature: None

30. Assume that a monopolist practices perfect price discrimination. The firm's marginal revenue curve will
    A) be perfectly elastic.
    B) be equal to its demand curve.
    C) will be perfectly inelastic.
    D) will lie below its demand curve.
    Answer: B
    Diff: 2   Type: MC   Page Ref: 515–7/515–7
    Topic: Perfect price discrimination
    Skill: Conceptual
    Objective: LO 2: Explain how a firm can increase its profits through price discrimination
    AACSB Coding: Reflective Thinking
    Special Feature: None

31. Assume that a monopolist practices perfect price discrimination. The firm will produce an output rate
    A) that is less than the efficient level of output.
    B) that is greater than the efficient level of output.
    C) that is equal to the efficient level of output.
    D) that converts consumers surplus into a deadweight loss.
    Answer: C
    Diff: 3   Type: MC   Page Ref: 515–7/515–7
    Topic: Perfect price discrimination
    Skill: Conceptual
    Objective: LO 2: Explain how a firm can increase its profits through price discrimination
    AACSB Coding: Reflective Thinking
    Special Feature: None

32. If a monopolist practices perfect price discrimination then
    A) the firm will break even in the long run.
    B) consumers surplus will be equal to the deadweight loss.
    C) producer surplus will equal consumer surplus.
    D) consumer surplus will be zero.
    Answer: D
    Diff: 2   Type: MC   Page Ref: 515–7/515–7
    Topic: Perfect price discrimination
    Skill: Conceptual
    Objective: LO 2: Explain how a firm can increase its profits through price discrimination
    AACSB Coding: Reflective Thinking
    Special Feature: None

33. Which of the following statements about perfect price discrimination is false?
    A) There is no consumer surplus if a firm engages in perfect price discrimination.
    B) Perfect price discrimination occurs when the seller charges the highest price each consumer would be willing to pay for the product.
    C) A condition for perfect price discrimination is that it must be costlier to service some customers than others.
    D) For the price discriminating firm, its marginal revenue curve coincides with its demand curve.
Answer: C
Diff: 2   Type: MC   Page Ref: 515–7/515–7
Topic: Perfect price discrimination
Skill: Conceptual
Objective: LO 2: Explain how a firm can increase its profits through price discrimination
AACSB Coding: Reflective Thinking
Special Feature: None

34. Suppose that a price–discriminating producer divides its market into two segments. If the firm sells its product at a price of $34 in the market segment with relatively less elastic customer demand, the price in the market segment with more elastic customer demand will be
    A) greater than $34.
    B) less than $34.
    C) less than marginal revenue in that market segment.
    D) equal to marginal revenue in that market segment.
Answer: B
Diff: 2   Type: MC   Page Ref: 510–1/510–1
Topic: Price discrimination
Skill: Conceptual
Objective: LO 2: Explain how a firm can increase its profits through price discrimination
AACSB Coding: Reflective Thinking
Special Feature: None

35. Publishers practice price discrimination when they sell books at high prices to
    A) early adopters.
    B) local bookstores.
    C) large chain bookstores.
    D) online book sellers.
Answer: A
Diff: 1   Type: MC   Page Ref: 517/517
Topic: Price discrimination across time
Skill: Conceptual
Objective: LO 2: Explain how a firm can increase its profits through price discrimination
AACSB Coding: Reflective Thinking
Special Feature: None

36. The term "early adopters" refers to
    A) firms that are the first to implement a new technology that is used to produce new goods or services.
    B) book clubs that are first to recommend best-selling books to their members.
    C) consumers who respond quickly to fads, seasonal changes, etc.
    D) consumers who are willing to pay high prices to be among the first to own new products.
    Answer: D
    Diff: 1   Type: MC   Page Ref: 517/517
    Topic: Price discrimination across time
    Skill: Definition
    Objective: LO 2: Explain how a firm can increase its profits through price discrimination
    AACSB Coding: Reflective Thinking
    Special Feature: None

37. Consumers who will pay high prices to be among the first to own certain new products are called
    A) savvy consumers.
    B) naive consumers.
    C) gullible.
    D) early adopters.
    Answer: D
    Diff: 1   Type: MC   Page Ref: 517/517
    Topic: Price discrimination across time
    Skill: Definition
    Objective: LO 2: Explain how a firm can increase its profits through price discrimination
    AACSB Coding: Reflective Thinking
    Special Feature: None

38. Which of the following antitrust laws forbade firms to engage in price discrimination if the effect would lessen competition or create a monopoly?
    A) The Sherman Act
    B) The Clayton Act
    C) The Robinson-Patman Act
    D) The Cellar-Kefauver Act
    Answer: C
    Diff: 1   Type: MC   Page Ref: 517/517
    Topic: Antitrust laws
    Skill: Fact
    Objective: LO 2: Explain how a firm can increase its profits through price discrimination
    AACSB Coding: Reflective Thinking
    Special Feature: None

39. Clarissa Kessler operates a store that sells recorded music. Her business suffered tremendously when a giant discount store chain opened a store in the area and is able to sell its products for less than Clarissa's wholesale cost. Is this evidence of illegal price discrimination on the part of the discount store chain?
    A) Yes, it is clearly a violation of the Robinson–Patman Act.
    B) No, because it can be argued that the discount store chain is justified in charging lower prices because it is a large-volume buyer and is able to purchase recorded music at a lower wholesale price than Clarissa.
    C) Yes, the discount store chain is engaging in predatory pricing.
    D) No, even if the price discrimination is based on differences in cost, the law states that it is not illegal.

Answer: B

Diff: 2   Type: MC   Page Ref: 517/517
Topic: Antitrust laws
Skill: Conceptual
Objective: LO 2: Explain how a firm can increase its profits through price discrimination
AACSB Coding: Reflective Thinking
Special Feature: None

Table 15–1

Potential Customer	Willingness to pay ($ per hour)
Arun	$8
Bernice	9
Cara	10
Dawn	12

Julie plans to start a pet–sitting service. She surveyed her neighborhood to determine the demand for this service. Assume that each person surveyed demands only one hour of pet sitting services per period. Table 15–1 below shows a portion of her survey results.

40. **Refer to Table 15–1.** If Julie charges $10 per hour, how many hours of pet sitting services will be purchased and by whom?
    A) 2 hours (1 hour by Cara and 1 hour by Dawn)
    B) 1 hour by Cara only
    C) 1 hour by Dawn only
    D) 3 hours (1 hour each by Arun, Bernice and Cara)
    Answer: A
    Diff: 2   Type: MC   Page Ref: 515–6/515–6
    Topic: Perfect price discrimination
    Skill: Analytical
    Objective: LO 2: Explain how a firm can increase its profits through price discrimination
    AACSB Coding: Analytic Skills
    Special Feature: None

41. **Refer to Table 15–1.** If Julie charges $10 per hour, what is the value of the consumer surplus received by Dawn?
    A) $2
    B) $12
    C) $10
    D) $22
    Answer: A
    Diff: 2   Type: MC   Page Ref: 515–6/515–6
    Topic: Perfect price discrimination
    Skill: Analytical
    Objective: LO 2: Explain how a firm can increase its profits through price discrimination
    AACSB Coding: Analytic Skills
    Special Feature: None

42. ***Refer to Table 15–1.*** Suppose Julie's marginal cost of providing this service is constant at $7 and she charges $7. How many hours will be purchased and what is her total revenue?

    A) 5 hours; total revenue = $35

    B) 4 hours; total revenue = $28

    C) 3 hours; total revenue = $21

    D) 2 hours; total revenue = $14

Answer: B

Diff: 2   Type: MC   Page Ref: 515–6/515–6

Topic: Perfect price discrimination

Skill: Analytical

Objective: LO 2: Explain how a firm can increase its profits through price discrimination

AACSB Coding: Analytic Skills

Special Feature: None

43. ***Refer to Table 15–1.*** Suppose Julie's marginal cost of providing this service is constant at $7 and she charges $7 per hour. What is her marginal revenue?

    A) It is $7 for the first hour and starts declining thereafter.

    B) It is $7 for the first hour and starts increasing thereafter.

    C) It is constant at $7

    D) It coincides with the figures in the table; $12 for the first hour, $10 for the second, $9 for the third and $8 for the fourth.

Answer: C

Diff: 2   Type: MC   Page Ref: 515–6/515–6

Topic: Perfect price discrimination

Skill: Conceptual

Objective: LO 2: Explain how a firm can increase its profits through price discrimination

AACSB Coding: Reflective Thinking

Special Feature: None

44. ***Refer to Table 15–1.*** Suppose Julie's marginal cost of providing this service is constant at $7 and she charges $7. What is the value of the consumer surplus enjoyed by her customers?

    A) $39

    B) $28

    C) $0

    D) $11

Answer: D

Diff: 2   Type: MC   Page Ref: 515–6/515–6

Topic: Perfect price discrimination

Skill: Analytical

Objective: LO 2: Explain how a firm can increase its profits through price discrimination

AACSB Coding: Analytic Skills

Special Feature: None

45. ***Refer to Table 15–1.*** Suppose Julie's marginal cost of providing this service is constant at $7 and she decides to charge each customer according to his or her willingness to pay. What is Julie's total revenue and how many hours of service will be purchased?

    A) 4 hours and her total revenue = $39

    B) 4 hours and her total revenue = $28

    C) 1 hour and her total revenue = $7

    D) 5 hours and her total revenue = $35

Answer: A

Diff: 3   Type: MC   Page Ref: 515–6/515–6
Topic: Perfect price discrimination
Skill: Analytical
Objective: LO 2: Explain how a firm can increase its profits through price discrimination
AACSB Coding: Analytic Skills
Special Feature: None

46. ***Refer to Table 15–1.*** Suppose Julie's marginal cost of providing this service is constant at $7 and she decides to charge each customer according to his or her willingness to pay. What is the value of consumer surplus by her customers?

    A) $39

    B) $28

    C) $11

    D) $0

Answer: D

Diff: 2   Type: MC   Page Ref: 515–6/515–6
Topic: Perfect price discrimination
Skill: Analytical
Objective: LO 2: Explain how a firm can increase its profits through price discrimination
AACSB Coding: Analytic Skills
Special Feature: None

47. ***Refer to Table 15–1.*** Suppose Julie's marginal cost of providing this service is constant at $7 and she charges each customer according to his or her willingness to pay instead of a uniform price of $7. Which of the following statements is true?

    A) Julie is worse off because the demand for her services is reduced.

    B) Julie has converted the consumer surplus (from a uniform price) into economic profit.

    C) Julie's customers are better off because their consumer surplus has increased.

    D) Julie's has converted the producer surplus (from a uniform price) into consumer surplus.

Answer: B

Diff: 2   Type: MC   Page Ref: 515–6/515–6
Topic: Perfect price discrimination
Skill: Conceptual
Objective: LO 2: Explain how a firm can increase its profits through price discrimination
AACSB Coding: Reflective Thinking
Special Feature: None

48. One requirement for a firm pursuing a price discrimination strategy is the ability to segment the market for its product. This means that
    A) the firm must set different prices for different regions where the product is sold.
    B) the firm must be willing to offer price discounts for senior citizens and children.
    C) the firm must be able to divide the market in a way that makes arbitrage impossible.
    D) the firm must choose a marketing strategy that appeals to different segments of the economy.
    Answer: C
    Diff: 2   Type: MC   Page Ref: 510–1/510–1
    Topic: Price discrimination
    Skill: Definition
    Objective: LO 2: Explain how a firm can increase its profits through price discrimination
    AACSB Coding: Reflective Thinking
    Special Feature: None

49. A perfectly competitive firm cannot practice price discrimination because
    A) a firm that breaks even in the long run cannot afford to engage in yield management.
    B) it does not advertise; this prevents the firm from marketing its product to different segments of the market.
    C) each consumer in a perfectly competitive market has the same willingness to pay.
    D) the firm can only charge the market price.
    Answer: D
    Diff: 2   Type: MC   Page Ref: 511/511
    Topic: Price discrimination
    Skill: Conceptual
    Objective: LO 2: Explain how a firm can increase its profits through price discrimination
    AACSB Coding: Reflective Thinking
    Special Feature: None

50. If price discrimination occurs in a market
    A) the law of one price does not hold.
    B) the firm earns arbitrage profits.
    C) consumers whose demand for the product sold is more elastic pay higher prices than consumers whose demand is less elastic.
    D) the marginal cost of production is constant.
    Answer: A
    Diff: 2   Type: MC   Page Ref: 510–1/510–1
    Topic: Price discrimination
    Skill: Conceptual
    Objective: LO 2: Explain how a firm can increase its profits through price discrimination
    AACSB Coding: Reflective Thinking
    Special Feature: None

51. Netflix, an online DVD rental service, engages in price discrimination by
    A) charging customers who rent the fewest movies per month a higher rental price than customers who rent the most movies per month.
    B) providing customers who rent the fewest movies per month better service than customers who rent the most movies per month.
    C) charging customers who rent the fewest movies per month a lower rental price than customers who rent the most movies per month.
    D) providing customers who rent the most movies per month better service than customers who rent the fewest movies per month.
    Answer: B
    Diff: 2   Type: MC   Page Ref: 518-9/518-9
    Topic: Price discrimination
    Skill: Fact
    Objective: LO 2: Explain how a firm can increase its profits through price discrimination
    AACSB Coding: Reflective Thinking
    Special Feature: Making the Connection: Price Discrimination with a Twist at Netflix

52. Netflix, an online DVD rental service, engages in price discrimination by separating its customers into two groups: those who have a relatively elastic demand and those who have a relatively inelastic demand for DVD rentals. Those who have a relatively elastic demand are customers who
    A) pay a monthly subscription fee; customers with a relatively inelastic demand pay for each DVD they rent.
    B) pay for each DVD they rent; customers with a relatively inelastic demand pay a monthly subscription fee.
    C) rent only a few DVDs per month; customers who rent many DVDs per month have a relatively inelastic demand.
    D) rent many DVDs per month; customers who rent only a few DVDs per month have a relatively inelastic demand.
    Answer: C
    Diff: 3   Type: MC   Page Ref: 518-9/518-9
    Topic: Price discrimination
    Skill: Fact
    Objective: LO 2: Explain how a firm can increase its profits through price discrimination
    AACSB Coding: Reflective Thinking
    Special Feature: Making the Connection: Price Discrimination with a Twist at Netflix

53. Early adopters are consumers who will pay a high price to be among the first to own new products.
    Answer: ⊚ True   False
    Diff: 2   Type: TF   Page Ref: 517/517
    Topic: Price discrimination across time
    Skill: Definition
    Objective: LO 2: Explain how a firm can increase its profits through price discrimination
    AACSB Coding: Reflective Thinking
    Special Feature: None

54. A successful strategy of price discrimination requires that a firm be a price-taker.
    Answer: True   ○ False
    Diff: 1   Type: TF   Page Ref: 510-1/510-1
    Topic: Price discrimination
    Skill: Conceptual
    Objective: LO 2: Explain how a firm can increase its profits through price discrimination
    AACSB Coding: Reflective Thinking
    Special Feature: None

55. The airline industry routinely engages in price discrimination across time.
    Answer: True   ○ False
    Diff: 2   Type: TF   Page Ref: 513-7/513-7
    Topic: Price discrimination
    Skill: Fact
    Objective: LO 2: Explain how a firm can increase its profits through price discrimination
    AACSB Coding: Reflective Thinking
    Special Feature: None

56. Perfect price discrimination will lead a firm to produce up to the point where price equals marginal cost, the efficient level of output.
    Answer: ○ True   False
    Diff: 2   Type: TF   Page Ref: 515-7/515-7
    Topic: Perfect price discrimination
    Skill: Conceptual
    Objective: LO 2: Explain how a firm can increase its profits through price discrimination
    AACSB Coding: Reflective Thinking
    Special Feature: None

57. The Clayton Act of 1936 outlawed price discrimination that reduced competition.
    Answer: True   ○ False
    Diff: 1   Type: TF   Page Ref: 517/517
    Topic: Antitrust laws
    Skill: Fact
    Objective: LO 2: Explain how a firm can increase its profits through price discrimination
    AACSB Coding: Reflective Thinking
    Special Feature: None

58. Hubbard and O'Brien refer to airlines as "The Kings of Price Discrimination." Why is price discrimination common in the airline industry?

Answer: When airlines fly with empty seats they lose the revenue that could have been earned from selling tickets for those seats that they can never recover. In addition, the marginal cost of flying one more passenger is very low. Therefore, airlines have an incentive to sell tickets for as many seats as they can, even if the price is low. This strategy will be profitable only if the airlines can prevent those who buy tickets at low prices from reselling them to other passengers at higher prices. Since the 1980s, airlines have used computer models to adjust prices for each seat on all of their flights. Airlines can divide their customers into two main categories: business travelers, who have inflexible schedules and often cannot book their flights very far in advance, and leisure travelers who are more flexible about when they travel and are more sensitive than business travelers to changes in price. By placing restrictions on who can purchase low-price tickets, airlines can force business travelers to pay high prices while attracting leisure travelers with low prices.

Diff: 2   Type: ES   Page Ref: 513-5/513-5
Topic: Price discrimination
Skill: Conceptual
Objective: LO 2: Explain how a firm can increase its profits through price discrimination
AACSB Coding: Reflective Thinking
Special Feature: None

59. What conditions are required for a firm to use a price discrimination strategy?

Answer: Three conditions must be met. First, a firm must possess market power. Second, some consumers must possess a greater willingness to pay for the product sold than other consumers and the firm must be able to identify these consumers by their willingness to pay. Third, the firm must be able to segment the market for the product in order to prevent arbitrage.

Diff: 2   Type: ES   Page Ref: 511/511
Topic: Price discrimination
Skill: Conceptual
Objective: LO 2: Explain how a firm can increase its profits through price discrimination
AACSB Coding: Reflective Thinking
Special Feature: None

60. What is the difference between price discrimination and other forms of discrimination?

Answer: Discrimination based on race or gender and other arbitrary characteristics is illegal under civil rights laws. Price discrimination generally is legal, although it could be illegal under the Robinson-Patman Act if its effect is to reduce competition in an industry. Price discrimination involves charging people different prices based on differences in their willingness to pay, when these differences are not due to differences in costs.

Diff: 2   Type: ES   Page Ref: 510-8/510-8
Topic: Price discrimination
Skill: Conceptual
Objective: LO 2: Explain how a firm can increase its profits through price discrimination
AACSB Coding: Reflective Thinking
Special Feature: None

61. Racial discrimination and other forms of discrimination based on irrelevant factors are illegal. Can price discrimination be illegal as well?

    Answer: In 1936 Congress passed the Robsinson–Patman Act which outlawed price discrimination if it resulted in less competition. However, the language used in the act made it seem that all price discrimination that was not based on differences in cost was illegal. Courts render judgments regarding violations of acts of Congress based on how they interpret the language used in these acts. In recent years, the courts have interpreted the Robinson–Patman Act narrowly; that is, price discrimination as practiced by the airlines, colleges and universities and other firms is not considered to be illegal.

Diff: 2   Type: ES   Page Ref: 517–8/517–8
Topic: Price discrimination
Skill: Conceptual
Objective: LO 2: Explain how a firm can increase its profits through price discrimination
AACSB Coding: Reflective Thinking
Special Feature: None

62. What is perfect price discrimination and why do economists believe that no firm is able to practice perfect price discrimination?

    Answer: Perfect price discrimination, also known as first–degree price discrimination, occurs when a firm knows every consumer's willingness to pay and is able to charge every consumer a different price – the maximum price each is willing to pay. The firm's marginal revenue curve in this situation is the same as its demand curve and the firm converts all potential consumer surplus into profits. It highly unlikely that any firm would be able to use yield management to determine each consumer's maximum willingness to pay. It is also unlikely that if the firm charged each consumer a different price it would prevent arbitrage, where a consumer who bought the product at a low price could sell the product to another consumer with a higher willingness to pay.

Diff: 2   Type: ES   Page Ref: 515–7/515–7
Topic: Perfect price discrimination
Skill: Conceptual
Objective: LO 2: Explain how a firm can increase its profits through price discrimination
AACSB Coding: Reflective Thinking
Special Feature: None

63. Book publishers use price discrimination routinely, but the form of price discrimination they use is different from the form used by airlines and other industries. Explain.

Answer: Some consumers in some markets are willing to pay a high price to be among the first to buy a new product. These consumers are called "early adopters." Book publishers offer new novels at high prices knowing that some consumers do not want to wait for a lower price before reading the book. Other consumers who are not early adopters will buy the novel in hardcover after time has elapsed and the novel's price is lower. Consumers who are content to wait for a paperback version of the book to be published will pay an even lower price. Publishers achieve higher profits from the books they sell by segmenting the market over time and charging a higher price to the segment with an inelastic demand (early adopters) and a lower price to the segment with a more elastic demand (paperback buyers).

Diff: 2   Type: ES   Page Ref: 517/517
Topic: Price discrimination across time
Skill: Conceptual
Objective: LO 2: Explain how a firm can increase its profits through price discrimination
AACSB Coding: Reflective Thinking
Special Feature: None

15.3   Other Pricing Strategies

1. When a firm charges $4.95 instead of $5.00, what do economists call this pricing strategy?
   A) Cost-plus pricing.
   B) Indirect pricing.
   C) Odd pricing.
   D) Unusual pricing.
   Answer: C
   Diff: 1   Type: MC   Page Ref: 519/519
   Topic: Odd pricing
   Skill: Definition
   Objective: LO 3: Explain how some firms increase their profits through the use of odd pricing cost-plus pricing, and two-part tariffs
   AACSB Coding: Reflective Thinking
   Special Feature: None

2. Odd pricing became common in the late 19th century. Although the origins of odd pricing are uncertain, several explanations for the practice have been given. Which of the following is one of these explanations?
   A) Odd pricing forced employees to give customers change. This made it more likely that employees would record sales rather than pocketing their customers' money.
   B) Odd pricing began in an era when it was difficult for owners and managers of firms to determine the marginal cost of the goods and services they sold. Odd prices were rough estimates designed to cover costs plus earn firms a profit.
   C) Odd pricing was begun in England in the 1700s when America was part of the British Empire. Members of the British Royal Court were given the task of pricing products. After independence, merchants in the United States carried on the practice of odd pricing.
   D) After the passage of the Sherman Act in 1890, merchants used odd pricing as a means of avoiding prosecution for antitrust violations.

Answer: A
Diff: 2   *Type: MC*   *Page Ref: 520/520*
Topic: Odd pricing
Skill: Fact
Objective: LO 3: Explain how some firms increase their profits through the use of odd pricing cost–plus pricing, and two–part tariffs
AACSB Coding: Reflective Thinking
Special Feature: None

3. Many firms use odd pricing – charging prices such as $.99 instead of $1.00 and $9.99 instead of $10.00. One reason for this pricing strategy is that consumers will somehow believe that the difference in price appears to be greater than it actually is. Researchers conducted consumer surveys to determine whether this is actually the case. What was the result of these surveys?
   A) The surveys found that small differences in price cause small differences in quantity demanded. There is no evidence that odd pricing makes economic sense.
   B) Although the results were not conclusive, there is some evidence that odd pricing makes economic sense.
   C) The surveys found indifference regarding this strategy among most consumers, but hostility among other consumers. The latter group resented what they viewed as attempt to fool them into buying products with odd prices. Researchers concluded that odd pricing is counterproductive.
   D) The survey results were inconclusive because most consumers gave unreliable responses to survey questions.

Answer: B
Diff: 2   *Type: MC*   *Page Ref: 520/520*
Topic: Odd pricing
Skill: Fact
Objective: LO 3: Explain how some firms increase their profits through the use of odd pricing cost–plus pricing, and two–part tariffs
AACSB Coding: Reflective Thinking
Special Feature: None

4. When firms price their products by adding a percentage markup to their average costs of production this is called
    A) average cost pricing.
    B) rounding up.
    C) break–even pricing.
    D) cost–plus pricing.
Answer: D
Diff: 1   Type: MC   Page Ref: 520/520
Topic: Cost–plus pricing
Skill: Definition
Objective: LO 3: Explain how some firms increase their profits through the use of odd pricing cost–plus pricing, and two–part tariffs
AACSB Coding: Reflective Thinking
Special Feature: None

5. Which of the following is *not* an advantage of cost–plus pricing?
    A) It is easy to calculate.
    B) It requires little information.
    C) If a firm is selling multiple products it ensures that the firm's prices will cover costs that are difficult to assign to one product.
    D) It ensures that the firm will maximize its profits.
Answer: D
Diff: 2   Type: MC   Page Ref: 520-2/520-2
Topic: Cost–plus pricing
Skill: Conceptual
Objective: LO 3: Explain how some firms increase their profits through the use of odd pricing cost–plus pricing, and two–part tariffs
AACSB Coding: Reflective Thinking
Special Feature: None

6. Which of the following firms is most likely to use cost–plus pricing?
    A) A firm that makes one product.
    B) A firm that sells one product and has a sizable research and development budget.
    C) A firm that makes several products and has a sizable research and development budget, the cost of which cannot be easily assigned to each product.
    D) A firm that makes many products but has a small research and development budget, the cost of which can be easily assigned to the different product lines.
Answer: C
Diff: 2   Type: MC   Page Ref: 520-2/520-2
Topic: Cost–plus pricing
Skill: Conceptual
Objective: LO 3: Explain how some firms increase their profits through the use of odd pricing cost–plus pricing, and two–part tariffs
AACSB Coding: Reflective Thinking
Special Feature: None

7. Cost-plus pricing would be consistent with selecting the profit-maximizing price when
    A) it results in a price that causes quantity sold to be where marginal revenue equals marginal cost.
    B) a firm has no difficulty estimating its demand curve.
    C) consumers value the product beyond its marginal cost.
    D) the demand for the firm's product is unitary elastic.
    Answer: A
    Diff: 2   Type: MC   Page Ref: 520-2/520-2
    Topic: Cost-plus pricing
    Skill: Conceptual
    Objective: LO 3: Explain how some firms increase their profits through the use of odd pricing cost-plus pricing, and two-part tariffs
    AACSB Coding: Reflective Thinking
    Special Feature: None

8. Cost-plus pricing may be a reasonable way to determine price when
    A) marginal cost and average fixed cost are roughly equal.
    B) marginal cost and average cost are about the same.
    C) marginal cost differs significantly from average cost.
    D) marginal cost is very low.
    Answer: B
    Diff: 1   Type: MC   Page Ref: 521-2/521-2
    Topic: Cost-plus pricing
    Skill: Conceptual
    Objective: LO 3: Explain how some firms increase their profits through the use of odd pricing cost-plus pricing, and two-part tariffs
    AACSB Coding: Reflective Thinking
    Special Feature: None

9. Book publishers often use a cost-plus pricing strategy. One reason for this is
    A) most publishers do not hire economists who can determine the number of books they must sell to equate marginal cost and marginal revenue.
    B) publishers do not want to incur the expense of determining the profit-maximizing strategy. They prefer cost-plus pricing because of its lower cost.
    C) much of the cost of publishing textbooks is difficult to assign to any particular book.
    D) bookstores, not publishers, ultimately determine how many books will be produced.
    Answer: C
    Diff: 2   Type: MC   Page Ref: 520-1/520-1
    Topic: Cost-plus pricing
    Skill: Conceptual
    Objective: LO 3: Explain how some firms increase their profits through the use of odd pricing cost-plus pricing, and two-part tariffs
    AACSB Coding: Reflective Thinking
    Special Feature: Making the Connection: Cost-Plus Pricing in the Publishing Industry

10. Cost-price pricing typically does not result in profit-maximization. As a result, economists have two views of cost-plus pricing. One of these views is
    A) cost-plus pricing is more likely to lead to profit-maximization for large firms than for small firms.
    B) cost-plus pricing is a good way to approximate the profit-maximizing price when marginal revenue or marginal cost is difficult to determine.
    C) cost-plus pricing is more likely to lead to profit-maximization for monopolistically competitive firms than for oligopoly firms.
    D) cost-plus pricing is more likely to result in profit-maximization the more elastic the firm's demand curve is.
    Answer: B
    Diff: 2   Type: MC   Page Ref: 521–2/521–2
    Topic: Cost-plus pricing
    Skill: Conceptual
    Objective: LO 3: Explain how some firms increase their profits through the use of odd pricing cost-plus pricing, and two-part tariffs
    AACSB Coding: Reflective Thinking
    Special Feature: None

11. Even though it often does not result in profit maximization, some small firms use a cost-plus pricing strategy anyway because
    A) it is easy to use.
    B) they do not understand what marginal revenue and marginal cost mean.
    C) it is expensive to hire an economist who can determine what the profit-maximizing price is.
    D) they sell several products, each of which sells for a different price. The time and expense involved in finding the profit-maximizing price for each product are not worth the effort.
    Answer: A
    Diff: 1   Type: MC   Page Ref: 521/521
    Topic: Cost-plus pricing
    Skill: Conceptual
    Objective: LO 3: Explain how some firms increase their profits through the use of odd pricing cost-plus pricing, and two-part tariffs
    AACSB Coding: Reflective Thinking
    Special Feature: None

12. Though large firms have the knowledge and resources to utilize a better pricing strategy, many choose to use cost–plus pricing. One reason for this is that
    A) large firms do not have to maximize their profits because they face little competition from other firms.
    B) there is less risk of violating antitrust laws if a cost–plus pricing strategy is used rather than a profit–maximizing pricing strategy.
    C) the additional revenue that would result from a profit–maximizing pricing strategy is an insignificant fraction of the firms' revenues.
    D) firms often adjust the markup they charge to reflect current demand.
    Answer: D
    Diff: 2   Type: MC   Page Ref: 522/522
    Topic: Cost–plus pricing
    Skill: Conceptual
    Objective: LO 3: Explain how some firms increase their profits through the use of odd pricing cost–plus pricing, and two–part tariffs
    AACSB Coding: Reflective Thinking
    Special Feature: None

13. Which of the following statements about two–part tariffs is false?
    A) Because each individual has a different individual demand curve, if there is just one entrance fee some consumers will be able to reap some consumer surplus.
    B) The producer cannot capture the entire consumer surplus because the entrance fee might discourage some potential consumers even though they would have been willing to pay a lesser entrance fee.
    C) Two–part tariff pricing allows a producer to capture the entire consumer surplus.
    D) For two–part tariff pricing to be successful, the producer must be able to identify two distinct customer groups.
    Answer: D
    Diff: 3   Type: MC   Page Ref: 522–4/522–4
    Topic: Two–part Tariffs
    Skill: Conceptual
    Objective: LO 3: Explain how some firms increase their profits through the use of odd pricing cost–plus pricing, and two–part tariffs
    AACSB Coding: Reflective Thinking
    Special Feature: None

14. Some firms require consumers to pay an initial fee for the right to buy their product and an additional fee for each unit of the product they purchase. This practice is referred to as
    A) odd pricing.
    B) dual pricing.
    C) a two–part tariff.
    D) intertemporal pricing.
    Answer: C
    Diff: 1   Type: MC   Page Ref: 522/522
    Topic: Two–part tariff
    Skill: Definition
    Objective: LO 3: Explain how some firms increase their profits through the use of odd pricing cost–plus pricing, and two–part tariffs
    AACSB Coding: Reflective Thinking
    Special Feature: None

15. The Walt Disney Company is in a position to use a two-part tariff by charging for admission and also charging for rides inside its two theme parks, Disneyland and Disney World. Which of the following statements regarding Disney's pricing strategy is true?
    A) At one time admission fees were charged at both parks but all rides were free. Disney has since changed its pricing policy; it earns higher profits by charging for both admission and rides.
    B) At one time customers had to pay for admission and rides at Disneyland and Disney World. Disney has since changed its pricing policy; it earns higher profits by charging for admission but not for rides.
    C) At one time customers had to pay for admission and rides at Disneyland and Disney World. Disney has since changed its pricing policy; it earns higher profits by charging for rides but not for admission.
    D) At one time fees for admission and rides at both parks were set at their profit-maximizing levels. Disney has since changed its pricing policy; it uses a cost-plus pricing strategy for admission and does not charge for rides.

    Answer: B
    Diff: 2   Type: MC   Page Ref: 522-4/522-4
    Topic: Two-part tariff
    Skill: Conceptual
    Objective: LO 3: Explain how some firms increase their profits through the use of odd pricing cost-plus pricing, and two-part tariffs
    AACSB Coding: Reflective Thinking
    Special Feature: None

16. The Walt Disney Company uses a two-part tariff policy in setting prices for admission and rides at Disney World. If this strategy resulted in maximum profit, Disney would convert all of consumer surplus into profit. Which of the following explains why Disney does not maximize its profits from admission and rides?
    A) To maximize its profits Disney would have to know the demand curves of each of its customers. Since this is not possible, Disney is not able to convert all of consumer surplus into profit.
    B) Disney purposely charges less than the profit-maximizing price for admission to Disney World because it does not want to risk alienating its customers.
    C) Disney purposely charges less than the profit-maximizing price for admission to Disney World in order to earn more profit from sales of food, lodging and other related services.
    D) Disney does not charge the profit-maximizing price for admission because it wants to keep admission affordable for children who will be more likely to visit Disney World when they become parents.

    Answer: A
    Diff: 2   Type: MC   Page Ref: 522-4/522-4
    Topic: Two-part tariff
    Skill: Conceptual
    Objective: LO 3: Explain how some firms increase their profits through the use of odd pricing cost-plus pricing, and two-part tariffs
    AACSB Coding: Reflective Thinking
    Special Feature: None

17. Many golf clubs charge members an annual membership fee as well as a fee each time they golf. One reason for this is
    A) golf clubs do not want their members to overuse their fairways. Charging for each round of golf played reduces fairway maintenance costs.
    B) charging both fees allows the clubs to transfer more consumer surplus into profit than charging only an admission fee.
    C) charging both fees allows the clubs to transfer more producer surplus into profit than charging only an admission fee.
    D) research has shown that charging both fees increases the likelihood that golfers will renew their memberships.
    Answer: B
    Diff: 2   Type: MC   Page Ref: 522-4/522-4
    Topic: Two-part tariff
    Skill: Conceptual
    Objective: LO 3: Explain how some firms increase their profits through the use of odd pricing cost-plus pricing, and two-part tariffs
    AACSB Coding: Reflective Thinking
    Special Feature: None

18. Consider a discount retailer such as Costco which uses a two-part tariff pricing strategy. The Costco membership fee
    A) buys the consumer the right to make future purchases at Costco.
    B) is a resalable asset to the consumer.
    C) is a resalable asset to the producer.
    D) is used by Costco to cover its fixed costs of production.
    Answer: A
    Diff: 1   Type: MC   Page Ref: 522-4/522-4
    Topic: Two-part tariff
    Skill: Conceptual
    Objective: LO 3: Explain how some firms increase their profits through the use of odd pricing cost-plus pricing, and two-part tariffs
    AACSB Coding: Reflective Thinking
    Special Feature: None

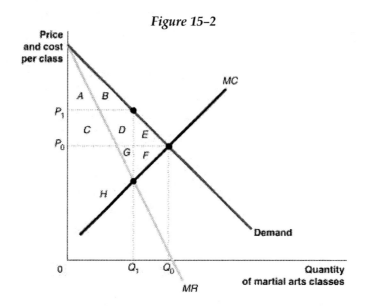

Figure 15-2

Watanabe Sensei operates the only martial arts school in Hartfield. For simplicity, assume that consumers have identical demand curves and that Sensei knows what this demand curve is. Figure 15-2 shows this demand curve.

19. *Refer to Figure 15-2.* If Sensei acts as a monopolist, his profit-maximizing price is _____ and the number of classes sold is _____.

   A) P_0; Q_0
   B) P_0; Q_1
   C) P_1; Q_0
   D) P_1; Q_1
   Answer: D
   Diff: 1   Type: MC   Page Ref: 522-4/522-4
   Topic: Two-part tariff
   Skill: Analytical
   Objective: LO 3: Explain how some firms increase their profits through the use of odd pricing cost-plus pricing, and two-part tariffs
   AACSB Coding: Analytic Skills
   Special Feature: None

20. ***Refer to Figure 15-2.*** If Sensei acts as a monopolist and charges the profit-maximizing price, what is the consumer surplus received by his customers?

    A) The area A + B + C + D.

    B) The area A + B + C + D + E.

    C) The area A + B.

    D) The area A + C + H.

Answer: C

Diff: 1   Type: MC   Page Ref: 522-4/522-4
Topic: Two-part tariff
Skill: Analytical
Objective: LO 3: Explain how some firms increase their profits through the use of odd pricing cost-plus pricing, and two-part tariffs
AACSB Coding: Analytic Skills
Special Feature: None

21. ***Refer to Figure 15-2.*** If Sensei acts as a monopolist and charges the profit-maximizing price, what is his producer surplus?

    A) The area B + D + G.

    B) The area A + B + C + D + H + G.

    C) The area C + D + H + G.

    D) The area A + C + H.

Answer: C

Diff: 1   Type: MC   Page Ref: 522-4/522-4
Topic: Two-part tariff
Skill: Analytical
Objective: LO 3: Explain how some firms increase their profits through the use of odd pricing cost-plus pricing, and two-part tariffs
AACSB Coding: Analytic Skills
Special Feature: None

22. ***Refer to Figure 15- 2.*** Sensei's friend, Marcel, suggests that he charge a one-time membership fee to use the martial arts school, in addition to a per-class charge. Suppose Sensei charges the monopoly price for each class and also imposes a one-time membership fee. What is the maximum amount of revenue from the membership fee he can collect from all his customers?

    A) An amount equal to the area A + B.

    B) An amount equal to the area E + F.

    C) An amount equal to the area H + G.

    D) An amount equal to the area A + C + H.

Answer: A

Diff: 2   Type: MC   Page Ref: 522-4/522-4
Topic: Two-part tariff
Skill: Analytical
Objective: LO 3: Explain how some firms increase their profits through the use of odd pricing cost-plus pricing, and two-part tariffs
AACSB Coding: Analytic Skills
Special Feature: None

23. *Refer to Figure 15- 2.* With a two–part pricing scheme – a monopoly price for classes and a one–time membership fee – what is the amount of producer surplus Sensei will earn?

    A) An amount equal to the area A + B + C + D.

    B) An amount equal to the area E + F.

    C) An amount equal to the area A + C + H.

    D) An amount equal to the area A + B + C + D + H + G.

Answer: D

Diff: 2   Type: MC   Page Ref: 522-4/522-4
Topic: Two–part tariff
Skill: Analytical
Objective: LO 3: Explain how some firms increase their profits through the use of odd pricing cost–plus pricing, and two–part tariffs
AACSB Coding: Analytic Skills
Special Feature: None

24. *Refer to Figure 15–2.* Suppose instead of charging the monopoly price for his classes, Sensei charges the competitive price. What is the competitive price and what is the quantity demanded at this price?

    A) P_0, Q_1

    B) P_0, Q_0

    C) P_1, Q_0

    D) P_1, Q_1

Answer: B

Diff: 1   Type: MC   Page Ref: 522-4/522-4
Topic: Two–part tariff
Skill: Analytical
Objective: LO 3: Explain how some firms increase their profits through the use of odd pricing cost–plus pricing, and two–part tariffs
AACSB Coding: Analytic Skills
Special Feature: None

25. *Refer to Figure 15–2.* If Sensei charges the competitive price for his classes, what is the maximum amount of admission fee that he can collect from his customers?

    A) The area A + B.

    B) The area A + B + C + D.

    C) The area A + B + C + D + E.

    D) The area A + C + D + G + H.

Answer: C

Diff: 1   Type: MC   Page Ref: 522-4/522-4
Topic: Two–part tariff
Skill: Analytical
Objective: LO 3: Explain how some firms increase their profits through the use of odd pricing cost–plus pricing, and two–part tariffs
AACSB Coding: Analytic Skills
Special Feature: None

26. **Refer to Figure 15- 2.** With this pricing scheme – a competitive price for the classes and a one–time membership fee – what amount of producer surplus will Sensei earn?

    A) The area A + B + C + D + E.

    B) The area E + F.

    C) The area H + G + F.

    D) The area A + B + C + D + E + F + G + H

Answer: D

Diff: 2   *Type: MC*   *Page Ref: 522–4/522–4*

Topic: Two–part tariff

Skill: Analytical

Objective: LO 3: Explain how some firms increase their profits through the use of odd pricing cost–plus pricing, and two–part tariffs

AACSB Coding: Analytic Skills

Special Feature: None

Figure 15–3

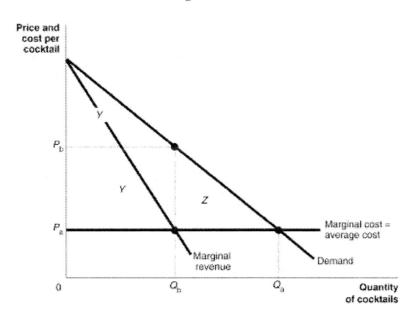

The Lizard Lounge is well known for its exotic cocktails. Figure 15–3 shows its estimated demand curve for cocktails.

27. *Refer to Figure 15–3.* The owners of the Lizard Lounge are considering the following four pricing options:
    a.   A single price scheme where the price of cocktails equals the monopoly price.
    b.   A single price scheme where the cocktail price equals the competitive price.
    c.   A two–part tariff: a monopoly price for cocktails and a cover charge that will generate total revenue equal to the area X.
    d.   A two–part tariff: a competitive price for cocktails and a cover charge that will generate total revenue equal to the area X + Y + Z.

    Which scheme will earn the largest profit?
      A) scheme a
      B) scheme b
      C) scheme c
      D) scheme d
    Answer: D
    Diff: 3   Type: MC   Page Ref: 522–4/522–4
    Topic: Two–part tariff
    Skill: Analytical
    Objective: LO 3: Explain how some firms increase their profits through the use of odd pricing cost–plus pricing, and two–part tariffs
    AACSB Coding: Analytic Skills
    Special Feature: None

28. *Refer to Figure 15–3.* The owners of the Lizard Lounge are considering the following four pricing options:
    a.   A single price scheme where the cocktail price equals the monopoly price.
    b.   A single price scheme where the cocktail price equals the competitive price.
    c.   A two–part tariff: a monopoly price for cocktails and a cover charge that will generate total revenue equal to the area X.
    d.   A two–part tariff: a competitive price for cocktails and a cover charge that will generate total revenue equal to the area X + Y + Z.

    Under which scheme are the Lounge customers better off?
      A) scheme b
      B) scheme a
      C) scheme c
      D) scheme d
    Answer: A
    Diff: 2   Type: MC   Page Ref: 522–4/522–4
    Topic: Two–part tariff
    Skill: Analytical
    Objective: LO 3: Explain how some firms increase their profits through the use of odd pricing cost–plus pricing, and two–part tariffs
    AACSB Coding: Analytic Skills
    Special Feature: None

29. *Refer to Figure 15-3.* The owners of the Lizard Lounge are considering the following four pricing options:
    a.   A single price scheme where the cocktail price equals the monopoly price.
    b.   A single price scheme where the cocktail price equals the competitive price.
    c.   A two-part tariff: a monopoly cocktail price and a cover charge that will generate total revenue equal to the area X.
    d.   A two-part tariff: a competitive cocktail price and whatever cover charge that will generate a total revenue equivalent to the area X + Y + Z.

    Which pricing scheme(s) achieve the economically efficient outcome?
    A) Schemes a and c.
    B) Scheme b.
    C) Schemes b and d.
    D) Scheme d only.
    Answer: C
    Diff: 3   Type: MC   Page Ref: 522-4/522-4
    Topic: Two-part tariff
    Skill: Analytical
    Objective: LO 3: Explain how some firms increase their profits through the use of odd pricing cost-plus pricing, and two-part tariffs
    AACSB Coding: Analytic Skills
    Special Feature: None

30. Movie theaters often charge different people different prices for admission. Why don't theaters charge different prices for popcorn and other food items?
    A) Although the elasticity of demand for admission differs among customers, most people have the same the elasticity of demand for food items.
    B) Concession stand personnel are too busy to ensure that different people pay different prices for food items.
    C) Once people are in the theater, concession stands have monopoly power and can charge everyone the same high prices for food.
    D) It is difficult to limit the resale of food items from those who pay low prices to those who would have to pay high prices from the concession stand.
    Answer: D
    Diff: 1   Type: MC   Page Ref: 525/525
    Topic: Price discrimination
    Skill: Conceptual
    Objective: LO 3: Explain how some firms increase their profits through the use of odd pricing cost-plus pricing, and two-part tariffs
    AACSB Coding: Reflective Thinking
    Special Feature: Economics in YOUR Life!: Why So Many Prices to See a Movie?

31. Assume that the demand for enrollment at George Borts University is elastic. George Borts University has decided to eliminate all merit-based scholarships in favor of increasing the number of its need-based scholarships. Which of the following is the most likely result of these actions?
    A) The cost of running George Borts University will increase and the revenue it receives from students from high income families will increase.
    B) Tuition revenues will increase.
    C) The total number of students who apply to George Borts University will increase.
    D) The total number of students who are accepted to George Borts University will increase.
    Answer: B
    Diff: 1   Type: MC   Page Ref: 526-7/526-7
    Topic: Price discrimination
    Skill: Analytical
    Objective: LO 3: Explain how some firms increase their profits through the use of odd pricing cost-plus pricing, and two-part tariffs
    AACSB Coding: Analytic Skills
    Special Feature: An Inside look: College Tuition: One Price Does Not Fit All

32. The Walt Disney Company uses cost-plus pricing to determine the prices it charges for admission and rides at Disneyland and Walt Disney World.
    Answer: True   ⊚ False
    Diff: 1   Type: TF   Page Ref: 522-4/522-4
    Topic: Two-part tariff
    Skill: Fact
    Objective: LO 3: Explain how some firms increase their profits through the use of odd pricing cost-plus pricing, and two-part tariffs
    AACSB Coding: Reflective Thinking
    Special Feature: None

33. There is no evidence that odd pricing succeeds in convincing consumers that prices are lower than they really are.
    Answer: True   ⊚ False
    Diff: 1   Type: TF   Page Ref: 520/520
    Topic: Odd pricing
    Skill: Fact
    Objective: LO 3: Explain how some firms increase their profits through the use of odd pricing cost-plus pricing, and two-part tariffs
    AACSB Coding: Reflective Thinking
    Special Feature: None

34. Economists believe that cost–plus pricing may be the best way for a firm to determine its optimal product price when the firm's marginal cost and average cost are about the same and when it is difficult to estimate the product's demand curve.

    Answer: ◎ True   False
    Diff: 1   Type: TF   Page Ref: 521–2/521–2
    Topic: Cost–plus pricing
    Skill: Fact
    Objective: LO 3: Explain how some firms increase their profits through the use of odd pricing cost–plus pricing, and two–part tariffs
    AACSB Coding: Reflective Thinking
    Special Feature: None

35. Firms engage in odd pricing when they charge prices that appear to be less than they really are; for example, charging a price of $4.95 instead of $5.00 and $.99 instead of $1.00. How have researchers tried to determine whether odd pricing is successful in convincing consumers that odd prices are less than they really are?

    Answer: Three researchers used surveys to answer this question. Survey results are inferior to actual purchasing behavior because surveys only determine what respondents state they will do, not what they actually do. Still, the surveys revealed that odd pricing may succeed in creating their intended illusion. The researchers asked survey respondents about their willingness to purchase six different products at a series of prices. Ten prices were odd prices. Out of the ten odd prices nine resulted in a quantity demanded that was greater than had been predicted using an estimated demand curve. This is evidence that charging odd prices makes sense for firms.
    Diff: 2   Type: ES   Page Ref: 520/520
    Topic: Odd pricing
    Skill: Conceptual
    Objective: LO 2: Explain how a firm can increase its profits through price discrimination
    AACSB Coding: Reflective Thinking
    Special Feature: None

36. What is cost–plus pricing? Why do some firms use cost–plus pricing even when the firms' managers have the resources to devise a pricing strategy that would result in greater profits?

    Answer: When a firm uses cost–plus pricing to set the price of a product it adds a percentage markup (for example, 10 percent or 30 percent) to its average cost at a particular level of production. If the firm sells more than one product the markup is intended to cover all costs, including those that cannot easily be assigned to a particular product. Economists believe that cost–plus pricing may be the best strategy for a firm, even a firm able to afford a more sophisticated pricing strategy, in two situations. First, when the firm's marginal cost and average cost are nearly equal. Second, when estimation of the firm's demand curve is difficult. Many large firms that use cost–plus pricing do not simply charge the marked–up price but alter the price based on the response of consumers in the market and the degree of competition in their industry.
    Diff: 2   Type: ES   Page Ref: 520–522/520–522
    Topic: Cost–plus pricing
    Skill: Conceptual
    Objective: LO 3: Explain how some firms increase their profits through the use of odd pricing cost–plus pricing, and two–part tariffs
    AACSB Coding: Reflective Thinking
    Special Feature: None

Chapter 16 The Markets for Labor and Other Factors of Production

16.1   The Demand for Labor

1. One difference between the labor market and markets for goods and services is
   A) the demand in the labor market is inelastic; the demand for goods and services may be elastic or inelastic.
   B) the supply of labor is perfectly inelastic because the quantity supplied is constant. The elasticity of supply for goods and services is different in different markets.
   C) concepts of fairness arise more frequently in labor markets than in the markets for goods and services.
   D) in the labor market firms are suppliers while households are demanders.
   Answer: C
   Diff: 1   Type: MC   Page Ref: 534–535/534–535
   Topic: Chapter Opener
   Skill: Conceptual
   Objective: LO 1: Explain how firms choose the profit-maximizing quantity of labor to employ
   AACSB Coding: Reflective Thinking
   Special Feature: Chapter Opener: Why Are the Chicago Cubs Paying Alfonso Soriano $18 Million per Year?

2. Alfonso Soriano and other star baseball players earn millions of dollars annually. These salaries are due to
   A) the greed of players and their agents.
   B) the demand and supply of labor in the market for baseball players.
   C) the elastic demand for jobs in Major League Baseball.
   D) the irrational behavior of team owners.
   Answer: B
   Diff: 1   Type: MC   Page Ref: 534–535/534–535
   Topic: Chapter Opener
   Skill: Conceptual
   Objective: LO 1: Explain how firms choose the profit-maximizing quantity of labor to employ
   AACSB Coding: Reflective Thinking
   Special Feature: Chapter Opener: Why Are the Chicago Cubs Paying Alfonso Soriano $18 Million per Year?

3. Major League Baseball teams are similar to other firms in that they use factors of production to produce a product (baseball games). An example of capital used by teams to produce their products is
   A) the money teams earn from television contracts and ticket sales.
   B) the land on which baseball games are played.
   C) the labor of baseball players.
   D) the ballparks where the games are played.

Answer: D
Diff: 1   Type: MC   Page Ref: 536/536
Topic: Factors of production
Skill: Conceptual
Objective: LO 1: Explain how firms choose the profit–maximizing quantity of labor to employ
AACSB Coding: Reflective Thinking
Special Feature: None

4. The demand for labor is different from the demand for final goods and services because
   A) the demand for labor is based on the demand for the good or service the labor is used to produce.
   B) it is a demand for people, not inanimate objects.
   C) the demand for labor is more inelastic than the demand for the goods and services produced with this labor.
   D) the law of demand does not apply to the demand for labor.

Answer: A
Diff: 1   Type: MC   Page Ref: 536/536
Topic: Derived demand
Skill: Conceptual
Objective: LO 1: Explain how firms choose the profit–maximizing quantity of labor to employ
AACSB Coding: Reflective Thinking
Special Feature: None

5. The demand for labor depends primarily on the additional output produced as a result of hiring an additional worker and
   A) the additional revenue received from selling the output produced as a result of hiring an additional worker.
   B) the payment made to the worker for producing the additional output.
   C) the elasticity of demand for the output produced by the worker.
   D) the number of workers willing to produce the additional output.

Answer: A
Diff: 1   Type: MC   Page Ref: 536–537/536–537
Topic: The demand for labor
Skill: Conceptual
Objective: LO 1: Explain how firms choose the profit–maximizing quantity of labor to employ
AACSB Coding: Reflective Thinking
Special Feature: None

6. The term "derived demand" refers to
    A) the demand for financial products called derivatives.
    B) the demand for a factor of production that is derived from the demand for the good the factor produces.
    C) a firm's estimated demand curve derived from sales data.
    D) a demand curve that derives from the availability of resources.
    Answer: B
    Diff: 1   Type: MC   Page Ref: 536/536
    Topic: Derived demand
    Skill: Definition
    Objective: LO 1: Explain how firms choose the profit-maximizing quantity of labor to employ
    AACSB Coding: Reflective Thinking
    Special Feature: None

7. An increase in the demand for orthodontic services leads to
    A) an increase in the supply of orthodontists.
    B) lower prices for orthodontic care.
    C) an increase in the demand for orthodontists.
    D) a rise in the rates of dental insurance.
    Answer: C
    Diff: 1   Type: MC   Page Ref: 536/536
    Topic: Derived demand
    Skill: Conceptual
    Objective: LO 1: Explain how firms choose the profit-maximizing quantity of labor to employ
    AACSB Coding: Reflective Thinking
    Special Feature: None

8. The marginal product of labor is
    A) the payment made to workers for their contribution to the output they produce.
    B) equal to the demand for labor.
    C) the change in a firm's revenue as a result of hiring one more worker.
    D) the additional output a firm produces as a result of hiring one more worker.
    Answer: D
    Diff: 2   Type: MC   Page Ref: 536/536
    Topic: Marginal product of labor
    Skill: Definition
    Objective: LO 1: Explain how firms choose the profit-maximizing quantity of labor to employ
    AACSB Coding: Reflective Thinking
    Special Feature: None

9. A firm should hire more workers to increase its profits if
    A) the marginal product of labor is greater than the wage the firm will pay these workers.
    B) the wage rate is less than the marginal revenue product of labor.
    C) there is enough capital and other resources for the workers to use.
    D) the demand for labor is elastic.
Answer: B
Diff: 2   Type: MC   Page Ref: 536–537/536–537
Topic: Marginal revenue product of labor
Skill: Conceptual
Objective: LO 1: Explain how firms choose the profit-maximizing quantity of labor to employ
AACSB Coding: Reflective Thinking
Special Feature: None

10. The demand curve for labor is also
    A) the demand curve for the output produced with labor since the demand for labor is a derived demand.
    B) the marginal product of labor curve.
    C) the marginal revenue product of labor curve.
    D) the supply curve for the output labor is used to produce.
Answer: C
Diff: 2   Type: MC   Page Ref: 538/538
Topic: Marginal revenue product of labor
Skill: Fact
Objective: LO 1: Explain how firms choose the profit-maximizing quantity of labor to employ
AACSB Coding: Reflective Thinking
Special Feature: None

11. Which of the following describes a difference between the marginal product of labor and the marginal revenue product of labor?
    A) The marginal product of labor declines as each additional worker is hired because of the law of diminishing returns. The marginal revenue product of labor declines as each additional worker is hired because of diseconomies of scale.
    B) The marginal product of labor declines as each additional worker is hired because of the law of diminishing returns. The marginal revenue product increases as each additional worker is hired because of increases the productivity of labor.
    C) The marginal product of labor is inelastic. The marginal revenue product of labor is elastic.
    D) The marginal product of labor measures the change in output as additional workers are hired. The marginal revenue product measures the change in revenue as additional workers are hired.
Answer: D
Diff: 2   Type: MC   Page Ref: 536–538/536–538
Topic: Marginal revenue product of labor
Skill: Definition
Objective: LO 1: Explain how firms choose the profit-maximizing quantity of labor to employ
AACSB Coding: Reflective Thinking
Special Feature: None

12. As more output is produced the marginal product of labor declines
    A) because of the law of diminishing returns.
    B) if firms reduce the wage paid to labor.
    C) if the firm's output supply curve is inelastic.
    D) because the firm's marginal revenue declines.
    Answer: A
    Diff: 2   Type: MC   Page Ref: 536/536
    Topic: Marginal product of labor
    Skill: Conceptual
    Objective: LO 1: Explain how firms choose the profit-maximizing quantity of labor to employ
    AACSB Coding: Reflective Thinking
    Special Feature: None

13. A firm's demand for labor curve slopes downwards because
    A) of the law of diminishing marginal returns.
    B) firms supply less labor as the wage rate rises.
    C) workers supply less labor services as the wage rate falls.
    D) of rising marginal product.
    Answer: A
    Diff: 1   Type: MC   Page Ref: 536–538/536–538
    Topic: The demand for labor
    Skill: Conceptual
    Objective: LO 1: Explain how firms choose the profit-maximizing quantity of labor to employ
    AACSB Coding: Reflective Thinking
    Special Feature: None

14. For a firm that is a price taker in the market for labor, the marginal revenue product of labor equals the
    A) marginal product of labor multiplied by the wage rate.
    B) marginal product of labor multiplied by the product price.
    C) marginal product of labor multiplied by the wage rate.
    D) marginal product of labor multiplied by the marginal cost of production.
    Answer: B
    Diff: 2   Type: MC   Page Ref: 536–537/536–537
    Topic: Marginal revenue product of labor
    Skill: Definition
    Objective: LO 1: Explain how firms choose the profit-maximizing quantity of labor to employ
    AACSB Coding: Reflective Thinking
    Special Feature: None

15. The change in a firm's revenue as a result of hiring one more worker is
    A) the definition of the marginal product of labor.
    B) is equal to the firm's marginal cost.
    C) is the definition of the marginal revenue product of labor.
    D) will be negative if the demand for the firm's output is inelastic.
    Answer: C
    Diff: 1   Type: MC   Page Ref: 536–537/536–537
    Topic: Marginal revenue product of labor
    Skill: Definition
    Objective: LO 1: Explain how firms choose the profit-maximizing quantity of labor to employ
    AACSB Coding: Reflective Thinking
    Special Feature: None

16. The marginal revenue product of labor is defined as
    A) the change in the firm's revenue as a result of selling one more unit of output.
    B) the change in the firm's output as a result of hiring one more worker.
    C) the change in the firm's profit as a result of hiring one more worker.
    D) the change in the firm's revenue as a result of hiring one more worker.
    Answer: D
    Diff: 1   Type: MC   Page Ref: 537/537
    Topic: Marginal revenue product of labor
    Skill: Definition
    Objective: LO 1: Explain how firms choose the profit-maximizing quantity of labor to employ
    AACSB Coding: Reflective Thinking
    Special Feature: None

17. The benefit to the firm from hiring one additional worker is called the
    A) marginal revenue product of labor.
    B) marginal revenue.
    C) marginal profit.
    D) total revenue.
    Answer: A
    Diff: 1   Type: MC   Page Ref: 536–537/536–537
    Topic: Marginal revenue product of labor
    Skill: Definition
    Objective: LO 1: Explain how firms choose the profit-maximizing quantity of labor to employ
    AACSB Coding: Reflective Thinking
    Special Feature: None

18. Holding the price of a firm's output constant, if the marginal product of labor increases
    A) the marginal revenue product of labor decreases.
    B) the marginal revenue product of labor also increases.
    C) the marginal products of other inputs also increase.
    D) the marginal revenue product of labor may increase or decrease.
    Answer: B
    Diff: 2   Type: MC   Page Ref: 536–537/536–537
    Topic: Marginal revenue product of labor
    Skill: Conceptual
    Objective: LO 1: Explain how firms choose the profit–maximizing quantity of labor to employ
    AACSB Coding: Reflective Thinking
    Special Feature: None

19. Hotspur Incorporated, a manufacturer of microwaves, is a price taker in both the input and output market. To maximize its profit, Hotspur will hire labor up to the point where
    A) the marginal product of labor is no longer positive.
    B) all economies of scale have been exhausted.
    C) the marginal revenue product of labor equals the wage rate.
    D) the marginal revenue product of labor equals the output price.
    Answer: C
    Diff: 2   Type: MC   Page Ref: 537–538/537–538
    Topic: Marginal revenue product of labor
    Skill: Conceptual
    Objective: LO 1: Explain how firms choose the profit–maximizing quantity of labor to employ
    AACSB Coding: Reflective Thinking
    Special Feature: None

20. Marginal revenue product falls as more labor is hired because
    A) the price of the product must fall for a perfectly competitive firm to sell more.
    B) the wage rate rises as more workers work more hours.
    C) the marginal product of labor is negative as additional units of labor are hired.
    D) the marginal product of labor falls as a result of the law of diminishing returns.
    Answer: D
    Diff: 2   Type: MC   Page Ref: 536–538/536–538
    Topic: Marginal revenue product of labor
    Skill: Conceptual
    Objective: LO 1: Explain how firms choose the profit–maximizing quantity of labor to employ
    AACSB Coding: Reflective Thinking
    Special Feature: None

Table 16–1

Number of workers	Output of microwaves ovens per week
1	30
2	55
3	75
4	90
5	100
6	105

Hotspur Incorporated, a manufacturer of microwave ovens, is a price taker in its input and output markets. The firm hires labor at a constant wage rate of $800 per week and sells microwave ovens at a constant price of $80. Table 16–1 shows the relationship between the quantity of labor it hires and the quantity of microwave ovens it produces.

21. *Refer to Table 16–1.* What is the amount of revenue added as a result of hiring the fourth worker?
    A) $1,200
    B) $7,200
    C) 15 microwaves
    D) 90 microwaves
    Answer: A
    Diff: 2   Type: MC   Page Ref: 536–538/536–538
    Topic: Marginal revenue product of labor
    Skill: Analytical
    Objective: LO 1: Explain how firms choose the profit–maximizing quantity of labor to employ
    AACSB Coding: Analytic Skills
    Special Feature: None

22. *Refer to Table 16–1.* What is the amount of profit added as a result of hiring the fourth worker?
    A) $7,200
    B) $1,200
    C) $800
    D) $400
    Answer: D
    Diff: 2   Type: MC   Page Ref: 536–538/536–538
    Topic: The demand for labor
    Skill: Analytical
    Objective: LO 1: Explain how firms choose the profit–maximizing quantity of labor to employ
    AACSB Coding: Analytic Skills
    Special Feature: None

23. ***Refer to Table 16–1.*** What is Hotspur's profit maximizing quantity of labor?
    A) 2 workers
    B) 3 workers
    C) 5 workers
    D) 6 workers
    Answer: C
    Diff: 2   Type: MC   Page Ref: 536–538/536–538
    Topic: The demand for labor
    Skill: Analytical
    Objective: LO 1: Explain how firms choose the profit-maximizing quantity of labor to employ
    AACSB Coding: Analytic Skills
    Special Feature: None

24. Which of the following is not held constant along a firm's demand for labor curve?
    A) The quantity of other inputs used by the firm.
    B) The wage rate.
    C) Changes in technology.
    D) The price of the product produced by the firm.
    Answer: B
    Diff: 1   Type: MC   Page Ref: 539–540/539–540
    Topic: The demand for labor
    Skill: Conceptual
    Objective: LO 1: Explain how firms choose the profit-maximizing quantity of labor to employ
    AACSB Coding: Reflective Thinking
    Special Feature: None

Table 16–2

Quantity of Labor	Output	MPL	Price	Total Revenue	$MRPL$	Wage
0	0	---	$200	$0	---	$500
1	6	6	180			500
2	11	5	160			500
3	15	4	140			500
4	18	3	120			500
5	20	2	100			500
6	21	1	80			500

25. ***Refer to Table 16–2.*** The table above lists data for the production of Apple iPods. Apple is assumed to be a price maker, so to increase the sales of iPods the firm must lower its price. MPL and $MRPL$ refer to the marginal product of labor and the marginal revenue product of labor, respectively. What is the price and quantity of workers that result in the maximum amount of revenue Apple would earn from selling iPods?
    A) $180; 1.
    B) $140; 2.
    C) $120; 2.
    D) $120; 4.
    Answer: D

Diff: 2   Type: MC   Page Ref: 538–539/538–539
Topic: The demand for labor
Skill: Analytical
Objective: LO 1: Explain how firms choose the profit–maximizing quantity of labor to employ
AACSB Coding: Analytic Skills
Special Feature: Solved Problem: Hiring Decisions by a Firm That is a Price Maker

26. *Refer to Table 16–2.* The table above lists data for the production of Apple iPods. Apple is assumed to be a price maker, so to increase the sales of iPods the firm must lower its price. MP_L and MRP_L refer to the marginal product of labor and the marginal revenue product of labor, respectively.   What are the price and quantity of workers that result in the maximum amount profit Apple would earn from selling iPods?
    A) $140; 2
    B) $160; 2
    C) $140; 3
    D) $180; 1
Answer: B
Diff: 3   Type: MC   Page Ref: 538–539/538–539
Topic: The demand for labor
Skill: Analytical
Objective: LO 1: Explain how firms choose the profit–maximizing quantity of labor to employ
AACSB Coding: Analytic Skills
Special Feature: Solved Problem: Hiring Decisions by a Firm That is a Price Maker

27. *Refer to Table 16–2.* The table above lists data for the production of Apple iPods. Apple is assumed to be a price maker, so to increase its sales of iPods the firm must lower its price. MP_L and MRP_L refer to the marginal product of labor and the marginal revenue product of labor, respectively. What are the quantity of labor and marginal revenue product of labor that will maximize the profit Apple would earn from selling iPods?
    A) 2; $160
    B) 3; $340
    C) 2; $680
    D) 2; $160
Answer: C
Diff: 3   Type: MC   Page Ref: 538–539/538–539
Topic: The demand for labor
Skill: Analytical
Objective: LO 1: Explain how firms choose the profit–maximizing quantity of labor to employ
AACSB Coding: Analytic Skills
Special Feature: Solved Problem: Hiring Decisions by a Firm That is a Price Maker

28. The market demand curve for labor
    A) is determined by adding up the quantity of labor demanded by each firm at each wage, holding constant the other variables that affect the willingness of firms to hire workers.
    B) is the same as the market demand curve for the product labor produces because it is a derived demand.
    C) is determined by adding up the demand for labor by each firm at each wage, holding constant the other variables that affect the willingness of firms to hire workers.
    D) is perfectly inelastic because there is a finite number of workers in the market for labor.
    Answer: A
    Diff: 1   Type: MC   Page Ref: 539/539
    Topic: The demand for labor
    Skill: Conceptual
    Objective: LO 1: Explain how firms choose the profit-maximizing quantity of labor to employ
    AACSB Coding: Reflective Thinking
    Special Feature: None

29. Which of the following factors will not cause the labor demand curve to shift?
    A) Increases in human capital.
    B) Changes in technology.
    C) Change in the price of the product produced with labor.
    D) The wage rate.
    Answer: D
    Diff: 1   Type: MC   Page Ref: 539-540/539-540
    Topic: The demand for labor
    Skill: Conceptual
    Objective: LO 1: Explain how firms choose the profit-maximizing quantity of labor to employ
    AACSB Coding: Reflective Thinking
    Special Feature: None

30. An increase in the price of grape juice causes an increase in the marginal revenue product of labor used to produce grape juice.
    Answer: ◉ True   False
    Diff: 1   Type: TF   Page Ref: 536-538/536-538
    Topic: Derived demand
    Skill: Conceptual
    Objective: LO 1: Explain how firms choose the profit-maximizing quantity of labor to employ
    AACSB Coding: Reflective Thinking
    Special Feature: None

31. The marginal product of labor curve is the demand curve for labor.
    Answer: True   ◉ False
    Diff: 1   Type: TF   Page Ref: 536/536
    Topic: Marginal product of labor
    Skill: Conceptual
    Objective: LO 1: Explain how firms choose the profit-maximizing quantity of labor to employ
    AACSB Coding: Reflective Thinking
    Special Feature: None

32.   *Table 16–3*

Number of hairdressers	Haircuts per day	Marginal Product	Marginal Revenue Product
1	8		
2	16		
3	23		
4	29		
5	34		
6	38		

Refer to Table 16–3. The Hair Cuttery, a new hair salon, is ready to start hiring. The table above shows the relationship between the number of hairdressers the firm hires and the quantity of haircuts it produces.

a. Suppose the price of haircuts is $8. Complete the table by filling in the values for marginal product and marginal revenue product.

b. The Hair Cuttery is an input price-taker. Suppose the wage paid to hairdressers is $40 per day: What is the profit-maximizing number of hairdressers?

c. Suppose the wage rate rises to $60 per day.
    (i) What happens to the firm's demand curve for hairdressers?
    (ii) What happens to the profit-maximizing quantity of hairdressers?

d. Suppose the wage rate is $40 per day and the price of haircuts is now $10.
    (i) What happens to the firm's demand curve for hairdressers?
    (ii) What happens to the profit-maximizing quantity of hairdressers?

Answer: a.

Number of hairdressers	Haircuts per day	Marginal Product	Marginal Revenue Product
1	8	8	$64
2	16	8	64
3	23	7	56
4	29	6	48
5	34	5	40
6	38	4	32

b. The profit-maximizing number of hairdressers is 5, where the marginal revenue product equals the wage rate.

c. (i) The demand curve does not change.
    (ii) The profit-maximizing quantity of hairdressers falls to 2.

d. (i) The demand curve shifts to the right.
    (ii) The profit-maximizing quantity of hairdressers increases to 6.

Diff: 3   Type: SA   Page Ref: 536–540/536–540
Topic: The demand for labor
Skill: Analytical
Objective: LO 1: Explain how firms choose the profit-maximizing quantity of labor to employ
AACSB Coding: Analytic Skills
Special Feature: None

33. Explain how the market for opticians is affected as a result of the development of laser technology which reduces the demand for glasses and contact lenses. In your explanation be sure to show the connection between the market for glasses and contact lenses and the market for opticians.

    Answer: Opticians are trained professionals who fit people with glasses and contact lenses. If the demand for glasses and contact lenses falls because more customers switch to lasik eye correction, the demand for opticians, which derives from the demand for glasses and contact lenses, will also fall.

    Diff: 2   Type: SA   Page Ref: 536–540/536–540
    Topic: The demand for labor
    Skill: Conceptual
    Objective: LO 1: Explain how firms choose the profit-maximizing quantity of labor to employ
    AACSB Coding: Reflective Thinking
    Special Feature: None

34. The demand for labor is a derived demand. Explain what is meant by the term "derived demand."

    Answer: A derived demand is the demand for a factor of production that is derived from the demand for the good or service the factor produces.

    Diff: 1   Type: SA   Page Ref: 536/536
    Topic: Derived demand
    Skill: Definition
    Objective: LO 1: Explain how firms choose the profit-maximizing quantity of labor to employ
    AACSB Coding: Reflective Thinking
    Special Feature: None

16.2   The Supply of Labor

1. The labor supply curve
   A) shows the relationship between the wage rate and the quantity of labor supplied.
   B) shows the quantity of jobs supplied at various wage rates.
   C) is unit–elastic.
   D) is U–shaped.
   Answer: A
   Diff: 1   Type: MC   Page Ref: 540–541/540–541
   Topic: The supply of labor
   Skill: Definition
   Objective: LO 2: Explain how people choose the quantity of labor to supply
   AACSB Coding: Reflective Thinking
   Special Feature: None

2. In general, the labor supply curve
   A) slopes downward because firms will hire fewer workers at higher wages.
   B) slopes upward because as the wage rises the opportunity cost of leisure increases.
   C) is vertical at the equilibrium wage rate.
   D) is perfectly elastic at the equilibrium wage rate.
   Answer: B
   Diff: 1   Type: MC   Page Ref: 540–541/540–541
   Topic: The supply of labor
   Skill: Conceptual
   Objective: LO 2: Explain how people choose the quantity of labor to supply
   AACSB Coding: Reflective Thinking
   Special Feature: None

3. The wage rate is the opportunity cost of
   A) working.
   B) working overtime.
   C) leisure.
   D) consumption.
   Answer: C
   Diff: 1   Type: MC   Page Ref: 540/540
   Topic: The supply of labor
   Skill: Conceptual
   Objective: LO 2: Explain how people choose the quantity of labor to supply
   AACSB Coding: Reflective Thinking
   Special Feature: None

4. Which of the following helps to explain why the supply curve of labor is upward sloping?
   A) The supply curve of labor is a derived supply curve; since the output supply curve is upward–sloping so is the labor supply curve.
   B) As the wage rate rises, the income effect causes the quantity of labor supplied to increase.
   C) The substitution effect of a price change makes a good more expensive relative to other goods.
   D) As the wage rate rises, the opportunity cost of leisure rises.
   Answer: D
   Diff: 2   Type: MC   Page Ref: 540–541/540–541
   Topic: The supply of labor
   Skill: Conceptual
   Objective: LO 2: Explain how people choose the quantity of labor to supply
   AACSB Coding: Reflective Thinking
   Special Feature: None

5. Which of the following statements is true?
    A) As the wage rate rises the substitution effect decreases the opportunity cost of leisure and causes a worker to devote more time to working and less time to leisure.
    B) As the wage rate rises the substitution effect increases the opportunity cost of leisure and causes a worker to devote more time to working and less time to leisure.
    C) As the wage rate rises, the income effect increases the opportunity cost of leisure and causes a worker to devote more time to working and less time to leisure.
    D) As the wage rate rises, the income effect causes a worker to devote more time to work and less time to leisure.

Answer: B
Diff: 3   Type: MC   Page Ref: 540–541/540–541
Topic: Substitution and income effects of a wage change
Skill: Conceptual
Objective: LO 2: Explain how people choose the quantity of labor to supply
AACSB Coding: Reflective Thinking
Special Feature: None

6. The typical labor supply curve is upward–sloping but it is possible for the curve to be backward bending – negatively sloped – at very high wage levels. Which of the following would cause a backward bending supply curve?
    A) This would occur when the income effect from an increase in the wage becomes larger than the substitution effect.
    B) This would occur when the substitution effect from an increase in the wage becomes larger than the income effect.
    C) This would occur if leisure is an inferior good.
    D) This would occur when a large number of workers choose leisure rather than employment at low wages; only a very large increase in the wage will lead these workers to prefer employment to leisure.

Answer: A
Diff: 2   Type: MC   Page Ref: 540–541/540–541
Topic: Backward bending labor supply curve
Skill: Conceptual
Objective: LO 2: Explain how people choose the quantity of labor to supply
AACSB Coding: Reflective Thinking
Special Feature: None

7. Because leisure is a normal good an increase in the wage rate will result in
   A) an increase in the quantity of labor supplied because of both the substitution effect and the income effect.
   B) a decrease in the quantity of labor supplied because of the substitution effect and an increase in the quantity of labor supplied because of the income effect.
   C) an increase in the quantity of labor supplied because of the substitution effect and a decrease in the quantity of labor supplied because of the income effect.
   D) an increase in the quantity of labor supplied because of the substitution effect.   At low wages the income effect causes an increase in the quantity of labor supplied, but at high wages the income effect causes a decrease in the quantity of labor supplied as the wage rises.
   Answer: C
   Diff: 3   Type: MC   Page Ref: 540–541/540–541
   Topic: Substitution and income effects of a wage change
   Skill: Conceptual
   Objective: LO 2: Explain how people choose the quantity of labor to supply
   AACSB Coding: Reflective Thinking
   Special Feature: None

8. In order for a labor supply curve to be backward bending at high wages
   A) leisure must be an inferior good.
   B) the substitution effect of wage increase must be greater than the income effect.
   C) workers must have an irrational response to wage increases.
   D) the income effect of a wage increase must be greater than the substitution effect.
   Answer: D
   Diff: 2   Type: MC   Page Ref: 540–541/540–541
   Topic: Backward bending labor supply curve
   Skill: Conceptual
   Objective: LO 2: Explain how people choose the quantity of labor to supply
   AACSB Coding: Reflective Thinking
   Special Feature: None

9. The market supply curve of labor is
   A) derived from the market supply curve for the output produced with labor.
   B) perfectly inelastic if leisure is an inferior good.
   C) determined by adding up the quantity of labor supplied by each worker at each wage, holding constant all other variables that affect the willingness of workers to supply labor.
   D) determined by adding up the wages each worker is willing to work at a given quantity supplied, holding constant all other variables that affect the willingness of workers to supply labor.
   Answer: C
   Diff: 2   Type: MC   Page Ref: 541–542/541–542
   Topic: The supply of labor
   Skill: Conceptual
   Objective: LO 2: Explain how people choose the quantity of labor to supply
   AACSB Coding: Reflective Thinking
   Special Feature: None

Figure 16–1

10. *Refer to Figure 16–1.* Which of the following is true if the wage rate increases from W_0 to W_1?

    A) The income effect is larger than the substitution effect.

    B) The substitution effect is larger than the income effect.

    C) The income effect and the substitution effect are equal.

    D) The supply curve is unit–elastic.

Answer: B

Diff: 2   *Type: MC*   *Page Ref: 540–541/540–541*
Topic: Substitution and income effects of a wage change
Skill: Analytical
Objective: LO 2: Explain how people choose the quantity of labor to supply
AACSB Coding: Analytic Skills
Special Feature: None

11. *Refer to Figure 16–1.* Which of the following is true at W_2?

    A) The income effect is larger than the substitution effect.

    B) The substitution effect is larger than the income effect.

    C) The income effect and the substitution effect are equal.

    D) The supply curve is positively sloped.

Answer: A

Diff: 3   *Type: MC*   *Page Ref: 540–541/540–541*
Topic: Substitution and income effects of a wage change
Skill: Analytical
Objective: LO 2: Explain how people choose the quantity of labor to supply
AACSB Coding: Analytic Skills
Special Feature: None

12. For most low-wage earners,
    A) the income effect of a wage rate increase is likely to be larger than the substitution effect.
    B) the substitution effect of a wage rate increase is likely to equal the income effect.
    C) the opportunity cost of leisure is high.
    D) the substitution effect of a wage rate increase is likely to be larger than the income effect.
    Answer: D
    Diff: 2   Type: MC   Page Ref: 540–541/540–541
    Topic: Substitution and income effects of a wage change
    Skill: Conceptual
    Objective: LO 2: Explain how people choose the quantity of labor to supply
    AACSB Coding: Reflective Thinking
    Special Feature: None

13. Francis Crawford recently received a 20 percent wage increase and desires to work less. We can conclude that at his current wage his supply of labor curve
    A) has a positive slope.
    B) has a negative slope.
    C) is U-shaped.
    D) is vertical.
    Answer: B
    Diff: 1   Type: MC   Page Ref: 540–541/540–541
    Topic: Backward bending labor supply curve
    Skill: Conceptual
    Objective: LO 2: Explain how people choose the quantity of labor to supply
    AACSB Coding: Reflective Thinking
    Special Feature: None

14. The income effect of a wage increase will cause a worker to devote
    A) more time to labor and more time to leisure.
    B) more time to labor and less time to leisure.
    C) less time to labor and more time to leisure.
    D) less time to labor and less time to leisure.
    Answer: C
    Diff: 2   Type: MC   Page Ref: 540–541/540–541
    Topic: Substitution and income effects of a wage change
    Skill: Conceptual
    Objective: LO 2: Explain how people choose the quantity of labor to supply
    AACSB Coding: Reflective Thinking
    Special Feature: None

15. Along an upward sloping labor supply curve, as the wage rate increases, the opportunity cost of leisure _____, causing individuals to supply a _____ quantity of labor.
    A) increases; greater
    B) increases; lower
    C) decreases; greater
    D) remains constant, constant
    Answer: A
    Diff: 2   Type: MC   Page Ref: 540–541/540–541
    Topic: The supply of labor
    Skill: Conceptual
    Objective: LO 2: Explain how people choose the quantity of labor to supply
    AACSB Coding: Reflective Thinking
    Special Feature: None

16. Leisure is
    A) an inferior good.
    B) a complementary good to labor.
    C) wasteful to society.
    D) a normal good.
    Answer: D
    Diff: 1   Type: MC   Page Ref: 540–541/540–541
    Topic: The supply of labor
    Skill: Conceptual
    Objective: LO 2: Explain how people choose the quantity of labor to supply
    AACSB Coding: Reflective Thinking
    Special Feature: None

17. Which of the following variables will *not* cause the market supply curve of labor to shift?
    A) Increases in population
    B) A favorable change in consumer tastes.
    C) A change in the labor participation rate of women.
    D) An increase in the number of people between the ages of 16 and 65.
    Answer: B
    Diff: 1   Type: MC   Page Ref: 542/542
    Topic: The supply of labor
    Skill: Conceptual
    Objective: LO 2: Explain how people choose the quantity of labor to supply
    AACSB Coding: Reflective Thinking
    Special Feature: None

18. How will an increase in population affect the labor market?
    A) It will shift the market supply curve.
    B) It will cause a decrease in the quantity of labor demanded.
    C) It will increase the supply of jobs.
    D) It will increase the opportunity cost of leisure.
    Answer: A
    Diff: 1   Type: MC   Page Ref: 542/542
    Topic: The supply of labor
    Skill: Conceptual
    Objective: LO 2: Explain how people choose the quantity of labor to supply
    AACSB Coding: Reflective Thinking
    Special Feature: None

19. In recent years unemployment rates in several European countries have been higher than unemployment rates in the United States. Many economists believe that European unemployment rates have been higher because
    A) of the different methods used to measure unemployment. If similar methods were used unemployment rates in Europe and the U.S. would be about the same.
    B) European firms hire many seasonal workers from other countries; this tends to inflate unemployment rates in their countries.
    C) unemployment benefits are more generous in Europe than in the United States.
    D) the size of the military is much higher in the United States and all military personnel are classified as employed.
    Answer: C
    Diff: 1   Type: MC   Page Ref: 542/542
    Topic: Unemployment
    Skill: Fact
    Objective: LO 2: Explain how people choose the quantity of labor to supply
    AACSB Coding: Reflective Thinking
    Special Feature: None

20. Which of the following factors has significantly increased the supply of labor in the United States since 1950?
    A) A large increase in the substitution effect as a result of higher wages.
    B) A low birth rate and an aging population.
    C) An increase in the number of people who have received college degrees.
    D) An increase in the labor force participation rate of women.
    Answer: D
    Diff: 1   Type: MC   Page Ref: 542/542
    Topic: The supply of labor
    Skill: Fact
    Objective: LO 2: Explain how people choose the quantity of labor to supply
    AACSB Coding: Reflective Thinking
    Special Feature: None

21. Increases in population shift the market supply curve for labor to the right.
    Answer: ⊙ True   False
    Diff: 1   Type: TF   Page Ref: 542/542
    Topic: Shifts in labor supply
    Skill: Conceptual
    Objective: LO 2: Explain how people choose the quantity of labor to supply
    AACSB Coding: Reflective Thinking
    Special Feature: None

22. In many European countries it is much easier than in the United States for unemployed workers to receive generous wage replacement income from their governments.
    Answer: ⊙ True   False
    Diff: 1   Type: TF   Page Ref: 542/542
    Topic: The supply of labor
    Skill: Conceptual
    Objective: LO 2: Explain how people choose the quantity of labor to supply
    AACSB Coding: Reflective Thinking
    Special Feature: None

23. What is the shape of the labor supply curve implied by the statements?
    a. "I'm sorry, kids, but now that I'm earning more, I just can't afford to come home early in the afternoon, so I won't be here when you get home from school."
    b. "They can pay me a lot or they can pay me a little. I'll still put in my 8 hours a day."
    c. "Now that I have received a salary increase, I am going to work 36 hours instead of 40 hours a week"
    Answer: a. Upward–sloping
            b. Vertical
            c. Backward–bending
    Diff: 1   Type: SA   Page Ref: 540–542/540–542
    Topic: The supply of labor
    Skill: Conceptual
    Objective: LO 2: Explain how people choose the quantity of labor to supply
    AACSB Coding: Reflective Thinking
    Special Feature: None

24. a. What are the two effects of an increase in the wage rate on an individual's labor supply decision? Briefly explain each effect?
    b. Explain how a labor supply curve could be backward-bending.

Answer: a. There are two effects of a wage rate increase: a substitution effect and an income effect. The substitution effect raises the price of leisure, which causes a worker to consume less leisure and supply more labor. Since leisure is a normal good, the income effect leads the worker to choose more leisure and supply less labor.

b. When the wage rate is low, an increase in the wage rate leads to an increase in the quantity of labor supplied because the substitution effect is greater than the income effect. Therefore, the labor supply curve slopes upward. When the wage rate is high, the income effect may be greater than the substitution effect. If this is so, the quantity of labor supplied will decrease as the wage increases and the labor supply curve would be backward-bending.

Diff: 2   Type: SA   Page Ref: 540-541/540-541
Topic: The supply of labor
Skill: Conceptual
Objective: LO 2: Explain how people choose the quantity of labor to supply
AACSB Coding: Reflective Thinking
Special Feature: None

16.3   Equilibrium in the Labor Market

1. If the labor supply is unchanged an increase in the demand for labor will
   A) increase the equilibrium wage and decrease the number of workers employed.
   B) increase the equilibrium wage and increase the quantity demanded of jobs.
   C) decrease the equilibrium wage and increase the number of workers employed.
   D) increase the equilibrium wage and increase the number of workers employed.

Answer: D

Diff: 1   Type: MC   Page Ref: 543/543
Topic: Labor market equilibrium
Skill: Analytical
Objective: LO 3: Explain how equilibrium wages are determined in labor markets
AACSB Coding: Analytic Skills
Special Feature: None

2. Michael Spence proposed the signaling hypothesis. According to this hypothesis
   A) workers signal their desire to work for a particular firm by the way they answer questions in job interviews.
   B) employers signal their preferences for the type of employee they wish to hire through job ads and the questions they ask during job interviews.
   C) employers view a college education as a signal that potential workers have certain desirable qualities.
   D) high wages are a signal that workers have skills that are highly valued by employers.

Answer: C
Diff: 1   Type: MC   Page Ref: 544–545/544–545
Topic: Signaling hypothesis
Skill: Conceptual
Objective: LO 3: Explain how equilibrium wages are determined in labor markets
AACSB Coding: Reflective Thinking
Special Feature: Making the Connection: Will Your future Income Depend on Which Courses You Take in College?

3. Daniel Hammermesh and Stephen Donald studied the determinants of the earnings of college graduates years after they graduated. Which of the following is one result of their study?
   A) The earnings of identical twins were about 9 percent higher than the earnings of all other students.
   B) Students, who had taken 15 credits of upper–division science and mathematics courses, and earned high grades in these courses, earned about 10 percent more than students who took no upper–division classes in these subjects.
   C) Students who took more Advanced Placement (AP) courses while still in high school earned significantly more income for each AP course they passed with a grade of 4 or 5.
   D) Students who took at least three economics courses earned more about 9 percent more income than students who took no college economics courses.

Answer: B
Diff: 1   Type: MC   Page Ref: 544–545/544–545
Topic: Explaining differences in wages
Skill: Fact
Objective: LO 3: Explain how equilibrium wages are determined in labor markets
AACSB Coding: Reflective Thinking
Special Feature: Making the Connection: Will Your future Income Depend on Which Courses You Take in College?

4. Which of the following summarizes the impact of population growth on the labor market?
    A) This will increase the labor supply, reduce the equilibrium wage and increase the quantity of labor demanded.
    B) There will be an increase in the demand for labor. As a result, the wage rate will rise and the quantity of workers supplied will decrease.
    C) There will be an increase in the demand for jobs. This will result in an increase in the equilibrium wage rate and a movement along the labor supply curve.
    D) There will be an increase in both the demand for labor and the supply of labor. As a result, the equilibrium wage will not change.
Answer: A
Diff: 2   Type: MC   Page Ref: 545–546/545–546
Topic: Labor market equilibrium
Skill: Analytical
Objective: LO 3: Explain how equilibrium wages are determined in labor markets
AACSB Coding: Analytic Skills
Special Feature: None

5. Which of the following would cause an increase in the equilibrium wage?
    A) The supply of labor increases more than the demand for labor.
    B) The supply of jobs increases more than the demand for jobs.
    C) The demand for labor increases faster than the supply of labor.
    D) The supply of labor increases and the demand for labor decreases.
Answer: C
Diff: 2   Type: MC   Page Ref: 545–546/545–546
Topic: Labor market equilibrium
Skill: Conceptual
Objective: LO 3: Explain how equilibrium wages are determined in labor markets
AACSB Coding: Reflective Thinking
Special Feature: None

6. Walt Disney's hit 1994 film *The Lion King* caused movie studios to produce more animated films. How did this affect the salaries of animators?
   A) The supply of animators increased more than the demand increased. As a result, there was a large decline in the salaries of animators. The continued popularity of animated films later increased the demand for animators; as a result, by 2002 salaries of the top animators exceeded $500,000.
   B) The demand for animators increased more than the supply. As a result, animators' salaries increased. After several animated firms between 1999 and 2001 failed to earn profits the demand for animators, and their salaries, decreased.
   C) Other movie studios increased production of animated films. The demand for animators increased and so did their salaries. The continued success of animated films at the box office after 1994 led to further increases in animators' salaries, some of which exceeded $500,000 by 2002.
   D) As other movie studies produced animated films, the supply of animators increased more than the demand. As a result, animators' salaries fell continually after 1994.
   Answer: B
   Diff: 2   Type: MC   Page Ref: 545–546/545–546
   Topic: Labor market equilibrium
   Skill: Fact
   Objective: LO 3: Explain how equilibrium wages are determined in labor markets
   AACSB Coding: Reflective Thinking
   Special Feature: None

7. Relative to its population, the largest wave of immigration occurred in the United States during which period of time?
   A) From 1990 to the present, mostly due to immigration from Central and South America
   B) From 1850 to 1870, mostly from Europe; many of these immigrants fought in the Civil War.
   C) From 1945 to 1955, mostly from Western Europe and South America.
   D) From 1900 to 1914.
   Answer: D
   Diff: 1   Type: MC   Page Ref: 546–547/546–547
   Topic: Shifts in labor supply
   Skill: Fact
   Objective: LO 3: Explain how equilibrium wages are determined in labor markets
   AACSB Coding: Reflective Thinking
   Special Feature: Making the Connection: Immigration and Wages, Then and Now

8. Despite an increase in immigration that led to a large increase in the supply of labor, wages in manufacturing rose in the United States between 1900 and 1914. Which of the following explains this fact?
    A) The demand for labor in manufacturing industries rose more than the supply of labor.
    B) Most of the workers who immigrated to the United States between 1900 and 1914 did not seek manufacturing jobs. Most of them found work in service industries.
    C) Many of the immigrants to the United States found jobs in agriculture because they had similar jobs in the countries they immigrated from.
    D) The demand for manufacturing jobs increased more than the supply of manufacturing jobs.
    Answer: A
    Diff: 1   Type: MC   Page Ref: 546–547/546–547
    Topic: Shifts in labor supply
    Skill: Fact
    Objective: LO 3: Explain how equilibrium wages are determined in labor markets
    AACSB Coding: Reflective Thinking
    Special Feature: Making the Connection: Immigration and Wages, Then and Now

9. In recent years illegal immigration into the United States has increased the supply of labor in some occupations. Which of the following occupations has experienced the biggest increase in the supply of labor from illegal immigration?
    A) Roofers.
    B) Dishwashers.
    C) Waiters and waitresses.
    D) Cooks.
    Answer: A
    Diff: 1   Type: MC   Page Ref: 546–547/546–547
    Topic: The supply of labor
    Skill: Fact
    Objective: LO 3: Explain how equilibrium wages are determined in labor markets
    AACSB Coding: Reflective Thinking
    Special Feature: Making the Connection: Immigration and Wages, Then and Now

10. Suppose the labor market is in equilibrium. Which of the following statements is *false*?
    A) The equilibrium wage rate is equal to the marginal revenue product of labor.
    B) At the equilibrium wage the quantity demanded of labor equals the quantity supplied of labor.
    C) Some workers will earn more than the equilibrium wage.
    D) At the equilibrium wage the demand for labor is equal to the supply of labor.
    Answer: D
    Diff: 2   Type: MC   Page Ref: 545–547/545–547
    Topic: Labor market equilibrium
    Skill: Conceptual
    Objective: LO 3: Explain how equilibrium wages are determined in labor markets
    AACSB Coding: Reflective Thinking
    Special Feature: None

11. If the demand for labor is unchanged, an increase in the supply of labor will lead to
    A) a decrease in the quantity demanded of labor and a decrease in the equilibrium wage.
    B) an increase in the quantity demanded of labor and a decrease in the equilibrium wage.
    C) an increase in the quantity demanded of labor and an increase in the equilibrium wage.
    D) a decrease in the quantity demanded of labor and an increase in the equilibrium wage.
    Answer: B
    Diff: 2   Type: MC   Page Ref: 545–547/545–547
    Topic: Shifts in labor supply
    Skill: Conceptual
    Objective: LO 3: Explain how equilibrium wages are determined in labor markets
    AACSB Coding: Reflective Thinking
    Special Feature: None

12. How will an increase in labor productivity affect equilibrium in the labor market?
    A) The supply of labor will increase and the equilibrium wage and quantity of labor will increase.
    B) The demand for jobs will increase and the equilibrium wage and quantity of labor will increase.
    C) The demand for labor will increase and the equilibrium wage and quantity of labor will increase.
    D) The demand for labor will decrease because fewer workers will be needed to produce the same output. The equilibrium wage and quantity of labor will decrease.
    Answer: C
    Diff: 2   Type: MC   Page Ref: 545–547/545–547
    Topic: Labor market equilibrium
    Skill: Conceptual
    Objective: LO 3: Explain how equilibrium wages are determined in labor markets
    AACSB Coding: Reflective Thinking
    Special Feature: None

13. If the demand for labor is unchanged, population growth will increase the supply of labor and increase the equilibrium wage.
    Answer: True   ◌ False
    Diff: 1   Type: TF   Page Ref: 545/545
    Topic: The supply of labor
    Skill: Conceptual
    Objective: LO 3: Explain how equilibrium wages are determined in labor markets
    AACSB Coding: Reflective Thinking
    Special Feature: None

14. Relative to its population, the largest wave of immigration into the United States occurred between 1900 and 1914.
    Answer: ◌ True   False
    Diff: 2   Type: TF   Page Ref: 546–547/546–547
    Topic: The supply of labor
    Skill: Fact
    Objective: LO 3: Explain how equilibrium wages are determined in labor markets
    AACSB Coding: Reflective Thinking
    Special Feature: None

15. Consider the market for nurses in a given city. In each of the following cases, explain what happens to the equilibrium wage rate and the quantity of nurses hired.

    a. One of the major hospitals in the city closes.
    b. A record number of students graduate with bachelor's degrees in nursing.
    c. Traditionally, nursing is a field that attracts women. However, changes in access to education and to the labor force participation rate by women have led to a greater demand for the services of women in a wide range of occupations. The demand for nurses, however, does not change.
    d. Advances in medical technology reduce the amount of time physicians must spend with patients in intensive care and increase the time that nurses spend with patients.

    Answer: a. The demand curve shifts to the left. The equilibrium wage decreases and the equilibrium quantity of nurses hired decreases.
    b. The supply curve shifts to the right. The equilibrium wage decreases and the equilibrium quantity of nurses hired increases.
    c. The supply curve shifts to the left. The equilibrium wage increases and the equilibrium quantity of nurses hired decreases.
    d. The demand curve shifts to the right. Both the equilibrium wage and the quantity of nurses hired increase.

    Diff: 2   Type: SA   Page Ref: 543–546/543–546
    Topic: Labor market equilibrium
    Skill: Analytical
    Objective: LO 3: Explain how equilibrium wages are determined in labor markets
    AACSB Coding: Analytic Skills
    Special Feature: None

16. Economist Michael Spence uses a concept called the "signaling hypothesis" to argue that college graduates don't earn high incomes because the skills they learned while in college serve to increase their productivity. Explain the signaling hypothesis. Is there evidence that the signaling hypothesis is not valid?

    Answer: Spence used the signaling hypothesis to argue that employers use college degrees as evidence that workers acquired or honed skills while they were in college that will make them good employees. Successful students must study, show up on time and occasionally work with other students in order to complete projects – all skills that will make them successful after graduation. The signaling hypothesis suggests that it is these skills, rather than skills acquired while taking specific subjects (calculus, U.S. history or accounting), that employers value most. Research by several economists has contradicted the signaling hypothesis because the studies have shown that earnings of colleges graduates vary based on the types and number of courses they take in specific disciplines (for example, science and mathematics).

    Diff: 2   Type: ES   Page Ref: 546–547/546–547
    Topic: Signaling hypothesis
    Skill: Analytical
    Objective: LO 3: Explain how equilibrium wages are determined in labor markets
    AACSB Coding: Analytic Skills
    Special Feature: None

16.4 Explaining Differences in Wages

1. One reason why the average salary of Major League Baseball players is higher than the average salary of college professors is
   A) the careers of most baseball players are much shorter than the careers of most college professors.
   B) the marginal revenue product of baseball players is greater than the marginal revenue product of college professors.
   C) college professors accept lower salaries in exchange for better working conditions.
   D) competition among baseball club owners forces player salaries to be much higher than the players' marginal revenue products.

   Answer: B
   Diff: 1   Type: MC   Page Ref: 548–549/548–549
   Topic: Explaining differences in wages
   Skill: Conceptual
   Objective: LO 4: Use demand and supply analysis to explain how compensating differentials, discrimination, and labor unions cause wages to differ
   AACSB Coding: Reflective Thinking
   Special Feature: None

2. Alfonso Soriano's marginal product as a baseball player would be about the same as a Chicago Cub and a Washington National. Why were the Cubs willing to pay Soriano a higher salary than he was paid as a Washington National?
   A) The Cubs play in Wrigley Field, an old ballpark that was paid for long ago. The Nationals have a new expensive ballpark. The Nationals could not afford to pay Soriano a higher salary while they were still paying for their ballpark.
   B) The Cubs play more home games than the Nationals. As a result, the Cubs earn more revenue from ticket sales that they can use to pay player salaries.
   C) Soriano's marginal revenue product is higher as a Cub that it was as a National.
   D) The owners of the Cubs were under more pressure from their fans and the Chicago media to pay Soriano a higher salary than the Nationals were willing to pay.

   Answer: C
   Diff: 1   Type: MC   Page Ref: 548–549/548–549
   Topic: Marginal revenue product of labor
   Skill: Conceptual
   Objective: LO 4: Use demand and supply analysis to explain how compensating differentials, discrimination, and labor unions cause wages to differ
   AACSB Coding: Reflective Thinking
   Special Feature: None

3. The total value to society of having garbage removed is greater than the value of baseball games. Why, then, are baseball players paid more than garbage collectors?
   A) Although the total value of garbage removal is greater than the total value of baseball, wages are determined by average values.
   B) Garbage removal results in significant external benefits that are not captured in the price paid for garbage removal. As a result, wages of garbage collectors do not reflect their social benefits.
   C) There is greater competition in the garbage collection industry than there is in Major League Baseball.
   D) Wages do not depend on total values but marginal values. The marginal revenue product of baseball players exceeds the marginal revenue product of garbage collectors.

Answer: D
Diff: 1   Type: MC   Page Ref: 549/549
Topic: Explaining differences in wages
Skill: Conceptual
Objective: LO 4: Use demand and supply analysis to explain how compensating differentials, discrimination, and labor unions cause wages to differ
AACSB Coding: Reflective Thinking
Special Feature: Don't let This Happen to YOU!: Remember That Prices and Wages Are Determined at the Margin

4. The difference between the salaries paid to movie stars and actors who play supporting roles is much greater today than it was in the 1930s and 1940s. What factor explains this increase in relative salaries over time?
   A) Technological advances in the entertainment industry increase the revenue that successful movies can earn. This has increased the movie studios' willingness to pay high salaries to movie stars.
   B) Agents of movies stars are effective in obtaining large salaries for their clients today. Few movie stars had agents to negotiate for them in the 1930s and 1940s.
   C) The studio system that dominated the industry in the 1930s and 1940s no longer exists. The studio system allowed movie studios to sign actors to long-term contracts that kept salaries down.
   D) There was no actors' union in the 1930s and 1940s. The rise of strong actors' unions has caused salaries of movies stars to be greater today than in previous years.

Answer: A
Diff: 1   Type: MC   Page Ref: 549-550/549-550
Topic: Explaining differences in wages
Skill: Conceptual
Objective: LO 4: Use demand and supply analysis to explain how compensating differentials, discrimination, and labor unions cause wages to differ
AACSB Coding: Reflective Thinking
Special Feature: Making the Connection: Technology and the Earnings of "Superstars"

5. Differences in marginal revenue products are the most important factor in explaining wage differences. Other factors that explain wage differences include all but one of the following. Which factor does not help explain differences in wages?
    A) Cognitive differentials.
    B) Compensating differentials.
    C) Discrimination.
    D) Labor unions.
Answer: A
Diff: 1   Type: MC   Page Ref: 550/550
Topic: Explaining differences in wages
Skill: Fact
Objective: LO 4: Use demand and supply analysis to explain how compensating differentials, discrimination, and labor unions cause wages to differ
AACSB Coding: Reflective Thinking
Special Feature: None

6. Most economists believe that a small amount of the gap between the wages of white males and the wages of other groups is due to discrimination. Which of the following factors is *not* another factor that explains part of this gap?
    A) Differences in education.
    B) Geographic location.
    C) Differences in experience.
    D) Differing preferences for jobs.
Answer: B
Diff: 2   Type: MC   Page Ref: 551/551
Topic: Explaining differences in wages
Skill: Conceptual
Objective: LO 4: Use demand and supply analysis to explain how compensating differentials, discrimination, and labor unions cause wages to differ
AACSB Coding: Reflective Thinking
Special Feature: None

7. An organization of employees that has the legal right to bargain with employers about wages and working conditions is called a
    A) closed shop.
    B) guild.
    C) labor union.
    D) monopsony.
Answer: C
Diff: 1   Type: MC   Page Ref: 556/556
Topic: Labor unions
Skill: Definition
Objective: LO 4: Use demand and supply analysis to explain how compensating differentials, discrimination, and labor unions cause wages to differ
AACSB Coding: Reflective Thinking
Special Feature: None

8. Competitive markets tend to eliminate economic discrimination, but there are many historical examples of firms that hired few, or no, black or female workers. Which of the following is not a reason for the persistence of this form of discrimination?
    A) In many cases, white workers refused to work with black workers.
    B) Some white consumers were unwilling to buy from companies that employed black workers.
    C) If discrimination makes it difficult for a member of a group to be hired in a particular occupation there is less incentive for members of the group to be trained to enter that occupation.
    D) Laws passed by the federal government made it more expensive to hire black or female workers. As a result, it was less expensive for employers to hire mostly white male workers.
Answer: D
Diff: 2   Type: MC   Page Ref: 554–556/554–556
Topic: Economic discrimination
Skill: Conceptual
Objective: LO 4: Use demand and supply analysis to explain how compensating differentials, discrimination, and labor unions cause wages to differ
AACSB Coding: Reflective Thinking
Special Feature: None

9. Paying a person a lower wage or excluding a person from an occupation on the basis of an irrelevant characteristic such as race or gender
    A) is economic discrimination.
    B) violates federal comparable worth laws.
    C) can be explained by negative feedback loops.
    D) creates differences in wages that economists call "compensating differentials."
Answer: A
Diff: 1   Type: MC   Page Ref: 551/551
Topic: Explaining differences in wages
Skill: Definition
Objective: LO 4: Use demand and supply analysis to explain how compensating differentials, discrimination, and labor unions cause wages to differ
AACSB Coding: Reflective Thinking
Special Feature: None

10. Larry and Mike are equally skilled construction workers employed by the Brown and Root Company. Larry's job is riskier because he typically works on a scaffold 1,000 feet above ground. Larry's higher wage rate is the result of
    A) economic discrimination.
    B) a compensating differential.
    C) a negative feedback loop.
    D) a higher marginal revenue product.
    Answer: B
    Diff: 1   Type: MC   Page Ref: 550/550
    Topic: Explaining differences in wages
    Skill: Conceptual
    Objective: LO 4: Use demand and supply analysis to explain how compensating differentials, discrimination, and labor unions cause wages to differ
    AACSB Coding: Reflective Thinking
    Special Feature: None

11. Wage differences can be explained by all of the following except
    A) compensating differentials.
    B) differences in marginal revenue products.
    C) economic discrimination.
    D) comparable worth.
    Answer: D
    Diff: 1   Type: MC   Page Ref: 550–554/550–554
    Topic: Explaining differences in wages
    Skill: Fact
    Objective: LO 4: Use demand and supply analysis to explain how compensating differentials, discrimination, and labor unions cause wages to differ
    AACSB Coding: Reflective Thinking
    Special Feature: None

12. According to two economists, George Ackerlof and William Dickens, how can cognitive dissonance affect workers' perceptions of their jobs?
    A) Cognitive dissonance makes workers believe that measures to improve their health and safety in the workplace are ineffective.
    B) Cognitive dissonance causes workers to perceive they are victims of discrimination when, in fact, they are not.
    C) Cognitive dissonance might cause workers to underestimate the true risks of their jobs.
    D) Cognitive dissonance causes a worker to believe his marginal revenue product is greater than it really is.
    Answer: C
    Diff: 3   Type: MC   Page Ref: 550–551/550–551
    Topic: Compensating differentials
    Skill: Conceptual
    Objective: LO 4: Use demand and supply analysis to explain how compensating differentials, discrimination, and labor unions cause wages to differ
    AACSB Coding: Reflective Thinking
    Special Feature: None

13. One implication of compensating differentials is that laws passed to protect the health and safety of workers may not make workers better off than they were prior to the passages of the laws. Why is this so?
    A) Workers may suffer from cognitive dissonance, which means that the perception workers have that their jobs are hazardous is not true.
    B) If the laws make the work environment safer, there is no reason to pay workers a compensating differential for the risk associated with their jobs.
    C) The principal–agent problem that exists in the workplace may cause workers to shirk more after the work environment becomes safer.
    D) In non–competitive markets workers are unlikely to receive a compensating differential to compensate for jobs with extra risk. As a result, after the laws are passed their wages will not change.
    Answer: B
    Diff: 2   Type: MC   Page Ref: 550–551/550–551
    Topic: Compensating differentials
    Skill: Conceptual
    Objective: LO 4: Use demand and supply analysis to explain how compensating differentials, discrimination, and labor unions cause wages to differ
    AACSB Coding: Reflective Thinking
    Special Feature: None

14. Phil Harrison is a welder who works on skyscrapers and extension bridges. Phil's brother William is also a welder but he works in a manufacturing plant where he does all of his welding on ground level. Which of the following would *not* explain why Phil earns a higher wage than his brother?
    A) Cognitive dissonance.
    B) Phil has greater experience as a welder than his brother has.
    C) Phil's marginal revenue product is greater than William's marginal revenue product.
    D) Phil's job is more hazardous than William's job.
    Answer: A
    Diff: 2   Type: MC   Page Ref: 550–551/550–551
    Topic: Compensating differentials
    Skill: Conceptual
    Objective: LO 4: Use demand and supply analysis to explain how compensating differentials, discrimination, and labor unions cause wages to differ
    AACSB Coding: Reflective Thinking
    Special Feature: None

15. Marsha Murphy complained, "Many jobs that are filled mostly by men offer higher wages than most jobs that are typically filled by women. In many cases, the jobs men have require the same education and skills as the jobs women have. This is clearly unfair. Women should be paid the same wages as men are paid for jobs that are equivalent in terms of their qualifications." Which of the following statements describes Marsha's position?
    A) Marsha believes that women's wages should include a compensating differential.
    B) Marsha believes employers assume that men and women have different job preferences.
    C) Marsha believes that employers are reluctant to hire women for certain jobs because of cognitive dissonance.
    D) Marsha endorses a concept called comparable worth.
    Answer: D
    Diff: 2   Type: MC   Page Ref: 553–554/553–554
    Topic: Comparable worth
    Skill: Conceptual
    Objective: LO 4: Use demand and supply analysis to explain how compensating differentials, discrimination, and labor unions cause wages to differ
    AACSB Coding: Reflective Thinking
    Special Feature: Solved Problem: Is "Comparable Worth" Legislation the Answer to Closing the Gap between Men's and Women's Pay?

16. Assume that a comparable worth law is passed that determines that kindergarten teachers and bricklayers have comparable jobs; therefore, workers in both of these occupations should be paid the same wages. Assume that prior to the law bricklayers were paid a higher wage than kindergarten teachers. Which of the following is the most likely result of the comparable worth law?
    A) The equilibrium wage will be the same for kindergarten teachers and bricklayers.
    B) Some former bricklayers will become kindergarten teachers and some former kindergarten teachers will become bricklayers.
    C) There will be a shortage in the market for bricklayers and a surplus in the market for kindergarten teachers.
    D) There will be surplus in the market for bricklayers and a shortage in the market for kindergarten teachers.
    Answer: C
    Diff: 2   Type: MC   Page Ref: 553–554/553–554
    Topic: Comparable worth
    Skill: Conceptual
    Objective: LO 4: Use demand and supply analysis to explain how compensating differentials, discrimination, and labor unions cause wages to differ
    AACSB Coding: Reflective Thinking
    Special Feature: Solved Problem: Is "Comparable Worth" Legislation the Answer to Closing the Gap between Men's and Women's Pay?

17. Many economists are critical of proposals to pass comparable worth legislation. Which of the following is the best explanation for this criticism?
    A) Comparable worth legislation will only lead to efficient market outcomes if women in low-paying jobs suffer from cognitive dissonance.
    B) Proposals for comparable worth legislation assume that wages for low-paying women's jobs should include compensating differentials. Economists believe that compensating differentials should be part of the wages for all jobs held by women.
    C) Proposals for comparable worth legislation call for increases in the wages of jobs held predominantly by women. Economists believe that this legislation should be used to increase the wages of all workers.
    D) Many economists believe that allowing markets to determine wages, rather than the rules required by comparable worth legislation, results in more efficient outcomes.
    Answer: D
    Diff: 2   Type: MC   Page Ref: 553–554/553–554
    Topic: Comparable worth
    Skill: Conceptual
    Objective: LO 4: Use demand and supply analysis to explain how compensating differentials, discrimination, and labor unions cause wages to differ
    AACSB Coding: Reflective Thinking
    Special Feature: Solved Problem: Is "Comparable Worth" Legislation the Answer to Closing the Gap between Men's and Women's Pay?

18. A number of economists have estimated the impact of unionization on workers' wages. Which of the following is one conclusion reached by these studies?
    A) Union workers earn less than they would if they were not unionized. This is because of the impact of workers' strikes, during which union members do not receive wages.
    B) Holding constant the impact of other factors that affect wages, being in a union has no impact on a worker's wages.
    C) Being in a union increases a worker's wages by about 10 percent, holding constant other factors that influence wages.
    D) The share of national income received by workers has increased significantly over time; unions have been responsible for about one-half of the increase in workers' share of national income from the end of World War II to 2000.
    Answer: C
    Diff: 2   Type: MC   Page Ref: 556–557/556–557
    Topic: Labor unions
    Skill: Fact
    Objective: LO 4: Use demand and supply analysis to explain how compensating differentials, discrimination, and labor unions cause wages to differ
    AACSB Coding: Reflective Thinking
    Special Feature: None

19. Compensating differentials are associated most closely with which of the following?
    A) Hazardous jobs.
    B) Comparable worth.
    C) Economic discrimination.
    D) Differences in education.

Answer: A
Diff: 1   Type: MC   Page Ref: 550/550
Topic: Compensating differentials
Skill: Conceptual
Objective: LO 4: Use demand and supply analysis to explain how compensating differentials, discrimination, and labor unions cause wages to differ
AACSB Coding: Reflective Thinking
Special Feature: None

20. Higher wages that compensate workers for unpleasant aspects of a job are called compensating differentials.

Answer: ⊙ True   False
Diff: 1   Type: TF   Page Ref: 550/550
Topic: Compensating differentials
Skill: Definition
Objective: LO 4: Use demand and supply analysis to explain how compensating differentials, discrimination, and labor unions cause wages to differ
AACSB Coding: Reflective Thinking
Special Feature: None

21. Most economists believe that only a small gap between the wages of white males and the wages of other groups is due to education; most of the gap is explained by discrimination.

Answer: True   ⊙ False
Diff: 1   Type: TF   Page Ref: 551/551
Topic: Economic discrimination
Skill: Conceptual
Objective: LO 4: Use demand and supply analysis to explain how compensating differentials, discrimination, and labor unions cause wages to differ
AACSB Coding: Reflective Thinking
Special Feature: None

22. The Equal Pay Act of 1963 requires that men and women be given equal pay for equal work in the same establishment. Most people agree that gender discrimination in the workplace is unfair, but many economists have criticized advocates of comparable worth. Is paying the same wages for jobs that have comparable worth mandated by the Equal Pay Act? Why don't most economists support proposals to force employers to pay their male and female employees based on comparable worth rules?

Answer: It would be hard to find anyone, economists included, who would argue against paying men and women equal pay for the same job in the same establishment. It is unfair, and illegal under the Equal Pay Act, to pay different wages to a male and a female employee who work next to each other on an assembly line doing similar tasks. A difficulty arises when the jobs performed by male and female workers are not the same, but have "comparable worth." The Equal Pay Act does not require employers to pay their male and female workers the same wages for different jobs that have comparable worth. Economists who disagree with comparable worth proposals argue that wages are determined in the market by the demand and supply for jobs that call for different skills. Mandating that jobs with different skills pay the same wages in effect argues for price controls to be used to either reduce wages that are "too high" (jobs that have traditionally been filled by males) or raise wages that are "too low" (jobs that have traditionally been filled by females) or both. Most economists believe that such controls will lead to outcomes that are less efficient than outcomes determined by markets without controls.

Diff: 2   Type: ES   Page Ref: 553–554/553–554
Topic: Comparable worth
Skill: Conceptual
Objective: LO 4: Use demand and supply analysis to explain how compensating differentials, discrimination, and labor unions cause wages to differ
AACSB Coding: Reflective Thinking
Special Feature: None

23. In the medical profession, pediatricians receive lower salaries than cardiologists. Suppose the government passes comparable worth legislation that requires hospitals to pay pediatricians the same salaries as cardiologists. Explain the effect of this legislation and illustrate your answer with demand and supply graphs for the following two scenarios:
   a.   hospitals respond by placing salaries at a level between the two existing salaries
   b.   hospitals respond by placing pediatricians' salaries at the initial level of cardiologists.

Answer: a.　　　Refer to the diagram below.

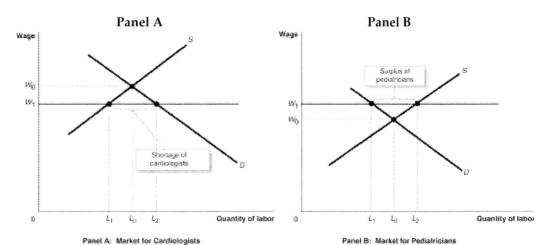

Panel A: Market for Cardiologists　　　Panel B: Market for Pediatricians

Panel A shows the market for cardiologists. Without comparable worth legislation, the equilibrium wage for cardiologists is W_0 per year, and the equilibrium number of cardiologists hired is L_0. Setting the wage for cardiologists below equilibrium at W_1 reduces the quantity who is willing to work in this occupation from L_0 to L_1 but increases the quantity demanded by employers from L_0 to L_2. The result is a shortage of cardiologists equal to $L_2 - L_1$, as shown in Panel A.

　　　Panel B shows the market for pediatricians. Without comparable worth legislation, the equilibrium wage for pediatricians is W_0 and the equilibrium quantity hired is L_0. Setting the wage for pediatricians above equilibrium at W_1 increases the number who want to work in this occupation from L_0 to L_2, but reduces the quantity demanded by employers from L_0 to L_1. The result is a surplus of pediatricians equal to $L_2 - L_1$, as shown in Panel B.

b.　　　Refer to the diagram below.

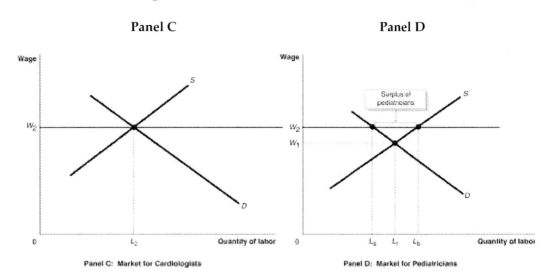

Panel C: Market for Cardiologists　　　Panel D: Market for Pediatricians

Panel C shows the market for cardiologists where the equilibrium wage is W_2 per year, and the equilibrium quantity of cardiologists hired is L_2. Panel D shows the market for pediatricians. Without comparable worth legislation, the equilibrium wage for pediatricians is W_1 per year and the equilibrium quantity hired is L_1. With comparable worth legislation, the wage for pediatricians is set at W_2 per year. Quantity supplied increases from L_1 to L_b, but quantity demanded by employers falls from L_1 to L_a, resulting in a surplus of pediatricians equal to $L_b - L_a$, as shown in Panel D.

Diff: 3   Type: SA   Page Ref: 553–554/553–554
Topic: Comparable worth
Skill: Analytical
Objective: LO 4: Use demand and supply analysis to explain how compensating differentials, discrimination, and labor unions cause wages to differ
AACSB Coding: Analytic Skills
Special Feature: None

16.5   Personnel Economics

1. The application of economic analysis to human resources issues is called
    A) resource economics.
    B) personnel economics.
    C) human economics.
    D) labor economics.
   Answer: B
   Diff: 1   Type: MC   Page Ref: 557/557
   Topic: Personnel economics
   Skill: Definition
   Objective: LO 5: Discuss he role personal economics can play in helping firms deal with human resources issues
   AACSB Coding: Reflective Thinking
   Special Feature: None

2. Mel's House of Cars is an automobile dealership that sells both new and used cars. Two other dealerships located nearer Mel's pay their salespeople a straight salary – they receive no commission for each car they sell. Mel has decided to pay all of his salespeople a commission on all car sales. Which of the following is most likely to occur as a result of Mel's decision?
    A) Mel will have difficulty finding salespeople. Research by labor economists has found that most employees prefer the security of a salary to the uncertainty of being paid based on how much revenue they generate for their employers.
    B) Mel will experience a principal–agent problem. Some of his salespeople will tend to shirk because they will not be paid if they sell no cars, regardless of how hard they work.
    C) Mel will be able to hire some of the most productive salespeople who work for the other two dealerships.
    D) Mel risks violation of federal law that regulates firms' compensation policies.
Answer: C
Diff: 2   Type: MC   Page Ref: 557–558/557–558
Topic: Compensation systems
Skill: Conceptual
Objective: LO 5: Discuss he role personal economics can play in helping firms deal with human resources issues
AACSB Coding: Reflective Thinking
Special Feature: None

3. Which of the following economists is best known for exploring the application of economic analysis to human resources issues?
    A) Edward Lazear
    B) Claudia Goldin
    C) David Hammermesh
    D) Alan Krueger
Answer: A
Diff: 1   Type: MC   Page Ref: 557/557
Topic: Personnel economics
Skill: Fact
Objective: LO 5: Discuss he role personal economics can play in helping firms deal with human resources issues
AACSB Coding: Reflective Thinking
Special Feature: None

4. The parent company of Safelite AutoGlass, the nation's largest installer of auto glass, changed the system it used to pay its glass installers in the mid–1990s. How did Safelite change its compensation system and what was the result?

    A) Safelite ended its system of paying workers on the basis of how many windows they repaired and replaced it with a system that paid workers hourly wages. As a result, productivity and worker morale improved.

    B) Safelite ended its system of paying workers hourly wages and replaced it with a system that determined wages on the basis of how many windows were repaired. As a result, productivity and worker morale suffered. Eventually, Safelite returned to its previous compensation system

    C) The new system has not been in place long enough to determine whether it is an improvement over the previous compensation system.

    D) Safelite ended its system of paying workers hourly wages and replaced it with a system that determined wages on the basis of how many windows were repaired. As a result, productivity and worker morale improved.

Answer: D

Diff: 2   Type: MC   Page Ref: 558–559/558–559
Topic: Compensation systems
Skill: Fact
Objective: LO 5: Discuss he role personal economics can play in helping firms deal with human resources issues
AACSB Coding: Reflective Thinking
Special Feature: Making the Connection: Raising Pay, Productivity, and Profits at Safelite AutoGlass

5. Edward Lazear analyzed data provided by the Safelite Group, the nation's largest installer of auto glass, after the company changed the way it paid its glass installers beginning in the mid–1990s. Instead of paying workers hourly wages, Safelite began to pay workers on the basis of how many windows they installed. Which of the following describes what Lazear concluded from his analysis of Safelite's data?

    A) Although workers installed more windows under the new system, Lazear found that there was also an increase in the number of workmanship–related defects. Lazear attributed this to workers taking short–cuts in order to earn higher wages. As a result, productivity did not improve and Safelite went back to paying hourly wages.

    B) Lazear found that worker productivity increased with the new system; about half of the increase in productivity was due to workers who continued with the company and half was due to new workers being more productive than those who left the company.

    C) Although worker productivity improved, the increase in hourly wages resulted in a significant decline in Safelite's profits.

    D) Because of a principal–agent problem, worker productivity was not affected by the new compensation system. However, Lazear attributed this to management problems that had nothing to do with Safelite's compensation system.

Answer: B

Diff: 2   Type: MC   Page Ref: 558–559/558–559
Topic: Making the Connection
Skill: Fact
Objective: LO 5: Discuss he role personal economics can play in helping firms deal with human resources issues
AACSB Coding: Reflective Thinking
Special Feature: Making the Connection: Raising Pay, Productivity, and Profits at Safelite AutoGlass

6. Despite evidence that companies will find it more profitable to use a commission system of compensation rather than a salary system, many companies continue to pay their workers salaries. Which of the following is one reason why firms choose a salary system?
    A) Most business owners and managers are not trained economists; therefore, they are unaware of the research that shows a commission system is more profitable than a salary system.
    B) Firms often use salary systems to overcome their principal–agent problems.
    C) Firms that have salary systems do not have to use compensating differentials to attract employees to do hazardous jobs.
    D) Many workers dislike risk and prefer to be paid a salary rather than to be paid by commission.
    Answer: D
    Diff: 2   Type: MC   Page Ref: 559/559
    Topic: Compensation systems
    Skill: Fact
    Objective: LO 5: Discuss he role personal economics can play in helping firms deal with human resources issues
    AACSB Coding: Reflective Thinking
    Special Feature: None

7. Which of the following is *not* a reason for firms to choose a salary system rather than a commission system to compensate their employees?
    A) Research has shown that most companies will find that a salary system will be more profitable than a commission system.
    B) It is often difficult to attribute output to particular workers.
    C) If workers are paid on the basis of the number of units of output they produce, they may become less concerned about quality.
    D) Commission compensation systems are riskier for employees than a salary system, and many workers dislike risk.
    Answer: A
    Diff: 2   Type: MC   Page Ref: 559/559
    Topic: Compensation systems
    Skill: Conceptual
    Objective: LO 5: Discuss he role personal economics can play in helping firms deal with human resources issues
    AACSB Coding: Reflective Thinking
    Special Feature: None

8. If it is difficult for a firm to attribute the output it produces to a particular worker then
    A) its employees are likely to form a union.
    B) a commission system of compensation will be preferable to a salary system.
    C) a salary compensation system will be preferable to a commission system.
    D) a piece-rate system of compensation will be preferable to a salary system.
    Answer: C
    Diff: 1   Type: MC   Page Ref: 559/559
    Topic: Compensation systems
    Skill: Fact
    Objective: LO 5: Discuss he role personal economics can play in helping firms deal with human resources issues
    AACSB Coding: Reflective Thinking
    Special Feature: None

9. Workers who dislike risk
    A) prefer to be paid monthly rather than weekly or daily.
    B) prefer a piece-rate compensation system to a salary system.
    C) prefer a salary system to a commission compensation system.
    D) prefer to be paid a salary rather than a wage.
    Answer: C
    Diff: 1   Type: MC   Page Ref: 559/559
    Topic: Compensation systems
    Skill: Fact
    Objective: LO 5: Discuss he role personal economics can play in helping firms deal with human resources issues
    AACSB Coding: Reflective Thinking
    Special Feature: None

10. One reason why firms would choose a salary system rather than a commission compensation system is that their employees might become less concerned about the quality of their work.
    Answer: ◉ True   False
    Diff: 2   Type: TF   Page Ref: 559/559
    Topic: Compensation systems
    Skill: Conceptual
    Objective: LO 5: Discuss he role personal economics can play in helping firms deal with human resources issues
    AACSB Coding: Reflective Thinking
    Special Feature: None

11. Wally, Vijay, Sandra and Consuela make up a software development team at Javasoft. The firm is considering implementing one of two incentive compensation schemes. In scheme A, each programmer receives an annual bonus if he or she meets all individual programming deadlines. In scheme B, members of the team share equally in a joint bonus if the team meets all of its product delivery deadlines. All four employees are equally talented but Wally is a slacker who does as little work as he can get away with. Which scheme might team members prefer? Which scheme will management prefer?

Answer: Team members (except Wally) prefer scheme A since it ensures that they are not denied the bonus because of one slacker. Team-based pay is only effective when the product is truly a team effort. In this case, scheme B may cause some resentment among team members especially since Wally is likely to be a "free-rider". Management favors scheme B because it is tied to the firm's goal of product delivery.

Diff: 2   Type: SA   Page Ref: 559/559
Topic: Compensation systems
Skill: Analytical
Objective: LO 5: Discuss he role personal economics can play in helping firms deal with human resources issues
AACSB Coding: Analytic Skills
Special Feature: None

16.6   The Market for Capital and Natural Resources

1. Marginal productivity theory implies that in a perfectly competitive market economy, a worker will receive income
    A) equal to the value of her marginal contribution to the production process.
    B) that is greater than the value of her marginal contribution to production process.
    C) that is less than the value of her marginal contribution to the production process.
    D) more, less or equal to the value of her marginal contribution to the production process, depending on her ability to negotiate with employers.

Answer: A
Diff: 1   Type: MC   Page Ref: 562–563/562–563
Topic: Marginal productivity theory of income distribution
Skill: Conceptual
Objective: LO 6: Show how equilibrium prices are determined in the markets for capital and natural resources
AACSB Coding: Reflective Thinking
Special Feature: None

2. Compared to a competitive market, a firm that has a monopsony in a labor market would
    A) hire fewer workers and pay higher wages.
    B) hire more workers and pay lower wages.
    C) hire fewer workers and pay lower wages.
    D) hire more workers and pay higher wages.
Answer: C
Diff: 1   Type: MC   Page Ref: 562/562
Topic: Monopsony
Skill: Conceptual
Objective: LO 6: Show how equilibrium prices are determined in the markets for capital and natural resources
AACSB Coding: Reflective Thinking
Special Feature: None

3. The labor market in Major League Baseball features
    A) a monopoly by the League in employing professional baseball players that is offset by the players' membership in a labor union.
    B) a monopsony by the League in employing professional baseball players that is offset by the players' membership in a labor union.
    C) an oligopoly by the League in employing professional baseball players that is offset by an oligopsony by the players in the labor market.
    D) monopolistic competition between the teams and professional baseball players.
Answer: B
Diff: 1   Type: MC   Page Ref: 562/562
Topic: Monopsony
Skill: Conceptual
Objective: LO 6: Show how equilibrium prices are determined in the markets for capital and natural resources
AACSB Coding: Reflective Thinking
Special Feature: None

4. The marginal productivity theory of income distribution was developed by
    A) Edward Lazear.
    B) George Akerlof.
    C) William Stanley Jevons.
    D) John Bates Clark.
Answer: D
Diff: 1   Type: MC   Page Ref: 563/563
Topic: Marginal productivity theory of income distribution
Skill: Fact
Objective: LO 6: Show how equilibrium prices are determined in the markets for capital and natural resources
AACSB Coding: Reflective Thinking
Special Feature: None

5. The marginal productivity theory of income distribution states that
    A) as more and more units of labor are added to a fixed quantity of capital, eventually labor's contribution to a firm's income will decrease.
    B) income distribution is determined by the marginal productivity of the factors of production that individuals own.
    C) factors of production in short supply command higher prices than those available in abundant quantities.
    D) capital owners receive the bulk of a nation's income because capital–intensive production generates productivity gains.
Answer: B
Diff: 1   Type: MC   Page Ref: 562–563/562–563
Topic: Marginal productivity theory of income distribution
Skill: Definition
Objective: LO 6: Show how equilibrium prices are determined in the markets for capital and natural resources
AACSB Coding: Reflective Thinking
Special Feature: None

6. A firm chooses its profit-maximizing quantity of capital by
    A) comparing the marginal revenue product of capital with the rental price of capital.
    B) comparing the price of capital with the price of labor.
    C) examining the total cost of capital equipment.
    D) determining the rate at which the firm can borrow funds to purchase plant and equipment.
Answer: A
Diff: 1   Type: MC   Page Ref: 560–561/560–561
Topic: The market for capital
Skill: Conceptual
Objective: LO 6: Show how equilibrium prices are determined in the markets for capital and natural resources
AACSB Coding: Reflective Thinking
Special Feature: None

7. The demand for capital is similar to the demand for labor in that
    A) the marginal product of labor is derived from the marginal product of capital.
    B) the marginal revenue product curve for labor is the same as the marginal revenue product curve for capital.
    C) both are derived demands.
    D) both are inelastic at high prices and elastic at low prices.
Answer: C
Diff: 1   Type: MC   Page Ref: 560–561/560–561
Topic: The market for capital
Skill: Conceptual
Objective: LO 6: Show how equilibrium prices are determined in the markets for capital and natural resources
AACSB Coding: Reflective Thinking
Special Feature: None

8. In general, the supply curve for a natural resource
    A) is vertical.
    B) is horizontal.
    C) slopes downward to reflect decreasing available quantities over time.
    D) slopes upward.
Answer: D
Diff: 1   Type: MC   Page Ref: 561–562/561–562
Topic: Supply of a resource
Skill: Conceptual
Objective: LO 6: Show how equilibrium prices are determined in the markets for capital and natural resources
AACSB Coding: Reflective Thinking
Special Feature: None

9. The price of a factor of production that is in fixed supply is called
    A) economic rent.
    B) economic profit.
    C) a compensating differential.
    D) opportunity cost.
Answer: A
Diff: 1   Type: MC   Page Ref: 561/561
Topic: Economic rent
Skill: Definition
Objective: LO 6: Show how equilibrium prices are determined in the markets for capital and natural resources
AACSB Coding: Reflective Thinking
Special Feature: None

10. Which of the following statements regarding equilibrium in the markets for capital and for a natural resource used in producing a good is true?
    A) The marginal revenue product of capital will equal the marginal revenue product of the natural resource.
    B) The rental price of capital will equal the price of the natural resource.
    C) The marginal product of capital will equal the rental price of capital and the marginal product of the natural resource will equal the price of the natural resource.
    D) The marginal revenue product of capital will equal the rental price of capital and the marginal revenue product of the natural resource will equal the price of the natural resource.
Answer: D
Diff: 2   Type: MC   Page Ref: 560–562/560–562
Topic: The market for natural resources
Skill: Conceptual
Objective: LO 6: Show how equilibrium prices are determined in the markets for capital and natural resources
AACSB Coding: Reflective Thinking
Special Feature: None

11. The Buda Agri Corporation is the sole employer in rural Hungary. In the labor market, Budi Agri is a
    A) monopolistic competitor.
    B) monopsony.
    C) monopoly.
    D) perfect competitor.
    Answer: B
    Diff: 1   Type: MC   Page Ref: 562/562
    Topic: Monopsony
    Skill: Fact
    Objective: LO 6: Show how equilibrium prices are determined in the markets for capital and natural resources
    AACSB Coding: Reflective Thinking
    Special Feature: None

12. If you were to ask your employer for a raise, which of the following would be your most effective argument?
    A) "I have a job offer at another firm that will pay me more than my current wage."
    B) "I am willing to work more hours each week."
    C) "Increases in my productivity have resulted in greater revenue and profits for your business."
    D) "My marginal product is greater than my current wage."
    Answer: C
    Diff: 1   Type: MC   Page Ref: 563/563
    Topic: Marginal revenue product of labor
    Skill: Conceptual
    Objective: LO 6: Show how equilibrium prices are determined in the markets for capital and natural resources
    AACSB Coding: Reflective Thinking
    Special Feature: Economics in YOUR Life!: Why Is It So Hard to Get a Raise?

13. In recent years members of auto racing pit crews have received higher salaries than pit crew members received prior to 1990. One explanation for the increase in salaries is
    A) the formation of a pit crew union in 1990 after a series of accidents that resulted in serious injuries to pit crew members.
    B) pit crew members spend more of their own money to become physically fit than pit crew members did before 1990.
    C) the realization of pit crew members that they deserved a compensating differential because of the hazardous nature of their work.
    D) NASCAR racing become more popular after 1990; as a result, the marginal revenue product of pit crew members increased.
    Answer: D
    Diff: 1   Type: MC   Page Ref: 564–565/564–565
    Topic: Marginal revenue product of labor
    Skill: Conceptual
    Objective: LO 6: Show how equilibrium prices are determined in the markets for capital and natural resources
    AACSB Coding: Reflective Thinking
    Special Feature: An Inside Look: Are Race Car Drivers Athletes? We Don't Know, but the Pit–Crew Members Are

14. A monopsony is a term used to refer to a firm that is the sole seller of a good or service.
    Answer: True   ◦ False
    Diff: 1   *Type: TF*   *Page Ref: 562/562*
    Topic: Monopsony
    Skill: Definition
    Objective: LO 6: Show how equilibrium prices are determined in the markets for capital and natural resources
    AACSB Coding: Reflective Thinking
    Special Feature: None

Chapter 17   The Economics of Information

17.1   Asymmetric Information

1. The difficulty insurance companies have in pricing their policies is due to
    A) an elastic demand for insurance.
    B) moral hazard.
    C) rational ignorance.
    D) asymmetric information.
    Answer: D
    Diff: 1   Type: MC   Page Ref: 574–5/574–5
    Topic: Asymmetric information
    Skill: Fact
    Objective: LO 1: Asymmetric Information
    AASCB Coding: Reflective Thinking
    Special Features: Chapter Opener: Why Does State Farm Charge Young Men So Much More Than Young Women for Auto Insurance?

2. The State Farm Insurance Company was founded by George Mecherle. Mercherle previously worked for another insurance company and decided to form his own company after
    A) he learned that his employer could charge clients lower insurance premiums and still make a profit.
    B) he realized that women had fewer accidents than men had.
    C) he realized that farmers had fewer accidents than people who lived in cities.
    D) he realized farmers were willing to pay more for insurance than people who lived in cities.
    Answer: C
    Diff: 1   Type: MC   Page Ref: 574–5/574–5
    Topic: The market for insurance
    Skill: Fact
    Objective: LO 1: Asymmetric Information
    AASCB Coding: Reflective Thinking
    Special Features: Chapter Opener: Why Does State Farm Charge Young Men So Much More Than Young Women for Auto Insurance?

3. George Mecherle started the State Farm Mutual Insurance Company. A key to the success of Mecherle's company was
    A) that his company could charge lower insurance rates to farmers because they had fewer accidents than people who lived in cities.
    B) the realization that State Farm could charge higher premiums than other companies were charging because the demand for car insurance is inelastic.
    C) selling more than one type of insurance (for example, automobile and home insurance) to the same customers.
    D) realizing that selling insurance could lead to adverse selection.

Answer: A
Diff: 1   Type: MC   Page Ref: 574-5/574-5
Topic: The market for insurance
Skill: Fact
Objective: LO 1: Asymmetric Information
AASCB Coding: Reflective Thinking
Special Features: Chapter Opener: Why Does State Farm Charge Young Men So Much More Than Young Women for Auto Insurance?

4. In recent years, insurance companies have changed the way they price their policies. How are automobile insurance policies priced differently today than in the past?
    A) Premiums are much lower for drivers who are under 25 years old.
    B) As a result of the use of computer models, there has been an increase in the number of different prices charged to drivers.
    C) Drivers who have the most elastic demand for insurance are charged the highest premiums.
    D) Farmers are charged lower prices than drivers who live in cities because farmers have fewer accidents.

Answer: B
Diff: 1   Type: MC   Page Ref: 574-5/574-5
Topic: The market for insurance
Skill: Fact
Objective: LO 1: Asymmetric Information
AASCB Coding: Reflective Thinking
Special Features: Chapter Opener: Why Does State Farm Charge Young Men So Much More Than Young Women for Auto Insurance?

5. In the market for insurance
    A) buyers often have more information than sellers.
    B) sellers often have better information than buyers.
    C) sellers are protected from lawsuits brought by buyers.
    D) demand is perfectly inelastic because, by law, home owners and automobile drivers must have insurance.

Answer: A
Diff: 1   Type: MC   Page Ref: 576/576
Topic: The market for insurance
Skill: Conceptual
Objective: LO 1: Asymmetric Information
AASCB Coding: Reflective Thinking
Special Features: None

6. What is the term that describes a situation in which one party to an economic transaction has less information than the other party?
    A) Inefficient market hypothesis
    B) Asymmetric information
    C) Unequal market structure
    D) Monopsony
Answer: B
Diff: 1   Type: MC   Page Ref: 576/576
Topic: Asymmetric information
Skill: Definition
Objective: LO 1: Asymmetric Information
AASCB Coding: Reflective Thinking
Special Features: None

7. The term that is used to refer to a situation in which one party to an economic transaction has less information than the other party is
    A) inefficient market hypothesis.
    B) moral hazard.
    C) information disparity.
    D) asymmetric information.
Answer: D
Diff: 1   Type: MC   Page Ref: 576/576
Topic: Asymmetric information
Skill: Definition
Objective: LO 1: Asymmetric Information
AASCB Coding: Reflective Thinking
Special Features: None

8. Pricing insurance policies is made difficult because buyers have more information than sellers. This difficulty is an example of
    A) moral hazard.
    B) adverse selection.
    C) asymmetric information.
    D) the free rider problem
Answer: C
Diff: 1   Type: MC   Page Ref: 576/576
Topic: Asymmetric information
Skill: Conceptual
Objective: LO 1: Asymmetric Information
AASCB Coding: Reflective Thinking
Special Features: None

9. The study of the problems due to asymmetric information was begun when economists analyzed which type of market?
    A) The market for citrus fruit.
    B) The market for insurance.
    C) Farmers' markets.
    D) The market for automobiles.
Answer: D
Diff: 1   Type: MC   Page Ref: 576/576
Topic: Asymmetric information
Skill: Conceptual
Objective: LO 1: Asymmetric Information
AASCB Coding: Reflective Thinking
Special Features: None

10. Which of the following Nobel laureates became known for the study of asymmetric information?
    A) Gary Becker
    B) Michael Spence
    C) George Ackerlof
    D) Ronald Coase
Answer: C
Diff: 1   Type: MC   Page Ref: 576/576
Topic: Asymmetric information
Skill: Fact
Objective: LO 1: Asymmetric Information
AASCB Coding: Reflective Thinking
Special Features: None

11. Adverse selection will occur in a market as a result of
    A) asymmetric information.
    B) moral hazard.
    C) the sale of "lemons."
    D) rational ignorance.
Answer: A
Diff: 1   Type: MC   Page Ref: 576–7/576–7
Topic: Adverse selection
Skill: Conceptual
Objective: LO 1: Asymmetric Information
AASCB Coding: Reflective Thinking
Special Features: None

12. Which of the following is an example of adverse selection?
    A) The odds of a fire rise after a building is insured because the person with fire insurance is likely to pay less attention to fire hazards.
    B) Someone who did not install fire alarms and a sprinkler system in a building he owns buys insurance for the building.
    C) Someone with automobile insurance drives more recklessly than someone without insurance.
    D) People prefer to buy new cars rather than used cars.
    Answer: B
    Diff: 1   Type: MC   Page Ref: 576–7/576–7
    Topic: Adverse selection
    Skill: Conceptual
    Objective: LO 1: Asymmetric Information
    AASCB Coding: Reflective Thinking
    Special Features: None

13. Adverse selection occurs in the market for used cars because used car buyers
    A) have more information than used car sellers.
    B) have less information than used car sellers.
    C) have less incentive to maintain the value of their cars than new car buyers.
    D) tend to have more accidents than new car buyers.
    Answer: B
    Diff: 1   Type: MC   Page Ref: 576–7/576–7
    Topic: The market for lemons
    Skill: Conceptual
    Objective: LO 1: Asymmetric Information
    AASCB Coding: Reflective Thinking
    Special Features: None

14. Why is the study of asymmetric information associated with the market for "lemons"?
    A) Sellers of citrus fruit – lemons, oranges, grapefruit – know the difference between bad fruit and good fruit; buyers do not have this information.
    B) Because there is little advertising in the market for lemons, buyers have difficulty determining the quality of lemons before they are purchased.
    C) Potential buyers of used cars have difficulty separating good used cars from bad used cars; bad used cars are often referred to as "lemons."
    D) Most sellers of used cars have less information about their cars than the dealers who buy them; used cars are often referred to as "lemons."
    Answer: C
    Diff: 1   Type: MC   Page Ref: 576/576
    Topic: The market for lemons
    Skill: Conceptual
    Objective: LO 1: Asymmetric Information
    AASCB Coding: Reflective Thinking
    Special Features: None

15. Because of asymmetric information, most used cars that are offered for sale will be sold for prices that are greater than their true value. Because of this fact, the used car market falls victim to
    A) the free rider problem.
    B) deadweight loss and economic inefficiency.
    C) a surplus of used cars.
    D) adverse selection.
Answer: D
Diff: 2   Type: MC   Page Ref: 576–7/576–7
Topic: The market for lemons
Skill: Conceptual
Objective: LO 1: Asymmetric Information
AASCB Coding: Reflective Thinking
Special Features: None

16. One way to reduce the problem of adverse selection in the used car market is
    A) for car manufacturers to provide warranties when cars are sold new.
    B) for car owners to donate their cars to charity, rather than to sell them as used cars.
    C) for used car dealers to buy insurance policies that protect them from lawsuits.
    D) for the federal government to impose a tax on each used car that is sold.
Answer: A
Diff: 2   Type: MC   Page Ref: 577/577
Topic: Adverse selection in the car market
Skill: Conceptual
Objective: LO 1: Asymmetric Information
AASCB Coding: Reflective Thinking
Special Features: None

17. "Lemon laws" are an attempt to reduce _____ in the used car market.
    A) the winner's curse
    B) adverse selection
    C) moral hazard
    D) uncertain information
Answer: B
Diff: 1   Type: MC   Page Ref: 577/577
Topic: Adverse Selection
Skill: Conceptual
Objective: LO 1: Asymmetric Information
AASCB Coding: Reflective Thinking
Special Features: None

18. Some states have passed "lemon laws" to reduce information problems in the market for cars. Most lemon laws have which of the following provisions?
    A) For each new car sold, a new car seller must pay the legal bills of a buyer who sues the seller if the car needs major repairs during the first year or two after the original purchase date.
    B) Sellers of new cars must pay a tax to the federal government for each car they sell. The tax revenue is used to compensate buyers whose cars need major repairs during the first year or two after their original purchase dates.
    C) New cars that need major repairs during the first year or two after the date of the original purchase may be returned to the manufacturer for a full refund.
    D) Sellers of new cars must make available to each potential car buyer the safety and repair records of the make and model of the car the buyer intends to purchase.
    Answer: C
    Diff: 2   Type: MC   Page Ref: 577/577
    Topic: Lemon laws
    Skill: Fact
    Objective: LO 1: Asymmetric Information
    AASCB Coding: Reflective Thinking
    Special Features: None

19. "Lemon laws" – laws passed by states to help reduce information problems in the market for cars – have been very popular with consumers. However, fewer than 20 states have enacted these laws. One reason for this is
    A) opposition from car manufacturers.
    B) most voters are rationally ignorant.
    C) the high cost of compliance with the laws.
    D) most state legislatures have spent their time passing other laws that are even more popular with their constituents.
    Answer: A
    Diff: 1   Type: MC   Page Ref: 577/577
    Topic: Lemon laws
    Skill: Conceptual
    Objective: LO 1: Asymmetric Information
    AASCB Coding: Reflective Thinking
    Special Features: None

20. To reduce information problems in the used car market, used car dealers can take steps to assure buyers that the cars they are selling are not lemons. One step taken by dealers to do this is
    A) lobbying the federal government to pass a "lemon law."
    B) by periodically holding special sales on their cars.
    C) by including free roadside emergency service for drivers when their cars break down.
    D) building a reputation for selling reliable used cars.
    Answer: D
    Diff: 1   Type: MC   Page Ref: 577/577
    Topic: Adverse selection in the car market
    Skill: Fact
    Objective: LO 1: Asymmetric Information
    AASCB Coding: Reflective Thinking
    Special Features: None

21. Adverse selection in the market for insurance arises because
    A) many insurance companies care more about profits than they do about providing services for their customers in the event of accident or illness.
    B) the federal government intervenes in insurance markets by controlling prices and reimbursement policies.
    C) insurance companies are not allowed to charge premiums that are high enough to insure against "worst-case" accidents or illness.
    D) buyers of insurance know more than insurance companies about the likelihood of an accident or illness for which buyers want insurance.
    Answer: D
    Diff: 2   Type: MC   Page Ref: 577/577
    Topic: The market for insurance
    Skill: Conceptual
    Objective: LO 1: Asymmetric Information
    AASCB Coding: Reflective Thinking
    Special Features: None

22. One reason why adverse selection problems arise in health insurance markets is that
    A) sick people are more likely to want health insurance than healthy people.
    B) because of advances in medical technology, people are living longer. These medical advances are costly and drive up the price of insurance for everyone.
    C) the average age of citizens of the United States has increased in recent years, and will continue to increase over the next 20 to 30 years. As older citizens retire, more and more of their medical bills will have to be paid by younger workers.
    D) fewer men and women are choosing medical careers because of the increase in the cost of malpractice insurance.
    Answer: A
    Diff: 1   Type: MC   Page Ref: 577/577
    Topic: The market for insurance
    Skill: Conceptual
    Objective: LO 1: Asymmetric Information
    AASCB Coding: Reflective Thinking
    Special Features: None

23. One reason why adverse selection problems arise in the market for automobile insurance is that
    A) a significant number of drivers have accidents because they use their cell phones while driving.
    B) the judicial system has not been able to keep drivers prone to accidents from continuing to drive and having more accidents.
    C) reckless drivers are more likely to want automobile insurance than careful drivers.
    D) only a few states have passed "lemon laws."
    Answer: C
    Diff: 2   Type: MC   Page Ref: 577/577
    Topic: The market for insurance
    Skill: Conceptual
    Objective: LO 1: Asymmetric Information
    AASCB Coding: Reflective Thinking
    Special Features: None

24. The situation in which one party to a transaction takes advantage of knowing more than the other party to the transaction is called
    A) asymmetric information.
    B) adverse selection.
    C) moral hazard.
    D) adverse hazard.
    Answer: B
    Diff: 1   Type: MC   Page Ref: 577/577
    Topic: Adverse selection
    Skill: Definition
    Objective: LO 1: Asymmetric Information
    AASCB Coding: Reflective Thinking
    Special Features: None

25. State governments reduce the adverse selection problem associated with automobile insurance by
    A) prosecuting drivers who have a history of reckless driving that leads to accidents.
    B) requiring all drivers to buy automobile insurance.
    C) placing a price ceiling on the premiums charged by insurance companies.
    D) mandating that automobile manufacturers include safety features in all of their new cars.
    Answer: B
    Diff: 1   Type: MC   Page Ref: 578/578
    Topic: Adverse selection in the car market
    Skill: Conceptual
    Objective: LO 1: Asymmetric Information
    AASCB Coding: Reflective Thinking
    Special Features: None

26. Insurance companies reduce their adverse selection problems by offering _____ to large firms. This practice is an example of _____.
    A) special discounts; economies of scale.
    B) comprehensive policies; whole insurance.
    C) group coverage; risk pooling.
    D) preferential treatment; risk management.
    Answer: C
    Diff: 1   Type: MC   Page Ref: 578/578
    Topic: The market for insurance
    Skill: Conceptual
    Objective: LO 1: Asymmetric Information
    AASCB Coding: Reflective Thinking
    Special Features: None

27. In addition to selling policies to individuals, insurance companies sell policies to large firms that cover all of the firm's employees. This type of insurance is referred to as
    A) comprehensive coverage.
    B) universal coverage.
    C) company coverage.
    D) group coverage.
    Answer: D
    Diff: 1   Type: MC   Page Ref: 578/578
    Topic: The market for insurance
    Skill: Fact
    Objective: LO 1: Asymmetric Information
    AASCB Coding: Reflective Thinking
    Special Features: None

28. Insurance companies sell health insurance policies to large firms that cover all of their employees. From the company's perspective, an advantage of this type of insurance is that because every employee must pay premiums
    A) the company avoids the problem of only sick people buying the insurance.
    B) the company maximizes its profits.
    C) no employee can be a "free rider."
    D) fewer people will have an incentive to file an insurance claim.
    Answer: A
    Diff: 2   Type: MC   Page Ref: 578/578
    Topic: The market for insurance
    Skill: Conceptual
    Objective: LO 1: Asymmetric Information
    AASCB Coding: Reflective Thinking
    Special Features: None

29. How many people in the United States do not have health insurance?
    A) Almost none. Those who do not have private health insurance plans are covered by government plans such as Medicare and Medicaid.
    B) About one-half of the population (close to 150 million).
    C) About 10 million.
    D) More than 45 million.
    Answer: D
    Diff: 1   Type: MC   Page Ref: 578-80/578-80
    Topic: The market for insurance
    Skill: Fact
    Objective: LO 1: Asymmetric Information
    AASCB Coding: Reflective Thinking
    Special Features: Making the Connection: Does Adverse Selection Explain Why Some People Do Not Have Health Insurance?

30. Research by economists has suggested that state government regulations may have worsened the adverse selection problem in the market for health insurance in the United States. The state regulations generally
    A) restrict the ability of insurance companies to charge higher premiums for employees of small firms who have existing health problems.
    B) place a limit on the premiums insurance companies can charge for group coverage.
    C) restrict the information insurance companies can request from policy holders. This information includes evidence of previous accidents and medical records.
    D) require insurance companies to offer private insurance to all individuals, regardless of their age or state of health.
    Answer: A
    Diff: 3   Type: MC   Page Ref: 578-80/578-80
    Topic: The market for insurance
    Skill: Fact
    Objective: LO 1: Asymmetric Information
    AASCB Coding: Reflective Thinking
    Special Features: Making the Connection: Does Adverse Selection Explain Why Some People Do Not Have Health Insurance?

31. Economists refer to the actions people take after they have entered into a transaction that makes the other party to the transaction worse off as
    A) bad faith.
    B) economic inefficiency.
    C) moral hazard.
    D) market failure.
    Answer: C
    Diff: 1   Type: MC   Page Ref: 580/580
    Topic: Moral hazard
    Skill: Definition
    Objective: LO 1: Asymmetric Information
    AASCB Coding: Reflective Thinking
    Special Features: None

32. In the 1973 movie *Save the Tiger*, Jack Lemon plays Harry Stoner, the CEO of a clothing manufacturer whose business has fallen on hard times. In one of the key scenes of the movie, Stoner tries to convince his partner that they should hire someone to burn one of their buildings in order to collect on their insurance policy. Harry Stoner's actions are an example of
    A) adverse selection.
    B) moral hazard.
    C) self-interest.
    D) asymmetric information.
    Answer: B
    Diff: 2   Type: MC   Page Ref: 580/580
    Topic: Moral hazard
    Skill: Conceptual
    Objective: LO 1: Asymmetric Information
    AASCB Coding: Reflective Thinking
    Special Features: None

33. In the 1973 movie *Save the Tiger*, Jack Lemon plays Harry Stoner, the CEO of a clothing manufacturer whose business has fallen on hard times. At one point in the movie Stoner convinces his partner to hire someone to burn one of their buildings to collect on their insurance policy. What term refers to the information problem that led the insurance company to sell a policy for this building to Stoner and his partner?
    A) Rational ignorance.
    B) The principal-agent problem.
    C) Adverse selection.
    D) Moral hazard.
    Answer: C
    Diff: 2   Type: MC   Page Ref: 577-8/577-8
    Topic: Adverse selection
    Skill: Conceptual
    Objective: LO 1: Asymmetric Information
    AASCB Coding: Reflective Thinking
    Special Features: None

34. Two consequences of asymmetric information are adverse selection and moral hazard. An important distinction between the two is
    A) adverse selection exists prior to the completion of a transaction while moral hazard occurs after the transaction is completed.
    B) moral hazard exists prior to the completion of a transaction while adverse selection occurs after the transaction is completed.
    C) adverse selection leads to an inefficient quantity while moral hazard leads to an efficient quantity.
    D) moral hazard leads to an inefficient quantity while adverse selection leads to an efficient quantity.

Answer: A
Diff: 1   Type: MC   Page Ref: 580/580
Topic: Adverse selection and moral hazard
Skill: Conceptual
Objective: LO 1: Asymmetric Information
AASCB Coding: Reflective Thinking
Special Features: Don't Let This Happen to YOU!: Don't Confuse Adverse Selection with Moral Hazard

35. The difference between adverse selection and moral hazard is that
    A) moral hazard happens at the time parties enter into a transaction; adverse selection occurs after the transaction takes place.
    B) adverse selection happens at the time parties enter into a transaction; moral hazard occurs after the transaction takes place.
    C) moral hazard is the motive that is behind one party entering into a transaction with another party. Adverse selection refers to the other party being harmed by the transaction.
    D) moral hazard refers to the likelihood that a transaction will lead one party to begetter off at the expense of the other party to the transaction. Adverse selection refers to the consequences of the transaction after it has occurred.

Answer: B
Diff: 2   Type: MC   Page Ref: 580/580
Topic: Adverse selection and moral hazard
Skill: Conceptual
Objective: LO 1: Asymmetric Information
AASCB Coding: Reflective Thinking
Special Features: Don't Let This Happen to YOU!: Don't Confuse Adverse Selection with Moral Hazard

36. _____ occurs when one party takes advantage of having more information than another party about the attributes of the good or service they will exchange.
   A) A negative externality
   B) Moral hazard
   C) A transaction cost
   D) Adverse selection
   Answer: D
   Diff: 2   Type: MC   Page Ref: 577/577
   Topic: Adverse selection
   Skill: Definition
   Objective: LO 1: Asymmetric Information
   AASCB Coding: Reflective Thinking
   Special Features: None

37. _____ occurs when actions taken by one party to a transaction are different from what the other party expected at the time of the transaction.
   A) Adverse selection
   B) Risk Aversion
   C) Fraud
   D) Moral hazard
   Answer: D
   Diff: 1   Type: MC   Page Ref: 580/580
   Topic: Moral hazard
   Skill: Conceptual
   Objective: LO 1: Asymmetric Information
   AASCB Coding: Reflective Thinking
   Special Features: None

38. Most home construction contracts include a clause that holds the building contractor liable for additional costs incurred beyond the original estimate. The purpose of this clause is to address
   A) moral hazard.
   B) adverse selection.
   C) loss minimization.
   D) building code regulations.
   Answer: A
   Diff: 1   Type: MC   Page Ref: 580/580
   Topic: Moral hazard
   Skill: Conceptual
   Objective: LO 1: Asymmetric Information
   AASCB Coding: Reflective Thinking
   Special Features: None

39. Many consumer items, such as cars and home entertainment systems, come with some form of warranty. Why do firms offer warranties?
    A) A warranty is essentially a form of price discrimination where the firm charges a higher price to some consumers without discouraging others.
    B) If firms do not offer warranties no one will buy high-priced consumer goods.
    C) Warranties serve as a form of consumer insurance.
    D) Firms want to encourage repeat customers.
    Answer: C
    Diff: 1   Type: MC   Page Ref: 577/577
    Topic: Asymmetric information
    Skill: Conceptual
    Objective: LO 1: Asymmetric Information
    AASCB Coding: Reflective Thinking
    Special Features: None

40. In some situations, parties to a transaction have the same information. In other cases, one party may have more information than the other party. Consider the following two scenarios:

    a.   Alex purchases a ticket from Jerry for an outdoor concert scheduled for six months in the future. Neither Alex nor Jerry know what the weather will be on the day of the concert.
    b.   Sven offers to sell Frank his 14-year old BMW. Sven is familiar with the car's maintenance records and accident history but Frank is not.

    Which of the following statements is true?
    A) Neither transaction involves the existence of asymmetric information.
    B) Scenario b involves the existence of asymmetric information while scenario a does not.
    C) Both transactions involve the existence of asymmetric information.
    D) Scenario a involves the existence of asymmetric information while scenario b does not.
    Answer: B
    Diff: 3   Type: MC   Page Ref: 576/576
    Topic: Asymmetric information
    Skill: Conceptual
    Objective: LO 1: Asymmetric Information
    AASCB Coding: Reflective Thinking
    Special Features: None

41. Suppose that in a market for used cars, there are good used cars and bad used cars (lemons). Consumers are willing to pay as much as $6,000 for a good used car but only $1,000 for a lemon. Sellers of good used cars ask $5,000 per car and sellers of lemons ask $800. Buyers cannot tell if a used car is reliable or is a lemon. Based on this information, what is the likely outcome in the market for used cars?
    A) Both good used cars and lemons will sell for $4,500 each.
    B) Only lemons will sell, for $800 each.
    C) Both good used cars and lemons will sell for $1,000 each.
    D) Most used cars offered for sale will be lemons.
Answer: D
Diff: 3   Type: MC   Page Ref: 576–7/576–7
Topic: Adverse selection in the car market
Skill: Analytical
Objective: LO 1: Asymmetric Information
AASCB Coding: Analytic Skills
Special Features: None

42. Suppose that in a market for used cars, there are good used cars and bad used cars (lemons). Consumers are willing to pay as much as $6,000 for a good used car but only $1,000 for a lemon. Sellers of good used cars ask $5,000 per car and sellers of lemons ask $800. Buyers cannot tell if a used car is reliable or is a lemon. Based on this information, what is the likely outcome in the market for used cars?
    A) Sellers of good used cars will drop out of the market.
    B) Sellers of good used cars will incur losses.
    C) Sellers of lemons will drop out of the market.
    D) Used cars will sell for $3,000.
Answer: A
Diff: 3   Type: MC   Page Ref: 576–7/576–7
Topic: Adverse selection in the car market
Skill: Analytical
Objective: LO 1: Asymmetric Information
AASCB Coding: Analytic Skills
Special Features: None

43. Health insurance markets have a problem with insuring people who are "poor health risks" while many people who are "good health risks" do not buy insurance. This problem is an example of
    A) moral hazard.
    B) adverse selection.
    C) market signaling.
    D) asymmetric information.
Answer: B
Diff: 2   Type: MC   Page Ref: 577–8/577–8
Topic: Adverse selection
Skill: Definition
Objective: LO 1: Asymmetric Information
AASCB Coding: Reflective Thinking
Special Features: None

44. Automobile insurance companies have a problem with people who buy insurance and then drive recklessly or take less care to avoid losses after being insured. In other words, the automobile insurance market is subject to

    A) asymmetric information.

    B) market signaling.

    C) moral hazard.

    D) adverse selection.

Answer: C

Diff: 2   Type: MC   Page Ref: 580/580

Topic: Moral hazard

Skill: Conceptual

Objective: LO 1: Asymmetric Information

AASCB Coding: Reflective Thinking

Special Features: None

45. Adverse selection is a situation in which one party to an economic transaction has less information than the other party.

Answer: True   False

Diff: 2   Type: TF   Page Ref: 576/576

Topic: Asymmetric information

Skill: Definition

Objective: LO 1: Asymmetric Information

AASCB Coding: Reflective Thinking

Special Features: None

46. One consequence of adverse selection in the market for used cars is that most used cars sold will be lemons.

Answer: True   False

Diff: 2   Type: TF   Page Ref: 576–7/576–7

Topic: The market for lemons

Skill: Conceptual

Objective: LO 1: Asymmetric Information

AASCB Coding: Reflective Thinking

Special Features: None

47. Insurance companies can reduce adverse selection problems in selling health insurance and life insurance by offering whole life policies to large firms, including colleges and universities.

Answer: True   False

Diff: 2   Type: TF   Page Ref: 578/578

Topic: Adverse selection

Skill: Conceptual

Objective: LO 1: Asymmetric Information

AASCB Coding: Reflective Thinking

Special Features: None

48. Insurance companies use deductibles and coinsurance to reduce moral hazard.
    Answer: ⊙ True   False
    Diff: 2   Type: TF   Page Ref: 580/580
    Topic: The market for insurance
    Skill: Conceptual
    Objective: LO 1: Asymmetric Information
    AASCB Coding: Reflective Thinking
    Special Features: None

49. Insurance companies can reduce adverse selection problems in selling medical insurance and life insurance by offering group coverage to large firms. Explain how this reduces adverse selection.
    Answer: As long as a group is large enough, it is likely to reflect the proportions of healthy and unhealthy people found in the general population. As a result, it is much easier for insurance companies to estimate the number of claims likely to be filed under a group policy than it would be to predict the number of claims filed under an individual policy. Because everyone in the group must pay premiums the company avoids the problem of selling insurance only to those with significant health risks.
    Diff: 3   Type: ES   Page Ref: 576–80/576–80
    Topic: The market for insurance
    Skill: Conceptual
    Objective: LO 1: Asymmetric Information
    AASCB Coding: Reflective Thinking
    Special Features: None

50. Explain why asymmetric information exists in the following situations. Explain the consequences of asymmetric information in these situations.
    a. The sale of life insurance.
    b. The sale of used computers.
    c. Hiring someone to manage the condominiums you own.
    Answer: a. Individuals know more about the health risks from their habits and life–styles than insurance companies do. The consequence of this is adverse selection: people with a greater risk of death are those most likely to buy life insurance.
    b. Owners of used computers know more about the characteristics of their computers than do potential buyers. The consequence is adverse selection: buyers fear buying defective computers which means that owners of reliable used computers will not be able to sell their products at the prices they want charge. This will result in dealers dropping out of the market. Another consequence is that some buyers interested in buying reliable computers will avoid the used computer market.
    c. The property manager acts as your agent since he is performing a service on your behalf. Because you, the principal, cannot perfectly monitor the agent's behavior, the agent has an incentive to use less effort in performing his job than you desire. The consequence of this asymmetric information is moral hazard: shirking or dishonest behavior by the agent.
    Diff: 3   Type: ES   Page Ref: 576–80/576–80
    Topic: Asymmetric information
    Skill: Analytical
    Objective: LO 1: Asymmetric Information

AASCB Coding: Analytic Skills
Special Features: None

51. Two key consequences of asymmetric information are adverse selection and moral hazard. Define each concept, provide one example of each and explain how the two concepts differ.

Answer: Adverse selection is the situation in which one party to a transaction takes advantage of knowing more than the other party to the transaction. Moral hazard refers to the actions people take after they enter into a transaction that makes the other party to the transaction worse off. An important difference between the two is that adverse selection refers to what happens at the time of entering into a transaction (for example, a reckless driver buys automobile insurance) while moral hazard refers to what happens after entering into the transaction (for example, the insured driver drives his car off a highway and into a tree).

Diff: 2   Type: ES   Page Ref: 576–80/576–80
Topic: Asymmetric information
Skill: Conceptual
Objective: LO 1: Asymmetric Information
AASCB Coding: Reflective Thinking
Special Features: None

17.2   Adverse Selection and Moral Hazard in Financial Markets

1. Investors
   A) prefer to buy stocks and bonds from relatively small firms, because the risk of large financial losses is less with small firms than with large firms.
   B) prefer to buy stocks and bonds from relatively small firms, because investors have more influence over small firms than they do over large firms.
   C) are reluctant to buy stocks and bonds from a firm unless there is a great deal of public information available about the firm.
   D) do not invest in large corporations unless they are guaranteed by these corporations that they won't suffer losses due to adverse selection or moral hazard.

Answer: C
Diff: 1   Type: MC   Page Ref: 581/581
Topic: Adverse selection and moral hazard in financial markets
Skill: Conceptual
Objective: LO 2: Adverse Selection and Moral Hazard in Financial Markets
AASCB Coding: Reflective Thinking
Special Features: None

2. For firms and investors the potential for adverse selection
   A) and moral hazard exists in the market for stocks, but not in the market for bonds.
   B) and moral hazard exists in the markets for stocks and bonds.
   C) but not moral hazard exists in the markets for stocks and bonds.
   D) but not moral hazard exists in the market for stocks. Neither adverse selection nor moral hazard are present in bond markets.

Answer: B
Diff: 1   Type: MC   Page Ref: 581/581
Topic: Adverse selection and moral hazard in financial markets
Skill: Conceptual
Objective: LO 2: Adverse Selection and Moral Hazard in Financial Markets
AASCB Coding: Reflective Thinking
Special Features: None

3. Asymmetric information is a key reason why
   A) large corporations are better able to raise funds by selling stocks and bonds than small firms.
   B) large corporations prefer to raise money by selling stocks rather than bonds.
   C) sole proprietorships face less financial risk than partnerships.
   D) the Securities and Exchange Commission regulates the premiums charged by insurance companies.

Answer: A
Diff: 2   Type: MC   Page Ref: 581/581
Topic: Adverse selection and moral hazard in financial markets
Skill: Analytical
Objective: LO 2: Adverse Selection and Moral Hazard in Financial Markets
AASCB Coding: Reflective Thinking
Special Features: None

4. Every firm knows more about its financial situation than any potential investor. Therefore,
   A) brokerage firms and investment companies prefer to buy and sell stocks of small firms rather than stocks of large firms.
   B) brokerage firms and investment companies prefer to buy and sell stocks of insurance companies rather than manufacturing companies.
   C) firms are better off selling their own stocks and bonds rather than depending on brokerage firms and investment companies to sell their stocks and bonds.
   D) adverse selection and moral hazard can create problems for investors in the market for stocks and bonds.

Answer: D
Diff: 1   Type: MC   Page Ref: 581/581
Topic: Adverse selection and moral hazard in financial markets
Skill: Conceptual
Objective: LO 2: Adverse Selection and Moral Hazard in Financial Markets
AASCB Coding: Reflective Thinking
Special Features: None

5. Moral hazard is one reason why investors are more likely to buy the stocks and bonds of large corporations than small corporations. The problem of moral hazard is not as great with large firms because
   A) the owners of large firms have greater incentive to ensure that their managers maximize the firms' profits.
   B) large firms have limited liability while small firms do not.
   C) more public information is available for large corporations than small corporations.
   D) most managers of large corporations are also stockholders, so they benefit directly when they maximize their firms' profits.

Answer: C
Diff: 1   Type: MC   Page Ref: 581/581
Topic: Adverse selection and moral hazard in financial markets
Skill: Conceptual
Objective: LO 2: Adverse Selection and Moral Hazard in Financial Markets
AASCB Coding: Reflective Thinking
Special Features: None

6. Moral hazard is a problem in financial markets because investors have trouble distinguishing between well-run and poorly-run firms before they buy stocks and bonds. After stocks and bonds are purchased,
   A) moral hazard is no longer a problem for investors.
   B) moral hazard is still a problem for investors because firms may use funds raised by selling stocks and bonds in ways that reduce profits.
   C) adverse selection is a problem for investors because firms may use funds raised by selling stocks and bonds in ways that reduce profits.
   D) moral hazard is still a problem for investors because firms may use funds raised by selling stocks and bonds to pay their workers higher than equilibrium wages or allow their employees to participate in a seniority system that reduces profits.

Answer: B
Diff: 2   Type: MC   Page Ref: 581/581
Topic: Adverse selection and moral hazard in financial markets
Skill: Conceptual
Objective: LO 2: Adverse Selection and Moral Hazard in Financial Markets
AASCB Coding: Reflective Thinking
Special Features: None

7. Congress established the Securities and Exchange Commission (SEC) in 1934 in response to
    A) complaints from investors that during the stock market crash of 1929 firms failed to provide them with accurate financial information.
    B) concerns that organized crime had infiltrated the management of many large firms in the late1920s.
    C) a large increase in the number of firms that organized as corporations, rather than sole proprietorships and partnerships, in the United States in the 1920s and early 1930s.
    D) lobbying by stockholders who complained that too much financial information was being made available by many new firms who tried to sell their stocks and bonds in the 1920s.

Answer: A
Diff: 2   Type: MC   Page Ref: 581/581
Topic: Adverse selection and moral hazard in financial markets
Skill: Fact
Objective: LO 2: Adverse Selection and Moral Hazard in Financial Markets
AASCB Coding: Reflective Thinking
Special Features: None

8. The Securities and Exchange Commission (SEC) was established by the U.S. Congress in 1934 to regulate stock and bond markets. The SEC requires that
    A) the top managers of corporations are legally responsible for the accuracy of their firms' financial statements.
    B) all corporations pay a tax on their profits, in addition to the taxes paid on dividends received by their shareholders.
    C) no proceeds from sales of stocks or bonds are used to make campaign contributions to candidates for office at the federal, state or local levels of government.
    D) firms register stocks and bonds they wish to sell with the SEC.

Answer: D
Diff: 2   Type: MC   Page Ref: 581/581
Topic: Adverse selection and moral hazard in financial markets
Skill: Fact
Objective: LO 2: Adverse Selection and Moral Hazard in Financial Markets
AASCB Coding: Reflective Thinking
Special Features: None

9. The government agency that requires firms to register the stocks and bonds they wish to sell and to provide potential investors with relevant financial information is
    A) the New York Stock Exchange.
    B) Standard & Poors.
    C) the Federal Reserve System.
    D) the Securities and Exchange Commission.

Answer: D
Diff: 1   Type: MC   Page Ref: 581/581
Topic: Adverse selection and moral hazard in financial markets
Skill: Fact
Objective: LO 2: Adverse Selection and Moral Hazard in Financial Markets
AASCB Coding: Reflective Thinking
Special Features: None

10. The Securities and Exchange Commission (SEC) requires firms to provide investors with a prospectus that contains relevant financial information about the firms. This requirement
    A) eliminates the risk that investors face from buying bonds and reduces the risk from buying stocks.
    B) makes top managers of the firms legally liable for the accuracy of the financial statements included in the prospectus.
    C) reduces adverse selection and moral hazard problems in financial markets.
    D) entitles those who receive the prospectus to buy stocks and bonds at discounted prices.
    Answer: C
    Diff: 2   Type: MC   Page Ref: 581/581
    Topic: Adverse selection and moral hazard in financial markets
    Skill: Conceptual
    Objective: LO 2: Adverse Selection and Moral Hazard in Financial Markets
    AASCB Coding: Reflective Thinking
    Special Features: None

11. During 2002 several financial scandals involving large corporations served as a reminder that
    A) investors and corporate managers care more about profits than people.
    B) adverse selection and moral hazard problems continue to exist in financial markets.
    C) the Securities and Exchange Commission has failed to adequately regulate financial markets.
    D) some firms violated the Sarbanes–Oxley Act.
    Answer: B
    Diff: 2   Type: MC   Page Ref: 581–2/581–2
    Topic: Adverse selection and moral hazard in financial markets
    Skill: Conceptual
    Objective: LO 2: Adverse Selection and Moral Hazard in Financial Markets
    AASCB Coding: Reflective Thinking
    Special Features: None

12. A financial statement that reports a firm's profits over a period of time is
    A) an income statement.
    B) a profit summary.
    C) a balance sheet.
    D) a prospectus.
    Answer: A
    Diff: 1   Type: MC   Page Ref: 582–3/582–3
    Topic: Adverse selection and moral hazard in financial markets
    Skill: Fact
    Objective: LO 2: Adverse Selection and Moral Hazard in Financial Markets
    AASCB Coding: Reflective Thinking
    Special Features: Making the Connection: Using Government Policy to Reduce Moral Hazard in Investments

13. All firms that issue stock to the public have their financial statements audited. Audited financial statements
    A) are required by the Internal Revenue Service, and become the firm's federal income tax statements.
    B) are certification from an independent accounting firm that the statements reflect the firm's true financial condition.
    C) are required by the Sarbanes-Oxley Act.
    D) guarantee that top managers will not be legally responsible for the accuracy of their financial statements.

Answer: B
Diff: 1   Type: MC   Page Ref: 582-3/582-3
Topic: Adverse selection and moral hazard in financial markets
Skill: Fact
Objective: LO 2: Adverse Selection and Moral Hazard in Financial Markets
AASCB Coding: Reflective Thinking
Special Features: Making the Connection: Using Government Policy to Reduce Moral Hazard in Investments

14. All firms that issue stock to the general public have their financial statements
    A) audited by their own accounting staff.
    B) audited by the Internal Revenue Service.
    C) audited by certified public accountants who are not employees of the firms they audit.
    D) audited by accountants who work for the Securities and Exchange Commission.

Answer: C
Diff: 1   Type: MC   Page Ref: 582-3/582-3
Topic: Adverse selection and moral hazard in financial markets
Skill: Fact
Objective: LO 2: Adverse Selection and Moral Hazard in Financial Markets
AASCB Coding: Reflective Thinking
Special Features: Making the Connection: Using Government Policy to Reduce Moral Hazard in Investments

15. In 2002 executives of the WorldCom corporation
    A) announced that the firm would merge with AT&T to form the largest provider of long-distance service in the world.
    B) announced that it would buy the remaining assets of Adelphia Communications, after Adelphia filed for bankruptcy.
    C) were found guilty of making illegal contributions during the 2000 presidential campaign.
    D) admitted to making errors in its financial statements that would cause it to file for bankruptcy.

Answer: D
Diff: 1   Type: MC   Page Ref: 582-3/582-3
Topic: Adverse selection and moral hazard in financial markets
Skill: Fact
Objective: LO 2: Adverse Selection and Moral Hazard in Financial Markets
AASCB Coding: Reflective Thinking
Special Features: Making the Connection: Using Government Policy to Reduce Moral Hazard in Investments

16. In 2002 the U.S. Congress passed a law that required chief executive officers and chief financial officers to personally certify the accuracy of their firms' financial statements. The law also raised the number of years violators of securities laws could be sentenced to prison. One result of the law is likely to be
    A) a reduction in the incidence of moral hazard in financial markets.
    B) a reduction in the number of managers who apply for positions as chief executive officers and chief financial officers.
    C) the elimination of adverse selection in financial markets.
    D) a reduction in the number of accountants hired by firms.
    Answer: A
    Diff: 1   Type: MC   Page Ref: 582–3/582–3
    Topic: Adverse selection and moral hazard in financial markets
    Skill: Conceptual
    Objective: LO 2: Adverse Selection and Moral Hazard in Financial Markets
    AASCB Coding: Reflective Thinking
    Special Features: Making the Connection: Using Government Policy to Reduce Moral Hazard in Investments

17. Asymmetric information is a key reason why only large corporations are able to raise funds by selling stocks and bonds.
    Answer: ◌ True   False
    Diff: 1   Type: TF   Page Ref: 581/581
    Topic: Asymmetric information
    Skill: Conceptual
    Objective: LO 2: Adverse Selection and Moral Hazard in Financial Markets
    AASCB Coding: Reflective Thinking
    Special Features: None

18. The Securities and Exchange Commission was formed to help restore confidence in the financial statements of corporations in the wake of several scandals that occurred in 2002.
    Answer: True   ◌ False
    Diff: 1   Type: TF   Page Ref: 581–3/581–3
    Topic: Adverse selection and moral hazard in financial markets
    Skill: Fact
    Objective: LO 2: Adverse Selection and Moral Hazard in Financial Markets
    AASCB Coding: Reflective Thinking
    Special Features: None

19. Consider the market for loans for the purpose of making capital investments. Suppose a lack of information about the credit worthiness of firms prevents lenders from charging different interest rates for their business loans. What is the nature of the adverse selection problem in this market? How does this problem affect the profits of lenders?

    Answer: Adverse selection occurs when the potential borrowers who are the most likely to produce an adverse outcome, the bad credit risks, are the ones who most actively seek loans. A lender's profit is likely to fall because the percentage of defaulted loans for this group of borrowers will be higher that it would be for firms that are better credit risks.

    Diff: 3   Type: ES   Page Ref: 581-3/581-3
    Topic: Adverse selection and moral hazard in financial markets
    Skill: Analytical
    Objective: LO 2: Adverse Selection and Moral Hazard in Financial Markets
    AASCB Coding: Analytic Skills
    Special Features: None

20. Why are large, well-established corporations likely to have access to securities markets (that is, they can borrow directly from lenders) to finance their activities while small, lesser-known firms tend to raise funds through a financial intermediary (for example, borrowing from a commercial bank)?

    Answer: The better known a corporation is the greater the amount of information there is about its activities. This information reduces the consequences of asymmetric information; namely, adverse selection and moral hazard. Therefore, investors will be willing to invest directly in the securities of these corporations. By the same reasoning, investors will be reluctant to invest directly in lesser-known firms. The cost of gathering information about the smaller firms is much lower for financial intermediaries than for private lenders.

    Diff: 2   Type: ES   Page Ref: 581-3/581-3
    Topic: Adverse selection and moral hazard in financial markets
    Skill: Conceptual
    Objective: LO 2: Adverse Selection and Moral Hazard in Financial Markets
    AASCB Coding: Reflective Thinking
    Special Features: None

21. Because corporations are not obligated to pay shareholders dividends and the prices of stocks fluctuate, stocks are a riskier investment than bonds. Corporations are obligated to pay the interest and principal on their bonds and if a corporation files for bankruptcy it must pay bondholders and other creditors with the proceeds of the sales of its assets before stockholders are paid. Does this mean that adverse selection and moral hazard pose problems for investors who purchase stocks but not for investors who buy bonds?

Answer: No. Adverse selection poses problems for investors when there is a lack of information about a firm. Investors will be reluctant to buy stocks *or* bonds from a company for which they have little information. Moral hazard poses problems for investors after they purchase either a corporation's stocks *or* its bonds. Because the managers of a corporation (the agents) can act in their own interests rather than the stockholders' (the principals) best interests, the funds raised from selling stocks or bonds can be used in ways that are inconsistent with profit maximization.

Diff: 2   Type: ES   Page Ref: 581–3/581–3
Topic: Adverse selection and moral hazard in financial markets
Skill: Conceptual
Objective: LO 2: Adverse Selection and Moral Hazard in Financial Markets
AASCB Coding: Reflective Thinking
Special Features: None

17.3   Adverse Selection and Moral Hazard in Labor Market

1. Once workers are hired by a firm there is potential for a principal–agent problem. This problem would result if
    A) workers acquire an agent – a union – that threatens to strike unless management agrees to its demands for higher wages and better working conditions.
    B) workers are paid by commission, rather than a certain wage per hour.
    C) workers are paid efficiency wages.
    D) workers shirk their obligations.

Answer: D

Diff: 2   Type: MC   Page Ref: 583/583
Topic: Principal–agent problem
Skill: Conceptual
Objective: LO 3: Adverse Selection and Moral Hazard in Labor Markets
AASCB Coding: Reflective Thinking
Special Features: None

2. Adverse selection in the labor market refers to a situation where
   A) employers have more information than employees about the terms of their employment contracts.
   B) an employer can observe certain qualities of a potential worker and decide on the basis of those qualities whether or not to hire that person.
   C) potential employees have more information about their abilities than employers.
   D) only below–average candidates will apply for a job.
   Answer: C
   Diff: 1   Type: MC   Page Ref: 583/583
   Topic: Adverse selection and moral hazard in labor markets
   Skill: Conceptual
   Objective: LO 3: Adverse Selection and Moral Hazard in Labor Markets
   AASCB Coding: Reflective Thinking
   Special Features: None

3. Dynasty Corp. is run by a team of managers who have been elected by the firm's stockholders. Dynasty is a corporation that manufactures security systems. A principal-agent relationship exists between
   A) Dynasty Corp. and its customers where Dynasty Corp. is the principal and its customers are the agents.
   B) Dynasty's stockholders and the management team; the stockholders are the principals and the managers are the agents.
   C) Dynasty's stockholders and the firm's employees where the stockholders are the agents and the employees are the principals.
   D) Dynasty's stockholders and its customers; the stockholders are the principals and the customers are the agents.
   Answer: B
   Diff: 2   Type: MC   Page Ref: 583/583
   Topic: Principal–agent problem
   Skill: Conceptual
   Objective: LO 3: Adverse Selection and Moral Hazard in Labor Markets
   AASCB Coding: Reflective Thinking
   Special Features: None

4. Some workers employed by the ACME Ball Bearing factory are known to take long lunch breaks (some take 1 1/2 hours, rather than the 1 hour they are allowed to take) and naps during work hours when their foreman and managers are not watching. As a result, productivity at the factory has fallen over the past two years. This is evidence that the factory has

   A) a principal–agent problem.
   B) an asymmetric information problem.
   C) a worker discrimination problem.
   D) a negative feedback loop.

   Answer: A
   Diff: 1   Type: MC   Page Ref: 583/583
   Topic: Principal-agent problem
   Skill: Conceptual
   Objective: LO 3: Adverse Selection and Moral Hazard in Labor Markets
   AASCB Coding: Reflective Thinking
   Special Features: None

5. An efficiency wage reduces shirking because employees who are

   A) fired for shirking will not be able to collect unemployment compensation.
   B) caught shirking will be forced to take a wage cut.
   C) paid an efficiency wage are more closely monitored.
   D) paid an efficiency wage are likely to work harder to keep their jobs.

   Answer: D
   Diff: 1   Type: MC   Page Ref: 583/583
   Topic: Adverse selection and moral hazard in labor markets
   Skill: Conceptual
   Objective: LO 3: Adverse Selection and Moral Hazard in Labor Markets
   AASCB Coding: Reflective Thinking
   Special Features: None

6. A firm that pays its workers wages that exceed the equilibrium wage

   A) gives its workers an incentive to work harder and shirk less.
   B) will create a shortage in the labor market.
   C) will suffer economic losses until it lowers its wages to the equilibrium level.
   D) will be at a disadvantage with respect to other firms in the same industry that earn higher profits by paying lower wages.

   Answer: A
   Diff: 2   Type: MC   Page Ref: 583/583
   Topic: Efficiency wages
   Skill: Conceptual
   Objective: LO 3: Adverse Selection and Moral Hazard in Labor Markets
   AASCB Coding: Reflective Thinking
   Special Features: None

7. "Shirking" is a problem associated with moral hazard in labor markets. Which of the following is an example of shirking?
   - A) Elliot refuses to work overtime when asked by his boss to do so. Instead, Elliot spends his day off watching a baseball game.
   - B) Mary decides to look for a full-time job after she graduates from high school, even though she received a partial scholarship to attend her hometown college.
   - C) About one-fourth of the employees at a chocolate factory regularly take naps and read newspapers and magazines during their shifts.
   - D) Workers at an auto parts factory in Milwaukee vote to form a union, despite opposition from the owners of the factory.

   Answer: C
   Diff: 1   Type: MC   Page Ref: 583/583
   Topic: Adverse selection and moral hazard in labor markets
   Skill: Conceptual
   Objective: LO 3: Adverse Selection and Moral Hazard in Labor Markets
   AASCB Coding: Reflective Thinking
   Special Features: None

8. Which of the following is *not* a measure used by firms to motivate their employees to work hard and avoiding shirking?
   - A) Paying efficiency wages.
   - B) Paying workers the same wages for jobs of comparable worth.
   - C) Using a seniority system to determine pay and benefits.
   - D) Profit- sharing.

   Answer: B
   Diff: 1   Type: MC   Page Ref: 583-4/583-4
   Topic: Principal-agent problem
   Skill: Conceptual
   Objective: LO 3: Adverse Selection and Moral Hazard in Labor Markets
   AASCB Coding: Reflective Thinking
   Special Features: None

9. A wage offer above the equilibrium wage that is intended to attract high-productivity workers is called
   - A) an efficiency wage.
   - B) a union wage.
   - C) economic rent.
   - D) a compensating differential.

   Answer: A
   Diff: 1   Type: MC   Page Ref: 583/583
   Topic: Efficiency wages
   Skill: Definition
   Objective: LO 3: Adverse Selection and Moral Hazard in Labor Markets
   AASCB Coding: Reflective Thinking
   Special Features: None

10. When a firm pays higher wages and benefits for workers the longer they work for the firm, this is called
    A) a commission compensation system.
    B) a system of compensating differentials.
    C) an efficiency wage compensation system.
    D) a seniority system.
    Answer: D
    Diff: 1   Type: MC   Page Ref: 583–4/583–4
    Topic: Adverse selection and moral hazard in labor markets
    Skill: Conceptual
    Objective: LO 3: Adverse Selection and Moral Hazard in Labor Markets
    AASCB Coding: Reflective Thinking
    Special Features: None

11. Many firms use a seniority system which awards higher pay and other benefits to workers who have been with the firm longer than other workers. The seniority system is one method a firm can use to
    A) pay workers an efficiency wage.
    B) satisfy federal labor laws.
    C) make a worker's job seem more valuable and reduce shirking.
    D) reward employees who also own shares of the firm's stock.
    Answer: C
    Diff: 1   Type: MC   Page Ref: 583–4/583–4
    Topic: Adverse selection and moral hazard in labor markets
    Skill: Conceptual
    Objective: LO 3: Adverse Selection and Moral Hazard in Labor Markets
    AASCB Coding: Reflective Thinking
    Special Features: None

12. Under a _____ plan the employees of a firm receive a share of the profits the firm earns.
    A) shareholders' compensation
    B) profit–sharing
    C) cooperative wage
    D) dividend distribution
    Answer: B
    Diff: 1   Type: MC   Page Ref: 584/584
    Topic: Adverse selection and moral hazard in labor markets
    Skill: Conceptual
    Objective: LO 3: Adverse Selection and Moral Hazard in Labor Markets
    AASCB Coding: Reflective Thinking
    Special Features: None

13. After a firm hires its workers it faces a moral hazard problem. Which of the following describes this problem?
    A) Much time and money can be spent training workers for their jobs only to have these workers quit to work for other firms.
    B) Workers can become dissatisfied with their working conditions and demand to form a union.
    C) Workers' jobs are outsourced because people from other countries are hired to do the same jobs at lower wages.
    D) Once hired, workers may shirk their obligations and not work hard.
    Answer: D
    Diff: 1   Type: MC   Page Ref: 583/583
    Topic: Adverse selection and moral hazard in labor markets
    Skill: Conceptual
    Objective: LO 3: Adverse Selection and Moral Hazard in Labor Markets
    AASCB Coding: Reflective Thinking
    Special Features: None

14. After workers are hired they may shirk their obligations and not work hard. This problem is an example of _____ that is a consequence of _____.
    A) asymmetric information; paying workers efficiency wages
    B) moral hazard; a principal-agent problem
    C) a seniority system; moral hazard
    D) cognitive dissonance; a principal-agent problem
    Answer: B
    Diff: 1   Type: MC   Page Ref: 583-4/583-4
    Topic: Adverse selection and moral hazard in labor markets
    Skill: Conceptual
    Objective: LO 3: Adverse Selection and Moral Hazard in Labor Markets
    AASCB Coding: Reflective Thinking
    Special Features: None

15. Jill Davis owns and manages a clothing store that has 20 employees. Jill's business has suffered recently because she cannot monitor all of her employees at all hours, and some workers do not make much effort to persuade customers to buy more clothes. Currently, Jill pays her workers an hourly wage. Jill is considering switching to a commission or piece-rate compensation system. If Jill makes this switch and the switch is successful

   A) she will reduce both her moral hazard and adverse selection problems.

   B) she will reduce her adverse selection problem, but only by creating a moral hazard problem.

   C) she will eliminate her moral hazard problem but will create an adverse selection problem.

   D) she will reduce her labor costs because she will have fewer than 20 employees.

   Answer: A

   Diff: 2   Type: MC   Page Ref: 583–4/583–4
   Topic: Adverse selection and moral hazard in labor markets
   Skill: Conceptual
   Objective: LO 3: Adverse Selection and Moral Hazard in Labor Markets
   AASCB Coding: Reflective Thinking
   Special Features: Solved Problem: Changing Workers' Compensation To Reduce Adverse Selection and Moral Hazard

16. Jill Davis owns and manages a clothing store that employs 20 workers. Jill is concerned that her business may suffer because she cannot monitor all of her employees at all hours. Currently, Jill pays her workers an hourly wage. Jill is considering switching to a compensation system that would pay her workers by commission. One of Jill's business associates recommended this change, adding "when you begin hiring new workers you will attract people who are willing to work hard to earn more income. They will earn more when they sell more and your revenues and profits will be greater as a result." Jill's business associate endorses paying workers on commission in order to solve which of the following problems?

   A) Moral hazard when hiring new workers.

   B) Asymmetric information when hiring new workers.

   C) Adverse selection when hiring new workers.

   D) Comparable worth when hiring new workers.

   Answer: C

   Diff: 2   Type: MC   Page Ref: 583–4/583–4
   Topic: Adverse selection and moral hazard in labor markets
   Skill: Conceptual
   Objective: LO 3: Adverse Selection and Moral Hazard in Labor Markets
   AASCB Coding: Reflective Thinking
   Special Features: Solved Problem: Changing Workers' Compensation To Reduce Adverse Selection and Moral Hazard

17. Jill Davis owns and manages a clothing store that has 20 employees. Currently, Jill pays her workers an hourly wage, but she is considering switching to a commission or piece-rate compensation system. She believes this switch will increase her store's profits. An advantage of making this switch is
    A) Jill's labor costs will be reduced when employees who prefer being paid by the hour quit.
    B) Jill will no longer have to pay her workers compensating differentials.
    C) Jill will no longer have to pay her workers benefits, such as health insurance, that she must pay under her current compensation system.
    D) Jill will attract people willing to work harder and sell more of her clothes.
    Answer: D
    Diff: 2   Type: MC   Page Ref: 584/584
    Topic: Adverse selection and moral hazard in labor markets
    Skill: Conceptual
    Objective: LO 3: Adverse Selection and Moral Hazard in Labor Markets
    AASCB Coding: Reflective Thinking
    Special Features: Solved Problem: Changing Workers' Compensation To Reduce Adverse Selection and Moral Hazard

18. Some firms pay efficiency wages in order to give their workers an incentive to work harder and shirk less.
    Answer: ⊙ True   False
    Diff: 1   Type: TF   Page Ref: 583/583
    Topic: Adverse selection and moral hazard in labor markets
    Skill: Conceptual
    Objective: LO 3: Adverse Selection and Moral Hazard in Labor Markets
    AASCB Coding: Use of Information Technology
    Special Features: None

19. Under a profit-sharing plan workers who have been with a firm longer receive higher pay and benefits.
    Answer: True   ⊙ False
    Diff: 1   Type: TF   Page Ref: 583-4/583-4
    Topic: Adverse selection and moral hazard in labor markets
    Skill: Conceptual
    Objective: LO 3: Adverse Selection and Moral Hazard in Labor Markets
    AASCB Coding: Reflective Thinking
    Special Features: None

20. An example of moral hazard in the workplace is a worker shirking his obligations and not working hard.
    Answer: ⊙ True   False
    Diff: 1   Type: TF   Page Ref: 583/583
    Topic: Adverse selection and moral hazard in labor markets
    Skill: Conceptual
    Objective: LO 3: Adverse Selection and Moral Hazard in Labor Markets
    AASCB Coding: Reflective Thinking
    Special Features: None

21. Kenny has just been hired as the manager of The Fennel Grill. This restaurant enjoys a good reputation for its food and service. Currently, the wait staff (servers) is not required to share their tips with the kitchen staff (cooks, dishwashers). Kenny feels that this is an unfair system and would like to replace tipping with a 15 percent service charge which will be shared equally among non-management restaurant staff. How will the new system affect the productivity of the wait staff? Will this scheme require less monitoring or more monitoring of the wait staff?

    Answer: Tipping gives servers an incentive to provide good service. If tipping were eliminated and replaced by a standard 15 percent service charge, the wages of servers are likely to fall and service will likely suffer. This scheme will require more monitoring in order to maintain the same quality of service.

    Diff: 2   Type: ES   Page Ref: 583-4/583-4
    Topic: Principal-agent problem
    Skill: Analytical
    Objective: LO 3: Adverse Selection and Moral Hazard in Labor Markets
    AASCB Coding: Analytic Skills
    Special Features: None

22. Assume that Adam Smith College is proposing an early retirement package in its next faculty contract. Full-time faculty who are 65 years old and have taught at the college for at least 20 years would be eligible for the retirement package, which entitles them to: (a) a one-time $100,000 payment (b) lifetime health care benefits under the college's group coverage plan. One of the vice-presidents of the college who is in favor of the retirement package argued that "In coming years we can eventually save money by hiring younger faculty who earn less than the faculty members they will replace." From the description of the early retirement plan and the vice president's comments explain why the compensation system at Adam Smith College an example of: (a) payment of efficiency wages (or, in this case, salaries) (b) a seniority system (c) profit sharing. If you believe there is no evidence that Adam Smith uses any of these systems, explain why.

    Answer: Although some colleges pay higher salaries to their faculty than other colleges, there is no evidence that Adam Smith College does so; therefore, the description of the retirement package and the vice president's comments do not provide evidence of the payment of efficiency wages or salaries. There is no evidence of a profit sharing plan. But the financial incentives in the retirement package and the vice president's comments suggest that there is a seniority system that offers faculty higher salaries (and possibly better benefits, although this is not clear) for faculty who have been with the college longer. Starting salaries for new faculty in some departments (but probably not in departments where there is a high demand for candidates for faculty positions outside of academia) are likely to be lower than the salaries of the faculty who accept the retirement package.

    Diff: 2   Type: ES   Page Ref: 582-4/582-4
    Topic: Adverse selection and moral hazard in labor markets
    Skill: Conceptual
    Objective: LO 3: Adverse Selection and Moral Hazard in Labor Markets
    AASCB Coding: Reflective Thinking
    Special Features: None

17.4   The Winner's Curse: When Is It Bad to Win an Auction?

1. An information problem that occurs in auctions is
    A) the artist's lament.
    B) cognitive dissonance.
    C) the principal–agent problem.
    D) the winner's curse

Answer: D

Diff: 1   Type: MC   Page Ref: 585/585
Topic: The winner's curse
Skill: Conceptual
Objective: LO 4: The Winners' Curse: When Is It Bad to Win an Auction?
AASCB Coding: Reflective Thinking
Special Features: None

2. In an auction of a common–value asset, such as an oil field, the winner of the auction
    A) will have more information about the value of the asset than the losers of the auction.
    B) may end up overestimating the value of the asset and end up worse off than the losers.
    C) will have a higher opportunity cost than the losers of the auction.
    D) will have a lower opportunity cost than the losers of the auction.

Answer: B

Diff: 1   Type: MC   Page Ref: 585/585
Topic: The winner's curse
Skill: Conceptual
Objective: LO 4: The Winners' Curse: When Is It Bad to Win an Auction?
AASCB Coding: Reflective Thinking
Special Features: None

3. The so-called "winner's curse" may occur when
    A) there is an auction of a common-value asset.
    B) a firm's board of directors pays its top management more than the value of the management's contribution to the profits of the firm.
    C) a firm agrees to a long–term contract for the rights to a common–value resource and then the price of the resource falls; the firm is still obligated to pay the higher price it agreed to pay in the contract.
    D) there is an auction of a private–value asset.

Answer: A

Diff: 1   Type: MC   Page Ref: 585/585
Topic: The winner's curse
Skill: Conceptual
Objective: LO 4: The Winners' Curse: When Is It Bad to Win an Auction?
AASCB Coding: Reflective Thinking
Special Features: None

4. When the U.S. government auctions off land for oil drilling the auction's winners may bid a price that is higher than the value of the oil sold from the land. The reason for this is
    A) the winners use the auction as a "loss leader" – they want to receive preferential treatment from the government in future auctions.
    B) the winners want to use the cost of the land to reduce their tax obligations, rather than to make a profit from selling oil.
    C) neither the government nor those who bid on the land know with certainty how much oil is in the land.
    D) the motive for the winners is to deprive other firms from having access to the land, rather than to make a profit from selling oil themselves.
Answer: C
Diff: 2   Type: MC   Page Ref: 585–6/585–6
Topic: The winner's curse
Skill: Conceptual
Objective: LO 4: The Winners' Curse: When Is It Bad to Win an Auction?
AASCB Coding: Reflective Thinking
Special Features: None

5. In an auction for a common–value asset, each of the firms that bid attempt to estimate the value of the asset using the best available information. Which of the following is most likely to be closest to the true value of the asset?
    A) The winning bid, since it must have been based on better information than the information available to those who made losing bids.
    B) The lowest bid; the "winner's curse" will cause the highest bid to be greater than the true value of the asset.
    C) The second highest bid; the "winner's curse" will cause the highest bid to be greater than the true value of the asset.
    D) The average bid; some bidders are likely to overestimate the value of the asset while other bidders will underestimate the value of the asset.
Answer: D
Diff: 2   Type: MC   Page Ref: 585–6/585–6
Topic: The winner's curse
Skill: Definition
Objective: LO 4: The Winners' Curse: When Is It Bad to Win an Auction?
AASCB Coding: Reflective Thinking
Special Features: None

6. Three Atlantic Richfield engineers examined bidding in government auctions of oil fields, which frequently resulted in the "winner's curse" – winning auction bids that exceeded the value of the oil recovered from the fields. Two conclusions resulted from this examination. One of these conclusions is:
   A) the greater the number of bidders, the greater the difference between the price paid for the oil fields and the profits received from selling oil from the fields.
   B) the greater the financial resources of the winning bidder, the greater the difference between the price paid for the oil fields and the profits received from selling oil from the fields.
   C) in competitive bidding, the winner tends to be the bidder who most overestimates the true value of the oil fields.
   D) the winning bidder in one auction is frequently the winning bidder in other auctions.
   Answer: C
   Diff: 2   Type: MC   Page Ref: 585–6/585–6
   Topic: The winner's curse
   Skill: Fact
   Objective: LO 4: The Winners' Curse: When Is It Bad to Win an Auction?
   AASCB Coding: Reflective Thinking
   Special Features: None

7. Three Atlantic Richfield engineers examined bidding in government auctions of oil fields, which frequently resulted in the "winner's curse" – winning auction bids that exceeded the value of the oil recovered from the fields. Two conclusions resulted from this examination. One of these conclusions is, in competitive bidding
   A) a bidder who bids what he thinks the oil field is worth will, in the long run, be "taken to the cleaners."
   B) those who submit losing bids tend to be those who know the least about the oil business. Therefore, the "winner's curse" affects bidders who know the most about the oil business.
   C) bidders who hire economists as consultants for their bids are those most likely to be the victims of the "winner's curse."
   D) the difference between the winning bid and the next highest bid is greater than the true value of the oil fields.
   Answer: A
   Diff: 2   Type: MC   Page Ref: 585–6/585–6
   Topic: The winner's curse
   Skill: Conceptual
   Objective: LO 4: The Winners' Curse: When Is It Bad to Win an Auction?
   AASCB Coding: Reflective Thinking
   Special Features: None

8. A consequence of the winner's curse is
    A) that by underestimating the value of the asset the winning bidder foregoes some profit from the asset.
    B) that by overestimating the value of the asset, the winning bidder is likely to reap lower-than-expected profits or incur a loss in the venture.
    C) that the winning bidder loses the asset to some unforeseen circumstances.
    D) that the tax liability for the asset far exceeds its true value.
Answer: B
Diff: 1   Type: MC   Page Ref: 585–6/585–6
Topic: The winner's curse
Skill: Conceptual
Objective: LO 4: The Winners' Curse: When Is It Bad to Win an Auction?
AASCB Coding: Reflective Thinking
Special Features: None

9. The winner's curse is more likely to occur when
    A) the value of a good being auctioned is known with certainty.
    B) the value of the good being auctioned is uncertain.
    C) the cost of gathering information about the item that is auctioned is low.
    D) there are more than five bidders for the item that is auctioned.
Answer: B
Diff: 1   Type: MC   Page Ref: 585–6/585–6
Topic: The winner's curse
Skill: Conceptual
Objective: LO 4: The Winners' Curse: When Is It Bad to Win an Auction?
AASCB Coding: Reflective Thinking
Special Features: None

10.   *Table 17–2*

Company	Bid
M	$40
N	30
O	20
P	15
Q	10

Refer to Table 17–2. The table above lists the bids (in millions) made by 5 companies for tracts of land in Louisiana. The winning bidder was granted the right to drill for oil on the land. All bids were based on the firms' best estimates of the value of the oil they expected to find. The value of the oil is most likely to equal
    A) the winning bid, since company M had the strongest incentive to make a bid that would give it drilling rights.
    B) company N's bid. Company N had a bid that was more accurate than the companies that had lower bids, but company M will likely be the victim of the winner's curse.
    C) the average bid of all five companies.
    D) the lowest bid, that of company Q. The other companies likely overestimated the value of the land.

Answer: C
Diff: 2   Type: MC   Page Ref: 585–6/585–6
Topic: The winner's curse
Skill: Analytical
Objective: LO 4: The Winners' Curse: When Is It Bad to Win an Auction?
AASCB Coding: Reflective Thinking
Special Features: None

11. ***Refer to Table 17–2.*** The table above lists the bids (in millions) made by 5 companies for tracts of land in Gulf of Mexico. The winning bidder was granted the right to drill for oil found from the land. All bids were based on the firms' best estimates of the value of the oil they expected to find. A winner's curse will result from this auction if
    A) the value of the oil found from the land is more than $30 million but less than $40 million.
    B) the average bid of all five companies is greater than the winning bid.
    C) the average bid of all five companies is less than the value of the oil found from the land.
    D) the winning bid is greater than the value of the oil found from the land.
    Answer: D
Diff: 1   Type: MC   Page Ref: 585–6/585–6
Topic: The winner's curse
Skill: Conceptual
Objective: LO 4: The Winners' Curse: When Is It Bad to Win an Auction?
AASCB Coding: Reflective Thinking
Special Features: None

12. Some economists have studied the process that men and women use to choose a marriage partner. Which of the following is one result from these studies?
    A) Because it is difficult to determine if a marriage will be successful until a couple is married, the winner's curse can help to explain why some marriages fail.
    B) Some choices people make, such as the choice of a marriage partner, cannot be analyzed by using positive economic analysis. The choice of a marriage partner is a normative choice.
    C) The average cost of a marriage, including the wedding ceremony, is greater when it is paid for by the bride's family than when the cost is shared by both families.
    D) Explaining why 43 percent of marriages end in divorce is simple if positive economic analysis is used, but not if normative economic analysis is used, as part of the explanation.
    Answer: A
Diff: 2   Type: MC   Page Ref: 586/586
Topic: The winner's curse
Skill: Fact
Objective: LO 4: The Winners' Curse: When Is It Bad to Win an Auction?
AASCB Coding: Reflective Thinking
Special Features: Making the Connection: Is There a Winner's Curse in the Marriage Market?

13. Some economists have studied the process that men and women use to choose a marriage partner. One result of these studies is that the winner's curse can apply to marriage
    A) when one marriage partner is much wealthier than the other marriage partner; there is a high probability that this marriage will end in divorce.
    B) when one marriage partner owns common-value resources that the other marriage partner cannot accurately value.
    C) when two partners marry for financial reasons only.
    D) when one person overestimates the value of the other person as a marriage partner.
    Answer: D
    Diff: 1   Type: MC   Page Ref: 585/586
    Topic: The winner's curse
    Skill: Conceptual
    Objective: LO 4: The Winners' Curse: When Is It Bad to Win an Auction?
    AASCB Coding: Reflective Thinking
    Special Features: Making the Connection: Is There a Winner's Curse in the Marriage Market?

14. Which of the following is a similarity that economists have identified between the choice of a marriage partner and bidding in an auction?
    A) A winner's curse may result from the choice of a marriage partner as well as from bidding in an auction for a private-value asset.
    B) Winning bidders in auctions for private-value assets are likely to overestimate the value of the assets they bid for, and marriage partners are likely to overestimate the value of their wedding ceremonies.
    C) A winner's curse may result from the choice of a marriage partner as well as from bidding in an auction for a common-value asset.
    D) A winner's curse can result from an auction as well as a marriage when decisions by auction bidders and marriage partners are based on normative analysis rather than positive analysis.
    Answer: C
    Diff: 2   Type: MC   Page Ref: 586/586
    Topic: The winner's curse
    Skill: Conceptual
    Objective: LO 4: The Winners' Curse: When Is It Bad to Win an Auction?
    AASCB Coding: Reflective Thinking
    Special Features: Making the Connection: Is There a Winner's Curse in the Marriage Market?

15. Why do economists believe that some failed marriages can be explained by the winner's curse?
    A) Many people who are" winners" in business are prone to make marriage decisions in the same way that they make business decisions.
    B) It is difficult to determine how good a marriage partner will be until you are actually married to this person.
    C) Many people who delay marriage to pursue their careers later make hasty decisions to marry before they are too old to have children.
    D) Marriage partners often fail to discuss whether they both want to have children before they marry.
    Answer: B
    Diff: 2   Type: MC   Page Ref: 586/586
    Topic: The winner's curse
    Skill: Conceptual
    Objective: LO 4: The Winners' Curse: When Is It Bad to Win an Auction?
    AASCB Coding: Reflective Thinking
    Special Features: Making the Connection: Is There a Winner's Curse in the Marriage Market?

16. The winner's curse does not apply to the auction of a private-value asset because
    A) the value of the asset to each bidder depends on the bidder's own preferences.
    B) auctions of these assets are perfectly competitive.
    C) these auctions are conducted privately, not publicly.
    D) each bid in this type of auction is the result of positive economic analysis rather than normative economic analysis.
    Answer: A
    Diff: 2   Type: MC   Page Ref: 586/586
    Topic: The winner's curse
    Skill: Conceptual
    Objective: LO 4: The Winners' Curse: When Is It Bad to Win an Auction?
    AASCB Coding: Reflective Thinking
    Special Features: None

17. In early 2007 a Honus Wagner baseball card from 1909 sold for over $2.3 million. Wagner, a Hall of Fame shortstop for the Pittsburgh Pirates, insisted that the tobacco company that sold the original cards stop selling them because he did not want to promote smoking. As a result, few of the cards have survived in mint condition. The $2.3 million price paid for the card
    A) proves that the winner's curse can be found in auctions of baseball cards as well as auctions of other common-value assets.
    B) reflects the value placed by the buyer on a private-value asset. The winner's curse does not apply.
    C) shows how a buyer can pay more than for an asset than it is worth.
    D) proves that the winner's curse can be found in auctions of baseball cards as well as auctions of other private-value assets.
Answer: B
Diff: 2   Type: MC   Page Ref: 586/586
Topic: The winner's curse
Skill: Conceptual
Objective: LO 4: The Winners' Curse: When Is It Bad to Win an Auction?
AASCB Coding: Reflective Thinking
Special Features: None

18. Recent advances in science and geology have increased the accuracy with which oil companies can predict how much oil will be found from a tract of land. Suppose that the U.S. Congress votes to allow increased exploration of oil in Alaska. Will the new technology cause an increase in the revenue the federal government receives from an auction of rights to drill for oil in Alaska?
    A) Yes, but only if the price of oil continues to rise.
    B) No, because the price of oil has risen too high for oil exploration in Alaska to be profitable, a fact that the new technology will verify.
    C) No, because the new technology will cause the auction's highest bid to be less that it otherwise would be.
    D) No, because the state government, not the federal government, is entitled to the revenue from the sale of drilling rights in Alaska.
Answer: C
Diff: 2   Type: MC   Page Ref: 587/587
Topic: The winner's curse
Skill: Analytical
Objective: LO 4: The Winners' Curse: When Is It Bad to Win an Auction?
AASCB Coding: Analytic Skills
Special Features: Solved Problem: Auctions, Available Information, and the Winner's Curse

19. The winner's curse results when the bidders in an auction for a common-value asset lack full information about what is being auctioned. Suppose that advances in technology resulted in a significant improvement in the ability of bidders in this type of auction to estimate the value of a common-value asset. The improvement in technology is most likely to produce which of the following results?
    A) An increase in the value of the winning auction bid.
    B) A decrease in the value of the winning auction bid, but an increase in the average value of all auction bids.
    C) A decrease in the number of auction bids.
    D) A decrease in the value of the winning auction bid.

Answer: D
Diff: 2   Type: MC   Page Ref: 587/587
Topic: The winner's curse
Skill: Conceptual
Objective: LO 4: The Winners' Curse: When Is It Bad to Win an Auction?
AASCB Coding: Reflective Thinking
Special Features: Solved Problem: Auctions, Available Information, and the Winner's Curse

20. In 1994, Pacific Telesis hired several economists to help plan the company's bidding strategy in auctions for licenses that would allow winning bidders to operate wireless communication networks. The strategy used by Pacific Telesis helped it to win the auctions with relatively low bids. Which of the following summarizes the company's strategy?
    A) Pacific Telesis took out ads that stressed its cost advantages over rival bidders and the risk that other firms would incur by overbidding for the licenses.
    B) Pacific Telesis made it widely known that it would bid very high prices for the licenses. This reduced the number of bids; the bids Pacific Telesis actually submitted were much lower than it said it would submit.
    C) Pacific Telesis kept a low profile and pretended not to be interested in bidding on the licenses. It kept its true intentions secret until the date of the auctions. As a result, other firms submitted lower bids than those submitted by Pacific Telesis.
    D) Pacific Telesis used the economists the firm hired to make detailed estimates of the value of the licenses. The economists recommended that Pacific Telesis submit bids that were lower than the bids the firm had planned to make. As a result, the firm won the auctions and avoided the winner's curse.

Answer: A
Diff: 2   Type: MC   Page Ref: 587-8/587-8
Topic: The winner's curse
Skill: Fact
Objective: LO 4: The Winners' Curse: When Is It Bad to Win an Auction?
AASCB Coding: Reflective Thinking
Special Features: None

21. Max Bazerman of Harvard University and William Samuelson of Boston University conducted experiments in their classrooms in which students bid on the value of paper clips and coins contained in glass jars. The purpose of these experiments was to determine if the winner's curse would result. What was the result of these experiments?
    A) The winning bids were all less than the value of the monetary value of the items in the jars. Bazerman and Samuelson concluded that the winner's curse applied to auctions of common-value assets, but not private-value assets.
    B) The winning bidders in the economics classes were not subject to the winner's curse, but the winning bidders in other classes were victims of the curse. Bazerman and Samuelson concluded that successful bidders used their economic knowledge to avoid making bids that would subject them to the winner's curse.
    C) The winning bids in all of the auctions were less than the value of the monetary value of the items in the jars. Bazerman and Samuelson concluded that the winner's curse applied only to auctions of common-value assets that have significant monetary value.
    D) Winning bidders in the auctions fell victim to the winner's curse.
    Answer: D
    Diff: 2   Type: MC   Page Ref: 588/588
    Topic: The winner's curse
    Skill: Conceptual
    Objective: LO 4: The Winners' Curse: When Is It Bad to Win an Auction?
    AASCB Coding: Reflective Thinking
    Special Features: Making the Connection: Want to Make Some Money? Try Auctioning a Jar of Coins

22. An individual who wishes to buy a used car can buy from a used car dealer or directly from the car's owner. Although asymmetric information is a problem with both types of transactions the price a used car owner gets is likely to be less than the price a used car dealer can get for the same type of car in the same condition. Which of the following offers the best explanation for this?
    A) The buyer knows that the used car's owner does not have much incentive to be honest in hopes of attracting future buyers. Car dealers have a greater incentive to deal honestly.
    B) The dealer has greater overhead costs that he will want to cover with the revenue he receives from car sales. A used car owner has little or no overhead costs so he will be willing to accept a lower price.
    C) Buying a used car from a dealer is similar to bidding on a common-value asset in an auction; the buyer is subject to the winner' curse and tends to pay a price that is greater than the used car is worth.
    D) Used car dealers want to sell at prices as high as they can get in order to maximize their profits. Car owners are not motivated by profit and are willing to sell at lower prices.
    Answer: A
    Diff: 2   Type: MC   Page Ref: 589/589
    Topic: Adverse selection in the car market
    Skill: Conceptual
    Objective: LO 4: The Winners' Curse: When Is It Bad to Win an Auction?
    AASCB Coding: Reflective Thinking
    Special Features: Economics in YOUR Life!: Have You Ever Tried to Sell a Car?

23. In recent years, insurance companies have used their customers' credit histories as a factor to help determine their premiums. Insurers believe that bad credit histories can indicate that drivers are likely to make bad decisions, including when they drive their cars. If, in fact, credit histories can be used to distinguish safe drivers from reckless drivers, how is the use of credit histories likely to affect the market for insurance?
    A) With better information about risks, insurance companies will offer fewer policies overall; drivers with good credit and safe driving records will be offered policies at the same premiums, but reckless drivers will not be offered insurance policies.
    B) With better information about risks, insurance companies will raise premiums for all of their customers, but reckless drivers with poor credit histories will experience the greatest increases.
    C) With better information about risks, insurance companies will be able to offer more policies, lower the price of polices and increase the quantity of insurance.
    D) With better information about risks, insurance companies will be able to eliminate moral hazard and increase their profits.
    Answer: C
    Diff: 3   Type: MC   Page Ref: 590–1/590–1
    Topic: Adverse selection and moral hazard
    Skill: Conceptual
    Objective: LO 4: The Winners' Curse: When Is It Bad to Win an Auction?
    AASCB Coding: Reflective Thinking
    Special Features: An Inside Look: Should Bad Credit Increase Your Car Insurance Rate?

24. The winner's curse can occur in auctions of common–value assets but not in auctions of private–value assets.
    Answer: ◔ True   False
    Diff: 1   Type: TF   Page Ref: 586/586
    Topic: The winner's curse
    Skill: Conceptual
    Objective: LO 4: The Winners' Curse: When Is It Bad to Win an Auction?
    AASCB Coding: Reflective Thinking
    Special Features: None

25. Suppose four oil companies bid for the right to drill on a tract of land auctioned by the U.S. government. Because the amount of oil contained in the tract is highly uncertain, the bids differ widely. The companies made the following estimates of net value of the tract of land:

Company A: $50 million
Company B: $90 million
Company C: $120 million
Company D: $200 million

a. Who is likely to win the bidding rights?
b. Suppose that after all the costs of drilling were accounted for there was $90 million worth of oil in the ground. Does the winning bidder earn a profit on the venture? What is this phenomenon called?
Answer: a. Firm D is likely to be the winning bidder.
b. The firm suffers a loss of $110 million. This phenomenon is called the winner's curse.

Diff: 2   Type: ES   Page Ref: 585-8/585-8
Topic: The winner's curse
Skill: Analytical
Objective: LO 4: The Winners' Curse: When Is It Bad to Win an Auction?
AASCB Coding: Analytic Skills
Special Features: None

26. Why does the winner's curse occur in auctions for common-value assets but not in auctions of private-value assets?
Answer: The problem that bidders have in auctions of common-value assets that can lead to a winner's curse is the inability to determine the monetary value of the assets prior to their purchase. This is why auctions for oil drilling rights, for example, can result in a winner's curse. There is uncertainty about how much oil can be recovered from the tracts of land that are purchased or leased as well as the price of oil after it is recovered and refined. But in auctions of private value assets the bidders know the items they bid on. You may be tempted to believe that paying millions of dollars for a rare stamp or painting is excessive, but this does not mean there is a winner's curse. Anyone who submits the winning bid for this type of asset must have placed a value on the asset that was greater than the price he was willing to pay.

Diff: 2   Type: SA   Page Ref: 585-6/585-6
Topic: The winner's curse
Skill: Conceptual
Objective: LO 4: The Winners' Curse: When Is It Bad to Win an Auction?
AASCB Coding: Reflective Thinking
Special Features: None

Chapter 18   Public Choice, Taxes, and the Distribution of Income

18.1   Public Choice

1. Some economists advocate cutting taxes on the dividends paid to shareholders. One reason for their position is that
   A) contrary to popular belief, most of the tax cut will provide relief to low-income, rather than high-income, taxpayers.
   B) cutting the tax on dividends will discourage speculation in financial markets.
   C) cutting this tax will reduce the double taxation of corporate profits.
   D) cutting this tax can be used to justify increasing income taxes on high-income citizens.
   Answer: C
   Diff: 1   Type: MC   Page Ref: 598-9/598-9
   Topic: The corporate income tax
   Skill: Fact
   Objective: LO 1: Public Choice
   AACSB Coding: Reflective Thinking
   Special Features: Chapter Opener: Should the Government Use the Tax System to Reduce Inequality?

2. Both presidents Kennedy and Reagan proposed significant cuts in income taxes because
   A) at the time of their proposals the federal government was experiencing budget surpluses; that is, tax revenue exceeded government expenditures.
   B) they wanted to offset their proposals to increase other taxes.
   C) state governments had increased their taxes and they believed the tax cuts they proposed would result in most citizens paying about the same total state and federal taxes.
   D) they believed that the tax cuts would enhance economic efficiency.
   Answer: D
   Diff: 1   Type: MC   Page Ref: 598-9/598-9
   Topic: Income taxes
   Skill: Fact
   Objective: LO 1: Public Choice
   AACSB Coding: Reflective Thinking
   Special Features: Chapter Opener: Should the Government Use the Tax System to Reduce Inequality?

3. Both presidents Kennedy and Reagan proposed significant cuts in income taxes. Opponents of these tax cut proposals argued that
   A) the tax cuts would benefit high–income taxpayers.
   B) cutting state sales taxes, rather than federal income taxes, would result in greater economic efficiency.
   C) while the tax cuts would result in greater economic efficiency, there was too much opposition to the tax cuts in Congress. As it turned out, Congress ultimately approved both tax cut proposals.
   D) it would be better to cut taxes on corporate profits.
   Answer: A
   Diff: 1   Type: MC   Page Ref: 598–9/598–9
   Topic: Income taxes
   Skill: Fact
   Objective: LO 1: Public Choice
   AACSB Coding: Reflective Thinking
   Special Features: Chapter Opener: Should the Government Use the Tax System to Reduce Inequality?

4. Economists often debate among themselves about the proper role of government in the U.S. economy and whether taxes should be increased or decreased. But there is little debate among economists that
   A) if taxes are cut, it is better to cut income taxes on the wealthy rather than to cut taxes on corporate profits.
   B) tax laws have important effects on economic incentives and economic activity.
   C) the rich do not pay enough of their incomes in taxes.
   D) increasing state sales taxes is a more efficient way to reduce deficits than increasing income taxes.
   Answer: B
   Diff: 1   Type: MC   Page Ref: 598–9/598–9
   Topic: Income taxes
   Skill: Fact
   Objective: LO 1: Public Choice
   AACSB Coding: Reflective Thinking
   Special Features: Chapter Opener: Should the Government Use the Tax System to Reduce Inequality?

5. Economists James Buchanam and Gordon Tullock are well–known for developing
   A) the impossibility theorem.
   B) the voting paradox.
   C) the public choice model.
   D) the concept of government failure.
   Answer: C
   Diff: 1   Type: MC   Page Ref: 600/600
   Topic: The public choice model
   Skill: Fact
   Objective: LO 1: Public Choice
   AACSB Coding: Reflective Thinking
   Special Features: None

6. The public choice model assumes that government policy makers
    A) must promote the public interest at the expense of their own self-interest in order to be re-elected.
    B) will pursue their self-interest in personal affairs but only if it does not conflict with the public interest.
    C) will often act irrationally in their personal affairs, but will act rationally when they promote the public interest.
    D) are likely to pursue their own self-interest, even if their self-interest conflicts with the public interest.
    Answer: D
    Diff: 2   Type: MC   Page Ref: 600/600
    Topic: The public choice model
    Skill: Conceptual
    Objective: LO 1: Public Choice
    AACSB Coding: Reflective Thinking
    Special Features: None

7. When members of Congress vote to pass new legislation they will
    A) always vote for the alternative favored by a majority of the voters.
    B) fail to consistently represent the underlying preferences of voters.
    C) always vote for the alternative favored by a plurality of the voters if there is no majority position.
    D) always fail to represent the underlying preferences of voters.
    Answer: B
    Diff: 2   Type: MC   Page Ref: 600-1/600-1
    Topic: Voting paradox
    Skill: Conceptual
    Objective: LO 1: Public Choice
    AACSB Coding: Reflective Thinking
    Special Features: None

8. Economist Kenneth Arrow has shown mathematically that no system of voting will consistently represent the underlying preferences of voters. This finding is called
    A) the Arrow impossibility theorem.
    B) Arrow's median voter model.
    C) Arrow's Amendment to the public choice model.
    D) Arrow's majority vote paradox.
    Answer: A
    Diff: 1   Type: MC   Page Ref: 600-1/600-1
    Topic: Arrow impossibility theorem
    Skill: Definition
    Objective: LO 1: Public Choice
    AACSB Coding: Reflective Thinking
    Special Features: None

9. The Arrow impossibility theorem explains
   A) why there is no system of voting that will consistently represent the underlying preferences of voters.
   B) why government regulation of private markets will always result in a reduction in economic efficiency in these markets.
   C) why voters are always rationally ignorant.
   D) why it is not possible to provide the economically efficient amount of any public good.
   Answer: A
   Diff: 2   Type: MC   Page Ref: 600–1/600–1
   Topic: Arrow impossibility theorem
   Skill: Conceptual
   Objective: LO 1: Public Choice
   AACSB Coding: Reflective Thinking
   Special Features: None

10. The proposition that the outcome of a majority vote is likely to represent the preferences of the voter who is in the political middle is called
    A) the mean (or average) voter theorem.
    B) the voting paradox.
    C) the Arrow impossibility theorem.
    D) the median voter theorem.
    Answer: D
    Diff: 1   Type: MC   Page Ref: 601–2/601–2
    Topic: The median voter model
    Skill: Definition
    Objective: LO 1: Public Choice
    AACSB Coding: Reflective Thinking
    Special Features: None

11.

Table 18–1

Policy	Ted Kenney	Nancy Polici	Bob Scranton
Homeland security	1st	2nd	3rd
Education	2nd	3rd	1st
Medical research	3rd	1st	2nd

Refer to Table 18–1. The table above lists three policy alternatives that the U.S. Senate will vote on, along with the ranking of these alternates the Senate must decide which of these alternatives should receive an additional $1 billion of funding, and that there is enough money in the federal budget for only one of these alternatives. If a series of votes is taken in which each pair of alternatives is considered (homeland security and education; homeland security and medical research; education and medical research) which of the following will result from these votes?

    A) When the vote is between homeland security and education, the Senators will vote for education to receive funding.

    B) The Senators' votes will demonstrate transitivity.

    C) The results will illustrate the voting paradox.

    D) The results from the voting will illustrate the median voter theorem.

Answer: C

Diff: 3   Type: MC   Page Ref: 600–1/600–1
Topic: Voting paradox
Skill: Conceptual
Objective: LO 1: Public Choice
AACSB Coding: Reflective Thinking
Special Features: None

12. The Arrow impossibility theorem

    A) explains why people can be rational as well as ignorant at the same time.

    B) explains why voting systems do not consistently represent the preferences of voters.

    C) explains why candidates for public office must represent the preferences of the political middle.

    D) explains why it is impossible, in most cases, to eliminate special interest legislation after it has become law.

Answer: B

Diff: 2   Type: MC   Page Ref: 600–1/600–1
Topic: Arrow impossibility theorem
Skill: Conceptual
Objective: LO 1: Public Choice
AACSB Coding: Reflective Thinking
Special Features: None

13. A common belief among political analysts is that someone running for his or her party's nomination for president of the United States must choose a different strategy once the nomination is secured. To be nominated the candidate must appeal to voters from one party – Democrat or Republican – but in a general election a party's nominee must appeal to voters from both parties as well as independent voters. Which of the following offers the best explanation for this change in strategy?
    A) The Arrow impossibility theorem.
    B) The voting paradox.
    C) The median voter theorem.
    D) Rent seeking.
Answer: C
Diff: 1   Type: MC   Page Ref: 601-2/601-2
Topic: The median voter model
Skill: Conceptual
Objective: LO 1: Public Choice
AACSB Coding: Reflective Thinking
Special Features: None

14. Congressman Gallstone seeks support from his colleagues for a bill he sponsors that will establish a new national park in his district. He offers to support Congresswoman Disrail's proposal to build a new library in her district in exchange for her vote for his national park bill. This is an example of
    A) regulatory capture.
    B) logrolling.
    C) rational ignorance.
    D) government failure.
Answer: B
Diff: 1   Type: MC   Page Ref: 603/603
Topic: Logrolling
Skill: Conceptual
Objective: LO 1: Public Choice
AACSB Coding: Reflective Thinking
Special Features: None

15. The political process is more likely to serve the interests of individuals whose preferences are in the middle, rather than individuals with preferences that are much to the left or right of the political center. This statement is best explained by which of the following?
    A) Logrolling.
    B) The voting paradox.
    C) The Arrow impossibility theorem.
    D) The median voter theorem.
Answer: D
Diff: 1   Type: MC   Page Ref: 601-2/601-2
Topic: The median voter model
Skill: Conceptual
Objective: LO 1: Public Choice
AACSB Coding: Reflective Thinking
Special Features: None

16. Which of the following is used to argue that the self-interest of public policymakers will often lead to actions that are inconsistent with the preferences of the voters they represent?
    A) The voting paradox.
    B) The median voter theorem.
    C) Rent seeking.
    D) Transitivity of voters' preferences.
    Answer: A
    Diff: 2   Type: MC   Page Ref: 600–1/600–1
    Topic: Voting paradox
    Skill: Conceptual
    Objective: LO 1: Public Choice
    AACSB Coding: Reflective Thinking
    Special Features: None

17. Some individuals seek to use government action to make themselves better off at the expense of others. The actions of these individuals
    A) are examples of fraud; but these individuals usually avoid prosecution because of logrolling and rational ignorance.
    B) are examples of rent seeking.
    C) offer proof that Adam Smith's "invisible hand" is not valid.
    D) are evidence of the voting paradox.
    Answer: B
    Diff: 2   Type: MC   Page Ref: 603/603
    Topic: Rent seeking
    Skill: Conceptual
    Objective: LO 1: Public Choice
    AACSB Coding: Reflective Thinking
    Special Features: None

18. Which of the following is an example of rent seeking behavior?
    A) Apple earned large profits from the development and sale of the iPod.
    B) Microsoft introduced the Zune to compete with the iPod. Microsoft was motivated by the desire to earn profits from the Zune but also increased the choice of digital music players available to consumers.
    C) U.S. sugar firms convinced Congress to impose a quota on imports of sugar.
    D) Recent increases in cigarette taxes faced little opposition from voters, many of whom were rationally ignorant with respect to the tax.
    Answer: C
    Diff: 2   Type: MC   Page Ref: 603/603
    Topic: Rent seeking
    Skill: Conceptual
    Objective: LO 1: Public Choice
    AACSB Coding: Reflective Thinking
    Special Features: None

19. Which of the following statements refers to rent seeking?
    A) "Laws passed by the federal government often provide benefits for a small number of individuals. These individuals, in turn, have an incentive to contribute to the campaigns of politicians who pass these laws."
    B) "The federal government should spend more money on programs that help low income citizens and less money on national defense."
    C) "The role of the federal government in the U.S. economy grew significantly after the Great Depression. Government spending and taxes are a much greater proportion of total income today than they were in 1929."
    D) "There is an opportunity cost whenever the federal government spends tax revenue. For example, an additional $1 billion spent on national defense means there will be less revenue for highway construction and maintenance or some other program."
    Answer: A
    Diff: 2   Type: MC   Page Ref: 603/603
    Topic: Rent seeking
    Skill: Conceptual
    Objective: LO 1: Public Choice
    AACSB Coding: Reflective Thinking
    Special Features: None

20. Rational ignorance
    A) explains why consumers ignore sunk costs when they vote.
    B) explains the Arrow impossibility theorem.
    C) refers to attempts by special interests to use government action to make themselves better off at the expense of others.
    D) helps to explain why rent seeking by special interest groups occurs.
    Answer: D
    Diff: 2   Type: MC   Page Ref: 603/603
    Topic: Rational ignorance
    Skill: Conceptual
    Objective: LO 1: Public Choice
    AACSB Coding: Reflective Thinking
    Special Features: None

21. Which of the following is a consequence of the voting paradox?
    A) A majority of voters elect a candidate that does not represent the preferences of the voter who is in the political middle.
    B) Politicians support small groups of individuals and firms that benefit from special interest legislation, rather than a much larger group of voters who pay the cost for this legislation.
    C) Individuals and firms who benefit from government actions engage in rent seeking.
    D) The collective preferences of voters are not transitive and voting outcomes are inconsistent.

Answer: D
Diff: 2   Type: MC   Page Ref: 600–1/600–1
Topic: Voting paradox
Skill: Conceptual
Objective: LO 1: Public Choice
AACSB Coding: Reflective Thinking
Special Features: None

22. What is the term that explains why voters often lack knowledge of pending legislation, and lack knowledge of the views of candidates for office on a range of issues that affect their own (the voters') welfare?
    A) The voting paradox.
    B) Logrolling.
    C) Rational ignorance.
    D) Regulatory capture.

Answer: C
Diff: 1   Type: MC   Page Ref: 603/603
Topic: Rational ignorance
Skill: Definition
Objective: LO 1: Public Choice
AACSB Coding: Reflective Thinking
Special Features: None

23. The public choice model can be used to examine voting models that contrast the manner in which collective decisions are made by governments (state, local and federal) and the manner in which individual choices are made in markets. Which of the following descriptions is consistent with the difference between collective decision-making and decision-making in markets?
    A) Everyone who votes must agree with a decision made collectively through government, but in markets individuals can make their own choices.
    B) Individuals are less likely to see their preferences represented in the outcomes of government policies than in the outcomes of markets.
    C) The cost of a government policy is determined by a majority vote of members of the public; decisions made in markets are based on individual willingness to pay.
    D) Choices made through government policies are more important than decisions individuals make through markets.
    Answer: B
    Diff: 2   Type: MC   Page Ref: 601-2/601-2
    Topic: The public choice model
    Skill: Conceptual
    Objective: LO 1: Public Choice
    AACSB Coding: Reflective Thinking
    Special Features: None

24. Economists often analyze the interaction of individuals and firms in markets. But economists also examine the actions of individuals and firms as they attempt to use government to make themselves better off at the expense of others, a process that is referred to as
    A) rent seeking.
    B) logrolling.
    C) government failure.
    D) the public choice initiative.
    Answer: A
    Diff: 2   Type: MC   Page Ref: 602-3/602-3
    Topic: Rent seeking
    Skill: Definition
    Objective: LO 1: Public Choice
    AACSB Coding: Reflective Thinking
    Special Features: None

25. Financial contributions to the campaigns of members of Congress, state legislators and other elected officials by firms that seek special interest legislation that make the firms better off are
    A) examples of rent seeking.
    B) illegal.
    C) the result of the voting paradox.
    D) irrational because elected officials will almost always act in the interest of the voters who have to pay the cost of the legislation.
    Answer: A
    Diff: 1   Type: MC   Page Ref: 603/603
    Topic: Rent seeking
    Skill: Conceptual
    Objective: LO 1: Public Choice
    AACSB Coding: Reflective Thinking
    Special Features: None

26. Congressman Flack votes for a program that will benefit the constituents of Congressman Walpole. Which of the following explanations for Flack's vote is most consistent with the public choice model?
    A) Congressman Flack did not have time to read and understand all of the legislation he voted on. Members of Congress often depend on their staffs to read proposed legislation and recommend how they should vote.
    B) Legislators such as Congressman Flack are similar to other decision-makers in that they sometimes make irrational choices.
    C) Congressman Flack will support programs of legislators from his own party, regardless of who benefits from these programs.
    D) Congressman Flack expects Congressman Walpole's support for programs that will benefit Flack's constituents.
    Answer: D
    Diff: 2   Type: MC   Page Ref: 603/603
    Topic: Logrolling
    Skill: Conceptual
    Objective: LO 1: Public Choice
    AACSB Coding: Reflective Thinking
    Special Features: None

27. Congressman Flack votes for a program that will benefit the constituents of Congressman Walpole. The public choice model suggests that Flack's vote is best explained by which of the following?
    A) Rational ignorance.
    B) Party loyalty.
    C) Logrolling.
    D) The voting paradox.
    Answer: C
    Diff: 1   Type: MC   Page Ref: 603/603
    Topic: Logrolling
    Skill: Conceptual
    Objective: LO 1: Public Choice
    AACSB Coding: Reflective Thinking
    Special Features: None

28. Some economists who use the public choice model to explain the ways government intervenes in the economy believe that regulatory capture results when an agency or commission is given authority over a particular industry or product. Which of the following is the best example of regulatory capture?
    A) The Food and Drug Administration (FDA) has increased the time and expense pharmaceutical firms incur to receive approval to market a new drug.
    B) A federal government agency hires more employees than it requires to regulate an industry because it does not seek to minimize costs or maximize the agency's profits.
    C) The head of an agency is required to testify before Congress because Congress controls the size of the agency's budget. Congress "captures" the agency because of its budget authority.
    D) Firms that were regulated by the Interstate Commerce Commission (ICC) attempted for many years to influence the ICC's actions.
    Answer: D
    Diff: 2   Type: MC   Page Ref: 603-4/603-4
    Topic: Regulatory capture
    Skill: Conceptual
    Objective: LO 1: Public Choice
    AACSB Coding: Reflective Thinking
    Special Features: None

29. Many economists believe that when the federal government establishes an agency to regulate a particular industry the regulated firms try to influence the agency, even if these actions do not benefit the public. Economists refer to this result of government regulation by which of the following terms?
    A) Regulatory capture.
    B) Logrolling.
    C) Special interest regulation.
    D) The regulatory paradox.
    Answer: A
    Diff: 2   Type: MC   Page Ref: 603–4/603–4
    Topic: Regulatory capture
    Skill: Conceptual
    Objective: LO 1: Public Choice
    AACSB Coding: Reflective Thinking
    Special Features: None

30. One result of the public choice model is that most economists believe that
    A) when market failure occurs government intervention will always lead to a more efficient outcome.
    B) government intervention will always result in a reduction in economic efficiency in regulated markets.
    C) policymakers may have incentives to intervene in the economy in ways that do not promote economic efficiency.
    D) the voting paradox will prevent voters from selecting the best person for public office.
    Answer: C
    Diff: 1   Type: MC   Page Ref: 603–4/603–4
    Topic: Government failure
    Skill: Conceptual
    Objective: LO 1: Public Choice
    AACSB Coding: Reflective Thinking
    Special Features: None

31. The public choice model raises questions about the government's ability to regulate economic activity efficiently. Which of the following statements represents the views of most economists with regard to the role of government?
    A) Congress should abolish the Food and Drug Administration, the Environmental Protection Agency and other agencies and commissions because the costs of their actions exceed the benefits they provide to the public.
    B) Government should do more to regulate markets. The public choice model has shown that rent seeking and rational ignorance affect more markets than are currently subject to regulation.
    C) U.S. citizens can afford more government regulation if the cost of this regulation is borne mostly by taxpayers with the highest incomes.
    D) Agencies such as the Food and Drug Administration and the Environmental Protection Agency can serve a useful purpose, but we need to take the costs of regulation into account along with the benefits.
    Answer: D
    Diff: 2   Type: MC   Page Ref: 603–4/603–4
    Topic: Government failure
    Skill: Conceptual
    Objective: LO 1: Public Choice
    AACSB Coding: Reflective Thinking
    Special Features: None

32. A key insight of the public choice model is that public policymakers are likely to pursue the public's interest, even if their self–interest conflicts with the public interest.
    Answer: True   ◎ False
    Diff: 1   Type: TF   Page Ref: 600/600
    Topic: The public choice model
    Skill: Conceptual
    Objective: LO 1: Public Choice
    AACSB Coding: Reflective Thinking
    Special Features: None

33. The median voter theorem states that the outcome of a majority vote is likely to represent the preferences of the voter who is in the political middle.
    Answer: ◎ True   False
    Diff: 1   Type: TF   Page Ref: 601/601
    Topic: The median voter model
    Skill: Definition
    Objective: LO 1: Public Choice
    AACSB Coding: Reflective Thinking
    Special Features: None

34. Logrolling refers to attempts by individuals to use government action to make themselves better off at the expense of others.
    Answer: True   ◦ False
    Diff: 1   Type: TF   Page Ref: 603/603
    Topic: Rent seeking
    Skill: Definition
    Objective: LO 1: Public Choice
    AACSB Coding: Reflective Thinking
    Special Features: None

35. A key assumption of the public choice model is that government policymakers will pursue their own self-interest. Economists assume that consumers and firms pursue their own self-interests when they interact in competitive markets and this interaction results in efficient economic outcomes. Does the pursuit of self-interest by policy markets makers result in efficient economic outcomes?

    Answer: The public choice model can be used to explain why the actions of self-interested policymakers often do not result in efficient economic outcomes. The model assumes that the self-interest motives of policymakers lead them to take actions that result in their being elected, or re-elected. Because elections are won by candidates who receive a majority (or, in some cases, a plurality) of the votes cast, candidates must appeal to the preferences of the voter who is in the political middle. Once in office, policymakers take actions that affect all of their constituents, not just those who agree with these actions. This is in contrast with private markets, where consumers are under no obligation to pay for a good or service they do not want. Other reasons why a policymaker's self-interest motives lead to economically inefficient outcomes are: (a) rent seeking by individuals and firms for the purpose of supporting special interest legislation that makes themselves better off at the expense of others, and (b) the rational ignorance of voters who pay the costs of this legislation. Since the benefits of legislation are concentrated among a small number of individuals and firms, they have an incentive to use resources to convince policymakers to support their interests. Most voters who must pay to support the legislation have little incentive to oppose it, since the cost to each individual voter is low. As a result, policymakers often support legislation that results in greater costs to taxpayers than the value of the benefits the legislation provides.
    Diff: 3   Type: ES   Page Ref: 600-3/600-3
    Topic: The public choice model
    Skill: Analytical
    Objective: LO 1: Public Choice
    AACSB Coding: Analytic Skills
    Special Features: None

36. Define logrolling. Explain why logrolling often results in legislation that benefits the economic interests of a few, while harming the interests of a larger group of people.

Answer: Logrolling refers to the situation where a member of Congress votes to approve a bill in exchange for votes from other members of Congress on other bills. Members of Congress often sponsor legislation that benefits constituents in their own districts; for example, a new highway. The costs of the highway are paid by taxpayers from all districts. Most of these taxpayers will see little or no benefit from the highway, which creates jobs and provides services mostly within a single Congressional district. Taxpayers outside of the district typically do not oppose the highway for two reasons. First, they often are rationally ignorant; the costs of the highway are spread widely so that each taxpayer incurs a very small part of the total cost. Second, taxpayers in other districts are the beneficiaries of their own projects, which receive, through logrolling, the votes of a majority of members of Congress.

Diff: 2   Type: ES   Page Ref: 603/603
Topic: Logrolling
Skill: Analytical
Objective: LO 1: Public Choice
AACSB Coding: Reflective Thinking
Special Features: None

37. Former Alabama Governor George Wallace ran for president several times, once as a third-party candidate in 1968. Wallace claimed there was "not a dime's worth of difference" between the Democratic and Republican parties during one of his campaigns. How does Wallace's comment relate to the median voter theorem?

Answer: To win his party's nomination for president a candidate can proclaim his support for the party's position on important domestic and foreign policy issues. But to be elected president a candidate must receive a majority of the states' electoral votes in a general election. This typically requires candidates from both the Democratic and Republican parties to reach out to voters from both parties as well independent voters. This is consistent with the median voter theorem and is one reason why many people believed that Wallace's observation was valid. Third-party candidates such as Wallace become popular because their views on important issues differentiate themselves from mainstream politicians but this places them away from the political middle in the general election. As a result, it is very difficult for a third-party candidate to win a general election.

Diff: 3   Type: SA   Page Ref: 603/603
Topic: The median voter model
Skill: Conceptual
Objective: LO 1: Public Choice
AACSB Coding: Reflective Thinking
Special Features: None

38.

Table 18-2

	Foreign Aid	*Post-Secondary Education*	*Roads and Bridges*
Tom	3rd	1st	2nd
Dick	2nd	3rd	1st
Harriet	1st	2nd	3rd

Refer to Table 18-2. The table above outlines the rankings of three members of the U.S. House of Representatives on three spending alternatives. Assume that Congress can spend additional revenue on only one of the three spending alternatives and that Tom, Dick and Harriet, all members of the House of Representatives, participate in a series of votes in which they are to determine which of two of the spending alternatives should receive funding. Three votes will be taken: (1) Foreign Aid and Post-Secondary Education (2) Foreign Aid and Roads and Bridges and (3) Post-Secondary Education and Roads and Bridges.

Determine whether the voting paradox will occur as a result of these votes.
Answer: First vote:

	Foreign Aid	*Post-Secondary Education*	*Selection*
Tom	3rd	1st	Post-Secondary Education
Dick	2nd	3rd	Foreign Aid
Harriet	1st	2nd	Foreign Aid

First vote: the majority votes for spending on Foreign Aid.

Second vote:

	Foreign Aid	*Roads and Bridges*	*Selection*
Tom	3rd	2nd	Roads and Bridges
Dick	2nd	1st	Roads and Bridges
Harriet	1st	3rd	Foreign Aid

Second vote: the majority votes for spending on Roads and Bridges.

Third vote:

	Post-Secondary Education	*Road and Bridges*	*Selection*
Tom	1st	2nd	Post-Secondary Education
Dick	3rd	1st	Roads and Bridges
Harriet	2nd	3rd	Post-Secondary Education

Third vote: the majority votes for spending on Post-Secondary Education.

The results of the voting process do illustrate the voting paradox because the preferences of Tom, Dick and Harriet are not transitive. If their preferences were transitive, we would find that if the voters prefer to spend on Foreign Aid rather than

Post-Secondary Education (the result of the first vote), and they prefer to spend on Roads and Bridges rather than Foreign Aid (the result of the second vote), they should prefer to spend on Roads and Bridges rather than Post-Secondary Education. If fact, they prefer to spend on Post-Secondary Education rather than Roads and Bridges (the result of the third vote). This is an example of the voting paradox, which is defined as the failure of majority voting to always result in consistent choices.

Diff: 3   Type: ES   Page Ref: 600-1/600-1
Topic: Voting paradox
Skill: Conceptual
Objective: LO 1: Public Choice
AACSB Coding: Reflective Thinking
Special Features: None

18.2   The Tax System

1. Which of the following is the largest source of revenue for the U.S. federal government?
    A) The individual income tax.
    B) Social insurance taxes.
    C) Sales taxes.
    D) Property taxes.
Answer: A
Diff: 1   Type: MC   Page Ref: 604-5/604-5
Topic: Income taxes
Skill: Fact
Objective: LO 2: The Tax System
AACSB Coding: Reflective Thinking
Special Features: None

2. In the United States the largest source of funds for public schools is
    A) the federal income tax.
    B) the property tax.
    C) the consumption tax.
    D) sales taxes.
Answer: B
Diff: 1   Type: MC   Page Ref: 605/605
Topic: Property taxes
Skill: Fact
Objective: LO 2: The Tax System
AACSB Coding: Reflective Thinking
Special Features: None

3. Which of the following is the source of revenue for Medicare and Social Security in the United States?
   A) Individual income taxes.
   B) Sales taxes.
   C) Social insurance taxes.
   D) Property taxes.
   Answer: C
   Diff: 1   Type: MC   Page Ref: 605/605
   Topic: Tax System
   Skill: Fact
   Objective: LO 2: The Tax System
   AACSB Coding: Reflective Thinking
   Special Features: None

4. A tax imposed by a state or local government on retail sales of most products is
   A) an excise tax.
   B) a social service tax.
   C) a consumption tax.
   D) a sales tax.
   Answer: D
   Diff: 1   Type: MC   Page Ref: 605/605
   Topic: Sales taxes
   Skill: Definition
   Objective: LO 2: The Tax System
   AACSB Coding: Reflective Thinking
   Special Features: None

5. The federal government and some state governments levy taxes on specific goods such as gasoline, cigarettes and beer. These are known as
   A) sales taxes.
   B) sin taxes.
   C) specific taxes.
   D) excise taxes.
   Answer: D
   Diff: 1   Type: MC   Page Ref: 605/605
   Topic: The tax system
   Skill: Definition
   Objective: LO 2: The Tax System
   AACSB Coding: Reflective Thinking
   Special Features: None

6. In 2006 over 75 percent of the revenue of the U.S. federal government was raised through
    A) individual income and social insurance taxes.
    B) property and social insurance taxes.
    C) sales and corporate income taxes.
    D) individual income and property taxes.
   Answer: A
   Diff: 1   Type: MC   Page Ref: 605/605
   Topic: The tax system
   Skill: Fact
   Objective: LO 2: The Tax System
   AACSB Coding: Reflective Thinking
   Special Features: None

7. In the United States, over the past 40 years federal revenues as a share of gross domestic product have
    A) risen steadily and now are about 40 percent.
    B) ranged between 17 and 23 percent.
    C) fallen below 20 because of rapid economic growth.
    D) been limited by law to no more than 20 percent.
   Answer: B
   Diff: 1   Type: MC   Page Ref: 606/606
   Topic: The tax system
   Skill: Fact
   Objective: LO 2: The Tax System
   AACSB Coding: Reflective Thinking
   Special Features: None

8. The term "payroll taxes" is often used to refer to
    A) individual income taxes that are withheld from paychecks.
    B) corporate income taxes.
    C) Social Security and Medicare taxes.
    D) sales taxes.
   Answer: C
   Diff: 2   Type: MC   Page Ref: 605/605
   Topic: The tax system
   Skill: Fact
   Objective: LO 2: The Tax System
   AACSB Coding: Reflective Thinking
   Special Features: None

9. The largest source of tax revenue for state and local governments in the United States in 2006 was
    A) sales taxes.
    B) the corporate income tax.
    C) the property tax.
    D) the individual income tax.
    Answer: A
    Diff: 1   Type: MC   Page Ref: 605/605
    Topic: The tax system
    Skill: Fact
    Objective: LO 2: The Tax System
    AACSB Coding: Reflective Thinking
    Special Features: None

10. A regressive tax is a tax for which people with lower incomes
    A) pay a lower percentage of their incomes in tax than do people with higher incomes.
    B) pay a higher percentage of their incomes in tax than do people with higher incomes.
    C) pay the same percentage of their incomes in tax as do people with higher incomes.
    D) do not have to pay unless their income exceeds a certain amount.
    Answer: B
    Diff: 1   Type: MC   Page Ref: 606/606
    Topic: Regressive tax
    Skill: Definition
    Objective: LO 2: The Tax System
    AACSB Coding: Reflective Thinking
    Special Features: None

11. A progressive tax is a tax for which people with lower incomes
    A) pay a higher percentage of their incomes in tax than do people with higher incomes.
    B) pay the same percentage of their incomes in tax as do people with higher incomes.
    C) pay a lower percentage of their incomes in tax than do people with higher incomes.
    D) receive most of the benefits from the services government provides.
    Answer: C
    Diff: 1   Type: MC   Page Ref: 606/606
    Topic: Progressive tax
    Skill: Definition
    Objective: LO 2: The Tax System
    AACSB Coding: Reflective Thinking
    Special Features: None

12. In reference to the federal income tax system a tax bracket is
    A) the estimated amount of federal income tax firms withhold from their employees' paychecks.
    B) the formula the federal government uses to determine the dollar amount of the personal exemption and the amounts taxpayers are allowed for deductions from their incomes.
    C) used to determine the average tax rate.
    D) the income range within which a tax rate applies.
    Answer: D
    Diff: 1   Type: MC   Page Ref: 606/606
    Topic: The tax system
    Skill: Definition
    Objective: LO 2: The Tax System
    AACSB Coding: Reflective Thinking
    Special Features: None

13. Which of the following is an example of a federal mandate?
    A) An excise tax.
    B) The Medicaid program.
    C) The personal tax exemption.
    D) The Food and Drug Administration (FDA).
    Answer: B
    Diff: 2   Type: MC   Page Ref: 606/606
    Topic: The tax system
    Skill: Fact
    Objective: LO 2: The Tax System
    AACSB Coding: Reflective Thinking
    Special Features: None

14. A proportional tax is a tax for which people with lower incomes
    A) pay a higher percentage of their incomes in tax than do people with higher incomes.
    B) pay a lower percentage of their incomes in tax than do people with higher incomes.
    C) pay the same percentage of their incomes in tax as do people with higher incomes.
    D) pay the same amount of taxes as people with higher incomes pay.
    Answer: C
    Diff: 1   Type: MC   Page Ref: 606/606
    Topic: Proportional tax
    Skill: Definition
    Objective: LO 2: The Tax System
    AACSB Coding: Reflective Thinking
    Special Features: None

15. In the United States taxpayers are allowed to exclude from taxation a certain amount of income, called
    A) the personal income exclusion.
    B) the income allowance.
    C) the income tax credit.
    D) the personal exemption.
Answer: D
Diff: 1   Type: MC   Page Ref: 606/606
Topic: The tax system
Skill: Definition
Objective: LO 2: The Tax System
AACSB Coding: Reflective Thinking
Special Features: None

Table 18–3

Income	Consumption Spending
$20,000	$18,000
24,000	20,700

Table 18–3 contains data on household spending at different income levels. Suppose that a 3 percent tax is levied on all consumption spending.

16. ***Refer to Table 18–3.*** Calculate the percent of income paid in taxes by a family with $20,000 income and by a family with $24,000 income.
    A) The family with a $20,000 income pays 2.7 percent of its income in consumption taxes and the family with a $24,000 income pays 2.6 percent of its income in consumption taxes.
    B) Each family pays 3 percent of their respective incomes in consumption taxes.
    C) The family with a $20,000 income pays 15 percent of its income in consumption taxes and the family with a $24,000 income pays 33.3 percent of its income in consumption taxes.
    D) There is insufficient information to make these calculations.
Answer: A
Diff: 3   Type: MC   Page Ref: 611/611
Topic: Consumption taxes
Skill: Analytical
Objective: LO 2: The Tax System
AACSB Coding: Analytic Skills
Special Features: Making the Connection: Should the United States Shift from an Income Tax to a Consumption Tax?

17. *Refer to Table 18-3.* The consumption tax is
    A) proportional.
    B) progressive.
    C) income neutral.
    D) regressive.
Answer: D
Diff: 2   Type: MC   Page Ref: 611/611
Topic: Consumption taxes
Skill: Conceptual
Objective: LO 2: The Tax System
AACSB Coding: Reflective Thinking
Special Features: Making the Connection: Should the United States Shift from an Income Tax to a Consumption Tax?

18.

Table 18–2

Taxable Income	Tax Payments
$10,000	$1,000
12,000	1,240
16,000	1,780
22,000	2,740

Table 18-4 shows the amount of taxes paid on various levels of income.

Refer to Table 18-4. The tax system is
    A) progressive throughout all levels of income.
    B) proportional throughout all levels of income.
    C) regressive throughout all levels of income.
    D) progressive between $10,000 and $12,000 of income and regressive between $16,000 and $22,000.
Answer: A
Diff: 1   Type: MC   Page Ref: 606/606
Topic: The tax system
Skill: Analytical
Objective: LO 2: The Tax System
AACSB Coding: Analytic Skills
Special Features: None

19. According to projections for 2007 by the Tax Policy Center, the 20 percent of U.S. taxpayers who make the highest incomes
    A) use loopholes and tax exemptions to reduce their share of federal income taxes to less than 20 percent.
    B) pay more than 80 percent of federal income taxes.
    C) pay about 60 percent of federal income taxes but only about 20 percent of Social Security and Medicare payroll taxes.
    D) pay more in excise and other taxes than they pay in Social Security and Medicare payroll taxes.

    Answer: B
    Diff: 2   Type: MC   Page Ref: 607–8/607–8
    Topic: Progressive tax
    Skill: Fact
    Objective: LO 2: The Tax System
    AACSB Coding: Reflective Thinking
    Special Features: Making the Connection: Which Groups Pay the Most in Federal Taxes?

20.   *Table 18–5*

Taxable Income	Tax Payments
$10,000	$1,000
12,000	1,080
16,000	1,360
22,000	1,760

Table 18–5 shows the amount of taxes paid on various levels of income.

Refer to Table 18–5. The tax system is
    A) progressive throughout all levels of income.
    B) proportional throughout all levels of income.
    C) regressive throughout all levels of income.
    D) progressive between $10,000 and $12,000 of income and regressive between $12,000 and $22,000.

    Answer: C
    Diff: 2   Type: MC   Page Ref: 606/606
    Topic: The tax system
    Skill: Analytical
    Objective: LO 2: The Tax System
    AACSB Coding: Analytic Skills
    Special Features: None

21. In the United States, the federal income tax is an example of a
    A) progressive tax.
    B) regressive tax.
    C) proportional tax.
    D) flat tax.
    Answer: A
    Diff: 1   Type: MC   Page Ref: 606/606
    Topic: Progressive tax
    Skill: Conceptual
    Objective: LO 2: The Tax System
    AACSB Coding: Reflective Thinking
    Special Features: None

22. The average tax rate is calculated as
    A) total income divided by the total tax paid.
    B) the change in total tax paid divided by the change in income.
    C) total tax paid divided by total income.
    D) the change in income divided by the change in total tax paid.
    Answer: C
    Diff: 1   Type: MC   Page Ref: 608/608
    Topic: Average tax rate
    Skill: Definition
    Objective: LO 2: The Tax System
    AACSB Coding: Reflective Thinking
    Special Features: None

23. When considering changes in tax policy, economists usually focus on
    A) the average tax rate.
    B) the marginal tax rate.
    C) people's willingness to pay taxes.
    D) people's ability to pay taxes.
    Answer: B
    Diff: 1   Type: MC   Page Ref: 608/608
    Topic: Marginal tax rate
    Skill: Conceptual
    Objective: LO 2: The Tax System
    AACSB Coding: Reflective Thinking
    Special Features: None

24. The marginal tax rate is
    A) the amount of taxes paid as a percentage of income.
    B) the amount of per capita taxes paid.
    C) the amount of taxes paid as a percentage of gross domestic product (GDP).
    D) the fraction of each additional dollar of income that must be paid in taxes.
    Answer: D
    Diff: 1   Type: MC   Page Ref: 608/608
    Topic: Marginal tax rate
    Skill: Definition
    Objective: LO 2: The Tax System
    AACSB Coding: Reflective Thinking
    Special Features: None

25. An income tax system is _____ if marginal tax rates increase as income increases.
    A) progressive
    B) regressive
    C) efficient
    D) equitable
    Answer: A
    Diff: 1   Type: MC   Page Ref: 606/606
    Topic: Progressive tax
    Skill: Conceptual
    Objective: LO 2: The Tax System
    AACSB Coding: Reflective Thinking
    Special Features: None

Table 18–6

Income Tax Bracket	Marginal Tax Rate
$0 to $6,000 of income	10%
$6,001 to $20,000 of income	15%
$20,001 to $44,500 of income	22%
$44,501 and over	30%

Table 18–6 shows the income tax brackets and tax rates for single taxpayers in Monrovia.

26. *Refer to Table 18–6.* Calculate the income tax paid by Sylvia, a single taxpayer with an income of $70,000.
    A) $21,000
    B) $15,740
    C) $13,475
    D) $15,400
    Answer: B
    Diff: 3   Type: MC   Page Ref: 606–8/606–8
    Topic: Progressive tax
    Skill: Analytical
    Objective: LO 2: The Tax System
    AACSB Coding: Analytic Skills
    Special Features: None

27. ***Refer to Table 18-6.***Sylvia is a single taxpayer with an income of $70,000. What is her marginal tax rate and what is her average tax rate?
    A) marginal tax rate = 30%; average tax rate = 30%
    B) marginal tax rate = 8%; average tax rate = 19.3%
    C) marginal tax rate = 30%; average tax rate = 22.5%
    D) marginal tax rate = 20%; average tax rate = 30%
    Answer: C
    Diff: 3   Type: MC   Page Ref: 606-8/606-8
    Topic: The tax system
    Skill: Analytical
    Objective: LO 2: The Tax System
    AACSB Coding: Analytic Skills
    Special Features: None

28. A tax is efficient if
    A) individuals with the lowest incomes pay proportionately lower taxes than individuals with the highest incomes.
    B) it is based on profits earned and not on wages.
    C) it encourages savings and investments.
    D) it imposes a small excess burden relative to the revenue it raises.
    Answer: D
    Diff: 1   Type: MC   Page Ref: 610/610
    Topic: Efficient tax
    Skill: Definition
    Objective: LO 2: The Tax System
    AACSB Coding: Reflective Thinking
    Special Features: None

29. The excess burden of a tax
    A) measures the efficiency loss to the economy that results from a tax causing a reduction in the quantity of goods and services produced.
    B) is measured by the administrative costs required to implement a tax system.
    C) is a measure of the hardship imposed on low-income individuals in a society.
    D) is a measure of the foregone consumption as a result of having to pay taxes.
    Answer: A
    Diff: 1   Type: MC   Page Ref: 610/610
    Topic: Excess burden of a tax
    Skill: Definition
    Objective: LO 2: The Tax System
    AACSB Coding: Reflective Thinking
    Special Features: None

30. A tax on interest earned from saving is an example of a tax with a high deadweight loss because
    A) it compels retired individuals to rely more heavily on Social Security.
    B) it encourages people to consume less and save more for their future expenditures.
    C) doing so amounts to double taxation since savings often come from income that has already been taxed once.
    D) the savings that are taxed could have been spent on capital goods which will benefit society.
    Answer: C
    Diff: 2   Type: MC   Page Ref: 611/611
    Topic: Consumption taxes
    Skill: Conceptual
    Objective: LO 2: The Tax System
    AACSB Coding: Reflective Thinking
    Special Features: Making the Connection: Should the United States Shift from an Income Tax to a Consumption Tax?

31. According to the ability-to-pay principle of taxation,
    A) individuals who receive the benefit of a good or service should bear a greater share of the tax burden.
    B) it is fair to expect a greater share of the tax burden to be borne by people who have a greater ability to pay.
    C) people in the same economic situation should bear an equal share of the tax burden.
    D) individuals who are willing to bear a greater share of the tax burden should be compensated with non-monetary benefits.
    Answer: B
    Diff: 1   Type: MC   Page Ref: 612/612
    Topic: Ability-to-pay principle
    Skill: Definition
    Objective: LO 2: The Tax System
    AACSB Coding: Reflective Thinking
    Special Features: None

32. For many U.S. individuals and households, replacing the federal income tax with a consumption tax would not make a major change in their tax liability – the amount they would be taxed. Which of the individuals described would be least affected by replacing the income tax with a consumption tax?
    A) A person in the lowest income bracket. This person would pay little or no tax under either system.
    B) A high-income individual who saves 35 percent of this income and uses his savings to purchase stocks and bonds.
    C) A female head of family, with no husband present.
    D) A taxpayer who puts part of her savings into a 401(k) retirement plan and in an Individual Retirement Account.
    Answer: D
    Diff: 2   Type: MC   Page Ref: 611/611
    Topic: Consumption taxes
    Skill: Analytical
    Objective: LO 2: The Tax System
    AACSB Coding: Analytic Skills
    Special Features: Making the Connection: Should the United States Shift from an Income Tax to a Consumption Tax?

33. Which of the following explains one difference between a consumption tax and an income tax?
    A) An income tax is a regressive tax; a consumption tax is a progressive tax.
    B) Under a consumption tax, households pay taxes only on the part of income they spend; under an income tax, households pay taxes on all income earned.
    C) Under an income tax, present consumption is taxed more heavily than future consumption; under a consumption tax, future consumption is taxed more heavily than present consumption.
    D) Savings are taxed more heavily under a consumption tax than under an income tax.
    Answer: B
    Diff: 1   Type: MC   Page Ref: 611/611
    Topic: Consumption taxes
    Skill: Conceptual
    Objective: LO 2: The Tax System
    AACSB Coding: Reflective Thinking
    Special Features: Making the Connection: Should the United States Shift from an Income Tax to a Consumption Tax?

34. U.S. taxpayers spend many hours during the year maintaining records for tax purposes and preparing their income tax returns. This administrative cost is
    A) part of the deadweight loss of taxation.
    B) equal to the value of consumer surplus associated with the income tax system.
    C) can be claimed as a deduction on income tax returns.
    D) larger for individuals in the lowest income quintile than for individuals in the highest income quintile.
    Answer: A
    Diff: 1   Type: MC   Page Ref: 611–2/611–2
    Topic: Excess burden of a tax
    Skill: Conceptual
    Objective: LO 2: The Tax System
    AACSB Coding: Reflective Thinking
    Special Features: None

35. According to the horizontal–equity principle of taxation,
    A) individuals who receive the benefits of a good or service should bear a greater share of the tax burden.
    B) individuals who are most able to pay should bear a greater share of the tax burden.
    C) people in the same economic situation should be treated equally.
    D) individuals who are willing to bear a greater share of the tax burden should be compensated with non–monetary benefits.
    Answer: C
    Diff: 1   Type: MC   Page Ref: 612/612
    Topic: Horizontal–equity principle
    Skill: Conceptual
    Objective: LO 2: The Tax System
    AACSB Coding: Reflective Thinking
    Special Features: None

36. The horizontal–equity principle of taxation is not easy to use in practice because
    A) some people engage in rent seeking to reduce their taxes below the level other people pay.
    B) people can use tax loopholes to reduce their incomes below the incomes of other taxpayers.
    C) different people receive different levels of government benefits even if their incomes are the same.
    D) it is difficult to determine whether people are in the same economic situation.
    Answer: D
    Diff: 2   Type: MC   Page Ref: 612/612
    Topic: Horizontal–equity principle
    Skill: Conceptual
    Objective: LO 2: The Tax System
    AACSB Coding: Reflective Thinking
    Special Features: None

37. According to the benefits–received principle of taxation
    A) individuals who receive the benefits from a government program should pay the taxes that support the program.
    B) because high income individuals receive the most benefits from government programs, they should pay more taxes than lower income individuals.
    C) people in the same economic situation should bear an equal share of the tax burden.
    D) the benefits of government programs such as national defense are shared equally by all people; therefore, the burden of paying for these programs should be shared equally.
    Answer: A
    Diff: 2   Type: MC   Page Ref: 612/612
    Topic: Benefits–received principle
    Skill: Conceptual
    Objective: LO 2: The Tax System
    AACSB Coding: Reflective Thinking
    Special Features: None

38. Vertical equity is most closely associated with which of the following goals or principles?
    A) The horizontal–equity principle.
    B) The goal of economic efficiency.
    C) The goal of attaining social objectives.
    D) The ability–to–pay principle.
    Answer: D
    Diff: 1   Type: MC   Page Ref: 612/612
    Topic: Ability–to–pay principle
    Skill: Conceptual
    Objective: LO 2: The Tax System
    AACSB Coding: Reflective Thinking
    Special Features: None

39. Suppose the government wants to finance housing for low–income families by placing a tax on the purchase of luxury homes. Assume the government defines a luxury home as a home that is purchased for at least $1 million. This tax is consistent with the
    A) benefits–received principle.
    B) social equity principle.
    C) ability–to–pay principle.
    D) horizontal–equity principle.
    Answer: C
    Diff: 1   Type: MC   Page Ref: 612/612
    Topic: Ability–to–pay principle
    Skill: Conceptual
    Objective: LO 2: The Tax System
    AACSB Coding: Reflective Thinking
    Special Features: None

40. According to the benefits-received principle, those who receive the benefits from a government program should pay the taxes that support the program.
    Answer: ◉ True   False
    Diff: 1   Type: TF   Page Ref: 612/612
    Topic: Benefits-received principle
    Skill: Definition
    Objective: LO 2: The Tax System
    AACSB Coding: Reflective Thinking
    Special Features: None

41. A change from an income tax to a consumption tax system would cause the greatest increase in taxes owed by those who currently put part of their savings into 401(k) retirement plans and Individual Retirement Accounts.
    Answer: True   ◉ False
    Diff: 2   Type: TF   Page Ref: 611/611
    Topic: Consumption taxes
    Skill: Conceptual
    Objective: LO 2: The Tax System
    AACSB Coding: Reflective Thinking
    Special Features: Making the Connection: Should the United States Shift from an Income Tax to a Consumption Tax?

42. A tax is efficient if it imposes a small excess burden relative to the tax revenue it raises.
    Answer: ◉ True   False
    Diff: 2   Type: TF   Page Ref: 610/610
    Topic: Efficient tax
    Skill: Conceptual
    Objective: LO 2: The Tax System
    AACSB Coding: Reflective Thinking
    Special Features: None

43. The complexity of the U.S. federal income tax system results in significant annual deadweight losses. The opportunity cost of the hours taxpayers spend on record keeping and completing their tax returns amounts to billions of dollars.
    a   If the tax system were simplified how would this benefit the economy?
    b   Why hasn't the tax system been simplified?
    Answer: a.   Reducing the time and effort now required for record keeping and completing tax returns could be used to produce additional goods and services. Firms and workers who produce these goods and services would receive additional income. Additional benefits would result because people would have less incentive to engage in activities for the purpose of avoiding or reducing their taxes, and more incentive to engage in activities that produce more goods and services.

    b.   The complexity of the current income tax system is largely the result of the inclusion of provisions that tax people at different rates and allow for income deductions and tax exemptions for specific purposes. For example, homeowners are allowed to deduct from their   income real estate taxes and interest paid on their mortgage loans. A simplified tax system that eliminated this and other provisions that reduced the tax liability of various special interest groups would face considerable opposition.

Diff: 3   Type: SA   Page Ref: 611–2/611–2
Topic: The tax system
Skill: Conceptual
Objective: LO 2: The Tax System
AACSB Coding: Reflective Thinking
Special Features: None

44. Last year, Anthony Millanti earned exactly $30,000 of taxable income. Assume that the income tax system used to determine Anthony's tax liability is progressive. The table below lists the tax brackets and the marginal tax rates that apply to each bracket.

    a.   Draw a new table that lists the amounts of income tax that Anthony is obligated to pay for each tax bracket, and the total tax he owes the government. (Assume that there are no allowable tax deductions, tax credits, personal exemptions or any other deductions that Anthony can use to reduce his tax liability).
    b.   Determine Anthony's average tax rate.

Tax Bracket	Marginal Tax Rate
$0–5,000	0.05 (5%)
5,001–10,000	0.10 (10%)
10,001–15,000	0.15 (15%)
15,001–20,000	0.20 (20%)
20,001–25,000	0.25 (25%)
25,001–30,000	0.30 (30%)

Answer: a

Tax Bracket	Marginal Tax Rate	Tax Liability
$0–5,000	0.05 (5%)	$250
$5,001–10,000	0.10 (10%)	$500
$10,001–15,000	0.15 (15%)	$750
$15,001–20,000	0.20 (20%)	$1,000
$20,001–25,000	0.25 (25%)	$1,250
$25,001–30,000	0.30 (30%)	$1,500
	Total	$5,250

B   The average tax rate is equal to the total tax paid divided by total income: $5,250/$30,000 = 0.175 (17.5 %)

Diff: 3   Type: ES   Page Ref: 606-8/606-8
Topic: Progressive tax
Skill: Analytical
Objective: LO 2: The Tax System
AACSB Coding: Analytic Skills
Special Features: None

18.3   Tax Incidence Revisited: The Effect of Price Elasticity

1. The term tax incidence refers to
    A) the degree of progression of a tax.
    B) the actual division of the burden of a tax between buyers and sellers in a market.
    C) the amount of revenue government collects from a tax imposed on a good or service.
    D) whether the burden of a tax rests more heavily on those with higher incomes or those with lower incomes.
Answer: B
Diff: 1   Type: MC   Page Ref: 612/612
Topic: Tax incidence
Skill: Definition
Objective: LO 3: Tax Incidence Revisited: The Effect of Price Elasticity
AACSB Coding: Reflective Thinking
Special Features: None

2. When the demand for a product is more elastic than the supply,
    A) consumers pay the majority of the tax on the product.
    B) consumers pay the entire tax on the product.
    C) firms pay the majority of the tax on the product.
    D) firms pay the entire tax on the product.
Answer: C
Diff: 2   Type: MC   Page Ref: 613/613
Topic: Tax incidence
Skill: Conceptual
Objective: LO 3: Tax Incidence Revisited: The Effect of Price Elasticity
AACSB Coding: Reflective Thinking
Special Features: None

3. When the demand for a product is less elastic than the supply,
    A) consumers pay the majority of the tax on the product.
    B) firms pay the majority of the tax on the product.
    C) firms pay the entire tax on the product.
    D) consumers pay the entire tax on the product.
Answer: A
Diff: 1   Type: MC   Page Ref: 613/613
Topic: Tax incidence
Skill: Conceptual
Objective: LO 3: Tax Incidence Revisited: The Effect of Price Elasticity
AACSB Coding: Reflective Thinking
Special Features: None

4. There is a difference between who is legally required to send a tax payment to the government and who bears the burden of the tax. Which of the following would have the most impact on who bears the burden of an excise tax?
    A) Whether the tax is imposed by the federal government or a state government.
    B) Whether the tax is based on the ability–to–pay principle or the benefits–received principle.
    C) The motive for the tax. If the tax is designed to raise revenue, more of the burden will fall on firms. If the tax is designed to achieve a social objective (for example, to discourage smoking) more of the burden will fall on consumers.
    D) The elasticity of demand for the item that is taxed.
Answer: D
Diff: 2   Type: MC   Page Ref: 612–3/612–3
Topic: Tax incidence
Skill: Conceptual
Objective: LO 3: Tax Incidence Revisited: The Effect of Price Elasticity
AACSB Coding: Reflective Thinking
Special Features: None

5. How would the elimination of a sales tax affect the market for a product that had been subject to the tax?
    A) The demand for the product would rise and the equilibrium price would fall by the amount of the tax.
    B) The equilibrium price for the product would fall by less than the amount of the tax.
    C) The reduction in government revenue from the tax would be made up by an increase in property taxes.
    D) The supply of the product would become more elastic.
Answer: B
Diff: 2   Type: MC   Page Ref: 613/613
Topic: Sales taxes
Skill: Conceptual
Objective: LO 3: Tax Incidence Revisited: The Effect of Price Elasticity
AACSB Coding: Reflective Thinking
Special Features: Don't Let This Happen to YOU!: Remember Not to Confuse Who Pays the Tax with Who Bears the Burden of the Tax

6. Which of the following statements concerning the federal corporate income tax is true?
    A) It is an efficient tax because it imposes a small excess burden relative to the tax revenue it raises.
    B) The incidence of the corporate income tax can be determined by using demand and supply analysis.
    C) Determining the incidence of the corporate income tax is complicated because it is not certain how corporations respond to the tax.
    D) The corporate income tax is an example of the benefits–received principle.
Answer: C
Diff: 2   Type: MC   Page Ref: 614/614
Topic: The corporate income tax
Skill: Conceptual
Objective: LO 3: Tax Incidence Revisited: The Effect of Price Elasticity
AACSB Coding: Reflective Thinking
Special Features: Making the Connection: Do Corporations Really Bear the Burden of the Federal Corporate Income Tax?

7. Most economists agree that some of the burden of the corporate income tax
    A) is reduced because the tax is progressive.
    B) is shared by the federal government.
    C) is reduced because the tax is used to attain a social objective.
    D) is passed on to consumers in the form of higher prices.
Answer: D
Diff: 1   Type: MC   Page Ref: 614/614
Topic: The corporate income tax
Skill: Conceptual
Objective: LO 3: Tax Incidence Revisited: The Effect of Price Elasticity
AACSB Coding: Reflective Thinking
Special Features: Making the Connection: Do Corporations Really Bear the Burden of the Federal Corporate Income Tax?

8. A study by the Congressional Budget Office (CBO) regarding the corporate income tax included the following statement: "A corporation may write its check to the Internal Revenue Service for payment of the corporate income tax, but the money must come from somewhere..." The comments that followed this statement argued that
    A) corporations pass on some of the burden of the tax to investors in the company, workers and consumers.
    B) the corporate income tax is a reliable source of revenue because corporations cannot avoid paying the tax.
    C) it is necessary to retain the tax because it is based on the ability–to–pay principle.
    D) the tax is more progressive than the individual income tax.
Answer: A
Diff: 2   Type: MC   Page Ref: 614/614
Topic: The corporate income tax
Skill: Conceptual
Objective: LO 3: Tax Incidence Revisited: The Effect of Price Elasticity
AACSB Coding: Reflective Thinking
Special Features: Making the Connection: Do Corporations Really Bear the Burden of the Federal Corporate Income Tax?

9. "For a given supply curve, the excess burden of a tax will be greater when the demand for a product is less elastic than when the demand is more elastic." This statement is
    A) Correct.
    B) Incorrect because the incidence of the tax, not the burden of the tax, is affected by the elasticity of demand.
    C) Incorrect. When demand is less elastic, the burden of the tax is smaller than when the demand is more elastic.
    D) Incorrect. The statement confuses demand with quantity demanded.
    Answer: A
    Diff: 2   Type: MC   Page Ref: 614–5/614–5
    Topic: Excess burden of a tax
    Skill: Conceptual
    Objective: LO 3: Tax Incidence Revisited: The Effect of Price Elasticity
    AACSB Coding: Reflective Thinking
    Special Features: Solved Problem: The Effect of Price Elasticity on the Excess Burden of a Tax

10. For a given supply curve, how does the elasticity of demand affect the burden of a tax imposed on a product?
    A) The excess burden of the tax will be minimized when the demand is unit–elastic.
    B) The excess burden of the tax will be greater when the elasticity of supply is greater than the elasticity of demand.
    C) The excess burden of the tax will be greater when the demand is less elastic than when it is more elastic.
    D) The excess burden of the tax will be greater when the demand is more elastic than when it is less elastic.
    Answer: C
    Diff: 2   Type: MC   Page Ref: 614–5/614–5
    Topic: Excess burden of a tax
    Skill: Conceptual
    Objective: LO 3: Tax Incidence Revisited: The Effect of Price Elasticity
    AACSB Coding: Reflective Thinking
    Special Features: Solved Problem: The Effect of Price Elasticity on the Excess Burden of a Tax

11. The actual division of a tax between buyers and sellers in a market is the excess burden of the tax.
    Answer: True   ○ False
    Diff: 1   Type: TF   Page Ref: 612/612
    Topic: Tax incidence
    Skill: Definition
    Objective: LO 3: Tax Incidence Revisited: The Effect of Price Elasticity
    AACSB Coding: Reflective Thinking
    Special Features: None

12. When the demand for a product is less elastic than the supply, consumers pay the majority of the tax on the product.

    Answer: ◉ True   False
    Diff: 1   *Type: TF*   *Page Ref: 613/613*
    Topic: Tax incidence
    Skill: Conceptual
    Objective: LO 3: Tax Incidence Revisited: The Effect of Price Elasticity
    AACSB Coding: Reflective Thinking
    Special Features: None

13. Explain why it is more difficult to determine the incidence of the corporate income tax than it is to determine the incidence of the tax on gasoline.

    Answer: You can determine the incidence of the gasoline tax if you know the elasticity of demand and the elasticity of supply of gasoline. If the demand for gasoline is less elastic than the supply, consumers will pay the majority of the tax. If the supply is less elastic than the demand, firms will pay the majority of the tax. Firms pass on some of the burden of the corporate income tax to consumers in the form of higher prices, but there is general agreement among economists that the tax also reduces the rate of return on investment in corporations. If a firm invests less with the tax than it would without the tax it will have a negative effect on productivity. This can result in lower wages for workers. All of these factors make it difficult to determine the impact of the corporate income tax on any one of the affected groups. A study by the Congressional Budget Office suggests that the total burden of the tax is significant, equal to as much as one-half of the revenue the tax raises.

    Diff: 3   *Type: SA*   *Page Ref: 614/614*
    Topic: Tax Incidence
    Skill: Conceptual
    Objective: LO 3: Tax Incidence Revisited: The Effect of Price Elasticity
    AACSB Coding: Reflective Thinking
    Special Features: None

14.

Table 18-7

Income Tax Bracket	Tax Rate
on the first $6,000 of taxable income	10%
on the next $14,000 of taxable income	15%
on the next $24,500 of taxable income	25%
on the next $30,500 of taxable income	30%

Table 18-7 shows the income tax brackets and tax rates for single taxpayers in Bauxhall

Refer to Table 18-7. A tax exemption is granted for the first $10,000 earned per year. Suppose you earn $75,000.
a. What is the amount of taxes you will pay?
b. What is your average tax rate?
c. What is your marginal tax rate?

Answer: a. $14,975

b. Approximately 20%

c. 30%

Diff: 3   Type: ES   Page Ref: 604–8/604–8
Topic: The tax system
Skill: Conceptual
Objective: LO 3: Tax Incidence Revisited: The Effect of Price Elasticity
AACSB Coding: Reflective Thinking
Special Features: None

15.   *Figure 18–1*

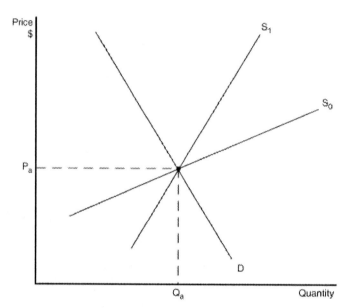

Refer to Figure 18–1. The figure above shows a demand curve and two supply curves, one more elastic than the other. Use Figure 18–1 to answer the following questions.

a.   Suppose the government imposes an excise tax of $1.00 on every unit sold. Use the graph to illustrate the impact of this tax.

b.   If the government imposes an excise tax of $1.00 on every unit sold, will the consumer pay more of the tax if the supply curve is S0 or S1? Refer to the graphs in your answer.

c.   If an excise tax of $1.00 on every unit sold is imposed, will the revenue collected by the government be greater if the supply curve is S_0 or S_1?

d.   If the government imposes an excise tax of $1.00 on every unit sold, will the deadweight loss be greater if the supply curve is S_0 or S_1?

Answer: a. The supply curve shifts up by the full amount of the tax. See below.

b. The consumer will pay more of the tax if the supply curve is S_0 (from P_a to P_b) than if the supply curve is S_1 (from P_a to P_f). See graph below.

c. The government will collect more revenue if the supply curve is S_1 ($1 x Q_f) than if the supply curve is S_1 ($1 x Q_b). See graph below.

d. The deadweight loss is greater under S_0 (represented by the area abe as opposed to the area afg under under S_1).

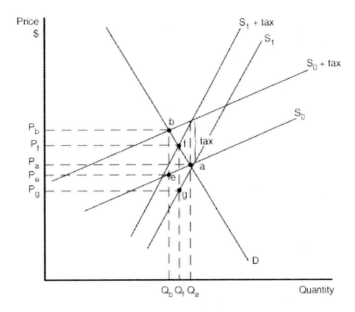

Diff: 3   Type: ES   Page Ref: 612-5/612-5
Topic: Tax Incidence
Skill: Analytical
Objective: LO 3: Tax Incidence Revisited: The Effect of Price Elasticity
AACSB Coding: Analytic Skills
Special Features: None

18.4   Income Distribution and Poverty

1. Which of the following statements about the distribution of income in the United States is
   true?
   A) The United States has the most unequal distribution of income of any high-income
      country in the world.
   B) The United States has a more unequal distribution of income than Bolivia and
      Botswana.
   C) The distribution of income in the United States is fairly equal and there have been no
      dramatic changes over time.
   D) The distribution of income in the United States is unequal and has become significantly
      more unequal over time.
   Answer: A
   Diff: 1   Type: MC   Page Ref: 621-2/621-2
   Topic: Income distribution
   Skill: Fact
   Objective: LO 4: Income Distribution and Poverty
   AACSB Coding: Reflective Thinking
   Special Features: None

2. Which of the following statements best represents the opinion of many economists regarding the impact that changes in tax laws have had on recent changes in income inequality in the United States?
   A) Reductions in income tax rates have favored high income individuals more than low income individuals. As a result, reductions in federal income tax rates have led to more income inequality.
   B) Reductions in income tax rates have created greater incentives for low-income individuals to work, save and invest. As a result, reductions in federal income tax rates have led to less income inequality.
   C) Reductions in income tax rates probably have had little impact on the distribution of income.
   D) Reductions in income tax rates have been offset by increases in corporate income tax rates and payroll taxes. As a result, greater income inequality in the 1990s has been followed by a more equal distribution of income since 2001.
   Answer: C
   Diff: 2   Type: MC   Page Ref: 618/618
   Topic: Income distribution
   Skill: Conceptual
   Objective: LO 4: Income Distribution and Poverty
   AACSB Coding: Reflective Thinking
   Special Features: None

3. The federal government defines the poverty line as
   A) a level of annual income equal to the amount necessary to purchase the minimal quantity of food required for adequate nutrition.
   B) a level of annual income equal to three times the amount of money necessary to purchase the minimal quantity of food required for adequate nutrition.
   C) the average income level of welfare recipients.
   D) an annual income of $12,000 in 2007.
   Answer: B
   Diff: 1   Type: MC   Page Ref: 616-7/616-7
   Topic:
   Skill: Definition
   Objective: LO 4: Income Distribution and Poverty
   AACSB Coding: Reflective Thinking
   Special Features: None

4. The poverty rate is defined as the percentage of the
   A) labor force that is poor according to the federal government's definition of poverty.
   B) population that is exempt from paying federal income taxes.
   C) population who qualify to receive welfare payments and food stamps.
   D) population that is poor according to the federal government's definition of poverty.
   Answer: D
   Diff: 1   Type: MC   Page Ref: 617/617
   Topic: Poverty rate
   Skill: Definition
   Objective: LO 4: Income Distribution and Poverty
   AACSB Coding: Reflective Thinking
   Special Features: None

5. Which of the following groups had the highest poverty rate in 2005 in the United States?
    A) Asians.
    B) White males.
    C) Hispanics.
    D) Female heads of families.
   Answer: D
   Diff: 1   Type: MC   Page Ref: 617/617
   Topic: Poverty rate
   Skill: Fact
   Objective: LO 4: Income Distribution and Poverty
   AACSB Coding: Reflective Thinking
   Special Features: None

6. What does a Lorenz curve illustrate?
    A) A comparison of the distribution of income in two different countries.
    B) The distribution of income within a country in a given time period.
    C) The share of taxes paid by different groups of households.
    D) The change over time in the percentage of households with incomes that place them below the poverty line.
   Answer: B
   Diff: 1   Type: MC   Page Ref: 618/618
   Topic: Lorenz curve
   Skill: Conceptual
   Objective: LO 4: Income Distribution and Poverty
   AACSB Coding: Reflective Thinking
   Special Features: None

7. Which of the following summarizes the information provided by a Lorenz curve?
    A) The Lorenz coefficient.
    B) The income distribution ratio.
    C) The Gini coefficient.
    D) The slope (the rise divided by the run) of the Lorenz curve at a particular point on the curve.
   Answer: C
   Diff: 2   Type: MC   Page Ref: 618–9/618–9
   Topic: Gini coefficient
   Skill: Conceptual
   Objective: LO 4: Income Distribution and Poverty
   AACSB Coding: Reflective Thinking
   Special Features: None

8. A Gini coefficient of _____ means that an income distribution is perfectly equal and a Gini coefficient of _____ means the income distribution is perfectly unequal.
    A) 0; 1
    B) 1; 0
    C) 0, 100
    D) 100, 0
    Answer: A
    Diff: 2   Type: MC   Page Ref: 618–9/618–9
    Topic: Gini coefficient
    Skill: Conceptual
    Objective: LO 4: Income Distribution and Poverty
    AACSB Coding: Reflective Thinking
    Special Features: None

9. Income inequality in the U.S. has increased somewhat over the past 25 years. Two factors that appear to have contributed to this are
    A) tax cuts on high income individuals and large increases in prices of stocks.
    B) strong economic growth and low inflation.
    C) rapid technological change and expanding international trade.
    D) outsourcing of jobs by U.S. firms and cuts in taxes on capital gains.
    Answer: C
    Diff: 1   Type: MC   Page Ref: 618/618
    Topic: Income distribution
    Skill: Conceptual
    Objective: LO 4: Income Distribution and Poverty
    AACSB Coding: Reflective Thinking
    Special Features: None

10. As a group, people with high incomes are likely to have
    A) greater-than-average family inheritance and greater than average SAT scores.
    B) greater-than-average holdings of stocks and bonds and lower-than-average productivity.
    C) greater-than-average productivity and greater-than-average amounts of capital.
    D) a stable marriage and no children.
    Answer: C
    Diff: 1   Type: MC   Page Ref: 618/618
    Topic: Income distribution
    Skill: Conceptual
    Objective: LO 4: Income Distribution and Poverty
    AACSB Coding: Reflective Thinking
    Special Features: None

11. Measures of poverty (for example, the poverty line) and the distribution of income (for example, the Lorenz curve and the Gini coefficient) are misleading for which of the following two reasons?
    A) First, these measures do not take into account income mobility over time. Second, these measures ignore the effects of government programs meant to reduce poverty.
    B) First, none of these measures are adjusted for inflation. Second, they do not measure income on a per capita basis.
    C) First, these measures fail to include the income U.S. citizens earn working for foreign firms that have operations located in the United States. Second, these measures fail to include income foreign citizens earn working for U.S. firms that have operations in foreign countries.
    D) First, these measures fail to include dividend and interest income earned on stocks and bonds. Second, these measures fail to include the value of goods and services citizens make for their own consumption that are not sold in markets.

Answer: A
Diff: 2   Type: MC   Page Ref: 619/619
Topic: Income distribution
Skill: Conceptual
Objective: LO 4: Income Distribution and Poverty
AACSB Coding: Reflective Thinking
Special Features: None

12. All Gini coefficients must lie between 0 and 1. The lower the value
    A) the more unequal is the income distribution.
    B) the closer the income distribution is to being equal.
    C) the greater the degree of poverty.
    D) the lower the degree of poverty according to the federal government's definition of poverty.

Answer: B
Diff: 2   Type: MC   Page Ref: 619/619
Topic: Gini coefficient
Skill: Conceptual
Objective: LO 4: Income Distribution and Poverty
AACSB Coding: Reflective Thinking
Special Features: None

13. If official poverty statistics for the United States included transfer payments individuals receive from the government, such as Social Security payments and other non-cash benefits such as food stamps,
    A) the poverty rate would be lower.
    B) poverty would be eliminated.
    C) income inequality would be greater.
    D) the poverty rate would be overstated.
Answer: A
Diff: 2   Type: MC   Page Ref: 621/621
Topic: Poverty rate
Skill: Conceptual
Objective: LO 4: Income Distribution and Poverty
AACSB Coding: Reflective Thinking
Special Features: None

14. Studies by the U.S. Census Bureau have shown that
    A) families remain below the poverty line for an average of five years.
    B) there is significant income mobility in the U.S. over time.
    C) income mobility in the U.S. is minimal.
    D) above half the people below the poverty line never move out of poverty.
Answer: B
Diff: 2   Type: MC   Page Ref: 619–20/619–20
Topic: Income mobility
Skill: Conceptual
Objective: LO 4: Income Distribution and Poverty
AACSB Coding: Reflective Thinking
Special Features: None

15. Which of the following is a transfer payment?
    A) The food stamp program.
    B) A tax deduction.
    C) Social Security payments.
    D) An income tax credit.
Answer: C
Diff: 1   Type: MC   Page Ref: 621/621
Topic: Income distribution
Skill: Conceptual
Objective: LO 4: Income Distribution and Poverty
AACSB Coding: Reflective Thinking
Special Features: None

16. The Gini coefficient for the United States in 1980 was 0.403. In 2005, the coefficient was equal to 0.469. This means that
    A) per capita income in the U.S. rose from 1980 to 2005.
    B) there was a decrease in the amount of government transfer payments from 1980 to 2005.
    C) cuts in federal income tax rates in the early 1980s and 2001 helped to reduce income inequality.
    D) income inequality increased from 1980 to 2005.

    Answer: D
    Diff: 2   Type: MC   Page Ref: 618–9/618–9
    Topic: Income distribution
    Skill: Analytical
    Objective: LO 4: Income Distribution and Poverty
    AACSB Coding: Analytic Skills
    Special Features: None

17. Sheldon Cleaver commented on the difficulty people have in overcoming poverty in the United States: "Most people whose incomes fall below the poverty line have difficulty pulling themselves above the line in future years. In this sense, poverty becomes a vicious cycle. I believe the psychological damage households face when they are branded with the 'poverty' label in our society is a major factor in their remaining in poverty. Despair is a major reason why the percentage of people with incomes that lie below the poverty line never falls below 10 percent." Which of the following correctly evaluates Cleaver's statement?
    A) Cleaver is correct. Economists often fail to take into account psychological factors when they analyze poverty and the distribution of income in the United States. Policies must take such factors into account if we are to make progress in eliminating poverty.
    B) Cleaver is correct when he notes that poverty is a chronic problem. The best way to reduce poverty is to force the poor to become better educated so that they can work their way out of poverty.
    C) Cleaver is correct, but he is looking at the wrong statistic. The official poverty line understates the true degree of poverty in the U.S.
    D) Cleaver assumes that all those with incomes below the poverty line in one year remain in poverty in subsequent years. In fact, research has shown that the number of people who remain in poverty for many years is much smaller than the number who are in poverty during any one year.

    Answer: D
    Diff: 2   Type: MC   Page Ref: 621/621
    Topic: Income mobility
    Skill: Analytical
    Objective: LO 4: Income Distribution and Poverty
    AACSB Coding: Reflective Thinking
    Special Features: Solved Problem: Are Many Individuals Stuck in Poverty?

Economists caution that conventional statistics used to estimate the extent of poverty in the United States fail to account for benefits people receive that, if considered, would reduce the
18. amount of poverty. Which of the following is an example of these benefits?
   A) Individuals can use tax credits and the personal exemption to reduce their taxable incomes. This reduces what they owe the government and increases their disposable incomes.
   B) The federal income tax system is progressive. As a result, the poor have higher after-tax incomes than they would have if the income tax system was proportional or progressive.
   C) Individuals with low incomes receive non-cash benefits such as free school lunches and food stamps.
   D) The federal minimum wage forces employers to pay workers with low skills an efficiency wage.
Answer: C
Diff: 2   Type: MC   Page Ref: 621/621
Topic: Poverty rate
Skill: Conceptual
Objective: LO 4: Income Distribution and Poverty
AACSB Coding: Reflective Thinking
Special Features: None

19. Which of the following statements is true?
   A) If transfer payments such as Social Security payments to the retired and disabled were excluded from official statistics used to estimate the percentage of people with incomes below the poverty line, the amount of poverty in the United States would be much greater.
   B) Because the federal income tax system is progressive, measuring poverty using after-tax incomes results in a higher poverty rate than if poverty is measured using before-tax incomes.
   C) If non-cash benefits such as food stamps and rent subsidies were added to the incomes of low-income families poverty would be eliminated.
   D) In the United States, income remaining after federal taxes are paid is more equally distributed than income before taxes.
Answer: D
Diff: 3   Type: MC   Page Ref: 621/621
Topic: Income distribution
Skill: Conceptual
Objective: LO 4: Income Distribution and Poverty
AACSB Coding: Reflective Thinking
Special Features: None

20. Between 1970 and 2000 the poverty rate in China declined while the poverty rate in Sub-Saharan Africa increased. The main reason for this is that
    A) the population growth rate decreased in China and increased in Sub-Saharan Africa.
    B) China's government increased transfer payments to poor families over this period of time. The governments of Sub-Saharan Africa have had practically no transfer payment programs from 1970 to 2000.
    C) China has a progressive income tax system. The countries of Sub-Saharan Africa all have regressive income tax systems.
    D) China experienced higher economic growth than Sub-Saharan Africa.
    Answer: D
    Diff: 2   Type: MC   Page Ref: 622/622
    Topic: Poverty rate
    Skill: Conceptual
    Objective: LO 4: Income Distribution and Poverty
    AACSB Coding: Reflective Thinking
    Special Features: None

21. The decision to make the U.S. income tax system progressive was
    A) a progressive decision.
    B) a positive decision.
    C) a decision that was needed to minimize the excess burden of taxation.
    D) a normative decision.
    Answer: D
    Diff: 1   Type: MC   Page Ref: 623/623
    Topic: Progressive tax
    Skill: Conceptual
    Objective: LO 4: Income Distribution and Poverty
    AACSB Coding: Reflective Thinking
    Special Features: Economics in YOUR Life!: How Much Tax Should You Pay?

22. In a 2007 speech Federal Reserve Chairman Ben Bernanke commented on income inequality in the United States. Which of the following policies did Bernanke advocate to reduce inequality?
    A) The U.S. should impose new restrictions on international trade and new regulations on labor markets.
    B) The U.S. should make greater use of the tax code to redistribute incomes.
    C) The U.S. should strengthen its economic safety net – for example, with portable and affordable health insurance – while investing in education and training.
    D) The U.S. government should encourage firms to develop new computer technology and do a better job of enforcing border security laws.
    Answer: C
    Diff: 1   Type: MC   Page Ref: 624-5/624-5
    Topic: Income distribution
    Skill: Conceptual
    Objective: LO 4: Income Distribution and Poverty
    AACSB Coding: Reflective Thinking
    Special Features: An Inside Look: Balancing Flexible Markets and a Government Safety Net

23. The federal income tax system is progressive. The payroll tax for Social Security is
    A) progressive as well.
    B) a proportional tax.
    C) not progressive.   The tax is not paid on labor earnings above a certain amount of income.
    D) progressive for individuals above a certain amount of income. Individuals with incomes below a certain amount do not pay any payroll tax.
    Answer: C
    Diff: 1   Type: MC   Page Ref: 624-5/624-5
    Topic: Regressive tax
    Skill: Conceptual
    Objective: LO 4: Income Distribution and Poverty
    AACSB Coding: Reflective Thinking
    Special Features: An Inside Look: Balancing Flexible Markets and a Government Safety Net

24. A Lorenz curve summarizes the information provided by a Gini coefficient.
    Answer: True   ⊚ False
    Diff: 1   Type: TF   Page Ref: 618-9/618-9
    Topic: Lorenz curve
    Skill: Conceptual
    Objective: LO 4: Income Distribution and Poverty
    AACSB Coding: Reflective Thinking
    Special Features: None

25. From 1970 to 2000 the poverty rate in China and south Asia fell dramatically but the level of poverty in sub-Saharan Africa rose.
    Answer: ⊚ True   False
    Diff: 1   Type: TF   Page Ref: 622/622
    Topic: Poverty rate
    Skill: Fact
    Objective: LO 4: Income Distribution and Poverty
    AACSB Coding: Reflective Thinking
    Special Features: None

Table 18-8

26.

Income quintile	Svetlana Percentage of Total Income	Grodsky Percentage of Total Income
Lowest 20%	8%	4%
Second quintile	12%	10%
Third quintile	16%	16%
Fourth quintile	20%	24%
Highest 20%	44%	46%

Table 18-8 shows income distribution data for two countries. Use this data to answer the following questions.

Refer to Table 18-8.
a. Draw a Lorenz curve for each country.
b. Which country has the more equal distribution of income?
c. Based on the Lorenz curve for the two countries, can you determine which country has the more progressive tax system? Explain your answer.

Answer: a. See diagram below.

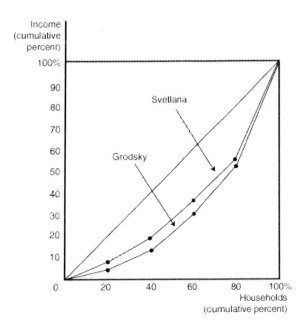

b. Svetlana
c. No, it is not possible to tell which country has the more progressive tax because the Lorenz curve is based on earned income not on after-tax income.

Diff: 3   Type: ES   Page Ref: 618-20-/18-20
Topic: Income distribution
Skill: Analytical
Objective: LO 4: Income Distribution and Poverty
AACSB Coding: Analytic Skills
Special Features: None